Lecture Notes in Information Systems and Organisation

Volume 80

Lecture Notes in Information Systems and Organization (LNISO) is a series of scientific books that explore the current state of information systems studies, in particular in the context of organizations, as well as behavioral and design aspects of information systems. The series offers an integrated publication platform for high-quality conferences, symposia and workshops proceedings. Books accepted for publication are selected based on a double-blind peer-review evaluation made by invited reviewers. The series is indexed in Scopus.

Michele Cipriano • Alessandra Lazazzara •
Leonardo Caporarello
Editors

Technologies for Organizations and Society

Balancing Sustainable Innovations and Social Implications

Springer

Editors

Michele Cipriano
Department of Economic and Social Sciences
Catholic University of the Sacred Heart
Piacenza, Italy

Alessandra Lazazzara
Department of Social and Political Sciences
University of Milan
Milano, Italy

Leonardo Caporarello
Department of Management and Technology
Bocconi University
Milano, Italy

ISSN 2195-4968 ISSN 2195-4976 (electronic)
Lecture Notes in Information Systems and Organisation
ISBN 978-3-032-01696-6 ISBN 978-3-032-01697-3 (eBook)
https://doi.org/10.1007/978-3-032-01697-3

This Springer imprint is published by the registered company Springer Nature Switzerland AG
The registered company address is: Gewerbestrasse 11, 6330 Cham, Switzerland

Contents

Contributors

Nico Abbatemarco SDA Bocconi School of Management, Milan, Italy

Davide Antonioli Università degli Studi di Ferrara, Ferrara, Italy

Gianluca Antonucci "G. d'Annunzio" University of Chieti-Pescara, Pescara, Italy

Pierpaolo Arquilla Azienda Sanitaria Locale Pescara, Pescara, Italy

Aurora Ascatigno School of Advanced Studies, University of Chieti-Pescara, Chieti, Italy

Bart Baesens KU Leuven, Leuven, Belgium
University of Southampton, Southampton, UK

Nicola Basile Department of Human Sciences, Innovation and Territory, University of Insubria, Como, Italy

Diego Boerchi Department of Psychology, Catholic University of the Sacred Heart, Milan, Italy

Sabrina Bonomi eCampus University, Novedrate, CO, Italy

Edgardo Bucciarelli University of Chieti-Pescara, Pescara, Italy

Andrea Caccialanza Università di Bologna, Bologna, Italy

Paolo Canonico Università degli Studi Federico II, Naples, Italy

Franca Cantoni Department of Economic and Social Sciences, Catholic University of the Sacred Heart, Piacenza, Italy

Leonardo Caporarello SDA Bocconi School of Management, Bocconi University, Milan, Italy
Department of Management and Technology, Bocconi University, Milan, Italy

Camilla Carpinelli Reykjavik University, Reykjavík, Iceland

Gianni Carvelli Dipartimento di Scienze Economiche e Sociali, Università Cattolica del Sacro Cuore, Piacenza, Italy

Walter Castelnovo Department of Human Sciences, Innovation and Territory, University of Insubria, Como, Italy

Michele Cipriano Department of Economic and Social Sciences, Catholic University of the Sacred Heart, Piacenza, Italy

Antonio D'Andreamatteo "G. d'Annunzio" University of Chieti-Pescara, Chieti, Italy

Ernesto De Nito Università degli Studi di Salerno, Fisciano, Italy

Leonardo Maria De Rossi SDA Bocconi School of Management, Milan, Italy

Armando Della Porta Dipartimento di Economia Aziendale, Università degli Studi G. d'Annunzio Chieti-Pescara, Pescara, Italy

Manuel Di Francesco Toto Holding S.p.A, Chieti, Italy

Olimpia Fontana Department of Agricultural and Food Economics, Catholic University of the Sacred Heart, Piacenza, Italy

Asia Guerreschi Università degli Studi di Ferrara, Ferrara, Italy

Michelle Grillo eCampus University, Novedrate, CO, Italy

Selini Natalia Hadjidimitriou Department of Sciences and Method for Engineering, University of Modena and Reggio Emilia, Reggio Emilia, Italy

Inga Karen Ingólfsdóttir Department of Computer Science, Reykjavik University, Reykjavik, Iceland

Anna Sigridur Islind Department of Computer Science, Reykjavik University, Reykjavik, Iceland

Valentina Langella Altis Advisory, Milan, Italy

Alessandra Lazazzara Dipartimento di Scienze Sociali e Politiche, University of Milan, Milan, Italy

Nidia Guadalupe López Flores Department of Computer Science, Reykjavik University, Reykjavik, Iceland

Antonio Lorena Magna Græcia University of Catanzaro, Germaneto, CZ, Italy

Massimo Magni SDA Bocconi School of Management, Bocconi University, Milan, Italy

Franca Maino Università degli Studi di Milano, Milan, Italy

Alessandro Margherita Università del Salento, Lecce, Italy

Francesca Mochi Università degli Studi di Milano, Milan, Italy

María Óskarsdóttir Department of Computer Science, Reykjavik University, Reykjavik, Iceland

Claudia Pelagatti School of Advanced Studies, University of Chieti-Pescara, Chieti, Italy

Haiat Perozzo LIUC – Cattaneo University, Castellanza, Italy

Paul Pierce Department of Informatics, School of Economics and Management, Lund University, Lund, Sweden

Pietro Previtali Department of Economics and Management, University of Pavia, Pavia, Italy

Beatrice Re Department of Economics and Management, University of Pavia, Pavia, Italy

Alessia Regnicoli School of Advanced Studies, University of Chieti-Pescara, Chieti, Italy

Rocco Reina Magna Græcia University of Catanzaro, Germaneto, CZ, Italy

Giulia Renzi Department of Sciences and Method for Engineering, University of Modena and Reggio Emilia, Reggio Emilia, Italy

Francesca Sanguineti Department of Economics and Management, University of Pavia, Pavia, Italy

Simon Michael Schmid University of St. Gallen, St. Gallen, Switzerland

Paolo Sckokai Department of Agricultural and Food Economics, Catholic University of the Sacred Heart, Piacenza, Italy

Marco Smacchia Department of Management and Business Administration, University "G. D'Annunzio", Pescara, Italy

Esli Spahiu Department of Management and Technology, Bocconi University, Milan, Italy

Odd Steen Department of Informatics, School of Economics and Management, Lund University, Lund, Sweden

Alessia Talarico Magna Græcia University of Catanzaro, Germaneto, CZ, Italy

Iuliia Trabskaia SDA Bocconi School of Management, Bocconi University, Milan, Italy

Paula Ungureanu Department of Sciences and Method for Engineering, University of Modena and Reggio Emilia, Reggio Emilia, Italy

Seppe Vanden Broucke University of Ghent, Ghent, Belgium
KU Leuven, Leuven, Belgium

Francesco Virili Department of Economic and Social Sciences, Catholic University of the Sacred Heart, Piacenza, Italy

Tiziano Volpentesta Department of Management, Luiss University, Rome, Italy

Shiting Wang Copenhagen Business School, Frederiksberg, Denmark

Stefano Za Department of Management and Business Administration, University "G. D'Annunzio", Pescara, Italy

Giacomo Zatini Università degli Studi G. d'Annunzio Chieti-Pescara, Chieti, Italy

Ludovica Zoccali Magna Græcia University of Catanzaro, Germaneto, CZ, Italy

List of Figures

List of Tables

Technologies for Organizations and Society: The Promise of Responsible Information Systems

Michele Cipriano, Alessandra Lazazzara, and Leonardo Caporarello

Abstract Digital technologies are increasingly pervasive, driving profound transformations across socio-economic and organizational landscapes. As rapid technological advancement intersects with intensifying global challenges, there is a growing priority to balance innovation with its social and environmental implications. This evolving context positions the Information Systems (IS) field at the forefront of addressing complex societal needs and shaping sustainable digital futures. This chapter focuses on the concept and development of Responsible IS, a research approach that refocuses IS scholarship on the common good by integrating ethical, theoretical, and practical considerations. It introduces the contributions of the volume to the discourse on how digital technologies can serve both organizations and society in a sustainable and socially responsible manner. The book collects 24 chapters from the Italian IS community that provide an interdisciplinary and multifaceted exploration of Responsible IS. The chapters are organized around four main thematic areas: the use of digital technologies to advance sustainability and the circular economy; the use of digital technologies for promoting social good, well-being, and digital inclusion; ethical and societal challenges related to the design and use of digital technologies; and digital ecosystems, organizational transformation, and stakeholder networks for responsible innovation. Collectively, these contributions exhibit how IS research can inform and guide digital innovation

M. Cipriano (✉)
Department of Economic and Social Sciences, Catholic University of the Sacred Heart, Piacenza, Italy
e-mail: michele.cipriano@unicatt.it

A. Lazazzara
Dipartimento di Scienze Sociali e Politiche, University of Milan, Milan, Italy
e-mail: alessandra.lazazzara@unimi.it

L. Caporarello
SDA Bocconi School of Management, Bocconi University, Milan, Italy

Department of Management and Technology, Bocconi University, Milan, Italy
e-mail: leonardo.caporarello@unibocconi.it

M. Cipriano et al. (eds.), *Technologies for Organizations and Society*,
Lecture Notes in Information Systems and Organisation 80,
https://doi.org/10.1007/978-3-032-01697-3_1

to maximize societal and environmental benefit while mitigating risks, advancing a more equitable and sustainable digital future.

Keywords Technologies · Organizations · Society · Responsible IS · Sustainable innovations · Social implications

1 Introduction

As rapid technological progress converges with escalating global challenges, organizations and societies are experiencing intense transformations driven by the pervasive integration of digital technologies. Emerging Technologies such as Artificial Intelligence (AI), blockchain, the Internet of Things (IoT), and big data analytics offer both transformative opportunities and complex risks, particularly concerning productivity goals, sustainability aims, and social equity [1]. Among other disciplines, the Information Systems (IS) field is increasingly called to move beyond deterministic views of technological development to engage with multiple, uncertain, and socially constructed digital futures, acknowledging the diverse pathways through which digital technologies might shape tomorrow's world [2].

In this regard, the role of IS research in contributing to a better world has received increasing attention in the last decade [3–5]. However, although a broader consensus in academia acknowledges the relevance that researchers have a moral obligation to improve society, only a few studies concretely echo this perspective [6–9]. A significant stimulus in this direction has directly questioned the extent to which IS research contributes to making the world a better place [6, 10].

From this perspective, various initiatives emerged aiming at fostering more engaged forms of research. For example, the virtual organization Responsible Research in Business and Management (RRBM) initiative was established to inspire, encourage, and support credible and valuable research in business and management disciplines [6]. At the same time, several calls for papers and editorials have been issued, inviting researchers to submit work explicitly addressing the theme of "making the world a better place" through IS research. Specifically, emphasis concerned practical and policy implications of the research, whether for academics and also for a wide array of practitioners and broader societal audiences (for example, including attention to the non-human world, referring to the "environment") [3, 6, 10].

Responsible IS research emerges as a distinct domain that transcends the traditional IS focus on economic metrics and organizational efficiency [6]. It is characterized by explicit theoretical and ethical objectives intended to increase the likelihood that IS produces positive outcomes for the world [11–13]. Accordingly, Responsible IS represents a different orientation towards a new paradigm for research in the field.

Adopting this perspective suggests overstepping traditional evaluation criteria and conventional scientific validity and reliability standards. Responsible IS studies should be assessed based on their inclusion of multiple perspectives, their capacity to address the complexity arising from conflicting objectives, their recognition of diverse stakeholder roles, and their specific attention to the needs of underserved communities [2, 6, 14, 15]. Hence, to achieve concrete contributions toward a better future for coming generations, it is posed to clarify the nature of the problems being addressed, articulate how IS can contribute to positive change, and inspire others to engage in this challenging domain [6].

These principles of Responsible IS become particularly relevant in the context of current digital transformation (DT) initiatives, which are profoundly reshaping socio-economic and organizational structures [1, 16]. For example, Augmented Intelligence, which emphasizes the synergistic integration of human judgment and AI capabilities, drives a paradigmatic shift [17]. Rather than replacing human agency, this model seeks to enhance decision-making processes through human-centric, ethically grounded, and socially informed AI systems designed to support sustainable development goals [9, 17]. However, this evolution is not without tensions and challenges, such as the potential increase in consumption linked to broader digital access [9]. Therefore, it becomes increasingly important to adopt a strategic approach that ensures DT initiatives align with sustainability goals [18].

In addition, digital ecosystems emerge as complex networks in which connected objects interact with each other and with people to create dynamic environments [19]. The proliferation of "smart" devices (e.g., smart homes, factories, and cities) has given rise to interconnected systems marked by complex behaviors and blurred boundaries, creating new opportunities and significant challenges for research and practice. Understanding the dynamics of these ecosystems, the interactions among various stakeholders, and the necessary organizational changes is fundamental to directing digital technologies toward social good and responsible impact [12, 13, 19, 20].

The IS field, traditionally rooted in an inherently multidisciplinary, data-driven, and socio-technical nature, is uniquely positioned to address the large-scale societal challenges emerging in this landscape [5]. IS research can serve as a key enabler of major transitions, such as the shift toward sustainable smart mobility [5], and generate not exclusively economic value but other forms of value, such as public value, social value (e.g., sustainable innovation, and social responsibility), ethical value [9, 21]. Future research directions should focus on advancing social good, promoting individual and collective well-being, enhancing digital inclusion, and analyzing the ethical and social dilemmas associated with the design and use of digital systems. Within the broader framework of Responsible IS, current research needs to address themes such as environmental sustainability, the circular economy, stakeholder engagement, and social impact assessment.

Despite its potential, the IS community has been described as a "relatively silent observer" in high-profile debates [5]. To contribute to advancing such a line of inquiry, this volume brings together a selection of contributions addressing these themes from diverse perspectives. It offers an updated and comprehensive overview of Responsible IS research and the role of digital ecosystems in tackling the challenges of building a better world.

2 Responsible IS Research: Five Fundamental Criteria

As highlighted in recent academic conversations on the subject, Responsible IS Research diverges from a narrow focus on efficiency or economic benefit for individual entities that historically characterized part of the IS discipline [10, 22]. Responsible IS Research characterizes a programmatic orientation toward a potential paradigm shift in the perspective of IS research [6], intended to advance knowledge and promote positive real-world outcomes concurrently (i.e., actively contributing to the common good).

To pursue this objective, Responsible IS Research integrates into its methodology and evaluative criteria elements that go beyond conventional scientific rigor and broad generalizability standards. Building upon the five criteria proposed by Davison et al. [6], we develop the following framework for Responsible IS research (where each subsection represents one of the five criteria).

Centrality of a Social or Environmental Good Context Research should focus on how IS are or can be designed and used to address social challenges, enhance collective or individual well-being, or promote environmental sustainability. The value of the IS under study is primarily assessed in relation to its capacity to generate positive impacts.

Consideration of a Multiplicity of Stakeholders Research should include analysis of the perspectives and needs of a wide range of actors, extending beyond those directly involved in economic transactions (such as businesses or traditional customers). This includes employees, ecosystem partners, individuals or groups who may be marginalized or adversely affected by digital systems ("*the underserved*"), and even the natural environment. The research must effectively manage the complexity arising from often divergent goals and the inherently "messy" nature of stakeholder roles.

Context-Specific Theoretical Development and Generalizability Research should consider the development of theories tailored to the specific context of social good under investigation. Such theories must account for complex interactions and the concerned needs of various stakeholders. Simultaneously, efforts should be made to abstract and connect the findings to the broader theoretical corpus of the IS discipline to inspire and guide future studies and help consolidate Responsible IS research as an integral component of the field.

Focus on Practical and Policy Implications Research should aim to provide concrete guidance. This translates into the articulation of design principles for

IS aimed at promoting the common good and the identification of implications for the academic community engaged in Responsible IS and, where possible, for policymakers. The goal is to translate knowledge into actions that support digital innovation with beneficial impacts.

Holistic and Impact-Oriented Evaluation Representative Responsible IS research is evaluated not only on data quality in the narrow sense but also on its ability to clarify the nature of the problems addressed, to explain how IS contributed to improving the world, and to stimulate further inquiry. Emphasis is placed on gathering data from multiple perspectives and on managing the inherent complexity of these contexts.

In light of this, we argue that Responsible IS Research is a dynamic field that can respond to the growing awareness of the pervasive and complex role of IS in shaping our future. Based on an explicit commitment to the common good and careful attention to multiple stakeholders, researchers are called to understand its core dimensions to navigate its various domains of application. From sustainability to healthcare, from ethics to digital ecosystems, Responsible IS research could provide the knowledge and tools necessary to direct digital innovation toward pathways that maximize social and environmental benefits while minimizing risks and inequalities, thereby contributing tangibly to the construction of a more equitable and sustainable future.

3 Researching Responsible IS

The above-introduced perspective translates into a wide variety of research fields in which IS plays a crucial role in shaping the future of organizations, society, and digital ecosystems. Many contemporary studies in the IS field, often discussed in prominent academic contexts, explore these issues through different analytical lenses.

In line with this rationale, the chapters collected in this volume offer a current and comprehensive overview of scholarly contributions to Responsible IS research developed by members of the interdisciplinary and international IS community in Italy. These chapters represent a selected set of the most compelling papers presented at the 2024 annual conference of the Italian Chapter of AIS, each having undergone a rigorous double-blind peer review process. Their inclusion in this book echoes their capacity to advance a multifaceted and interdisciplinary understanding of key themes such as social good, stakeholder engagement, impact evaluation, and the ongoing dynamics shaping digital ecosystems. The volume includes 24 papers exploring a broad spectrum of challenges and opportunities within this domain. The contributions are grouped into four main thematic areas: the use of digital technologies to advance sustainability and circular economy; the use of digital technologies for the promotion of social good, individual and collective well-being, and digital inclusion; the ethical and societal challenges related to the design and use of digital technologies; and the evolution of digital ecosystems, stakeholder engagement, and organizational transformation aimed at generating responsible and impactful innovation.

3.1 *Digital Technologies for Sustainability and Circular Economy*

The first thematic area explores the intersection of digital transformation with pressing environmental and economic sustainability challenges. The research collected in this section examines how IS can support the adoption of sustainable practices within organizations, facilitate the transition to circular economy models, improve natural resource management, and contribute to impact measurement and reporting (e.g., ESG metrics). It also includes reflections on the environmental footprint of digital technologies themselves and on how to steer their development and use in more eco-friendly directions (e.g., "Green IS").

A total of 10 chapters contribute to advancing the dialogue on how sustainability and digital transformation are increasingly intertwined. These contributions engage with key topics such as the environmental impacts of digital technologies, the promotion of circular economy principles, and the broader pursuit of organizational and ecological sustainability. While this research area has recently gained momentum in the IS field, it responds to urgent global priorities and aligns with the growing scholarly focus on the environmental implications of digital innovation. Moreover, these studies resonate strongly with the elaborated criteria outlined in Sect. 2, particularly regarding social good, stakeholders impact, context-specific theoretical development and the generalizability of Responsible IS research.

From this perspective, with their study, Giacomo Zatini and Armando Della Porta in Chap. "Global Trends and Collaborative Dynamics in Environmental Management Accounting: A Comparative Analysis" examine the evolution of Environmental Management Accounting (EMA) in light of global sustainability initiatives such as the European Green Deal [23]. Using bibliometric and semi-systematic review methods, the chapter highlights both the theoretical progress and the limited practical adoption of EMA, particularly within Europe. The study highlights the need for stronger policy support and international collaboration to foster more widespread and effective use of EMA tools in corporate sustainability strategies.

In Chap. "Digital Innovations and Sustainability: A 5-year Panel Analysis" Tiziano Volpentesta, Esli Spahiu, and Gianni Carvelli investigate the relationship between digital innovation and firms' sustainability performance [24]. Drawing on a global, cross-industry panel dataset (2018–2022), the study uses ESG metrics and patent data to assess impacts across environmental, social, and governance dimensions. While findings vary by methodological approach, results suggest that digital innovation may play a complementary role in advancing sustainable value creation, highlighting the complexity of these dynamics and calling for continued empirical exploration.

Chapter "Metaverse: An Environmental Sustainability Tool?" by Sabrina Bonomi and Michelle Grillo, explore the potential of the Metaverse to support environmental sustainability in the fashion industry [25]. Drawing on four detailed case studies, the chapter examines whether digital fashion can serve as a viable alternative to traditional fashion, reducing environmental impacts associated with overproduction, material waste, and resource consumption. The analysis highlights emerging sustainable practices within digital fashion and also uncovers contradictions such as the material demands of digital infrastructure and the persistence of consumption-driven models. The study includes implications of digital innovation in fashion and calls for a nuanced understanding of sustainability in virtual ecosystems.

In. Chap. "Circular Business Models and Organisational Networks in the Italian Agri-Food Ecosystem" Michele Cipriano, Olimpia Fontana, Paolo Sckokai, and Francesco Virili explore the design of Circular Business Models (CBM) and the role of organizational networks in the agri-food ecosystem for the circular transition in Emilia-Romagna region [26]. Selecting two representative organizations operating in such an industry, the study extensively draws on the literature on the role and characteristics of organizational networks, setting the groundwork for empirically investigating how this contributes to the design of circular practices.

Paul Pierce and Odd Steen, with their study in Chap. "Talking The Talk but Not Walking the Walk: Is the Use of Sustainability Keywords in IS/IT Job Ads "Greenwashing"?" investigate the presence of sustainability-related keywords in over 230,000 Swedish IS/IT job advertisements [27]. Through a large-scale textual analysis, the study examines whether such language reflects authentic strategic needs or serves as superficial signaling. The findings reveal that sustainability references are predominantly associated with operational-level roles rather than tactical or strategic competencies. This suggests a possible misalignment between the strategic importance of sustainability and how it is operationalized in recruitment practices, raising questions about the sincerity of corporate commitments and the potential for "greenwashing."

The study by Francesca Sanguineti, Beatrice Re, and Pietro Previtali in Chap. "The Organizational Features of Circular Platforms: Balancing Digital Transformation and Sustainability" analyses the organizational features of circular platforms and their balance between digital transformation and sustainability [28]. A multiple case study approach is conducted to examine 28 circular platforms across various industries and geographical locations. The major contribution of the study lies in a framework that categorizes platforms into B2B, B2C, C2B, and C2C models, emphasizing the balancing role of interaction complexity and organizational integration dimensions.

Chapter "Optimizing Sustainability: Benchmarking Time-Series Forecasting Models on Purchasing Data to Reduce Overproduction" by Camilla Carpinelli, Seppe Vanden Broucke, Bart Baesens, Anna Sigridur Islind, and María Óskarsdóttir explore the potential of advanced AI forecasting models to enhance sustainable production planning [29]. Drawing on purchasing data from a major Icelandic supermarket chain, the authors benchmark multiple predictive approaches, including regression, LLMs, and foundation models, across different levels of data aggregation. The results shows how improved demand forecasting can reduce overproduction, minimize waste, and support more efficient resource allocation, offering practical implications for sustainability in supply chain and production systems.

Chapter "Planting Digital Seeds: Treedom's Technological Approach to Sustainable Development" by Paolo Canonico, Ernesto De Nito, Andrea Caccialanza, and Valentina Langella examines the role of digital innovation to support sustainability-oriented transitions through an in-depth case study of Treedom, a startup committed to global reforestation [30]. The chapter explores the company's technological infrastructure, managerial strategies, and market positioning as tools for habitat restoration and climate change mitigation. It also identifies key enablers, challenges, and implications for advancing research and practice in technology-enabled environmental stewardship.

In Chap. "Systematic Review and Organizational Insight: Navigating Digital Healthcare and Environmental Sustainability" Antonio Lorena, Ludovica Zoccali, Alessia Talarico, and Rocco Reina investigate the interplay between digital healthcare innovations and environmental sustainability through the lens of institutional theory [31]. Drawing on a systematic review of existing literature, the chapter analyzes how healthcare organizations integrate digital solutions (e.g., electronic health records, telemedicine, and IoMT) while responding to institutional pressures and environmental challenges. The study offers evidence-based insights into how healthcare systems can align technological innovation with sustainability goals (especially concerning policy and organizational adaptation).

Finally, Edgardo Bucciarelli, Alessia Regnicoli, and Aurora Ascatigno focus in Chap. "The ESG Rating Conundrum: A Bibliometric Analysis" on the challenges and inconsistencies in ESG evaluations, exploring the divergence among rating agencies and the pressing need for standardization [32]. By developing a bibliometric analysis of academic literature, the chapter identifies key themes and trends in ESG research, revealing growing concerns about the reliability of current methodologies and the risk of information asymmetry for stakeholders. The study highlights the importance of greater alignment and transparency in ESG assessments to support more accurate and meaningful sustainability evaluations.

3.2 Digital Technologies for Social Good, Well-Being and Inclusion

This second thematic area focuses on the application of IS to address specific social challenges and generate positive outcomes for individuals and communities. The contributions in this section examine how digital technology can promote inclusion, enhance access to essential services (such as healthcare), foster individual and organizational well-being, and empower traditionally marginalized groups. Particularly attention is given to understanding and meeting the needs of users and stakeholders - especially those in vulnerable conditions - thus aligning closely with the first two evaluation criteria outlined in Sect. 2: social good and impacted stakeholders.

Four chapters contribute to this area, advancing our understanding of how digital technologies can be designed and deployed to tackle social challenges, enhance well-being, foster inclusion, and respond explicitly to the needs of users and stakeholders. These studies highlight the importance of context-sensitive approaches that prioritize user needs and social impact, reinforcing the role of IS as an enabler of social good.

Michele Cipriano, Francesco Virili and Stefano Za in Chap. "How to Measure the Social Impact of Renewable Energy Communities?" explore how IS discipline can contribute to evaluating the social impact of Renewable Energy Communities (RECs) [33]. The chapter offers a critical review of existing literature and proposes a Design Science Research (DSR) approach for the development of an IT artefact. The study advances the conceptual and methodological groundwork for a system aimed at supporting REC stakeholders in monitoring and improving their social value contributions. This work contributes to a more holistic understanding of sustainability in IS by emphasizing community-oriented metrics and participatory energy models.

The study by Francesca Mochi, Alessandra Lazazzara, Franca Maino, Asia Guerreschi, Alessandro Margherita and Davide Antonioli in Chap. "Toward a Data-Driven Social Intelligence System: Bridging Societal and Organizational Well-being" conduct a comprehensive review of the social dimension of well-being as a pillar of sustainability [34]. The study systematizes existing literature from both social and organizational well-being domains to develop a shared conceptual foundation. It outlines key constructs and indicators, revealing gaps between HR practices and societal impact, and proposes a citizen science-based intelligence system to guide inclusive, data-driven well-being strategies. This work offers valuable guidance for organizations and policymakers committed to fostering social good through evidence-based and participatory frameworks.

Chapter "Misalignments in the Digitalization of Proximity Health Care Services. A Case Study Upon Reforms in Italy", by Gianluca Antonucci, Antonio D'Andreamatteo, and Pierpaolo Arquilla, analyze the implementation gaps within Italy's policy-driven digital healthcare reforms [35]. Drawing on a mixed-method case study, the chapter reveals a misalignment between top-down telemedicine initiatives and the readiness of both healthcare professionals and patients. The authors remark that digital transformation requires more than innovation; it depends on user education, inclusive co-production and the active involvement of general practitioners as change agents. The study highlights the need for ecosystem-level engagement to ensure policy objectives translate into effective, user-centered digital health services.

Chapter "Developing Social Sustainability in Higher Education: Evidence from a Framed Field Experiment with Causal Inference Analysis" by Claudia Pelagatti, Manuel Di Francesco, Aurora Ascatigno, and Alessia Regnicoli, investigates the social and educational outcomes of the "Impresa IN Accademia" (IINA) project [36]. Through a framed field experiment comparing participants and non-participants, the chapter analyzes the project's effects on students' employment prospects and engagement with entrepreneurial activities. The study highlights broader benefits for students, professors, and entrepreneurs, aligning with SDGs and demonstrating the project's potential to enhance the university workplace interface.

3.3 *Addressing the Ethical and Social Challenges of Design and Use of Digital Technologies*

The third thematic area engages with a core strand of Responsible IS Research that focuses on the unintended consequences and ethical dilemmas arising from the design, implementation, and diffusion of digital technology. This includes issues such as algorithmic bias, particularly in the context of AI, privacy and data protection in the era of big data, the demand for transparency and accountability, and the broader societal implications of technology diffusion. Rather than treating technology adoption as a purely technical matter, the contributions in this section approach it as a process that reshapes social practices, power relations, and institutional norms.

Five chapters contribute to this area by examining the diffusion of disruptive digital technologies and the ethical, social, and organizational challenges they raise. These include concerns around biases, privacy, transparency, and the broader societal challenges of digital systems. The studies reflect the ongoing interest in the "dark side" of information technologies and the critical need to identify who may be harmed by technological change. This section emphasizes the role of IS research in highlighting how adoption processes redefines business models, organizational routines, and social dynamics – aligning particularly with the criteria elaborated in Sect. 2 relate to design principles, and policy implications of Responsible IS research.

In Chap. "The Impact of Network Expansion, Developer's Activity and Seasonality on the Adoption of Cryptocurrencies" Leonardo Maria De Rossi and Nico Abbatemarco explore the drivers of cryptocurrency adoption, shifting focus from price speculation to broader adoption patterns [37]. Using a seasonal autoregressive model on Bitcoin data, the study highlights the influence of miners, developers, and seasonal dynamics on end-user engagement. By shedding lights on how technical and temporal factors shape adoption, the chapter contributes to fintech research and informs ongoing debates about the societal and environmental implications of digital currencies.

In Chap. "Design in the Wild: Novel Insights into High School Students Identification and Perception of Misleading Data Visualisations", Nidia Guadalupe López Flores, Inga Karen Ingólfsdóttir, Anna Sigridur Islind, and María Óskarsdóttir investigate how high school students perceive and interpret misleading elements in data visualizations [38]. Drawing on a four-module case study, the research highlights limited student awareness of deceptive visual and textual cues, raising important ethical questions around digital literacy, responsible information design, and the societal implications of visual communication in digital environments.

In Chap. "Developing a Framework for Shared Responsibility: The Role of Digital Technology", Shiting Wang and Haiat Perozzo examine how digital technologies such as IoT and Generative AI shape the evolving concept of shared responsibility in IS [39]. Drawing on a systematic literature review and Gioia methodology, the study identifies three core dimensions: technological adoption and resistance, information control and power dynamics, and trust and transparency. The analysis reveals that IoT can enhance operational transparency and can reinforce hierarchical control, whereas Generative AI introduces accountability challenges due to its opaque outputs. This work offers a structured framework for understanding how different technologies mediate responsibility, emphasizing the ethical and organizational implications of emerging digital systems.

The chapter, "Entrepreneurial Perspective of AI Bias: A Preliminary Investigation" by Marco Smacchia, Michele Cipriano, and Stefano Za, examine how entrepreneurs perceive and interpret bias in AI systems, distinguishing between technical (computational) and societal (systemic) forms [40]. Based on a preliminary case study of Italian firms, the research shows varied awareness of AI bias, with responses ranging from performance-focused mitigation to broader ethical and communication concerns. The authors propose a matrix to map how different types of bias impact organizational decision-making. This work highlights the need for greater awareness and structured approaches among SMEs to address AI bias and underscores the importance of socio-technical perspectives for fostering responsible AI adoption.

Chapter "(Ir)Responsible Uses of Digital Technologies in Business Education. Interruptions or Engagement?" by Leonardo Caporarello, Massimo Magni, and Iuliia Trabskaia, explores the ethical and pedagogical implications of digital technology integration in business education [41]. Based on a student survey and structural equation modeling, the study reveals the complex role of digital tools, enhancing engagement while also contributing to distraction. The study underlines the need for a nuanced understanding of responsible technology use in education, making a valuable contribution to the discourse on the societal impacts of digital system design and implementation.

3.4 Digital Ecosystems, Stakeholders, and Organizational Change for a Responsible Impact

The fourth thematic area explores Responsible IS Research within the context of complex digital ecosystems understood as interconnected networks of technologies, organizations, and individuals. The contributions in this section examine the dynamics that shape these ecosystems, the interactions and power relations among diverse stakeholders, and the organizational changes necessary to navigate DT toward responsible outcomes, such as social good and responsible impact. Topics addressed include cross-sector collaboration (including partnership between researchers and practitioners), data sharing in multi-stakeholder environments, and the influence of institutional and regulatory frameworks on the direction and impact of technological change.

This section includes five chapters that particularly align with the evaluation criteria outlined in Sect. 2, specifically the development of theory in social context and impact-oriented assessment in Responsible IS research.

Among these, the study by Walter Castelnovo and Nicola Basile in Chap. "Organizational Change in Social Cooperatives: Implementing the Shared Administration Paradigm in Italy" investigates how social cooperatives are adapting to Italy's shared administration model, a governance shift that emphasizes collaboration between public and third-sector organizations [42]. Based on interviews with experienced cooperative leaders, the study highlights the organizational transformations needed to align with this paradigm, including the development of planning capabilities, lateral communication, and managerial practices. The authors emphasize the delicate balance cooperatives must strike between embracing management tools and preserving their social mission, underscoring the need for responsible governance in hybrid organizational contexts.

Chapter "Bridging the Gap: Analyzing Collaboration Between Practitioners and Researchers Across Different Stages of the Design Science Research Process" by Simon Michael Schmid, investigates how collaboration unfolds across Design Science Research (DSR) phases [43]. The study aligns with the broader ethos of Responsible IS by highlighting how research can deliver both theoretical and practical value. Initial findings indicate that collaboration between researchers and practitioners is often unevenly distributed and poorly documented, where room for further investigations concerns how to ensure more integrated, transparent, and impactful co-creation processes within complex digital ecosystems.

In Chap. "Unveiling the Behaviour: Analysing Isomorphic Forces in the Emilia-Romagna Industrial Ecosystem" by Michele Cipriano, Francesco Virili, Franca Cantoni, and Diego Boerchi authors examines how regional industrial ecosystems are responding to emerging sustainability regulations such as the EU Taxonomy [44]. Drawing on institutional theory and isomorphism, the study investigates how normative, coercive, and mimetic forces could shape organizational behavior in non-financial accounting. While still in a preliminary phase, the work underscores the managerial and digital implications of aligning with ESG metrics, laying the foundation for future empirical research into how digital technologies and accountability frameworks interact to support sustainable transformation.

Chapter "Motivation and Risk-Opportunity Dynamics in Big Data Ecosystems" by Giulia Renzi, Paula Ungureanu, and Selini Natalia Hadjidimitriou investigates the motivations and perceptions that shape data-sharing behaviors in complex, multi-stakeholder ecosystems [45]. The study identifies three distinct sharing practices, diving, scaffolding, and pushing, driven by actors' cognitive and social evaluations of risks and opportunities, and whether their motivations are utilitarian or socially oriented. The work highlights that data-sharing is not binary but influenced by nuanced risk-benefit assessments, with socially motivated actors more inclined to share despite uncertainties.

Finally, Giulia Renzi, Paula Ungureanu, and Selini Natalia Hadjidimitriou in Chap. "Collaborative Data Sharing Partnership in Mobility: Transformations, Sustainability, and Hidden Challenges" focus on examining the dynamics of data sharing in the transport sector [46]. Focusing on trust, risk, and perceived benefits, the study explores how stakeholder attitudes shape strategies, ranging from refraining to improving or maintaining engagement. The authors highlight the complex interplay of motivations and perceptions in fostering sustainable, cross-sectoral data collaborations.

Disclosure of Interests The authors have no competing interests to declare that are relevant to the content of this article.

References

1. Ncube, T., Murray, U., & Dennehy, D. (2023). Digitalising social protection systems for achieving the sustainable development goals: Insights from Zimbabwe. *Communications of the Association for Information Systems, 53*, 138–161. https://doi.org/10.17705/1CAIS.05306
2. Schlagwein, D., Currie, W., Leimeister, J. M., & Willcocks, L. (2025). Digital futures: Definition (what), importance (why) and methods (how). *Journal of Information Technology, 40*, 2–8. https://doi.org/10.1177/02683962241301544
3. Qureshi, S. (2015). Are we making a better world with information and communication technology for development (ICT4D) research? Findings from the field and theory building. *Information Technology for Development, 21*, 511–522. https://doi.org/10.1080/02681102.2015.1080428
4. George, G., Howard-Grenville, J., Joshi, A., & Tihanyi, L. (2016). Understanding and tackling societal grand challenges through management research. *Academy of Management Journal, 59*, 1880–1895. https://doi.org/10.5465/amj.2016.4007
5. Ketter, W., Schroer, K., & Valogianni, K. (2023). Information systems research for smart sustainable mobility: A framework and call for action. *Information Systems Research, 34*, 1045–1065. https://doi.org/10.1287/ISRE.2022.1167
6. Davison, R. M., Majchrzak, A., Hardin, A., & Ravishankar, M. N. (2023). Special issue on responsible IS research for a better world. *Information Systems Journal*. https://doi.org/10.1111/isj.12405
7. Voegtlin, C., Scherer, A. G., Stahl, G. K., & Hawn, O. (2021). Grand societal challenges and responsible. *Innovation*. https://doi.org/10.1111/joms.12785

8. Ferraro, F., Etzion, D., & Gehman, J. (2015). Tackling grand challenges pragmatically: Robust action revisited. *Organization Studies, 36*, 363–390. https://doi.org/10.1177/0170840614563742
9. Saba, P., Harfouche, A., Fosso Wamba, S., Kumar Sharma, S., & Cranefield, J. (2025). Special issue-call for papers: Emerging technologies for sustainable development? The grand challenge special issue guest editors. *Communications of the Association for Information Systems, 55.*
10. Walsham, G. (2012). Are we making a better world with Icts? Reflections on a future agenda for the IS field. *Journal of Information Technology, 27*, 87–93. https://doi.org/10.1057/jit.2012.4
11. Maruping, L.: Quantitative behavioral IS research—a look back and a look forward. (2025).
12. Wang, Q., Pienta, D., Jiang, S., Ngai, E. W. T., & Thatcher, J. B. (2025). Do good and do no harm too: Employee-related corporate social (Ir)responsibility and information security performance. *Journal of the Association for Information Systems, 26*, 171–204. https://doi.org/10.17705/1jais.00908
13. Virto, L. R., Saba, P., Thielens, A., Czerwiński, M., Noumba, P., & The U., Bank, W. (2025). Digital sustainability trade-offs: Public perceptions of mobile radiation and green roofs radiation and green roofs. *Communications of the Association for Information Systems.*
14. Mini, T., & Widjaja, T. (2019). Tensions in digital platform business models: A literature review. In *40th international conference on information systems, (ICIS)*, Munich, Germany.
15. Kouhizadeh, M., Zhu, Q., & Sarkis, J. (2020). Blockchain and the circular economy: Potential tensions and critical reflections from practice. *Production Planning & Control, 31*, 950–966. https://doi.org/10.1080/09537287.2019.1695925
16. Wessel, L., Mosconi, E., Indulska, M., & Baiyere, A. (2025). Digital transformation: Quo Vadit? *Information Systems Journal*. https://doi.org/10.1111/isj.12578
17. Harfouche, A., Quinio, B., Saba, M., & Saba, P. B. (2023). The recursive theory of knowledge augmentation: Integrating human intuition and knowledge in artificial intelligence to augment organizational knowledge. *Information Systems Frontiers, 25*, 55–70. https://doi.org/10.1007/s10796-022-10352-8
18. Kotlarsky, J., Corbett, J., Sutanto, J., Kude, T., & Tim, Y. (2024). Digital sustainability and information systems research: New challenges and theoretical perspectives. JAIS Call for papers: Digital Sustainability and Information Systems Research.
19. Braccini, A. M., Ricciardi, F., & Virili, F. (2024). Digital eco-systems, change, and organising. In *Lecture notes in information systems and organisation* (pp. 1–9). Springer Science and Business Media Deutschland GmbH. https://doi.org/10.1007/978-3-031-75586-6_1
20. Püchel, L., Wang, C., Buhmann, K., Brandt, T., von Schweinitz, F., Edinger-Schons, L. M., vom Brocke, J., Legner, C., Teracino, E., & Mardahl, T. D. (2024). On the pivotal role of data in sustainability transformations: Challenges and opportunities. *Business and Information Systems Engineering*. https://doi.org/10.1007/s12599-024-00904-4
21. Chen, W., & Zhang, Q. (2025). Can corporate climate risk drive digital transformation? Evidence from Chinese heavy-polluting enterprises. *Technological Forecasting and Social Change, 212*, 123990. https://doi.org/10.1016/j.techfore.2025.123990
22. Piccoli, G., Rodriguez, J., & Grover, V. (2022). Digital strategic initiatives and digital resources: Construct definition and future research directions. *MIS Quarterly, 46*, 2289–2316. https://doi.org/10.25300/MISQ/2022/17061
23. Zatini, G., & Della Porta, A. (2025). Global trends and collaborative dynamics in environmental management accounting: A comparative analysis. In M. Cipriano, A. Lazazzara, & L. Caporarello (Eds.), *Technologies for organizations and society*. Lecture notes in information systems and organisation (Vol. 80). Cham: Springer.
24. Volpentesta, T., Spahiu, E., & Carvelli, G. (2025). Digital innovations and sustainability: A 5-year panel analysis. In M. Cipriano, A. Lazazzara, & L. Caporarello (Eds.), *Technologies for organizations and society*. Lecture notes in information systems and organisation (Vol. 80). Cham: Springer.
25. Bonomi, S., & Grillo, M. (2025). Metaverse: An environmental sustainability tool? In M. Cipriano, A. Lazazzara, & L. Caporarello (Eds.), *Technologies for organizations and society*. Lecture notes in information systems and organisation (Vol. 80). Cham: Springer.

26. Cipriano, M., Fontana, O., Sckokai, P., & Virili, F. (2025). Circular business models and organisational networks in the Italian agri-food ecosystem. In M. Cipriano, A. Lazazzara, & L. Caporarello (Eds.), *Technologies for organizations and society*. Lecture notes in information systems and organisation (Vol. 80). Cham: Springer.
27. Pierce, P., & Steen, O. (2025). Talking the talk but not walking the walk: Is the use of sustainability keywords in IS/IT job ads "Greenwashing"? In M. Cipriano, A. Lazazzara, & L. Caporarello (Eds.), *Technologies for organizations and society*. Lecture notes in information systems and organisation (Vol. 80). Cham: Springer.
28. Sanguineti, F., Re, B., & Previtali, P. (2025). The organizational features of circular platforms: Balancing digital transformation and sustainability. In M. Cipriano, A. Lazazzara, & L. Caporarello (Eds.), *Technologies for organizations and society*. Lecture notes in information systems and organisation (Vol. 80). Cham: Springer.
29. Carpinelli, C., Vanden Broucke, S., Baesens, B., Islind, A. I., & Òskarsdóttir, M. (2025). Optimizing sustainability: benchmarking time-series forecasting models on purchasing data to reduce overproduction. In M. Cipriano, A. Lazazzara, & L. Caporarello (Eds.), *Technologies for organizations and society*. Lecture notes in information systems and organisation (Vol. 80). Cham: Springer.
30. Canonico, P., De Nito, E., Caccialanza, A., & Langella, V. (2025). Planting digital seeds: Treedom's technological approach to sustainable development. In M. Cipriano, A. Lazazzara, & L. Caporarello (Eds.), *Technologies for organizations and society*. Lecture notes in information systems and organisation (Vol. 80). Cham: Springer.
31. Lorena, A., Zoccali, L., Talarico, A., & Reina, R. (2025). Systematic review and organizational insight: Navigating digital healthcare and environmental sustainability. In M. Cipriano, A. Lazazzara, & L. Caporarello (Eds.), *Technologies for organizations and society*. Lecture notes in information systems and organisation (Vol. 80). Cham: Springer.
32. Bucciarelli, E., Regnicoli, A., & Ascatigno, A. (2025). The ESG rating conundrum: A bibliometric analysis. In M. Cipriano, A. Lazazzara, & L. Caporarello (Eds.), *Technologies for organizations and society*. Lecture notes in information systems and organisation (Vol. 80). Cham: Springer.
33. Cipriano, M., Virili, F., & Za, S. (2025). How to measure the social impact of renewable energy communities? In M. Cipriano, A. Lazazzara, & L. Caporarello (Eds.), *Technologies for organizations and society*. Lecture notes in information systems and organisation (Vol. 80). Cham: Springer.
34. Mochi, F., Lazazzara, A., Maino, F., Guerreschi, A., Margherita, A., & Antonioli, D. (2025). Toward a data-driven social intelligence system: Bridging societal and organizational well-being. In M. Cipriano, A. Lazazzara, & L. Caporarello (Eds.), *Technologies for organizations and society*. Lecture notes in information systems and organisation (Vol. 80). Cham: Springer.
35. Antonucci, G., D'Andreamatteo, A., & Arquilla, P. (2025). Misalignments in the digitalization of proximity health care services. A case study upon reforms in Italy. In M. Cipriano, A. Lazazzara, & L. Caporarello (Eds.), *Technologies for organizations and society*. Lecture notes in information systems and organisation (Vol. 80). Cham: Springer.
36. Pelagatti, C., Di Francesco, M., Ascatigno, A., & Regnicoli, A. (2025). Developing social sustainability in higher education: Evidence from a framed field experiment with causal inference analysis. In M. Cipriano, A. Lazazzara, & L. Caporarello (Eds.), *Technologies for organizations and society*. Lecture notes in information systems and organisation (Vol. 80). Cham: Springer.
37. De Rossi, L. M., & Abbatemarco, N. (2025). The impact of network expansion, developer's activity and seasonality on the adoption of cryptocurrencies. In M. Cipriano, A. Lazazzara, & L. Caporarello (Eds.), *Technologies for organizations and society*. Lecture notes in information systems and organisation (Vol. 80). Cham: Springer.
38. López Flores, N. G., Ingólfsdóttir, I. K., Islind, A. S., & Óskarsdóttir, M. (2025). Design in the wild: Novel insights into high school students identification and perception of misleading data visualisations. In M. Cipriano, A. Lazazzara, & L. Caporarello (Eds.), *Technologies for organizations and society*. Lecture notes in information systems and organisation (Vol. 80). Cham: Springer.

39. Wang, S., & Perozzo, H. (2025). Developing a framework for shared responsibility: The role of digital technology. In M. Cipriano, A. Lazazzara, & L. Caporarello (Eds.), *Technologies for organizations and society*. Lecture notes in information systems and organisation (Vol. 80). Cham: Springer.
40. Smacchia, M., Cipriano, M., & Za, S. (2025). Entrepreneurial perspective of AI bias: A preliminary investigation. In M. Cipriano, A. Lazazzara, & L. Caporarello (Eds.), *Technologies for organizations and society*. Lecture notes in information systems and organisation (Vol. 80). Cham: Springer.
41. Caporarello, L., Magni, M., & Trabskaia, I. (2025). (Ir)Responsible uses of digital technologies in business education. Interruptions or engagement? In M. Cipriano, A. Lazazzara, & L. Caporarello (Eds.), *Technologies for organizations and society*. Lecture notes in information systems and organisation (Vol. 80). Cham: Springer.
42. Castelnovo, W., & Basile, N. (2025). Organizational change in social cooperatives: Implementing the shared administration paradigm in Italy. In M. Cipriano, A. Lazazzara, & L. Caporarello (Eds.), *Technologies for organizations and society*. Lecture notes in information systems and organisation (Vol. 80). Cham: Springer.
43. Schmid, S. M. (2025). Bridging the gap: Analyzing collaboration between practitioners and researchers across different stages of the design science research process. In M. Cipriano, A. Lazazzara, & L. Caporarello (Eds.), *Technologies for organizations and society*. Lecture notes in information systems and organisation (Vol. 80). Cham: Springer.
44. Cipriano, M., Virili, F., Cantoni, F., & Boerchi, D. (2025). Unveiling the behaviour: Analysing isomorphic forces in the Emilia-Romagna Industrial Ecosystem. In M. Cipriano, A. Lazazzara, & L. Caporarello (Eds.), *Technologies for organizations and society*. Lecture notes in information systems and organisation (Vol. 80). Cham: Springer.
45. Renzi, G., Ungureanu, P., & Hadjidimitriou, S. N. (2025). Motivation and risk-opportunity dynamics in big data ecosystems. In M. Cipriano, A. Lazazzara, & L. Caporarello (Eds.), *Technologies for organizations and society*. Lecture notes in information systems and organisation (Vol. 80). Cham: Springer.
46. Renzi, G., Ungureanu, P., & Hadjidimitriou, S. N. (2025). Collaborative data sharing partnership in mobility: Transformations, sustainability, and hidden challenges. In M. Cipriano, A. Lazazzara, & L. Caporarello (Eds.), *Technologies for organizations and society*. Lecture notes in information systems and organisation (Vol. 80). Cham: Springer.

Global Trends and Collaborative Dynamics in Environmental Management Accounting: A Comparative Analysis

Giacomo Zatini and Armando Della Porta

Abstract This study offers a comprehensive examination of Environmental Management Accounting (EMA) trends and collaborative dynamics, focusing on the impact of the European Green Deal and other global initiatives. By employing a combination of bibliometric and semi-systematic review methodologies, this study investigated the development of EMA practices, particularly in response to institutional pressures and new sustainability reporting standards. Despite extensive research on EMA worldwide, there is a noticeable concentration of scholarly activity in certain countries, with European nations excluding Germany showing limited engagement. This research emphasizes the progression of EMA in effectively managing environmental impacts within the corporate sector, revealing that while significant theoretical advancements have been made, the practical applications of EMA remain relatively underexplored. These findings underscore the need for increased research efforts and more effective policy frameworks, particularly in the European context, to facilitate the integration of EMA practices in line with recent legislative changes. This study aims to provide a clearer understanding of global EMA trends, the state of collaborative research, and implications for policy and practice in environmental accounting.

Keywords Environmental management accounting · Integrated reporting · European Green Deal

G. Zatini (✉)
Università degli Studi G. d'Annunzio Chieti-Pescara, Chieti, Italy
e-mail: giacomo.zatini@phd.unich.it

A. Della Porta
Dipartimento di Economia Aziendale, Università degli Studi G. d'Annunzio Chieti-Pescara, Pescara, Italy
e-mail: armando.dellaporta@unich.it

M. Cipriano et al. (eds.), *Technologies for Organizations and Society*,
Lecture Notes in Information Systems and Organisation 80,
https://doi.org/10.1007/978-3-032-01697-3_2

1 Introduction

Environmental Management Accounting (EMA) has emerged as a significant branch of accounting and gained notable prominence in the scientific community in recent years. Concurrently, managers' awareness of environmental impacts has increased [1]. Despite the European Green Deal, announced by the European Commission in December 2019, highlighting the commitment to reduce carbon emissions by at least 50% by 2030 and achieve carbon neutrality by 2050 [2], companies have adapted to these directives by implementing Integrated Reporting (IR) as a means of externally communicating their environmental and social practices [3]. IR aims to convey to various stakeholder groups the financial and business indicators, how the company creates value, and how it manages sustainability [4]. However, IR does not inherently focus exclusively on informing stakeholders about environmental impacts; thus, there is no immediate reason or obligation for companies to develop an accounting system that accurately measures environmental performance and related emissions.

In fact, the need for an accounting system suitable for measuring the environmental impacts of businesses became apparent only in 2023, following Directive 2023/2772, which introduced the new European Sustainability Reporting Standards (ESRS) [5].

Considering the recent Directive 2023/2772, which will fundamentally alter the approach to reporting, it is necessary to evaluate, through a literature review, the current state of EMA and, particularly, the development of new accounting practices to prepare companies for ongoing changes. Both EMA and Integrated Reporting (IR) are responses to institutional pressures [6], as companies are not inclined to invest in new practices aimed at reducing emissions and environmental costs without such pressures, despite the proven key role of EMA in cost optimization [7].

As the new Directive 2023/2772 affects European Union countries, it is essential to understand how scientific research within these nations has progressed in recent years to develop Environmental Management Accounting Practices (EMAPs). Previous reviews [1, 8, 9] have focused on generalized analyses of the state of the art in EMA, employing bibliometric analyses to frame the topic from a broad perspective. However, the aim of this study is to adopt a quantitative approach to discern EMA trends across different countries and a qualitative approach, through a semi-systematic review, to explore the quality, themes, and methodologies addressed in the most significant papers from various nations.

The main goal of this study is to investigate the progress of EMAPs and measurement approaches across various regions worldwide. This research endeavors to determine whether specific countries or regions, such as the European Union, exhibit a particular emphasis on EMAPs or whether researchers globally are concentrating their efforts on other environmental accounting aspects. By analyzing a wide range of international contributions and collaborations, this study seeks to deliver a comprehensive overview of the current state and trends in EMA research globally. The following research questions guide this study:

RQ1: Which countries are most engaged with EMA and which produce the most scholarly material?
RQ2: What types of collaborative relationship exist between countries?
RQ3: What kinds of publications are produced within EU countries of the European Union?

The main contributions of our study are twofold: first, it enhances the academic understanding of EMA trends, offering a specific insight into the state of the art of EMA across different countries; second, it provides businesses with a clear framework on the nature of EMA as an essential measurement tool for keeping pace with current European directives in reporting.

2 Methods

2.1 Bibliometric Analysis

This study adopts a bibliometric approach to analyze the scientific literature on EMA. The use of bibliometric methods stems from the necessity to map the field accurately using data that are minimally subject to significant bias [10]. Through this initial step, it will be possible to develop a semi-systematic review that is as free of misleading interpretations as possible.

To develop a comprehensive analysis, before conducting the bibliometric analysis on a geographic basis, we performed a brief descriptive analysis to explore the field. Subsequently, we mapped the EMA production through co-authorship [11] and citation analysis [12]. The research protocol is illustrated in Fig. 1.

Based on previous reviews [9, 13, 14] and prior knowledge of the subject, it was possible to conceptualize the literature. Data were collected through the "Scopus" platform, currently the largest scientific literature database in the world [15]. The query used by Scopus to search for documents is as follows.

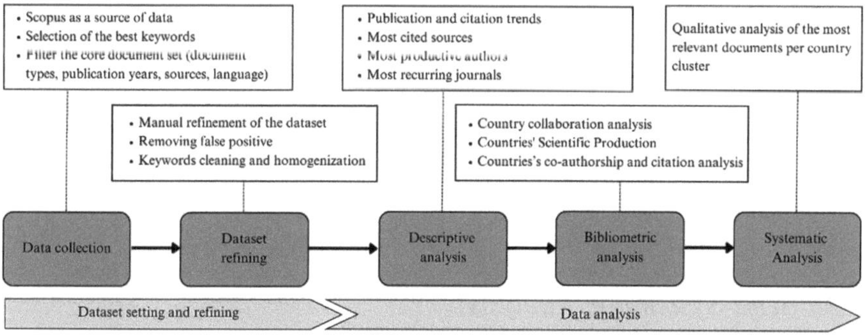

Fig. 1 Research protocol (adapted) [17]

Table 1 Refined set of most recurrent keywords

Original keywords	Revised keywords
Competitive advantage	Competitive advantages
Competitive advantages	
Environmental management accounting (ema)	Environmental management accounting
Environmental management accounting ema	
ema	
Full cost accounting	Full-cost accounting
Full-cost accounting	
Institutional pressure	Institutional pressures
Institutional pressures	
Material cost flow accounting (mfca)	Material flow cost accounting
Material flow cost accounting (mfca)	
Material flow cost accounting(mfca)	
Material flow cost accounting	
emas	Environmental management accounting system
Environmental management accounting system (emas)	
Environmental management accounting systems	
Environmental management accounting system	

TITLE-ABS ("environmental management accounting") OR AUTHKEY ("environmental management accounting") AND (LIMIT-TO (LANGUAGE, "English") OR EXCLUDE (LANGUAGE, "Moldavian") OR EXCLUDE (LANGUAGE, "Moldovan") OR EXCLUDE (LANGUAGE, "Romanian")).

Given that EMA is an emerging topic, reviews, book chapters, and conference papers were also considered. After the initial selection, Scopus returned 316 articles. To proceed with the exploratory phase, the dataset was cleaned by removing 20 false positives, reducing the number of articles to 296. Subsequently, the homogenization of keywords was conducted using either singular or plural forms or by merging keywords with the same meaning, acronyms, or combinations thereof. Consequently, the keywords were replaced, yielding a cleaner and more usable output. Table 1 displays the homogenization of the most frequent keywords.

To effectively develop the review, R (bibliometrix package) and VosViewer were employed as analysis tools [16].

2.2 Semi-Systematic Analysis

Once the dataset has been analyzed through bibliometric analysis, we will conduct a semi-systematic review with the aim of examining, via content analysis [18], the fundamental themes and the most common question archetypes in the most significant papers for each country or group of countries [19]. By analyzing the content of the most relevant articles, it is possible to understand the nature of the documents and their theoretical, empirical, or case study orientation.

3 Main Findings

3.1 Descriptive Analysis

The initial papers on EMA were published in the early 2000s, as depicted in Fig. 2, but there was irregular growth in the number of publications. 2020 and 2023 witnessed the highest number of publications, with 38 and 35 publications, respectively. From 2019 to 2024 (ongoing), 53% of the papers were published, whereas the remaining 47% were published over a span of 19 years (2000–2018).

The analysis of the most cited papers, as shown in Table 2, allows for an understanding of which studies have had a greater impact within the scientific literature. The paper with the highest number of citations is by Latan et al. (2018), which demonstrated through empirical evidence that specific organizational resources, such as management commitment and environmental strategies, have a significant and positive impact on the adoption of EMA. This, in turn, can lead to improved environmental performance within companies [20].

Other authors, such as Burritt et al. (2002), focused on the relationship between EMA and business actors, developing a framework that categorizes the two main components of EMA: Monetary Environmental Management Accounting (MEMA) and Physical Environmental Management Accounting (PEMA) [21]. Others have

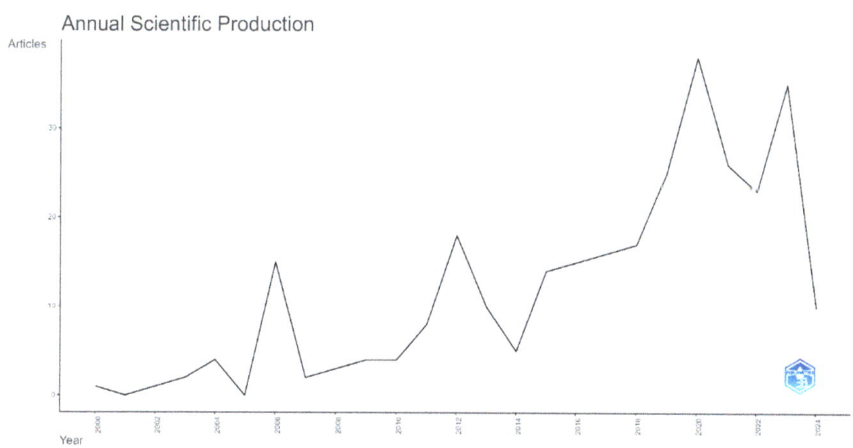

Fig. 2 Number of publications per year by 2000

Table 2 Top 10 papers by total citations

Paper	Total citations	TC per year
LATAN H, 2018, J CLEAN PROD	313	44,71
BURRITT RL, 2002, AUST ACCOUNT REV	281	12,22
SCHALTEGGER S, 2012, J CLEAN PROD-a	220	16,92
FERREIRA A, 2010, ACCOUNT AUDIT ACCOUNT J	211	14,07
JASCH C, 2003, J CLEAN PROD	182	8,27
BARTOLOMEO M, 2000, EUR ACC REV	174	6,96
HENRI J-F, 2008, J ENVIRON MANAGE	156	9,18
QIAN W, 2011, ACCOUNT AUDIT ACCOUNT J	150	10,71
CHRIST KL, 2013, J CLEAN PROD	138	11,50
BURRITT RL, 2006, J CLEAN PROD	136	7,16

Table 3 Top 10 authors per number of articles

Author	Articles	Articles fractionalized
BURRITT RL	20	8,75
SCHALTEGGER S	15	5,62
CHRIST KL	7	3,67
VAN DER POLL HM	7	3,17
JASCH C	6	4,70
LEE K-H	6	3,67
VIERE T	6	1,75
ZVEZDOV D	6	2,03
GIBASSIER D	5	3,83
DOORASAMY M	4	3,00

concentrated on the relationship between EMA and innovation, finding a positive association between EMA and product innovation but not process innovation [22].

An initial review suggests that there is still an effort to map the field, its boundaries, and its limits far from developing operational processes that enable the transformation of internal processes within the business context.

Table 3 displays the 10 authors with the most publications. It is evident that there is a disparity in the number of publications among Burritt, Schaltegger, and the rest of the authors, with the first two accounting for 35 out of a total of 82 articles, representing 42.68% of the publications.

Table 4 displays the ranking of leading journals based on the volume of publications and provides, for each journal, the number of papers, the Scimago Journal & Country Rank Rating (SJR Rating) [23], the H-index, and the field of study.

The Journal of Cleaner Production (JClePro) is the most prolific journal, accounting for 36.36% of the publications in the top 10.

Table 4 Most recurring journals

Journal	N° papers	SJR rating	H-index	Field of studies
Journal of Cleaner Production	36	2058	309	Business, Management and Accounting
International Journal of Energy Economics and Policy	14	0,310	53	Economics, Econometrics and Finance
Sustainability	13	0,672	169	Computer Science
Accounting, Auditing and Accountability Journal	8	1847	121	Business, Management and Accounting
Business Strategy and the Environment	6	3666	147	Business, Management and Accounting

Table 5 Top 10 countries per articles

Author	Articles
MALAYSIA	104
AUSTRALIA	76
INDONESIA	73
GERMANY	61
CHINA	54
SOUTH AFRICA	43
ROMANIA	29
ITALY	24
JAPAN	24
UK	23

3.2 *Country Bibliometric Analysis*

An initial examination of the worldwide distribution of publications on EMA is shown in Table 5 and Fig. 3. Except for Germany, no European country ranks high in the production of scientific articles. This is somewhat discouraging, considering the Union's efforts concerning emission measurements and impact calculations. Moreover, European countries, despite the limited number of publications, do not show multiple country production (MCP), which implies a significant degree of isolation that does not facilitate the consistent development of EMA.

This situation appears to have improved from the perspective of citations. Table 6 lists the 10 countries with the highest number of citations. Despite having fewer publications than countries such as Malaysia, Indonesia, South Africa, and Australia, European countries seem to produce high-quality articles that are frequently cited.

On the other hand, the map of collaborations between countries, as shown in Fig. 4, confirms impressions regarding the isolation of European countries in research. Only Germany maintains active collaboration with foreign countries, particularly Australia. The rest of the countries remain isolated, with virtually no collaborative relationships, even within the Union itself.

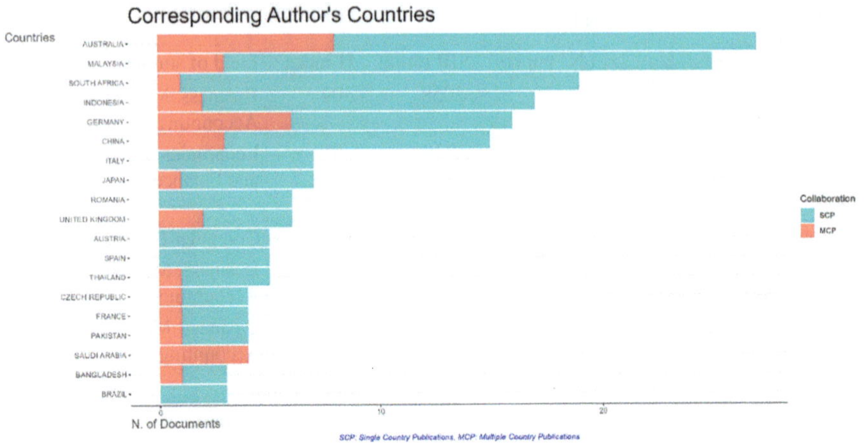

Fig. 3 Corresponding Author's Countries

Table 6 Top 10 countries per number of citations

Region	Citations	Average articles citations
AUSTRALIA	1761	65,20
GERMANY	699	43,70
INDONESIA	627	36,90
MALAYSIA	362	14,50
AUSTRIA	322	64,40
SPAIN	270	54,00
CANADA	235	117,50
CHINA	198	13,20
NETHERLANDS	175	87,50
ITALY	163	23,30

Figure 5 displays the co-authorship network among countries and highlights the international collaborative relationships in the field of research under examination. The size of the nodes reflects the number of publications, while the thickness of the links indicates the intensity of collaborations. Australia, Germany, and Malaysia emerge as major centers of collaboration. Australia shows a broad network of international collaborations, connecting with countries across various continents. There are also regional clusters, such as that between Malaysia and Indonesia, and specific bilateral partnerships, such as between South Africa and the United Kingdom.

The graph in Fig. 6 represents the citation network among countries. The size of the nodes corresponds to the number of citations received, while the thickness of the links indicates the frequency of citations between countries.

Australia, Germany, and Malaysia have emerged as the main centers of citations, reflecting their prominent role and influence in the global scientific landscape. The network also highlights a broad interconnection among countries, with Australia

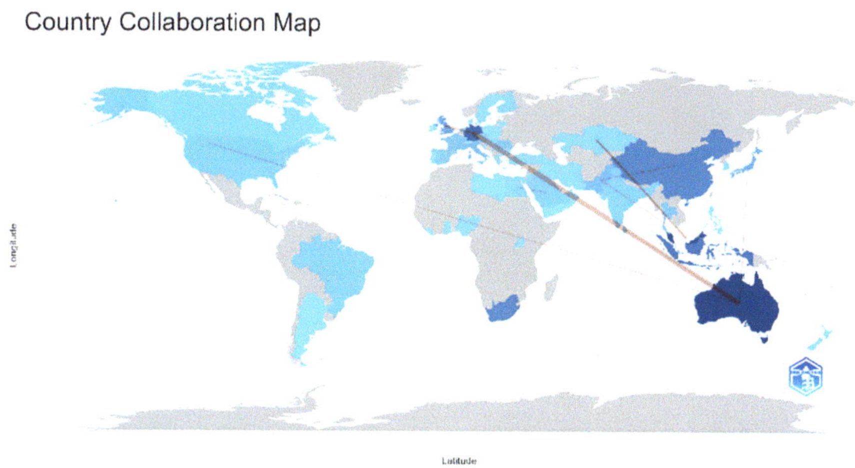

Fig. 4 Countries' collaboration world map

Fig. 5 Co-authorship network based on countries

demonstrating numerous links with various nations, including the United States, United Kingdom, and Italy, underscoring its significance as a central node in the network. Additionally, distinct regional clusters were observed, such as between Malaysia, Indonesia, and Pakistan, indicating strong citation interactions within specific geographical areas.

It is important to acknowledge that the bibliometric analysis largely relied on the corresponding author's affiliation, which may have led to an imbalance in country allocation by favoring the locations of the lead researchers over the contributions of all institutions. Furthermore, it is crucial to consider the limited number of multiple-country publications, as demonstrated in Fig. 3, particularly when the corresponding author hails from an EU country.

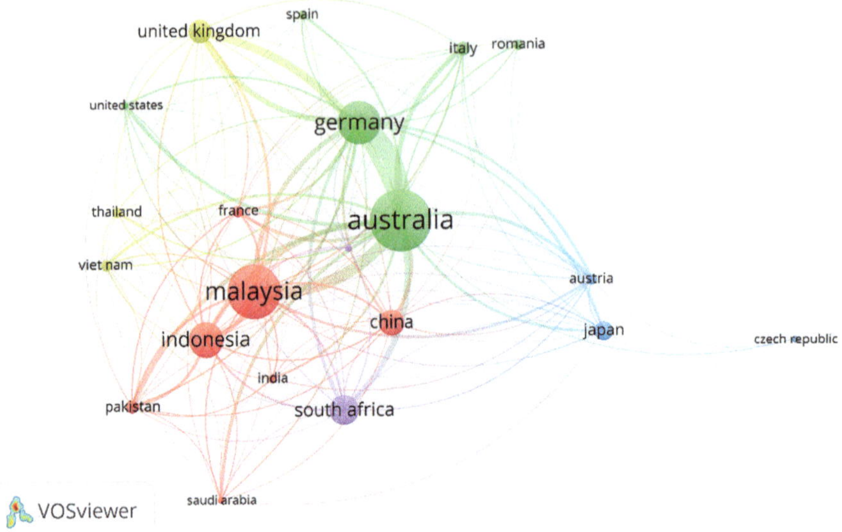

Fig. 6 Country citation network

4 Content Analysis

Content analysis, employed as a method within semi-systematic analysis, is based on clusters identified through bibliometric analysis, aiming to understand the state of the art of research in regional clusters.

- Indonesia-Malaysia: Strong regional collaboration with Pakistan, India, and Thailand, highlighting shared knowledge production.
- South Africa: A central node with significant connections to the United Kingdom and Australia, reflecting targeted and high-quality collaboration.
- Australia-Germany: An influential cluster with extensive international collaborations involving the United States, the United Kingdom, China, and various European countries, demonstrating strong capacity for attraction and influence.
- European Countries: Italy, Spain, Austria, Romania, and the United Kingdom, show intra-European collaborations and connections with other clusters, integrating into global research networks.

Subsequent sections delve into the most relevant papers for each cluster, with a particular focus on the strategies of European countries.

4.1 Indonesia-Malaysia cluster

The Indonesia-Malaysia cluster provides a comprehensive analysis of how EMA can improve corporate environmental performance. These studies delve into the relationships between EMA and organizational factors such as environmental strategies, institutional pressures, and green intellectual capital, offering a detailed perspective on how these elements collectively impact corporate sustainability practices.

The research conducted by Latan et al. (2018) offer a compelling analysis of how corporate environmental strategy coupled with management commitment and environmental uncertainty impacts environmental performance. Their study used an online survey to demonstrate that effective management can leverage EMA to significantly enhance corporate environmental outcomes [20].

Further enriching the discourse, Solovida and Latan (2017) scrutinized a conceptual framework that intricately links environmental strategies with environmental accounting and performance. Their analysis, based on data from executives at ISO 14001 certified companies in Indonesia, employs advanced statistical methods, such as partial least squares and bootstrap analysis, confirming that strategic environmental planning facilitates improved environmental results through EMA [24].

Extending the geographical scope, Latif et al. (2020) delved into the manufacturing sector in Pakistan, examining how institutional pressures shape the adoption of EMA practices. Their findings highlight the positive effects of coercive, normative, and mimetic pressures on embracing EMA, underscoring the influence of institutional frameworks on environmental accounting practices [25].

Asiaei et al. (2022) introduce a novel concept of "natural resource orchestration," investigating the symbiotic relationship between green intellectual capital and EMA. By analyzing responses from 106 CFOs in Iran, they discovered a positive correlation between the facets of green intellectual capital, human, structural, and relational, and both EMA adoption and environmental performance, suggesting that intellectual capital is a vital asset in environmental strategy [26].

Research within the Indonesia-Malaysia cluster emphasizes the empirical and theoretical advantages of survey-based methodologies. It explores frameworks, such as natural capital-based resource theory and institutional theory, enhancing theoretical understanding and offering practical insights into implementing EMA in various Asian contexts and beyond to improve environmental performance. This study contributes significantly to both the theoretical and operational aspects of environmental management, presenting extensive empirical research, practical applications, and strategic considerations for corporate sustainability practices.

4.2 *South Africa Cluster*

The principal papers from the "South Africa" cluster predominantly address EMA and its implications in business practices, addressing both theoretical and empirical aspects. The content analysis of these articles revealed a combination of theoretical research, empirical studies, case studies, and conceptual frameworks, primarily focusing on operational and strategic practices.

Several studies have concentrated on theoretical development and conceptual frameworks through the adoption of various EMA practices, such as Material Flow Cost Accounting (MFCA), Life Cycle Costing (LCC), and Activity-Based Costing (ABC) [27], while others have examined decision-making frameworks to address the environmental impacts of the coal industry in South Africa [28].

There is a significant emphasis on quantitative analyses, as evidenced by Iredele et al. (2020) and Mukwarami et al. (2023), who analyze EMA practices among listed companies in Nigeria and South Africa [29], explore the challenges in implementing environmental accounting in the manufacturing sector of emerging economies, identify barriers through a literature review, and propose a framework for cleaner production [30].

Case studies have received considerable attention in recent years. Doorasamy (2015) examined various case studies to demonstrate the role of MFCA in identifying non-productive costs and improving organizational profitability [31]. Mbedzi et al. (2018) developed an informative framework to facilitate cost savings on environmental impacts in the South African coal industry and proposed a practical and operational approach to enhance transparency in material use and identify hidden costs [32].

Overall, the papers from the South African cluster address both the operational and strategic aspects of the EMA. Operational practices are explored through the implementation and use of EMA tools, such as MFCA, LCC, and ABC, highlighting the importance of managing environmental costs and transparency in production processes. Strategic aspects are addressed through the analysis of institutional pressures, policy formulation, and proposal of conceptual frameworks to improve business practices and promote environmental sustainability.

4.3 Australia-Germany Cluster

Regarding the Australia-Germany cluster, the articles predominantly addressed EMA and its implications for sustainable business management. The content analysis of these articles revealed a blend of theoretical approaches, exploratory studies, and conceptual frameworks, with a strong emphasis on strategic rather than operational practices. A notable point is that many of the most influential articles are dated, primarily from the 2000s and the early 2010s, focusing on theoretical or exploratory analyses of the state-of-the-art.

Several articles in this cluster focus on the development of conceptual frameworks and theoretical analysis of EMA practices. Burritt et al. (2002) develop a comprehensive framework for EMA, linking business actors and EMA tools [21]. Similarly, Schaltegger and Csutora (2012) provide an overview of the state of carbon accounting in the context of sustainability management [33].

Other authors adopt an exploratory approach to investigate the use of EMA in business practices but do not delve into technical or operational applications. Ferreira et al. (2010) explored the relationship between EMA use and innovation in large Australian companies through a survey and found that EMA is positively associated with process innovation, but not with product innovation [22].

The articles from the Australia-Germany cluster are dated and predominantly deal with theoretical or exploratory analyses of the state of the art rather than detailed practical or technical applications. This emphasis on theory and exploration suggests that, while there is a solid conceptual foundation for EMA and carbon accounting, there is a lack of studies focused on specific technical and operational implementations.

4.4 European Countries

The principal articles from the remaining European countries primarily focus on environmental accounting and circular economy, blending theoretical and empirical approaches with a strong emphasis on strategic practices. Some articles provide theoretical analysis and develop conceptual frameworks to better understand environmental accounting practices within the context of a circular economy. Scarpellini et al. (2020) analyze the environmental capabilities of companies using a structural equation model, highlighting the relationship between environmental accounting practices and business performance [34]. Gibassier and Alcouffe (2018) discuss the link between environmental accounting and sustainability and propose future research directions [35]. Various studies have adopted empirical approaches to explore the implementation of circular economy practices in business. Aranda-Usón et al. (2020) analyzed the adoption process of the circular economy in a Spanish region, providing practical indicators to measure the introduction of circular practices in businesses [36]. These studies offer practical models and operational tools for resource management and measurement of environmental impacts. The article also discusses the strategic implications of environmental accounting and the circular economy. Scarpellini et al. (2019) analyze the implementation of the circular economy at the regional level, identifying barriers and suggesting incentives to promote sustainable practices. These studies emphasize the importance of corporate policies and regulations to facilitate the adoption of a circular economy and improve stakeholder relations.

Overall, these studies provide a theoretical and empirical basis for understanding the dynamics of environmental accounting and the circular economy. While some articles are predominantly theoretical, others provide operational approaches and practical tools to help businesses effectively measure and manage their environmental impact.

5 Discussion

The findings highlight a range of interesting and sometimes concerning dynamics in the field of EMA. Regarding RQ1, the most active countries in the EMA are Australia, Indonesia, Malaysia, Germany, and China, highlighting the geographical research distribution. Notably, Europe is underrepresented, with only Germany being in the top five. This absence could be concerning given the EU's ambitious environmental goals, necessitating increased efforts to integrate sustainability into business strategies [37].

5.1 *Barriers to EMA Adoption in the EU*

Regarding international collaboration (RQ2), Germany stands out as the sole European country with notable interactions, mainly with Australia. This isolation among European countries is unexpected, given the EU's push for stronger environmental sustainability commitments [38]. The limited representation of European nations in EMA research, excluding Germany, may be attributed to several structural and institutional obstacles that are analogous to those observed worldwide. Despite the dearth of studies focusing on the EU context, barriers such as inadequate government backing, financial limitations, and the lack of guidance, combined with an urgent need for heightened awareness and comprehension of EMA benefits, could be obstructing EMA implementation within the EU [39, 40]. Fahad et al.'s systematic review highlights the significance of stringent legislation and adaptable financing for SMEs in fostering EMA adoption, a development that has been mirrored in EU policy through the introduction of the Corporate Sustainability Reporting Directive (CSRD) [41]. The CSRD mandates "limited assurance" for sustainability reports and establishes the European Sustainability Reporting Standard (ESRS), specifically tailored for SMEs to facilitate compliance and comparability [42]. These legislative changes are poised to address the previously identified barriers and drive a more extensive adoption of EMA practices across European enterprises.

5.2 *Critical Issues and Future Directions in EMA Implementation*

Regarding RQ3, research in EMA within the European Union predominantly comprises theoretical papers and state-of-the-art reviews highlighting EMA's significance and applications in sustainable business management. These studies, mostly dated, focus on conceptual or exploratory analyses [22, 34–36]. Despite a strong theoretical base, more recent studies on specific technical and operational applications are lacking, which are essential for guiding businesses in practical sustainability policy implementation.

In contrast, non-European countries like Australia and Germany have developed conceptual frameworks integrating EMA and carbon accounting, yet lack research on practical applications [21, 33]. Other non-European countries, such as South Africa, Malaysia, and Indonesia, are increasingly interested in the technical aspects of EMA, including material flow cost accounting and activity-based costing [26–32].

A critical issue in the implementation of EMA is that a defensible, coherent, and complete account of sustainable development is still far off and depends on much more experimentation and imagination [35]. To date, EMA appears to be more a collection of practices already in use in traditional accounting, which suggests the need for a profound revision of EMA tools to include more effective considerations of time and space, an approach highlighted as essential by Bebbington [43]. This deconstruction of current tools should aim not only to integrate environmental considerations more thoroughly but also to facilitate transparency and accountability within environmental management.

Incorporating the research of Van der Poll [44], it is clear how the contexts of developed and developing countries differently influence the adoption of EMA practices. In developed countries, strong institutions exert isomorphic pressure that promotes the adoption of these practices, whereas in developing countries, the lower isomorphic pressure and mimetic and normative forces play a less significant role [44]. This distinction is crucial for understanding how to promote the adoption of EMA practices in a targeted manner, overcoming specific barriers and leveraging contextual drivers, ultimately contributing to sustainable development and achieving the United Nations Sustainable Development Goals.

5.3 Limitations

The study's global examination of EMA trends and cooperative patterns faces limitations that could affect the generalizability and interpretation of its findings. The underrepresentation of some regions, especially non-European ones, could distort the perceived global engagement with EMA practices. The bibliometric analysis's reliance on Scopus data might overlook pertinent studies published in non-English languages or regional journals not indexed by Scopus, potentially limiting the analysis's comprehensiveness. The study's dependence on bibliometric and semi-systematic review methods emphasizes quantitative metrics rather than research quality, which might not fully capture the research's impact or innovative aspects.

5.4 Implications and Future Directions

The results of this investigation generate significant ramifications for policy, managerial practice, and scholarship on EMA within the European Union and worldwide. From a policy standpoint, the persistent under-representation of most EU member states, Germany being the conspicuous exception, signals the need for concrete interventions that broaden participation in EMA initiatives. Legislators could, for example, introduce fiscal instruments such as subsidies or targeted tax relief to encourage firms that demonstrably integrate EMA into their decision-making. Such measures would not only accelerate the diffusion of EMA but also fortify the EU's leadership in setting environmental benchmarks at a global scale (see Table 7).

Operationally, the worldwide shift toward more demanding environmental disclosure regimes obliges European enterprises to embed EMA tools more swiftly and comprehensively into their organisational routines. Early adoption will facilitate compliance with emerging regulations while simultaneously enhancing competitive advantage in markets where sustainability credentials increasingly influence investor and consumer preferences. Yet the practical uptake of EMA still lags behind its theoretical promise, underscoring a pressing research agenda: empirical studies must move beyond abstract frameworks to examine, in situ, the organisational hurdles and performance benefits of EMA. By interrogating real-world applications, scholars can refine extant models and furnish evidence-based guidance for both managers and regulators.

Looking ahead, EU member states must renew their commitment to the systematic study and implementation of EMA, especially as the regulatory landscape evolves under instruments such as Directive 2023/2772 [5]. Universities and research centres should prioritise projects that close the gap between conceptual development and technical deployment, thereby fostering an operationally robust and technologically advanced approach to environmental accounting. Equally vital is enhanced collaboration among member countries; sharing resources, expertise, and data will enable the Union to respond to global environmental challenges with greater coordination and efficacy. Only through such a concerted effort can the European Union sustain its capacity to guide the world toward a more sustainable future.

Table 7 Regional EMA research clusters with representative studies

Cluster	Research description	Main studies
Indonesia-Malaysia	• Studies on how EMA enhances corporate environmental performance • Explore relationships between EMA, environmental strategies, and institutional pressures • Utilize surveys to provide insights in Asian contexts	Latan et al. (2018), Solovida and Latan (2017), Latif et al. (2020), Asiaei et al. (2022)
South Africa	• Theoretical and empirical focus on EMA in business practices • Emphasis on operational practices using EMA tools and strategic aspects influenced by institutional pressures • Case studies and quantitative analyses highlight challenges and propose frameworks for cleaner production	Iredele et al. (2020), Mukwarami et al. (2023), Doorasamy (2015), Mbedzi et al. (2018)
Australia-Germany	• Predominantly theoretical and exploratory studies on EMA and sustainable management • Emphasis on strategic practices with less focus on recent practical applications • Developed conceptual frameworks but highlight the need for updated practical research	Burritt et al. (2002), Schaltegger and Csutora (2012), Ferreira et al. (2010)
Other European Countries	• Focus on environmental accounting within the circular economy • Blend of theoretical and empirical studies with strategic emphasis • Provide practical tools for resource management and measuring environmental impacts • Address policies and stakeholder relations to promote sustainability	Scarpellini et al. (2020), Gibassier and Alcouffe (2018), Aranda-Usón et al. (2020)

Disclosure of Interest The authors declare that they have no financial or non-financial conflicts of interest relevant to the content of this manuscript.

References

1. Thottoli, M. (2022). Two decades of environmental accounting: A bibliometric analysis. *Institutions and Economies, 14*, 83–113. https://doi.org/10.22452/IJIE.vol14no4.4
2. Sikora, A. (2021). European Green Deal—legal and financial challenges of the climate change. *ERA Forum, 21*, 681–697. https://doi.org/10.1007/s12027-020-00637-3
3. Hahn, R., & Kühnen, M. (2013). Determinants of sustainability reporting: a review of results, trends, theory, and opportunities in an expanding field of research. *Journal of Cleaner Production, Volume, 59*, 5–21., ISSN 0959-6526. https://doi.org/10.1016/j.jclepro.2013.07.005
4. Morros, J. (2016). The integrated reporting: A presentation of the current state of art and aspects of integrated reporting that need further development. *Intangible Capital, 12*(1). https://doi.org/10.3926/ic.700
5. Commission Delegated Regulation (EU) 2023/2772 of 31 July 2023 supplementing Directive 2013/34/EU of the European Parliament and of the Council as regards sustainability reporting standards. Official Journal of the European Union, L 2772, 31 July 2023, (pp. 1–12). http://data.europa.eu/eli/reg_del/2023/2772/oj
6. Contrafatto, M. (2014). The institutionalization of social and environmental reporting: An Italian narrative. *Accounting, Organizations and Society, 39*(6), 414–432, ISSN 0361-3682. https://doi.org/10.1016/j.aos.2014.01.002
7. Nyide, C. (2019). A Qualitative investigation of the environmental management accounting practices for the optimisation of environmental costs in the South African hotel sector. https://doi.org/10.20472/BMC.2019.010.004.
8. Mochamad Fahru Komarudin Agus Hasanudin Imam Hanifah Windu Mulyasari Year: 2023 bibliometric analysis of literatures on environmental management accounting between 2017-end off Aug 2021 ICOSTELM EAI DOI: https://doi.org/10.4108/eai.4-11-2022.2328658.
9. Setiawan, D., Rahmawati, I. P., & Santoso, A. (2023). A bibliometric analysis of evolving trends in climate change and accounting research. *Cogent Business & Management, 10*(3). https://doi.org/10.1080/23311975.2023.2267233
10. Zupic, I., & Cater, T. (2015). Bibliometric methods in management and organization. *Organizational Research Methods, 18*(3), 429–472.
11. Chen, K., Zhang, Y., & Xiaolan, F. (2019). International research collaboration: An emerging domain of innovation studies? *Research Policy, 48*(1), 149–168., ISSN 0048-7333. https://doi.org/10.1016/j.respol.2018.08.005
12. Donthu, N., Kumar, S., Mukherjee, D., Pandey, N., & Lim, W. M. (2021). How to conduct a bibliometric analysis: An overview and guidelines. *Journal of Business Research, 133*, 285–296., ISSN 0148-2963. https://doi.org/10.1016/j.jbusres.2021.04.070
13. Schaltegger, S., Gibassier, D., & Zvezdov, D. (2013). Is environmental management accounting a discipline? A bibliometric literature review. *Meditari Accountancy Research, 21*(1), 4–31. https://doi.org/10.1108/medar-12-2012-0039
14. Guenther, E., Endrikat, J., & Guenther, T. W. (2016). Environmental management control systems: a conceptualization and a review of the empirical evidence. *Journal of Cleaner Production, 136*(Part A), 147–171., ISSN 0959-6526. https://doi.org/10.1016/j.jclepro.2016.02.043
15. Schotten, M., El Aisati, M., Meester, W. J. N., Steiginga, S., & Ross, C. A. (2017). In F. J. A. Cantu-Ortiz (Ed.), *A brief history of Scopus: The world's largest abstract and citation database of scientific literature in research analytics, boosting university productivity and competitiveness through scientometrics.*

16. Moral-Muñoz, J. A., Herrera-Viedma, E., Santisteban-Espejo, A., & Cobo, M. J. (2020). Software tools for conducting bibliometric analysis in science: An up-to-date review. *Profesional De La información, 29*(1). https://doi.org/10.3145/epi.2020.ene.03
17. Za, S., & Braccini, A. M. (2017). Tracing the roots of the organizational benefits of IT services. In S. Za, M. Drăgoicea, & M. Cavallari (Eds.), *Exploring services science. IESS 2017. Lecture notes in business information processing* (Vol. 279). Springer. https://doi.org/10.1007/978-3-319-56925-3_1
18. Braun, V., & Clarke, V. (2006). Using thematic analysis in psychology. *Qualitative Research in Psychology, 3*, 77–101. https://doi.org/10.1191/1478088706qp063oa
19. Snyder, H. (2019). Literature review as a research methodology: An overview and guidelines. *Journal of Business Research, 104*, 333–339., ISSN 0148-2963. https://doi.org/10.1016/j.jbusres.2019.07.039
20. Latan, H., Jabbour, C. J. C., de Sousa Jabbour, A. B. L., Wamba, S. F., & Shahbaz, M. (2018). Effects of environmental strategy, environmental uncertainty and top management's commitment on corporate environmental performance: The role of environmental management accounting. *Journal of Cleaner Production, 180*, 297–306., ISSN 0959-6526. https://doi.org/10.1016/j.jclepro.2018.01.106
21. Burritt, R. L., Hahn, T., & Schaltegger, S. (2002). Towards a comprehensive framework for environmental management accounting—links between business actors and environmental management accounting tools. *Australian Accounting Review, 12*, 39–50. https://doi.org/10.1111/j.1835-2561.2002.tb00202.x
22. Ferreira, A., Moulang, C., & Hendro, B. (2010). Environmental management accounting and innovation: An exploratory analysis. *Accounting, Auditing & Accountability Journal, 23*(7), 920–948. https://doi.org/10.1108/09513571011080180
23. Michael Hall, C. (2011). Publish and perish? Bibliometric analysis, journal ranking and the assessment of research quality in tourism. *Tourism Management, 32*(1), 16–27., ISSN 0261-5177. https://doi.org/10.1016/j.tourman.2010.07.001
24. Solovida, G. T., & Latan, H. (2017). Linking environmental strategy to environmental performance: Mediation role of environmental management accounting. *Sustainability Accounting, Management and Policy Journal, 8*(5), 595–619. https://doi.org/10.1108/SAMPJ-08-2016-0046
25. Latif, B., Mahmood, Z., Tze San, O., Mohd Said, R., & Bakhsh, A. (2020). Coercive, normative and mimetic pressures as drivers of environmental management accounting adoption. *Sustainability, 12*, 4506. https://doi.org/10.3390/su12114506
26. Asiaei, K., Bontis, N., Alizadeh, R., & Yaghoubi, M. (2022). Green intellectual capital and environmental management accounting: Natural resource orchestration in favor of environmental performance. *Business Strategy and the Environment, 31*(1), 76–93. https://doi.org/10.1002/bse.2875
27. Nyakuwanika, M., van der Poll, H. M., & van der Poll, J. A. (2021). A conceptual framework for greener goldmining through environmental management accounting practices (EMAPs): The case of Zimbabwe. *Sustainability, 13*(18), 10466. https://doi.org/10.3390/su131810466
28. Mbedzi, M. D., van der Poll, H. M., & van der Poll, J. A. (2020). Enhancing a decision-making framework to address environmental impacts of the South African coalmining industry. *Energies, 13*(18), 4897. https://doi.org/10.3390/en13184897
29. Iredele, O. O., Tankiso, M., & Adelowotan, M. O. (2020). The influence of institutional isomorphism and organisational factors on environmental management accounting practices of listed Nigerian and South African firms. *South African Journal of Accounting Research, 34*(3), 183–204. https://doi.org/10.1080/10291954.2019.1675254
30. Mukwarami, S., Nkwaira, C., & van der Poll, H. M. (2023). Environmental management accounting implementation challenges and supply chain management in emerging economies' manufacturing sector. *Sustainability, 15*(2), 1061. https://doi.org/10.3390/su15021061
31. Doorasamy, M. (2015). Theoretical developments in environmental management accounting and the role and importance of MFCA. *Foundations of Management, 7*. https://doi.org/10.1515/fman-2015-0024

32. Mbedzi, M. D., Van der Poll, H. M., & Van der Poll, J. A. (2018). An information framework for facilitating cost saving of environmental impacts in the coal mining industry in South Africa. *Sustainability, 10*(6), 1690. https://doi.org/10.3390/su10061690
33. Schaltegger, S., & Csutora, M. (2012). Carbon accounting for sustainability and management. Status quo and challenges. *Journal of Cleaner Production, 36*, 1–16., ISSN 0959-6526. https://doi.org/10.1016/j.jclepro.2012.06.024
34. Scarpellini, S., Marín-Vinuesa, L. M., Aranda-Usón, A., & Portillo-Tarragona, P. (2020). Dynamic capabilities and environmental accounting for the circular economy in businesses. *Sustainability Accounting, Management and Policy Journal, 11*(7), 1129–1158. https://doi.org/10.1108/SAMPJ-04-2019-0150
35. Gibassier, D., & Alcouffe, S. (2018). Environmental management accounting: The missing link to sustainability? *Social and Environmental Accountability Journal, 38*(1), 1–18. https://doi.org/10.1080/0969160X.2018.1437057
36. Aranda-Usón, A., Portillo-Tarragona, P., Scarpellini, S., & Llena-Macarulla, F. (2020). The progressive adoption of a circular economy by businesses for cleaner production: An approach from a regional study in Spain. *Journal of Cleaner Production, 247*, 119648., ISSN 0959-6526. https://doi.org/10.1016/j.jclepro.2019.119648
37. Goucha Soares, A. (2024). The European green deal. *Revista Jurídica Portucalense*, 44–67. https://doi.org/10.34625/issn.2183-2705(35)2024.ic-03
38. García-Sánchez, I.-M., Ortiz-Martínez, E., Marín-Hernández, S., & Aibar-Guzmán, B. (2023). How does the European Green Deal affect the disclosure of environmental information? *Corporate Social Responsibility and Environmental Management, 30*(6), 2766–2782. https://doi.org/10.1002/csr.2514
39. Nyahuna, T., Baldavoo, K., & Doorasamy, M. (2023). Barriers to implementation of environmental management accounting in South African small and medium enterprises for sustainable performance. *Indonesian Journal of Social and Environmental Issues (IJSEI), 4*(3), 258–266. https://doi.org/10.47540/ijsei.v4i3.995
40. Alkisher, A. O. (2021). The influence of technological factors on environmental management accounting adoption in Libyan oil firms. https://doi.org/10.59743/jau.v34i1.1652.
41. Javed, F., Yusheng, K., Iqbal, N., Fareed, Z., & Shahzad, F. (2022). A systematic review of barriers in adoption of environmental management accounting in Chinese SMEs for sustainable performance. *Frontiers in Public Health, 10*, 832711. https://doi.org/10.3389/fpubh.2022.832711
42. European Union. (2022). Directive (EU) 2022/2464 of the European Parliament and of the Council of 14 December 2022 amending Regulation (EU) No 537/2014, Directive 2004/109/EC, Directive 2006/43/EC and Directive 2013/34/EU, as regards corporate sustainability reporting. *Official Journal of the European Union, L, 322*, 15–74.
43. Bebbington, J., & Gray, R. (2001). An account of sustainability: Failure, success and a reconceptualization. *Critical Perspectives on Accounting, 12*(5), 557–587. https://doi.org/10.1006/cpac.2000.0450
44. Van der Poll, H. M. (2022). The barriers and drivers of environmental management accounting practices' adoption in developed and developing countries for sustainable development. *Sustainable Development, 30*(5), 1222–1234. https://doi.org/10.1002/sd.2312

Digital Innovations and Sustainability: A 5-Year Panel Analysis

Tiziano Volpentesta, Esli Spahiu, and Gianni Carvelli

Abstract This research investigates the relationship between digital innovations and sustainability performance, utilizing a firm-level, cross-industry global panel dataset from 2018 to 2022. We measure digital innovation by the number of digital patents filed, and we further capture the environmental, social, and governance (ESG) sustainability metrics. Our methodological approach employs a panel regression analysis incorporating a fixed effect model and a dynamic panel data (DPD) estimator. Our findings reveal mixed effects of digital innovation on sustainability. Specifically, the fixed effects model indicates a negative impact on environmental and governance aspects. In contrast, the dynamic estimator consistently shows a positive effect across all ESG pillars.

Keywords Digital innovation · Sustainability · ESG · Panel data · System-GMM

1 Introduction

Today's organisations are at the crossroads of two critical imperatives: navigating the always-evolving digital transformation while embracing sustainability goals [1, 2]. These demands compel organisations to engage extensively with digital inno-

T. Volpentesta (✉)
Department of Management, Luiss University, Rome, Italy
e-mail: tvolpentesta@luiss.it

E. Spahiu
Department of Management and Technology, Bocconi University, Milan, Italy
e-mail: esli.spahiu@unibocconi.it

G. Carvelli
Dipartimento di Scienze Economiche e Sociali, Università Cattolica del Sacro Cuore, Piacenza, Italy
e-mail: gianni.carvelli@unicatt.it

M. Cipriano et al. (eds.), *Technologies for Organizations and Society*,
Lecture Notes in Information Systems and Organisation 80,
https://doi.org/10.1007/978-3-032-01697-3_3

vation while endorsing sustainability within the company strategy, operations, and culture. While digital innovations offer opportunities for addressing sustainability challenges [3] by enabling smarter and optimised production processes [4], circular business models [5], and reducing resource use, their contribution to environmental, social, and economic performances is not unequivocal. Indeed, digital innovation can also undermine sustainability, leading to ethical issues [6], social injustices, or opaque resource consumption [7]. While considerable research has been conducted into conceptualizing the core digital innovation phenomenon, studies aiming to understand the complex and multifaceted relationship between digital innovation and today's most pressing sustainability issues are still nascent.

Sustainability encompasses any development that strives to satisfy the current needs without hindering the needs of future generations [8]. In the organisational realm, the Environmental, Social, and Governance (ESG) framework is the most widely used method for quantifying and assessing corporate performance in sustainability matters across environmental, social, and governance aspects [9, 10]. Research at the intersection of digital phenomena and ESG is proliferating [11–15]. However, the results are contrasting. While digital innovation has set new standards for social impact and corporate responsibilities towards sustainability [3, 16–18], the literature also reports downsides resulting from the diffusion of digital innovations [18–20]. Indeed, digital innovation has also been shown to raise ethical concerns [6], lead to excessive resource consumption, and contribute to social injustice [7]. Furthermore, it remains unclear whether digital innovations contribute positively across the Environmental (E), Social (S), or Governance (G) pillars.

Assessing the influence on Environmental (E), Social (S), and Governance (G) sustainability practices can help disentangle digital innovations' multifaceted implications for both organisations and societies at large. To pursue the call for more comprehensive studies, this paper focuses on assessing the relationship between digital innovation and sustainability. More specifically, we pose the following question: Does digital innovation impact environmental issues (as measured by the E pillar score), social issues (S pillar score), and governance issues (G pillar score) to a different extent?

To answer this research question, we retrieve a longitudinal firm-level panel dataset of cross-industry and global organisations spanning from 2018 to 2022. We collect information on yearly patenting activity, ESG ratings, and financial measures for these companies. We utilize the ORBIS database to obtain patents related to digital innovations to reflect the organisation's digital savviness by filtering patents according to their Cooperative Patent Classification (CPC) [21]. To complement patent and organisational data, we retrieve ESG ratings from the MSCI database. This allows us to assess how companies effectively manage ESG across specific E, S, and G pillar scores. To fully exploit and account for the longitudinal nature of the dataset, we employ panel data approaches in the quantitative analysis. Specifically, we estimate two models: a fixed effects model and a system GMM model [22]. The fixed effects model allows us to account for time-invariant and potentially unobserved characteristics of the firms, allowing us to assess the impact of digital innovations over time. The system GMM model addresses potential endogeneity issues by using lagged variables as instruments, providing more robust estimates. This methodological approach enables us to rigorously investigate the differential impacts of digital innovation on environmental (E), social (S), and governance (G) performance, thereby disentangling the multifaceted implications of digital innovations.

We find inconclusive effects related to the relationship between digital innovation and sustainability. Specifically, the fixed-effects model shows increased heterogeneity in the impact of digital innovation across ESG pillars, estimating a negative effect on environmental and governance aspects. In contrast, a positive and significant coefficient appears for the social pillar. This result is surprising given the research design employed. We use patent data as a proxy for digital innovation, which entails a more technical perspective. This approach typically favours digital innovation solutions focused on technical concerns such as waste management optimization, process and resource optimization. Therefore, finding significant coefficients for the social pillar suggests that digital innovations might be linked to higher social performance. When employing the dynamic estimator, we found a more consistent and positive effect across all ESG pillars, with the social pillar retaining its significance and relative strength compared to others.

With this study, we propose the following contributions. Firstly, we investigate the interconnections between digital innovation and sustainability by examining the degree to which they converge [17, 23], thereby disentangling the multifaceted implications of digital innovation. As scholars are increasingly calling for assessments of the tangible impact of digital transformation on sustainability, this study aims to provide valuable insights into these matters [18]. Moreover, to the best of our knowledge, this study is the first to use patent data as a reliable measure of digital innovativeness and intersect it with ESG metrics. Additionally, we employ a five-year longitudinal, cross-industry, and global analysis using sophisticated panel data approaches. This comprehensive methodology allows us to provide novel and robust insights into the relationship between digital innovation and sustainability.

2 Background

2.1 Digital Innovation

Digital innovations are pervasively diffusing in societies and organisations, carrying different characteristics and logic when compared to material innovations [24]. The digital objects at the core of digital innovations are more easily malleable and continuously evolving than their material counterparts. Digital innovation, even after being deployed in an organisational setting, remains always in the making, due to its proclivity to easily fit multiple contexts, scopes, users, and trajectories. As a consequence, digital innovation is characterized by a more uncertain and fluid innovation process [25–29].

In the rapidly transforming domain of digital transformation, the notion of digital innovation has surfaced as an important driving factor in reshaping organisational strategies, business models, and broader societal interactions [1, 26, 30]. By fostering digital innovation, organisations can navigate emerging challenges, drive sustainable growth, and foster progress, making it therefore an important element in steering the complexities of today's digital era [31, 32]. Moreover, a landscape continually disrupted by the emergence of new technologies like the Internet of Things, artificial intelligence, big data, and blockchain, profoundly alters the nature and expected outcomes of innovation. Hence, understanding the intricate impact of digital innovation on societal-wide matters has become increasingly paramount.

Digital innovations leverage digital technology to drive significant changes in products or operational paradigms [33]. Fichman [34] elevates the concept of digital innovation by emphasizing that not every modification qualifies as digital innovation; rather, it is the transformations necessitating substantial shifts that truly embody it. Consequently, they take an outcome view and define digital innovation as a novel product, process, or business model that demands notable adjustments and significant organisational changes propelled by information technology. Similarly, Nambisan [2] embraces both a process and outcome perspective and refers to digital innovation as the utilisation of digital technology throughout the innovation process leading to new ways of developing products and services and creating value. Henfridsson [35] on the other hand, emphasized users and consumers and underlined the need to look at digital innovation beyond the confines of organisations and industries alone but as an iterative process between the needs of users and an evolving digital landscape that demands a re-evaluation of such needs.

The initial wave of research literature on digital innovation primarily focused on the innovation processes and the information technologies involved [34]. Accordingly, the first avenues of research encompassed investigations on the antecedents and adoption [36] and the development of digital innovation [37]. More recently, there has been a shift towards additional important aspects such as digitised artefacts and service innovation [38], paradoxes and dilemmas in managing digital innovation [39]. As a result, the scope of studies on digital innovation is expanding, but is still limited in understanding the whole breadth of digital innovation due to the accelerated pace at which technologies are developing and the competitive pressure to integrate them. In terms of outcomes, most scholarly articles have been predominantly concerned with how digital innovation processes materialise digitisation [40, 41]. As a process, digital innovation has been mostly investigated based on how innovation is created [1, 33, 42].

Nevertheless, the rapidly changing nature of digital innovation processes requires more novel lenses to study the phenomena that go beyond digitisation and the accepted theories of innovation [2, 42, 43]. Although extant research focused on describing the phenomena, there is still more exploration needed to understand how it aligns with various forms of value creation [44]. Such a need can be attributed to the evolving nature of digital innovations that demand constant adaptation to ethical frameworks and policies distributed against all segments of society [29, 45]. In addition, organisations are also becoming more conscious of the need to gain new knowledge on digital innovation and its implications as a result of increasing pressure to renew their business models concerning today's most pressing issues [1]. To pursue the call for more comprehensive studies, this paper focuses on digital innovation and sustainability to better understand the relationship between these two important phenomena in today's world. Hence, studying digital innovation is paramount in understanding its multifaceted dimensions and the level of transformative impact, especially when assessed against specific sustainability indicators.

2.2 Digital Innovation and Sustainability

Organisations are embracing the strategic deployment of emerging digital innovations not only to optimize their operations but also to set new standards for social impact and corporate responsibilities [16, 17]. This shift underlines how digital innovations are steering towards pioneering innovative solutions to have a more tangible impact on society and to drive a positive change towards sustainability [30; 45]. Ultimately, organisations are recognizing that harnessing the power of digital technologies requires a more profound sense of purpose to confront critical sustainability challenges [17]. As a consequence, sustainability is moving to the forefront to address more effectively not only economic challenges but also societal and environmental ones [46–48].

Sustainability represents a holistic concept that encompasses any development that strives to satisfy the current needs without hindering the needs of future generations [8]. Organisations are increasing their focus on the importance of not only generating economic value but also addressing social and environmental challenges [49, 50]. As a result, digital innovation and digital transformation make up two persisting trends in value creation and appropriation [18, 51] that have inspired extensive research on their potential to transform the corporate world and society in general. The implementation of sustainability and digital innovation has the potential to complement each other and generate extra value for organisations [7, 52, 53]. Furthermore, a strategic blend between sustainability, technology adoption, and digitisation has already been shown to be a driving force in achieving positive environmental and societal impact [54, 55].

Nevertheless, while there is general optimism about the potential of new technologies and innovation to enhance sustainability, it is crucial to also recognise the disruptive force and adverse effects of digital innovation on sustainability [18–20]. Digital innovation poses not only opportunities but also risks to sustainability, which ought to be recognised [56]. In this regard, research shows that digital innovation could undermine sustainability by raising ethical concerns [6] and lead to excessive resource consumption and social injustice [7]. Such dual implications concerning digital innovation make it important to further investigate its interconnection with sustainability by looking at the degree to which they converge [17, 23]. Moreover, while digital innovation has out to have huge transforming power, the business world and organisations are still struggling to leverage this power to support addressing sustainability issues [57]. There remains scepticism about the tangible impact of digital transformation and innovation on sustainability that calls for more investigation [18]. From a scholarly perspective, a more effective analysis is needed to bridge the gap between the two concepts [58].

As sustainability is a multifaceted notion, there exist different indices that offer measurable variables aimed at quantifying organisations' efforts and practices. In this regard, the Environmental, Social, and Governance (ESG) framework is considered an important metric in measuring sustainability standards and corporate social performance [9, 10]. The framework stems as an evaluation tool for analysing corporate behaviour and financial performance in accordance with the sustainable development of enterprises. Two decades after their formal introduction, the ESG principles have gained considerable attention from both scholars and practitioners and have become a mainstream tool in assessing sustainability and the social impact of organisational processes and activities [59, 60]. As it concerns digital innovation, most studies have previously only looked at the ESG pillars by considering the digital technology applications in terms of digitisation [11, 15] and digital transformation [12–14]. Only recently has the literature shifted to also studying it individually in relation to ESG performance. Huang [61] showcases how digital innovation can have the most noticeable effect on ESG performance in competitive and service-oriented firms. Wang & Tang [62] infer that digital innovation has the most improving effect on the governance pillar and has stimulating consequences on the social pillar but find no evidence of boosting effects on the environmental aspect. Dai & Zhu [63] look at the role of ESG performance on green innovation and reason how the former can play a boosting role in fostering significant advancements in bridging technological innovation and environmental protection. While these studies provide a valuable initial foundation in shedding light on the role of digital innovation and ESG, it should also be noted that these investigations are based on cases originating from nation-specific databases. This highlights the need to broaden the research and understand the phenomenon from various societal landscapes and offer more applicable insights. Furthermore, given the recent emergence of the topic, the enablement of additional study contexts could also address the calls for new perspectives and analysis on the intersection between digital innovation and sustainability.

3 Methodology

3.1 Data Sample

To unpack the relationship between digital innovations and sustainability, we comprised a sample of 12,256 cross-industry and cross-country companies between 2018 and 2022 (see Appendix for more details). We draw data from two databases:

the MSCI for the sustainability indicators, and the ORBIS for organisational and patent data. The MSCI (Morgan Stanley Capital International) is a financial market data provider collecting information related to the ESG (Environmental, Social, and Governance) ratings of companies. The ORBIS database, a global database of company information provided by Bureau van Dijk (Moody's Analytics), was used to extract financial data and control variables. We merged the two databases using a fuzzy name-matching algorithm to retrieve most of the companies from both databases.

The procedure resulted in an unbalanced panel (70.89% where 100% is a fully balanced panel) of 12,256 unique firms with 43,440 firm-year observations for the analysis. The retrieved sample provides several advantages. First, it relies on patent data rather than surveys, which allows it to overcome potential respondent biases. Second, the unbalanced nature allows for mitigating organisational survivorship bias. Moreover, given that the sample comprises only listed firms, it avoids systemic differences between private and listed firms [64].

3.2 *Variable Specification*

3.2.1 ESG Ratings

To measure sustainability, we use ESG ratings as a proxy for sustainability. The ESG is a three-factor framework widely adopted to assess organisational efforts towards sustainability-related themes. The ESG framework comprehensively considers factors related to three types of sustainability issues: the environment, the social, and the governance. The environmental aspects are concerned, among others, with themes related to the preservation of natural resources and linked issues such as carbon emission, pollution, and water use. The social aspect refers to issues related to human relationships, such as rights, privacy, and inclusiveness, among others. Lastly, the governance pillar reflects sustainability themes centred around regulations, lobbying, and governance mechanisms, among others.

We chose the MSCI ESG database as it appears to be one of the most comprehensive in terms of coverage of indicators [65]. MSCI employs a rule-based method that determines the extent to which companies are exposed to, and how effectively they manage ESG risks, setting in place strategies. MSCI identifies a list of industry-specific key issues and then aggregates these issues in specific E, S, and G pillar scores. The weighted average of the score pillars comprises an overall one-to-ten rank ranging from the worst rating (0) to the best rating (10) with a continuous scale. Of note, ratings are industry-adjusted according to industry peers across markets, so that the rating does not depend on local context, and it is meaningful to compare company-level ESG across different industries [66]. Since the overall ESG score represents a unified and averaged measure of how well a company performs in E, S, or G, a company might be contributing differently to each of the sub-factors [67]. Hence, we retrieved both the unified ESG score but also the individual E, S, and G pillar components to propose a fine-grained analysis and unpack the impacts of digital innovation on the different ESG themes.

3.2.2 Digital Patents

Digital patents embody and reflect the organisational capacity to convert knowledge on digital resources (data, artefacts, software, hardware) into new-to-the-world digital innovations [13]. That is, digital patenting activity represents the firm's mastery of turning knowledge on digital activities into innovations that are deemed useful and amenable to protection. Despite the longstanding debates on patents as innovation indicators, patenting activity is a reasonable proxy for innovativeness. Indeed, a patent needs to demonstrate novelty, non-triviality, and utility to be accepted and granted protection [68, 69].

We retrieved the firm's patenting activity from the ORBIS dataset. We use the application filing date rather than the granting date to document it as early as possible [69]. Indeed, the application date is the earliest time when the innovation is ready for review, and the issue dates may vary between patent agencies and other characteristics. Consistent with previous research, we define patents as digital if they involve digital components (algorithms, software, standards, communication interfaces) at their core. The approach is in line with other studies in the Information Systems discipline [13, 21, 70]. In line with previous research, we identified patents related to the digital realm by following the Cooperative Patent Classification (CPC) patent classification system, which has been officially endorsed and supported by patent agencies since 2013 and provides a way to classify patents according to their technological functionalities. The CPC is suitable for cross-time comparison, as contrary to other classification systems, it has been retrospectively reclassified to avoid time-historic incompatibilities. Moreover, being assigned by the patent office, it avoids biases and influences from applicants.

3.2.3 Control Variables

We retrieved from the ORBIS database a wide array of control variables, commonly used in innovation studies, to account for firms and industry characteristics. As large-sized firms typically have more slack for patenting activity, we account for organisation size by retrieving the number of employees and the revenue. To control for operating performance, we retrieve Tobin's Q, which represents the extent to which the market perceives the firm to have growth potential. We retrieved R&D Intensity, which influences decisions to patent but is not related to IT [70] (Table 1).

Table 1 Variable descriptions and sources

Variable	Description	Source
Dependent variables		
ESG - overall	Score measuring the overall ESG performance	MSCI
ESG - environment	Environmental pillar score	MSCI
ESG - governance	Corporate governance pillar score	MSCI
ESG - social	Social pillar score	MSCI
Independent variable		
Digital innovation	Number of digital patents filed by the firm	ORBIS
Control variables		
Tobin's Q	Performance measure indicating firm value	ORBIS
R&D investments	Total investments in research and development activities	ORBIS
Employees	Total number of employees in the firm	ORBIS
Revenues	Total revenues generated by the firm	ORBIS

3.3 Model Specification

The investigation of our research question builds on two-panel specifications—i.e., a static regression and a dynamic model, which are defined in Eq. 1 and Eq. 2, respectively:

$$ESG_{i,t}=\beta_0+\beta_1\ln(\text{Digital Innovation})_{i,t-1}+\beta_2\ln(\text{Revenue})_{i,t-1} +\beta_3\ln(\text{TobinQ})_{i,t-1}+\beta_4\ln(\text{R\&D})_{i,t-1}+\beta_5\ln(\text{Employees})_{i,t-1}+\alpha_i +\gamma Year+\varepsilon_{i,t} \quad (1)$$

$$ESG_{i,t}=\rho ESG_{i,t-1}+\beta_0\ln(DI)_{i,t-1}+\beta_1\ln(\text{Revenue})_{i,t-1}+\beta_2\ln(\text{TobinQ})_{i,t-1} +\beta_3\ln(\text{R\&D})_{i,t-1}+\beta_4\ln(\text{Employees})_{i,t-1}+\alpha_i+\gamma Year+\varepsilon_{i,t} \quad (2)$$

Where:

- ESG: Environmental, Social, and Governance rating for firm i at time t
- ln(Digital Innovation): Natural logarithm of the number of digital patents (independent variable) filed by firm i in year t-1 (lagged by one period). The coefficient β0 captures how digital patenting activities relate to ESG performances.
- ln(Revenue) i, t − 1: Natural logarithm of revenues (control variable) for firm i at year t-1 (lagged by one period)
- ln(Tobin Q) i, t − 1: Natural logarithm of Tobin's Q (control variable) for firm i at year t-1 (lagged by one period)
- ln(R&D) i,t − 1: Natural logarithm of Research and Development Expenses (control variable) for firm i in year t-1 (lagged by one period)

- ln(Employees) i,t − 1: Natural logarithm of the number of employees (control variable) for firm i in year t-1 (lagged by one period)
- Year: Time fixed effects, with γ as the associated coefficient which represents the firm-invariant time effects
- α_i: Firm-specific fixed effects
- $\varepsilon\_(i,t)$: Error term clustered at the industry level (NACE 1)

The dependent variable ESG is our measure of sustainability performance, while the regressor DI stands to represent the organisational digital savviness. We include a set of controls, as well as firm-fixed effects captured by the individual-varying constant α_i and the time dummy to control for the temporal effects. The term ε is thus our idiosyncratic error.

The panel approach with fixed time and entity effects offers several economic and inferential advantages [71]. In other words, the specification represented in Eq. 1 is the two-way fixed effects model (2FE). Such a specification allows us to control for time and entity-invariant unobserved heterogeneity, such as unmeasured firm attributes, ultimately mitigating several sources of bias, especially, in our case, the issue of omitted variables. By using firm- and year-effects, we ensure that results are not due to differences in patentability or firm-specific time-invariant predispositions to apply for patents. Our main empirical issue is the identification of the coefficient β_0, which aims to capture the effect of changes in the digital sustainability variables on the ESG ratings. Given our objective of understanding how and whether digital innovations affect the environmental, social, or governance pillars, we propose four different models, one for the overall ESG and one for each of the three sustainability pillars, to capture any heterogeneous effects across our measures of pillars. The explanatory variables enter the model with a one-year lag to partially address potential simultaneity problems and to account for the fact that it takes longer for firms to receive the ESG rating after the application for patents.

Whilst the 2FE model is particularly appealing under the assumption of uncorrelation of the variable ESG with its own past and independence between the covariates and the current innovations in the model, some extensions are needed due to the complexities behind the relationship we are trying to investigate. For that purpose, in the second model specification (Eq. 2), we use a dynamic panel approach to account for potential endogeneity and to accommodate the autoregressive behaviour of ESG that likely characterises the true data-generating process. Considering that our panel is characterised by the condition $N > T$ and that the errors can be assumed to be orthogonal across the units, we employ the System-GMM (SGMM) estimator developed in [22, 72]. The implementation of the SGMM technique appears to be proper in our case when the response variable is modelled as autoregressive. In fact, considering that our T is fixed, applying the 2FE model to the dynamic scenario would translate into severe bias of the autoregressive variable [73]. Moreover, SGMM can be a valid candidate to tackle the endogeneity issue associated with our key independent variable, i.e., the digital patents. Moreover, it may be significantly correlated with observable or unobservable factors that affect the ESG score and that, at the same time, are not controlled in the model.

The SGMM estimator is employed as an instrument of the endogenous variables in levels of their past first differences. Thus, such a moment condition can be considered valid in our context if the lagged variations in our measure of digital patents are uncorrelated with the current unpredicted variations in the ESG scores. Moreover, the past variations of digital patents should explain their current level. Although our time dimension is limited, there might still exist the risk of internal instrument proliferation, which would weaken the instruments [74]. To avoid such a problem, we collapse the matrix of the internal instruments as suggested by Roodman [74]. Considering that all the covariates enter the model with one lag, we use as instruments the variations of the endogenous variable starting from their second lag. The variance-covariance matrix of the standard errors is adjusted by employing the procedure proposed by [75]. Since our N is large, we employ the two-step version of the SGMM technique as it gains efficiency relative to its one-step counterpart in large samples [61]. Assessing the validity of the internal instrument is a non-trivial issue. However, the outcomes of the Hansen test for the overidentifying restrictions, jointly with the results of the Arellano-Bond test for serial correlation [76], can provide useful insights into both the validity of the internal instruments and the correctness of the overall model specification. The analyses are performed using STATA 18 through the package xtabond2 proposed by [77].

4 Findings

We report the results derived from the two model specifications (Tables 2 and 3).

The tests associated with the SGMM regressions suggest that the overall performance of the models is encouraging. The presence and absence of autocorrelation

Table 2 2FE. Robust standard errors are in parentheses. *** $p < 0.01$, ** $p < 0.05$, * $p < 0.1$

	(1)	(2)	(3)	(4)
	ESG	Environment	Social	Governance
Digital innovation (ln)	0.0884***	−0.0117	0.0285*	−0.0301
	(0.0108)	(0.0110)	(0.0142)	(0.0181)
Revenue (ln; t-1)	0.0448	0.0323	−0.0184	−0.0196
	(0.0496)	(0.0396)	(0.0153)	(0.0135)
R&D (ln; t-1)	−0.0798*	−0.0525	0.0006	−0.0345
	(0.0422)	(0.0471)	(0.0235)	(0.0226)
Employees (ln; t-1)	0.2751**	0.1985**	0.1928	−0.2032
	(0.0990)	(0.0697)	(0.1182)	(0.1413)
Tobin's Q (ln; t-1)	−0.0085	−0.0204	−0.2810**	−0.1330
	(0.0981)	(0.1329)	(0.1091)	(0.1242)
Observations	3209	3209	3209	3209
No. of firms	1254	1254	1254	1254
R-squared	0.1060	0.0365	0.0646	0.1164

Table 3 SGMM. Windmeijer's SE in parentheses. *** p < 0.01, ** p < 0.05, * p < 0.1

	(1) ESG	(2) Environment	(3) Social	(4) Governance
Lagged dependent variable	0.8985*** (0.0735)	0.9130*** (0.0547)	0.9390***(0.1112)	0.7576*** (0.0832)
Digital innovation (ln)	0.2103 (0.1803)	0.0729 (0.1343)	0.2626* (0.1516)	0.0012 (0.1494)
Revenue (ln; t-1)	0.0665 (0.0698)	0.0393 (0.0539)	0.0948 (0.0590)	−0.0358 (0.0562)
R&D (ln; t-1)	−0.0947 (0.0778)	−0.0498 (0.0611)	−0.1072 (0.0677)	−0.0021 (0.0651)
Employees (ln; t-1)	−0.0636 (0.0912)	0.0010 (0.0661)	−0.1270* (0.0767)	0.0245 (0.0733)
Tobin's Q (ln; t-1)	0.0652 (0.0743)	0.1301** (0.0544)	−0.0260 (0.0589)	0.0987 (0.0614)
Observations	3213	3213	3213	3213
No. of firms	1255	1255	1255	1255
No. of instruments	14	14	14	14
AR(1)p-value	0.0000	7.65e-08	4.23e-08	0.0000
AR(2)p-value	0.3910	0.0569	0.1050	0.3160
Hansen J- test(p-value)	0.00123	0.2200	0.0549	0.0538

of orders one and two, respectively, indicate that the model specification properly tackles any autocorrelation issue. Except for the regression reported in column one, the Hansen test of overidentifying restrictions rejects the null hypothesis of no validity of the internal instruments and, at the same time, its p-values are not too high, which would be a sign of trouble rather than strong evidence against the null hypothesis [77]. The number of instruments remains well below the number of groups across all the specifications, thus implying that our instrumentation process is not affected by over-instrumentation issues.

5 Discussion

The rapidly proliferating implications of digital innovation for organisations and societies call for novel lenses to study the phenomena that extend beyond mere digitisation [2, 42, 43]. The intersection of sustainability and digital innovation has far-reaching implications and entails unique opportunities. Literature has investigated how digital innovations resulted in multifaceted consequences, both with positive and negative implications. Beyond local and context-specific claims, it is crucial to assess the average effect digital innovation might have on sustainability. This broader perspective enables a more comprehensive understanding of the overall impact of digital innovation on sustainability.

The fixed effects model (2FE) shows mixed results regarding the impact of digital innovations across ESG pillars. The coefficients of our main variable of interest are highly significant for overall ESG performance. However, despite its high significance level, the magnitude of the coefficient (0.0884) is relatively modest. This indicates that while digital innovation appears to be positively associated with overall ESG performance, its influence is not overwhelming. Contrary to our expectations, the coefficient for environmental performance is negative (−0.0117) and not statistically significant. Given that we are dealing with patent data and, hence, technical innovations, we expected to find a stronger effect on environmental concerns, as patents are more likely to have technical implications (e.g., waste reduction, process optimization) than societal or governance ones. For social performance, the coefficient of digital innovation is 0.0285, which is moderately significant at the 10% level. This is surprising as it indicates that digital innovation positively influences social performance aspects, such as community engagement, employee relations, and diversity. For the governance performance pillar, the coefficient for digital innovation is −0.0301 and not statistically significant, implying that governance practices do not appear to be significantly influenced by digital innovation.

The second model specification (SGMM) reveals a strong persistence of ESG scores over time, indicating that ESG scores largely depend on previous realizations. Furthermore, results show a generally positive influence of digital innovation across ESG pillars, in contrast to the 2FE model. In the overall ESG model, the coefficient for digital innovation indicates a positive relationship, although not statistically significant, suggesting that while digital innovation may contribute to ESG performance, the evidence is not strong enough to be conclusive. In the environmental model, the coefficient for digital innovation is also positive but not significant, while the social model shows a significant coefficient, indicating that digital innovation positively influences social performance. Lastly, the governance model presents a positive but not significant coefficient, suggesting no strong evidence that digital innovation impacts governance performance. Overall, while digital innovation appears to positively influence the social aspects of ESG, its effect on environmental and governance aspects remains inconclusive.

As with any study, this research has limitations. Our analysis primarily relied on patent data as a proxy for innovation, which, while common in innovation research [69], may not fully capture all types of innovation or the adoption of digital technologies that can still have implications for sustainability. Moreover, previous studies have pointed out that the propensity to file patents varies considerably across industries [78], which could introduce biases into our sample composition and affect the generalizability of our findings. Additionally, another potential limitation of this study arises from the variability in ESG ratings across different data sources. As noted by [65], there are significant divergences in ESG ratings, which may influence the consistency and reliability of sustainability measurements.

To address these limitations, future research could enhance and test the robustness of our findings by incorporating alternative proxies for digital innovation, such as annual investments in information technology (IT). Additionally, applying industry-specific weights could better account for the varying importance of patents across sectors. Lastly, cross-validating with other ESG databases would further strengthen the reliability of sustainability assessments, providing a more comprehensive view of the impact of digital innovation on sustainability.

6 Conclusion

To explore the interplay between sustainability and digital innovation, we utilized a global, cross-industry panel dataset and applied robust fixed-effects and dynamic panel data models. Our fixed effect model specification shows heterogeneous results across ESG pillars, presenting both negative and positive coefficients. In contrast, the second model specification supports the perspective that digital innovation has the potential to complement sustainability efforts and generate additional value for organisations and broader societies [52, 53, 79]. Acknowledging the limitations of this study, we encourage future research to untangle the complex relationship between sustainability and digital technologies.

Acknowledgments This study was funded by the European Union - NextGenerationEU, Mission 4, Component 2, in the framework of the GRINS- Growing Resilient, INclusive and Sustainable project (GRINS PE00000018—CUP B43C22000760006). The views and opinions expressed are solely those of the authors and do not necessarily reflect those of the European Union, nor can the European Union be held responsible for them.

Disclosure of Interests The authors have no competing interests to declare that are relevant to the content of this article.

Appendix

Data Sources MSCI (Morgan Stanley Capital International) is an independent provider of financial market data. MSCI ESG (Environmental, Social, and Governance) datasets refer to information related to the ESG performance of companies. ORBIS is a global database of company information. It is provided by Bureau van Dijk, a Moody's Analytics company. ORBIS includes financial data, corporate structures, ownership details, and various financial ratios (Tables 4 and 5).

Table 4 Dependent variable descriptive statistics

Variable	Obs.	Mean	Std. dev.	Min	Max
ESG	43,440	4.578645	2.252473	0	10
Environment	43,440	4.772788	2.205408	0	10
Social	43,440	4.414705	1.628592	0	10
Governance	43,440	4.944296	1.658693	0	9.5

Table 5 Independent variable descriptive statistics

Statistic	DI	R&D	Tobin's Q	Age	Employees	Revenues
Mean	23	15,632,688	1.5	42.8	17,106	2,449,705,251
N	43,440	30,029	41,200	43,023	36,860	39,913
Max	19,508	19,589,430,199	100	370	2,300,000	572,754,000,000
Min	0	0	0	1	0	0
SD	345	311,108,664	2.8	35.8	52,456	12,727,530,073
Mean	23	15,632,688	1.5	42.8	17,106	2,449,705,251

Panel Data Descriptive Statistics There are 43,440 time-by-individual observations, covering 12,256 unique individuals. The time dimension spans from 2018 to 2022, with a maximum range of 5 years. On average, each individual is observed for 3.54 periods. The panel is 70.89% complete, where 100% would indicate a fully balanced panel. On average, each individual has 0.01 gaps in their observation periods, with an average gap size of 1.29 years. The largest observed gap is 3 years.

References

1. Kohli, R., & Melville, N. P. (2019). Digital innovation: A review and synthesis. *Information Systems Journal, 29*(1), 200–223.
2. Nambisan, S., Lyytinen, K., Majchrzak, A., & Song, M. (2017). Digital innovation management. *MIS Quarterly, 41*(1), 223–238.
3. Kotlarsky, J., Oshri, I., & Sekulic, N. (2023). Digital sustainability in information systems research: Conceptual foundations and future directions. *Journal of the Association for Information Systems, 24*, 936–952. https://doi.org/10.17705/1jais.00825
4. Aubert, B. A., Schroeder, A., & Grimaudo, J. (2012). IT as enabler of sustainable farming: An empirical analysis of farmers' adoption decision of precision agriculture technology. *Decision Support Systems, 54*(1), 510–520. https://doi.org/10.1016/j.dss.2012.07.002
5. Akarsu, T. (2023). Digital transformation towards a sustainable circular economy: Can it be the way forward? *Journal of Information Technology Teaching Cases*, 20438869231178036. https://doi.org/10.1177/20438869231178036
6. De Moya, J.-F., & Pallud, J. (2020). From panopticon to heautopticon: A new form of surveillance introduced by quantified-self practices. *Information Systems Journal, 30*(6), 940–976. https://doi.org/10.1111/isj.12284
7. Sedlmeir, J., Buhl, H. U., Fridgen, G., & Keller, R. (2020). The energy consumption of blockchain technology: Beyond myth. *Business and Information Systems Engineering, 62*(6), 599–608. https://doi.org/10.1007/s12599-020-00656-x
8. Brundtland Commission. (1987). Opening address by Gro Harlem Brundtland on the occasion of the launch of the report "Our Common Future", London, England, 27 April 1987. *World Commission on Environment and Development.*
9. Friede, G., Busch, T., & Bassen, A. (2015). ESG and financial performance: Aggregated evidence from more than 2000 empirical studies. *Journal of Sustainable Finance & Investment, 5*(4), 210–233.
10. Halbritter, G., & Dorfleitner, G. (2015). The wages of social responsibility—where are they? A critical review of ESG investing. *Review of Financial Economics, 26*, 25–35.

11. Eliwa, Y., Aboud, A., & Saleh, A. (2021). ESG practices and the cost of debt: Evidence from EU countries. *Critical Perspectives on Accounting, 79*, 102097.
12. Fang, M., Nie, H., & Shen, X. (2023). Can enterprise digitization improve ESG performance? *Economic Modelling, 118*, 106101.
13. Hanelt, A., Firk, S., Hildebrandt, B., & Kolbe, L. M. (2021). Digital M&A, digital innovation, and firm performance: An empirical investigation. *European Journal of Information Systems, 30*(1), 3–26. https://doi.org/10.1080/0960085X.2020.1747365
14. Hu, J., Han, Y., & Zhong, Y. (2023). How corporate digital transformation affects corporate ESG performance. *Indian Economic Review, 54*(1), 105–123.
15. Mu, W., Liu, K., Tao, Y., & Ye, Y. (2023). Digital finance and corporate ESG. *Finance Research Letters, 51*, 103426.
16. Di Vaio, A., Palladino, R., Pezzi, A., & Kalisz, D. E. (2021). The role of digital innovation in knowledge management systems: A systematic literature review. *Journal of Business Research, 123*, 220–231.
17. George, G., Merrill, R. K., & Schillebeeckx, S. J. (2021). Digital sustainability and entrepreneurship: How digital innovations are helping tackle climate change and sustainable development. *Entrepreneurship Theory and Practice, 45*(5), 999–1027.
18. Guandalini, I. (2022). Sustainability through digital transformation: A systematic literature review for research guidance. *Journal of Business Research, 148*, 456–471.
19. Andriushchenko, K., Buriachenko, A., Rozhko, O., Lavruk, O., Skok, P., Hlushchenko, Y., Kondarevych, V.: Peculiarities of sustainable development of enterprises in the context of digital transformation (2020).
20. Flyverbom, M., Deibert, R., & Matten, D. (2019). The governance of digital technology, big data, and the internet: New roles and responsibilities for business. *Business & Society, 58*(1), 3–19.
21. Bockelmann, T., Werder, K., Recker, J., Lehmann, J., & Bendig, D. (2024). Configuring alliance portfolios for digital innovation. *The Journal of Strategic Information Systems, 33*(1), 101808. https://doi.org/10.1016/j.jsis.2023.101808
22. Arellano, M., & Bover, O. (1995). Another look at the instrumental variable estimation of error-components models. *Journal of Econometrics, 68*(1), 29–51.
23. Mäkitie, T., Hanson, J., Damman, S., & Wardeberg, M. (2023). Digital innovation's contribution to sustainability transitions. *Technology in Society, 73*, 102255.
24. Orlikowski, W. J., & Iacono, C. S. (2001). Research commentary: Desperately seeking the "IT" in IT research—a call to theorizing the IT artifact. *Information Systems Research, 12*(2), 121–134.
25. Faulkner, P., & Runde, J. (2019). Theorizing the digital object. *Management Information Systems Quarterly, 43*(4), 1278–1302. https://doi.org/10.25300/MISQ/2019/13136
26. Hanseth, O., & Lyytinen, K. (2010). Design theory for dynamic complexity in information infrastructures: The case of building internet. *Journal of Information Technology, 25*(1), 1–19. https://doi.org/10.1057/jit.2009.19
27. Kallinikos, J., Aaltonen, A., & Marton, A. (2013). The ambivalent ontology of digital artifacts. *Management Information Systems Quarterly, 37*(2), 357–370. https://doi.org/10.25300/MISQ/2013/37.2.02
28. Lyytinen, K., Yoo, Y., & Boland, R. J., Jr. (2016). Digital product innovation within four classes of innovation networks. *Information Systems Journal, 26*(1), 47–75.
29. Nambisan, S., Lyytinen, K., & Yoo, Y. (2020). Digital innovation: Towards a transdisciplinary perspective. In *Handbook of digital innovation* (pp. 2–12). Edward Elgar Publishing.
30. Heikka, J., Baskerville, R., & Siponen, M. (2006). A design theory for secure information systems design methods. *Journal of the Association for Information Systems, 7*(11), 31.
31. Akter, S., Michael, K., Uddin, M. R., McCarthy, G., & Rahman, M. (2022). Transforming business using digital innovations: The application of AI, blockchain, cloud and data analytics. *Annals of Operations Research*, 1–33.
32. Nylén, D., & Holmström, J. (2015). Digital innovation strategy: A framework for diagnosing and improving digital product and service innovation. *Business Horizons, 58*(1), 57–67.

33. Yoo, Y., Lyytinen, K.J., Boland, R.J., Berente, N.: The next wave of digital innovation: Opportunities and challenges: A report on the research workshop 'Digital Challenges in Innovation Research' (2010).
34. Fichman, R. G., Dos Santos, B. L., & Zheng, Z. (2014). Digital innovation as a fundamental and powerful concept in the information systems curriculum. *MIS Quarterly, 38*(2), 329–A15.
35. Henfridsson, O., Nandhakumar, J., Scarbrough, H., & Panourgias, N. (2018). Recombination in the open-ended value landscape of digital innovation. *Information and Organization, 28*(2), 89–100.
36. Fichman, R. G. (2004). Going beyond the dominant paradigm for information technology innovation research: Emerging concepts and methods. *Journal of the Association for Information Systems, 5*(8), 1.
37. Markus, M. L., Majchrzak, A., & Gasser, L. (2002). A design theory for systems that support emergent knowledge processes. *MIS Quarterly*, 179–212.
38. Nambisan, S. (2013). Information technology and product/service innovation: A brief assessment and some suggestions for future research. *Journal of the Association for Information Systems, 14*(4), 1.
39. Tilson, D., Lyytinen, K., & Sørensen, C. (2010). Research commentary—digital infrastructures: The missing IS research agenda. *Information Systems Research, 21*(4), 748–759.
40. Lee, J., & Berente, N. (2012). Digital innovation and the division of innovative labor: Digital controls in the automotive industry. *Organization Science, 23*(5), 1428–1447.
41. Majchrzak, A., & Malhotra, A. (2017). Effect of knowledge sharing trajectories on innovative outcomes in temporary online crowds. *Information Systems Research*. https://doi.org/10.1286/isre.2016.0669
42. Hund, A., Drechsler, K., Reibenspiess, V. A. (2019). The current state and future opportunities of digital innovation: A literature review.
43. Svahn, F., Mathiassen, L., & Lindgren, R. (2017). Embracing digital innovation in incumbent firms. *MIS Quarterly, 41*(1), 239–254.
44. Frey, J., Holotiuk, F., & Beimborn, D. (2020). Debating digital innovation: A literature review on realizing value from digital innovation. *Wirtschaftsinformatik (Zentrale Tracks)*, 812–827.
45. Nambisan, S. (2018). Architecture vs. ecosystem perspectives: Reflections on digital innovation. *Information and Organization, 28*(2), 104–106.
46. Cillo, V., Petruzzelli, A. M., Ardito, L., & Del Giudice, M. (2019). Understanding sustainable innovation: A systematic literature review. *Corporate Social Responsibility and Environmental Management, 26*(5), 1012–1025.
47. Schneider, S. (2019). The impacts of digital technologies on innovating for sustainability. In *Innovation for sustainability: Business transformations towards a better world*. (pp. 415–433).
48. Shahzad, M., Qu, Y., Zafar, A. U., Rehman, S. U., & Islam, T. (2020). Exploring the influence of knowledge management process on corporate sustainable performance through green innovation. *Journal of Knowledge Management, 24*(9), 2079–2106.
49. Rauter, R., Jonker, J., & Baumgartner, R. J. (2017). Going one's own way: Drivers in developing business models for sustainability. *Journal of Cleaner Production, 140*, 144–154.
50. Starik, M., & Kanashiro, P. (2013). Toward a theory of sustainability management: Uncovering and integrating the nearly obvious. *Organization and Environment, 26*(1), 7–30.
51. Castro, G. D. R., Fernandez, M. C. G., & Colsa, A. U. (2021). Unleashing the convergence amid digitalization and sustainability towards pursuing the sustainable development goals (SDGs): A holistic review. *Journal of Cleaner Production, 280*, 122204.
52. Brenner, B., & Hartl, B. (2021). The perceived relationship between digitalization and ecological, economic, and social sustainability. *Journal of Cleaner Production, 315*, 128128.
53. Chauhan, C., Parida, V., & Dhir, A. (2022). Linking circular economy and digitalization technologies: A systematic literature review of past achievements and future promises. *Technological Forecasting and Social Change, 177*, 121508.
54. Martínez-Peláez, R., Ochoa-Brust, A., Rivera, S., Félix, V. G., Ostos, R., Brito, H., & Mena, L. J. (2023). Role of digital transformation for achieving sustainability: Mediated role of stakeholders, key capabilities, and technology. *Sustainability, 15*(14), 11221.

55. Piccarozzi, M., Silvestri, C., Aquilani, B., & Silvestri, L. (2022). Is this a new story of the 'Two Giants'? A systematic literature review of the relationship between industry 4.0, sustainability and its pillars. *Technological Forecasting and Social Change, 177*, 121511.
56. Kunkel, S., & Matthess, M. (2020). Digital transformation and environmental sustainability in industry: Putting expectations in Asian and African policies into perspective. *Environmental Science & Policy, 112*, 318–329.
57. von Kutzschenbach, M., & Daub, C. H. (2020). Digital transformation for sustainability: A necessary technical and mental revolution. In *New trends in business information systems and technology: Digital innovation and digital business transformation* (pp. 179–192). Springer.
58. El Hilali, W., El Manouar, A., & Idrissi, M. A. J. (2020). Reaching sustainability during a digital transformation: A PLS approach. *International Journal of Innovation Science, 12*(1), 52–79.
59. Li, T. T., Wang, K., Sueyoshi, T., & Wang, D. D. (2021). ESG: Research progress and future prospects. *Sustainability, 13*(21), 11663.
60. Widyawati, L. (2020). A systematic literature review of socially responsible investment and environmental social governance metrics. *Business Strategy and the Environment, 29*(2), 619–637.
61. Huang, Q., Fang, J., Xue, X., & Gao, H. (2023). Does digital innovation produce better ESG performance? An empirical test of Shenzhen a-listed firms in China. Empir. Test Shenzhen a-listed firms China.
62. Wang, Z., & Tang, P. (2024). Substantive digital innovation or symbolic digital innovation: Which type of digital innovation is more conducive to corporate ESG performance? *International Review of Economics and Finance.*
63. Dai, J., & Zhu, Q. (2024). ESG performance and green innovation in a digital transformation perspective. *American Journal of Economics and Sociology, 83*(1), 263–282.
64. Miroshnychenko, I., Miller, D., De Massis, A., & Le Breton-Miller, I. (2024). Are family firms green? *Small Business Economics*. https://doi.org/10.1007/s11187-024-00907-1
65. Berg, F., Kölbel, J. F., & Rigobon, R. (2022). Aggregate confusion: The divergence of ESG ratings. *Review of Finance, 26*(6), 1315–1344. https://doi.org/10.1093/rof/rfac033
66. Crace, L., & Gehman, J. (2023). What really explains ESG performance? Disentangling the asymmetrical drivers of the triple bottom line. *Organization and Environment, 36*(1), 150–178.
67. Humphrey, J. E., Lee, D. D., & Shen, Y. (2012). The independent effects of environmental, social and governance initiatives on the performance of UK firms. *Australian Journal of Management, 37*(2), 135–151. https://doi.org/10.1177/0312896211410081
68. Hagedoorn, J., & Cloodt, M. (2003). Measuring innovative performance: Is there an advantage in using multiple indicators? *Research Policy, 32*(8), 1365–1379. https://doi.org/10.1016/S0048-7333(02)00137-3
69. Li, G. Y., Ascani, A., & Iammarino, S. (2024). The material basis of modern technologies. A case study on rare metals. *Research Policy, 53*(1), 104914. https://doi.org/10.1016/j.respol.2023.104914
70. Bendig, D., Wagner, R., Piening, E.P., Foege, J.N.: Attention to digital innovation: Exploring the impact of a chief information officer in the top management team (2023).
71. Mundlak, Y. (1978). On the pooling of time series and cross section data. *Econometrica*, 69–85.
72. Blundell, R., & Bond, S. (1998). Initial conditions and moment restrictions in dynamic panel data models. *Journal of Econometrics, 87*(1), 115–143.
73. Nickell, S. (1981). Biases in dynamic models with fixed effects. *Econometrica*, 1417–1426.
74. Roodman, D. (2009). A note on the theme of too many instruments. *Oxford Bulletin of Economics and Statistics, 71*(1), 135–158.
75. Windmeijer, F. (2005). A finite sample correction for the variance of linear efficient two-step GMM estimators. *Journal of Econometrics, 126*(1), 25–51.
76. Arellano, M., & Bond, S. (1991). Some tests of specification for panel data: Monte Carlo evidence and an application to employment equations. *The Review of Economic Studies, 58*(2), 277–297.

77. Roodman, D. (2009). How to do xtabond2: An introduction to difference and system GMM in Stata. *The Stata Journal, 9*(1), 86–136.
78. Park, Y., Yoon, B., & Lee, S. (2005). The idiosyncrasy and dynamism of technological innovation across industries: Patent citation analysis. *Technology in Society, 27*(4), 471–485. https://doi.org/10.1016/j.techsoc.2005.08.003
79. Seele, P., & Lock, I. (2017). The game-changing potential of digitalization for sustainability: Possibilities, perils, and pathways. *Sustainability Science, 12*, 183–185.

Metaverse: An Environmental Sustainability Tool?

Sabrina Bonomi and Michelle Grillo

Abstract To be genuinely competitive today, organizations cannot ignore ethical issues and their impact on the environment and the community. In the fashion industry specifically, the issue of sustainability has become central as the socio-environmental impact of the industry is enormous. The fast fashion model adopted by so many companies operating on the global market is the exact opposite of the ethical dimension of fashion that has been needed in recent years. Can innovation and the opportunities the Metaverse offers be the way to a more sustainable fashion? In recent years, many start-ups have sprung up that exclusively produce digital fashion, and many other companies whose core business is mainly in real life (IRL) have integrated digital fashion into their business strategies. Through the investigation of four case studies, the paper aims to investigate the lights and shadows of digital fashion in the Metaverse, trying to clarify whether this model is compatible with the need for a more sustainable fashion, especially from an environmental point of view.

Keywords Metaverse · Fashion industry · Digital transformation · Sustainability

1 Introduction

Organizations have the power to adapt business models to innovation, which consequently impacts various internal aspects of the organization, changing internal functions and processes, and the general environment. To be truly competitive, they must act with economic, environmental, and social sustainability in mind [1].

In the specific case of fashion companies, the issue of environmental protection has become central. Indeed, the textile and clothing industry occupies a large share of the global economy, both in terms of employment and investment [2]; it

S. Bonomi (✉) · M. Grillo
eCampus University, Novedrate, CO, Italy
e-mail: sabrina.bonomi@uniecampus.it; michelle.grillo@studenti.uniecampus.it

M. Cipriano et al. (eds.), *Technologies for Organizations and Society*,
Lecture Notes in Information Systems and Organisation 80,
https://doi.org/10.1007/978-3-032-01697-3_4

represents the third largest manufacturing industry in the world, after automotive and electronics [3]. However, it remains among the most polluting sectors after oil due to its significant consumption of water, use of chemicals, and waste generation [4].

The COVID-19 pandemic has and made even more urgent the need to redesign the future according to a radical rethinking and re-founding of values such as caring for people, time of life, priorities in production choices [5]; in other words, to give a soul to business' [6]. Today, there is an increasing need for fashion production not to clash with the values of social life to achieve a balance between sustainability and commercial pressures [7]. From an environmental point of view, which is the focus of this work, according to the U.N. report, the fashion industry contributes around 10% of global greenhouse gas emissions. It produces around 20% of global wastewater [8]. Moreover, the fast fashion model that has been imposing itself in recent years and carried out by so many companies operating on the global market is the exact opposite of the ethical dimension of fashion that has been needed in recent years [4]. It is estimated that 85% of textiles are thrown into landfills yearly [9] and has a negative impact on the environment because, among other things, many of the clothes produced in these commercial models contain plastic fibres [10].

Emissions are expected to increase by 30% by 2030 [11], and those most affected by the consequent devastation of climate change will be countries such as Bangladesh, China, India and Vietnam that play a central function in the value chain, exporting an estimated $65 billion worth of clothing [12].

As a sublimated expression of the most advanced capitalism, fashion can also question itself [13]. Last December 2023, the fashion industry renewed its commitment to sustainability by joining the Cop28 in Dubai on climate change[1]. The assessment made during Cop 28 highlighted the need to reduce global gas emissions by 2023 and by 60 percent by 2050; these plans follow on from the Glasgow Plan of 2021, which set the fashion industry's goals to tackle climate change by zero emissions by 2050 [14]; to do this, fashion companies need to develop and implement capabilities that can create alternative business models to reduce environmental impact [7].

In this context, technology and innovation drive strategic change forces and enable organizations to adapt to the global environment [15]. According to Kohli and Merville [16], digital transformation concerns adopting technologies within business operations to transform physical and digital processes. Digital transformation in the fashion industry, mainly digital fashion, appears to realize the dream of fashion that can cut costs and waste by being more sustainable.

With the emergence of the Metaverse, we are witnessing a new way of expressing and experiencing fashion. Thanks to the technology of augmented reality (A.R.), virtual reality (V.R.), and extended reality (X.R.) technologies, in recent years, we are facing a dematerialization of the fashion industry\vadjust{\pagebreak} and its production stages, which should reduce negative impacts on both the environment

[1] https://www.consilium.europa.eu/it/policies/climate-change/paris-agreement/cop28/.

and the community. According to Periyasamy et al., the Metaverse has the potential to promote innovation in sustainable fashion [2].

This perspective suggests that, thanks to the adaptability and personalization of digital content, it will be possible to hyper-personalize the product, promptly responding to customers' demands and thus reducing the global fashion overpopulation, which one study estimates at around 27% [17]. Digital fashion is expected to enhance traceability in the supply chain, fully meeting demand and optimising the use of raw materials. Furthermore, considering that global polyester fiber production reached 63.3 million metric tonnes by 2022 [18], digital fashion could significantly reduce wasted energy, water, and chemicals, leaving a 97% smaller CO2 footprint [19].

From 2019, many start-ups have sprung up that exclusively produce digital fashion, such as the Dutch The Fabricant and the Americans RTFKD and DressX; the latter, in particular, show a clear vocation of sustainability, enunciated by the slogan Don't shop less, shop digital fashion [20], with a clear invitation to keep consumption hight while paying attention to the issue of sustainability.

A narrative that looks at digital as a viable route to zero-impact fashion but at the same time one that does not stop the economy around it, continuing to satisfy the need to consume fashion.

However, what we are witnessing today is a use of the Metaverse by the fashion industry, mainly oriented toward marketing and communication, instead of an actual digitalization process to increase sustainability [2], with the danger of being faced with classic greenwashing [21] or, in the case of social, "soulwashing". One wonders, in fact, how far this narrative is reflected in reality.

Considering the growing importance of sustainability in the fashion industry, and recognizing that it is a widely debated field with extensive literature addresses its economic, social, and environmental aspects, this paper aims to explore both the positive and negative facets of digital fashion in the metaverse. The goal is to assess how organizations, society, and the environmental can genuinely benefit from this emerging trend. While keeping in mind the threefold nature of sustainability, and considering the vastness of the topic, this exploratory study specifically on the environmental aspect, given the broad scope of topic. Specifically, we will try to answer the following research question: if the digital fashion model is destined to grow [22], how much will the sector's sustainability improve at an environmental level?

This paper contributes to the existing literature on Metaverse-oriented business models by examining whether those carried out by fashion organizations contribute to environmental sustainability and is structured as follows: after a literature review, the case studies Adidas, Dolce & Gabbana, DressX, The Fabricant will be examined, adopting a mixed qualitative methodology that combines the multiple case study techniques, i.e., an empirical investigation that aims to investigate a contemporary phenomenon in its real-world context, with the use of various sources of evidence [23], with a netnographic analysis [24, 25]. In particular, business models will be investigated to analyze mechanisms for creating and capturing value

[26] and determine whether they improve environmental sustainability. At the end, conclusions with limitations and implications of the study will be presented.

2 Theoretical Background

The tragedy of the commons [27] and the effect of climate change are increasingly important, and the issue of environmental sustainability in the fashion industry has become a priority. In recent years, there has been a visible green strand institutionalized by the LVMH group, which implemented a series of procedures inspired by eco-responsibility in the 1990s, well in advance of the recent focus of the issue [14].

Considering the growing attention and topicality of the topic, academia is also increasingly focusing on the different aspects of sustainability in the fashion industry by linking it to innovation. Cutting-edge resources can improve sustainability by offering different solutions for production cycles, maximizing the use of already utilized resources, and thus reducing the extraction of raw materials [28].

As Karaosman [7] noted, environmental practices by organizations are mostly product-oriented through the use of biological materials. Reuter [29] notes that from a sustainability perspective, business models should not be limited to recycling or reuse but should also address resource efficiency to avoid waste. For example, the article by Wagner et al. [30] examines the possibility and challenges of sustainable value creation by addressing the issue of Digital Twins (DTs) to virtually test fashion collections, thus avoiding the use and waste of raw materials. D.T.s are exceptionally functional because their use allows for real-time data feedback, which enables modification directly at the design stage. Environmental pioneer Viktor Papanek [31] argues that thinking about what you design and why is the basis of ethical thinking that looks at sustainability.

However, the topic of sustainability is much broader. Sustainable innovation is a systemic approach that integrates all levels of the company, ranging from products to technology to services to stakeholder relations [32]. According to Brezet and van Hemel [33], the levels of innovation are as follows: incremental, i.e., making small improvements to existing products; redesigning existing products; product alternatives, i.e., new product or service concepts; and system innovation and design for a sustainable society.

Today, fashion efforts in the Metaverse are mainly oriented towards the third level, with the risk, very often, of being faced with real greenwashing operations [21].

Companies can often use the sustainability theme as a marketing ploy to court [34], applying labels indicating the percentage of recycled material in a product without adopting a genuinely sustainable vision and design of the various processes. Marketing and communication, moreover, continue to be the aspects that find easy application of the Metaverse to influence brand value and purchase intention [35–39].

The same analyses on business models applied to the Metaverse are more concerned with strategic aspects to increase brand value [40, 41]. Periyasami et al.[42] dwell on the use of AR/VR filters to reduce waste, but few contributions dwell on the investigation of business models applied to the Metaverse; among them, Huynt [43] presents some empirical evidence on how fashion companies can adopt digital innovations and business models to improve sustainability.

2.1 Business Models in the Metaverse and Sustainability

Business Model (BM) provides an abstract construct that conceptualizes the way an organization conducts business, reducing complexity [44]. According to a traditional approach, a B.M. is based on the financial return on investment [45]. This model is based on the assumption of allocating resources to achieve a result [46]. Undoubtedly, it is impossible to grow when some essential resources are limited; therefore, adopting B.M.s capable of creating value while considering the need for an environmental sustainability approach is necessary. The literature on B.M. in the last 20 years has become increasingly popular and has led to the evolution of many definitions. A significant contribution is provided by Shafer, Smith, and Linder [47], who 2005 defined the business model as representing a company's underlying rationale and strategic choices for creating and capturing value within a value network.

According to Osterwalder et al. [48] "[...] a business model is a conceptual tool containing a set of objects, concepts and their relationships to express the business logic of a specific company. It describes the logic by which an organization creates, distributes, and captures value. [...] Therefore, we have to consider which concepts and relationships allow us to describe and represent in a simplified way the value provided to customers, how it is realized, and the financial consequences".

According to Teece [49], B.M. describes an architecture for how an organization creates and delivers value to customers and the mechanisms used to capture a portion of the value. In the academic field, the concept of value capture in business models refers to the ability of a company to retain a portion of the value created through its economic activities [26, 47, 49]. This value can be monetary but can also include non-monetary benefits such as corporate reputation, social capital, and environmental sustainability, so the analysis of how companies capture value, therefore, offers a lens through which one can assess whether the sustainability practices adopted by a company are substantive or merely communicative. Companies can capture value from new technologies in two ways: by incorporating technology into their current operations or by launching new initiatives that exploit technology in new business areas [26].

Value can be defined as an individual's perception of the satisfaction of a basic need and can be assessed using monetary, psychological, utilitarian, physiological, or aesthetic criteria [50].

The Metaverse takes the form of an immersive world within virtual environments in which, with the help of A.R., V.R. technologies, and devices that replicate three-dimensional environments, avatars interact and perform virtual activities such as playing games, purchasing products, and professional activities [2, 22, 39, 40].

Recent studies on B.M. in the Metaverse have mostly focused on value creation and value capture mechanisms to gain a competitive advantage, create new ways of interaction [51], and create new communities around brands [52]. These studies have used cryptocurrencies and Non-Fungible Tokens (NFT) as enablers to enhance transactions [53, 54].

However, many of the digital fashion companies, thus present on the metaverse platforms, advocate greener fashion by claiming that digital fashion can be substituted for tangible fashion [20, 33], significantly reducing waste at the design stage and facilitating choice for online shopping by decreasing returns and waste.

3 Aims and Methodology

In light of what has emerged from the theoretical framework and the context in which digital fashion moves, exploratory research is needed to shed light on the creation and value-capture mechanisms realized by organizations operating in the digital fashion sector; we try to understand whether the digital fashion business model supported by metaverse platforms is really environmentally sustainable.

A mixed qualitative methodology was applied, combining two methodologies to answer this question.

Firstly, the case study was used [23] since an empirical investigation studying a contemporary phenomenon, still in its primordial phase, within its real-life context seemed particularly appropriate as the boundaries between the phenomenon and context seemed particularly appropriate as the boundaries between the phenomenon and the context were not yet evident; a multiple case study was chosen because it was considered more significant due to the reliability of the data collected, which can lend greater rigor to the study of the phenomenon observed [55]. Four cases were chosen: Adidas, Dolce e Gabbana, DressX, and The Fabricant because the first two companies have their core business in real life (IRL), while the other two operate exclusively in the Metaverse, and it was felt that this gave a broader and more complete view of the object of study (Table 1).

The multiple case study method was supplemented by a netnographic analysis, an adaptation of qualitative methods used in anthropology and cultural studies, to study consumer behavior in virtual communities [24].

Referring to the analysis model of Mancuso et al. [40], the paper intends to explore how digital fashion production favors or does not favor sustainability through the study of the four cases, observing two aspects for each of them: the mechanisms of value creation, which are transformative, and those of value capture, which are linked to communicative elements.

Table 1 Value creations and capture mechanisms

Adidas	Dolce & Gabbana	DressX	The Fabricant
Using metaverse platforms to create interaction between users Linking physical and virtual products Customization of avatars	Innovation and offerings to enrich the customer experience in virtual worlds Building an online community through immersive experiences, fashion shows, and pop-up shops in metaverse platforms	Users' possibility to be fashionable even in online spaces Proposal of a democratic space where emerging designers can propose their digital collections Through the use of generative A.I., it allows all users to participate in the creative process	Digital fashion proposal to wear in online spaces Democratization of fashion through co-creation by users offering a fashion that is non-polluting because it does not produce waste and overproduction
Direct earnings from the sale of digital and NFT products Building a solid community to increase awareness of the brand Data from avatar customization provide information on styles and trends	Sale of digital luxury and NFT goods related to clothing and accessories in IRL Data from interactions on metaverse platforms will be used to learn about users' tastes and preferences	Offering B2B and B2C services and products Sale of digital and NFT clothes and accessories on their marketplace	Offering B2B and B2C services and products Sale of digital and NFT clothes and accessories on their marketplace

Data on each individual case was collected from multiple secondary sources, including company websites and academic articles [52, 56–58]. Information from the official social pages, LinkedIn, Meta, Youtube, and X, was also used. The data was then cross-referenced with information from business magazines (Sole24Ore, Forbes, Vogue Business, Milano Finanza).

At the same time, netnographic analysis was carried out with a participatory approach on the metaverse platforms Roblox, Decentraland, and The Sandbox.[2]

[2] They are three metaverse platforms easily accessible from PCs or smartphones. They allow users to create, explore, and interact in virtual worlds. Each platform has its unique characteristics and objectives and allows companies to evaluate the success of their projects in the Metaverse.

3.1 Analysis

3.1.1 The Adidas Case

Adidas is a leading sportswear company. It has recently extended its focus to digital and the Metaverse. This effort involves integrating technology into the consumer experience and internal processes to improve efficiency and reduce environmental impact through supply chain optimization. In this way, the company intends to optimize demand and inventory and minimize waste (an example is the 1% reduction in air travel in 2023) [59]. In 2021, Adidas collaborated with Coinbase [60] for exploration and integration in the Metaverse. Coinbase is a cryptocurrency exchange platform founded in 2012 that allows users to buy, sell, and store various types of cryptocurrency, such as Bitcoin and Ethereum; it offers solutions for businesses and facilitates the acceptance of cryptocurrency payments [61]. In 2021, it entered the Metaverse, collaborating with The Sandbox; the partnership included purchasing virtual land and creating exclusive content and experiences. In the same year, it launched the Adidas Originals Into the Metaverse (AOIM) project, which includes the sale of NFT and exclusive products for the Metaverse [62]. In December 2023, it launched a shop on Roblox and is also deepening its expertise in the Metaverse through initiatives promoting collective ownership and social responsibility; it collaborates with Prada in the "Adidas for Prada resource" (AfPr) project, which involves the community in the creation of digital art in NFT [63].

Adidas' business model in the Metaverse involves three value creation mechanisms that relate to interacting with users, especially those belonging to Gen Z, within virtual and personalized worlds, connecting digital products to physical ones, and personalization. The former can be found in both The Sandbox and Roblox universe and aims to create connections with a new audience while offering added value to the brand's fans. The exact sharing mechanism can be found in both the 'Adidas for Prada resource project, which aims at involvement in the creation of digital art in NFT, and the 'Into the Metaverse project, with which the brand intends to reconnect with the younger generation. In AOIM, the second value creation mechanism also emerges, which concerns the link between digital clothes in NFT made in collaboration with other companies such as Bored Ape Yacht Club, Gmoney and Punks Comic, and the physical twins [64]. The personalization mechanism was made possible by the 'Oz World' collection and the metaverse platform dedicated to it (Oz World Experience), in which users could create a personalized avatar from the information provided based on specific questions that reflected their personality [65]. Creating value through customization is also present in the Roblox experiences, where users can collect and create official user generation content (U.G.C.) thanks to the new avatar customization options.

On the other hand, Adidas's business model in the Metaverse involves three value-capture mechanisms involving direct revenue through the sale of NFT and virtual products on Roblox [66]. Digital items included the oversized Trefoil shoulder bag and digital hair looks. Prices for Adidas X Rush X packages include a range of limited edition U.G.C.s made in collaboration with Roblox creator Rush Bogin (Rush X); they cost between 85 and 500 Robux[67], allowing users to assert their virtual identity by purchasing low-cost virtual products. The second value capture mechanism involves building a community to increase brand awareness. To increase co-capture, Adidas created the Into the Metaverse project in three phases; in the first phase, users were granted access to the exclusive physical collection through the purchase of NFTs; in the second phase, users could personalize the Oz World collection through the use of the metaverse platform dedicated to it where users could create a personalized avatar based on some questions reflecting their personality [63]. The initiative involved 250,000 unique users, and 480,000 avatars were generated. The third phase concerned the Virtual Gear project launched on November 16, 2022: a limited digital collection consisting of 16 exclusive NFT pieces, revealed following a teaser campaign with the Adidas community on the Discord platform and available in the wallets of the NFT capsule holders of phase two. Finally, the AfPr project focuses on the creation of a collective digital artwork in NFT, part of the proceeds of which go to support non-profit organizations working on social sustainability education and the creation of more inclusive communities [68]. The third value capture mechanism comes from the data on users' tastes and preferences that interact on metaverse platforms. This data is invaluable in enabling companies to make increasingly personalized, mainstream fashion products in line with tastes and trends.

The Dolce and Gabbana Case

Dolce & Gabbana is a luxury fashion house with its core business in IRL, founded in 1985 by Stefano Dolce and Domenico Gabbana. The brand is distinguished by a style that combines classic elegance with modern influences, often inspired by Italian cultural heritage. In recent years, it has explored the Metaverse for brand expansion and interaction with a younger demographic. In September 2021, he launched NFT's 'Genesis collection, which included digital fashion pieces [56] showcasing the powerful combination of NFT, tangible fashion, and the luxury brand experience connected to the NFT purchase [57].

Acknowledging the growing importance of environmental sustainability, Dolce & Gabbana has undertaken several initiatives to integrate sustainable practices into its business model to contribute to the creation of social value while protecting the natural ecosystem through the definition of a sustainability plan, in which the company has identified seven priorities as the basis of its commitment. Among these, the objectives related to environmental sustainability are Net Zero Carbon, Zero Waste, Materials & Circularity. Priorities include the reduction of the carbon footprint of emissions to the transition to 100% renewable energy, waste recovery, and land conservation [68]. In this sense, the development of digital fashion collections and the NFT offer partly follows the logic of a more sustainable fashion that allows consumers to express their identity while reducing their environmental impact.

The value creation mechanisms pursued in the Metaverse focus on innovation and offerings that enrich the customer experience, increasing customer engagement and brand perception, and include digital clothes and accessories that bypass the need for physical production and the creation of NFTs that create new forms of artistic and personal expression for consumers. Furthermore, with the help of metaverse platforms and campaigns for the launch of NFT, Dolce & Gabbana aims to build a strong community. In detail, Dolce & Gabbana, on the occasion of the 2021 haute couture event in Venice, launched a collection of nine NFT dresses inspired by Venetian history and traditions.

Each NFT purchased was accompanied by an original sketch signed by Stefano Dolce and Domenico Gabbana, a private tour of the atelier, and an exclusive invitation to the fashion show in real life [69].

Dolce & Gabbana created immersive experiences with virtual fashion shows as a sustainable alternative to physical events, with a collection of 20 wearables for the first Metaverse Fashion Week hosted on Decentraland, in collaboration with UNXD, and available on Dolce & Gabbana's exclusive pop-up in the Luxury Fashion District [70]. The brand then launched the DGFamily community to offer NFT owners a range of benefits, such as access to exclusive drops, physical and digital events, and collaborations. For the second edition of MVFW, it launched Future Rewind, a digital competition to promote young talent [70].

In exploring the Metaverse, Dolce & Gabbana has adopted strategic approaches to value capture that align with its luxury and innovation positioning. At the heart of this strategy is the sale of digital goods, including virtual clothes and accessories, often made in NFT, generating new revenue streams from consumers who want to stand out in the virtual environment. NFT not only attracts a technologically advanced audience willing to spend on exclusive digital objects but also offers the brand a new revenue channel with potentially high margins: the Genesis collection presented in Venice in 2021 was sold in 10 days of auction for the sum of 1885.73 ETH, or about six million dollars [69]. Although some pieces of the collection were physically realized, the heart of the inner project was the digital version. Often launched as limited editions, such products can acquire value over time, increasing their appeal as collector's items. In addition to direct sales, Dolce & Gabbana capitalizes on its presence in the Metaverse through partnerships with Metaverse platforms and the sale of exclusive products and experiences. These collaborations increase the brand's visibility and attract a younger, international audience. In addition, another essential value capture mechanism involves using user interaction data on metaverse platforms that can offer valuable insights into customers' tastes and preferences.

3.1.2 The DressX Case

DressX is a digital fashion store founded by Daria Shapovalova and Natalia Modenova in California [71]. The vision on the site reads: "We strongly believe that the amount of clothing produced today is way greater than humanity needs. We share the beauty and excitement that physical fashion creates, but we believe there are ways to produce less, more sustainably, and not produce at all. At the current stage of DRESSX development, we aim to show that some clothes can only be in their digital versions. Don't shop less, shop digital fashion" [72]. In the section of the website dedicated to environmental sustainability, the advantages of digital fashion over traditional fashion that inspire DressX's work are listed: 'The fashion industry is considered one of the largest polluters in the world, according to the U.N. Conference on Trade and Development. The environmental damage only increases as the industry grows. The production and distribution of the fibers and garments used in fashion contribute to different forms of environmental pollution, including water, air, and soil pollution. Some of the main factors that create pollution are vast overproduction, overconsumption of fashion items, and synthetic fibers. At DressX, we are making the garments of the future that eliminate waste and chemicals during production and minimize carbon footprint [73].

The DressX business model is characterized by value-creation mechanisms that focus on the possibility of people being fashionable online using digital fashion. The pay-off "don't buy less, shop digital fashion" represents the synthesis of the business model adopted by the Californian company, which is based on a virtual world connected to the offer of digital clothes and accessories, offering the possibility for users to build their own digital identity within digital environments thanks to the use of clothes made with A.R. filters. The idea stems from the observation and a study carried out by the company's two founders, in which it emerged that many people buy fast fashion clothes that they use only once to show off their outfits within social networks [74]. Furthermore, DressX creates value from a fashion democratization perspective by acting as a space where emerging designers can create and sell digital fashion. The latest innovation concerns the possibility for all users to participate in the creative process of digital clothes and accessories with the help of generative AI [75], enabling people to design and wear their digital garments quickly. DressX Gen AI allows people to send a photo and be digitally dressed in seconds with a dress generated based on text instructions.

The mechanisms that enable DressX to capture value concern B2B and B2C digital product and service offerings. B2B offerings concern the digitalization of clothes in IRL, A.R. mirrors for companies, event management, and strategy in the Metaverse of Decentraland. Furthermore, DressX projects range from partnerships with media companies, as in the case of L'Officiel [76], for a series of archive looks presented on The Sandbox platform to various partnerships with brands operating in the traditional fashion industry and wishing to enter the Metaverse. Examples are the collaboration with Lacoste, for whom DressX created 10 looks, five of which can be purchased on Zepeto and another five on Roblox. DressX then collaborated with Diesel to create a collection on the Meta Avatar Store. With the digital fashion company, they made a 3D campaign led by sustainability ambassador, actress, and activist Maisie Williams, which consisted of a capsule collection of three exclusively virtual looks: an oversized waistcoat made from impossible materials paired with a jumpsuit, an orange braided knitted dress with sparkles; and baggy trousers in pink, paired with a hoodie. The virtual looks were available exclusively for the three winners of the company's virtual fashion competition [77]. It then worked with the G.A.P. brand to bring the winning designs of the #GapLogoRemix challenge into the digital world. Previously, G.A.P. had announced its #GapLogoRemix challenge, inviting its community to reimagine the brand's logo. DRESSX then recreated the iconic sweatshirts in 3D, making the limited edition looks available for purchase as digital collectibles on gap.com. Owners received exclusive access to their hoodies in A.R. on the DRESSX app [78]. With the e-commerce platform FARFETCH, it created the platform's first innovative editorial and influencer marketing campaign for the pre-order collection, then digitized 20 menswear and womenswear looks from the new collections of brands Burberry, Off-White, Balenciaga, Palm Angels, Dolce & Gabbana, Khaite and Nanushka [79]. Another value-capture mechanism in the B2B-based metaverse concerns consultancy and courses for traditional fashion companies wishing to have a touchpoint in the virtual world. One example is the Sup de Luxe certification, a program designed for professionals who want to improve their knowledge in the Web 3 and Metaverse and refine their strategies in the digital world; participants in the certification also have the opportunity to make their NFTs, all for the price of EUR1428,10.

The B2C offer ranges from the sale of clothes and accessories in A.R. to being used on social networks also thanks to a service called Metaarmadio, a desktop application that allows people to wear digital fashion during video calls on Google Meet, Skype, Teams, Zoom, to the sale of digital clothes and accessories on the DressX platform where there are both digital garments made by brands whose core business is in the Metaverse and garments made for brands whose core business is in IRL and who have decided to re-propose their physical creations in the virtual world. Purchasing on DressX is done via P.C. or a smartphone app and involves choosing a digital garment and sending a photo. Thanks to the collaboration with Roblox's metaverse platform, DressX earns revenue from the sale of digital clothes and accessories such as corsets, necklaces, scarves, blazers, or U.G.C. such as mugs, pillows to be attached to avatars on the platform. A further value capture mechanism regarding the sale of NFT[3] on the company's marketplace, such as the Hape®X Drop collection, an exclusive collection created by Hape and DressX, or Mavion x Rebecca Minkoff, a collection of NFT bags whose proceeds from each bag support WINWEB3, a non-profit organization that uses art and technology to help women and girls in war-torn countries.

3.1.3 The Fabricant Case

The Fabricant is a digital fashion house that only makes digital fashion. Its goal is to "Digitally build a new fashion industry where everybody participates and profits [80]. The Fabricant, like DressX, intends to change the fashion industry by changing the very idea of fashion linked to the materiality of fabrics while helping to reduce

[3] https://onchain.dressx.com/marketplace/nft/.

environmental impact by eliminating the manufacturing process [81]. The company was founded in 2018 with a 'green friendly' mission; its webpage announced that it is a Digital Fashion House that produces digital-only clothing that wastes nothing but data and uses nothing but imagination [81]. In 2019, The Fabricant was in the spotlight after auctioning a digital dress at the Ethereal Summit blockchain event in New York for a cryptocurrency value of $9500 [82].

In recent years, the digital fashion house has changed a lot, shifting its mission focused on environmental sustainability to a more inclusive and participatory vision that focuses on the co-creation of digital fashion, thanks to an online design platform, The Fabricant Studio, where users can create, wear and exchange clothes in the Metaverse, hoping to be the thought-leading digital fashion house, dressing 100 million people by 2025 [80]. Within the same platform, a 12-piece collection was created for the Metaverse Fashion Week held last March on the Decentraland platform [83].

The Fabricant is open to collaborating with several traditional fashion houses that want to explore the Metaverse and digital fashion.

The value creation mechanisms for the metaverse concern the participation of users in the digital fashion creation process with the help of The Fabricant Studio's platform that allows all users to participate in the creation of digital fashion on an equal footing with the big fashion houses, disrupting the professional authority of traditional fashion in an environment where designers share knowledge among members of the online community [80] and where each user becomes an active part of the story of each digital or NFT garment, creating a broader emotional involvement.

In addition, The Fabricant, being a digital company, creates value through environmental sustainability by eliminating fabric waste and the use of natural resources for fabrication. Thus, it is less polluting than traditional fashion and promotes a new approach to fashion that makes The Fabricant a leader in fashion innovation, differentiating itself from traditional competitors.

Value capture mechanisms are closely linked to the company's ability to enter an untapped market and gain a competitive advantage. This strategy has enabled the company to establish itself in the fast-growing market and create strategic partnerships that have allowed The Fabricant to expand and capture value. Specifically, it has partnered with the metaverse platforms Ready Player Me, Spatial, The Sandbox [80], and Decentraland as partners of the first and second Metaverse Fashion Weeks. In addition, in recent years, it has been providing services and collaborations with traditional fashion houses wishing to enter the Metaverse and the digital fashion market, among them Maison Margiela, who with the MetaTABI digital collection has brought the iconic Tabi Boot into the Metaverse, the purchase of each piece of which grants several benefits such as exclusive product access in IRL, access to Ready Player Me and The Sandbox wearable gaming devices, as well as exclusive entry to Web3 brand events [84].

The Fabricant also captures value through the direct sale of digital fashion by various digital fashion designers, such as the emerald-colored elven cloak inspired by fantasy books the Primal Rave or Adventure Top & Paradigm collections.

4 Discussion and Conclusion

Underlying this study is the shared idea that technological advances and digital override the material dimension, thus representing an opportunity for companies to maintain environmental sustainability through the use of digital. The idea proposed by the case studies is that digital fashion represents a sustainable alternative as it consumes data, reducing the environmental impact related to waste, fast fashion, and the consumption of natural resources needed to make fabrics [71, 72, 74].

This exploratory study aimed to investigate the lights and shadows of digital fashion in the metaverse through the analysis of business models, to shed light on the positive and negative aspects of digital fashion.

As the analysis of the business models of the fashion houses in the metaverse revealed, the digitization of the fashion industry presents both benefits and disadvantages regarding sustainability.

While the companies analyzed are mainly active from the point of view of environmental sustainability, promoting initiatives within the meta-verse in favor of greater awareness [57, 71, 73, 80], the study of the mechanisms of creation and value capture also revealed how much more complex the issue is. Digital fashion fits within the intensive consumption of this speed-based time.

Now, the study found that the companies examined only partially replace tangible fashion by limiting the waste of materials and resources, but that the creation and value capture models support and galvanize both digital and traditional fashion consumption. The analysis of the creation and value capture business model of Adidas shows that fashion projects for the Metaverse do not replace digital fashion but are tools for accessing and purchasing exclusive collections in IRL, thus supporting traditional fashion. The exact mechanism emerged for Dolce & Gabbana's Genesi collection and Maison Margiela's collection by The Fabricant.

Furthermore, DressX offers digital fashion by proposing that users not consume less but consume digitally [72]. At the same time, the company draws its economic sustainability from partnerships with brands present in IRL that intend to explore the Metaverse to enrich the customer experience, increasing customer engagement and brand perception through the creation of NFT and new forms of immersive fashion experiences; the latter do not replace tangible fashion, but reinforce brand perception and enable the creation of strong communities through co-creation initiatives, to continue to support traditional fashion consumption.

However, it would be reductive to consider it thoroughly 'greenwashing'; as this study has shown, the cases analyzed express their commitment to environmental sustainability, especially outside the virtual experience. Dolce & Gabbana has embarked on a decarbonization program that addresses Scope 1 and 2 emissions and includes measures to ensure that the electricity used comes from certified renewable sources [85].

Adidas maintains its commitment to reducing pollution caused by plastic by replacing virgin polyester with recycled polyester from 2024, where possible. By 2025, it will commit to reducing carbon emissions by an average of 15%. The study also shows an essential aspect for the benefit of more sustainable fashion: using data on tastes and trends from avatar interactions and customizations. Such data could be used for production increasingly in line with customers' demands and tastes, resulting in increasingly customized tangible fashion and reduced overproduction.

Finally, as people surround themselves with smart devices, clouds, email, and every system equipped with sensors and circuits, the era of the Internet of Things requires an increasing amount of hardware, which is more and more hidden [86], so it is necessary to question the materiality of the digital and whether the myth of immateriality and dematerialization [87]. Kittler's studies underlie this perspective [88] that calls for a focus on hardware. In this sense, Jussi Parikka [89] emphasizes the material aspect of digital devices by focusing on the inner workings of digital devices and networks, from production, distribution, and disposal. Moreover, theories of media ecologies and Marxist approaches emphasize digital materiality and political economy, emphasizing the unsustainability of the growth model proposed by digital network capitalism [90–96.

These approaches aim to counter the common perception of digital fashion's immateriality by focusing on the shadows concerning infrastructure, mechanisms of technological devices, and socio-economic implications.

The research enriches the literature debate on sustainability in the fashion industry, paving the way for the academic debate on the sustainability of digital fashion.

Furthermore, the research has some limitations. First, the very exploratory nature of the survey work, which does not present, now, an in-depth qualitative or quantitative analysis to support it, but which, given the initial results, has stimulated the desire to continue and enrich the investigation in the future.

Secondly, the fact that, although we are aware of the threefold nature of sustainability, it has been decided to focus only on the environmental issue, both to reduce the vastness of the topic and for the more significant amount of research related to it given the high impact the fashion industry has in this area.

In the future, it is intended to enrich the study by incorporating a more in-depth qualitative and quantitative analysis, and address the social sustainability of digital fashion, as the sector is equally impactful on people and communities and is still part of the systemic vision of sustainability. In addition, it is hoped to deepen the study by addressing the issues of technology and digital consumption, the environmental impact in terms of carbon emissions and hardwires, investigating the contradictions of digital fashion, and critique the idea of dematerialization of fashion and its production processes.

In fact, the metaverse requires the use of technologies such as augmented and virtual reality devices, artificial intelligence, volumetric scanning, 3D modeling, Internet of Things, Blockchain, cryptocurrencies, and NFT, which represent the dark side of a fashion that claims to be environmentally sustainable.

However, it is believed that the study offers interesting insights to be developed in the future, not least because of the organizational implications of these issues.

Funding This research received no external funding.

Disclosure of Interests The authors have no competing interests to declare that are relevant to the content of this article.

References

1. Elkington, J. (1998). Partnerships from cannibals with forks: The triple bottom line of 21st-century business. *Environmental Quality Management, 8*(1), 37–51.
2. Periyasamy, A. P., & Periyasami, S. (2023). Rise of digital fashion and Metaverse: Influence on sustainability. *Digital Economy and Sustainable Development, 1*(1), 16.
3. Ditty, S. (2015). It's time for a fashion revolution; white paper; fashion revolution: Derbyshire, UK.
4. Periyasamy, A. P., & e J. Militky. (2020). LCA (Valutazione del ciclo di vita) sul poliestere riciclato. In S. S. Muthu (Ed.), *Impronta ambientale del poliestere riciclato* (pp. 1–30). Springer.
5. Algayerova, O. (2018). Moda e SDG: quale ruolo per le Nazioni Unite? In *UNECE*. https://unece.org/fileadmin/DAM/RCM_Website/RFSD_2018_Side_event_sustainable_fashion.pdf.
6. Bonomi, S., & Giorgetti, A. (2023). The sense of impact assessment through the lens of civil economy. Impresa progetto. *Electronic Journal of Management, 1*.
7. Karaosman, H., Morales-Alonso, G., & Brun, A. (2016). From a systematic literature review to a classification framework: Sustainability integration in fashion operations. *Sustainability, 9*(1), 30. https://doi.org/10.3390/su9010030
8. United Nations Framework Convention on Climate Change. (2018, September 6). U.N. helps the fashion industry shift to low carbon. UNFCCC. https://unfccc.int/news/un-helps-fashion-industry-shift-to-low-carbon.
9. Calefato, P. (2021). La moda e il corpo, Roma, Carocci Editore.
10. Barnes, L., & Lea-Greenwood, G. (2006). Fast fashioning the supply chain: Shaping the research agenda. *Journal of Fashion Marketing and Management: An International Journal, 10*, 259–271.
11. Janmark, J., Magnus, K.-H., Marcos, I., & Wiener, E. (2024, 28 March). Sustainable style: How fashion can afford and accelerate decarbonisation. McKinsey & Company. Retrieved August 14, 2024, from https://www.mckinsey.com/industries/retail/our-insights/sustainable-style-how-fashion-can-afford-and-accelerate-decarbonization.
12. McKinsey & Company. (2023, 29 November). The State of Fashion 2024: Finding pockets of growth while uncertainty reigns. McKinsey & Company. Retrieved 14 August 2024, from https://www.mckinsey.com/industries/retail/our-insights/the-state-of-fashion-2024-finding-pockets-of-growth-as-uncertainty-reigns.
13. Barile, N. (2022). Dress Coding: Moda e stili dalla strada al Metaverso. Mimesis.
14. United Nations Climate Change. (2021, November 5). Fashion industry charter for climate action. UNFCCC. https://unfccc.int/sites/default/files/resource/Fashion%20Industry%20Carter%20for%20Climate%20Action_2021.pdf.
15. Abell, D. F. (2014). The past, present, and future of strategy: Broadening challenges; advancing insight. *Iberoamerican Journal of Strategic Management (IJSM), 13*(3), 07–18.
16. Kohli, R., & Melville, N. P. (2019). Digital innovation: A review and synthesis. *Information Systems Journal, 29*(1), 200–223.
17. Rauturier, S. (2022). Perché alcuni marchi di moda distruggono e bruciano i vestiti invenduti? https://goodonyou.eco/fashion-brands-burn-unsold-clothes/.
18. Statista. (2021). Production of polyester fibers worldwide from 1975 to 2021. Retrieved from https://www.statista.com/statistics/912301/polyester-fiber-production-worldwide/.
19. Ellen MacArthur Foundation. (2021, November 23). *A digital-only, multi-brand fashion platform: DRESSX*. Retrieved from https://www.ellenmacarthurfoundation.org/circular-examples/dressx.

20. DRESSX. (n.d.). Sustainability. More Dash Inc. dba DRESSX. Recuperato il [03/04/2024], da https://dressx.com/pages/sustainability
21. Adamkiewicz, J., Kochańska, E., Adamkiewicz, I., & Łukasik, R. M. (2022). Greenwashing and sustainable fashion industry. *Current Opinion in Green and Sustainable Chemistry, 38*, 100710.
22. Belardinelli, R. (2021, November 18). Per Morgan Stanley il metaverso può valere 50 miliardi per la moda. Milano Finanza. https://www.milanofinanza.it/fashion/per-morgan-stanley-il-metaverso-puo-valere-50-miliardi-per-la-moda-202111171112595093.
23. Yin, R. K. (1993). *Application of case study research*. Sage Publications.
24. Kozinets, R. V. (1998). On netnography: Initial reflections on consumer research investigations of cyberculture. A.C.R. North American Advances.
25. Kozinets, R. V. (2002). The field behind the screen: using netnography for marketing research in online communities. *Journal of Marketing Research, 39*, 61–72.
26. Chesbrough, H. W., & Rosenbloom, R. S. (2002). The role of the business model in capturing value from innovation: evidence from Xerox Corporation's technology spinoff companies. *Industrial and Corporate Change, 11*, 533–534.
27. Hardin, G. (1968). The tragedy of the commons: the population problem has no technical solution; it requires a fundamental extension in morality. *Science, 162*(3859), 1243–1248.
28. Dantas, T., de Souza, E., Destro, I., Hammes, G., Rodriguez, C., & Soares, S. (2021). How the combination of circular economy and industry 4.9 can contribute towards achieving the sustainable development goals. *Sustainable Production and Consumption, 26*, 213–227. https://doi.org/10.1016/j.spc.2020.10.005
29. Reuter, E. (2022). Hybrid business models in the sharing economy: The role of business model design for managing the environmental paradox. *Business Strategy and the Environment, 31*(2), 603–618. https://doi.org/10.1002/bse.2939
30. Wagner, R., & Kabalska, A. (2023). Sustainable value in the fashion industry: A case study of value construction/destruction using digital twins. *Sustainable Development, 31*(3), 1652–1667.
31. Papanek, V. (1995). *The green imperative. Ecology and ethics in design and architecture*. Thames and Hudson.
32. K. Niinimäki, (Ed.). (2013). Sustainable fashion: New approaches. Hel sinki: Aalto ARTS Books. https://aaltodoc.aalto.fi/handle/123456789/13769. Accessed 1 October 2014.
33. Brezet, H., & Van Hemel, C. (1997). *Ecodesign: A promising approach to sustainable production and consumption*. UNEP.
34. Goworek, H., Hiller, A., Fisher, T., Cooper, T., & Woodward, S. (2013). Consumers' attitudes towards sustainable fashion. In M. Gardetti & A. Torres (Eds.), *Sustainability in fashion and textiles* (pp. 377–392). Greenleaf Publishing.
35. Rathore, B. (2023). Digital transformation 4.0: Integration of artificial intelligence & Metaverse in marketing. *Eduzone: International Peer Reviewed/Refereed Multidisciplinary Journal, 12*(1), 42–48.
36. Noris, A., Nobile, T. H., Kalbaska, N., & Cantoni, L. (2021). Digital fashion: A systematic literature review. A perspective on marketing and communication. *Journal of Global Fashion Marketing, 12*(1), 32–46.
37. Arya, V., Sambyal, R., Sharma, A., & Dwivedi, Y. K. (2023). Brands are calling your AVATAR in Metaverse—a study to explore XR-based gamification marketing activities & consumer-based brand equity in virtual world. *Journal of Consumer Behaviour*.
38. Temperino, E. (2023). The Perks of being digital. Nikeland: A case study. Springer Nature Switzerland, In International conference on fashion communication: between tradition and future digital developments. (pp. 88–95).
39. Mogaji, E., Dwivedi, Y. K., & Raman, R. (2023). Fashion marketing in the Metaverse. *Journal of Global Fashion Marketing*, 1–16.
40. Mancuso, I., Petruzzelli, A. M., & Panniello, U. (2023). Digital business model innovation in Metaverse: How to approach virtual economy opportunities. *Information Processing & Management, 60*(5), 103457.

41. Venturini, A., & Columbano, M. (2023). 'Fashioning'the Metaverse: A qualitative study on consumers' value and perceptions of digital fashion in virtual worlds. *Journal of Global Fashion Marketing*, 1–17.
42. Periyasamy, A. P., & Periyasami, S. (2023). Rise of digital fashion and Metaverse: influence on sustainability. *Digital Economy and Sustainable Development, 1*(1), 1–26.
43. Huynh, P. H. (2021). Enabling circular business models in the fashion industry: The role of digital innovation. *International Journal of Productivity and Performance Management, 71*(3), 870–895.
44. Kraus, S., Kanbach, D. K., Krysta, P. M., Steinhoff, M. M., & Tomini, N. (2022). Facebook and the creation of the Metaverse: radical business model innovation or incremental transformation? *International Journal of Entrepreneurial Behavior & Research, 28*(9), 52–77.
45. Larrinaga-González, C., Carrasco, F., Correa, C., Llena, F., & Moneva, J. (2002). Accountability and accounting regulation: The case of the Spanish environmental disclosure standard. *European Accounting Review, 11*(4), 723–740. https://doi.org/10.1080/09638180220000001000
46. Conway, E. (2018). Sustainability, the triple bottom line, and corporate social responsibility. *Contemporary issues in accounting: The current developments in accounting beyond the numbers*, 15–35.
47. Shafer, S. M., Smith, J. H., & Linder, J. C. (2005). The power of business models. *Business Horizons, 48*, 199–207.
48. Osterwalder, A., Pigneur, Y., & Tucci, C. L. (2005). Clarifying business models: origins, present, and future of the concept. *Communications of the Association for Information Systems, 16*(1), 1–38.
49. Teece, D. J. (2018). Business models and dynamic capabilities. *Long Range Planning, 51*(1), 40–49.
50. Upward, A., & Jones, P. (2016). An ontology for strongly sustainable business models: Defining an enterprise framework compatible with natural and social science. *Organization & Environment, 29*(1), 1–27. https://doi.org/10.1177/1086026615592933
51. Anagondanahalli, S., Chong, W. K., & Pismeya, I. (2023). Digital fashion: Influence of K-Pop and go-to market strategy in the Metaverse. *International Journal of Design, Analysis & Tools for Integrated Circuits & Systems, 12*(1).
52. Joy, A., Zhu, Y., Peña, C., & Brouard, M. (2022). Digital future of luxury brands: Metaverse, digital fashion, and non-fungible tokens. *Strategic Change, 31*(3), 337–343.
53. Park, H., & Lim, R. E. (2023). Fashion and the Metaverse: Clarifying the domain and establishing a research agenda. *Journal of Retailing and Consumer Services, 74*, 103413.
54. Sung, E., Kwon, O., & Sohn, K. (2023). NFT luxury brand marketing in the Metaverse: Leveraging blockchain-certified NFTs to drive consumer behavior. *Psychology & Marketing, 40*(11), 2306–2325.
55. Concoran, P. B., Walker, K. E., & Wals, A. E. J. (2004). Case studies, make-your-ca-se studies, and case stories: A critique of case-study methodology in sustanability in higher education. *Environmental Education Research*, 7–21.
56. Segura, L. Z. (2022). ¿ Qué son y cómo se utilizan actualmente los NFT? Investiga. TEC.
57. Grillo, M., & Bonomi, S. (2023). Digital transformation in the fashion industry: Metaverse as an additional business platform or a new innovative stakeholder interaction model. In A. Lerro, D. Carlucci, & G. Schiuma (Eds.), *Proceeding of IFKAD2023. Managing knowledge for sustainability distribution*. Institute of Knowledge Asset Management. Matera 7–9 June. ISBN 978-88-96687-16-1; ISSN 2280-787X.
58. Kirjavainen, E. (2022). The future of luxury fashion brands through NFTs.
59. Adidas Group. (2023). Environmental impacts. 2023 Adidas Group Annual Report. Retrieved May 9, 2024, from https://report.adidas-group.com/2023/en/group-management-report-our-company/sustainability/environmental-impacts.html.
60. Iqbal, M. Z. (2023). Metaverse as tech for good: Current progress and emerging opportunities. In Virtual worlds (Vol. 2, 4). MDPI.
61. Capoti, D. (2018). *Tutto su bitcoin: guida pratica per investire in criptovalute*. Hoepli Editore.

62. Adidas Originals. (2021, December 16). Into the Metaverse: How we got here and where we are headed. Adidas News. Retrieved in 02/05/2024 from https://news.adidas.com/originals/into-the-metaverse%2D%2Dhow-we-got-here-and-where-we-are-headed/s/6ccb61cb-2135-453e-8626-ac3d56faab30.
63. Adidas Originals. (2022, January 20). Adidas Originals and Prada announce a first-of-its-kind open Metaverse & user-generated NFT project. Adidas News. Retrieved May 2, 2024, from https://news.adidas.com/originals/adidas-originals-and-prada-announce-a-first-of-its-kind-open-metaverse%2D%2D-user-generated-nft-project/s/30a29dad-6ded-4302-ae40-f9f2338e7298.
64. Hartwich, E. O. (2024). Probably something: A multi-layer taxonomy of non-fungible tokens. *Internet Research, 34*(1), 216–238.
65. Adidas. (2022, April 5). Adidas originals introduces first-of-its-kind digital OZWORLD experience. Adidas News Retrieved in May 3, 2024. https://news.adidas.com/originals/adidas-originals-introduces-first-of-its-kind-digital-ozworld-experience/s/c29e6fdd-2c70-4362-b84a-c46c279d8faf.
66. Hirschmiller, S. (2023, December 9). Why Adidas is selling limited edition march on gaming platform Roblox. Forbes. Retrieved May 2, 2024, from https://www.forbes.com/sites/stephaniehirschmiller/2023/12/09/why-adidas-is-selling-limited-edition-merch-on-gaming-platform-roblox/.
67. Belardinelli, R. (2022, 18 April). Adidas originals porta la collezione Ozworld nel metaverso. Milano Finanza. https://www.milanofinanza.it/fashion/adidas-originals-porta-la-collezione-ozworld-nel-metaverso-202204181244487653.
68. Dolce & Gabbana. (2022, December). Un futuro all'insegna della sostenibilità. Retrieved May 6, 2024.
69. Dolce & Gabbana. (2022, March). Dolce & Gabbana approda nel Metaverso. Dolce & Gabbana. https://world.dolcegabbana.com/it/news/dolcegabbana-approda-nel-metaverso.
70. Dolce & Gabbana. (2023, March). Dolce & Gabbana partecipa alla seconda edizione della Metaverse Fashion Week. Dolce & Gabbana. https://world.dolcegabbana.com/it/news/dolce-gabbana-metaverse-fashion-week-collezione.
71. Rodrigues, E. C. Moda digital e Sentidos da Sustentabilidade; una anàlise semiòtica das marcas DressX e Studio ACCI.
72. DressX. (n.d.). Our vision. Retrieved May 1, 2024, from https://dressx.com/pages/about.
73. DressX. (n.d.). Environmental impacts: Traditional fashion vs digital fashion. Retrieved May 1, 2024, from https://dressx.com/pages/sustainability.
74. Bellini, E. P. (2020, December 2). Moda sostenibile: gli abiti virtuali di Dress-X. Vogue Italia. Retrieved May 1, 2024, from https://www.vogue.it/vogue-talents/article/moda-sostenibile-vestiti-virtuali-intervista-creatrici-ecommerce-dressx.
75. Vogue Business. (2024, March 26). Dressed in seconds: Testing fashion's latest generative A.I. tool. Retrieved May 1, 2024, from https://www.voguebusiness.com/story/technology/dressed-in-seconds-testing-fashions-latest-generative-ai-tool.
76. Hirschmiller, S. (2022, June 16). LVMH Innovation Award 2022 Finalist DressX wants to be the Google Cloud of digital fashion. Forbes. Retrieved May 5, 2024, from https://www.forbes.com/sites/stephaniehirschmiller/2022/06/16/lvmh-innovation-award-2022-finalists-dressx-on-the-future-of-digital-fashion/?sh=50029eb33b22.
77. DRESSX. (n.d.). Maisie Williams X H&M X The Fabricant. Recuperato il 12 aprile 2024, da https://pro.dressx.com/maisie_williams/.
78. DRESSX. (n.d.). Case Studies: G.A.P. Recuperato il 12 aprile 2024, da https://pro.dressx.com/gap/.
79. DRESSX. (n.d.). Case Studies: Farfetch. Recuperato il 12 aprile 2024, da https://pro.dressx.com/farfetch/.
80. The Fabricant. (n.d.). Our mission. Retrieved May 5, 2024, from https://www.thefabricant.com/about.
81. Särmäkari, N. (2021). Digital 3D fashion designers: Cases of Atacac and the fabricant. *Fashion Theory*, 1–30.

82. Renwick, F. (2019). In the future your clothes will be made out of pixels: Inside the 'Wild West' World of Digital Fashion." Esquire, December 31. Accessed September 10, 2020. https://www.esquire.com/uk/style/fashion/a30150947/digital-fashion-the-fabricanmenswearfuture-trends/.
83. Grillo, M. (2022). Fashion and Metaverse: an expository study on the first MVTW. *Visual Review: International Visual Culture Review/Revista Internacional de Cultura Visual, 9*, 37.
84. The Fabricant. (n.d.). MetaTABI. Retrieved May 5, 2024, from https://www.thefabricant.com/collection/maison-margiela-metatabi.
85. D'Auria, G. (2023, November 7). Il prossimo capitolo di Dolce&Gabbana: una conversazione con il CEO Alfonso Dolce. McKinsey & Company. Retrieved May 7, 2024, from https://www.mckinsey.com/industries/retail/our-insights/dolcegabbanas-next-chapter-a-conversation-with-ceo-alfonso-dolce.
86. Tirino, M. (2017). Il materialismo digitale. Approcci e prospettive mediologiche. Scienza E. *Filosofia, 18*(18).
87. Chun, W. H. K. (2011). *Programmed visions: Software and memory*. MIT Press.
88. Kittler, F. There is no software. In *CTheory*. October 18, 1995. http://ctheory.net/ctheory_wp/there-is-no-software-2/. Retrieved May 9, 2024.
89. Parikka, J. (2012). New materialism as media theory: Medianatures and dirty matter. *Communication and Critical/Cultural Studies, 9*(1), 95–100.
90. Casemajor, N. (2015). Digital materialisms: Frameworks for digital media studies. In *Westminster papers in culture and communication*. (Vol. 10, p. 1).
91. van den Boomen, M. (2014). *Transcoding the digital: How metaphors matter in new media*. Institute of Network Cultures.
92. Fuchs, C. (2008). The implications of new information and communication technologies for sustainability. In Environment, development and sustainability. (Vol. 10, p. 3).
93. Fuchs, C. (2011). *Foundations of critical media and information studies*. Taylor & Francis.
94. Id. (2014). Digital labour and Karl Marx. New York: Routledge.
95. Bennett, J. (2009). *Vibrant matter: A political ecology of things*. Duke University Press.
96. Dyer Witheford, N. (1999). *Cyber-Marx: Cycles and circuits of struggle in high-technology capitalism*. University of Illinois Press.

Circular Business Models and Organisational Networks in the Italian Agri-Food Ecosystem

Michele Cipriano, Olimpia Fontana, Paolo Sckokai, and Francesco Virili

Abstract This study investigates circular business models (CBMs) within the "ECOSISTER: Ecosystem for Sustainable Transition in Emilia-Romagna" project, aligned with and funded by the NextGeneration EU plan. Focusing on the circular economy (CE) sub-area, we explore how CBMs contribute to the circular transition of Emilia-Romagna organisations operating in the agri-food ecosystem. Despite growing interest in CE, the comprehension of the role of organisational networks in new CBMs, remains limited due to limited theoretical grounds and scarce empirical investigations. This study aims to address such a gap by designing and conducting theory-grounded empirical research based on case study analysis, focusing on the representative cases of Parmigiano Reggiano and Mutti. Drawing on extant literature, we design semi-structured interviews, aiming to unfold the characteristics of organisational relationships and the role of organisational networks in innovative CBMs. This preliminary study lays the groundwork for data collection and analysis, proposing a semi-structured interview structure aimed at developing theoretical propositions on the role and characteristics of organisational networks in CBMs. Our findings contribute to the understanding and development of new network-based business models for implementing CE in agri-food industries.

Keywords Circular business models · Networks · Circular economy · Agri-food

M. Cipriano (✉) · F. Virili
Department of Economic and Social Sciences, Catholic University of the Sacred Heart, Piacenza, Italy
e-mail: michele.cipriano@unicatt.it; francesco.virili@unicatt.it

O. Fontana · P. Sckokai
Department of Agricultural and Food Economics, Catholic University of the Sacred Heart, Piacenza, Italy
e-mail: olimpia.fontana@unicatt.it; paolo.sckokai@unicatt.it

M. Cipriano et al. (eds.), *Technologies for Organizations and Society*,
Lecture Notes in Information Systems and Organisation 80,
https://doi.org/10.1007/978-3-032-01697-3_5

1 Introduction

The Italian region Emilia-Romagna boasts one of Europe's most influential innovation ecosystems. This dynamic network, characterised by a live interplay of resources, institutions, organisations, and projects, serves as a powerful catalyst for regional growth. By fostering collaboration, supporting research and development (R&D), and nurturing entrepreneurship, the regional innovation ecosystem not only benefits Italy but also extends its impact beyond national borders [1, 2].

Recently, the Ecosister project emerged within this context. Supported by the NextGeneration EU plan and Italy's "Piano Nazionale Ripresa e Resilienza" (PNRR), Ecosister represents a flagship research endeavour. It connects key research institutions, including six universities, four public research centres, and 13 private research and innovation hubs. With over 800 researchers participating, the project aims to invest €110 million over 3 years to leverage the innovation ecosystem for Emilia-Romagna's sustainable transition. Research activities span critical areas such as materials for sustainability, clean energy production, green manufacturing, intelligent mobility solutions, and ecological transition driven by high-performance computing and data technology. The Ecosister project dedicates a sub-area to exploring circular economy principles. Among various definitions, Murray et al. [3] describe circular economy as an economic model that aims to maximise ecosystem functioning and human well-being sustainably.

Scholars have delved into practical and political aspects related to circular economy [4]. Additionally, they have examined the three pillars of sustainability (economic, environmental, and social), investigating how circular economy models can foster sustainable businesses and contribute to achieving development goals [5, 6]. Furthermore, researchers have explored innovations and digitalisation processes, emphasising digital technologies and strategies for achieving sustainable outcomes [7, 8].

Despite growing interest in CE, the comprehension of the role of organisational networks in new CBMs, remains narrowed due to limited theoretical grounds and scarce empirical research. Our research aims to address this gap by designing and conducting theory-grounded empirical research based on case study analysis, focusing on the representative cases of Parmigiano Reggiano and Mutti.

Thus, the underlying research question is: What is the role of organisational networks in developing new circular business models in the Italian agri-food ecosystem?

On the grounds of extant literature, we design semi-structured interviews, aiming to unfold the characteristics of organisational relationships and the role of social networks in innovative CBMs.

The paper unfolds as follows. The next section provides the literature analysis on CBMs in the agri-food ecosystem, evidencing the evolution of the business model frameworks in circular economy, their specificity and applications in such a domain, and evidencing the potential role of organisational relationships and networks for implementing circularity (in agri-food). Notably, extant CBM frameworks do not explicitly take into account organisational networks, and this study aims to cover this gap.

In Sect. 3, the methodological underpinnings of the data collection and analysis are proposed. Two relevant case studies are selected, and semi-structured interview schemes are developed on the basis of extant CBM models, integrated with a new section on organisational relationships and networks. Expected outcomes, final remarks and conclusions close the paper.

2 Literature Review

In recent years, particular scholarly attention has been given to examining the dynamics enabling circular economy (CE), recognising the potential of closed-loop systems for minimising waste and maximising resource efficiency as a sustainable alternative to the traditional linear economy [1, 2]. A circular economy approach draws on principles such as valorising by-products and adopting regenerative practices to transform an ecosystem, leading to improved environmental outcomes and enhanced resilience [9]. The relevance of this approach is given to its potential for supporting different stakeholders to address sustainability challenges while fostering economic growth [4].

Among other aspects, innovative business models that facilitate the circulation of resources, products, and services within an ecosystem are central to a circular approach [5]. In particular, business models based on a circular approach usually enhance collaboration, resource sharing, and value chain integration [6]. In addition, the intersection of information systems and circular economy disciplines [7] has received growing attention in this scientific debate [1, 8, 10–12]. For example, several scholars discuss the emergence of collaborative platforms and sharing models, enabling different stakeholders to share equipment, knowledge, and resources to optimise production and reduce waste [1, 8, 10, 11, 13]. At the same time, further studies reveal different types of barriers (e.g., cultural, regulatory, economic, and technical) that hinder the implementation of specific circular business model dimensions (e.g., value proposition, creation, delivery, and capture) [14].

The following four subsections present relevant theoretical underpinning on CE and business models, especially exploring the discussions concerning such a new paradigm in the agri-food sector [15]. Moreover, the fourth subsection provides insights into the role of organisational networks.

2.1 Circular Business Models

Focusing on the scientific literature examining circular business models (CBM), scholars have widely explored this innovative paradigm in terms of the sustainable competitive advantage it could offer organisations [16]. In particular, the last decade has seen a growing increase in the number of publications proposing theoretical conceptualisation and related frameworks [17], as well as focusing on several research areas such as archetypes, classification methods, adoption-oriented challenges, and decision-support tools (to mention some) [18].

Given the intersection of different aspects seemingly contributes to the development of circular business models in organisations, recent studies emphasise the role played by digital technologies surrounding advanced manufacturing practices in the Industry 4.0 era [19]. Interestingly, the multidisciplinary nature characterising the innovation of such business models is often based on the triple bottom line foundation, considering it a basis for achieving a sustainable society through circular economy practices [20]. Then, digital technologies present the potential for leveraging value creation across social, economic, and environmental dimensions [18], accelerating novel ways of collaboration toward the transition to resource-efficient and circular production systems [7].

Accordingly, some research analyses the benefits coming from the implementation of CE [21] and the aspects that could influence the implementation of circular business models (e.g., resource flow management, considerations on surpluses, system orientation, challenges, system design, company size, rebound effects, customers, company's culture and behaviour, and capacity building) [22]. Foroozanfar et al. [23] also recognise regulatory and institutional aspects as pivotal as the environmental, economic and social ones when organisations integrate circularity in their organisational design.

By rethinking the organisational design in addition to supply chain management practices [24], Sarja et al. [25] explore the types of catalysts, obstacles, and ambivalent factors affecting CE in organisations. Uhrenholt et al. [26] focus on the financial performance of organisations adopting a CE by examining the factors affecting product take-back systems. Ding et al. [27] examine opportunities and risks of digital technologies in CBM, remarking that room for further investigation concerns empirical evidence of the virtualise, exchange, and regenerate CBM.

In comparison, while some scholars delve deeper into the impact of CE on companies' value chain processes [28], further academics examine the adoption and implementation of CE practices in particular contexts or industries. Among others, significant research progression has advanced with regard to construction [29], product-service systems (SSPSS) [30], e-waste [31], bio-residuals [32], biogas production [33], plastic consumption [34], photovoltaics and energy production [35].

Focusing on production ecosystems, the agriculture ecosystem represents one of the key sectors in which much of the assumptions beyond circularity could be applied. As a matter of fact, increasing attention is given to the potential of CE applied in such a context where the value generated could significantly enrich and enhance the cumulative effort toward social sustainability [36]. However, in reviewing the literature, we acknowledged that only 10 out of 718 documents included the keyword "Agriculture" by running the following query search on the Scopus database (last update early May 2024) *TITLE-ABS-KEY (circular* AND business AND model*) AND (ISSN (. . .) OR ISSN (. . .))*. Specifically, we decided to target our research by selecting all the ISSN codes of the Journals ranked in the AJG2021 established by the Chartered Association of Business Schools.[1] In light of this, the following sections provide a thorough exploration of CE and CBM research strictly discussing topics connected to such a sector (in line with the objective of this paper).

2.2 *Circular Economy in the Agri-Food Ecosystem*

In recent years, the agri-food sector has paid considerable attention to issues such as food safety, product quality, and respect for the environment in particular [30]. The high demand for food at global levels, coupled with climate change and environmental degradation, has emphasised the importance of developing sustainable agriculture, with the transition to a circular economy approach resulting a key strategy [37]. Environmental challenges present a major opportunity for developing innovative technologies (i.e., the application of scientific knowledge and innovations to enhance practices) and profitable business practices to address the utilisation of agricultural wastes and by-products. From this perspective, a CE approach can reduce the negative impacts of resource extraction and use on the environment, simultaneously contributing to restoring biodiversity and natural capital [38].

Focusing on the agriculture sector, among other definitions provided by the literature, Velasco-Muñoz et al. [39] conceptualise CE applied to agriculture as "the set of activities designed to ensure economic, environmental, and social sustainability in agriculture through practices that pursue the efficient and effective use of resources in all phases of the value chain and also guarantee the regeneration of biodiversity in agroecosystems and the surrounding ecosystems". Specifically, a CE approach is mainly based on three principles driven by design [9], that is: i.) eliminate waste and pollution; ii.) circulate products and materials at their highest value (i.e., keeping materials in use, either as a product or, when that can no longer be used, as components or raw materials; iii.) regenerate nature (i.e., the transition from a linear to a circular economy approach consist in shifting the focus from extraction to regeneration).

Exploring strictly such literature, it also appears that further CE principles are based on the representation of the process as a combination of biological and technical flows of the economic system [40]. These flows are generally conceived as two cycles: organic materials circulating in open-loop systems via the environment and inorganic materials circulating in closed-loop systems within society [41]. Drawing on these assumptions, the biological circle is primarily relevant, as agro-waste and by-product valorisation concerns the biological sphere, mainly through two reverse cycles (i.e., cascading and repurposing and organic feedstock conversion) [24].

[1] https://charteredabs.org/academic-journal-guide.

Regarding cascading and repurposing, it refers to the sequential use of resources for different purposes, first exploiting these materials as components and finally producing energy [42]. Cascading is associated with resource efficiency through consecutive resource circulation. Once all feasible cascades are exploited, organic residuals can be processed via biomass conversion, like anaerobic digestion. In comparison, organic feedstock conversion refers to the conversion processes that simultaneously transform biomass into chemical products and one or more forms of energy, thereby closing the loop by providing inputs for other processes [24].

Waste management represents a further peculiar pillar concerning circularity in agri-food ecosystems. Receiving particular scholarly attention is the shift from the traditional philosophy based on the "3Rs" framework (i.e., Reduce, Reuse, and Recycle) towards a "zero waste" philosophy, based on the idea of managing materials in ways that preserve value, reduce environmental impact, and conserve natural resources [43]. This expanded philosophy has been conceptualised through the introduction of two further aspects, Refuse and Repurpose, originating a "5Rs" framework [44]. According to Papargyropoulou et al. [44], the "5Rs" framework is conceived in a hierarchical logic, meaning that the first four actions (Rs) should be sequentially taken, if possible, before the final potential action (the fifth R) of recycling [44]. Precisely, such a cycle consists of the sequential undertaking of the following: first action, "Refuse" (i.e., avoid materials or products not necessarily needed), second action, "Reduce" (i.e., reduction of wasteful, harmful, and non-recyclable materials), third action, "Reuse" (i.e., several use of products or materials), fourth action, "Repurpose" (i.e., reuse of products in new transformation), eventually a fifth action, "Recycle" (i.e., converting waste and other used materials into reusable products) [44].

Among others, Jurgilevich et al. [45] shed light on the concept of circular economy in the food ecosystem. These authors adopt the lens of sociotechnical transition theory, implying long-term and fundamental transformation processes through which established sociotechnical systems shift to more sustainable modes of production and consumption [45]. According to Jurgilevich et al. [45], a CE approach offers solutions along the entire system circle, which includes three interconnected stages: i.) food production; ii.) food consumption; iii) food waste and surplus management. Food waste and surplus management refer to both the production (i.e., the utilisation of by-products and food waste) and consumption phases (i.e., the reuse of food and surplus avoidance). Interestingly, up to 40% of losses in developed countries occur during consumption, mainly because of consumer behaviours and food standards.

From a strategic point of view, to implementing CE in the agricultural sector, Bocken et al. [46] provide a framework that classifies specific strategies according to the mechanisms by which resources flow through a system. Based on these assumptions, to assess the applicability and effectiveness of such strategies in measuring agricultural systems' circularity, Velasco-Muñoz et al. [39] extend these latter assumptions [46] by proposing the following conceptualisation (that we arranged summarizing it through different subsections).

Slowing Resource Loop Strategies are defined as "a set of measures to extend the life of products within the agri-food system" [39 , p.4]. This strategy aims to keep nutrients within the food chain in order to be in use for the longest possible to satisfy the purpose of feeding people (e.g., avocados that present any deficiency are used for the production of guacamole).

Closing Resource Loop Strategies (corresponding to resource cascading) include "all those operations aimed at recycling agricultural materials, including the production of energy with waste materials" [39 , p. 5] (e.g., on the basis of the previous example, concerning this strategy, after the transformation process, the stone and skin of the avocado are used in producing animal feed, while bio-elements are extracted and destined to the cosmetics and nutraceutical industries).

Narrowing Resource Loop Strategies are defined as "all those measures aimed at optimising the use of bio-resources" [39 , p. 4]. Solutions that reduce resource intensity and the environmental impacts per unit of product belong to this category (e.g., the use of drip irrigation to minimise water use in the cultivation phase of avocado or the installation of solar panels to provide the energy required.

Regenerating Resource Loop Strategies include "all actions aimed at preserving and enhancing natural capital" [39 , p. 5] (e.g., again based on the first example, concerning this strategy, the residues of avocado that can no longer be reused in another process are used in the production of bio-fertiliser for cultivation farms, which returns nutrients to the soil.

2.3 Circular Business Models in the Agri-Food Ecosystem

Agriculture shows peculiar characteristics, not only in terms of the biological cycle of CE but also in aspects like family ownership, the diffuse and seasonal nature of production, and the link between the production process and the quality and safety of products [47]. In this perspective, food loss and waste in the supply chain and the business model and organisation management [31] are the most investigated topics in the literature, while room for further investigation concerns the specific aspects driving the implementation of circularity with the agri-food ecosystem (and related implications affecting the different stakeholders involved).

Interestingly, sustainability and CE are often acknowledged as two related issues for organisations operating in the agri-food ecosystem, where the latter is conceived as an approach useful to foster sustainable development [48]. Exploring deeper into the peculiarities of such association, however, it appears that few empirical evidence supports an understanding of the sustainable characteristics of such new business model configurations. In other words, it seems unclear how and what circular practices contribute to facilitate organisations in improving sustainability aspects. Moreover, such research is often based on the analysis of new organisational configurations (building on circularity foundation), rather than implementing circularity into existing organisational configurations. For example, Franceschelli et al. [49] investigate how a food start-up leveraged innovations through its business model. These authors highlight certain sustainable characteristics for each business model component, especially focusing on social and environmental issues. Furthermore, claiming that research in this domain is yet to offer a proper theoretical lens for investigating the relationship between sustainability and circularity (resulting in business model configurations), Barth et al. [47] suggest that a conceptual framework for sustainable business model innovation in the agri-food sector should explicitly include the sustainability aspects of its building blocks. Evans et al. [50] identify and further classify sustainable business models into 14 unique categories, among the others agri-food and circular economy foundation. However, these studies do not explicitly integrate CE issues into sustainable business models.

One exemption is Donner et al. [13], who developed a "combined" theoretical framework to understand business model innovations to convert agro-waste and by-products into valuable products. These authors identify different cases of circular business models (biogas plant, upcycling entrepreneurship, environmental biorefinery, agricultural cooperative, agro park and support structure) according to the type of organisational structure, resources, transformation processes, value propositions, key partners, customers, strategic approaches and innovation. They find that successfully implementing circular business models in the agricultural domain responds to internal organisational redefinition and proper response to external challenges, like policies and regulations. Then, it is worth noting that a business model based on cascading, repurposing, and organic feedstock conversion can lead to extended relationships with business partners and consumers due to the need for various and repeated delivery and take-back activities as part of the value creation processes [24].

2.4 The Missing Link: Organisational Networks

A few recent studies are acknowledging the hypothesis that organisational networks and relationships could play a crucial role in the development and operation of circular business economies: for example, a specific investigation focused on supply chains was proposed by Marques and Manzanares [51]. Organisational networks encompass various stakeholders, including farmers, suppliers, manufacturers, distributors, retailers, consumers, and waste management organisations [6, 11]. By fostering collaboration and information exchange, these networks enable the efficient flow of resources and facilitate the implementation of circular practices [15].

While specific studies are still scarce, some relevant concepts for circular networks have been object of attention. For example, effective stakeholder collaboration can be paramount to promote circularity in an ecosystem [8]. By engaging stakeholders across value chains, organisations are able to identify opportunities for waste reduction, resource optimisation, and innovation [10]. The importance of these collaborations is underscored by the fact that information sharing among stakeholders is critical for coordinating activities, aligning incentives, and overcoming barriers to circularity [11, 12]. Moreover, other scholars further underline the importance of information transparency and trust among stakeholders, representing a condition for enabling circular business models [13, 14]. As a result, a circular economy approach requires a collective effort that is beneficial and necessary for the successful implementation of the different practices enabling circularity [52, 53].

Besides, government policies and regulatory frameworks also play a significant role in shaping circular ecosystems [54]. Policies that incentivise sustainable practices, promote circular business models and regulate waste management can create an enabling environment for circularity [40]. However, it is essential to ensure that these policies are coherent and aligned with the goals of stakeholders across a value chain [55].

Thus, relationships that generate networks among different stakeholders are pivotal in crafting circular business economies, where digital technologies could play a significant role in facilitating such transition [7]. By fostering collaboration, information sharing, and stakeholder engagement, these networks enable the implementation of circular practices and drive sustainable innovation.

In their study, Tate et al. [56] propose a biomimicry lens to frame circular systems. Drawing inspiration from natural ecosystems, they identify four critical roles: producers, consumers, scavengers, and decomposers. The ecosystem's balance relies on producers providing enough food for consumers without resource depletion. The authors explore visual diagrams, using Social Network Analysis (SNA), to connect circular economy principles with supply networks. They emphasise introducing new actors (i.e., scavengers and decomposers) to enhance circularity.

To summarise, the analysis of the existing literature shows that organisational networks could play a crucial role in shaping new circular economy business models within the agri-food sector. However, despite this recognition, a notable gap remains: the absence of well-defined frameworks and empirical field studies that delve into the intricate interplay between network presence, configuration, and dynamics. Understanding how these factors impact innovative circular business models in the agri-food industry remains an area ripe for exploration.

3 Methodology

This section comprises three subsections. The first consists of the multiple case study design, outlining the specific theoretical propositions underpinning the development of a semi-structured interview format. The second presents the semi-structured interview protocol, encompassing its structure, inquiries, and pertinent details regarding the data collection procedure. Lastly, the third subsection provides a concise overview of the selected cases, encompassing their legal classification and primary objectives.

3.1 Case Study Design

This study employs an exploratory qualitative methodology [57] to investigate the dynamics contributing to developing circular business models within the agri-food ecosystem, drawing on Yin's [58] recommendations for multiple-case studies. Our aim is to delve into how various stakeholders within the agri-food ecosystem design and develop circular practices to achieve diverse business objectives, examining both commonalities and unique aspects across selected cases. We seek to qualitatively explore the effects of circular economy practices on organisations operating within this ecosystem, as well as the resultant organisational transformations [58].

In addition to qualitative analysis, this study includes a multi-dimensional quantitative examination of the organisational, social, and environmental factors influencing circular economy practices. Through triangulation of data from multiple sources across diverse cases within the agri-food ecosystem, we aim to derive insights that can be generalised beyond the specific cases studied. Our analysis also includes a research journal developed by the present authors, sustainability reports, non-financial statements provided by the two organisations, and further documents retrieved for secondary sources.

In order to develop investigations, we adopt and adapt Donner and de Vries' [59] assumptions to guide our data collection and analysis to examine two food organisations within the Italian agri-food sector. At the same time, in line with the proposed literature review, we acknowledge that there could be general agreement among scholars in acknowledging the so-called "R's" of circularity. In contrast, assumptions and conceptualisations of how to investigate the transition from linear to circular business models (given the practices and needs characterising a case) could vary due to the specific context (i.e., a micro field in such an ecosystem), in addition to the overarching circularity approach being adopted or implemented by a specific company [39]. For this reason, we have designed a tailored semi-structured interview protocol based on three areas of investigation.

The rationale is to cover the different areas of inquiry (arranged among macro- and micro-level aspects for examining circular business practices), aligning with the *"new conceptual framework for circular business model innovation in the agri-food ecosystem"* suggested by Donner and de Vries [59]. However, this research contemplates only "closing resource loop strategies" representing one particular circularity approach (among the practices along the entire system circle characterising the agri-food ecosystem). Therefore, to avoid assuming a default bias (i.e., avoid assuming that a case understudied is supposed to refer to a closed loop strategy [39] and the related approach of circularity, as in [59]), we integrate two further areas of investigation. The first area intended to develop an understanding of the specific circularity approach (characterising the agri-food business case). An additional area concerns organisational networks to explore how relationships among different stakeholders contribute to designing and developing circular practices (with regard to the specific business case).

Table 1 Macro and micro aspects as interview guide adopted by Donner and de Vries [59]

Aspect of the investigation	Objective(es) of the investigation
Macro-level Environmental Aspects	
1. Political-legal	Policies, laws and regulations
2. Economic	Markets and subsidies
3. Social, technological and environmental conditions	"not specified"
Micro-level Business Aspects	
4. Historical	Origin, triggers and development of the initiative
5. Organisational	Governance, partnerships and logistics
6. Technological	Type and maturity of technologies used, examples of by-product valorisation and outputs (for this study, we also considered Velasco-Muñoz et al. [39] for this objective).
7. Marketing and financial elements	Investments and cost-benefit structure

From this perspective, each area would serve as a focal point for investigation, drawing from previously established assumptions and conceptualisations (considering not only the peculiarities of the circularity discourse but also the one characterising the agri-food ecosystem and established theories in organisational studies). In other words, the selected framework [59] is adapted to suit our objective of exploring CE as a sociotechnical transition [45] within the agri-food ecosystem, focusing on the interconnection with sustainability practices [48, 49], investigating the role of relationships and networks contributing to the development of CBMs (in this specific ecosystem).

3.2 *Data Collection and Analysis*

Drawing on the adopted theoretical framework [59], we have developed a tailored interview protocol to explore the organisations' operational practices and daily activities while also investigating their engagement with CE practices. The interviews are semi-structured, allowing participants to respond openly to questions or share insights, typically lasting between 60 min to 2 h. Our focus within these interviews is to investigate the transition process of a business model to a circular one as outlined by Donner and de Vries [59], in addition to exploring circularity network aspects (that we integrate in this research). In particular, Table 1 reports the relevant macro- and micro-level business aspects [59] to consider when examining the flows of the operations and practices generated through the implementation of a circularity approach [59].

Besides, drawing on the foundations grounded in social network theory, we intend to examine the underlying structures and dynamics shaping relationships and networks in this research. Several authors in the literature adopt social network theory as a robust framework for analysing the interconnections and interactions among various actors in a given system [60, 61]. Accordingly, we leverage concepts such as nodes and ties to examine entities and their relationships within the specific agri-food ecosystem under investigation [60, 62]. Then, we adopt the meaning of two significant measures, *Density* and *Centrality*, using nodes referring to organisations and ties to signify interactions or transactions among them (which stand for the intricate connections contributing to the development of circular practices) [63, 64].

As a way of explanation, density is a measure of the interconnectedness of nodes within a network and could be helpful to investigate the extent of collaboration and exchange within an ecosystem [64]. Then, high density indicates a tightly knit network with frequent interactions, while low density suggests a more fragmented network. In comparison, we refer to the centrality metric, considering it as a measure that, in this case, could allow us to identify key actors or organisations exerting significant influence within the network. Considering centrality metrics such as degree centrality, betweenness centrality, and closeness centrality, we elaborate on the idea that we could be able to identify pivotal nodes that play crucial roles in facilitating circular economy initiatives [63, 64].

By quantifying the number of transactions among different organisations, the quantity of product exchange, and the frequency of such transactions, we are supposed to be able to gain insights into the density and centrality of such networks. Focusing on the idea of analysing nodes and ties, we aim to interpret the patterns of interaction and identify key actors driving the transition towards a more sustainable and circular agri-food ecosystem (also considering that this could impact other productive ecosystems).

To this end, in analysing how organisational networks influence the application of circular business models within the agri-food ecosystem, we acknowledge significative assumptions in three essential network properties [65, 66]. Among other pioneers in theorising a social network approach [67–70], Tichy et al. [66] propose a comprehensive model grounded in network theory aimed at effectively understanding social and organisational processes. Specifically, these authors argue *transactional content*, *nature of the link* (i.e., relationship nature), and *structural characteristics* (i.e., attribute) as the central properties of networks in order that organisational settings can be examined, and comparative analyses can be conducted [66]. Accordingly, the first property, *transactional content*, concerns examining what is exchanged within the network, such as knowledge, resources, or support. The second property, the *nature of the links*, consists of examining the strength and quality of relationships among network members, which influences collaboration. Lastly, the *structural characteristics* property, refers to examining the overall network configuration, including factors like clustering, density, and the presence of central nodes, all of which determine interaction patterns and network dynamics (and effectiveness) [66].

As a result, we crafted open-ended questions arranged in three distinct areas of investigation. The first Area 1, “Understanding the circularity approach”, refers to

Table 2 Structure of the interview protocol

Area	Focus and number of questions (for sections if included)
1. Understanding the circularity approach [39]	Four approaches/loop strategies (slowing 3, closing 2, narrowing 3, regenerating 3) CoP & IO statutes - 2
2. Understanding the transition from linear to circular business models [59]	Section A (experiences, changes, and practices from a sustainable point of view) – 4 Section B (key characteristics of the business case) – 6
	Section C (external drivers, market-pull or outside-in) – 6 Section D (stakeholders involved and internal drivers) – 2 Section E (innovation in circular business models) – 15
3. Understanding the organisational network [66]	Section F 1. Transactional content - 4 2. Nature of the link – 4 3. Structural characteristics - 12

the possibility of targeting the business case and recognising the cycle(s) of circularity fostered by the organisation. It is based on a set of different circular economy strategies [39], supposed to be also characterised by the Code of Practice (CoP) for the cheese case [71] and the statute of the Inter-Branch Organisation (IO) for the tomato case [72]. The second Area 2, "Understanding the transition from linear to circular business models", refers to the dynamics and key dimensions where changes are commonly made in the agri-food ecosystem [59]. It consists of six sections, intending to explore how the business case adapted or is adapting to these changes (along with the presentation of the characteristics of the business case). Furthermore, considering the significance of relationships among stakeholders in facilitating the development of effective and efficient circular economy practices, the third Area 3, "Understanding the organisational network", refers to the circularity network aspects we design for exploring the networks that might have influenced and/or driven/supported the pursuit of circularity practices within the business case. Through an "interaction approach" [66], this area refers to the understanding of the key properties and dynamics of an organisational network by examining aspects of interactions and transactions generated between entities and business stakeholders [59]. Accordingly, each area is relevant to the case study design, accompanied by corresponding questions intended for participants. The structure of such interview protocol is summarised in Table 2, while the complete questionnaire protocol (and questions for each area) is reported in Appendix.

To ensure participant comfort during the interview process, we aimed to initiate discussions in a welcoming and approachable manner. This involved initiating conversations about the participants themselves and their roles within the organisations.

3.3 Business Cases Description

To identify suitable organisations for our case study, we considered identifying organisations operating in the same sectors as the one mostly explored in the specific literature rooted in the agri-food ecosystem (considering this could allow us to perform cross-national comparisons). Specifically, considering the specific project requirements upon which this research is founded and conducted, we selected organisations producing cheese and tomato products [73–76].

The cheese and tomato sectors in the Emilia Romagna region are two cases in point according to the Localized Agri-food Systems (LAFs) [72, 74, 77–79]. LAFs are defined as a type of organisation of agri-food activities in which territorial dynamics play a decisive role in terms of the coordination between stakeholders and the development of production activities [80].

The Parmigiano Reggiano is a Protected Designation of Origin (PDO) cheese produced in five provinces on the south bank of the Po River in Italy that are Parma, Reggio Emilia, Modena, part of Bologna and Mantua [81]. It is produced following strict rules defined by the producer association named *Consorzio del Formaggio Parmigiano Reggiano,*[2] according to the PDO quality schemes for specific agricultural products with a strong link to the geographical area where it is produced.

Previous works investigate the environmental impact of Parmigiano Reggiano production in terms of water, energy consumption and packaging material [82, 83]). Arfini et al. [74, 77–79] and Mancini et al. [73] assessed the evolution of sustainability in Parmigiano Reggiano's organisation over the period 2000–2018. In these studies, the co-authors stress the interaction between the territory and the value chain and find that Parmigiano Reggiano Protected Designation of Origin (PDO) cheese is a product with a long history but with a slow and progressive evolution, as it is tightly regulated in the technical and managerial aspects. Habli et al. [71] investigate the effective adoption of CE principles in three cheese value chains with geographical indication, putting emphasis on the role of the specific CoP and on the nature of practice to understand circularity in the specific context of PDO productions. Their questionnaire includes a session on the "5Rs" framework, where for each "R", the interviewer asks about the adoption of the practice within the production phase of the value chain, whether the practice is traditional or innovative, and whether it is specified in such a CoP.

Besides, Mutti S.p.A. is a leading Italian processing firm specialising in the tomato sector. The company was founded in the 1950s, and since the early 2000s, Mutti has set up different projects related to the company's environmental sustainability [84]. Italy is the third largest tomato producer in the world (12% of global tomato processing), after California (26%) and China (18%).[3]

---

[2] https://www.parmigianoreggiano.com/consortium-specifications-and-legislation.

[3] https://oipomodoronorditalia.it/dati/#dati_filiera.

In this context, tomato wastes are generated along the whole production chain, from cultivation to transformation, ranging from immature and damaged fruits to residues like peels, seeds and pomaces [85]. Rajan et al. [86] review different by-products associated with tomato processing at various processing stages and their utilization in all the possible ways to provide solutions for effective waste utilization. Moreover, emerging from previous work are also estimations about the amount of food lost and waste generated along the tomato-sauce supply chain [75], as well as the water footprint of tomato production and processing [87].

Regarding the interviewee, for such an exploratory first wave of interviews confirming participation in our project are the sustainability manager for the Mutti S.p.A. and the general manager for the Parmigiano Reggiano group (consortium).

4 Expected Results and Preliminary Discussion

The analysis of the two case studies should give an answer to our research question: *What is the role of organisational networks in developing new circular business models in the Italian agri-food ecosystem?*

In particular, the basic Circular Business Model Framework recently proposed by Donner and de Vries [59] is depicted in Fig. 1 here below. As presented in the previous sections, the interview design, data collection, and data analysis for the two case studies are designed based on this framework. In particular, the "External trends and drivers" in the top left part of the figure are the Macro-level Environmental Aspects, and the Internal drivers depicted in the bottom left part of the figure are the Micro-level Business Aspects (as presented in Table 1). In addition, the different sections of Area 2, presented in Table 2, are intended to investigate the flows and dynamics affecting a business model. In particular, Section A focuses on the central horizontal flow starting from business core activities, the control quadrant, backwards and forward to the appreciate quadrant. Section B focuses on the central vertical flow intended to examine how "sustainable needs" generate new dynamics and practices implemented in the business (developing along and through the red quadrants). Section C investigates the flow characterising the external trends and drivers shaping the business ecosystems level (dark blue quadrants), while section D focuses on the stakeholders involved and the internal drivers contributing to innovations and cocreation practices shaping the "circular" business level (light blue quadrants). In addition to sections C and D, Section E aims to examine how the business model of the case understudied evolved in response to circularity practices given the typical elements of innovation as outlined in the Business Model Canvas (BMC) framework [88] (that is, through the red quadrants).

The data collection and analysis are expected to show from actual on-the-field observations how these aspects are affecting the creation of new parts of the business models towards achieving circularity.

In addition, we expect that the information collected about organisational networks can be introduced in this model as a new component. Specifically, Section

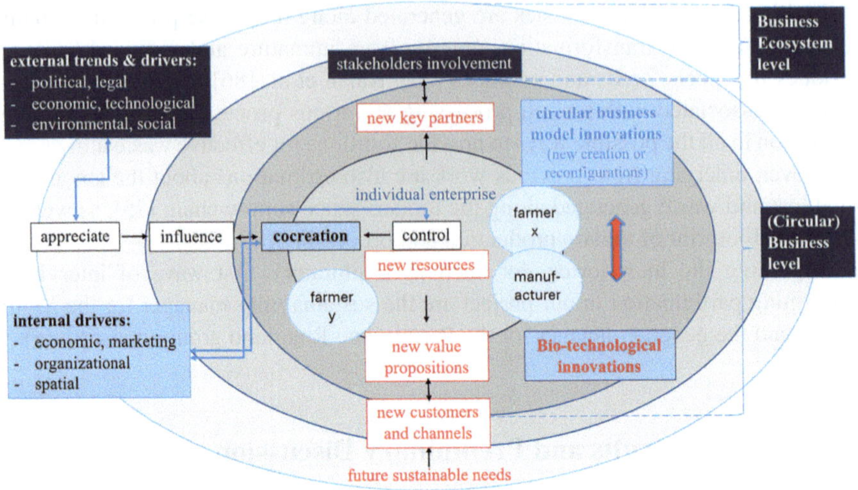

Fig. 1 The conceptual framework for Circular Business Model Innovation in the agri-food domain adapted from Donner and de Vries [59]

F in Table 2, integrating the "missed link" characterising this research, intends to investigate the role and influence of the organisational network with respect to the circularity change and related dynamics. The analysis of the existence, configuration and structure of the social network can shed new light on how circular business models could be enabled by different types of social networks.

5 Conclusion

This work-in-progress paper lays the groundwork for data collection and analysis, proposing a semi-structured interview structure aimed at developing theoretical propositions on the role and characteristics of organisational networks in CBMs. Our expected findings contribute to the understanding and development of new network-based business models for implementing CE in agri-food industries.

From a theoretical point of view, this study offers an overview of the state of the art based on relevant reviews on circular business models, considering the most cited publications, the most recent, and the once interconnected with the agriculture field of study. Moreover, this work intends to provide foundations for investigating the pivotal role of organisational networks in catalysing business model circularity in the Italian agri-food arena.

From a practical perspective, we propose a tailored protocol to conduct semi-structured interviews to develop a theoretical proposition that will help explore the relationships unfolding in the network catalysing circular business models. In particular, we place significant emphasis on considering that the peculiarities of a specific geographical area are likely to affect the structure of a circular network. Then, the main contribution (as a long-term ambition) of this research is to develop a conceptual proposition and provide empirical evidence that could support organisations, managers, and other stakeholders (such as third-sector entities) in designing and developing their circularity (enhancing and strengthening the network).

This research is not without limitations. Although we are arranging in-depth interviews to corroborate the analysis, the present work does not provide an exhaustive analytical generalisation of the results. As a future step, we plan to code and classify the interviews through an in-depth analysis in order to recognise the main characteristics of the relationships generating circularity among the cases analysed. Accordingly, we intend to compare the cases to identify differences and similarities given the different sizes and structures of the networks, as well as the stakeholders involved (and their roles). Furthermore, since we compare organisations operating under different contexts and branches, this work might ignore economic, cultural, and organisational factors that could influence the results. For this reason, we could increase the number of participants and organisations in additional steps. In particular, we are supposed to collect information that could lay the groundwork to design, refine, and run, at least, a second wave of interviews with the same respondents, enriching the number of respondents for each case, also informing about the suitability to select specific/ or a broader number of cases to be studied. From this perspective, a comparison with other ecosystems with different meso and macro attributes (that could affect social relationships) represents room for further investigations.

In addition, it could also be interesting to focus deeply on the technological aspects, given its relevance in promoting collaborations and social interaction in the supply chain of businesses [19, 89]. For example, industrial clusters and motivations for collaborations, besides digital technologies, are emerging items that contribute to the development of such networks toward circular economy transition [89].

Acknowledgments This study was funded by the "National Recovery and Resilience Plan (NRRP), Mission 04 Component 2 Investment 1.5 – NextGenerationEU, Call for tender n. 3277 dated 30/12/2021, Award Number: 0001052 dated 23/06/2022".

Disclosure of Interests The authors have no competing interests to declare that are relevant to the content of this article.

A.1 Appendix: Questionnaire

Area 1. Understanding the circularity approach (among the practices along the entire system circle characterising the agri-food business case).

The circular economy in the agri-food sector encompasses various practices primarily designed to enhance sustainability by reusing resources, reducing waste, and optimising resource use. This first area of investigation intends to explore the practices that could be aligned with circularity principles and sustainability. To this

Table 3 Understanding the circularity approach

Strategy	Question(s)
1. Slowing resource loop strategies This approach involves measures to extend the lifespan of products within the supply chain. For instance, avocados with imperfections are used to produce guacamole	*Does your organisation implement measures to extend the life of products within your supply chain?* *Can you describe these measures?* *Who are the stakeholders involved?*
2. Closing resource loop strategies This approach refers to recycling agricultural materials, including energy production from waste. For example, avocado pits and skins are used for animal feed production, while bio elements are extracted for the cosmetic and nutraceutical industries	*Does your organisation adopt measures for recycling agricultural materials, including energy production from waste?* *Can you describe these measures, and the stakeholders involved?*
3. Narrowing resource loop strategies This approach aims to optimise the use of bio-resources. Examples include drip irrigation to minimise water usage for avocado cultivation or installing solar panels to meet energy needs	*Does your organisation implement measures to optimize the use of bio-resources?* *Can you describe these measures?* *Who are the stakeholders involved?*
4. Regenerating resource loop strategies. This approach involves measures to preserve and enhance natural capital. For example, avocado residues that cannot be reused in other processes are used to produce biofertilizers, which return nutrients to the soil	*Does your organisation implement measures to preserve and enhance natural capital?* *Can you describe these measures?* *Who are the stakeholders involved?*
5. In addition	*Have any of these practices been implemented historically in your organisation?* *Are there some of these practices considered innovative in your organisation?*

end, hereafter, a set of different circular economy strategies is proposed, exemplified by some examples from the avocado industry [39]. Accordingly, this first area of investigation refers to the possibility of targeting the business case and recognising the approach(es) of circularity fostered by the organisation. Then, based on the example, please feel free to describe whether and how, if it is the case, these (or similar) practices are adopted in your organisation (Table 3).

Area 2. Understanding the transition from linear to circular business models (along with the presentation of the characteristics of the business case).

According to Donner et al. [13], the shift from a linear business model to a circular one involves several key changes in a company. The second area of the questionnaire consists of six sections, intending to explore how the business case adapted or is adapting to these changes.

To develop an understanding of how the company is shifting from traditional business practices to more sustainable, circular models, hereafter are presented some key dimensions where changes are commonly made in the agri-food ecosystem. These dimensions include, for example, managing waste or by-products, collaborating with new partners, sharing resources, and expanding the specific market reach through innovative practices.

Figure 1 is an explicative (and adapted) depiction of a conceptual framework for Circular Business Model Innovation in the agri-food domain proposed by Donner and de Vries [59]. Starting from the assumptions claimed by these authors, the following sections are intended to investigate the flows and dynamics affecting a business model. In particular, Section A focuses on the central horizontal flow starting from business core activities, the control quadrant, backwards and forward to the appreciate quadrant. Section B focuses on the central vertical flow intended to examine how "sustainable needs" generate new dynamics and practices implemented in the business (developing along and through the red quadrants). Section C investigates the flow characterising the external trends and drivers shaping the business ecosystems level (dark blue quadrants), while section D focuses on the stakeholders involved and the internal drivers contributing to innovations and cocreation practices shaping the "circular" business level (light blue quadrants). In addition to sections C and D, Section E aims to examine how the business model of the case understudied evolved in response to circularity practices given the typical elements of innovation as outlined in the Business Model Canvas (BMC) framework (Osterwalder and Pigneur [88]; that is, through the red quadrants). Finally, integrating the "missed link" characterising this research, we include Section F as Area 3, intended to investigate the role and influence of the organisational network with respect to the circularity change and related dynamics.

To this end, the following first group of questions adopt a top-down approach with the aim to start reasoning about experiences and practices in the context of such dimensions, and therefore, intending to easily identify changes and practices related to how your organisation is embracing circular economy principles. Explicit questions are then proposed. Meanwhile, for this purpose, please feel free to share any example that is believed to be aligned with such objectives.

Section A (experiences, changes, and practices from a sustainable point of view) (Table 4).

From a sustainable point of view, the previous questions have focused on specific dimensions contributing to the investigation of the circular economy changes and practices, focusing on expanding control, introducing cocreation, establishing a broader influence cycle, and reinforcing appreciation of the business case.

Then, delving deeply into the typical dynamics and changes contributing to the development of Circular Business Model Innovation in the agri-food domain, the following questions will examine the characteristics, external and internal drivers, and stakeholders that affected or are affecting the business case understudied (adopting a contraposing logic as a bottom-up approach).

Table 4 Understanding the transition from linear to circular business models (section A)

Area of change	Question(s)
1. Expanding control Implementing circularity, the traditional control cycle of a company is often expanded to include new "elements" such as:	
Agricultural waste or by-products	*How does your organisation manage agricultural waste and by-products? Are there specific relationships or transactions focused on waste management and by-product utilisation? Please describe them and identify the stakeholders involved*
Biotechnology	*Is your organisation engaging with partners that provide bio (or other) technological solutions? How are these technologies integrated into such (circular) practices? Describe the partnerships and the role of such "technology" in daily operations*
Complementary skills	*Does your organisation collaborate with partners who offer complementary skills necessary for such (circular) practices? How do these collaborations enhance (circular economy) initiatives? Please provide examples of these collaborations*
2. Introducing cocreation A new cycle between control and influence, typically acknowledged as "cocreation", is often introduced. This involves joint activities and synergies with cluster partners, leading to new value propositions:	
Shared resources and synergies	*Does your organisation participate in joint management of key resources, shared logistics, or common infrastructures with other partners? Can you describe these collaborations? How do these partnerships contribute to the circular business model of the organisation?*
Cross-sectoral networks and training	*Are there cross-sectoral networks or shared training events that your organisation is involved in? How do these contribute to the pooling of knowledge and complementary know-how? Please describe the nature of these interactions and their impact*
3. Expanding influence The Influence cycle is often broadened to cover a wider area due to the creation of clusters that reach new customers, channels, segments, and markets	
Cluster expansion and market reach	*How has the creation of clusters influenced your organisation's reach to new markets or customer segments? Can you describe any joint responsibilities or interactive efforts made with partners to achieve sustainable solutions? Who are the key stakeholders involved?*
4. Reinforcing appreciation The Appreciation cycle remains focused on the macroeconomic context and the business ecosystem but with a stronger emphasis on sustainability	
Sustainability	*How does your organisation integrate sustainability into its broader business ecosystem? In what ways has the focus on sustainability shaped your macroeconomic strategies? Can you provide examples of how this shift has influenced your business model?*

Several foundational elements could be explored to understand the key characteristics that define the business case. Accordingly, the first questions aim to identify the main actors, resources, and strategic approaches that are essential to the case's circularity practices, offering insights into how these components contribute to redesigning a business model.

Table 5 Understanding the transition from linear to circular business models (section B)

Foundational element	Question(s)
1. Main actors	*Do you recognise any main actors involved in the core processes of the business case?*
2. Resources and transformation processes	*What resources are required to pursue such circularity practices? Can you describe the transformation processes related to these practices?*
3. Value proposition	*Can you summarise the primary value proposition of the business case?*
4. Key partners	*Can you recognise key partners involved in such circularity practices?*
5. Customers	*Who are the main customers of such practices?*
6. Strategic approach	*Can you describe the strategic approach driving such circularity practices?*

Section B (key characteristics of the business case) (Table 5).

In addition to exploring the key characteristics shaping circular practices, external factors might trigger or influence such practices. The following questions are designed to identify any political, legal, economic, social, technological, and environmental drivers that could impact adopting and implementing (circular) business models. These external elements are critical in understanding the broader context in which the business case operates.

Section C (external drivers, market-pull or outside-in) (Table 6).

Various stakeholders and internal drivers could also be significant in triggering or promoting circularity practices that are developed and sustained within an organisation. Both directly and indirectly involved stakeholders could play a significant role in influencing and implementing circular practices. These can include local actors like farmers, processing companies, suppliers, grid operators, consumers, and various public and private entities. Additionally, the internal drivers, such as the motivations behind adopting circularity practices, often stem from economic, environmental, social, or legal considerations. This section aims to delve into these two dimensions to understand their impact on the circular business model of the business case. In other words, these questions are designed to identify the key players and motivations that drive the circularity efforts within such a business, taking into account the internal dynamics that contribute to the transition toward a circular business model.

Section D (stakeholders involved and internal drivers) (Table 7).

Table 6 Understanding the transition from linear to circular business models (section C)

External factor	Question(s)
1. Political trends/drivers	*Can you recognise any political or policy-level factors that push the organisation to adopt circularity practices? For example, how have European or national strategies and policies for circularity impacted your traditional business?*
2. Legal	*Have there been any regulations or legal frameworks that have played a role in shaping circularity practices? Consider, for example, agro-waste management regulations*
3. Economic	*Can you identify any economic pressure that has driven the adoption of circularity practices? Consider aspects such as market demand, cost-effectiveness for bio-based products, investments in technology and agro-logistic networks*
4. Social	*Can you identify any social factors contributing to the adoption of circularity practices? For instance, consider changes in consumer habits and awareness, the general involvement of civil society in promoting sustainability, or Corporate Social Responsibility initiatives*
5. Technological	*Can you identify any technological advancements that triggered or played a significant role in adopting circularity practices? For example, consider the impact of new technological developments in agro-waste conversion.*
6. Environmental	*Can you identify any environmental factors that have influenced the adoption of circularity practices? For instance, how have climate change and soil conditions affect-ed the management and sensitivity of agro-waste in your organisation?*

Table 7 Understanding the transition from linear to circular business models (section D)

Internal factor	Question(s)
1. Stakeholders involved	*Could you distinguish stakeholders directly or indirectly involved in some circularity practices? For the first type of stakeholders, consider, for example, actors such as farmers, suppliers, processing companies, grid operators, consumers, and other relevant entities*
2. Internal drivers	1. *Could you recognise specific reasons behind the decision to introduce circularity practices in your organisation? Do you believe these have been pushed primarily by economic, environmental, social, or legal forces/dynamics? Or was it a combination of the latter?*

To fully investigate the transformative effects of circularity on business models, the focus of the interview is now pleased on understanding if and how "innovations" are integrated and impact organisational practices. The following section intends to examine how the case business model evolved in response to circularity practices (according to Donner et al. (2020)). Here, considering the various elements of innovation as outlined in the Business Model Canvas (BMC) framework (Osterwalder and Pigneur, 2010), whether these changes constitute entirely new models or modifications of existing settings is questioned. Then, it investigates the nature and extent of innovation and the strategic motivations driving the adoption of circular practices.

Section E (innovation in circular business models) (Table 8).

Area 3. Understanding the organizational network (along with the presentation of the characteristics of the business case).

This final area of the questionnaire aims to investigate the organisational networks that might have influenced and/or driven/supported the pursuit of circularity practices within a business. Understanding the dynamics characterising a network includes examining aspects of interactions and transactions generated between entities and business stakeholders.

Key elements are often represented by the types and characteristics of transactions, the nature of relationships among network members, and the structural characteristics of the network itself. From this perspective, organisational networks could contribute to effectively implementing circularity and related practices. Specifically, according to Tichy et al. [66], the key properties of an organisational network are:

1. Transactional content: this involves identifying the types of exchanges occurring within the network, including emotional connections, influence attempts, information sharing, and the exchange of goods or services.
2. Nature of the link: this focuses on the strength, reciprocity, clarity of expectations, and multiplexity of relationships between network members.
3. Structural characteristics: this encompasses various network properties such as size, density, clustering, openness, stability, reachability, centrality, and specific roles like star, liaison, bridge, gatekeeper, and isolate.

Section F (organisational networks and network properties) (Table 9).

Table 8 Understanding the transition from linear to circular business models (section E)

Area of change	Question(s)
1. Innovation of the business model:	
New creation or reconfiguration	*Can you give an example of how the adoption of circularity practices affected your business model? Consider new creations or a reconfiguration of a previous setting/ existing model*
2. Elements of business model innovation (according to the element of the BMC):	
New key partners	*Can you identify new key partners that have been introduced in the business in order to/as a result of adopting circularity practices?*
New key activities	*Can you make an example of some key activities that have been incorporated into the organisational settings/operations due to the adoption of circularity practices?*
New key resources	*Can you make an example of key resources that are now part of the business as a consequence of adopting circularity practices?*
New value proposition	*Can you recognise a new value proposition that has emerged in the business, given the implementation and adoption of circularity practices?*
New customer relationships	*Can you identify new customer relationships that have been established in the business as a result of implementing or adopting circularity practices?*
New channels	*Given the implementation and adoption of circularity practices, what new channels have been introduced in the business?*
New customer segments	*Can you identify new customer segments that have been targeted in the business as a result of implementing and adopting circularity practices?*
Cost Structure	*Can you recognise or make an example of the disadvantages and costs associated with implementing or adopting circularity practices in the business?*
Revenue Streams	*Can you recognise or give an example of the advantages and revenue streams generated by adopting or implementing circularity practices in the business?*
3. Innovation type	
Innovation type	*Does the adopted or implemented circularity practice require developing or acquiring technological, organisational, or social innovation?*
4. Degree of innovation	
Degree of innovation	*Based on your expertise, do you believe the innovation associated with such circularity practices is incremental or radical?*
5. Innovation strategy	
Defensive strategies	*Is the adoption or implementation of circularity practices (in your organisation) driven primarily by the need to comply with legislation?*
Accommodative strategies	*Is the adoption or implementation of circularity practices motivated by the need to enhance and improve the business by addressing environmental and/or social objectives?*
Proactive strategies	*Is the adoption or implementation of circularity practices driven by the desire to re-design and/or fully address sustainability concerns related to the business's products/processes?*

Table 9 Understanding the organizational network (section F)

Property	Question(s)
1. Transactional content (four types of exchange)	
Expression of Affect	*Could you identify or make an example of the types of emotional or relational exchanges (e.g., friendship, collaboration) that occur between entities (in the business network) involved in circularity practices?*
Influence Attempt	*Could you identify or make an example of how entities in the business network attempt to influence one another in the context of circularity practices?*
Exchange of Information	*Could you identify or make an example of what kinds of information regarding circularity practices are exchanged between entities within the business network?*
Exchange of Goods or Services	*Could you identify or make an example of what goods or services are exchanged among entities in the business network (as part of circularity practices)?*
2. Nature of the link	
Intensity (the strength of the relation between individuals)	*How would you describe the strength of the relationships between entities involved in circularity practices within the business network?*
Reciprocity (the degree to which a relation is commonly perceived and agreed on by all parties to the relation, that is, the degree of symmetry)	*To what extent are relationships in the business network perceived as mutual and symmetrical by all parties involved in circularity practices?*
Clarity of Expectations (the degree to which every pair of individuals has clearly defined expectations about each other's behaviour in the relation)	*How clearly defined are the expectations between pairs of entities regarding each other's behaviour in circularity practices?*
Multiplexity (the degree to which pairs of individuals are linked by multiple relations)	*How many different types of relationships (e.g., informational, transactional) link pairs of entities could you identify within the business network?*
3. Structural characteristics	
Size (the number of individuals participating in the network)	*What is the number of entities participating in the business network that are related to circularity practices?*
Density (Connectedness) (the number of actual links in the network as a ratio of the number of possible links)	*What is the ratio of actual links to possible links within the business network?*

(continued)

Table 9 (continued)

Property	Question(s)
Clustering (the number of dense regions in the network)	*Could you identify how many dense regions or clusters exist within the business net-work?*
Openness (the number of actual external links of a social unit as a ratio of the number of possible external links)	*What is the ratio of actual external links to possible external links for entities in the network?*
Stability (the degree to which a network pattern changes over time)	*How stable is the network pattern over time in the context of circularity practices?*
Reachability (the average number of links between any two individuals in the network)	*What is the average number of links between any two entities in the business network?*
Centrality (the degree to which relations are guided by the formal hierarchy)	*How does the formal hierarchy influence the relations within the business network?*
Star (the individual with the highest number of nominations)	*Who are the individuals with the highest number of connections within the business network related to circularity practices?*
Liaison (An individual who is not a member of a cluster but links two or more clusters)	*Are there any individuals who link two or more clusters within the business network without being a member of any cluster?*
Bridge (An individual who is a member of multiple clusters in the network, such as a "linking pin")	*Are there any individuals who belong to multiple clusters in the business network, facilitating connections between them?*
Gatekeeper (A star who also links the social unit with external domains)	*Are there any individuals who act as gatekeepers, linking the network with external domains?*
Isolate (An individual who has uncoupled from the network)	*Have there been any individuals who have become disconnected from the business network?*

References

1. Acquier, A., Carbone, V., & Ezvan, C. (2024). Scaling circular economy business models: A capability perspective. *Business Ethics, the Environment and Responsibility.*https://doi.org/10.1111/beer.12658
2. Kanda, W., Geissdoerfer, M., & Hjelm, O. (2021). From circular business models to circular business ecosystems. *Business Strategy and the Environment, 30*, 2814–2829. https://doi.org/10.1002/bse.2895

3. Murray, A., Skene, K., & Haynes, K. (2017). The circular economy: An interdisciplinary exploration of the concept and application in a global context. *Journal of Business Ethics, 140*, 369–380. https://doi.org/10.1007/s10551-015-2693-2
4. Savaget, P., Geissdoerfer, M., Kharrazi, A., & Evans, S. (2018). The theoretical foundations of sociotechnical systems change for sustainability: A systematic literature review. *Journal of Cleaner Production*. https://doi.org/10.1016/j.jclepro.2018.09.208
5. Geissdoerfer, M., Pieroni, M. P. P., Pigosso, D. C. A., & Soufani, K. (2020). Circular business models: A review Circular business model business model innovation sustainable business model circular economy review. https://doi.org/10.1016/j.jclepro.2020.123741.
6. Krishnan, R., Yen, P., Agarwal, R., Arshinder, K., & Bajada, C. (2021). Collaborative innovation and sustainability in the food supply chain-evidence from farmer producer organisations. *Conservation & Recycling, 168*, 105253. https://doi.org/10.1016/j.resconrec.2020.105253
7. Neligan, A., Baumgartner, R. J., Geissdoerfer, M., & Schöggl, J. P. (2023). Circular disruption: Digitalisation as a driver of circular economy business models. *Business Strategy and the Environment, 32*, 1175–1188. https://doi.org/10.1002/bse.3100
8. Jayakodi, S., Senaratne, S., & Perera, S. (2024). Circular economy business model in the construction industry: A systematic review. *Buildings*. https://doi.org/10.3390/buildings14020379
9. Ellen MacArthur Foundation. (2019). How the circular economy tackles climate change.
10. Otasowie, O. K., Aigbavboa, C. O., Oke, A. E., & Adekunle, P. (2024). Mapping out focus for circular economy business models (CEBMs) research in construction sector studies—a bibliometric approach. *Journal of Engineering, Design and Technology*. https://doi.org/10.1108/JEDT-10-2023-0444
11. Dodzi Bissadu, K., Sonko, S., & Hossain, G. (2024). Society 5.0 enabled agriculture: Drivers, enabling technologies, architectures, opportunities, and challenges. *Information Processing in Agriculture*. https://doi.org/10.1016/j.inpa.2024.04.003
12. Adelekan, A., & Sharmina, M. (2024). Collaborative digitally-enabled business models for a circular economy: Sustaining, managing and protecting value in the UK plastics sector. *Journal of Cleaner Production, 438*, 140770. https://doi.org/10.1016/j.jclepro.2024.140770
13. Donner, M., Gohier, R., & de Vries, H. (2020). A new circular business model typology for creating value from agro-waste. *Science of the Total Environment, 716*, 137065. https://doi.org/10.1016/j.scitotenv.2020.137065
14. Baldassarre, B., & Calabretta, G. (2024). Why circular business models fail and what to do about it: A preliminary framework and lessons learned from a case in the European Union (Eu). *Circular Economy and Sustainability, 4*, 123–148. https://doi.org/10.1007/s43615-023-00279-w
15. Urbinati, A., Chiaroni, D., & Chiesa, V. (2017). Towards a new taxonomy of circular economy business models. *Journal of Cleaner Production*. https://doi.org/10.1016/j.jclepro.2017.09.047
16. Geissdoerfer, M., Vladimirova, D., & Evans, S. (2018). Sustainable business model innovation: A review. *Journal of Cleaner Production, 198*, 401–416. https://doi.org/10.1016/j.jclepro.2018.06.240
17. Geissdoerfer, M., Pieroni, M. P. P., Pigosso, D. C. A., & Soufani, K. (2020). Circular business models: A review. *Journal of Cleaner Production, 277*, 123741. https://doi.org/10.1016/j.jclepro.2020.123741
18. Rosa, P., Sassanelli, C., & Terzi, S. (2019). Towards circular business models: A systematic literature review on classification frameworks and archetypes. *Journal of Cleaner Production, 236*, 117696. https://doi.org/10.1016/j.jclepro.2019.117696
19. Kerin, M., & Pham, D. T. (2019). A review of emerging industry 4.0 technologies in remanufacturing. *Journal of Cleaner Production, 237*, 117805. https://doi.org/10.1016/j.jclepro.2019.117805
20. Khan, I. S., Ahmad, M. O., & Majava, J. (2021). Industry 4.0 and sustainable development: A systematic mapping of triple bottom line, circular economy and sustainable business models perspectives. *Journal of Cleaner Production, 297*, 126655. https://doi.org/10.1016/j.jclepro.2021.126655
21. Rosa, P., Sassanelli, C., & Terzi, S. (2019). Circular business models versus circular benefits: An assessment in the waste from electrical and electronic equipments sector. *Journal of Cleaner Production, 231*, 940–952. https://doi.org/10.1016/j.jclepro.2019.05.310

22. Salvador, R., Barros, M. V., da Luz, L. M., Piekarski, C. M., & de Francisco, A. C. (2020). Circular business models: Current aspects that influence implementation and unaddressed subjects. *Journal of Cleaner Production, 250*, 119555. https://doi.org/10.1016/j.jclepro.2019.119555
23. Foroozanfar, M. H., Imanipour, N., & Sajadi, S. M. (2022). Integrating circular economy strategies and business models: A systematic literature review. *Journal of Entrepreneurship in Emerging Economies, 14*, 678–700. https://doi.org/10.1108/JEEE-10-2021-0411
24. Lüdeke-Freund, F., Gold, S., & Bocken, N. M. P. (2019). A review and typology of circular economy business model patterns. *Journal of Industrial Ecology, 23*, 36–61. https://doi.org/10.1111/jiec.12763
25. Sarja, M., Onkila, T., & Mäkelä, M. (2021). A systematic literature review of the transition to the circular economy in business organizations: Obstacles, catalysts and ambivalences. *Journal of Cleaner Production, 286*, 125492. https://doi.org/10.1016/j.jclepro.2020.125492
26. Uhrenholt, J. N., Kristensen, J. H., Rincón, M. C., Jensen, S. F., & Waehrens, B. V. (2022). Circular economy: Factors affecting the financial performance of product take-back systems. *Journal of Cleaner Production, 335*, 130319. https://doi.org/10.1016/j.jclepro.2021.130319
27. Ding, S., Tukker, A., & Ward, H. (2023). Opportunities and risks of internet of things (IoT) technologies for circular business models: A literature review. *Journal of Environmental Management, 336*, 117662. https://doi.org/10.1016/j.jenvman.2023.117662
28. Eisenreich, A., Füller, J., Stuchtey, M., & Gimenez-Jimenez, D. (2022). Toward a circular value chain: Impact of the circular economy on a company's value chain processes. *Journal of Cleaner Production, 378*, 134375. https://doi.org/10.1016/j.jclepro.2022.134375
29. Obi, L., Arif, M., Daniel, E. I., Oladinrin, O. T., & Goulding, J. S. (2023). Establishing underpinning concepts for integrating circular economy and offsite construction: a bibliometric review. *Built Environment Project and Asset Management, 13*, 123–139. https://doi.org/10.1108/BEPAM-01-2022-0009
30. Roman, P., Thiry, G., Muylaert, C., Ruwet, C., & Maréchal, K. (2023). Defining and identifying strongly sustainable product-service systems (SSPSS). *Journal of Cleaner Production, 391*, 136295. https://doi.org/10.1016/j.jclepro.2023.136295
31. Islam, M. T., Huda, N., Baumber, A., Shumon, R., Zaman, A., Ali, F., Hossain, R., & Sahajwalla, V. (2021). A global review of consumer behavior towards e-waste and implications for the circular economy. *Journal of Cleaner Production, 316*, 128297. https://doi.org/10.1016/j.jclepro.2021.128297
32. Gregg, J. S., Jürgens, J., Happel, M. K., Strøm-Andersen, N., Tanner, A. N., Bolwig, S., & Klitkou, A. (2020). Valorization of bio-residuals in the food and forestry sectors in support of a circular bioeconomy: A review. *Journal of Cleaner Production, 267*, 122093. https://doi.org/10.1016/j.jclepro.2020.122093
33. Nasrin, A. B., Abdul Raman, A. A., Bukhari, N. A., Sukiran, M. A., Buthiyappan, A., Subramaniam, V., Aziz, A. A., & Loh, S. K. (2022). A critical analysis on biogas production and utilisation potential from palm oil mill effluent. *Journal of Cleaner Production, 361*, 132040. https://doi.org/10.1016/j.jclepro.2022.132040
34. Borg, K., Lennox, A., Kaufman, S., Tull, F., Prime, R., Rogers, L., & Dunstan, E. (2022). Curbing plastic consumption: A review of single-use plastic behaviour change interventions. *Journal of Cleaner Production, 344*, 131077. https://doi.org/10.1016/j.jclepro.2022.131077
35. Rabaia, M. K. H., Semeraro, C., & Olabi, A.-G. (2022). Recent progress towards photovoltaics' circular economy. *Journal of Cleaner Production, 373*, 133864. https://doi.org/10.1016/j.jclepro.2022.133864
36. Haque, F., Fan, C., & Lee, Y.-Y. (2023). From waste to value: Addressing the relevance of waste recovery to agricultural sector in line with circular economy. *Journal of Cleaner Production, 415*, 137873. https://doi.org/10.1016/j.jclepro.2023.137873
37. Duque-Acevedo, M., Belmonte-Ureña, L. J., Plaza-Úbeda, J. A., & Camacho-Ferre, F. (2020). The management of agricultural waste biomass in the framework of circular economy and bioeconomy: An opportunity for greenhouse agriculture in Southeast Spain. *Agronomy, 10*. https://doi.org/10.3390/agronomy10040489

38. European Commission: A New Circular Economy Action Plan. (2020).
39. Velasco-Muñoz, J. F., Mendoza, J. M. F., Aznar-Sánchez, J. A., & Gallego-Schmid, A. (2021). Circular economy implementation in the agricultural sector: Definition, strategies and indicators. *Resources, Conservation and Recycling, 170*. https://doi.org/10.1016/j.resconrec.2021.105618
40. Kumar, R., Verma, A., Shome, A., Sinha, R., Sinha, S., Jha, P. K., Kumar, R., Kumar, P., Shubham, Das, S., Sharma, P., & Prasad, P. V. V. (2021). Impacts of plastic pollution on ecosystem services, sustainable development goals, and need to focus on circular economy and policy interventions. *Sustainability*. https://doi.org/10.3390/su13179963
41. Macarthur, E. (2013). Towards the circular economy, economic and business rationale for an accelerated transition.
42. Campbell-Johnston, K., Vermeulen, W. J. V., Reike, D., & Brullot, S. (2020). The circular economy and cascading: Towards a framework. *Resources, Conservation & Recycling: X*. https://doi.org/10.1016/j.rcrx.2020.100038
43. Khawar Balwan, W., Singh, A., & Kour, S. (2022). 5R's of zero waste management to save our green planet: A narrative review. *European Journal of Biotechnology and Bioscience, 10*, 7–11.
44. Papargyropoulou, E., Lozano, R., Steinberger, J. K., Wright, N., & Ujang, Z. B. (2014). The food waste hierarchy as a framework for the management of food surplus and food waste. *Journal of Cleaner Production, 76*, 106–115. https://doi.org/10.1016/j.jclepro.2014.04.020
45. Jurgilevich, A., Birge, T., Kentala-Lehtonen, J., Korhonen-Kurki, K., Pietikäinen, J., Saikku, L., & Schösler, H. (2016). Transition towards circular economy in the food system. *Sustainability, 8*. https://doi.org/10.3390/su8010069
46. Bocken, N. M. P., de Pauw, I., Bakker, C., & van der Grinten, B. (2016). Product design and business model strategies for a circular economy. *Journal of Industrial and Production Engineering, 33*, 308–320. https://doi.org/10.1080/21681015.2016.1172124
47. Barth, H., Ulvenblad, P. O., & Ulvenblad, P. (2017). Towards a conceptual framework of sustainable business model innovation in the agri-food sector: A systematic literature review. *Sustainability, 9*. https://doi.org/10.3390/su9091620
48. Ghisellini, P., Cialani, C., & Ulgiati, S. (2016). A review on circular economy: The expected transition to a balanced interplay of environmental and economic systems. *Journal of Cleaner Production, 114*, 11–32. https://doi.org/10.1016/j.jclepro.2015.09.007
49. Franceschelli, M. V., Santoro, G., & Candelo, E. (2018). Business model innovation for sustainability: A food start-up case study. *British Food Journal, 120*, 2483–2494. https://doi.org/10.1108/BFJ-01-2018-0049
50. Evans, S., Vladimirova, D., Holgado, M., Van Fossen, K., Yang, M., Silva, E. A., & Barlow, C. Y. (2017). Business model innovation for sustainability: Towards a unified perspective for creation of sustainable business models. *Business Strategy and the Environment, 26*, 597–608. https://doi.org/10.1002/bse.1939
51. Marques, L., & Manzanares, M. D. (2023). Towards social network metrics for supply network circularity. *International Journal of Operations & Production Management, 43*, 595–618. https://doi.org/10.1108/IJOPM-02-2022-0139
52. Luoma, P., Toppinen, A., & Penttinen, E. (2021). The role and value of data in realising circular business models—a systematic literature review. *Journal of Business Models, 9*, 44–71. https://doi.org/10.5278/JBM.V9I2.3448
53. Hina, M., Chauhan, C., Kaur, P., Kraus, S., & Dhir, A. (2022). Drivers and barriers of circular economy business models: Where we are now, and where we are heading. *Journal of Cleaner Production, 333*, 130049. https://doi.org/10.1016/j.jclepro.2021.130049
54. Kazancoglu, I., Sagnak, M., Kumar Mangla, S., & Kazancoglu, Y. (2021). Circular economy and the policy: A framework for improving the corporate environmental management in supply chains. *Business Strategy and the Environment, 30*, 590–608. https://doi.org/10.1002/bse.2641
55. Rodríguez-Espíndola, O., Cuevas-Romo, A., Chowdhury, S., Díaz-Acevedo, N., Albores, P., Despoudi, S., Malesios, C., & Dey, P. (2022). The role of circular economy principles and sustainable-oriented innovation to enhance social, economic and environmental performance:

Evidence from Mexican SMEs. *International Journal of Production Economics*. https://doi.org/10.1016/j.ijpe.2022.108495
56. Tate, W. L., Bals, L., Bals, C., & Foerstl, K. (2019). Seeing the forest and not the trees: Learning from nature's circular economy. *Resources, Conservation and Recycling, 149*, 115–129. https://doi.org/10.1016/j.resconrec.2019.05.023
57. Venkatesh, V., Brown, S. A., & Bala, H. (2013). Bridging the qualitative-quantitative divide: Guidelines for conducting mixed methods research in Information systems. *MIS Quarterly, 37*, 21–54.
58. Yin, R. K. (2018). *Case study research and applications: Design and methods*. Cambridge University Press.
59. Donner, M., & de Vries, H. (2021). How to innovate business models for a circular bio-economy? *Business Strategy and the Environment, 30*, 1932–1947. https://doi.org/10.1002/bse.2725
60. Otte, E., & Rousseau, R. (2002). Social network analysis: A powerful strategy, also for the information sciences. *Journal of Information Science, 28*, 441–453.
61. Kleinberg, J. M. (1999). Authoritative sources in a hyperlinked environment. *Journal of the ACM, 46*, 604–632.
62. Castriotta, M., Loi, M., Marku, E., & Naitana, L. (2019). What's in a name? Exploring the conceptual structure of emerging organizations. *Scientometrics, 118*, 407–437. https://doi.org/10.1007/s11192-018-2977-2
63. Zupic, I., & Čater, T. (2015). Bibliometric methods in management and organization. *Organizational Research Methods, 18*, 429–472. https://doi.org/10.1177/1094428114562629
64. Cobo, M. J., López-Herrera, A. G., Herrera-Viedma, E., & Herrera, F. (2011). An approach for detecting, quantifying, and visualizing the evolution of a research field: A practical application to the Fuzzy Sets Theory field. *Journal of Informetrics, 5*, 146–166. https://doi.org/10.1016/j.joi.2010.10.002
65. Tichy, N., & Fombrun, C. (1979). Network analysis in organizational settings. *Human Relations, 32*, 923–965. https://doi.org/10.1177/001872677903201103
66. Tichy, N. M., Tushman, M. L., & Fombrun, C. (1979). Social network analysis for organizations. *Academy of Management Review, 4*, 507–519. https://doi.org/10.5465/amr.1979.4498309
67. Betts, S. C., & Stouder, M. D. (2004). The network perspective in organization studies: Network organizations or network analysis? *Academy of Strategic Management Journal, 3*, 1–20.
68. Ahuja, G., Soda, G., & Zaheer, A. (2012). The genesis and dynamics of organizational networks. *Organization Science, 23*, 434–448. https://doi.org/10.1287/orsc.1110.0695
69. Zappa, P., & Lomi, A. (2016). Knowledge sharing in organizations: A multilevel network analysis. In *Multilevel Network analysis for the social sciences* (pp. 333–353). Springer. https://doi.org/10.1007/978-3-319-24520-1_14
70. Reagans, R., & Zuckerman, E. W. (2001). Networks, diversity, and productivity: The social capital of corporate R&D teams. *Organization Science, 12*, 502–517. https://doi.org/10.1287/orsc.12.4.502.10637
71. Habli, K., Dumitras, D. E., Schmitt, E., Maglietti Smith, I., & Barjolle, D. (2023). Circular economy in mountain value chains: The case of three PDO cheeses. *Foods, 12*, 3954. https://doi.org/10.3390/foods12213954
72. Mantino, F., & Forcina, B. (2018). Market, policies and local governance as drivers of environmental public benefits: The case of the localised processed tomato in Northern Italy. *Agriculture, 8*, 34. https://doi.org/10.3390/agriculture8030034
73. Mancini, M. C., Arfini, F., & Guareschi, M. (2019). Innovation and typicality in localised agri-food systems: The case of PDO Parmigiano Reggiano. *British Food Journal, 121*, 3043–3061. https://doi.org/10.1108/BFJ-10-2018-0662
74. Arfini, F., Cozzi, E., Mancini, M. C., Ferrer-Perez, H., & Gil, J. M. (2019). Are geographical indication products fostering public goods? Some evidence from Europe. *Sustainability., 11*, 272. https://doi.org/10.3390/su11010272

75. Secondi, L., Principato, L., Ruini, L., & Guidi, M. (2019). Reusing food waste in food manufacturing companies: The case of the tomato-sauce supply chain. *Sustainability., 11*, 2154. https://doi.org/10.3390/su11072154
76. Muchnik, J. (2009). Localised agrifood systems: Concept development and diversity of situations. In *Informing possibilities for the future of food and agriculture-joint annual meeting of AFHVS & ASFS*, May 2009, State College, Pennsylvanie, United States.
77. Arfini, F., Bellassen, V. (2019). Sustainability of European food quality schemes: Multi-performance, structure, and governance of PDO, PGI, and organic agri-food systems. Sustainability of European food quality schemes: Multi-performance, structure, and governance of PDO, PGI, and organic agri-food systems. (pp. 1–567). https://doi.org/10.1007/978-3-030-27508-2/COVER.
78. Arfini, F., Antonioli, F., Cozzi, E., Donati, M., Guareschi, M., Mancini, M. C., & Veneziani, M. (2019). Sustainability, innovation and rural development: The case of Parmigiano-Reggiano PDO. *Sustainability, 11*, 4978. https://doi.org/10.3390/su11184978
79. Arfini, F., Antonioli, F., Donati, M., Gorton, M., Mancini, M. C., Tocco, B., & Veneziani, M. (2019). Conceptual framework. In *Sustainability of European Food Quality Schemes* (pp. 3–21). Springer. https://doi.org/10.1007/978-3-030-27508-2_1
80. Muchnik, J. (2010). Sistemi agroalimentari localizzati/localised agri-food systems. Sviluppo Locale. 35/2010.
81. Battini, F., Agostini, A., Tabaglio, V., & Amaducci, S. (2016). Environmental impacts of different dairy farming systems in the Po Valley. *Journal of Cleaner Production, 112*, 91–102. https://doi.org/10.1016/j.jclepro.2015.09.062
82. Borghesi, G., Stefanini, R., & Vignali, G. (2022). Life cycle assessment of packaged organic dairy product: A comparison of different methods for the environmental assessment of alternative scenarios. *Journal of Food Engineering, 318*, 110902. https://doi.org/10.1016/j.jfoodeng.2021.110902
83. Puglia, M., Allesina, G., Pedrazzi, S., & Raguzzoni, F. (2022). Energy cost and parmesan cheese. An overview in the different energy fluxes needed to produce a parmesan wheel. *IOP Conference Series: Earth and Environmental Science, 1106*, 012012. https://doi.org/10.1088/1755-1315/1106/1/012012
84. Marrucci, L., Daddi, T., & Iraldo, F. (2024). Creating environmental performance indicators to assess corporate sustainability and reward employees. *Ecological Indicators, 158*, 111489. https://doi.org/10.1016/j.ecolind.2023.111489
85. Boccia, F., Di Donato, P., Covino, D., & Poli, A. (2019). Food waste and bio-economy: A scenario for the Italian tomato market. *Journal of Cleaner Production, 227*, 424–433. https://doi.org/10.1016/j.jclepro.2019.04.180
86. Rajan, K., Samykano, M., Kadirgama, K., Harun, W. S. W., & Rahman, M. M. (2022). Fused deposition modeling: process, materials, parameters, properties, and applications. *The International Journal of Advanced Manufacturing Technology., 120*, 1531–1570. https://doi.org/10.1007/s00170-022-08860-7
87. Santini, M., & Valentini, R. (2015). Calculating the water footprint of an agri-food company's supply chain: The Mutti case. In M. Antonelli & F. Greco (Eds.), *The water we eat* (pp. 243–256). Springer Water. https://doi.org/10.1007/978-3-319-16393-2_18
88. Osterwalder, A., & Pigneur, Y. (2010). *Business model generation: A handbook for visionaries, game changers, and challengers*. Wiley.
89. Muzamwese, T. C., Franco-Garcia, L., & Heldeweg, M. (2024). Industrial clusters as a vehicle for circular economy transition: A case study of networks in four industrial clusters in Zimbabwe. *Journal of Cleaner Production, 447*, 141479. https://doi.org/10.1016/j.jclepro.2024.141479

Talking the Talk But Not Walking the Walk: Is the Use of Sustainability Keywords in IS/IT Job Ads "Greenwashing"?

Paul Pierce and Odd Steen

Abstract This paper explores the intersection of corporate sustainability and recruitment perspectives in Swedish companies, examining the use of one hundred and seven sustainability keywords in more than 230,000 IS/IT job ads collected from the Swedish Public Employment Service. The study emphasizes the pressing need for a new breed of computing professionals to address environmental challenges and climate change. Despite the strategic nature of sustainability issues, the analysis reveals a surprising focus on operational occupations in both IS and Engineering job ads. The study suggests that companies are signaling an interest in sustainability, maybe even "greenwashing", but often seek operational/micro rather than tactical/meso or strategic/macro business level competencies. Future work proposes a deeper content analysis using suitable AI applications and interviews with companies to study the contextual use of sustainability keywords and more nuanced perspectives of recruiters.

Keywords Sustainability · IS/IT job ads · IS/IT employer studies · IS/IT green-washing

1 Introduction

In a world facing unprecedented environmental challenges and the ever-growing urgency of climate change, we also see the global population burgeoning, the consumption of finite resources escalating, and ecosystems facing irreversible degradation [1, 2]. The consequences of unsustainable behaviour have transcended the boundaries of scientific discourse and now touch every facet of our existence –

P. Pierce (✉) · O. Steen
Department of Informatics, School of Economics and Management, Lund University, Lund, Sweden
e-mail: paul.pierce@ics.lu.se; odd.steen@ics.lu.se

M. Cipriano et al. (eds.), *Technologies for Organizations and Society*,
Lecture Notes in Information Systems and Organisation 80,
https://doi.org/10.1007/978-3-032-01697-3_6

from the ecological systems that sustain life to the socioeconomic stability of societies worldwide [3].

In this era marked by, among other things, unprecedented environmental challenges and the escalating urgency of climate change, the imperative to prioritize sustainable practices has reached a critical juncture [4]. One example of this is that in February of 2022, the European commission adopted a proposal for Corporate Sustainability Due Diligence Directive (CSDD) which in effect will hold companies responsible for their entire supply chain [5]. This move underscores the growing expectation for businesses to embed sustainability at the core of their operations, including their workforce strategies.

One critical area where this shift is evident is in the recruitment of IS/IT professionals. As companies navigate the complexities of sustainability, there is an ever-increasing need for a new breed of computing professionals who possess not only technical expertise but also a deep understanding of environmental, social, and economic factors. In the pursuit of sustainability, organizations will require visionary workers as well as leaders who understand how these three factors interact. We would argue that this workforce must possess the ability to navigate the complex landscape of sustainable practices and spearhead initiatives that not only mitigate environmental impact but also contribute positively to societal well-being.

If organizations are to meet this challenge, they must actively seek out innovators and problem-solving individuals who can devise sustainable solutions through cutting-edge technologies, resource-efficient processes, or novel business models. The dynamic nature of sustainability challenges demands professionals who are adaptable, forward-thinking, and capable of cultivating a culture of innovation within their organizations [6].

Moreover, collaboration becomes crucial in this endeavor; companies need team players who can foster cross-disciplinary partnerships, bridging gaps between scientific expertise, policy advocacy, and business acumen. Effective communication skills become paramount as individuals work towards aligning diverse stakeholders and communities for a shared vision of sustainable progress [7, 8].

Given the significance of the competences mentioned, this paper sets out to explore how Swedish companies are integrating sustainability into their recruitment processes for IS/IT professionals, as reflected in job advertisements. By examining and analyzing these job ads, the paper strives to give some answers to the present state of affairs in regard to organizations' sustainability readiness both in terms of what they are looking for in employees, if there are different sustainability requirements for different occupations and for IS and IS/IT Engineering education backgrounds of the job seekers, and what this could entail for the IS community. This analysis will provide valuable insights for the IS community, as well as academia as we navigate the evolving demands of sustainability in the digital age.

2 Sustainability and Green IS/IT

Having established the need for companies to integrate sustainability principles in everyday operations, this chapter delves into the concept of Green IS, exploring factors for implementation as well as trying to understand organizational implementations as well as the strategic significance of Green IS for organizations.

In [9] the authors argue that the successful implementation of Green IS hinges upon several key factors, including leader commitment, government policy, customer awareness, and the demand for green services. These elements collectively shape the organizational landscape and influence decision-making processes regarding sustainability initiatives. This notion is further supported by [10] whose research underscores the significance of ecological messages in job advertisements, highlighting a positive correlation with organizational attractiveness and a positive ecological footprint. We would argue that this finding reinforces the notion that public perceptions and environmental messaging play pivotal roles in shaping organizational image and recruitment outcomes.

If the concept of organizational sustainability is pivotal in job ads, then it lends itself to reason that organizations need to adopt Green IS thinking in the formulation of comprehensive strategies and policies, otherwise it is very easy to talk the talk, but not walk the walk. This argumentation has been noted by [11], who argue that companies must establish green IT strategies and policies to guide employee actions and align organizational practices with sustainability goals. They go further and claim that strategic alignment extends beyond mere rhetoric; it necessitates the integration of corporate social responsibility (CSR) and green IT into the organizational mission statement.

If we accept the argumentation that all organizations need to both formulate and adhere to sustainable strategies and policies, then we also need to understand and distinguish the difference between Green IT and Green IS. Their respective roles in mitigating environmental impact is elucidated in [12]. While Green IT focuses on reducing the direct environmental effects of IS use, Green IS leverages IS to promote eco-sustainability in businesses and society. This distinction underscores the multifaceted nature of sustainability efforts within the IS domain.

Despite the recognition of Green IS within operations, [13] argues that there is a gap in strategic integration within organizations. This disparity underscores the challenges associated with implementing Green IS, which often transcends traditional operational procedures and requires a strategic organizational approach. As [13] suggests, the successful integration of Green IS hinges upon the formulation of appropriate goals, policies, and organizational structures. Echoing this sentiment, [14] underscores the transformative potential of Green IS, positing it as a catalyst for organizational change and competitive advantage. By enabling organizational sense-making and sustainable practices, Green IS initiatives can drive innovation and position organizations as leaders in sustainability.

In conclusion, we argue that the integration of sustainability principles into IS practices is a multifaceted endeavor that requires strategic alignment, organizational commitment, and a holistic understanding of environmental issues. Moving forward, organizations must be able to both talk the talk of sustainability and Green IS as well as know how to walk the walk and prioritize the adoption of Green IS strategies to navigate the complexities of the modern business landscape and drive sustainable growth.

3 Method and Dataset

The dataset for this study is a local database with job ads fetched from Platsbanken ("The Position Bank") administered by the Swedish Public Employment Service (Arbetsförmedlingen – AF) government agency and shared as open data. AF is responsible for the Swedish public service to match job seekers with employers looking for hires. According to AF, Platsbanken is Sweden's largest and most visited employment website.

Job advertisements/postings as a source to discover employer expectations has been used several times before and in several different countries and contexts (in IS/IT, see e.g., [15–24]) and also to study sustainability/pro-environmental messages in job ads [10]. This method makes it is easier to achieve a big data volume and good coverage and is considered unobtrusive [25]. In addition, job ads "[. . .] are a major means by which employers indicate, more or less effectively, what they want from potential employees." [16, p. 340].

Employers create job ads that get published in Platsbanken. Everyone in Sweden can look for jobs there via the AF web page: https://arbetsformedlingen.se/other-languages/english-engelska. All the ads are also visible in the Eures portal (https://eures.ec.europa.eu/index_en) in the EU/EES and Switzerland, and all job seekers and employers in these countries can therefore use the service to apply for the positions or post job ads.

The data were fetched using several REST services published by the AF subsidiary JobTech Development (https://jobtechdev.se/en) and were then cleansed and stored in a local MS SQL Server database for data coding and analysis.

This study is a population study, meaning than we analyse the full populations of collected job ads and *not* randomised and representative samples from these populations. The full population is the total amount of IS/IT job ads that we have collected and stored locally. Two subpopulations in the study specify different education backgrounds of the job seekers (see Appendix 1 for selection criteria):

1. Business and society oriented 'IS' and hence specifying an IS or equivalent type of education, and
2. Technically oriented 'IS/IT Engineering' and hence specifying an IS/IT Engineering type of education.

When we refer to 'sample' and 'n' and 'N' in the rest of the text, a sample is either all the ads tagged with 'IS', all the ads tagged with 'IS/IT Engineering', or all ads tagged with one of the sustainability keywords and as such they are parts of or samples from all the collected ads. These samples represent ‘n’, and all the collected job ads represent ‘N’.

Because of this, there is little point in statistical inference from sample to population using various statistical tests like a t-test, since ‘IS’ and ‘IS/IT Engineering’ are subpopulations of the IS/IT job ads in the study. In addition, without engaging in the debate about statistical inference and its assumptions, we acknowledge more statistically schooled researchers’ discussions (see e.g., [26–28]) about common misconceptions about P-values, confidence levels, etc. and the requirements for all the parts of the full model being true (e.g., randomised sampling) for them to be valid, meaningful, or useful.

This ultimately led us to use the entire sample instead of using a randomized sampling study with e.g., n ‘IS’ ads from the population of ‘IS’ ads, instead all the ads tagged with e.g., ‘IS’ have been analyzed, making the ‘IS’ ads a subpopulation of all the IS/IT job ads and thus not a randomised sample.

3.1 Occupation Types

Each job ad is tagged with an occupation label by the ad author. The occupation label is selected from a list of occupations classified by SCB (Statistiska Centralbyrån – Statistics Sweden) [29] according to the four level classification hierarchy of *Standard för svensk yrkesklassificering* (SSYK 2012). SSYK 2012 matches the International Standard Classification of Occupations (ISCO-08) [30] and the European Skills, Competences, Qualifications and Occupations (ESCO) classification [31]. In addition to this, AF provides its own fifth occupation level, which partly matches the ESCO level 5. The occupation labels tagged to the job ads are of AF level 5 occupations (see Appendix 2).

In this study, the job ads are tagged with occupation that belong to the ESCO level 2 occupation fields in Table 1. Only ads for occupations that might attract IS/IT job seekers have been collected. Most of the job ads (88.50%) are tagged with an occupation that belongs to the ESCO level 4 occupation groups in Table 2.

Table 1 ESCO level 2 occupation fields in the study

ESCO level 2	Label	%
25	Information and communications technology professionals	58.21%
35	Information and communications technicians	34.25%
13	Production and specialized services managers	4.66%
24	Business and administration professionals	2.68%
23	Teaching professionals	0.14%
21	Science and engineering professionals	0.06%
		100.00%

Table 2 The majority of the ESCO level 4 occupation groups in the study

ESCO level 4	Label	%
3512	Information and communications technology user support technician	31.48%
2511	Systems analysts	27.26%
2512	Software developers	14.28%
2522	Systems administrators	5.53%
2519	Software and applications developers and analysts not elsewhere classified	5.25%
1330	Information and communications technology service managers	4.66%
		88.50%

Apart from various job ad fields such as company name, place of work, and number of positions, the primary ad content is the ad text of up to 6000 characters in length describing whatever the employer wants to convey to the job seeker.

At the time of writing, the database contained 234 584 IS/IT job ads with publication dates between 2017-05-02 and 2024-04-03. These ads are for 318 047 positions at 10 790 workplaces representing all of Sweden's 290 municipalities. Almost a quarter (24.59%) of the workplaces are found in the three major city regions of Stockholm (15.95%), Gothenburg (6.48%), and Malmö (2.16%).

3.2 Data Analysis

We used ChatGPT to generate a list of the most important and current sustainability keywords (see Appendix 3 for the keywords). The list started with keywords from the job ads. Then we did google searches for e.g., "sustainability keywords". All the different keywords were collected and synthesized, whereafter we fed the entire list into ChatGPT with different prompts to get a more manageable list of keywords in relation to IS/IT. This list contains one hundred and seven unique keywords. We translated these into Swedish to have one hundred and seven pairs of English and Swedish keywords since most of the job ads are written in Swedish.

We used the keywords in SQL LIKE statements to create a table with ad texts using any of the keywords. This served as descriptive coding of the data. Next, we categorized the ads according to each sustainability keyword pair and created another table for this.

The two tables constitute the first steps of coding and categorization. For the subsequent data analysis, we used spreadsheet software to calculate descriptive statistics and generate relevant displays.

4 Findings

Of the 234 584 IS/IT ads, 140 811 mention or use sixty-seven sustainability keywords. This means that 60.0% of the job ads mention or use any of the one hundred and seven sustainability keywords and that 62.6% of these keywords are used. No outlying keywords were found, i.e., as far as we can tell we have not missed any sustainability keywords within the set of the 107 keywords used.

4.1 The Most Frequently Used Sustainability Keywords in the Ads

Ten sustainability keywords in the job ads comprise 96.32% of the used keywords in this sample and 57.82% of the total number of ads. The most recurring keyword is the all-encompassing and rather indistinct, or even fluffy, keyword of 'Environment' which is used in 81.73% in the sample and 49.06% of all the ads (see Table 3).

It occurs almost eleven times more often than the next most frequent keyword of 'Sustainability', which itself is a rather "inclusive" concept. Table 3 shows that the other keywords mostly refer to either social or societal aspects: 'Corporate social responsibility', 'Community engagement', 'Social Responsibility', or technical/technology aspects: 'Autonomous Vehicles', 'Electric Vehicles', 'Renewable Energy'.

Table 3 The top ten sustainability keywords used in the ads

Rank	Keyword	n	% of $\sum$n	% of n Cumul.	% of N	% of N Cumul.
1	Environment	115,084	81.73%	81.73%	49.06%	49.06%
2	Sustainability	10,699	7.60%	89.33%	4.56%	53.62%
3	Telecommuting	3481	2.47%	91.80%	1.48%	55.10%
4	Sustainable development	1938	1.38%	93.18%	0.83%	55.93%
5	Corporate social responsibility	1116	0.79%	93.97%	0.48%	56.41%
6	Community engagement	1066	0.76%	94.73%	0.45%	56.86%
7	Autonomous vehicles	657	0.47%	95.19%	0.28%	57.14%
8	Electric vehicles	614	0.44%	95.63%	0.26%	57.40%
9	Renewable energy	494	0.35%	95.98%	0.21%	57.61%
10	Social responsibility	487	0.35%	96.32%	0.21%	57.82%
		135,636	96.32%		57.82%	

4.2 The Expected Education Background in Relation to the Keywords

Looking at the educational expectations, none of the ads specify any formal environmental or sustainability training. Little more than half of the ads, 54.0% (126706) specify any higher education expectations and, consequently, 46.0% do not (107878). Of the ads expecting any higher education, 64.5% (81695) specifically expect a higher IS/IT education of the job seekers, of which 11.2% (14129) are IS (information system, informatics, information management, etc., cf. Appendix 1) educations and 52.2% (66082) are IS/IT Engineering (computer science, software engineering, ICT, electrical engineering, etc., cf. Appendix 1) educations. This means that IS/IT Engineering ads outnumber IS ads by 4.6 times. Ads for IS use 40 (38.1%) and ads for IS/IT Engineering use 58 (55.2%) keywords.

We analysed for any differences in sustainability keyword frequency between these two groups, since it would be reasonable, considering the different foci of IS and IS/IT Engineering educations, to assume that IS ads would use sustainability keywords of more business and societal types, like 'CSR', 'Social Responsibility', and 'Circular Economy', and IS/IT Engineering ads more technical and engineering ones, like 'Autonomous Vehicles', 'Electric Vehicles', and 'Renewable Energy'.

We found that the four most recurring keywords ('Environment', 'Sustainability', 'Telecommuting', and 'Sustainable Development') are the same for both IS and IS/IT Engineering, and they account for 93.8% of the occurrences in IS and 92.2% in IS/IT Engineering, which is not a noteworthy difference. Apart from this, we found only smaller differences of the expected kind mentioned above. Hence, there are only very small differences between the frequency of sustainability keywords in ads targeting job seekers with an IS compared to an IS/IT Engineering education background and the differences found are consistent with our expectations.

4.3 Sustainability Keywords and Occupations

Since there were no noteworthy differences between IS and IS/IT Engineering job ads in general, we decided to break down the two groups of ads into occupation types. In this analysis we excluded the overarching and indistinct keyword of 'Environment' giving a sample of 1923 IS and 8874 IS/IT Engineering job ads.

In the top twenty combinations of occupations and sustainability keyword in IS ads, which accounts for 45.55% in the sample, we found six distinct level 5 occupations (see Table 4).

The occupation of 'IT Strategist' is ranked thirteen for 'Sustainability' and fourteen for 'Sustainable Development'. This means that almost all ads (eighteen out of twenty) in the top twenty IS ads list specify an occupation which is either systems development related or related to systems administration.

Table 4 Six distinct IS level 5 occupations in the top twenty occupation and keyword combinations

ESCO level 5	AF level 5	Label	%
2511.15	2419	ICT system developer	21.43%
2522.1	2918, 2919	ICT system administrator	9.29%
1330.7	5388	ICT project manager	5.04%
2511.17	6626	Integration engineer	4.75%
2512.4	80	Software developer	3.92%
n.a.	5432	IT strategist (Translated AF and not an ESCO occupation title)	1.12%
			45.55%

Table 5 Ten distinct IS/IT Engineering level 5 occupations in the top twenty occupation and keyword combinations

ESCO level 5	AF level 5	Label	%
2512.4	80	Software developer	19.34%
2511.15	2419	ICT system developer	16.36%
1330.7	5388	ICT project manager	3.30%
n.a.	6509	Civil engineer, systems development[2]	1.54%
2434.2	7661	ICT business development manager	1.49%
n.a.	7632	Back-end developer (Translated AF and not ESCO occupation titles)	1.25%
2519.7.4	5422	ICT system tester	1,23%
2511.17	6626	Integration engineer	1,15%
n.a.	5432	IT Strategist[2]	0,85%
2512.5	7633	User interface developer	0,59%
			47.10%

We compared this to the top twenty combinations of occupation and keyword in IS/IT Engineering ads, which accounts for 47.10% in the sample, and found ten distinct occupations (see Table 5).

'ICT business development manager' is ranked nine and 'IT Strategist' fourteen for 'Sustainability'. As with the analysis of IS ads above, it is striking that eighteen out of twenty occupations are related to either systems or software development.

IS/IT occupations of more strategic and tactical nature in the IS and IS/IT Engineering ads are 'ICT business development manager', 'IT Strategist'[2], 'Business architect'[2], 'Business consultant – IT'[2], 'Enterprise Architect'[2], 'Business analyst', and 'ICT business analysis manager'.

In the IS ads, the occupation of 'IT Strategist' is used in 76 ads (3.95%), 'Business consultant – IT' in 16 ads (0.83%) and 'Enterprise Architect' in seven ads (0.36%). This can be compared to 'ICT system developer' and 'Software developer' that together are used in 661 ads (34.37%).

In the IS/IT Engineering ads, the occupation of 'IT Strategist' is used in 188 ads (2.12%), 'ICT business development manager' in 135 ads (1.52%), and 'Enterprise

Architect' in 22 ads (0.25%). 'ICT system developer' and 'Software developer' together appear in 4192 (47.24%) of the ads in the sample.

It is thus obvious that the sustainability keywords, except for 'Environment', appear much more frequently in ads for systems and software development occupations and hence operational architectures and levels of the business, than in ads for occupations concerned with more strategic and tactical architectures and business levels.

5 Discussion

Looking at the content analysis of job ads we would argue that companies at least know they need to showcase an interest in sustainability behaviour. The word 'Environment' is mentioned in 49.1% of the all the job ads. This finding is in accordance with the conclusions in [10] that ecological messages in job ads have a positive relationship with organizational attractiveness. To put it bluntly, sustainability keywords could be used to "greenwash" the job ads to signal a potentially attractive employer and workplace.

Despite the difference in foci between IS and IS/IT Engineering educations, there are only small differences in the frequency of sustainability keywords in ads specifying these education backgrounds. Hence, more business and society oriented IS does not seem to value sustainability more or in other ways than technically oriented IS/IT Engineering.

In the top twenty combinations of occupation and keyword for IS ads, most occupations are related to systems development or systems administration, which aligns with operational architectures and levels of the business. From a Zachman EA Framework (ZEF or ZEFA) [32–34] perspective, the six distinct IS occupations above, except for 'IT Strategist', are relevant for rows four and five and thus the operational architectures and levels of the business rather than for any strategic or tactical architecting or development in row one to three. This strikes us as surprising, given that sustainability issues are relevant for both strategic, tactical, and operational levels as discussed in Sect. 2, or macro, meso, and micro [12] levels in business and not just the operational or micro level.

In the case of ICT systems administrators, it is even fair to say that the interest is not on an architectural level of ZEF at all, but on the instantiated architectural artefacts in the form of the functioning organization, its running systems, the actual geographical places of the organization, etc. Hence, the interest is partly the very operations of the business rather than the planning of it, and therefore instantiations rather than architecture. This will normally entail day-to-day problems and issues of immediate concerns and hence the micro level rather than the macro and meso business levels.

In the top twenty combinations of occupation and keyword for IS/IT Engineering, most occupations are also related to operational architecture or micro levels of the business rather than strategic or tactical architecture or macro or meso business levels. Sustainability keywords, excluding 'Environment', are more prevalent in ads for systems and software development occupations (operational architectures and business levels) than in ads for occupations related to strategic and tactical architectures and business levels.

6 Conclusions

Even if the previous literature review showed that sustainability is relevant and important to all levels in organizations, it also showed that sustainability should be a strategic initiative and interest. Yet our findings point to ads wanting operational rather than strategic and/or tactical personnel and specify occupations on an operational and micro level of business and architecture, and not strategic/macro or tactical/meso business levels. What we mean is that since sustainability is strategically important, we expected that IS/IT occupations of a more strategic and tactical character would have higher relative frequencies of sustainability keywords, which is not the case.

This could be explained by a sustainability keyword like Green IS as well-known on the operational but not on the strategic level. But there is also a risk, as we see it, that IS/IT employers in their ads want to appear to be interested in sustainability merely to increase the attractiveness of the position and organization. That would mean that sustainability appearance could be more important than genuine care for sustainability, hence turning the sustainability keywords into embellishment.

Another possible conclusion could of course be that sustainability is something that *must* be mentioned in the job ads, or else the employer and organization seem out of touch with sustainability issues and dilemmas facing the world and people. However, since 40% of the ads do not use any of the one hundred and seven sustainability keywords, the support for this conclusion is relatively weak. In any event, it could still mean that sustainability keywords are used as embellishment to increase the attractiveness of the job and organization more than for a genuine interest in sustainability.

If the presupposition holds that companies need to start thinking strategically about sustainability, it means that there is a misalignment between recruitment being carried out with expectations, as manifest in the job ads, and real needs in accordance with the changes we see with for instance the Corporate Sustainability Due Diligence Directive.

7 Future Work

The job ads data we have collected in the database are of a manifest nature and might not represent a nuanced view of the needs of the recruiters. In addition, job ads might not reflect senior managers' but lower level recruiters' perspectives [19], or the view of HR representatives that are maybe not as knowledgeable in the actual work conditions and specific details of the very job seeking new employees. Hence, the content analysis in this paper is perhaps a bit shallow and scratches the surface of important concepts and issues. Still, we have analysed more than 230,000 job ads to distil findings and reach conclusions, which carries weight.

As we have discussed above, we find it noteworthy that the top occupations tagged to the ads are of an operational rather than tactical or strategic kind, which is contrary to our expectations. We therefore see the need to go beyond mere descriptive coding for a deeper analysis of the data to find out how the ad texts use the sustainability keywords and what they seem to mean in the ads.

To do this, we plan use a random or a stratified (on sustainability keyword frequency) sample of ads per important occupations from the database using an SQL statement and using suitable AI tools, like a GPT application for NLP, to analyse the context of the keywords in the ads and whether the ads are connected to sustainability in any other way than just dutifully sprinkling the ads with the keywords, i.e., embellishment and "greenwashing."

In additions to this, to better understand the revised material, we plan to do twenty to thirty in-depth interviews with a random selection of the companies that have job ads listed. This would enable us to discuss what different parts of their ads are implied to mean, as well as to verify if they indeed are looking for operational/micro rather than tactical/meso and strategic/macro business level competencies. We would also have a better chance of understanding in what capacity they view sustainability and what role ICT and IS play in refence to sustainability goals.

8 Limitations and Bias

One of the limitations of this study that we have already touched upon, is the manifest nature of the job ads and the surface level of content analysis we have done. The study is broad rather than deep and might through this miss nuances and deeper meanings. At the same time, it does analyse a very large number of job ads and thus favour quantity over deeper insights. In addition, the job ads might express "typical" or "expected" views in job ads in the Swedish IS/IT sector, or the views of recruiters and HR representatives rather than the professionals needing new colleagues. We are aware of these potential shortcomings and hence plan to go from breadth to depth in subsequent studies.

Considering bias, we are the ones who have constructed the coding of education backgrounds specified in the ads based on analysis of ads samples and our own understanding of various education programmes and degree labels based on our experience as scholars at Lund University, which is a kind of bias. We might have misunderstood or wrongly understood various textual specifications, especially ads specifying a more technical education background in IS/IT Engineering, which is not our own field. Apart from this, we have no specific bias to report.

Acknowledgments This study has not received any special funding.

Disclosure of Interests The authors have no competing interests to declare that are relevant to the content of this article.

Appendix 1: Phrases for IS and IS/IT Engineering Education Coding

IS Education	'%[Aa]kademisk utbildning inom [Ss]ystemutveckling%', '%[Dd]egree%[Ii]nformatics%', '%[Dd]egree%[Ii]nformation [Mm]anagement%', '%[Dd]egree%[Ii]nformation [Ss]ystems%', '%[E][Ee]xamen%[Ss]ystemutvecklare%', '%[Ee]xamen i%[Ii]nformationssystem%', '%[Ee]xamen%systemutvecklare%', '%[Hh]ögskoleutbildning i%[Ii]nformationssystem%', '%[Ii]nformatik%', '%[Mm]aster%[Ii]nformatics%', '%[Mm]aster%[Ii]nformation [Mm]anagement%', '%[Mm]aster%[Ii]nformation [Ss]ystems%', '%[Pp]ost [Gg]raduate%[Ii]nformatics%', '%[Pp]ost [Gg]raduate%[Ii]nformation [Mm]anagement%', '%[Pp]ost [Gg]raduate%[Ii]nformation [Ss]ystems%', '%[Ss]ystemvet%', '%[Uu]niversitets%i%[Ii]nformationssystem%', '%3 eller 5 årig datautbildning%', '%akademisk utbildning inom systemutveckling%', '%B.Sc%[Ii]nformatics%', '%B.Sc%[Ii]nformation [Mm]anagement%', '%Bachelor%[Ii]nformatics%', '%Bachelor%[Ii]nformation [Mm]anagement%', '%Bachelor%[Ii]nformation [Ss]ystems%', '%BS.c%[Ii]nformation [Ss]ystems%', '%BSc%[Ii]nformatics%', '%BSc%[Ii]nformation [Mm]anagement%', '%BSc%[Ii]nformation [Ss]ystems%', '%högskoleutbildning i%[Ii]nformationssystem%', '%IT-[Dd]egree%', '%M.Sc%[Ii]nformatics%', '%M.Sc%[Ii]nformation [Mm]anagement%', '%M.Sc%[Ii]nformation [Ss]ystems%', '%MSc%[Ii]nformatics%', '%MSc%[Ii]nformation [Mm]anagement%', '%MSc%[Ii]nformation [Ss]ystems%'

Engineering education	'%[Aa]kademisk utbildning inom [Ss]ystemutveckling%', '%[Cc]ivil[Ii]ngenjör%', '%[Cc]omputer [Ee]ngineer%', '%[Cc]omputer [Ss]cience%', '%[Dd]atatekni%', '%[Dd]atavetenskap%', '%[Dd]egree%[Ee]ngineer%', '%[Dd]egree%[Ss]cience%', '%[Ee]ftergymnasial%teknisk%', '%[Ee]l[Ii]ngenjör%', '%[Ee]lectrical [Ee]ngineer%', '%[Ee]lectroni%[Ee]ngineer%', '%[Hh]igher [Ee]ducation%[Ee]ngineering%', '%[Hh]ögre [Uu]tbildning%inom%datakom/telekom%', '%[Hh]ögre [Uu]tbildning%inom%teknik%', '%[Hh]ögre utbildning%inom%teknik%', '%[Hh]ögskole- eller [Uu]niversitetsutbildning%elektronik%', '%[Hh]ögskole- eller Civil[Ii]ngenjör%', '%[Hh]ögskole%[Ii]ngenjör%', '%[Hh]ögskole[Ii]ngenjör%', '%[Hh]ögskoleutbildning för teknisk kompetens%', '%[Hh]ögskoleutbildning inom det tekniska%området%', '%[Hh]ögskoleutbildning%[Dd]atalogi%', '%[Hh]ögskoleutbildning%teknisk inriktning%', '%[Ii]ngenjör%', '%[Ii]ngenjör%[Dd]ata%', '%[Ii]ngenjör%IT/[Dd]atateknik%', '%[Ii]ngenjörsutbildning%', '%[Mm]aster of [Ss]cience E/D/IT/Z%', '%[Mm]aster%[Dd]egree%mechatronic%', '%[Mm]aster%[Dd]egree%technical discipline%', '%[Mm]aster%[Ee]ngineer%', '%[Mm]aster%[Ss]cience%', '%[Mm]asters of [Ss]cience E/D/IT/Z%', '%[Mm]echanical%[Ee]ngineer%', '%[Pp]ost [Gg]raduate%[Ee]ngineer%', '%[Pp]ost [Gg]raduate%[Ss]cience%', '%[Ss]oftware [Ee]ngineer%', '%[Tt]eknisk akademisk utbildning%', '%[Uu]niversitets- eller [Hh]ögskoleutbildning%[Ii]ngenjörer%', '%[Uu]niversity [Ee]ducation%[Ee]ngineering%', '%[Uu]niversity [Ee]ducation%[Ss]cience%', '%3 eller 5 årig datautbildning%', '%B.Sc%[Ee]ngineer%', '%B.Sc%[Ss]cience%', '%B.Sc.%[Cc]omputer%', '%B.Sc.%[Ee]lectrical%', '%B.Sc.%Computer%', '%Bachelor%[Ee]ngineer%', '%Bachelor%[Ss]cience%', '%BE, BTECH, ME, MTECH, MCA%', '%BSc%[Ee]ngineer%', '%BSc%[Ss]cience%', '%el[Ii]ngenjör%', '%Högskole- eller Civil[Ii]ngenjör%', '%inriktning mekanik / elektronik / mjukvara%', '%IT-[Dd]egree%', '%M.Sc%[Ee]ngineer%', '%M.Sc%[Ss]cience%', '%MSc%[Ee]ngineer%', '%MSc%[Ss]cience%', '%MSc%[Tt]echnical [Dd]iscipline%', '%teknisk [Hh]ögskole-/[Uu]niversitetsutbildning%', '%teknisk [Hh]ögskoleutbildning%', '%teknisk akademisk utbildning%'

Appendix 2: AF Level 5 Occupations (Verbatim Translation from Swedish)

Administrative developer; Agile coach; Application consultant; Application developer; Application developer/App developer; Back-End developer; Business analyst; Business architect; Business consultant, IT; Business developer; Civil engineer, systems development; Communication technician; Computer linguist; Computer operator; Computer pedagogue/IT pedagogue/Computer educator; Computer security manager; Configuration Manager/CM; Data Warehouse specialist; Database administrator; Database analyst; Database designer; Database developer; Database technician; Dispatcher; Enterprise Architect; Front-End developer; Full Stack developer; Game tester; GIS developer; Help desk technician/Support technician; Infrastructure architect; Interaction designer; IT architect/Solutions architect; IT coordinator; IT forensic; IT investigator; IT methodology manager; IT security manager; IT strategist; IT technician/Computer technician; Methodology analyst, IT; Mobile application developer; Network administrator; Network designer; Network manager; Network operator; Network technician; Operating technician, computing; Operations manager, IT; Organizational consultant; Process manager, ITIL; Project manager, IT; Requirement analyst; Researcher, IT; Scrum master; Security administrator, IT; Security analyst, IT; Security manager, IT; Service designer; Software developer; Software tester; System administrator; System analyst/System investigator; System architect; System manager; System operator; System tester; System tester/Functionality tester; Systems designer; Systems developer/Programmer; Test developer; Test lead/QA lead; Test manager; Usability designer; Usability expert; UX designer; Web designer; Web manager/Web strategist; Web master; Web technician

Appendix 3: Sustainability Keywords

English	Swedish
Air Quality Monitoring; Autonomous Vehicles; Biodiversity; Biomimicry; Carbon Footprint; Circular Building Design; Circular Business Models; Circular Economy; Circular Economy Hubs.; Circular Economy Incubators; Circular Logistics; Circular Materials Management; Circular Procurement; Circular Supply Chains; Circular Urban Metabolism+C30; Citizen Participation; Clean Tech; Clean Technology; Climate Change; Closed-Loop Systems; Collaborative Consumption; Community Engagement; Conservation; Corporate Social Responsibility; Corporate Sustainability; Cradle To Cradle; Decentralized Energy Systems; Digital Circular Economy; Digital Ethics; Digital Sustainability; Digital Twins; E-Waste Management; Eco-Design; Eco-Friendly; Eco-Innovation; Eco-Labeling; Electric Vehicles; Energy Efficiency; Energy Management Systems; Energy-Efficient Data Centers; Energy-Efficient Hardware; Environment; Environmental Management Systems; Ethical Consumption; Extended Producer Responsibility; Fair Trade; Green Certifications; Green Computing; Green Data Centers; Green Infrastructure; Green IS; Green IT; Green Marketing; Green Procurement; Green Space; Green Supply Chain Management; Greenhouse Gases; Industrial Symbiosis; Information Systems; Intelligent Transportation Systems; Life Cycle Assessment; Material Recovery; Natural Resources; Organic Farming; Predictive Maintenance; Product Stewardship; Product-Service Systems (PSS); Regenerative Agriculture; Remanufacturing; Renewable Energy; Renewable Energy Integration; Resource Efficiency; Resource Management; Resource-Efficient Urban Planning; Shared Mobility Solutions; Sharing Economy Platforms; Smart Buildings; Smart Cities; Smart Grid; Smart Grids; Smart Homes And Buildings; Smart Waste Management; Social Justice; Social Responsibility; Stakeholder Engagement; Sustainability; Sustainable Business Models; Sustainable Consumption; Sustainable Development; Sustainable Finance; GSCM; Sustainable ICT Services; Sustainable Information Management; Sustainable Product Design; Sustainable Software Development; Sustainable Sourcing; Sustainable Supply Chain Management; Sustainable Transportation; Telecommuting; Upcycling; Urban Agriculture; Urban Mining; Urban Planning; Urban Resilience; Waste Management; Water Conservation; Zero Waste	Övervakning av luftkvalitet; Autonoma fordon; Biologisk mångfald; Biomimik; Koldioxidavtryck; Cirkulär byggnadsdesign; Cirkulära affärsmodeller; Cirkulär ekonomi; Circular Economy Hubs.; Inkubatorer för cirkulär ekonomi; Cirkulär logistik; Cirkulär materialhantering; Cirkulär upphandling; Cirkulära försörjningskedjor; Cirkulär Urban Metabolism+C30; Medborgarmedverkan; Ren teknik; Ren teknik; Klimatförändring; Slutna system; Samverkande konsumtion; Samhällsengagemang; Bevarande; Företagens sociala ansvar; Företagens hållbarhet; Vagga till vagga; Decentraliserade energisystem; Digital cirkulär ekonomi; Digital etik; Digital hållbarhet; Digitala tvillingar; E-avfallshantering; Ekodesign; Miljövänlig; Ekoinnovation; Miljömärkning; Elektriska fordon; Energieffektivitet; Energiledningssystem; Energieffektiva datacenter; Energieffektiv hårdvara; Miljö; Miljöledningssystem; Etisk konsumtion; Utökat producentansvar; Rättvis handel; Gröna certifieringar; Grön datoranvändning; Gröna datacenter; Grön infrastruktur; Grön IS; Grön IT; Grön marknadsföring; Grön upphandling; Grön yta; Grön supply chain management; GSCM; Växthusgaser; Industriell symbios; Informationssystem; Intelligenta transportsystem; Livscykelanalys; Materialåtervinning; Naturliga resurser; Ekologiskt jordbruk; Prediktivt underhåll; Produkthantering; Produktservicesystem (PSS); Regenerativt jordbruk; Återtillverkning; Förnybar energi; Integrering av förnybar energi; Resurseffektivitet; Resurshantering; Resurseffektiv stadsplanering; Lösningar för delad mobilitet; Delningsekonomiplattformar; Smarta byggnader; Smarta städer; Smarta elnät; Smarta nät; Smarta hem och byggnader; Smart avfallshantering; Social rättvisa; Socialt ansvar; Engagemang av intressenter; Hållbarhet; Hållbara affärsmodeller; Hållbar konsumtion; Hållbar utveckling; Hållbar ekonomi; Hållbara IKT-tjänster; Hållbar informationshantering; Hållbar produktdesign; Hållbar mjukvaruutveckling; Hållbara inköp; Hållbar supply chain management; Hållbara transporter; Distansarbete; Upcycling; Urbant jordbruk; Urban gruvdrift; Stadsplanering; Urban resiliens; Avfallshantering; Vattenbesparing; Noll avfall

References

1. Giovannoni, E., & Fabietti, G. (2013). What is sustainability? A review of the concept and its applications. In C. Busco, M. Frigo, A. Riccaboni, & P. Quattrone (Eds.), *Integrated reporting: Concepts and cases that redefine corporate accountability* (pp. 21–40). Springer.
2. IPCC: Sections. (2023). Accessed.
3. UN Environment: Global Environment Outlook (GEO-6): Healthy Planet, Healthy People. (2019). Accessed.
4. Freitag, C., Berners-Lee, M., Widdicks, K., Knowles, B., Blair, G. S., & Friday, A. (2021). The real climate and transformative impact of ICT: A critique of estimates, trends, and regulations. *Patterns, 2*.
5. European Commission: Corporate Sustainability Due Diligence (n.d.), https://commission.europa.eu/business-economy-euro/doing-business-eu/corporate-sustainability-due-diligence_en. Accessed November 15, 2023.
6. Chen, A., & Roberts, N. (2023). *Joint drivers of different shades of green IT/IS practices: A strategic cognition perspective*. Information Technology & People ahead-of-print.
7. Leidner, D. E., Sutanto, J., & Goutas, L. (2022). Multifarious roles and conflicts on an Interorganizational green IS. *MIS Quarterly, 46*.
8. Steen, O., & Pierce, P. (2023). Do IS curricular guidelines match employer expectations in Swedish IS Job Ads? In: 31st international conference on information systems development (ISD 2023).
9. Sahu, G. P., & Singh, M. (2016). Green information system adoption and sustainability: A case study of select Indian Banks. In: Social Media: The Good, the Bad, and the Ugly: 15th IFIP WG 6.11 Conference on e-Business, e-Services, and e-Society, I3E 2016, Swansea, UK, September 13–15, 2016, Proceedings 15, (pp. 292–304). Springer.
10. Coelho, M. P., Cesário, F., Sabino, A., & Moreira, A. (2022). Pro-environmental messages in job advertisements and the intentions to apply—the mediating role of organizational attractiveness. *Sustainability, 14*, 3014.
11. Chou, D. C., Chen, H.-G., & Lin, B. (2023). Green IT and corporate social responsibility for sustainability. *Journal of Computer Information Systems, 63*, 322–333.
12. Pan, S. L., Carter, L., Tim, Y., & Sandeep, M. (2022). Digital sustainability, climate change, and information systems solutions: Opportunities for future research. *International Journal of Information Management, 63*, 102444.
13. Harnischmacher, C., Herrenkind, B., & Weilbier, L. (2020). Yesterday, today, and tomorrow—perspectives on green information systems research streams. In *European conference on information systems*.
14. Zeng, F., Lee, S. H.-N., & Lo, C. K. Y. (2020). The role of information systems in the sustainable development of enterprises: A systematic literature network analysis. *Sustainability*.
15. Gallivan, M. J., Truex, D. P., III, & Kvasny, L. (2004). Changing patterns in IT skill sets 1988-2003: A content analysis of classified advertising. *ACM SIGMIS Database: The DATABASE for Advances in Information Systems, 35*, 64–87.
16. Kennan, M. A., Willard, P., Cecez-Kecmanovic, D., & Wilson, C. S. (2007). IS early career job advertisements: A content analysis. In: PACIS 2007. (p. 51).
17. Litecky, C., Igou, A. J., & Aken, A. (2012). Skills in the management oriented IS and enterprise system job markets. In *The 50th annual conference on computers and people research* (pp. 35–44). Association for Computing Machinery.
18. Prabhakar, B., Litecky, C. R., & Arnett, K. (2005). IT skills in a tough job market. *Communications of the ACM, 48*, 91–94.
19. Todd, P. A., McKeen, J. D., & Gallupe, R. B. (1995). The evolution of IS job skills: A content analysis of IS job advertisements from 1970 to 1990. *MIS Quarterly, 19*, 1–27.
20. Aldenhoven, C. M., Brosch, D. K., Prommegger, B., & Krcmar, H. (2021). *Differences in skill requirements for agile workers in the German and the US IT industries* (pp. 582–595). Springer.

21. Burns, T. J., Gao, Y., Sherman, C., & Klein, S. (2018). Do the knowledge and skills required by employers of recent graduates of undergraduate information systems programs match the current ACM/AIS information systems curriculum guidelines? *Information Systems Education Journal, 16*, 56.
22. Dong, T., & Triche, J. (2020). A longitudinal analysis of job skills for entry-level data analysts. *Journal of Information Systems Education, 31*, 312.
23. Mardis, M. A., Ma, J., Jones, F. R., Ambavarapu, C. R., Kelleher, H. M., Spears, L. I., & McClure, C. R. (2018). Assessing alignment between information technology educational opportunities, professional requirements, and industry demands. *Education and Information Technologies, 23*, 1547–1584.
24. Steen, O., & Pierce, P. (2020). Swedish undergraduate information systems curricula: A comparative study. In A. Siarheyeva, C. Barry, M. Lang, H. Linger, & C. Schneider (Eds.), *Advances in information systems development: Information systems beyond 2020* (pp. 131–145). Springer Nature.
25. Litecky, C. R., Arnett, K. P., & Prabhakar, B. (2004). The paradox of soft skills versus technical skills in IS hiring. *Journal of Computer Information Systems, 45*, 69–76.
26. Greenland, S., & Poole, C. (2011). Problems in common interpretations of statistics in scientific articles, expert reports, and testimony. *Jurimetrics*, 113–129.
27. Greenland, S., Senn, S. J., Rothman, K. J., Carlin, J. B., Poole, C., Goodman, S. N., & Altman, D. G. (2016). Statistical tests, P values, confidence intervals, and power: A guide to misinterpretations. *European Journal of Epidemiology, 31*, 337–350.
28. Rafi, Z., & Greenland, S. (2020). Semantic and cognitive tools to aid statistical science: Replace confidence and significance by compatibility and surprise. *BMC Medical Research Methodology, 20*, 1–13.
29. SCB: Standard för svensk yrkesklassificering (SSYK). Statistiska centralbyrån/Statistics Sweden. (2023). https://www.scb.se/dokumentation/klassifikationer-och-standarder/standard-for-svensk-yrkesklassificering-ssyk/. Accessed March 8, 2023.
30. International Labour Organization (ILO): The International Standard Classification of Occupations (ISCO). (2023). https://www.ilo.org/public/english/bureau/stat/isco/index.htm. Accessed March 8, 2023.
31. European Commission: European Skills, Competences, and Occupations (ESCO). European Commission (2023). https://esco.ec.europa.eu/en. Accessed March 28, 2023.
32. Finkelstein, C. (2015). *Enterprise architecture for integration: Rapid delivery methods and technologies*. Information Engineering Services Pty Ltd.
33. Kappelman, L. A., & Zachman, J. A. (2013). The enterprise and its architecture: Ontology & challenges. *Journal of Computer Information Systems, 53*, 87–95.
34. Zachman, J. A. (1987). A framework for information systems architecture. *IBM Systems Journal, 26*, 276–292.

The Organizational Features of Circular Platforms: Balancing Digital Transformation and Sustainability

Francesca Sanguineti, Beatrice Re, and Pietro Previtali

Abstract Circular platforms, digital business models designed to prioritize circular economy principles, are transforming how we approach sustainability. In an era where digital platforms and environmental consciousness are reshaping markets, circular platforms are striving to survive and success. This study investigates the organizational features that enable circular platforms to balance digital transformation and sustainability. Employing a qualitative multiple case study approach, it examines 28 circular platforms across various industries and geographical locations. The analysis identifies interaction complexity and organizational integration as important dimensions for balancing digital transformation and sustainability, proposing a framework which categorizes platforms into B2B, B2C, C2B, and C2C models. Key challenges linked with digital transformation include market penetration, logistics, and regulatory barriers, while benefits encompass enhanced transparency and resource optimization. The proposed framework provides a first step to the categorization of circular platforms and its key managerial implications.

Keywords Circular platforms · Digital transformation · Sustainability

1 Introduction

In a world where digitalization is reshaping the market, and environmental concerns are growing, a new way of doing business is emerging. Individuals, firms, and governments seem all engaged in efforts to reduce pollution and waste by finding new ways of reusing existing materials and regenerating natural resources. This has given rise to the circular economy (CE), an economic system that represents a shift from the traditional linear "take, make, waste" model of production [1, 2]. The

F. Sanguineti (✉) · B. Re · P. Previtali
Department of Economics and Management, University of Pavia, Pavia, Italy
e-mail: francesca.sanguineti@unipv.it; beatrice.re@unipv.it; pietro.previtali@unipv.it

M. Cipriano et al. (eds.), *Technologies for Organizations and Society*,
Lecture Notes in Information Systems and Organisation 80,
https://doi.org/10.1007/978-3-032-01697-3_7

CE promotes the reduction, reuse, recycling, and recovery of materials throughout production, distribution, and consumption processes [1].

At the same time, the digitalization process of the past three decades has facilitated the creation of digital platforms [3, 4]. These platforms create value through the interaction between two or more groups of users with shared business interests [5–7]. Unlike traditional businesses, digital platforms provide an infrastructure for users without controlling the entire production process, making them highly scalable and suitable for rapid expansion [6].

Given their scalability and reach, digital business platforms are an ideal channel to foster and promote the CE globally [8, 9]. For example, the Ellen MacArthur Foundation & McKinsey Center for Business and Environment [10] estimate that the CE business will grow by 3% by 2030, generating total annual benefits of €1.8 trillion [11]. In fact, we are witnessing the emergence of multiple circular—digital-platforms (e.g., Close the Loop, Lablaco, and Globechain) specifically designed to facilitate the transition to circularity [12] by enabling interactions among economic actors and promoting circular activities, information, and best practices. This intersection of digital platforms and CE principles represents a research area with significant implications for CE business practices as it may help address the critical challenges of climate change, resource depletion, and the need for more resilient, sustainable economic models.

While digital platforms have become integral to modern society [13], shaping economic interactions and facilitating social exchanges globally, there is an area that needs further attention and that concerns the organizational features of circular platforms (CPs), specifically with regards to the success balance of digital transformation and sustainability initiatives [14, 15]. Previous studies have primarily focused on classifying business models for circularity adopted by innovative firms [2, 14, 16, 17] or traditional companies [18], as well as exploring barriers and enablers of circularity at the SME level [19] and within industrial symbiosis contexts [9]. A recent study [20] highlights the roles of digital platforms in enabling a CE. Yet, one identified under-researched area in the literature regards the specific organizational features that are fundamental for CPs to successfully balance digital transformation and sustainability initiatives [20]. Addressing this gap can introduce novel perspectives on the organizational features essential for the success of CPs, thus contributing to the discourse about business models in the CE context, a substream of business model research that aim to understand how business models could be structured and designed to pursue CE-related principles and strategies [20–22]. Thus, the current study aims to address the following research question: "What organizational features enable CPs to balance digital transformation and sustainability?" Through the secondary data analysis of 28 CPs, this research highlights the factors driving their success and the challenges they face. Our findings provide timely insights that can guide businesses, policymakers, and researchers in developing and implementing effective strategies for CPs, contributing to the theoretical and practical knowledge of how CPs can operate and thrive in an increasingly digital and sustainable economy.

The paper is organized as follows. After introducing the relevant literature, we present the methodology and sample identified. Subsequently, we report our results, proposing a framework that highlights the main organizational features, and we present the analysis on the benefits and challenges faced by CPs in their digital transformation journey. Finally, we discuss the implications of our findings and suggest directions for future research.

2 Theoretical Background

This section provides an overview of the key concepts underlying our study, i.e., digital transformation and sustainability, CE and digital platforms, and challenges and opportunities for CPs.

2.1 Digital Transformation and Sustainability

The intersection of digital transformation and sustainability has become an increasingly important point for modern organizations, particularly those adopting CE business models [23]. Digital platforms, which leverage technology to enable interactions between multiple user groups, have the potential to significantly impact sustainability initiatives [24]. Thanks to very recent studies, we now know that online platforms have an active role in enabling the CE, with roles that include coordinating market interactions, operating product-service systems, and facilitating co-creation processes [20]. Therefore, these platforms can be leveraged to balance digital transformation and sustainability. Yet, one identified under-investigated area concerns the specific organizational features of CPs to balance digital transformation and sustainability initiatives. Understanding the organizational features that enable CPs to effectively balance on those, is essential for guiding decision-making, resource allocation, and strategic planning in the context of CE initiatives [20].

Organizational features such as culture, strategy, and operations play a crucial role in shaping digital transformation strategies [25]. Industry 4.0 technologies, such as the Internet of Things (IoT) and Artificial Intelligence (AI), are pivotal in integrating digital transformation with CE principles, thereby promoting operational efficiencies and sustainability [20, 26]. Digital platforms enable better resource flow and empower consumers to make informed decisions, enhancing the sustainability of circular business models [27]. Furthermore, the orchestration mechanisms within platform-based meta-organizations are essential for economic value creation and sustainability [28].

However, achieving widespread adoption of CPs necessitates addressing barriers such as global awareness, education, and supportive legal frameworks [29]. The concept of "digital sustainability" underscores the importance of leveraging digitalization to achieve sustainability goals, highlighting the thematic connections between these domains [30].

2.2 Circular Economy and Digital Platforms

The circular economy (CE) represents a reverse approach to the traditional linear "take, make, waste" model of production, instead promoting the reduction, reuse, recycling, and recovery of materials throughout the production, distribution, and consumption processes [1, 2]. The integration of digital platforms within this paradigm creates opportunities for scaling up sustainability efforts by enhancing resource efficiency and enabling new forms of economic interactions [26]. CE-related studies gained importance in the second decade of the 2000s, facilitating the sharing of best practices among scholars [1, 31] and practitioners [10, 32, 33].

At the same time, the digitalization process has facilitated the creation of digital platforms [3, 4]. These platforms generate value through interactions between two or more user groups with shared business interests [5–7]. Examples of successful digital platforms are AirBnB and Couchsurfing in the tourism industry, both offering competitive-priced accommodations across the world through the use of sharing privately-owned resources (rooms or apartments) [34]; Uber in the automotive industry, which adopts a similar sharing system for urban mobility in more than 60 countries [35]; and BlaBlaCar in the car-sharing industry, offering users the possibility to enjoy others' company while splitting the costs of the car usage when traveling in 21 different countries. These examples demonstrate how digital platforms can disrupt traditional business models by leveraging shared resources to create value, a principle that aligns well with the CE. Online platforms have become integral to modern society, shaping economic interactions and facilitating social exchanges on a global scale [13].

Within the context of the CE, leveraging online platforms is essential for promoting sustainability and resource efficiency [36]. As a result, in recent years, we are witnessing the emergence of multiple circular digital platforms (e.g., Depop, Too Good To Go, and Rheaply), whose main aim is to favor the transition to circularity [12] by facilitating the interaction among the economy's main actors, and the promotion of circularity-related activities, information, and good practices.

While representative of a rising phenomenon, "circular platforms" (CPs), that we define as digital business platforms pursuing circularity as their primary objective, have yet to reach their full potential. Despite their increasing prevalence and clear advantages in terms of resource value and positive externalities generated, CPs have not yet replaced traditional linear -platform- models, thus much still needs to be done to see CPs becoming the dominant economic models.

2.3 Challenges and Opportunities for Circular Platforms

Limited knowledge and logistical issues seem to be among the principal factors limiting the diffusion or expansion of CPs. Interested users may be unaware of their existence, the associated opportunities, or how to properly utilize and exploit them.

A "lack of information about the benefits of the CE" [19] may be a significant barrier CPs face at the individual level, despite increasing global awareness of environmental concerns. Furthermore, the lack of information regarding sources, amounts, and availability of goods, combined with limited knowledge of potential sustainability and feasibility, may prevent the adoption of circular business models at the market/firm level [8].

Trust within the platform is another important issue, as platforms should ensure confidence that all the parties involved in the transactions will behave appropriately [8]. This, in turn, may translate into lower transaction volumes, making it even harder to gain users' trust. Moreover, high transaction costs for secondary materials and recycling markets persist [8, 9], discouraging firms—especially small and medium-sized enterprises (SMEs)—from switching to more circular-based business models. Finally, there is still a lack of consensus, and few academic studies, on the drivers and dynamics of CPs' international expansion, as some markets may not be conducive for these platforms to survive and grow successfully [9].

However, CPs also offer significant advantages. Due to their waste management purpose, they may include reduced fixed costs and an increased pool of potential customers [37, 38]. For example, industries that previously purchased new materials now can buy the same raw materials derived from the waste of other industries, reducing both costs and waste in a win-win scenario—the industrial symbiosis CP case. According to Chertow and Park [39] "industrial symbiosis construed as networks of organizations cooperatively sharing wastes has created irresistible imagery and high hopes for a time when virtually all water, energy, and materials will be used more than once, and not to do will have become socially unacceptable." Additionally, the digital nature of CPs makes them less dependent on physical borders [37, 38].

Thus, CPs, which facilitate resource reduction, reuse, and recycling, are increasingly recognized for their potential to drive sustainable business models [40]. The adoption of circular business models is influenced by various determinants, including market conditions, regulatory frameworks, and collaborative efforts [41]. Therefore, this study aims to address the following research question: "What organizational features enable circular platforms to balance digital transformation and sustainability?". By analyzing these factors, the research aims to better understand the elements that drive the success of CPs in navigating digital transformation and sustainability pursuits.

3 Methodology

The current study aims to investigate the organizational features that enable CPs to balance digital transformation and sustainability. The exploratory nature of our research, aiming for an in-depth exploration of the organizational features, processes, and impacts of CPs calls for a qualitative methodological approach [42, 43]. In particular, we opted for collecting data from secondary data sources

Table 1 Data collection

Source type	Data items	Data content	Data details
Company Reports	Annual reports, sustainability reports	Detailed organizational practices, financial data, and sustainability impacts	52 company reports 4 sustainability reports
Academic Articles	Peer-reviewed articles and case studies published in academic journals	Theoretical frameworks, case studies, and empirical research	120 case studies of the CPs included in the sample
Industry Publications	Reports from industry associations, white papers	Industry trends, best practices, and market analysis	5-Deloitte (e.g., circular goes digital), Ellen MacArthur Foundation, Forbes, McKinsey & Company, UNEP circularity platform
Online Resources	Company websites, social media, news articles	Real-time updates, organizational announcements, and additional data	28 websites and related social media pages (that link to the news articles)

[44], which included company reports, academic articles and case studies, industry publications, and online resources.

The triangulation of multiple data sources enhances the validity and reliability of the findings [45, 46]. Data was collected from February to November 2023. The use of secondary data as a reliable source of information in case studies has been well-established, particularly when there is the availability of many sources of information [22, 44, 47]. To further support the validity of secondary data, extant studies have utilized sources such as published historical accounts, newspapers, public materials (e.g., annual reports), and archival documents—relying exclusively on secondary data [44]. Additionally, information gathered from multiple sources increases data triangulation, which is fundamental in ensuring internal validity [48].

A summary of the data collection is presented in Table 1.

3.1 Data Collection

The sample was selected through a systematic process involving several steps. Initially, a broad search identified digital platforms with potential relevance to the CE from academic databases, industry reports, and online resources. In order to select the sample that best addresses our purpose, we performed an extensive online search to identify the potential cases [20]. We found two main platforms with a focus on CE, i.e., Ellen MacArthur Foundation and the European Circular Economy Networks. In these platforms, we searched for firms adopting circular business models and showing publicly available information regarding our research themes. Each identified case was then evaluated following specific inclusion and exclusion criteria that were set a priori to determine their eligibility. We ended up with 28 case firms to be analyzed. The choice to opt for a secondary data analysis also supports the feasibility of analyzing a larger number of cases without compromising analytical depth, enabling us to capture the broad spectrum of organizational features and impacts relevant to our research question [49].

Thus, before selecting the cases for this study, the authors identified specific inclusion and exclusion criteria to ensure the relevance and quality of the data. The aim was to identify digital platforms that exemplify the integration of digital transformation and sustainability within the framework of the CE—what we refer to as circular platforms (CPs).

The inclusion criteria applied are the following:

- The platforms were included if they were adopting one or more of the different circular business models introduced by Lacy and Rutqvisot [2], i.e., circular supply chain, resource recovery and recycling, product life extension, sharing, product as a service.
- Eligible platforms facilitate interaction among key economic actors (businesses, consumers, policymakers) to promote circularity-related activities, information, and best practices, fostering a collaborative circular ecosystem [50]
- Platforms included in the study have documented social, economic, or environmental impacts, as evidenced by case studies, company reports, or academic articles.

The criteria for exclusion were, instead, the following:

- Platforms without a clear adoption of a circular business model as their main objective were excluded to maintain relevance to the core of the research.
- Platforms lacking sufficient publicly available data for analysis were also excluded, as comprehensive data is essential for an in-depth examination of organizational features, processes, and impacts.

Eligible platforms underwent a more detailed analysis, including a review of available documentation such as company reports, impact assessments, and relevant publications whenever available. All authors firstly checked the list on their own and then discussed those cases that were on the edge, choosing on whether to maintain them or not in the final dataset. Platforms that passed this whole process were included in the final sample. This approach to case selection aims at ensuring that the study focuses on relevant and data-rich platforms, enhancing the validity and reliability of the findings.

Table 2 reports the analyzed cases, with information about the CPs regarding (1) its name, (2) the headquarter's country, (3) the main industry in which it operates, and (4) a description of the platform.

Table 2 Cases selected for the analysis

CP name	HQ	Main industry	Description
Back Market	France	Electronics	Marketplace for refurbished electronics.
Close the Loop	Australia	Electronics	Offers recycling solutions for various types of waste.
Depop	UK	Fashion	Social marketplace for buying and selling fashion items among individuals.
Etsy	USA	Various	Online marketplace for handmade, vintage, and unique factory-manufactured items, supporting small businesses and promoting sustainable shopping.
Fairphone	Netherlands	Electronics	Creates modular smartphones designed for easy repair and recycling.
Fruitleather Rotterdam	Netherlands	Materials	Converts leftover fruit into durable leather-like materials.
Globechain	UK	Various	Facilitates redistribution of unneeded items among businesses, charities, and individuals.
iFixit	USA	Electronics	Provides repair guides and parts to promote product longevity.
innovan-dotech.com	Italy	Industrial	Connects industrial supply and demand for waste materials.
Lablaco	Italy	Fashion	Promotes circular fashion through a blockchain-based system for tracking and reselling clothing.
Loop	USA	Consumer Goods	Delivers products in reusable packaging, returned for cleaning and reuse.
Material reuse portal	USA	Construction	Platform for recycling and reusing construction materials.
Mud Jeans	Netherlands	Fashion	Offers a leasing model for jeans, promoting recycling and reuse.
OfferUp	USA	Various	Mobile marketplace for buying and selling locally.
OLIO	UK	Food	Food-sharing app connecting neighbors and local businesses to share surplus food.
Patagonia Worn Wear	USA	Fashion	Allows customers to trade in used Patagonia gear for store credit and purchase refurbished items.
Poshmark	USA	Fashion	Social commerce marketplace for new and secondhand fashion, home goods, and electronics.
Re-Tek	UK	Electronics	IT asset management and refurbishment services, promoting reuse and recycling of electronics.
Reflaunt	Singapore	Fashion	Allows users to resell luxury fashion items across multiple marketplaces.
Rent the Runway	USA	Fashion	Allows users to rent designer clothing and accessories.

(continued)

Table 2 (continued)

CP name	HQ	Main industry	Description
Rheaply	USA	Industrial	Connects businesses to exchange materials, reducing waste and keeping resources in use.
Swap.com	USA	Various	Online consignment and thrift store for secondhand goods.
The RealReal	USA	Fashion	Luxury consignment store for authenticated luxury items.
ThredUP	USA	Fashion	Online consignment and thrift store for secondhand clothes.
Too Good To Go	Denmark	Food	Connects consumers with businesses that have surplus food to prevent food waste.
Trove	USA	Various	Helps brands implement re-commerce programs to buy back and resell used items.
Vigga	Denmark	Fashion	Subscription service for baby and children's clothing, allowing returns for new sizes.
Vinted	Lithuania	Fashion	Online marketplace for buying, selling, and swapping secondhand clothes and accessories.

Description of the Sample The circular digital platforms included in the final sample are headquartered in various countries, and are mainly active in industries such as fashion, electronics, and food. These platforms are primarily based in the United States, the United Kingdom, and several European countries, including the Netherlands, Denmark, and Italy. The geographical distribution of the sample highlights the global nature of the CE movement.

Upon closer examination, the platforms can be grouped into different categories based on their primary functions and the industries they serve. The fashion industry, in particular, is well-represented in the sample, with platforms such as Lablaco (Italy), Reflaunt (Singapore), and ThredUP (USA). These platforms share a strong commitment to promoting sustainable practices within the fashion sector, including the resale, leasing, and recycling of clothing items. By facilitating the redistribution and reuse of fashion items, these platforms play a crucial role in reducing waste and fostering a more circular approach to fashion consumption.

Another key sector represented in the sample is the electronics industry. Platforms like Back Market (France) and Re-Tek (UK) have emerged as leaders, focusing their efforts on repairing, refurbishing, and recycling electronic devices. These platforms recognize the importance of extending the lifecycle of electronic products and minimizing the environmental impact of electronic waste. By leveraging advanced digital technologies and innovative business models, these platforms are able to optimize resource use and promote more sustainable practices within the electronics industry.

In addition to fashion and electronics, the sample also includes several platforms operating in the food sector. Companies like Too Good To Go (Denmark) and OLIO (UK) have made it their mission to reduce food waste by connecting consumers with businesses or other consumers that have surplus food. These platforms rely on strong community engagement and efficient logistics to ensure that leftovers, but perfectly preserved food, is redistributed rather than wasted. By addressing the pressing issue of food waste, these platforms demonstrate the potential for CPs to create positive social and environmental impact.

The diverse range of companies, industries, and geographical locations represented underscores the growing importance of the CE and the role that digital platforms can play in promoting sustainability and resource efficiency also on a global scale.

3.2 Data Analysis

Our data analysis involves coding the collected data according to three key variables/dimensions of interest: (1) organizational features, (2) main challenges of digital transformation, and (3) main benefits of digital transformation. Subsequently, we identify the most frequent themes emerging across cases, which lead us to the development of the framework presented in Fig. 1. Here, we categorize platforms along the two dimensions of interaction complexity and organizational integration. Through this process, we were able to synthesize our findings to identify the main

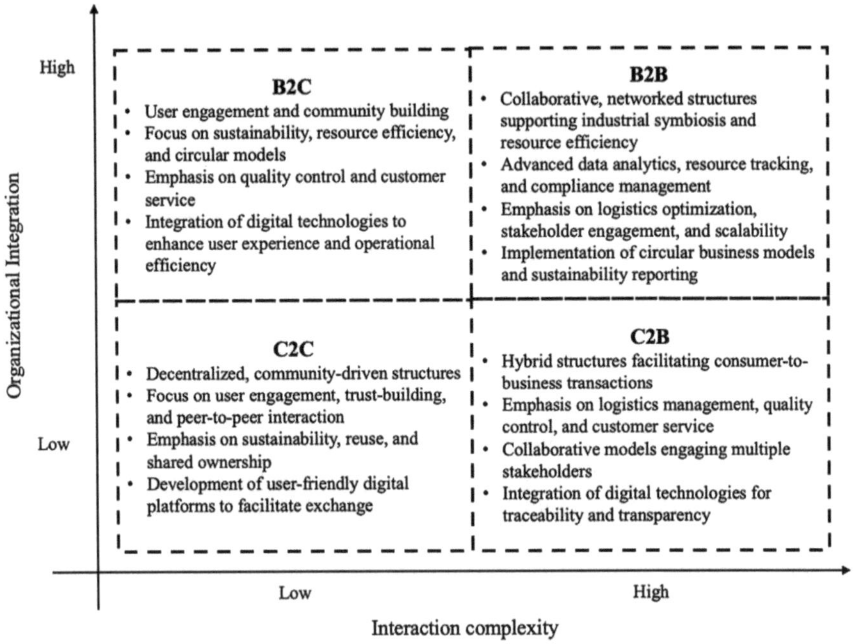

Fig. 1 Resulting framework. Source: own elaboration

organizational features, challenges, and benefits across different types of circular digital platforms.

4 Findings

The analysis of secondary data concerning our sample of 28 circular digital platforms reveals several patterns and insights that shed light on the organizational features enabling these platforms to balance digital transformation and sustainability effectively (see Table 3 for details on organizational features per CP). To systematically examine these features, we propose a framework that categorizes platforms based on two key dimensions: interaction complexity and organizational integration.

In the context of our study, interaction complexity refers to the intricacy and dynamism of the interactions occurring within digital ecosystems, influenced by factors such as the number and diversity of stakeholders, the nature of the processes involved, and the volume and variety of data exchanged. Organizational integration, on the other hand, refers to the seamless coordination and collaboration among various stakeholders within a digital ecosystem to achieve CE objectives.

As explained in the data analysis, we consider the two dimensions of interaction complexity (x-axis) and organizational integration (y-axis), and we position the main themes emerging from the data analysis into four distinct quadrants: B2B, B2C, C2B, and C2C. We adopt this clusterization to have a holistic perspective on digital platforms by including all the four typologies advanced in the literature [46].

B2B platforms, such as Close the Loop, innovandotech.com, and Rheaply, are characterized by high organizational integration and high interaction complexity. These platforms prioritize collaborative and integrative structures that support industrial symbiosis, enabling businesses to exchange resources, materials, and waste products efficiently. They focus on supply chain optimization, resource management, and scalability, which require advanced data analytics, resource tracking, and compliance management. The complex interactions among multiple stakeholders necessitate robust coordination and information sharing.

B2C platforms, like Mud Jeans, Too Good To Go, and Vigga, demonstrate high organizational integration and low interaction complexity. These platforms emphasize logistics, quality control, and customer service, indicating a more centralized and formalized structure. For instance, Mud Jeans, a B2C platform, emphasizes its logistics and customer service integration through its unique "Lease A Jeans" model. According to their company reports, this model requires a sophisticated reverse logistics system to handle returns and repairs, demonstrating high organizational integration. Similarly, Too Good To Go's platform necessitates inventory management and efficient logistics to connect consumers with businesses having surplus food, showcasing how B2C platforms in the circular economy require streamlined processes despite lower interaction complexity compared to B2B models. They facilitate straightforward transactions between businesses and

Table 3 Data analysis of circular platforms. Source: own elaboration

Platform name	Organizational features	Main challenges of digital transformation	Main benefits of digital transformation
Back Market	Structure organized for quality control, warranty offerings. Focus on reducing electronic waste.	Ensuring consistent product quality.	Comprehensive quality checks, warranty integration.
Close the Loop	Logistics management, stakeholder collaboration, sustainability focus.	E-waste handling regulations.	Efficient logistics for e-waste, stakeholder engagement.
Depop	User engagement, community building, digital marketplace.	Building trust among users.	Social engagement features, mobile app interface.
Etsy	Community-focused platform, support for small businesses or independent sellers, emphasis on sustainability.	Ensuring product quality, user trust.	Enhanced reach for small businesses, digital marketing tools, sustainability focus.
Fairphone	Ethical sourcing, sustainability, consumer empowerment.	Market penetration, customer adoption.	Modular design for easy repair, ethical and sustainable brand image.
Fruitleather Rotterdam	Innovation in material use, sustainability, resource optimization.	Scaling production.	Innovative material use, sustainability branding.
Globechain	Networked structure, efficient logistics management, stakeholder engagement.	Logistic challenges, awareness.	Efficient matching of supply and demand, data analytics.
iFixit	Global community support, repair advocacy.	Access to repair parts, regulatory barriers.	Comprehensive repair guides, community-driven support.
innovandotech.com	Industrial symbiosis, resource efficiency, digital integration.	Market awareness, regulatory issues.	Efficient matching of industrial waste supply and demand.
Lablaco	Decentralized structure, collaboration with brands and consumers, technology integration.	Adoption and scalability issues.	Enhanced transparency and traceability through blockchain.

(continued)

Table 3 (continued)

Platform name	Organizational features	Main challenges of digital transformation	Main benefits of digital transformation
Loop	Circular supply chain, customer engagement, reusable packaging logistics.	Logistics of returns and cleaning.	Efficient reusable packaging logistics, sustainability branding.
Material reuse portal	Resource optimization, sustainability in construction, logistics management.	Regulatory compliance, logistics.	Efficient recycling logistics, optimization of construction waste.
Mud Jeans	Customer engagement, sustainability, leasing model, resource efficiency.	Customer retention, logistics.	Leasing model for continuous use and recycling, sustainability branding.
OfferUp	User-friendly interface, local focus, community engagement.	Local trust issues.	Easy-to-use mobile app, local community focus.
OLIO	Community engagement, digital platform for sharing, sustainability focus.	User trust, food safety concerns.	Community-building features, user-friendly app interface.
Patagonia Worn Wear	Emphasis on product longevity, resource efficiency, customer engagement.	Scaling refurbishment operations.	Promotion of sustainability values, efficient trade-in system.
Poshmark	Social engagement features, community-driven, sustainability in resale.	User trust, shipping logistics.	Social features for user engagement, streamlined resale processes.
Re-Tek	Efficient refurbishment and resale operations, sustainability, IT asset management.	Managing logistics of returned items.	Streamlined IT asset management and refurbishment processes.
Reflaunt	Digital integration for managing listings, sales, logistics, sustainable fashion promotion.	Trust in luxury resale market, logistics.	Multi-channel integration, streamlined resale process.
Rent the Runway	Logistics and customer service integration, rental model, sustainable consumption.	High logistics costs, inventory management.	Efficient rental logistics, customer relationship management.

(continued)

Table 3 (continued)

Platform name	Organizational features	Main challenges of digital transformation	Main benefits of digital transformation
Rheaply	Collaborative structure, focus on industrial symbiosis, resource optimization.	Limited awareness, regulatory barriers.	Optimization of resource flows, improved network collaboration.
Swap.com	Large-scale operations, quality control, emphasis on reuse and recycling.	Logistics and inventory management.	Efficient consignment processes, quality control measures.
The RealReal	Rigorous authentication, efficient resale operations, digital integration.	Authentication costs, trust in resale.	Advanced authentication technology, high-value item management.
ThredUP	Large-scale operations, sorting, listing, shipping pre-owned clothing, hybrid structure.	Quality control, logistics.	Large-scale sorting and inventory management, user-friendly resale platform.
Too Good To Go	Digital platform for coordinating supply and demand, sustainability focus, robust logistics.	Consumer trust, food safety regulations.	Real-time inventory management, efficient logistics.
Trove	Support for circular business models, logistics management, sustainability integration.	Brand partnerships, logistics.	Efficient recommerce logistics, data-driven inventory management.
Vigga	Efficient logistics network, reuse and recycling focus, subscription model.	Logistics of returns and exchanges.	Subscription model for continuous use and recycling.
Vinted	Community-focused platform, strong user engagement, sustainability focus.	Ensuring product quality, user trust.	Large community engagement, easy-to-use platform.

consumers, which typically involve fewer complex interactions compared to other types of platforms.

C2B platforms, such as Patagonia Worn Wear, The RealReal and Back Market align with low organizational integration and high interaction complexity. These platforms focus on decentralized structures that support peer-to-peer exchanges and rely on user engagement and trust-building mechanisms. The interactions on these platforms can be more complex, as they involve multiple individual consumers interacting with businesses, requiring significant coordination and management of various stakeholders.

C2C platforms, like OLIO, OfferUp and Vinted are characterized by low organizational integration and low interaction complexity. These platforms primarily facilitate direct exchanges between individuals, enabling peer-to-peer sharing, swapping, and second-hand trading of goods. They rely on decentralized structures and user-driven interactions, with minimal intermediation from the platform itself. The interactions on these platforms are typically less complex compared to B2B or B2C platforms.

It is important to note that some platforms, such as ThredUP and Globechain, exhibit features of more than one interaction model, as they facilitate consumer-to-consumer transactions while also involving business-to-consumer or consumer-to-business elements. These hybrid platforms have a mix of organizational integration and interaction complexity levels, depending on the specific aspects of their operations. This led them to be at the edge of two quadrants, highlighting the peculiarity of each CP and the difficulty in categorizing them.

In addition to the organizational features and interaction types, the analysis also highlights the main challenges and benefits that CPs face in their digital transformation efforts. Platforms like Fruitleather Rotterdam, Mud Jeans and Fairphone deal with adoption and scalability issues, as well as challenges related to market penetration and customer acquisition. Logistics and supply chain management emerge as key issues for platforms such as Globechain, Loop, and Rent the Runway. For example, Globechain, a platform facilitating the redistribution of unneeded items, faces significant logistical challenges due to the diverse nature of items exchanged and countries in which they operate. According to Globechain's report,[1] they managed over five million items across 14 countries in 2022, highlighting the complexity of their supply chain management.

Building and maintaining consumer trust is another critical challenge, particularly for platforms dealing with sensitive industries such as food (e.g., Too Good To Go, OLIO) or high-value items (e.g., The RealReal). Regulatory barriers and compliance issues pose additional obstacles for platforms operating in highly regulated sectors, such as e-waste management (e.g., Close the Loop) or construction (e.g., Material reuse portal).

Additionally, platforms across all quadrants face technology-specific challenges. Data security is a critical concern, especially for platforms handling sensitive information. The RealReal, which deals with luxury goods, reported investing $2.5 million in cybersecurity measures in 2022 to protect customer data and maintain trust. Systems interoperability is another challenge, particularly for B2B platforms like Rheaply that need to integrate with various enterprise systems. It is evident from their business model that they must invest significantly in developing integrations

[1] https://www.applytosupply.digitalmarketplace.service.gov.uk/g-cloud/services/330138812881573

to ensure seamless data exchange with clients' existing inventory management systems. This challenge is common among B2B platforms in the circular economy, as they often need to connect with diverse IT infrastructures across multiple organizations.

Despite these challenges, the analysis also reveals the significant benefits that digital transformation brings to circular digital platforms. These benefits include enhanced transparency and traceability (e.g., Lablaco), efficient matching of supply and demand (e.g., Globechain), optimization of resource flows (e.g., Rheaphy), and the development of innovative business models such as rental (e.g., Rent the Runway), leasing (e.g., Mud Jeans), and subscription (e.g., Vigga). Moreover, digital transformation enables platforms to implement advanced features such as real-time inventory management (e.g., Too Good To Go), multi-channel integration (e.g., Reflaunt), and user-friendly interfaces (e.g., OLIO, OfferUp) that enhance the user experience and drive engagement.

It is also important to clarify that the challenges and benefits of digital transformation can influence the positioning of circular digital platforms within the framework's quadrants. Platforms facing higher levels of complexity in their digital transformation efforts, such as those dealing with regulatory barriers or logistical challenges, may require more sophisticated organizational structures and processes to manage these complexities effectively. This could push them towards higher levels of organizational integration and interaction complexity, potentially shifting their position within the framework.

The framework's quadrants, therefore, not only reflect the organizational features of circular digital platforms but also encompass the challenges and benefits they face in their digital transformation efforts. By understanding how these factors interplay and influence the positioning of platforms within the framework, practitioners and researchers can gain valuable insights into the strategies and approaches needed to successfully balance digital transformation and sustainability in the context of the CE.

5 Conclusions, Limitations and Future Research Avenues

Overall, the current study presents findings aimed at providing a comprehensive understanding of the organizational features, interaction types, challenges, and benefits that shape the ability of circular digital platforms to balance sustainability and technological innovation. The interplay of these factors influences the platforms' capacity to drive CE objectives and create sustainable value. The insights gained from this analysis are presented as a framework that positions circular digital platforms along the dimensions of interaction complexity and organizational integration. This framework is a first attempt to offer a guide for the design, operation, and evaluation of circular digital platforms across various industries and contexts, contributing to the growing body of knowledge in this emerging field.

5.1 Theoretical Contribution

This study contributes to the growing body of literature on CE and digital platforms by proposing a framework for understanding the organizational features of CPs. The framework, which categorizes CPs based on interaction complexity and organizational integration, expands our theoretical understanding [51] of how digital platforms might balance digital transformation and sustainability initiatives.

Our framework builds upon existing platform theories [5–7] by addressing some challenges and opportunities faced by CPs. This contributes to a more nuanced understanding of how different types of platforms (B2B, B2C, C2B, and C2C) may operate within the context of the CE. The study also explores connections between digital transformation literature and sustainability research [14, 15], providing initial insights into how these areas might intersect in the context of CPs.

By focusing on the organizational features of CPs, we add to the discussion on how organizations might implement CE principles [1, 2]. It provides a theoretical basis for understanding the role of digital platforms in facilitating resource reduction, reuse, and recycling. Finally, the proposed framework could serve as a starting point for future research on CP design and operation. It provides a basis for understanding how different organizational features and interaction types can influence a platform's ability to balance digital transformation and sustainability.

5.2 Managerial Implications

The findings of our study also suggest some practical implications for businesses, policymakers, and platform developers seeking to leverage different technologies for CE purposes.

The framework can provide guidance for organizations designing or operating CPs. Understanding the implications of different interaction types (B2B, B2C, C2B, C2C) could help organizations make decisions about their platform's structure and features when balancing digital transformation and sustainability goals [36]. The challenges identified, such as market penetration, logistics, and regulatory barriers, offer insights for CP operators, potentially supporting organizations to anticipate and address obstacles in their CE journey [8, 9]

The study highlights potential benefits of CPs, including enhanced transparency, efficient resource matching, and innovative business models. Practitioners can use these insights when developing their digital CE initiatives [40, 41]. The findings also suggest the importance of stakeholder management in CPs. Organizations consider this when developing strategies for engaging and coordinating diverse stakeholders, from suppliers to end-users [34].

For policymakers, this study provides initial insights into some of the challenges faced by CPs, particularly in areas such as e-waste management and food safety. This information could be considered in the development of regulatory frameworks that facilitate the growth of CPs while addressing environmental and social responsibilities [29].

By implementing these practical implications, organizations can enhance their ability to create sustainable value through digital platforms, contributing to the broader CE goals.

5.3 Limitations and Avenues for Future Research

While this study provides valuable insights, it is important to acknowledge its limitations which are linked to potential avenues for future research. The first limitation of this study is its reliance on secondary data sources. Although secondary data have been established as a valid and valuable source of information for case studies [44, 45], future research could benefit from incorporating qualitative primary data to further investigate the organizational features of CPs. Conducting interviews with platform CEOs, stakeholders, and users could provide deeper insights into the nuances and challenges of balancing digital transformation and sustainability in practice. Such primary data could also help validate and refine the findings derived from secondary sources.

Another limitation is the focus on a specific set of circular digital platforms, primarily based in developed countries. While this sample provides a diverse range of industries and interaction types, future research could explore circular digital platforms in emerging economies and different cultural contexts. Investigating how organizational features and strategies may differ in varying socio-economic and institutional environments could yield valuable insights into the context-specific factors that influence the success of circular digital platforms.

The proposed framework, based on the dimensions of interaction complexity and organizational integration, offers a useful starting point for understanding the features of circular digital platforms. However, future research could further refine and expand this framework by considering additional dimensions or variables that may impact the balance between digital transformation and sustainability. For example, researchers could explore the role of platform governance, organizational culture, or data management practices in shaping the effectiveness of circular digital platforms.

Finally, the findings of this study are based on data gathered at a specific point in time. Future research could adopt a longitudinal approach to examine how organizational features and strategies evolve over time as platforms mature and adapt to changing market and regulatory conditions. Tracking the development of circular digital platforms over an extended period could provide insights into the dynamic processes of organizational learning, innovation, and transformation.

By addressing these limitations and exploring new research directions, scholars can continue to advance knowledge in this emerging field and support the development of more sustainable and resilient digital platforms.

Disclosure of Interests The authors have no competing interests to declare that are relevant to the content of this article.

References

1. Kirchherr, J., Reike, D., & Hekkert, M. (2017). Conceptualizing the circular economy: An analysis of 114 definitions. *Resources, Conservation and Recycling, 127*(April), 221–232.
2. Lacy, P., & Rutqvist, J. (2015). *Waste to wealth: The circular economy advantage*. Palgrave Macmillan.
3. Cennamo, C., & Santalo, J. (2013). Platform competition: Strategic trade-offs in platform markets. *Strategic Management Journal, 34*, 1331.
4. Hänninen, M., Smedlund, A., & Mitronen, L. (2018). Digitalization in retailing: Multi-sided platforms as drivers of industry transformation. *Baltic Journal of Management, 13*, 152.
5. Kretschmer, T., Leiponen, A., Schilling, M., & Vasudeva, G. (2020). Platform ecosystems as meta-organizations: Implications for platform strategies. *Strategic Management Journal, 43*, 1–20.
6. Parker, G., Van Alstyne, M., & Choudary, S. (2016). *Platform revolution: How networked markets are transforming the economy and how to make them work for you*. W.W. Norton & Company.
7. Stummer, C., Kundisch, D., & Decker, R. (2018). Platform Launch strategies. *Business and Information Systems Engineering, 60*, 167.
8. Berg, H., & Wilts, H. (2018). Digital platforms as market places for the circular economy—Requirements and challenges. *NachhaltigkeitsManagementForum | Sustainability Management Forum, 27*, 1–9.
9. Fraccascia, L., & Yazan, D. M. (2018). The role of online information-sharing platforms on the performance of industrial symbiosis networks. *Resources, Conservation and Recycling, 136*, 473–485.
10. MacArthur, E., & Environment, M. C. for B., SUN. (2015). *Growth within: A circular economy vision for a competitive Europe*. Ellen MacArthur Foundation.
11. Rizos, V., Tuokko, K., & Behrens, A. (2017). The circular economy: A review of definitions, processes and impacts.
12. Franco, M. A. (2017). Circular economy at the micro level: A dynamic view of incumbents' struggles and challenges in the textile industry. *Journal of Cleaner Production, 168*, 833.
13. Van Dijck, J., Poell, T., & De Waal, M. (2018). *The platform society: Public values in a connective world*. Oxford University Press.
14. Bocken, N. M. P., Short, S. W., Rana, P., & Evans, S. (2014). A literature and practice review to develop sustainable business model archetypes. *Journal of Cleaner Production, 65*, 42.
15. Tukker, A. (2015). Product services for a resource-efficient and circular economy–A review. *Journal of Cleaner Production, 97*, 76–91.
16. Kortmann, S., & Piller, F. (2016). Open business models and closed-loop value chains. *California Management Review, 58*, 88.
17. Pieroni, M. P. P., McAloone, T. C., & Pigosso, D. C. A. (2019). Business model innovation for circular economy and sustainability: A review of approaches. *Journal of Cleaner Production, 215*, 198.
18. Gusmerotti, N. M., Testa, F., Corsini, F., Pretner, G., & Iraldo, F. (2019). Drivers and approaches to the circular economy in manufacturing firms. *Journal of Cleaner Production, 230*, 314–327.
19. Rizos, V., Behrens, A., van der Gaast, W., Hofman, E., Ioannou, A., et al. (2016). Implementation of circular economy business models by small and medium-sized enterprises (SMEs): Barriers and enablers. *Sustainability (Switzerland), 8*(11).

20. Blackburn, O., Ritala, P., & Keränen, J. (2023). Digital platforms for the circular economy: Exploring meta-organizational orchestration mechanisms. *Organization & Environment, 36*(2), 253–281.
21. Bocken, N. M., & Ritala, P. (2022). Six ways to build circular business models. *Journal of Business Strategy, 43*(3), 184–192.
22. Geissdoerfer, M., Morioka, S. N., de Carvalho, M. M., & Evans, S. (2018). Business models and supply chains for the circular economy. *Journal of Cleaner Production, 190*, 712–721.
23. Chauhan, C., Parida, V., & Dhir, A. (2022). Linking circular economy and digitalisation technologies: A systematic literature review of past achievements and future promises. *Technological Forecasting and Social Change, 177*, 121508.
24. Gregori, P., & Holzmann, P. (2020). Digital sustainable entrepreneurship: A business model perspective on embedding digital technologies for social and environmental value creation. *Journal of Cleaner Production, 272*, 122817.
25. Kodithuwakku, H. Y. A., & Wickramarachchi, R. (2023). Determining the relationship between organizational characteristics and digital transformation strategies—A systematic literature review. In *2023 3rd international conference on advanced research in computing (ICARC)* (pp. 328–333). IEEE.
26. Ada, E., Sezer, M. D., & Khaleel, R. (2023). Towards the smart sustainable and circular food supply chains through digital technologies. *International Journal of Mathematical, Engineering & Management Sciences, 8*(3), 374.
27. Mbanefo, C., & Grobbelaar, S. S. S. (2022). A systematic review of concepts and future directions of platform ecosystem development. In *2022 IEEE 28th international conference on engineering, technology and innovation (ICE/ITMC)* (pp. 1–11). IEEE.
28. Guandalini, I. (2022). Sustainability through digital transformation: A systematic literature review for research guidance. *Journal of Business Research, 148*, 456–471.
29. Quiroz-Flores, J. C., Aguado-Rodriguez, R. J., Zegarra-Aguinaga, E. A., Collao-Diaz, M. F., & Flores-Perez, A. E. (2023). Industry 4.0, circular economy and sustainability in the food industry: A literature review. *International Journal of Industrial Engineering and Operations Management, 6*, 1–24.
30. Akarsu, T. N. (2023). Digital transformation towards a sustainable circular economy: Can it be the way forward? *Journal of Information Technology Teaching Cases, 14*, 186.
31. Gallaud, D., & Laperche, B. (2016). Circular economy, industrial ecology and short supply chain. In *Circular economy, industrial ecology and short supply chain*. Wiley.
32. EY. (2018). *EY Sustainability Summit 2018: Challenges and trends*. Ernst & Young.
33. MacArthur, E. (2013). *Towards the circular economy: Opportunities for the consumer goods sector*. Ellen MacArthur Foundation.
34. Nambisan, S., Zahra, S. A., & Luo, Y. (2019). Global platforms and ecosystems: Implications for international business theories. *Journal of International Business Studies, 50*(9), 1464–1486.
35. Garud, R., Kumaraswamy, A., Roberts, A., & Xu, L. (2020). Liminal movement by digital platform-based sharing economy ventures: The case of Uber Technologies. *Strategic Management Journal, 43*, 1–29.
36. Konietzko, J., Bocken, N., & Hultink, E. J. (2020). Circular ecosystem innovation: An initial set of principles. *Journal of Cleaner Production, 253*, 119942.
37. Nachum, L., & Zaheer, S. (2005). The persistence of distance? The impact of technology on MNE motivations for foreign investment. *Strategic Management Journal, 26*(8), 747–767.
38. Zhang, Y., Li, J., & Tong, T. W. (2020). Platform governance matters: How platform gatekeeping affects knowledge sharing among complementors. *Strategic Management Journal, 43*, 1–28.
39. Chertow, M., & Park, J. (2016). Scholarship and practice in industrial symbiosis: 1989–2014. In *Taking stock of industrial ecology* (pp. 87–116). Springer.
40. Valcozzena, S., Attanasio, G., Battistella, C., & Cantele, S. (2023). Exploring the sustainable business model of digital platforms. In *New business models conference proceedings 2023*. Maastricht University Press.

41. Assmann, I. R., Rosati, F., & Morioka, S. N. (2023). Determinants of circular business model adoption—A systematic literature review. *Business Strategy and the Environment, 32*(8), 6008–6028.
42. Denzin, N. K. (1978). *The research act: A theoretical introduction to sociological methods*. McGraw-Hill.
43. Patton, M. Q. (1990). *Qualitative evaluation and research methods*. Sage.
44. Johnston, M. P. (2014). Secondary data analysis: A method of which the time has come. *Qualitative and Quantitative Methods in Libraries, 3*(3), 619–626.
45. Ruggiano, N., & Perry, T. E. (2019). Conducting secondary analysis of qualitative data: Should we, can we, and how? *Qualitative Social Work, 18*(1), 81–97.
46. Ritala, P., Golnam, A., & Wegmann, A. (2014). Competition-based business models: The case of Amazon.com. *Industrial Marketing Management, 43*(2), 236–249.
47. Rusko, R. (2011). Exploring the concept of coopetition: A typology for the strategic moves of the Finnish forest industry. *Industrial Marketing Management, 40*, 311–320.
48. Shankar, V., Grewal, D., Sunder, S., Fossen, B., Peters, K., & Agarwal, A. (2022). Digital marketing communication in global marketplaces: A review of extant research, future directions, and potential approaches. *International Journal of Research in Marketing, 39*(2), 541–565.
49. Voss, C., Tsikriktsis, N., & Frohlich, M. (2002). Operations management case research. *International Journal of Operations & Production Management, 22*(2), 195–219.
50. Aarikka-Stenroos, L., Ritala, P., & Thomas, L. D. (2021). Circular economy ecosystems: A typology, definitions, and implications.
51. Colquitt, J. A., & Zapata-Phelan, C. P. (2007). Trends in theory building and theory testing: A five-decade study of the Academy of Management Journal. *Academy of Management Journal, 50*(6), 1281–1303.

Optimizing Sustainability: Benchmarking Time-Series Forecasting Models on Purchasing Data to Reduce Overproduction

Camilla Carpinelli, Seppe Vanden Broucke, Bart Baesens, Anna Sigridur Islind, and María Òskarsdóttir

Abstract This study delves into computational sustainability, leveraging AI methods to address sustainable consumption and production challenges. Utilizing historical purchasing data from a prominent Icelandic supermarket chain spanning from 2018 to 2023, the study explores various dimensions of data aggregation, including macro-categories, micro-categories, and product labels. Six distinct forecasting methodologies are employed: regression-based, LLM, foundation models, and statistical approaches. Evaluating these models using Root-Mean-Squared-Error reveals different findings dependent on dataset aggregation. As a result, datasets with finer aggregation exhibit higher predictive accuracy, with the LLM model consistently outperforming others across macro and micro-category datasets. While one of the foundation models demonstrates comparable performances, LLM's efficiency is notable despite GPU utilization and longer processing times. The regressor emerges as the most effective predictor for datasets categorized by product labels, with LLM and one foundation model also displaying commendable performance. These findings offer valuable insights for reducing overproduction

C. Carpinelli (✉)
Reykjavik University, Reykjavík, Iceland
e-mail: camillac@ru.is

S. Vanden Broucke
University of Ghent, Ghent, Belgium

KU Leuven, Leuven, Belgium
e-mail: seppe.vandenbroucke@ugent.be

B. Baesens
KU Leuven, Leuven, Belgium

University of Southampton, Southampton, UK
e-mail: bart.baesens@kuleuven.be

A. S. Islind · M. Òskarsdóttir
Department of Computer Science, Reykjavik University, Reykjavík, Iceland
e-mail: annasi@ru.is; mariaoskars@ru.is

M. Cipriano et al. (eds.), *Technologies for Organizations and Society*,
Lecture Notes in Information Systems and Organisation 80,
https://doi.org/10.1007/978-3-032-01697-3_8

and optimizing production planning in the production industry, underscoring the importance of leveraging advanced forecasting models to promote sustainability. Further details and implications are discussed in the paper.

Keywords Forecasting · Data science · Machine learning · Benchmark · Sustainability

1 Introduction

In today's dynamic market landscape, the societal impact of balancing customers' demands with environmental protection is deep [1]. One of the main obstacles to face is overproduction, a problem that arises when industries produce more goods than customers actually buy [2]. The consequences of overproduction go far beyond the excess stock on shop shelves. Excess products often end up as waste, discarded due to spoilage, obsolescence, or simply because they are not sold [3]. These surpluses contribute to the growing global waste crisis, adding to the mountains of discarded items that fill landfills around the world [4]. When these products decompose, they release harmful pollutants into the air, soil, and water, exacerbating environmental degradation and endangering ecosystems [5].

The environmental impact of overproduction extends beyond discarded products. This includes the enormous amount of resources, such as water, energy, and raw materials, consumed during the production process [6, 7]. Every wasted product represents a dissipation of these precious resources, further straining our planet's limited resources and accelerating climate change. Overproduction produces excess goods and perpetuates a cycle of environmental damage, underlining the urgent need for companies to adopt sustainable production practices [8, 9].

Meeting this challenge requires a comprehensive strategy, of which accurate demand forecasting is a crucial component [10]. Accurate demand forecasts are essential for the production industry seeking to find the delicate balance between satisfying consumer needs and minimizing environmental impact [11]. By accurately forecasting future demand, companies can strategically optimize their production schedules, ensuring they produce enough to meet market demands without exceeding them [12]. This helps minimize excess inventory and streamlines stock management processes, reducing the need for costly storage facilities and the risk of perishable products going to waste [10]. Such a forecast requires a thorough understanding of market dynamics, consumer behavior, and industry trends [13]. From traditional statistical methods to state-of-the-art machine learning algorithms, the choice of forecasting model can determine the accuracy of forecasts [14]. Companies must, therefore, engage in robust forecasting methodologies and adapt them to their specific operational needs, laying the foundation for sustainable production practices and responsible resource management.

This paper delves into time-series forecasting, shedding light on its fundamental role in sustainability efforts to decrease overproduction and waste [15, 16]. We delve into the complexities of forecasting models, using different levels of aggregation of historical purchasing data as a guide and identifying fitting models and, therefore, identifying the most accurate model through meticulous benchmarking based on root mean square error (RMSE) [17]. We tested six forecasting models based on four different structures and three different data types to achieve our goal. Further information will be provided in the methods section. Unlike traditional benchmarks driven solely by marketing objectives, our study is oriented towards a higher purpose: promoting sustainable practices in supply chain management. We aim to balance business objectives and environmental protection, recognizing that the two are not mutually exclusive but intrinsically linked [18]. By advocating sustainability in our forecasting methodologies, we aim to empower companies to make informed decisions that optimize efficiency and profitability and uphold environmental integrity. Against that backdrop, we pose the following research question (RQ): "*Which forecasting models provide the most accurate predictions for consumer purchasing behavior in a supermarket chain, and how do these models vary in effectiveness across different levels of data granularity in order to minimize overproduction and waste?*".

Through our analysis, we aspire to pave the way for a future where economic prosperity coexists harmoniously with ecological resilience.

2 Related Works

2.1 *The Overproduction Problem and Its Environmental Consequences*

Overproduction represents a multifaceted challenge with far-reaching environmental repercussions [19]. It occurs when goods are produced in quantities exceeding market demand, resulting in surplus stocks and waste of resources. This surplus strains financial resources and exerts immense pressure on natural resources and ecosystems [20].

The environmental consequences of overproduction are manifold and include increased energy consumption, increased emissions of greenhouse gases and pollutants, and extensive waste generation during production and distribution processes [21–23]. Every supply chain step contributes to environmental degradation, from raw material extraction to production, transport, and disposal.

Regarding the food industry, the problem seems to be even more serious [24]. This occurs when more food is produced than is needed to meet demand, resulting in excess stocks that often remain unused, rot, or expire and are then wasted [25]. Several factors contribute to food overproduction, including market fluctuations, agricultural subsidies, inefficient supply chain management, and consumer preferences [26]. Food overproduction strains natural resources such as land, water, and energy and exacerbates environmental problems such as deforestation, soil degradation, and greenhouse gas emissions [25, 27].

To reduce food waste throughout the supply chain, measures include promoting sustainable farming practices, improving distribution networks, and raising consumer awareness of the importance of conscious consumption [28, 29]. In addition, promoting collaboration between stakeholders, including farmers, politicians, businesses, and consumers, is essential to develop practical solutions to combat food overproduction and build a more sustainable food system [29].

2.2 Times Series Forecasting

Forecasting is crucial in mitigating overproduction by enabling better inventory management and production planning in various sectors, including agriculture, production, and retail [30, 31]. It supports sustainability initiatives by promoting resource efficiency and waste reduction [32]. By accurately predicting future demand for goods and services, forecasts help companies optimize their production schedules, optimize inventory levels, and minimize the risk of overproduction of unsold items [33]. This can lead to decreased use of natural resources, energy, and materials associated with production processes.

A key aspect of forecasting is its ability to anticipate fluctuations in consumer demand, seasonal trends, and market dynamics [34]. With reliable forecasts, companies can adjust their production levels accordingly, ensuring they meet demand without generating excess inventory [35, 36]. By aligning production with demand forecasts, companies can reduce the likelihood of excess goods that can lead to waste [37, 38].

However, if a forecast is incorrect, it can result in significant losses through overproduction or underproduction, which carry their own costs and environmental impacts [39, 40]. Companies can identify the most accurate and reliable approaches for predicting future demand by evaluating and comparing multiple forecasting models [41]. This allows them to reduce the risk of overproduction or underproduction.

Over the years, several studies have explored demand forecasting for sustainability purposes using various models, from basic statistical methods to more advanced machine learning approaches and neural networks [42–48]. Some studies assert that the fuzzy time series model is the most accurate machine learning model for forecasting electricity consumption [46]; others assume that statistical models like ARIMA are the best to perform food consumption [47]. Another study from [48] finds the best model to predict wheat prices in China in artificial neural networks.

Each study focuses on specific contexts and data sets, making it difficult to generalize the effectiveness of any single prediction model in all scenarios. The diversity of approaches reflects ongoing research efforts to identify the most suitable forecasting techniques for different industries and applications [49].

As research surfaces on this impactful topic, researchers will likely explore new and refine existing methods to improve predictive accuracy and address the unique challenges associated with sustainability-driven demand forecasting.

2.3 Benchmarking for Forecasting Models Evaluation

Benchmarking involves comparing the effectiveness of different forecasting models in predicting future outcomes [50]. This process is crucial in evaluating prediction models because it provides a standardized basis for assessing their accuracy and reliability [51]. By setting benchmarks, researchers and practitioners can identify the strengths and weaknesses of each model, enabling informed decisions on which to use in specific contexts [52]. Benchmarking facilitates the comparison of new models with existing ones, guiding innovation and improving forecasting methodologies over time [53].

The variability in datasets and study objectives underscores the importance of benchmarking in selecting the most suitable prediction models for specific problems. Since different forecasting models may excel in various contexts, benchmarking is a valuable tool for identifying the most effective models tailored to the unique characteristics of each dataset and research question [52, 53]. Researchers can gain insights into their strengths and limitations by systematically comparing the performance of various prediction models against common metrics. This empirical approach enables data-driven decision-making, allowing practitioners to make informed choices about which models to employ in their forecasting endeavors.

3 Methods

In this section, we delve into the dataset utilized for our analysis and outline the forecasting models employed to benchmark and compare their performance.

3.1 Experimental Setup

In our study, we worked with three distinct datasets, each offering a different level of aggregation and insight into purchasing trends. These datasets span from 2018 to 2023, with a daily granularity, corresponding to 1820 data entries, and were provided from one of the most prominent Icelandic supermarket chains.

The first dataset focused on broad product categories, encompassing macro categories such as Meat and Fish, Dry Products, and Milk Products, for a total of 9 features. This level of aggregation allowed us to analyze overarching trends within these product groups and understand general consumer behavior patterns.

Moving to a finer level of aggregation, the second dataset zoomed in on micro categories, including specific items like Meat, Fish, Bread, Pasta, Milk, and Yogurt. This dataset was comprehensive of 20 features. By narrowing our focus to these individual product categories, we gained more profound insights into consumers' preferences and purchasing habits at a more granular level.

The third dataset took a different approach by categorizing products based on labels the supermarket chain provided us, such as Green, Vegan, Organic, and Healthy (including items with no added sugar or deemed keto-friendly). This dataset had 8 features in total and aimed to uncover trends related explicitly to labeled products, providing valuable insights into evolving consumer preferences and the demand for products with specific attributes.

We partitioned each dataset into a training set comprising 70% of the data and a separate test set containing the remaining 30%. For forecasting purposes, we projected 60 days ahead. This duration was selected to maintain the accuracy of our models while also allowing for effective management of production and inventory levels [54]. By forecasting this time frame, we aimed to balance capturing future demand trends and mitigating the risk of overproduction or excess ordering.

By analyzing datasets that span macro-categories, micro-categories, and labeled products, we aimed to understand how different forecasting models behave in response to these different data structures [55]. The diverse range of aggregation allowed us to assess the strengths and weaknesses of each forecasting model in capturing trends and patterns at different levels of detail. By systematically comparing the performance of each model across these datasets, we can provide valuable insights into their suitability for different forecasting tasks [56].

By understanding how these models perform under different conditions, we can offer informed recommendations that help businesses optimize their forecasting processes and make data-driven decisions. Through this approach, we can provide the manufacturing industry with the necessary tools and insights to anticipate market trends and avoid overproduction.

3.2 Forecasting Models

In our quest to select forecasting methods, we searched several different models with the aim of comprehensive exploration and comparison. Our selection criteria emphasized models with different architectures, including regressor, statistical, and deep learning models, to ensure a wide spectrum of forecasting methodologies were represented. We carefully examined the latest advances in forecasting technology, prioritizing models released between 2021 and 2024 and checking their validation and availability to ensure the reliability of our analysis. We specifically sought validated models that were publicly available and not in beta version, ensuring reliability and robustness in our analysis. Our initial focus was identifying the most recent models that met our criteria. The top contenders, in chronological order, were Chronos developed by Amazon [57], Lag-LLama [58], TimeGPT [59], and linear-tree [60]. In addition to the latest models, we also incorporated seminal models to provide a benchmark for comparison. Among these, we included Gradient Booster [61], which utilizes regression similar to linear-tree, and the classic ARIMA model [62], which has long been a staple in time series forecasting due to its simplicity and effectiveness.

Table 1 Comparison between the forecasting models

Model feature	Chronos	Lag-LLama	TimeGPT	Linear tree	Gradient booster	ARIMA
Supports Multiple Time Series	✗	✓	✓	✗	✗	✗
Requires GPU	✓	✗	✗	✗	✗	✗
Requires Online Token	✓	✗	✓	✗	✗	✗
Pre-Trained Model	✓	✓	✓	✗	✗	✗
Year of Publication	2024	2023	2023	2021	2001	1970

Table 1 provides an overview of the chosen forecasting models, detailing the respective year of publication.

Using this set of forecasting models at different levels of aggregation within the dataset, we sought to analyze their performance and identify the most accurate model in terms of RMSE.

3.2.1 Root Mean Squared Error (RMSE)

RMSE is characterized by the following equation:

$$\text{RMSE}(y, \hat{y}) = \sqrt{\frac{\sum_{i=0}^{N-1}(y_i - \hat{y}_i)^2}{N}}$$

The error measure works as follows: First, subtract the predicted value from the actual value for each data point. This gives the error or residual. Second, square each of the calculated differences. This removes negative values. Third, add up all the squared differences and divide by the number of data points. This gives the Mean Squared Error (MSE). Finally, the square root of the MSE is calculated to get the RMSE.

RMSE is a commonly used metric for evaluating the accuracy of time series forecasting models, as we can read in [63–65].

This approach allows us to understand which models perform best for forecasting at different levels of aggregation within the supermarket chain's product offering, thereby informing future forecasting efforts and helping to improve decision-making on quantities to be produced and distributed to avoid unnecessary waste.

3.2.2 Chronos

Chronos is a large language model (LLM) designed by Amazon developers specifically for time series prediction tasks, representing the convergence of state-of-the-art language model architectures with the requirements of sequential data analysis [57]. Unlike natural language, characterized by discrete tokens drawn from a finite vocabulary, time series data present a continuous sequence of real-valued observations [66]. This dichotomy necessitates modifying existing language modeling frameworks to make them suitable for time series analysis. Chronos addresses this challenge by adapting transformer-based architectures and training procedures, taking advantage of the remarkable success of these models in natural language processing tasks [57].

One of the distinguishing features of Chronos is its inherent probabilistic nature. By exploiting autoregressive sampling from predicted distributions, Chronos facilitates the generation of multiple future realizations, offering a comprehensive view of potential outcomes [67]. These sampling paths, represented as ID tokens, are subjected to a meticulous transformation process to recover the actual predicted values, ensuring fidelity to the underlying time series data [57].

By synthesizing mixup augmentations from real datasets and supplementing training with synthetic data, Chronos seeks to enrich the diversity and quality of training data. This augmentation process improves the robustness and generalization capabilities of Chronos models and enables them to excel in zero-shot forecasting scenarios, where access to large and diverse training data is crucial [68].

3.2.3 Lag-LLama Zero-Shot

Lag-Llama is introduced as a foundational model for univariate probabilistic forecasting, mainly focusing on the complexities of tokenization and architecture within this domain [58]. The model operates within the univariate time series forecasting framework, addressing the challenge of predicting future values based on past observations and covariates [58]. Lag-Llama tokenizes time series data by considering a comprehensive set of lag indices and constructing lagged features that capture temporal dependencies and patterns. This tokenization scheme enables the model to adapt to varying frequencies and combinations of seen frequencies in downstream datasets without directly relying on specific dataset characteristics. Lag-Llama's architecture is built upon the decoder-only transformer-based architecture LLaMA, featuring multiple decoder layers for processing the tokenized sequences [69]. These sequences, comprising the time series data and associated covariates, are transformed through shared linear projection layers before being processed by attention modules [69].

In the field of Lag-LLama modeling, there are two distinct approaches: zero-shot and fine-tuning. In our current study, we chose to use the zero-shot variant due to its robustness and established performance, while the fine-tuning variant is still in the beta-testing phase. The zero-shot Lag-LLama variant directly applies a pre-trained model to a new prediction task without further training, exploiting the learned knowledge to make predictions in novel contexts. In contrast, Lag-Lama tuning involves further training of a pre-trained model on a related task or dataset to adapt it to the specifics of the new task, a process still being refined in our research.

Therefore, in the present investigation, we used zero-shot Lag-Lama to assess the accuracy and efficiency of the prediction results in our target domain.

3.2.4 TimeGPT

TimeGPT stands out as a state-of-the-art foundation model characterized by integrating self-attention mechanisms. Its intricate architecture boasts an encoding-decoding structure strengthened by multiple layers, residual connections, and layer normalization, ensuring robust performance across diverse datasets [59]. In particular, TimeGPT enhances its predictive capabilities by incorporating local positional encoding, thus enriching input data and enabling a more nuanced understanding of temporal patterns [70]. Designed with adaptability, TimeGPT can handle time series data with different characteristics, such as frequency, trend, seasonality and heteroscedasticity [59]. This versatility is supported by training on a huge dataset comprising over 100 billion data points from different sectors, from finance to economics, healthcare to weather. The training process, meticulously executed on high-performance NVIDIA A10G GPUs, involves extensive exploration and optimization of hyper-parameters to perfect model performance. In addition, TimeGPT embraces conformal prediction for uncertainty quantification, providing forecast ranges with specific coverage accuracy to facilitate informed decision-making and risk assessment [59].

In addition to its core functionalities, TimeGPT offers the advantage of simultaneously supporting multiple time series predictions. Furthermore, as a pre-trained model for fine-tuning, TimeGPT allows users to adapt and optimize its parameters to suit specific forecasting tasks or datasets, exploiting its pre-existing knowledge and improving performance in targeted domains.

3.2.5 Linear-Tree

Linear-tree Regressor is a unique approach to forecasting in time series analysis that blends the interpretability of linear models with the adaptability of decision trees [71]. Unlike traditional decision trees that assign constant values to each leaf node, linear-tree regression assigns linear functions to these nodes [60]. This means that instead of approximating the target variable with step functions, the regressor approximates it with linear functions, resulting in more flexible and nuanced predictions. Building a linear-tree regression model involves recursively partitioning the feature space based on the input variables, similar to traditional decision trees. Still, the regressor fits a linear function to the data within each leaf [72]. This enables the model to capture more complex relationships between the features and the target variable, allowing for better adaptation to the underlying data patterns [73].

One of the main advantages of linear-tree is its interpretability. Since each leaf node is associated with a linear function, it is easier to understand how changes in the input variables affect the predicted outcome. linear-tree regression is particularly useful in scenarios where interpretability is crucial, such as financial forecasting or risk analysis.

However, linear-tree regression also has its limitations. It may struggle to capture highly non-linear relationships in the data, as linear functions may not adequately represent these patterns [74]. Also, building and interpreting linear-tree regression models can be computationally expensive, especially for large datasets with high-dimensional feature spaces [75].

3.2.6 Gradient Boosting Regressor

Gradient Boosting Regressor (GBR) is a popular machine learning algorithm known for its effectiveness in predicting future values based on historical data. It belongs to the family of ensemble learning techniques, which means it combines multiple weaker models, typically decision trees, to create a stronger predictive model.

GBR builds a sequence of decision trees iteratively, with each tree focusing on the prediction errors of the previous ones [76]. This iterative process allows it to gradually improve its predictions by emphasizing the areas where the model performs poorly. By iteratively minimizing prediction errors, the model can capture complex relationships and patterns in the data, making it particularly useful for time series forecasting tasks [77].

As a regression model, it is very flexible and robust. It can handle various data types and is less sensitive to outliers than other machine learning algorithms. Additionally, GBR does not require the data to be preprocessed extensively, making it relatively easy to implement and deploy [61]. However, it may struggle with very noisy or irregular data, and it can be computationally expensive, especially when dealing with large datasets or complex models [75]. Moreover, GBR does not provide explicit insights into the underlying relationships in the data, which may limit its interpretability.

3.2.7 ARIMA

Autoregressive Integrated Moving Average (ARIMA), is a classical time series forecasting model widely used for decades due to its simplicity and effectiveness [62]. ARIMA captures the linear relationships in time series data, making it particularly well-suited for stationary or near-stationary processes [78]. The "AR" in ARIMA refers to the autoregressive component, which models the dependency between observation and several lagged observations, also known as the autoregressive terms. This component captures the linear relationship between the current value of the time series and its previous values [79]. The "I" stands for integrated, indicating that the time series data may need differencing to achieve stationarity. Differencing involves taking the difference between consecutive observations to remove trends or seasonality in the data [80]. The "MA" denotes the moving average component, which models the dependency between an observation and a residual error from a moving average model applied to lagged observations. This component captures the short-term effects present in the time series data that are not accounted for by the autoregressive component [81]. ARIMA models are typically identified using a process known as model selection, where different combinations of the autoregressive (p), differencing (d), and moving average (q) parameters are tested to find the model that best fits the data [62]. This process often involves examining diagnostic plots and statistical tests to ensure that the chosen model adequately captures the underlying patterns in the data. While ARIMA involves estimating coefficients similar to regression models, it operates within a different framework and relies on different assumptions [82]. ARIMA models are commonly used for univariate time series forecasting and effectively capture linear and stationary data trends.

4 Results

In this section, we analyze the performances of the forecasting methods by examining their RMSE values according to the considered dataset.

Figure 1 illustrates the RMSE values obtained for each model across the three datasets. Further details will be given in the next paragraphs.

In evaluating the best forecasting model, we also considered the running time a crucial factor. It is worth noting that not all models supported multiple time series forecasting, necessitating individual runs for each time series in those cases. This process naturally consumed more time. However, on average, the duration of a

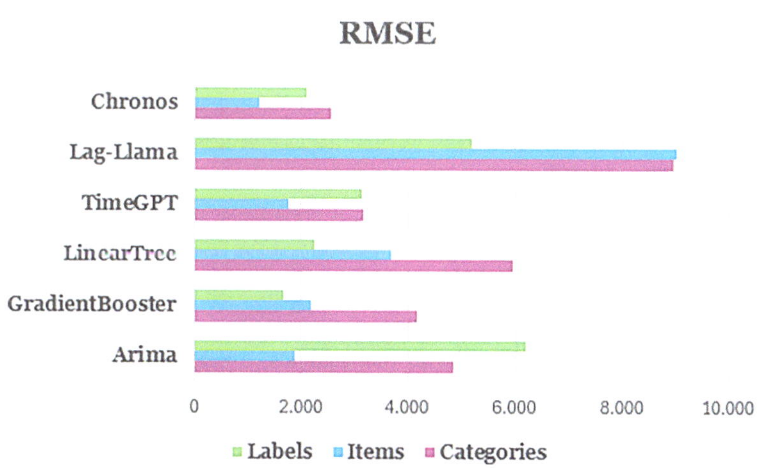

Fig. 1 RMSE for each model across each dataset used

Table 2 Average running time for a single run, on a single or multiple time series according to the model

Model	Average running time
Chronos	8 min
Lag-LLama	20 min
TimeGPT	50 s
Linear Tree	5 min
Gradient Booster	15 s
ARIMA	2 s

single run for each model (whether for a single or multiple time series) is outlined in Table 2.

4.1 Chronos

Chronos exhibited very good performance across all three datasets, boasting an RMSE of 2547,1086 for macro-categories, 1201.0829 for micro-categories, and 2085.3362 for labeled products.

Despite its accuracy, Chronos lacked support for forecasting multiple time series simultaneously and necessitated GPU usage due to its model complexity, resulting in a somewhat time-consuming forecasting process.

4.2 Lag-LLama Zero-Shot

Lag-LLama turned out to be the least favorable model in our analysis, demonstrating consistently subpar performance across all three datasets. Specifically, it exhibited an RMSE of 8935.9425 for macro-categories, 9015.4867 for micro-categories, and 5206.6180 for the labeled dataset. This result is particularly disappointing considering Lag-LLama's advantage in supporting multiple time series forecasting simultaneously.

4.3 TimeGPT

TimeGPT delivered notable results in our analysis, exhibiting consistent performance across all three datasets. With an RMSE of 3175.8053 for the macro-categories dataset, 1762.1944 for the micro-categories, and 3135.4592 for the labeled dataset, TimeGPT demonstrated its effectiveness in predicting future purchasing trends. Its ability to simultaneously support multiple time series analysis further adds to its practical utility.

Additionally, TimeGPT turned out to be the fastest model used in our study, with a running time of only a few seconds, highlighting its suitability for real-world forecasting tasks.

4.4 Linear-Tree

The linear-tree regressor demonstrated promising performance in the labels dataset, achieving an RMSE of 2263.815. However, its effectiveness decreased as the aggregation of the datasets increased. In the micro-categories dataset, the RMSE rose to 3688.2905, and this trend continued with a further increase in RMSE to 5954.243 for the macro-categories dataset. This observation underscores the need for careful consideration when selecting models, ensuring they align with the complexity of the dataset at hand.

4.5 Gradient Boosting Regressor

The Gradient Booster regressor, boasting a comparable architecture to the linear-tree model, exhibited similar trends in the results but demonstrated superior performance. The macro-categories dataset achieved an RMSE of 4168.165, while the micro-categories dataset improved to 2187.1058. Notably, the labels dataset yielded an impressive RMSE of 1667.0848.

Both Gradient Booster and linear-tree are not able to perform multiple time series forecasting.

4.6 ARIMA

The classical ARIMA model demonstrated performance consistent with other models, yielding an RMSE of 4855.1974 for the macro-categories dataset. Particularly noteworthy is its commendable forecasting accuracy for the micro-categories dataset, which achieved a value of 1889.9318, comparable to TimeGPT. However, its performance faltered with the labeled dataset, recording the highest RMSE among the models at 6204.9487.

Despite being the fastest model for individual runs, it is important to note that ARIMA does not support multiple time series forecasting. Therefore, for each time series, a separate run was required. This additional requirement increased the overall processing time, neutralizing its speed advantage for single runs.

5 Discussion

In the context of sustainability and overproduction prevention, our study's findings offer valuable insights into the effectiveness of various forecasting models in mitigating waste and environmental impact.

First, it should be noted that the dataset featuring micro-categories exhibited the lowest average RMSE, suggesting that forecasting at a finer aggregation can enhance accuracy, as shown in the study of [83]. This finding underscores the potential for industries, particularly manufacturing, to adopt a product-specific forecasting approach to optimize production levels. By forecasting on a product-by-product basis, businesses can gain more precise insights into demand fluctuations and adjust production accordingly. For grocery chains, our study provides valuable guidance on order quantities from suppliers, enabling them to align production with demand more effectively and mitigate overproduction. This strategic approach reduces waste and promotes sustainability by minimizing resource consumption and environmental impact.

Across all the datasets, Chronos emerged as the most accurate forecasting model, demonstrating its potential to contribute significantly to overproduction prevention and sustainability efforts. Its robust performance suggests that businesses adopting Chronos can optimize production schedules and inventory management more effectively, reducing the risk of excess production and waste. However, Chronos turned out to be very time-consuming; it does not support multiple time series forecasting and requires the use of a GPU.

TimeGPT also showcased promising results, particularly considering its support for multiple time series forecasting and relatively faster processing times than Chronos. While not as accurate as Chronos, TimeGPT's performance suggests it can still be a viable option for businesses seeking sustainable forecasting solutions, especially considering its versatility and efficiency.

On the other hand, Lag-LLama exhibited poor performance across all datasets, indicating limitations in its ability to provide accurate forecasts for sustainable decision-making [84].

Models like Gradient Boosting Regressor and linear-tree Regressor yielded mixed results, demonstrating varying degrees of effectiveness across different datasets. For example, Gradient Booster was the best predictor for the label-based dataset, but the results were still not good enough for the other two datasets.

ARIMA did not stand out as exceptional in our analysis. While it performed adequately in some instances, particularly for the micro-categories dataset, its overall performance was not significantly better than other models. This suggests that while ARIMA may still have its place in specific forecasting scenarios, it may not offer a substantial advantage over more advanced models, especially regarding accuracy and adaptability to different datasets. As such, businesses looking to implement more sustainable forecasting practices may find exploring alternative models that offer superior performance and capabilities beneficial.

Given the diverse characteristics of the models outlined in Table 1, the varying running times detailed in Table 2, and the results depicted in Fig. 1, we hesitate to recommend a singular model for sustainable forecasting. While Chronos and TimeGPT emerged as frontrunners across all datasets, their adoption comes with specific technological requirements and limitations. TimeGPT, for instance, necessitates an online connection, while Chronos relies on GPU support and lacks the capability for multiple time series forecasting.

We advocate for selecting either Chronos or TimeGPT based on the available technological infrastructure and dataset characteristics to optimize demand prediction and minimize overproduction and waste.

Leveraging highly accurate models is essential in mitigating excesses and waste, fostering more sustainable forecasting practices over the long run [85]. By harnessing the predictive power of advanced forecasting models such as Chronos and TimeGPT, businesses can make more informed decisions regarding production schedules, inventory management, and resource allocation. This helps minimize the risk of overproduction and reduces waste throughout the supply chain.

5.1 Limitations

Despite the comprehensive approach of this study, several limitations should be acknowledged. The data, sourced from a leading Icelandic supermarket chain, may not represent other regions or retail environments, potentially affecting the generalizability of our findings. While diverse, selecting forecasting models is not exhaustive, and including other models might yield different results. Additionally, the inability of specific models to support multiple time series forecasting simultaneously increases computational load.

6 Conclusions

Our research yields novel insights that hold significant implications for the evolution of forecasting practices and, notably, for advancing sustainability within information systems.

The key findings of our study underscore the critical role of accurate forecasting in sustainability within supply chain management. By benchmarking various forecasting models, we identified the most effective approaches for predicting consumer demand and reducing overproduction and waste. Our analysis revealed that models such as Chronos and TimeGPT exhibited superior performance across different datasets, highlighting their potential for enabling more sustainable forecasting practices.

Accurate forecasting is critical to aligning production with actual demand, thereby minimizing excessive production and waste throughout the supply chain

[86]. By harnessing advanced forecasting models, companies can optimize resource utilization, simplify inventory management, and reduce the environmental impact of overproduction and unnecessary production processes [87, 88].

6.1 Future Work

The limitations discussed in Sect. 5.1 open avenues for future research, where similar analyses can be conducted with an expanded set of models, diverse datasets, and alternative error metrics. Exploring these variations can provide a more comprehensive understanding of forecasting model performance across different contexts and improve the robustness and applicability of findings in the pursuit of sustainable supply chain management.

Disclosure of Interests The authors have no competing interests to declare that are relevant to the content of this article.

References

1. Shimell, P. (1991). Corporate environmental policy in practice. *Long Range Planning, 24*, 10–17.
2. Ai, H. (2000). Boosting economy and constructing sustainable development consumption mode. *Journal of Tianjin University of Commerce.*
3. Darlington, R., Staikos, T., & Rahimifard, S. (2009). Analytical methods for waste minimisation in the convenience food industry. *Waste Management, 29*(4), 1274–1281.
4. Gaur, V., Sharma, P., Sirohi, R., Awasthi, M., Dussap, C., & Pandey, A. (2020). Assessing the impact of industrial waste on environment and mitigation strategies: A comprehensive review. *Journal of Hazardous Materials, 398*, 123019.
5. Domínguez, J., & Gómez-Brandón, M. (2012). Vermicomposting: Composting with earthworms to recycle organic wastes.
6. Cockborne, A., Vallès, V., Bruckler, L., Sevenier, G., Cabibel, B., Bertuzzi, P., & Bouisson, V. (1999). Environmental consequences of apple waste deposition on soil. *Journal of Environmental Quality, 28*, 1031–1037.
7. Uniyal, S., Paliwal, R., Kaphaliya, B., & Sharma, R. (2017). Human overpopulation: Impact on environment, 1–11.
8. Poore, J., & Nemecek, T. (2018). Reducing food's environmental impacts through producers and consumers. *Science, 360*, 987–992.
9. Crenna, E., Sinkko, T., & Sala, S. (2019). Biodiversity impacts due to food consumption in Europe. *Journal of Cleaner Production, 227*, 378–391.
10. Adhikari, N., Domakonda, N., Chandan, C., Gupta, G., Garg, R., Teja, S., Das, L., & Misra, A. (2018). An intelligent approach to demand forecasting. In *International Conference on Computer Networks and Communication Technologies.*
11. Suki, N. (2015). Customer environmental satisfaction and loyalty in the consumption of green products. *International Journal of Sustainable Development and World Ecology, 22*, 292–301.
12. Prusa, P., & Chocholáč, J. (2015). Demand forecasting in production logistics of food industry. *Applied Mechanics and Materials, 803*, 63–68.

13. Bayus, B., Hong, S., & Labe, R. (1989). Developing and using forecasting models of consumer durables: The case of color television. *Journal of Product Innovation Management*, *6*, 5–19.
14. Verma, P., Reddy, S., Ragha, L., & Datta, D. (2021). Comparison of time-series forecasting models. In *2021 International Conference on Intelligent Technologies (CONIT)* (pp. 1–7).
15. Ali, S., & Ahmad, A. (2019). Forecasting MSW generation using artificial neural network time series model: A study from metropolitan city. *SN Applied Sciences*, *1*.
16. Yang, Y., Zhang, J., & Feng, W. (2010). A prediction on electronic waste resource with time series model. In *2010 International Conference on Computer Application and System Modeling (ICCASM)* (Vol. 2, pp. V2-551–V2-555).
17. Kelley, K., & Lai, K. (2011). Accuracy in parameter estimation for the root mean square error of approximation: Sample size planning for narrow confidence intervals. *Multivariate Behavioral Research*, *46*, 1–32.
18. Ince, F. (2018). International Businesses and Environmental Issues, 86–111.
19. Mazur, N., Nowak, D., & Zalizko, V. (2021). Problems of sustainable development and challenges related to production. In *Production–Operation Management: The Chosen Aspects*.
20. Hannah, L., Roehrdanz, P., K., Fraser, E., Donatti, C., Sáenz, L., Wright, T., Hijmans, R., Mulligan, M., Berg, A., & Soesbergen, A. (2020). The environmental consequences of climate-driven agricultural frontiers. *PLoS One*, **15**.
21. Ai, H. (2000). Boosting economy and constructing sustainable development consumption mode. *Journal of Tianjin University of Commerce*.
22. Donohoe, M. (2003). Causes and health consequences of environmental degradation and social injustice. *Social Science & Medicine*, *56*(3), 573–587.
23. Taghikhah, F., Voinov, A., & Shukla, N. (2019). Extending the supply chain to address sustainability. *Journal of Cleaner Production*.
24. Clark, M., & Tilman, D. (2017). Comparative analysis of environmental impacts of agricultural production systems, agricultural input efficiency, and food choice. *Environmental Research Letters*, *12*.
25. Messner, R., Richards, C., & Johnson, H. (2020). The "Prevention Paradox": Food waste prevention and the quandary of systemic surplus production. *Agriculture and Human Values*, 1–13.
26. Taghikhah, F., Voinov, A., Shukla, N., Filatova, T., & Anufriev, M. (2020). Integrated modeling of extended agro-food supply chains: A systems approach. *European Journal of Operational Research*, *288*, 852–868.
27. Cockborne, A., Vallès, V., Bruckler, L., Sevenier, G., Cabibel, B., Bertuzzi, P., & Bouisson, V. (1999). Environmental consequences of apple waste deposition on soil. *Journal of Environmental Quality*, *28*, 1031–1037.
28. Raak, N., Symmank, C., Zahn, S., Aschemann-Witzel, J., & Rohm, H. (2017). Processing- and product-related causes for food waste and implications for the food supply chain. *Waste Management*, *61*, 461–472.
29. Kasza, G., Szabó-Bódi, B., Lakner, Z., & Izsó, T. (2019). Balancing the desire to decrease food waste with requirements of food safety. *Trends in Food Science & Technology*.
30. Nissim, D. (2019). The valuation implications of overproduction. *Columbia: Accounting (Topic)*.
31. Goltsos, T., Syntetos, A., Glock, C., & Ioannou, G. (2021). Inventory - forecasting: Mind the gap. *European Journal of Operational Research*, *299*, 397–419.
32. Aihua, D., Liangxing, Y., Tangyou, L., & Qingying, M. (2010). A simulation study of a two-echelon apparel supply chain with forecasting error. In *2010 8th International Conference on Supply Chain Management and Information* (pp. 1–6).
33. Garrone, P., Melacini, M., Perego, A., & Sert, S. (2016). Reducing food waste in food manufacturing companies. *Journal of Cleaner Production*, *137*, 1076–1085.
34. Zimmer, J., Raabe, A., & Lemberg, T. (2012). Increasing grid stability through accurate infeed forecasts of renewable energies, 1–4.
35. Korpela, J., & Tuominen, M. (1996). Inventory forecasting with a multiple criteria decision tool. *International Journal of Production Economics*, *45*, 159–168.

36. Babai, M., Boylan, J., & Tabar, B. (2021). Demand forecasting in supply chains: A review of aggregation and hierarchical approaches. *International Journal of Production Research, 60*, 324–348.
37. Gružauskas, V., Gimžauskienė, E., & Navickas, V. (2019). Forecasting accuracy influence on logistics clusters activities: The case of the food industry. *Journal of Cleaner Production, 240*, 118225.
38. Filimonau, V., Todorova, E., Mzembe, A., Sauer, L., & Yankholmes, A. (2020). A comparative study of food waste management in full service restaurants of the United Kingdom and the Netherlands. *Journal of Cleaner Production.*
39. Xie, J., Lee, T., & Zhao, X. (2004). Impact of forecasting error on the performance of capacitated multi-item production systems. *Computers & Industrial Engineering, 46*, 205–219.
40. Poore, J., & Nemecek, T. (2018). Reducing food's environmental impacts through producers and consumers. *Science, 360*, 987–992.
41. Steenbergen, R., & Mes, M. (2020). Forecasting demand profiles of new products. *Decision Support Systems, 139*, 113401.
42. Feizabadi, J. (2020). Machine learning demand forecasting and supply chain performance. *International Journal of Logistics Research and Applications, 25*, 119–142.
43. Carbonneau, R., Laframboise, K., & Vahidov, R. (2008). Application of machine learning techniques for supply chain demand forecasting. *European Journal of Operational Research, 184*, 1140–1154.
44. BalajiPrabhu, B. V., & Dakshayini, M. (2020). Computational performance analysis of neural network and regression models in forecasting the societal demand for agricultural food harvests. *International Journal of Grid and High Performance Computing, 12*, 35–47.
45. Chen, Y., Sun, E., & Lin, Y. (2020). Machine learning with parallel neural networks for analyzing and forecasting electricity demand. *Computational Economics, 56*, 569–597.
46. Lee, M., Ser, Y., Selvachandran, G., Thong, P., Cuong, L., Son, L., Tuan, N., & Gerogiannis, V. (2022). A comparative study of forecasting electricity consumption using machine learning models. *Mathematics.*
47. Maas, M., & Bisognin, C. (2020). Forecast of the historical series of revenues of the Brazilian food industry using forecasting techniques. *Revista Brasileira de Gestão de Negócios, 42*, 47.
48. Zou, H., Xia, G., Yang, F., & Wang, H. (2007). An investigation and comparison of artificial neural network and time series models for Chinese food grain price forecasting. *Neurocomputing, 70*, 2913–2923.
49. Kahraman, C., Kaya, I., Ulukan, H., & Uçal, I. (2010). Economic forecasting techniques and their applications, 16–44.
50. Hubrich, K., & West, K. (2008). Forecast evaluation of small nested model sets. *ERN: Simulation Methods (Topic).*
51. Gerds, T., Cai, T., & Schumacher, M. (2008). The performance of risk prediction models. *Biometrical Journal, 50.*
52. Luo, Y., Randerson, J., Abramowitz, G., Bacour, C., Blyth, E., Carvalhais, N., Ciais, P., Dalmonech, D., Fisher, J., Fisher, R., et al. (2012). A framework for benchmarking land models. *Biogeosciences, 9*, 3857–3874.
53. Frasier-Sleyman, K. (1992). Benchmark your way to forecasting excellence. *The Journal of Business Forecasting Methods & Systems, 11*, 6.
54. Franch, B., Vermote, E., Becker-Reshef, I., Claverie, M., Huang, J., Zhang, J., Justice, C., & Sobrino, J. (2015). Improving the timeliness of winter wheat production forecast in the United States of America, Ukraine and China using MODIS data and NCAR Growing Degree Day information. *Remote Sensing of Environment, 161*, 131–148.
55. Netto, C., Brei, V., Hyndman, R. (2023). Forecasting system's accuracy: A framework for the comparison of different structures. *Applied Stochastic Models in Business and Industry.*
56. Tian, Z., Li, H., & Li, F. (2021). A combination forecasting model of wind speed based on decomposition. *Energy Reports, 7*, 1217–1233.
57. Ansari, A. F., Stella, L., Turkmen, C., Zhang, X., Mercado, P., Shen, H., et al. (2024). Chronos: Learning the language of time series. arXiv preprint arXiv:2403.07815.

58. Rasul, K., Ashok, A., Williams, A. R., Khorasani, A., Adamopoulos, G., et al. (2023). Lag-llama: Towards foundation models for time series forecasting. arXiv preprint arXiv:2310.08278.
59. Garza, A., & Mergenthaler-Canseco, M. (2023). TimeGPT-1. arXiv preprint arXiv:2310.03589.
60. Cerliani, M. (2021). Linear-tree: The perfect mix of Linear Model and Decision Tree. *Towards Data Science*, Medium.
61. Friedman, J. (2001). Greedy function approximation: A gradient boosting machine. *Annals of Statistics*, *29*, 1189–1232.
62. Gilbert, K. (2005). An ARIMA supply chain model. *Management Science*, *51*, 305–310.
63. Yamak, P., Yujian, L., & Gadosey, P. (2019). A comparison between ARIMA, LSTM, and GRU for time series forecasting. In *Proceedings of the 2019 2nd International Conference on Algorithms, Computing and Artificial Intelligence*.
64. Memmedli, M., & Ozdemir, O. (2010). An application of fuzzy time series to improve ISE forecasting. *WSEAS Transactions on Mathematics*, *9*, 12–21.
65. Hill, P., Biggs, J., Ponce-López, V., & Bull, D. (2021). Time-series prediction approaches to forecasting deformation in Sentinel-1 InSAR data. *Journal of Geophysical Research: Solid Earth*, *126*.
66. Brown, T. B., Mann, B., Ryder, N., Subbiah, M., Kaplan, J., et al. (2020). Language models are few-shot learners. arXiv preprint arXiv:2005.14165.
67. Xu, Y., Song, Y., Garg, S., Gong, L., Shu, R., et al. (2021). Anytime sampling for autoregressive models via ordered autoencoding. arXiv preprint arXiv:2102.11495.
68. Sharami, J., Shterionov, D., Blain, F., Vanmassenhove, E., Sisto, M., Emmery, C., & Spronck, P. (2023). Tailoring domain adaptation for machine translation quality estimation, 9–20.
69. Touvron, H., Lavril, T., Izacard, G., Martinet, X., Lachaux, M.-A., et al. (2023). Llama: Open and efficient foundation language models. arXiv preprint arXiv:2302.13971.
70. Vaswani, A., Shazeer, N., Parmar, N., Uszkoreit, J., Jones, L., et al. (2017). Attention is all you need. In *Advances in Neural Information Processing Systems* (Vol. 30).
71. Zhang, H., Nettleton, D., & Zhu, Z. (2019). Regression-enhanced random forests. arXiv preprint arXiv:1904.10416.
72. Ilic, I., Gorgulu, B., Cevik, M., & Baydogan, M. G. (2020). Explainable boosted linear regression for time series forecasting. arXiv preprint arXiv:2009.09110.
73. Bobrowski, L., & Kretowski, M. (2000). Induction of multivariate decision trees by using dipolar criteria, 331–336.
74. Grambsch, P., & O'Brien, P. (1991). The effects of transformations and preliminary tests for non-linearity in regression. *Statistics in Medicine*, *10*(5), 697–709.
75. Vanli, N., & Kozat, S. (2013). A comprehensive approach to universal piecewise nonlinear regression based on trees. *IEEE Transactions on Signal Processing*, *62*, 5471–5486.
76. Wang, J., Li, P., Ran, R., Che, Y., & Zhou, Y. (2018). A short-term photovoltaic power prediction model based on the gradient boost decision tree. *Applied Sciences*, *8*, 689.
77. Aguilar-Palacios, C., Muñoz-Romero, S., & Rojo-Álvarez, J. (2020). Cold-start promotional sales forecasting through gradient boosted-based contrastive explanations. *IEEE Access*, *8*, 137574–137586.
78. Maravall, A. (1986). Revisions in ARIMA signal extraction. *Journal of the American Statistical Association*, *81*, 736–740.
79. Corduas, M., & Piccolo, D. (2008). Time series clustering and classification by the autoregressive metric. *Computational Statistics & Data Analysis*, *52*, 1860–1872.
80. Cavaliere, G., & Taylor, A. (2005). Stationarity tests under time-varying second moments. *Econometric Theory*, *21*, 1112–1129.
81. Álvarez-Ramírez, J., Rodriguez, E., & Echeverría, J. (2005). Detrending fluctuation analysis based on moving average filtering. *Physica A: Statistical Mechanics and Its Applications*, *354*, 199–219.
82. Krämer, W. (1986). Least squares regression when the independent variable follows an ARIMA process. *Journal of the American Statistical Association*, *81*, 150–154.

83. Dong, R., & Pedrycz, W. (2008). A granular time series approach to long-term forecasting and trend forecasting. *Physica A: Statistical Mechanics and Its Applications*, *387*, 3253–3270.
84. Zhang, L., & Wen, J. (2019). A systematic feature selection procedure for short-term data-driven building energy forecasting model development. *Energy and Buildings*.
85. Fan, G., Wei, X., Li, Y., & Hong, W. (2020). Forecasting electricity consumption using a novel hybrid model. *Sustainable Cities and Society*, *61*, 102320.
86. Kourentzes, N., Trapero, J., & Barrow, D. (2019). Optimising forecasting models for inventory planning. *ERN: Model Construction & Estimation (Topic)*.
87. Aktepe, A., Yanık, E., & Ersöz, S. (2021). Demand forecasting application with regression and artificial intelligence methods in a construction machinery company. *Journal of Intelligent Manufacturing*, *32*, 1587–1604.
88. Teng, S., & Jaramillo, H. (2005). Linking tactical and operational decision-making to strengthen textile/apparel supply chains. *International Journal of Logistics Systems and Management*, *1*, 244.
89. Shariffdeen, R., Munasinghe, D., Bhathiya, H., Bandara, U., & Bandara, H. (2016). Adaptive workload prediction for proactive auto scaling in PaaS systems. In *2016 2nd International Conference on Cloud Computing Technologies and Applications (CloudTech)* (pp. 22–29).
90. Zhou, H., Zhang, S., Peng, J., Zhang, S., Li, J., Xiong, H., & Zhang, W. (2021). Informer: Beyond efficient transformer for long sequence time-series forecasting. *Proceedings of the AAAI Conference on Artificial Intelligence*, *35*(12), 11106–11115.
91. Student, Su, J., Lu, Y., Pan, S., Wen, B., & Liu, Y. (2021). Roformer: Enhanced transformer with rotary position embedding. arXiv preprint arXiv:2104.09864.
92. Wang, W., Chau, K., Xu, D., & Chen, X. (2015). Improving forecasting accuracy of annual runoff time series using ARIMA based on EEMD decomposition. *Water Resources Management*, *29*, 2655–2675.
93. Jiang, J., Lerman, K., & Ferrara, E. (2022). Zero-shot meta-learning for small-scale data from human subjects. In *2023 IEEE 11th International Conference on Healthcare Informatics (ICHI)* (pp. 311–320).
94. Lu, Y., Kandula, S., König, A., & Chaudhuri, S. (2021). Pre-training summarization models of structured datasets for cardinality estimation. *Proceedings of the VLDB Endowment*, *15*, 414–426.

Planting Digital Seeds: Treedom's Technological Approach to Sustainable Development

Paolo Canonico, Ernesto De Nito, Andrea Caccialanza, and Valentina Langella

Abstract This study explores Treedom's role in advancing technology-led sustainability transitions. By examining Treedom's innovative approaches to global reforestation and sustainable development, it highlights how technology can foster environmental stewardship and promote sustainable practices. Treedom's contributions to environmental sustainability through technology-driven reforestation and habitat conservation are analysed, demonstrating how technological innovations can support global efforts in these areas and further sustainable development (Sreenivasan & Suresh, Management Research Review, 47(3), 390–405, 2024). The research investigates sustainability orientation as an emerging factor in evaluating startups, considering performance, communication, and technological managerial practices as sources of market competitiveness (Carle & Rayna, Journal of Management & Organization, 30, 1–17, 2023). It also assesses their capability to preserve natural resources, promote biodiversity, and mitigate climate change impacts. The research questions (RQs) are:

- RQ1: How has the startup engaged in the preservation and restoration of habitats?
- RQ2: What are the identified barriers to implement sustainability-oriented technological solutions?

P. Canonico
Università degli Studi Federico II, Naples, Italy
e-mail: pcanonic@unina.it

E. De Nito
Università degli Studi di Salerno, Fisciano, Italy
e-mail: edenito@unisa.it

A. Caccialanza (✉)
Università di Bologna, Bologna, Italy
e-mail: andrea.caccialanza@unibo.it

V. Langella
Altis Advisory, Milan, Italy
e-mail: valentina.langella@altisadvisory.com

M. Cipriano et al. (eds.), *Technologies for Organizations and Society*,
Lecture Notes in Information Systems and Organisation 80,
https://doi.org/10.1007/978-3-032-01697-3_9

- RQ3: What managerial practices has the startup employed for the sustainability-oriented transition?

This research employs a case study approach, reconstructing the current debate on sustainable startups as discussed by Trautwein (Journal of Cleaner Production, 281, 125330, 2021). An analysis of online, offline, and confidential internal sources has been conducted.

The study offers both theoretical and practical implications. Theoretically, it highlights the evolution of literature on the topic and the challenges of promoting sustainability in startups (Di Vaio et al., Journal of Cleaner Production, 378, 134469, 2022). Practically, it identifies developmental elements and obstacles to the growth of sustainability orientation, along with suitable technological solutions to operationalize it (Horne and Fichter, Journal of Cleaner Production, 349, 131163, 2022).

Keywords Startup · Sustainability · Biodiversity · Reforestation · Technology · Climate change

1 Introduction

The urgency of sustainable development is increasingly recognized, and entrepreneurs, along with the spread of entrepreneurial mindsets, are pivotal in driving this agenda by linking entrepreneurial processes with market transformations and large-scale societal changes (e.g., [1, 2]). Within entrepreneurship studies, sustainable entrepreneurship has emerged as a significant and established concept that aims to equally prioritize economic, social, and environmental objectives (e.g., [3, 4]). The term 'sustainability impact' highlights the meaningful contributions of sustainable entrepreneurship across these three dimensions of value creation (e.g., [5, 6]). These studies actively contribute to achieving sustainable development goals (e.g., [1]), with varying mechanisms and efforts depending on the scale of the ventures involved (e.g., [7]).

In particular, startups are crucial in this context due to their potential for radical innovation, which allows them to exploit significant opportunities and improve social and environmental conditions [8]. These emerging and fast-growing ventures, with their innovative products and services, possess unique characteristics that set them apart from established firms. They drive societal and environmental shifts towards sustainability through their transition-oriented business models and innovative practices (e.g., [9, 10]). Furthermore, Hockerts & Wüstenhagen [11] emphasize that startups are instrumental during the initial and early growth stages of market development, while larger, established companies become more influential during the growth and mature stages of an industry. In addition, sustainable entrepreneurship and the proactive role of start-ups are essential in addressing the urgent need for sustainable development, fostering innovations that balance economic, social, and environmental objectives, and catalysing significant positive changes within society (e.g., [12]).

Consequently, it is important to understand from the outset the impacts an organisation generates, not only to appreciate the achieved internal efficiency but also to ensure transparency and accreditation for various categories of stakeholders (e.g., [13]). According to several scholars, such as Di Vaio [5] and Venturelli et al. [14], the development of innovative and sustainable business models has been proven to be key in fostering innovation and minimising impacts through the integration of sustainability-oriented processes.

In light of this, and recognising the importance of the topic, this chapter aims to present a case study of a successful startup in this domain. Specifically, it seeks to understand the startup engagement in the preservation and restoration of habitats (RQ1), identify and systematise the recognised and discussed barriers to the implementation of these technological solutions (RQ2), and analyse the managerial practices employed for this purpose (RQ3).

The remainder of the chapter is the following. The next section provides an overview of the background of the debate, followed by a presentation of the methodological aspects of the review. Subsequently, the results and discussion are covered. Finally, the contributions to the debate and the conclusion are outlined.

2 Background

2.1 Startups and Sustainability

The growing interest in the literature on entrepreneurship for sustainable development highlights the capacity of individuals (i.e., entrepreneurs) and new ventures to serve as agents of change, particularly on social and environmental fronts (e.g., [8]). Johnson & Schaltegger [1] identify two common traits in this body of literature: (i) the depiction of processes and (ii) the description of challenges and opportunities at multiple levels. This literature focuses on the co-creation of value processes that contribute to macro-level targets and examines how entrepreneurial activities address market failures and the co-evolution of players to create value collaboratively.

Start-ups, as mentioned in the introduction, are promoting sustainability transitions and evolving business models towards a sustainability-oriented perspective. Scholars such as Bidmon & Knab [15] and Broccado et al. [16] explore the connections between business models and transition theory, emphasizing the role of start-ups as successful agents if they adapt their technological solutions to sustainable business models. Their propensity for innovation must be grounded in feasibility studies and include an assessment of their ability to achieve equilibrium within socio-technical systems (e.g., [17]). Achieving this equilibrium can be particularly challenging for start-ups, even if only temporarily. To address this, both the literature and practice have developed various strategies to improve start-up performance in the initial phases of business development.

For instance, Deyanova et al. [18] systematically analysed the role of business incubators in addressing resource and strategy formulation challenges. Additionally, investors increasingly consider the sustainability orientation of business models when evaluating startup positioning and strategy (e.g., [19]). In particular, some institutional investors specifically target investments focused on sustainability issues (e.g., [20], with sustainable finance literacy emerging as a crucial determinant of such investment preferences [21]). On the behavioural-individual side, Boar-Boar & Oliveras-Villanueva [22] previously discussed the characteristics of entrepreneurs and investors related to their propensity to invest in sustainability-oriented start-ups, especially those with a social focus, and proposed an analysis of existing start-ups and the impact of institutional support.

Financial and institutional support is also relevant for sustainable start-ups but market demand and resilience are equally important in the long term. Hockerts & Wüstenhagen [11] examined the strategies of sustainable new entrants compared to incumbent firms, while Parrish [23] identified drivers of sustainability-driven entrepreneurship based on contextual values and motives. Despite the recognized urgency to orient businesses towards sustainability criteria, both from investor and market-demand perspectives, the debate on identifying, quantifying, and disclosing impact remains unresolved.

2.2 Startups and the Assessment of Sustainable Development Performance

To enhance both the theoretical and practical discourse, numerous studies have focused on under-standing the definitions, processes, and dynamics of sustainability assessment in the context of startups. Trautwein [24] identifies several challenges in establishing effective assessment tools: (i) informal and rapidly changing management structures that hinder replicability; (ii) resource limitations that restrict the thoroughness of assessments and the communication of results; (iii) business model and value chain volatility due to unpredictable changes; (iv) a lack of historical performance data since startups are new to the market; and (v) limited specific knowledge, leading to the use of overly simplistic assessment tools.

These emerging market players face a significant contradiction. Their small, informal, and agile organisational structures make them highly responsive to changes, yet they are also pressured to formalise procedures and business models and report performance without historical benchmarks (e.g., [25]).

Therefore, it is crucial for a startup to promote sustainable development effectively through a thorough and motivated approach to sustainability management (e.g., [22]). This approach must consider and assess both positive and negative impacts on all stakeholders (e.g., [26]). Additionally, the focus should extend beyond reporting to include all activities involved in value creation, ensuring transparency in how value is maintained, unlocked, and shared (e.g., [27]). These processes are intrinsically linked to sustainability impact assessment, which evaluates past, present, and anticipated future performances (e.g., [7]).

2.3 Hypothesis Development and Research Questions

Albeit the review proposed by Trautwein [24] mapped and discussed 23 original assessments approaches in literature for the sustainability impact assessment of startups performances, the variety of activities, sectors, dimensions and impacts still requires a reduction in the fragmentation of approaches and a deeper understanding of specific contexts (e.g., [5]). Furthermore, in line with this reasoning, Fichter et al. [28] stressed that the sustainability assessment of startups impacts is still a neglected area of intervention and study, albeit the performance evaluation, value distribution and impact of incumbent firms has been a key topic of sustainability-led research for long time. In fact, as mentioned above, our opinion is that sustainability orientation is one of the emerging factors in the evaluation of startups, both from a perspective of their performance and the quality of corporate disclosure and communication, and for an assessment of current and prospective competitiveness in the market in a broad sense (e.g., [7]). Startups could promote ecosystem preservation and reforestation, as suggested by the Food and Agriculture Organization of the United Nations [29] and The Economics of Ecosystems and Biodiversity [30] reports. These sources estimate that startup initiatives could have a substantial impact on environmental conservation and the expansion of forested areas.

Furthermore, this is also reflected in their current (or potential) ability to exploit resources, nor promote circular initiatives, proving more or less resilience to the impacts of climate change. Consequently, those previous evidence led to our research gap and the development of our research questions (RQs). Therefore, we formulated the following RQs:

RQ1: How has the startup engaged the preservation and restoration of habitats?
RQ2: Can the recognized and discussed barriers to implement sustainability-oriented technological solutions be identified and systematized?
RQ3: What managerial practices has the startup employed for the sustainability-oriented transition?

2.4 Case Study Selection and Presentation: Treedom

As mentioned above, several startups attempted to foster the integration of responsible technological practices in the attempt to promote sustainable development. Treedom, a pioneering B-Lab certified startup at the intersection of technology and environmental conservation, exemplifies how responsible technologies can drive positive societal and environmental change. This commitment to transparency not only builds trust among users but also amplifies the impact of reforestation projects by fostering a sense of ownership and connection to the sustainability-oriented vision that this startup proposes.

Furthermore, Treedom leverages technology to monitor and track the environmental impact of tree planting activities, enabling data-driven decision-making for sustainable land management. By restoring degraded landscapes, conserving habitats, and promoting biodiversity, Treedom contributes to ecosystem resilience and climate change mitigation. Additionally, Treedom's model creates economic opportunities for local communities involved in tree planting and agroforestry projects, thereby fostering sustainable livelihoods and empowering marginalized populations. At the same time, they also support agroforestry projects, which blend tree planting with agricultural practices, benefiting both the environment and local communities. This approach not only helps restore ecosystems and conserve habitats but also promotes biodiversity and provides sustainable livelihoods for farmers. In this way, in addition to a predominantly environmental impact, an equally important social impact is achieved in relation to the local communities involved.

Consequently, as single case study, Treedom offers valuable insights into how technology can amplify reforestation efforts, enhance habitat conservation, and drive sustainable development. Its successful integration of digital innovation and environmental sustainability makes Treedom a compelling example for exploring the broader phenomenon of technology-led sustainability transitions.

In particular, in Table 1 we propose a synthesis of the achievement reached by the startup in which they confirm their leading role in the achievement and promotion of sustainable-development-led initiatives.

Table 1 Ranking and reports on Treedom achievements

Ranking or Report	Achievement
Top 100 Startups [31]	In 2021, the startup raised €13 million, stemming from an initial funding round of €3 million with Banca Generali as the lead investor. Followed by a subsequent capital increase of €10 million, thanks to a series of investors, including former Formula 1 world champion Nico Rosberg and Italian national team captain Giorgio Chiellini.
Best For The World—top 5% according to B Lab (Treedom - Impact report, 2021)	The B Lab publishes a list that rewards the most performance-certified B Corporations both overall and within each impact area. In 2021, Treedom was awarded in the Governance and Workers category. It is recognized as "The Best For The World" in the Governance impact area and Workers impact area, striving daily through exemplary practices, scoring in the top 5% among all B Corps worldwide.
Leaders of the Growth [32]	It ranked 32nd in the "Leader della crescita 2023" ranking, which is the list of the 500 self-nominated Italian companies that achieved the highest revenue growth between 2018 and 2021, compiled by Sole 24 Ore and Statista.

Source: Authors' elaboration on external data sources

Once the analysed case study is introduced, the following section presents the data sources process adopted.

3 Methodology

With reference to methodological aspects, we employ a qualitative methodology [33] to explore the key technological factors contributing to the enhancement and measurement of actual performance within sustainability-oriented ecosystems [34]. To accomplish this, we propose an exploratory single-case research design to examine their successful experiences, akin to the approach adopted by previous scholars in evaluating best practices [35–37]. Indeed, a case study approach is conducive to abductive reasoning and facilitates the reconciliation of general theories with the specific contextual nuances that may arise from individual cases [38]. Furthermore, a case-based design forms the foundation for a more comprehensive and systematic approach, which can, in subsequent stages, yield more grounded, robust, and generalizable results when compared to isolated case studies [37].

Furthermore, this article applies the discussed document analysis framework to the case study as proposed by Bowen [39], thus exploring the role of several 'external' and 'confidential' documents in understanding its technological innovations and sustainability initiatives, following best practices for evidence-informed management research as outlined by Tranfield et al. [40]. By examining the nature and forms of documents utilized by Treedom, assessing their advantages and limitations, and providing concrete examples, this study elucidates how document analysis enhances our comprehension of Treedom's operations within the context of sustainable development.

The rationale for grouping the aforementioned technological aspects is to present Treedom as a case study illustrating various applications and facilitating roles that have had an impact not only within the dimensions already explored in academic debate (e.g., [9, 17, 34]) but also in monitoring the trends of the most prevalent and emerging themes in recent years. We adopted different information sources. First of all, internal and official documents (the most important one is the impact analysis conducted on the 2023 performance and published on the website www.treedom.net), and then a report realized by an external consultancy organization (ALTIS Advisory, a university spin-off set up as a benefit company, which realized a social impact report of the start-up). Adopting an external view provided a more objective picture and was useful to reduce bias risks.

In the impact analysis conducted on the 2023 performance, Treedom chose to undertake a path aimed at creating a model for monitoring and measuring the impact of its agroforestry projects in the world. This model and the impact assessment that emerged was used in this paper as a direct source of the impact assessment of the technologies in Treedom's business model. The model is characterised by its replicability over time and its adherence to the different environmental and socio-cultural contexts of all the countries in which Treedom operates, as well as being dimensionally suitable for the context of a startup (See sub-section 2.2).

The adoption of a social impact report means changing one's paradigm, abandoning performance assessment alone in favour of a more organic system of evaluating one's work. What catalyses the attention is the need to measure the effects generated by the activities of an organisation, on the territory and on the community of concern, through a quantification of the relative importance that the relevant stakeholders attribute to the changes experienced by each of them in their own lives thanks to its work [5, 8, 41]. A preliminary context analysis carried out with Treedom's contact persons has identified three countries—Kenya, Madagascar, Nepal—and their projects for which to carry out the work of impact measurement, with an initial trial phase that may subsequently be extended to all countries in which Treedom operates. This choice was dictated by the need to identify different dynamics and cultures that are representative of the globality of active projects and significant for the definition of the evaluation framework to be shared with Treedom.

In order to operationalise the different theoretical frameworks, each theme is associated with one or more indicators, populated thanks to the data collection tools, through the items of a survey. For synthesis purposes, only the analyses relating to the technological aspects between the various themes estimated will be proposed.

The questions were formulated with the aim of attributing the causal link between the changes in the lives of the beneficiaries and Treedom's projects, noting a direct correlation between the local partners and Treedom ('Thanks to the collaboration with Treedom') and a direct correlation between local farmers and staff and the local partners ('Thanks to the participation in the project with'—'Thanks to my work with the organisation'). The questions were posed in such a way that the answers could be normalised on a scale from 1 to 7, providing a range from 'Very decreased/Very much disagree/not at all relevant/Very worsened' to 'Very increased/Very much agree/Extremely relevant/Very improved' as a response possibility. The results of the textual analysis and impact assessment are discussed in the next section.

4 Results and Discussion

As mentioned above, Treedom stands out as a significant case study for examining the convergence of technology, environmental sustainability, habitat conservation, and reforestation. Established with a vision to create a greener planet, Treedom employs advanced technology to spearhead global tree-planting initiatives. Its digital platform enables users to easily participate in tree planting, providing transparency and engagement through real-time project tracking and detailed updates on tree growth. What sets Treedom apart is its innovative approach that combines environmental action with digital tools, making reforestation accessible to individuals and organizations worldwide. By offering the ability to plant trees remotely, Treedom democratizes environmental stewardship, fostering a global community committed to sustainability (e.g., [7]). Each tree planted through Tree-

Table 2 Technology and managerial practices in Treedom

Technology	Managerial practice	Source
Technological education as enabling factor for sustainability	Assessment of the stakeholders' knowledge of technological instruments and development of the skills needed to manage that knowledge.	Table 4—Variable tested of the impact generated. (p. 26, internal use impact report 2023)
Education as target for development of sustainable agriculture	"Technological access" as emerged indicator in the materiality assessment in the impact evaluation. Company will invest in technological education of users (farmers) to ensure the reliability of data entry process.	Table 14—materiality assessment for sustainability report (internal use impact report 2023)
Technology as tools—Firm side	Variety of instruments and tools adopt-ed for monitoring the effectiveness of activities and increase the internal efficiency (use of geo-localization of interventions and photos).	www.Treedom.net
Technology as tools—Subscriber side	Subscriber authentication in the "MyTreedom" login area to access to: the ID of the tree(s) planted; monitor the Co2 absorbed by the tree, a follow up section to the linked initiatives and enable "personalization" of this donation (e.g., give a name to the tree or leave a message).	www.Treedom.net
Technology as source of trust and legitimization to institutions and followers/supporters	Digital communication channels and digital accessibility to sustainability reports or impact reports as instruments legitimization to (external) stakeholders.	www.Treedom.net
Digital technologies enabling factors for key sources of finance	Within the website you can subscribe to their packages of products and services with a high sustainability impact and the final goal to preserve and restore rural areas.	www.Treedom.net

Source: Authors' elaboration

dom is geotagged and photographed, ensuring transparency and allowing donors to follow the progress of their contributions. Treedom's digital platform serves as a catalyst for global reforestation efforts by providing individuals and organizations with a transparent and engaging way to participate in tree planting initiatives; through real-time updates, geotagged photos, and interactive storytelling, Treedom ensures transparency, accountability, and community engagement throughout the tree planting process (e.g., [5]). In Table 2 it has been summarized the main results linked with the impact of technology in Treedom activities.

The startup has heavily invested in the development of its own technological applications to become more accountable and appealing to both internal and external stakeholders. Specifically, it achieves a dual purpose in this regard; on one hand, it gains the trust and a good reputation of corporate and retail customers who purchase the offered packages and solutions, and on the other hand, it enhances its attractiveness to institutional investors during the fundraising rounds. This is in line with previous studies on the subject. In fact, Di Lauro et al. [42] observe how this orientation towards non-financial objectives enhances the management of internet-based technologies, specifically social media, fundraising campaigns. While the impact on social capital fundraising can be relatively estimated as a measure of the startup's ability to finance itself through technological innovation, the contribution and quantification of its social impact are not as straightforward. As analysed by Humphries et al. [43], it is essential to understand which activities and managerial practices in forest management have had externalities on the impacted context or the areas subject to replanting by the local community (e.g., cooperatives or local farmers). These groups are then operationally responsible for the transplanting, monitoring, and maintenance of the introduced local biomass. In this context the Treedom philosophy demonstrates its uniqueness. According to the last impact report 2023 (p. 15—translated from the Italian original internal document): "Treedom's philosophy is to create sustainable ecosystems by directly involving thousands of farmers in different parts of the world. This approach provides concrete support in covering the initial costs of tree planting, enabling the development of resources over time that are essential for protecting the local ecosystem and creating continuous income opportunities. This journey going beyond mere financial transfers; it became a moment sharing and the construction of methods and production processes. It involves raising awareness of their resources, planning a development and care plan projected for the medium and long term, because 'trees do not plant themselves'."

Within this broad scope of intervention, the impact assessment system was also consistently adapted. As described above, the impact dimensions that drive the theoretical framework for farmers are three: personal well-being, economic well-being, and training and education in sustainable agriculture. When completing the questionnaires, respondents were asked to rate the change they perceived in relation to the indicators representative of each dimension. Within the three dimensions, the last one was specifically embedding the evaluation of technological-led perceptions.

Since these criteria are not widely discussed in the literature, it is important to highlight that technology and "Access to technology" are key elements in Treedom's framework for evaluating external stakeholders. Each intervention proposed by Treedom and implemented in a developing context has unique characteristics, necessitating a context-specific approach that varies with the availability of technologies (both agronomic and information technology). This approach is essential to maximize the utility, efficiency, and effectiveness of the intervention. In Table 3 are summarized those elements.

Finally, within this aspect linked to "Access to technology" in Treedom Framework, we report the impact of the Indices estimated in Table 4.

Such a high score suggests not only the materiality of the issue in terms of materiality matrix in an impact assessment perspective, but also further strategic and

Table 3 The evaluation framework for the stakeholder Personnel of partners

Dimension of impact	Aspect	Theme
Agroforestry Training and Education	Management Capacity of Agroforestry Projects	Specialized support in managing new issues that may arise
	Access to Technology	Access to new tools (e.g., water tank)
	Soil Quality Skills	Perception of increased knowledge about soil quality (synergies between crops, fertilizers, etc.)
	Biodiversity Knowledge and Protection	Perception of increased knowledge about biodiversity
	Knowledge on Prevention of Consequences Related to Extreme Weather Events	Perception of increased knowledge of risks related to extreme weather events
	Management Capacity of Agroforestry Projects	Specialized support in managing new issues that may arise

Source: Impact report – Treedom (2023, p. 15)

Table 4 Indexes estimated for aspects led to the "Access to technology" in Treedom Framework

Aspect	Indicator	Index theme	Index aspect
Access to technology	Variety of new cultivation tools and technologies that I have become aware of and used	5.48 out of 7	5.43 out of 7
Access to technology	Ability to use new tools and technologies for cultivation that I was previously unaware of	5.68 out of 7	

Source: Impact report – Treedom (2023, p. 26)

long-term considerations. In particular, it emerges as for Treedom it is important to monitor the evolution of the perception of technologies as this seems to be a driver of their ability to promote sustainable-development-led and broadly sustainability-oriented initiatives. Further considerations are outlined in the implications section.

5 Implications

5.1 Theoretical Implications

This contribution has both theoretical and practical implications. On the theoretical front, this study advances the literature on sustainable entrepreneurship by highlighting the challenges and opportunities unique to start-ups in the sustainability domain [44]. It underscores the need for a massive diffusion (and application of) sustainability impact assessment tools tailored to the dynamic and resource-constrained environments of startups [24]. The case of Treedom illustrates how innovative business models can integrate digital technologies to achieve sustainability goals, providing a foundation for future research on the intersection of technology and sustainability in entrepreneurial contexts [15, 16].

Additionally, this study contributes to the understanding of how startups can effectively balance economic, social, and environmental objectives [5]. By examining Treedom's model, it reinforces the concept that sustainability-driven business models are not only viable but essential for fostering long-term societal and environmental benefits [9, 10].

5.2 Managerial Implications

From a managerial perspective, the findings emphasize the importance of integrating technology into sustainability strategies. For startup founders and managers, Treedom's approach offers a blueprint for leveraging digital tools to enhance transparency, accountability, and community engagement. Key managerial practices such as the use of geotagging, real-time updates, and interactive platforms can significantly improve the effectiveness and impact of sustainability initiatives [1].

Furthermore, this case highlights the necessity of comprehensive stakeholder engagement. By involving local communities in tree planting and agroforestry projects, startups can build trust and foster sustainable livelihoods, thereby enhancing their social license to operate. Managers can learn from Treedom's experience to develop strategies that not only address environmental issues but also create economic opportunities for marginalized populations [11].

5.3 Societal Implications

The societal implications of this study are profound, particularly concerning the preservation of habitats and biodiversity for future generations. Treedom's model demonstrates how technology can play a crucial role in environmental conservation efforts, contributing to the restoration of degraded landscapes and the conservation of biodiversity. This has direct benefits for local communities, promoting ecosystem resilience and sustainable agriculture [8].

Moreover, Treedom's initiatives help mitigate climate change impacts by increasing carbon sequestration through reforestation. By fostering a global community committed to sustainability, Treedom sets a precedent for future generations to prioritize environmental stewardship. The integration of technology in these efforts ensures that such initiatives are scalable and replicable, offering a pathway for widespread adoption of sustainable practices [17].

6 Conclusions

This chapter highlights the importance of understanding the impacts of sustainable startups, using Treedom as a single case study to exemplify the effective use of technology for sustainable development. The urgency of sustainable development is increasingly recognized, and the pivotal role of startups in this context cannot be overstated. Their potential for radical innovation and agility allows them to address significant social and environmental challenges, driving societal and market shifts towards sustainability.

Treedom's innovative approach combines digital tools with environmental action, making reforestation accessible and transparent for a global audience. The startup's use of geotagging and real-time updates ensures accountability and fosters a sense of ownership among its users. By leveraging technology, Treedom not only enhances the impact of its reforestation efforts but also contributes to ecosystem resilience and climate change mitigation, promoting sustainable livelihoods for local communities involved in its projects.

The case study of Treedom underscores the necessity of comprehensive sustainability management for startups. It demonstrates how digital innovation can facilitate the effective assessment and communication of sustainability impacts, addressing both positive and negative externalities for all stakeholders. This approach aligns with the broader discourse on sustainability impact assessment, which evaluates the past, present, and future performance of ventures.

In conclusion, the insights gained from Treedom's experience provide valuable lessons for other startups aiming to integrate technology with sustainability. This case study reinforces the need for robust sustainability assessments and highlights the role of start-ups in advancing sustainable development goals. By showcasing Treedom's achievements, this chapter contributes to the theoretical and practical understanding of technology-driven sustainability transitions, offering a successful case-study for other ventures to emulate in their pursuit of sustainable innovation.

Acknowledgments The authors would like to express their gratitude to the members of the scientific and organizing committee of the ITAIS Conference 2024—"Growing in a Digital and Sustainable Society," held at Università Cattolica del Sacro Cuore on October 10–12, 2024. Specifically, they thank the co-chairs of the "T08 Responsible Technologies for Digital and Sustainable Organizations and Society" track: A. Tursunbayeva (Parthenope University of Naples), L. Moschera (Parthenope University of Naples), V. Fernandez Alarcon (Universitat Politècnica de Catalunya), and Ž. Stankevičiūtė (Kaunas University of Technology).

Disclosure of Interests The authors have no competing interests to declare that are relevant to the content of this article.

References

1. Johnson, M. P., & Schaltegger, S. (2020). Entrepreneurship for sustainable development: A review and multilevel causal mechanism framework. *Entrepreneurship Theory and Practice, 44*(6), 1141–1173. https://doi.org/10.1177/1042258719885368
2. Volkmann, C., Fichter, K., Klofsten, M., & Audretsch, D. B. (2021). Sustainable entrepreneurial ecosystems: An emerging field of research. *Small Business Economics, 56*(3), 1047–1055. https://doi.org/10.1007/s11187-019-00253-7
3. Hörisch, J., Johnson, M. P., & Schaltegger, S. (2015). Implementation of sustainability management and company size: A knowledge-based view. *Business Strategy and the Environment, 24*(8), 765–779. https://doi.org/10.1002/bse.1844
4. Loprevite, S. (2020). Vocazione sociale, profitto e nuovi modelli ibridi d'impresa: Paradigmi e realtà in prospettiva economico-aziendale. *Vocazione sociale, profitto e nuovi modelli ibridi d'im-presa*, 1–148.
5. Di Vaio, A., Hassan, R., Chhabra, M., Arrigo, E., & Palladino, R. (2022). Sustainable entrepreneur-ship impact and entrepreneurial venture life cycle: A systematic literature review. *Journal of Cleaner Production, 378*, 134469.
6. Figge, F., & Hahn, T. (2004). Sustainable value added—measuring corporate contributions to sustainability beyond eco-efficiency. *Ecological Economics, 48*(2), 173–187. https://doi.org/10.1016/j.ecolecon.2003.08.005
7. Carle, A., & Rayna, T. (2023). Where to start? Exploring how sustainable startups integrate sustainability impact assessment within their entrepreneurial process. *Journal of Management & Organization, 30*, 1–17. https://doi.org/10.1017/jmo.2023.46
8. Cohen, B., & Winn, M. I. (2007). Market imperfections, opportunity and sustainable entrepreneurship. *Journal of Business Venturing, 22*(1), 29–49. https://doi.org/10.1016/j.jbusvent.2004.12.001
9. Schaltegger, S., & Wagner, M. (2011). Sustainable entrepreneurship and sustainability innovation: categories and interactions. *Business Strategy and the Environment, 20*(4), 222–237. https://doi.org/10.1002/bse.682
10. Sreenivasan, A., & Suresh, M. (2024). Start-up sustainability: Does blockchain adoption drives sustainability in start-ups? A systematic literature reviews. *Management Research Review, 47*(3), 390–405. https://doi.org/10.1108/MRR-07-2022-0519
11. Hockerts, K., & Wüstenhagen, R. (2010). Greening Goliaths versus emerging Davids—Theorizing about the role of incumbents and new entrants in sustainable entrepreneurship. *Journal of Business Venturing, 25*(5), 481–492. https://doi.org/10.1016/j.jbusvent.2009.07.005
12. Bacq, S., & Wang, S. (2024). The lean impact start-up framework: Fueling innovation for positive societal change. *Journal of Management, 48*(4), 1123–1145. https://doi.org/10.1177/01492063241240713
13. Davidsson, P., Recker, J., & Von Briel, F. (2020). External enablement of new venture creation: A framework. *Academy of Management Perspectives, 34*(3), 311–332. https://doi.org/10.5465/amp.2017.0163
14. Venturelli, A., Caputo, F., Leopizzi, R., Mastroleo, G., & Mio, C. (2017). How can CSR identity be evaluated? A pilot study using a Fuzzy Expert System. *Journal of Cleaner Production, 141*, 1000–1010. https://doi.org/10.1016/j.jclepro.2016.09.172
15. Bidmon, C. M., & Knab, S. F. (2018). The three roles of business models in societal transitions: New linkages between business model and transition research. *Journal of Cleaner Production, 178*, 903–916. https://doi.org/10.1016/j.jclepro.2017.12.198
16. Broccardo, L., Vola, P., Zicari, A., & Alshibani, S. M. (2023). Contingency-based analysis of the drivers and obstacles to a successful sustainable business model: Seeking the uncaptured value. *Technological Forecasting and Social Change, 191*, 122513. https://doi.org/10.1016/j.techfore.2023.122513
17. Elzen, B., & Wieczorek, A. (2005). Introduction: transitions towards sustainability through system innovation. *Technological Forecasting and Social Change, 72*, 651e661. https://doi.org/10.1016/j.techfore.2005.04.002

18. Deyanova, K., Brehmer, N., Lapidus, A., Tiberius, V., & Walsh, S. (2022). Hatching start-ups for sustainable growth: a bibliometric review on business incubators. *Review of Managerial Science, 16*(7), 2083–2109. https://doi.org/10.1007/s11846-022-00525-9
19. Joyce, A., & Paquin, R. L. (2016). The triple layered business model canvas: A tool to design more sustainable business models. *Journal of Cleaner Production, 135*, 1474–1486. https://doi.org/10.1016/j.jclepro.2016.06.067
20. Bocken, N. M. (2015). Sustainable venture capital–catalyst for sustainable start-up success? *Journal of Cleaner Production, 108*, 647–658. https://doi.org/10.1016/j.jclepro.2015.05.079
21. Auzepy, A., Bannier, C. E., & Gärtner, F. (2024). *Looking beyond ESG preferences: The role of sustainable finance literacy in sustainable investing*. Center for Financial Studies Working Paper, (719). https://doi.org/10.2139/ssrn.4773211
22. Boar-Boar, A., & Oliveras-Villanueva, M. (2019). Systematic literature review: Sustainability practices in start-ups. *European Accounting and Management Review, 6*(1), 53–80. https://ssrn.com/abstract=3486127
23. Parrish, B. D. (2010). Sustainability-driven entrepreneurship: Principles of organization design. *Journal of Business Venturing, 25*(5), 510–523. https://doi.org/10.1016/j.jbusvent.2009.05.005
24. Trautwein, C. (2021). Sustainability impact assessment of start-ups–Key insights on relevant assessment challenges and approaches based on an inclusive, systematic literature review. *Journal of Cleaner Production, 281*, 125330. https://doi.org/10.1016/j.jclepro.2020.125330
25. Comin, L. C., Aguiar, C. C., Sehnem, S., Yusliza, M. Y., Cazella, C. F., & Julkovski, D. J. (2020). Sustainable business models: a literature review. *Benchmarking: An International Journal, 27*(7), 2028–2047. https://doi.org/10.1108/BIJ-12-2018-0384
26. Hörisch, J., Freeman, R. E., & Schaltegger, S. (2014). Applying stakeholder theory in sustainability management: Links, similarities, dissimilarities, and a conceptual framework. *Organization & Environment, 27*(4), 328–346. https://doi.org/10.1177/1086026614535786
27. Lüdeke-Freund, F., Froese, T., Dembek, K., Rosati, F., & Massa, L. (2024). What makes a business model sustainable? Activities, design themes, and value functions. *Organization & Environment, 37*, 194. https://doi.org/10.1177/10860266241235212
28. Fichter, K., Lüdeke-Freund, F., Schaltegger, S., & Schillebeeckx, S. J. (2023). Sustainability impact assessment of new ventures: An emerging field of research. *Journal of Cleaner Production, 384*, 135452. https://doi.org/10.1016/j.jclepro.2022.135452
29. FAO - Food and Agriculture Organization of the United Nations. (2020). State of the World's Forests 2020. Retrieved from https://www.fao.org/state-of-forests/en/
30. TEEB - The Economics of Ecosystems and Biodiversity. (2010). The economics of ecosystems and biodiversity: Mainstreaming the economics of nature: A synthesis of the approach, conclusions and recommendations of TEEB. Retrieved from https://teebweb.org/publications/teeb-for/synthesis/
31. Startup Italia. (2021). Top 100 startups to watch. Retrieved from https://startupitalia.eu/startup/top-100-le-migliori-startup-del-2021-chi-sono-e-come-crescono/
32. Il Sole 24 Ore & Statista. (2023). *Leader della crescita 2023* (5th ed.). Retrieved from https://lab24.ilsole24ore.com/leader-crescita/2023
33. Barratt, M., Choi, T. Y., & Li, M. (2011). Qualitative case studies in operations management: Trends, research outcomes, and future research implications. *Journal of Operations Management, 29*(4), 329–342. https://doi.org/10.1016/j.jom.2010.06.002
34. DiVito, L., & Ingen-Housz, Z. (2021). From individual sustainability orientations to collective sustainability innovation and sustainable entrepreneurial ecosystems. *Small Business Economics, 56*(3), 1057–1072.
35. Crossley, R. M., Elmagrhi, M. H., & Ntim, C. G. (2021). Sustainability and legitimacy theory: The case of sustainable social and environmental practices of small and medium-sized enterprises. *Business Strategy and the Environment, 30*(8), 3740–3762.
36. Eisenhardt, K. M. (1989). Building theories from case study research. *Academy of Management Review, 14*(4), 532–550.
37. Yin, R. K. (2018). *Case study research: Design and methods* (6th ed.). SAGE Publications. Available at: www.books.google.co.uk/books?id=OgyqBAAAQBAJ

38. Ketokivi, M., & Choi, T. (2014). Renaissance of case research as a scientific method. *Journal of Operations Management, 32*(5), 232–240. https://doi.org/10.1016/j.jom.2014.03.004
39. Bowen, G. A. (2009). Document analysis as a qualitative research method. *Qualitative Research Journal, 9*(2), 27–40. https://doi.org/10.3316/QRJ0902027
40. Tranfield, D., Denyer, D., & Smart, P. (2003). Towards a methodology for developing evidence-informed management knowledge by means of systematic review. *British Journal of Management, 14*(3), 207–222. https://doi.org/10.1111/1467-8551.00375
41. Di Vaio, A., Hasan, S., Palladino, R., & Hassan, R. (2023). The transition towards circular economy and waste within accounting and accountability models: A systematic literature review and conceptual framework. *Environment, Development and Sustainability, 25*(1), 734–810.
42. Di Lauro, S., Tursunbayeva, A., & Antonelli, G. (2019). How nonprofit organizations use social media for fundraising: A systematic literature review. *International Journal of Business and Management, 14*(7), 1. https://doi.org/10.5539/ijbm.v14n7p1
43. Humphries, S., Holmes, T., de Andrade, D. F. C., McGrath, D., & Dantas, J. B. (2020). Searching for win-win forest outcomes: Learning-by-doing, financial viability, and income growth for a community-based forest management cooperative in the Brazilian Amazon. *World Development, 125*, 104336.
44. Horne, J., & Fichter, K. (2022). Growing for sustainability: Enablers for the growth of impact startups–A conceptual framework, taxonomy, and systematic literature review. *Journal of Cleaner Production, 349*, 131163. https://doi.org/10.1016/j.jclepro.2022.131163

Systematic Review and Organizational Insight: Navigating Digital Healthcare and Environmental Sustainability

Antonio Lorena, Ludovica Zoccali, Alessia Talarico, and Rocco Reina

Abstract This study examines the intersection of digital healthcare innovations and environmental sustainability within the framework of Institutional Theory. It systematically reviews literature to identify how healthcare organizations adapt to and integrate digital technologies and sustainable practices under institutional pressures. This research employs a comprehensive systematic review methodology, synthesizing findings from a broad range of studies to offer a nuanced understanding of the challenges and opportunities at this nexus. The core objective is to uncover the dynamics between technological advancements and environmental strategies within healthcare systems, highlighting the roles of institutional pressures and organizational responses. Our analysis delves into several key areas, including the adoption of electronic health records (EHRs), telemedicine, and the Internet of Medical Things (IoMT), all within the context of striving for environmental sustainability. Results indicate a significant trend towards digitalization, driven by both the pursuit of enhanced patient care and the need to meet increasingly stringent environmental standards. However, the transition poses unique challenges, such as ensuring data security, managing the environmental footprint of digital solutions, and aligning with complex regulatory frameworks. This study contributes to the literature by providing evidence-based insights and strategic recommendations for integrating digital health solutions with environmental sustainability efforts. It underscores the importance of institutional alignment and adaptive strategies in achieving these integrations, suggesting that future policy directions and organizational practices should consider these dual objectives to enhance the overall effectiveness and sustainability of healthcare delivery.

Keywords Digital healthcare · Environmental sustainability · Institutional theory

A. Lorena (✉) · L. Zoccali · A. Talarico · R. Reina
Magna Græcia University of Catanzaro, Germaneto, CZ, Italy
e-mail: a.lorena@unicz.it; ludo.zoccali@gmail.com; alessiatalarico@hotmail.it; rreina@unicz.it

M. Cipriano et al. (eds.), *Technologies for Organizations and Society*,
Lecture Notes in Information Systems and Organisation 80,
https://doi.org/10.1007/978-3-032-01697-3_10

1 Introduction

As healthcare continues to evolve, the integration of digital technologies has emerged as a transformative force, reshaping service delivery and enhancing patient care efficiency. Innovations such as electronic health 8records (EHRs), telemedicine, and mobile health (mHealth) applications are pivotal, bringing substantial improvements in patient outcomes and operational efficiencies [1, 2]. This evolution is part of a broader trend marked by the fourth and emerging fifth industrial revolutions, characterized by their emphasis on human-centricity and intelligent automation. These revolutions integrate cutting-edge technologies to enhance healthcare delivery, focusing on environmental sustainability and empowering human workers [3, 4]. Employing Institutional Theory, this research explores the convergence of digital health technologies and environmental sustainability within healthcare systems. The main objective is to identify the opportunities and challenges associated with integrating digital technologies and to provide evidence-based recommendations for enhancing environmental sustainability in healthcare organizations [5, 6]. This study focuses on how healthcare organizations respond to institutional pressures—including regulatory requirements, market demands, and normative expectations—and leverage digital innovation to achieve specific environmental sustainability goals [7, 8]. Institutional Theory offers a robust framework for examining the complexities involved in adopting sustainable digital practices. Meyer and Rowan [9] introduced the concept of institutionalized organizations, illustrating how organizations adopt structured practices that reflect institutional rules rather than the demands of their work activities. Di Maggio and Powell [10] further elaborated on this concept by discussing institutional isomorphism, which highlights how organizations become homogeneous over time through coercive, mimetic, and normative pressures. This framework is instrumental in analyzing the adoption of digital technologies in healthcare, emphasizing the influence of institutional forces in shaping organizational practices and strategies. A key aspect of this study is understanding how the transition from traditional to digital healthcare delivery is influenced by institutional demands for environmental sustainability. This involves examining how organizational choices impact this transition and how healthcare systems can integrate digital innovations while adhering to sustainability goals [2, 11]. The methodological framework of this study is anchored in a systematic review, rigorously examining the intersecting domains of digital healthcare and environmental sustainability. This research is guided by precisely defined keywords: 'Institutional Theory', 'Digital Healthcare', and 'Environmental Sustainability'. The choice of Institutional Theory as a guiding framework allows for a focused exploration of how institutional pressures shape the adoption and implementation of sustainable digital technologies in healthcare settings. This structured approach enables us to synthesize findings from a broad spectrum of literature, identifying gaps and drawing connections that are not immediately apparent, providing a deep and nuanced understanding of how digital advancements and sustainability challenges are being addressed within healthcare systems [12, 13]. By systematically examining the dynamics at the intersection of institutional pressures and technological advancements, this study aims to uncover critical insights that could drive future policy and organizational strategies aimed at sustainable healthcare delivery. The methodology, known for its comprehensiveness and analytical rigor, positions us to offer robust, evidence-based recommendations and strategic insights that help healthcare systems navigate the complex interplay between technological innovation and institutional frameworks, enhancing the capability to meet environmental sustainability goals effectively [14–17].

2 Methodology

This study employs a systematic literature review methodology [13] to thoroughly explore the integration of digital health technologies and environmental sustainability within healthcare systems, with a focus on Institutional Theory as the guiding framework. Celebrated for its comprehensiveness and rigor, this methodological approach enables us to critically synthesize existing research findings and identify gaps in the literature, thus providing a nuanced understanding of the subject matter [12].

2.1 Research Strategy

We conducted an exhaustive search across several prominent databases including PubMed, Scopus, Web of Science, and Google Scholar. The search strategy was carefully designed to encompass a broad spectrum of relevant literature using a combination of refined keywords and Boolean operators. The revised terms used were "Digital Health*", "Environmental Sustainability", and "Institutional Theory". This adjustment ensures that our review captures studies that specifically address the interplay between digital health innovations and sustainability practices through the lens of institutional dynamics. Below, we detail how each keyword combination aligns with the objectives of our project:

1. "Digital Health*" and "Environmental Sustainability": This combination specifically targets literature that explores how digital healthcare technologies contribute to environmental sustainability. It focuses on identifying studies that address the environmental impacts or strategies of digital healthcare, helping to uncover how technological advancements can directly contribute to environmental conservation efforts.
2. "Digital Health*" "Environmental Sustainability" and "Institutional Theory": Incorporating "Institutional Theory" into this combination allows us to delve deeper into understanding how institutional frameworks influence or facilitate the integration of environmental sustainability within digital healthcare settings. This

approach is particularly relevant to our study as it bridges theoretical frameworks with practical implementations in the healthcare sector, offering insights into both the structural and operational aspects of sustainability.

3. "Digital Health*" and "Institutional Theory": This keyword combination explores how institutional forces shape the adoption and implementation of digital technologies in healthcare settings. Analyzing this intersection provides insights into the organizational and regulatory challenges and opportunities that influence digital transformation in healthcare. By focusing on "Institutional Theory," we gain a deeper understanding of how governance, norms, and organizational cultures impact the strategic decisions and operational practices associated with digital healthcare innovations. This combination highlights the role of institutional pressures in fostering or hindering the adoption of digital technologies, thus offering a more nuanced perspective on the organizational dynamics at play.

This structured approach enables us to systematically explore the complex dynamics among digitalization, environmental sustainability, and institutional frameworks in the healthcare sector. Utilizing these specific combinations ensures exhaustive coverage of the research field, maximizing the likelihood of capturing pertinent works that provide insights into how these areas intersect and influence each other. This meticulous selection of keyword combinations is essential for conducting a comprehensive and in-depth systematic review. By investing time and resources in analyzing these intersections, we are better positioned to generate evidence-based recommendations for policy and organizational strategy formulation in the healthcare sector. This systematic and well-structured research approach aligns with the expectations for an ambitious and rigorous project like ours, ensuring that we address the multifaceted challenges and opportunities presented by digital health technologies and environmental sustainability within an institutional context.

2.2 Inclusion and Exclusion Criteria

Inclusion and exclusion criteria were meticulously defined to ensure the relevance and academic rigor of the literature included in our review. We exclusively focused on peer-reviewed scientific articles published in English that provide empirical data or substantial theoretical analysis pertinent to the integration of digital health technologies and environmental sustainability within healthcare systems, guided by Institutional Theory. This selective focus allows us to concentrate our analysis on high-quality research that specifically explores the interaction of these areas under institutional pressures. Non-peer-reviewed works, conference abstracts, and articles that solely focus on digital health or environmental sustainability without examining their integration within an institutional framework were excluded. This stringent criterion reinforces our commitment to academic validity and maintains the specific scope of our analysis [18].

2.3 Data Extraction and Synthesis

Upon identifying relevant articles through our systematic search strategy, we embarked on a meticulous process of data extraction and synthesis. Initially, key information was extracted from each article, including the study's objectives, theoretical frameworks, methodologies, main findings, and implications for practice and policy. This foundational step allowed us to systematically analyze the literature, appreciating both the depth and breadth of each study while assessing its direct relevance to the overarching themes of our research. To further refine our literature pool and ensure maximum relevance to our study's research question, we conducted a rigorous content analysis. This involved a detailed review of the manuscripts to ascertain their alignment with the core topics of digital healthcare, environmental sustainability, and institutional dynamics within healthcare systems. Through this process, we methodically excluded articles that did not directly contribute to addressing our research question, thereby sharpening the focus and enhancing the quality of our review. This stage of content analysis was crucial in ensuring that all studies included in the final analysis were directly linked to the thematic exploration of integrating digital health technologies with sustainability practices within an institutional context. Following the content analysis, we conducted thematic synthesis to categorize the findings into coherent themes. This synthesis was both analytical and aggregative, designed to identify prevalent themes, methodologies, and outcomes across the studies. The themes were meticulously developed to reflect the critical aspects of integrating digital health with sustainability practices within an institutional framework, allowing us to comprehensively map the research landscape in this area. This process highlighted both convergences and divergences among the studies examined. Through the interconnected processes of data extraction, content analysis, and thematic synthesis, we developed a nuanced understanding of the current state of research. This methodology not only spotlighted the existing knowledge but also uncovered gaps and areas ripe for further exploration. Ultimately, our systematic review provides a robust platform for drawing insightful conclusions and implications for practice and policy in the realm of sustainable digital healthcare. This structured approach ensures the credibility and relevance of our findings, offering significant contributions to the academic discourse on digital healthcare and environmental sustainability, viewed through an institutional lens.

2.4 Quality Assessment

To assess the quality of studies included in our review, we utilized the Critical Appraisal Skills Programme (CASP) checklist [19]. This appraisal involved scrutinizing each study's objectives, methodological rigor, reliability of findings, and the overall significance of the conclusions drawn. The incorporation of the CASP checklist into our review process ensured that our analysis was built on research with the highest levels of credibility and relevance.

This evaluation was performed after the initial selection of studies, which was based on an analysis of titles, keywords, and abstracts. This sequence ensured that only methodologically sound and pertinent studies formed the foundation of our review. Our methodology underscores a structured approach to investigating how digital health initiatives align with environmental sustainability goals within an institutional framework. By methodically reviewing the literature, we aim to provide a comprehensive overview of the current research landscape, highlighting best practices, pinpointing challenges, and proposing future research directions. Our methodological framework is designed for transparency and replicability, offering a robust basis for ongoing investigations into this critical intersection in healthcare research.

3 Descriptive Analysis

The analysis of selected literature illuminates the confluence of digital healthcare, environmental sustainability, and institutional theory. Our meticulous methodology, as detailed in Table 1, distills an extensive body of research into 97 high-quality articles, establishing a solid foundation for our thematic exploration. This process entailed a rigorous application of inclusion and exclusion criteria, data extraction, synthesis, and quality assessment conducted across major academic databases—Google Scholar, Web of Science, PubMed, and Scopus. The search strategy was carefully designed to leverage each database's unique capabilities, ensuring the comprehensive retrieval of relevant, recent, and peer-reviewed literature up to April 2024. This methodological rigor facilitates a detailed mapping of the scholarly landscape, enhancing our understanding of how digital healthcare innovations are integrated within an institutional framework. This structured approach ensures that our findings provide insightful contributions to the fields of healthcare technology and sustainability.

Table 2 displays the distribution of studies across various databases using selected keywords related to digital healthcare, environmental sustainability, and institutional theory. Our comprehensive data collection, totaling 1365 results, highlights the varied focus of different academic databases. Scholar yielded the highest number of results (678), followed by Web of Science (290), PubMed (211), and Scopus (186). The keyword combinations explored included "Digital Health* and Environmental Sustainability", "Digital Health* and Institutional Theory" and "Digital Health* and Environmental Sustainability and Institutional Theory" providing insights into the specific intersection of these themes.

To ensure the accuracy and integrity of our analysis, a systematic method was employed to identify and eliminate duplicate entries. We utilized an Excel spreadsheet to organize articles by author, year, and title, facilitating the visual identification of duplicates. By overlaying entries from various databases, we

Table 1 Database search options

Database	Search options
Google Scholar	Search: anywhere in the article Data range: all years to April 2024 Document type: article Language: English
Web of Science	Search: topic Document type: article Citation databases: all Data range: all years to April 2024 Language: English
PubMed	Search: full text, abstract and free full text Language: English Other: excluded preprints Species: Human Data range: all years to April 2024
Scopus	Search: article title, abstract, keywords Data range: all years to April 2024 Language: English Document type: Article

Table 2 Distribution of studies by database and keywords

Keywords	Scholar	Web of Science	PubMed	Scopus	Total results
Digital Health*, Environmental Sustainability	607	136	31	122	
Digital Health*, Environmental Sustainability, Institutional Theory	7	3	6	8	
Digital Health*, Institutional Theory	64	151	174	56	
Total results for Database	678	290	211	186	1365

were able to detect and remove any duplicates, ensuring that each study was represented uniquely in our dataset. This rigorous approach to data management mitigated the issue of overlapping sources and maintained the precision of the research findings presented in Table 2. The application of inclusion and exclusion criteria filtered the initial pool to focus on peer-reviewed articles that provided empirical data or substantial theoretical analysis pertinent to the integration of digital health and environmental sustainability. A meticulous data extraction and synthesis process followed, with key information such as objectives, theoretical frameworks, methodologies, findings, and implications systematically recorded. A rigorous content analysis ensured the studies were directly relevant to our research question, refining our selection further.

Finally, a quality assessment using the CASP checklist assessed the methodological rigor and reliability of the remaining studies. This rigorous approach refined our selection from 1365 articles to 97 high-quality studies, offering valuable insights into the integration of digital healthcare and sustainability within institutional

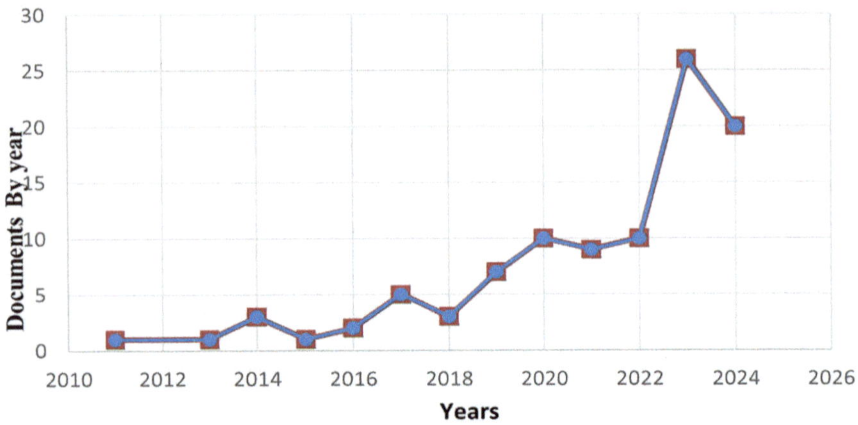

Fig. 1 Trends in Research Publication from 2011 to 2024

contexts. This methodological rigor underscores the robustness of our research and supports the foundational elements of our analysis (Fig. 1).

Figure 1 above, illustrates the annual number of studies published over the period from 2010 to 2024. The data exhibit a gradual increase in the volume of research publications starting from 2011, with minor fluctuations observed in the initial years. A significant upward trend begins around 2016 and continues through 2023, which is marked as the year with the highest number of publications. The apparent decline observed in 2024 is not indicative of a decrease in interest or output but rather reflects partial data for the year, only accounting for publications up to April. This suggests that the total publications for 2024 might exceed those of 2023 once full-year data are available, reinforcing the notion that the field is attracting increasing interest. This analysis underscores the continued growth and relevance of this research area, highlighting its expanding footprint in academic literature (Fig. 2).

The bar graph in Fig. 2 below, provides a comparative overview of the number of research documents produced by various countries, clearly illustrating global disparities in research output. The United States leads, followed by other developed nations such as the United Kingdom, China, Italy, France, Germany, and Australia. In contrast, countries like Saudi Arabia, Turkey, India, Malaysia, and Pakistan show lower publication numbers. The "Others" category at the end of the graph represents a collection of countries that each contributed one or two studies. This grouping was made to streamline the presentation and maximize clarity, covering a range of smaller or less research-intensive nations. This visual distribution highlights the varied research landscapes across different regions, reflecting a broad spectrum of outputs that contribute to the global research community. This varied distribution of Global Distribution of Research Publications by Country sets the stage for a deeper exploration of the thematic trends and strategic focuses highlighted in Tables 3, 4, and 5 below. In these latter tables, we engage in a systematic synthesis of

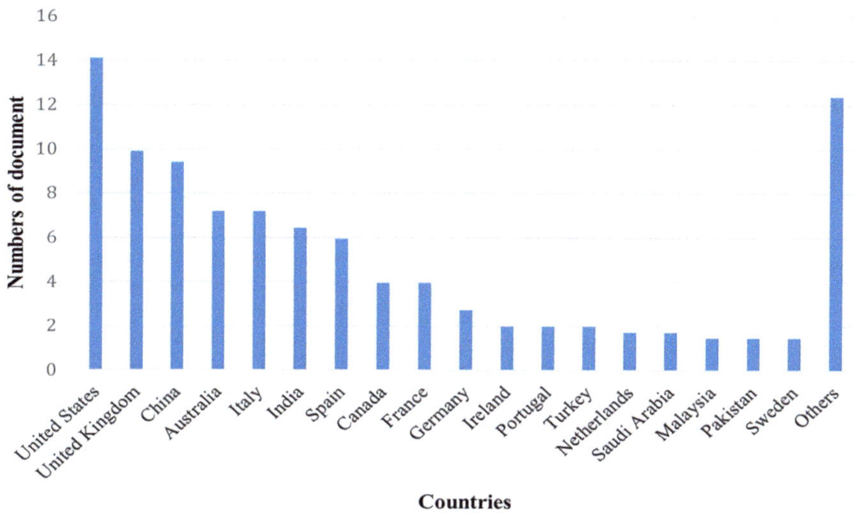

Fig. 2 Global distribution of research publications by country

key themes, which emerges from a comprehensive content analysis of selected scholarly papers. This approach ensures that each keyword and associated concept is deeply rooted in the literature, reflecting critical areas of study that include technological innovations in healthcare, strategies for ecological preservation, and adaptive practices within institutional frameworks [31, 67, 79, 98].

Each keyword was meticulously selected based on its frequency in the literature and its crucial role in framing the discourse within these areas. This method was uniformly applied to all tables to guarantee consistency and to demonstrate the strategic focus of our review, clearly linking the keywords to the thematic content they represent.

Table 3 outlines pivotal digital technologies transforming healthcare delivery. It highlights key technologies such as EHR, Telemedicine, mHealth, and the Internet of Medical Things (IoMT), which are essential for modernizing healthcare. This table not only discusses the implementation of these technologies—like EHR systems, telemedicine services, and mHealth apps—but also emphasizes forward-looking innovations such as predictive analytics and AI-driven chatbots, showcasing their potential to revolutionize healthcare practices.

Table 4 focuses on the environmental strategies integrated within healthcare practices. It stresses keywords such as Green IT Solutions, Life Cycle Assessment (LCA), and Carbon Footprint Reduction, each selected for their role in minimizing the environmental impacts of healthcare operations. The interventions, including green IT deployments and the adoption of renewable energy sources, are derived from best practices and case studies, illustrating active efforts toward environmental sustainability. The table also features innovative elements like smart grids and

Table 3 Digitalization in Healthcare

Category	Details	Authors
Keyword	• EHR, Telemedicine, mHealth, IoMT, Artificial Intelligence (AI), Big Data Analytics, Blockchain Wearable Devices, Virtual Health Clinics (VHC), Telehealth, Health Information Systems (HIS)	Menachemi and Collum [20]; Kourou et al. [21]; Piwek et al. [22]; Bashi et al. [23]; Jiang et al. [24]; Sardi et al. [25]; Conte et al. [26]; Gamache et al. [27]; Agbo et al. [28]; de Los Reyes [29]; Nadarzynski et al. [30]; Oftedal et al. [31]; Greenhalgh et al. [32]; Moro Visconti and Morea [33]; Smith et al. [34]; Webster [35]; Canfell et al. [16]; Kamarudin et al. [36]; Pley et al. [37]; Brown et al. [38]; Alfieri et al. [39]; Nair et al. [40]; Caelli et al. [15]; Godinho et al. [41]; Lehoux et al. [42]; Mezei et al. [43]; Ndejjo et al. [44]; Oo et al. [45]; Thomas et al. [46]; Tsagkaris et al. [47]; Vărzaru et al. [48]; Ansari et al. [49]; Chen et al. [50]; Eckelman et al. [51]; Ijiga et al. [52]; Mani et al. [53]; Skogman–Lindqvist et al.[54].
Interventions	• Implementation of EHR Systems: Transitioning from paper-based records to electronic systems to enhance data accuracy, accessibility, and patient care; • Telemedicine Services: Providing remote consultation, diagnosis, and treatment via digital platforms, reducing the need for in-person visits; • mHealth Apps: Developing applications for health monitoring, patient engagement, and chronic disease management; • IoMT Integration: Utilizing interconnected devices to monitor patient health in real-time, improving responsiveness and care; • AI in Diagnostics: Employing machine learning algorithms to enhance diagnostic accuracy and predict patient outcomes; • Blockchain for Data Security: Implementing blockchain technology to ensure the security and integrity of patient data; • Wearable Health Monitors: Using devices to track vital signs and health metrics continuously; • Virtual Consultations: Establishing virtual clinics to facilitate access to healthcare specialists remotely; • Telehealth Platforms: Expanding the scope of healthcare services available through digital means, including mental health support;	

(continued)

Table 3 (continued)

Category	Details	Authors
Innovative elements	• Predictive Analytics: Leveraging big data to forecast health trends and personalize patient care; • AI-driven Chatbots: Using AI to provide immediate health advice and triage patients; • Remote Patient Monitoring: Continuous monitoring of patient health data to enable proactive interventions; • Digital Therapeutics: Developing software-based interventions for disease management and treatment; • Robotic Process Automation (RPA): Automating routine administrative tasks to increase efficiency; • Interoperable Systems: Ensuring that different health information systems can communicate and share data seamlessly;	

green building designs, highlighting ongoing initiatives to foster environmental stewardship.

Table 5 explores the application of institutional theory within healthcare, examining how organizations adapt to and integrate regulatory, mimetic, and normative pressures. Keywords like Institutional Isomorphism and Regulatory Compliance underscore adaptation strategies that align organizational practices with broader institutional norms. This table further investigates strategic interventions such as policy development and leadership adaptation, essential for maintaining legitimacy and achieving strategic conformity under institutional pressures. This comprehensive overview links the technological, environmental, and theoretical frameworks guiding contemporary healthcare. It offers a detailed examination of the interconnectedness of interventions and innovations across these domains, providing a robust framework for understanding the complex interplay that defines modern healthcare systems. The objective is to provide readers with a nuanced perspective on how integrated efforts in digital innovation, sustainability practices, and institutional adherence are crucial for advancing effective healthcare policies and practices.

Table 4 Environmental Sustainability

Category	Details	Authors
Keyword	• Green IT Solutions, Life Cycle Assessment (LCA), Carbon Footprint Reduction Renewable Energy, Sustainable Healthcare Practices, Energy-efficient Technologies	McGain and Naylor [55]; Moore and Hawarden [56]; Virgolino et al. [57]; Ye [58]; Münzel et al. [59]; Chute et al. [60]; Lokmic–Tomkins et al. [61]; Saisó et al. [62]; Samuel and Lucassen [2]; Vărzaru et al. [48]; Agnello et al. [63]; Berniak-Woźny and Rataj [64]; Hameed and Hameed [65]; Lapão et al. [66]; Li et al. [67]; Rayan et al. [68]; Sun et al. [69]; Almasri et al. [70]; Bevere and Faccilongo [71]; Mountford and Geiger [72]; Rowan [73]; Sepetis et al. [74]; Tarpani and Gallego-Schmid [75].
Interventions	• Implementing Green IT Solutions: Adopting energy-efficient technologies and practices to reduce the environmental impact of healthcare IT systems; • Conducting Life Cycle Assessments: Evaluating the environmental impact of healthcare products and services from production to disposal; • Reducing Carbon Footprint: Initiatives to lower greenhouse gas emissions from healthcare facilities and operations; • Utilizing Renewable Energy Sources: Transitioning to solar, wind, and other renewable energy sources to power healthcare facilities; • Promoting Sustainable Practices: Encouraging the use of reusable materials, recycling programs, and eco-friendly products; • Optimizing Energy Use: Implementing energy-efficient lighting, heating, and cooling systems;	
Innovative elements	• Green Building Designs: Constructing healthcare facilities with sustainable materials and energy-efficient designs; • Eco-friendly Innovations: Deployment of environmentally friendly innovations that reduce the environmental impact of healthcare delivery; • Smart Grids: Integrating smart grid technologies to manage energy use more efficiently; • Sustainable Transportation: Promoting the use of electric vehicles and public transport for healthcare logistics; • Telemedicine for Sustainability: Reducing travel-related emissions by providing remote healthcare services; • Digital Health Technologies: Utilizing digital health solutions to minimize physical resource consumption and waste.	

Table 5 Institutional theory

Category	Details	Authors
Keyword	• Institutional Isomorphism, Regulatory Compliance, Mimetic Adoption, Normative Alignment	Liverani et al. [76]; Huang et al. [77]; Wallin and Fuglsang [78]; Lennox et al. [79]; Sadoughi et al. [80]; Ahmed et al. [81]; Burton–Jones et al. [82]; Moro Visconti and Morea [33]; Heinsch et al. [83]; Münzel et al. [59]; Steinhauser [84]; Chute et al [60]; Vărzaru [85]; Alami et al. [14]; Carswell et al. [86]; Denicolai et al. [87]; Carboni et al. [88]; Chatterjee et al. [17]; Godinho et al. [41]; Konopik and Blunck [89]; Mishra and Pandey [90]; Priyadarshini et al. [91]; Mountford and Geiger [72]; Price et al. [92]; Rahat et al. [93]; Schmitt [94]; Tan et al. [95]; Tetteh et al. [96]; Tenggono et al. [97].
Interventions	• Strategic Alignment with Institutional Norms: Implements adaptive strategies that align organizational practices with broader institutional norms and values to maintain legitimacy; • Development of Institutional Policies: Crafts policies that are reflective of institutional theories, aiming to encapsulate regulatory, mimetic, and normative insights for comprehensive governance; • Adaptation to Institutional Pressures: Deploys tactical measures to navigate and mitigate external pressures, ensuring organizational resilience and strategic conformity;	
Innovative elements	• Leadership Approaches to Institutional Adaptation: Engages in leadership tactics that effectively maneuver through institutional pressures, fostering a culture of innovation and adherence to institutional frameworks; • Application of Theoretical Frameworks to Strategic Decisions: Utilizes institutional theory as a strategic lens for organizational decision-making, emphasizing the role of theoretical insights in driving sustainable change; • Engagement of Stakeholders in Shaping Institutional Practices: Facilitates comprehensive stakeholder involvement to refine institutional practices, ensuring that operations align with both internal ambitions and external expectations.	

4 Discussion, Conclusions and Future Research Directions

This section synthesizes the principal findings from our research and proposes directions for future inquiries. The ensuing discussion seeks to elucidate the complex interplay among digital health technologies, environmental sustainability, and institutional frameworks within healthcare systems. Drawing from a comprehensive review encompassed in this study, we aim to address several critical areas identified through the analysis of current literature. This discussion will articulate how digital innovations not only support but also drive sustainable practices within healthcare, all while responding to the multifaceted pressures imposed by institutional demands

[91]. Central to our discourse are four pivotal themes that emerged from the review:

1. Exploration of the convergence between digital health technologies and environmental sustainability within healthcare settings, assessing how this synergy can be harnessed to foster more sustainable healthcare environments [99].
2. Examination of the opportunities and challenges associated with integrating digital technologies, providing evidence-based recommendations that aim to enhance environmental sustainability in healthcare organizations [71].
3. Analysis of how healthcare organizations respond to institutional pressures, including regulatory requirements, market demands, and normative expectations, using digital innovation to meet specific environmental sustainability goals effectively [88, 100].
4. Consideration of the transition from traditional to digital healthcare delivery, exploring how this shift is influenced by institutional demands for environmental sustainability and what this means for the future of healthcare practices [101].

By structurally unpacking these themes, the following sections will demonstrate how our findings not only respond to but also advance the conversation on integrating digital health solutions with sustainable practices under the guidance of institutional theory. This approach provides a multifaceted view of the potential transformations within the healthcare sector, highlighting both strategic innovations and the challenges they entail.

4.1 Digital Health and Environmental Sustainability: A Synergistic Approach

In the evolving nexus between digital health technologies and environmental sustainability, advanced tools such as predictive analytics and AI-driven systems are pivotal in elevating healthcare efficiency while promoting environmentally sustainable practices. These technologies enhance diagnostic precision and patient outcomes by optimizing resource use, thus reducing unnecessary procedures and waste, crucial for sustainability in healthcare [88]. As stated by Doo et al. [102], AI applications in healthcare are transforming resource management, enabling facilities to decrease energy consumption and waste. For instance, AI algorithms capable of predicting patient admission rates can adjust energy usage dynamically, ensuring that hospital operations are environmentally sustainable [40, 41]. This integration of digital tools bridges the gap between innovative healthcare services and eco-friendly operations, setting new standards for the sector.

mHealth applications also play a critical role in enhancing patient engagement and self-management, indirectly fostering sustainability. By enabling patients to monitor their health conditions from home, these technologies minimize the need for frequent in-person visits, thereby reducing the carbon emissions associated with patient travel [33, 36, 44]. Additionally, these apps aid in large-scale data collection, which can be leveraged to optimize population health management and curtail the overall resource consumption within healthcare systems. Furthermore, several studies [95, 103, 104] highlight that telemedicine platforms extend these benefits further by facilitating virtual consultations, which conserve resources and reduce the carbon footprint associated with traditional healthcare delivery models. The adoption of telemedicine has been shown to decrease the number of physical office visits, lower vehicle emissions, and reduce the physical space requirements for healthcare facilities, contributing to a reduction in energy and material usage [23, 29, 38]. The push towards EHRs complements these sustainability efforts by eliminating the need for paper-based records, thereby reducing waste and improving the efficiency of healthcare data management. EHRs enable better coordination among healthcare providers, reduce duplicate tests and procedures, and support the effective analysis of patient data for improved clinical decision-making and resource allocation [20, 21, 53]. However, as digital health solutions are integrated with sustainability initiatives, it is imperative to address potential ethical, privacy, and security concerns diligently. Safeguarding data and managing the environmental impact of digital infrastructures are essential to maintain as healthcare systems continue to evolve [30, 91]. Overall, the amalgamation of digital health with environmental sustainability outlines a progressive approach that not only advances healthcare delivery but also mitigates significant environmental issues. By adopting such integrative strategies, healthcare systems can simultaneously promote planetary health and deliver high-quality, efficient, and accessible healthcare [47, 54]. This approach emphasizes the necessity for ongoing innovation and strict adherence to environmental and regulatory frameworks, ensuring that the healthcare sector remains at the forefront of medical excellence and environmental stewardship [69, 74, 80, 93].

4.2 Navigating the Challenges and Opportunities in Digital Healthcare Integration

Navigating the Challenges and Opportunities in Digital Healthcare Integration presents a complex landscape that healthcare systems globally must address. As noted by Münzel et al. [59], the integration of digital technologies in healthcare brings significant benefits, including improved patient outcomes and resource efficiencies. However, these advancements also pose new challenges such as data privacy concerns and the need for robust cybersecurity measures [60]. The shift towards a more digitalized healthcare environment necessitates an overarching framework that accommodates both technological advancements and the ethical considerations they entail. Furthermore, successful integration of digital health technologies requires adaptive leadership and strategic alignment with existing healthcare policies [61]. This is further supported by Saisó et al. [62], who argue for the importance of establishing equitable access to these technologies to ensure no patient demographic is disproportionately disadvantaged. Furthermore, the transition involves not just the adoption of new technologies but also the transformation of healthcare professionals' roles and patient engagement strategies. Training and continuous education of healthcare staff on new technologies become crucial [66]. This professional development is necessary to harness the full potential of innovations such as telemedicine and AI-driven diagnostics, which, as [48] suggest, can drastically alter treatment pathways and patient interaction models. Moreover, the integration of digital health solutions often requires significant investment in infrastructure, which can be a formidable barrier, especially in lower-resource settings. Nti et al. [105] highlight the financial challenges involved in upgrading systems to support digital health initiatives. Yet, the long-term sustainability of healthcare systems may hinge on overcoming these hurdles to leverage the efficiencies and enhanced care coordination that digital health promises [68]. The opportunities for improving environmental sustainability through digital healthcare are particularly compelling. Digital tools can reduce the carbon footprint of healthcare delivery by minimizing the need for physical materials and optimizing building energy use [70]. For instance, Bevere and Faccilongo [71] discuss how cloud-based technologies can decrease the energy consumption of data management and storage, offering a more sustainable alternative to traditional methods. Each of these aspects underscores the necessity of a thoughtful approach to digital healthcare integration, one that balances the promise of innovation with the practicalities of implementation and the ethical imperatives of equity and privacy. As healthcare systems evolve, they must navigate these challenges thoughtfully, ensuring that technological advancements enhance rather than impede the provision of care [87].

4.3 Institutional Pressures and Digital Innovation in Healthcare

In the context of modern healthcare, the response to institutional pressures—such as regulatory requirements, market demands, and normative expectations—is critically shaped by the strategic deployment of digital innovations. As Liverani et al. [76] and Huang et al. [77] argue, healthcare organizations face a complex landscape where conforming to regulations, satisfying market expectations, and adhering to ethical norms are paramount for sustainability and operational success. Digital technologies offer transformative potential to address these challenges effectively. According to Burton-Jones et al. [82], the implementation of advanced digital systems like EHRs and telemedicine platforms enables healthcare institutions to meet stringent regulatory standards while enhancing care delivery efficiency. These technologies facilitate real-time data monitoring and management, ensuring compliance with healthcare regulations and policies [33]. Market demands also shape how institutions adopt digital innovations. In a competitive healthcare landscape, organizations leverage technologies such as AI and big data analytics to gain strategic advantages. Heinsch et al. [83] and Steinhauser [84] highlight how these technologies not only optimize clinical outcomes but also drive patient satisfaction and retention by offering personalized and efficient healthcare services. As Carswell et al. [86] note, the integration of such innovations aligns with market trends towards personalized medicine, responding adeptly to patient needs and preferences. Furthermore, responding to normative expectations involves aligning with ethical standards and societal values. Digital tools play a crucial role here by promoting transparency and accountability. Denicolai et al. [87] and Carboni et al. [88] discuss how blockchain and secure data-sharing platforms ensure that patient data is handled ethically, fostering trust and adhering to societal expectations regarding privacy and data security. The synergy between digital technology and environmental sustainability goals is particularly noteworthy. Implementing green IT solutions and energy-efficient practices reduces the carbon footprint of healthcare facilities, aligning with global sustainability goals [41]. Moreover, as Konopik and Blunck [89] and Mishra and Pandey [90] elucidate, digital health innovations like remote patient monitoring reduce the need for physical travel, thereby decreasing environmental impacts associated with traditional healthcare delivery models. In navigating these institutional pressures, healthcare organizations not only enhance their capacity to meet regulatory and market demands but also contribute to environmental sustainability. The strategic integration of digital technologies thus serves as a dual-purpose tool that promotes operational efficiency and sustainability, illustrating a progressive approach to healthcare management [72, 81]. By addressing these multifaceted pressures through digital innovation, healthcare organizations position themselves at the forefront of sustainable practice, ready to meet the challenges of a dynamic healthcare environment while fostering a sustainable future. This adaptation and integration highlight the importance of a strategic and informed approach to institutional dynamics in healthcare [92, 94].

4.4 From Traditional to Digital: Transforming Healthcare Delivery through Institutional Demands

The transition from traditional to digital healthcare delivery, fundamentally driven by institutional demands for environmental sustainability, represents a crucial evolution in the healthcare sector. This shift not only aims to enhance healthcare delivery efficiency but also aligns with broader environmental goals, significantly reducing healthcare's ecological footprint [106]. Institutional frameworks, particularly regulatory and normative, have increasingly emphasized sustainability, compelling healthcare organizations to integrate digital technologies that offer substantial environmental benefits. As Ramírez-Saltos et al. [107] observe, regulatory mandates aimed at decreasing carbon footprints have spurred the adoption of digital systems that minimize the use of physical resources and reduce waste. Further illustrating this point, Tsagkaris et al. [108] discuss how digital health applications, by lessening the necessity for physical patient transport and diminishing reliance on paper-based systems, markedly reduce greenhouse gas emissions and lessen deforestation pressures, thereby meeting sustainability targets. The core digital tools, such as EHRs and telemedicine platforms, are pivotal not only in streamlining operations but also in achieving these environmental objectives. EHRs significantly cut down on paper use, leading to a dramatic reduction in waste and resource use, as highlighted by Verdejo Espinosa et al. [109]. Telemedicine also reduces travel-related emissions by allowing patients to receive care remotely, minimizing the environmental impacts traditionally associated with healthcare delivery [110]. Additionally, the incorporation of cutting-edge technologies like AI and big data analytics advances the sustainability agenda by optimizing resource allocation and enhancing operational efficiency. These technologies enable precision medicine approaches that are less wasteful and more targeted, thereby conserving resources across healthcare systems [111]. Mostepaniuk et al. [112] emphasize how predictive analytics can optimize energy use in healthcare facilities by dynamically adjusting energy consumption to match actual needs rather than adhering to fixed schedules. However, this shift towards digital healthcare, while beneficial, introduces new challenges, including increased energy demands primarily driven by the data centers and network infrastructures that support these digital technologies [45]. Ohalete et al. [113] underline the importance of considering the environmental costs of digitalization, which include energy consumption and electronic waste. It is crucial that digital healthcare solutions are designed and operated sustainably to truly fulfill both healthcare efficiency and environmental sustainability goals. This evolving landscape necessitates continual adaptation and innovation to ensure that healthcare delivery not only progresses in terms of technological advancements but also adheres to sustainable practices [43]. This transition exemplifies the complex interplay between digital innovations and institutional environmental demands, showcasing a strategic approach to integrate ecological considerations into the fabric of healthcare delivery. This holistic view emphasizes the necessity of a balanced integration where technological advancements and environmental sustainability are pursued concurrently, guiding healthcare towards a more sustainable future.

4.5 Conclusions and Future Research Directions

This study provides an in-depth analysis and synthesis of existing research at the intersection of digital health technologies, environmental sustainability, and institutional theory within healthcare systems. By examining these interlinked areas, the research highlights significant opportunities and challenges that have critical implications for various stakeholders including patients, healthcare providers, policymakers, and medical and paramedical staff [114]. For patients, the integration of digital health technologies such as EHRs, telemedicine, and mHealth applications promises more accessible, efficient, and tailored healthcare services. These technologies reduce the need for physical visits, which is particularly beneficial for patients in remote or underserved areas, thereby improving healthcare equity.

Healthcare providers and medical staff can leverage these digital tools to enhance diagnostic accuracy, streamline administrative processes, and improve patient engagement and outcomes. However, the transition requires careful consideration of the digital divide and the training needs of healthcare professionals to ensure smooth implementation and adoption. Policymakers and government officials must consider the regulatory frameworks that support the adoption of these technologies while ensuring they align with environmental sustainability goals. This involves crafting policies that incentivize the adoption of green technologies in healthcare and rigorously assessing the environmental impact of new digital health solutions. In terms of scholarly implications, this study furnishes a comprehensive state-of-the-art framework that can serve as a foundation for future research. Future studies should explore the quantifiable benefits and drawbacks of digital health solutions in reducing the carbon footprint of healthcare operations, focusing on life-cycle assessments of these technologies to understand their full environmental impacts.

Nevertheless, this study is not without limitations. The rapidly evolving nature of digital technologies and environmental standards means that continuous updating of data and strategies is necessary to keep abreast of new developments and their implications. Future research should also delve into the socioeconomic dynamics that influence the adoption of these technologies. Studies could examine how different demographic groups adapt to and benefit from digital health innovations and identify barriers to their wider acceptance. Additionally, more research is needed to explore how digital health can be scaled sustainably without exacerbating existing healthcare disparities. Overall, this study underscores the need for a holistic approach to integrate digital health with environmental and institutional objectives, ensuring that the advancement of healthcare systems contributes positively to both health outcomes and sustainability goals [75, 85]. This comprehensive approach will ensure that healthcare delivery evolves to meet the demands of modern society while adhering to global sustainability standards.

Disclosure of Interests The authors have no competing interests to declare that are relevant to the content of this article.

References

1. Rehman, A., & Farrakh, A. (2022). A systematic review: Towards a smarter approach to healthcare 5.0. *International Journal of Advanced Sciences and Computing, 1*(2), 28–37.
2. Samuel, G., & Lucassen, A. M. (2022). The environmental sustainability of data-driven health research: A scoping review. *Digital Health, 8*, 20552076221111297.
3. Sharifi, A., Khavarian-Garmsir, A. R., & Kummitha, R. K. R. (2021). Contributions of smart city solutions and technologies to resilience against the COVID-19 pandemic: A literature review. *Sustainability, 13*(14), 8018.

4. Venkataraman, A., Fatma, N., Edirippulige, S., & Ramamohan, V. (2024). Facilitators and barriers for telemedicine systems in India from multiple stakeholder perspectives and settings: A systematic review. *Telemedicine and e-Health, 30*, 1341.
5. Hermes, S., Riasanow, T., Clemons, E. K., Böhm, M., & Krcmar, H. (2020). The digital transformation of the healthcare industry: Exploring the rise of emerging platform ecosystems and their influence on the role of patients. *Business Research, 13*(3), 1033–1069.
6. Wang, X., Li, C., Chen, Y., Zheng, C., Zhang, F., Huang, Y., & Birch, S. (2022). Relationships between job satisfaction, organizational commitment, burnout and job performance of healthcare professionals in a district-level health care system of Shenzhen, China. *Frontiers in Psychology, 13*, 992258.
7. Zengin, Ş., & Yontar, E. (2022). Reflections of digital transformation in the health sector in the Covid 19 Pandemic with the effect of Industry 4.0. *Tarsus Üniversitesi İktisadi ve İdari Bilimler Fakültesi Dergisi, 3*(2), 136–152.
8. Zhang, G., Chen, Y., Zhou, W., Chen, C., & Liu, Y. (2023). Bioenergy-based closed-loop medical systems for the integration of treatment, monitoring, and feedback. *Small Science, 3*(10), 2300043.
9. Meyer, J. W., & Rowan, B. (1977). Institutionalized organizations: Formal structure as myth and ceremony. *American Journal of Sociology, 83*(2), 340–363.
10. DiMaggio, P. J., & Powell, W. W. (1983). The iron cage revisited: Institutional isomorphism and collective rationality in organizational fields. *American Sociological Review, 48*(2), 147–160.
11. Mubarak, F. S. (2023). Sustainable healthcare to provide quality care in the surgical industry in the United Kingdom. *Cureus, 15*(4).
12. Higgins, J. P. T., & Green, S. (2011). *Cochrane handbook for systematic reviews of interventions (Version 5.1.0)*. The Cochrane Collaboration. Available from www.handbook.cochrane.org
13. Tranfield, D., Denyer, D., & Smart, P. (2003). Towards a methodology for developing evidence-informed management knowledge by means of systematic review. *British Journal of Management, 14*(3), 207–222.
14. Alami, H., Rivard, L., Lehoux, P., Ag Ahmed, M. A., Fortin, J. P., & Fleet, R. (2023). Integrating environmental considerations in digital health technology assessment and procurement: Stakeholders' perspectives. *Digital Health, 9*, 20552076231219113.
15. Caelli, C., Tamburrino, F., Brondi, C., Razionale, A. V., Ballarino, A., & Barone, S. (2023). Sustainability in healthcare sector: The dental aligners case. *Sustainability, 15*(24), 16757.
16. Canfell, O. J., Littlewood, R., Burton-Jones, A., & Sullivan, C. (2021). Digital health and precision prevention: Shifting from disease-centred care to consumer-centred health. *Australian Health Review, 46*(3), 279–283.
17. Chatterjee, S., Chaudhuri, R., Gupta, S., Mangla, S. K., & Kamble, S. (2023). Examining the influence of industry 4.0 in healthcare supply chain performance: Moderating role of environmental dynamism. *Journal of Cleaner Production, 427*, 139195.
18. Mays, D. C., & Hunt, J. R. (2005). Hydrodynamic aspects of particle clogging in porous media. *Environmental Science & Technology, 39*(2), 577–584.
19. Critical Appraisal Skills Programme: CASP qualitative checklist.
20. Menachemi, N., & Collum, T. H. (2011). Benefits and drawbacks of electronic health record systems. *Risk Management and Healthcare Policy*, 47–55.
21. Kourou, K., Exarchos, T. P., Exarchos, K. P., Karamouzis, M. V., & Fotiadis, D. I. (2015). Machine learning applications in cancer prognosis and prediction. *Computational and Structural Biotechnology Journal, 13*, 8–17.
22. Piwek, L., Ellis, D. A., Andrews, S., & Joinson, A. (2016). The rise of consumer health wearables: Promises and barriers. *PLoS Medicine, 13*(2), e1001953.
23. Bashi, N., Karunanithi, M., Fatehi, F., Ding, H., & Walters, D. (2017). Remote monitoring of patients with heart failure: An overview of systematic reviews. *Journal of Medical Internet Research, 19*(1), e18.

24. Jiang, F., Jiang, Y., Zhi, H., Dong, Y., Li, H., Ma, S., Wang, Y., Dong, Q., Shen, H., & Wang, Y. (2017). Artificial intelligence in healthcare: Past, present and future. *Stroke and Vascular Neurology, 2*(4), 230–243. https://doi.org/10.1136/svn-2017-000101
25. Sardi, L., Idri, A., & Fernández-Alemán, J. L. (2017). A systematic review of gamification in e-Health. *Journal of Biomedical Informatics, 71*, 31–48.
26. Conte, K. P., & Hawe, P. (2018). Will E-monitoring of policy and program implementation stifle or enhance practice? How would we know? *Frontiers in Public Health, 6*, 243.
27. Gamache, R., Kharrazi, H., & Weiner, J. P. (2018). Public and population health informatics: The bridging of big data to benefit communities. *Yearbook of Medical Informatics, 27*(01), 199–206.
28. Agbo, F. J., Oyelere, S. S., Suhonen, J., & Adewumi, S. (2019, November). A systematic review of computational thinking approach for programming education in higher education institutions. In *Proceedings of the 19th Koli calling international conference on computing education research* (Koli Calling'19). Association for Computing Machinery, Article 12, 1–10.
29. de Los Reyes, G., Jr. (2019). Institutional entrepreneurship for digital public health promotion: Challenges and opportunities. *Health Education & Behavior, 46*(2_suppl), 30S–36S.
30. Nadarzynski, T., Miles, O., Cowie, A., & Ridge, D. (2019). Acceptability of artificial intelligence (AI)-led chatbot services in healthcare: A mixed-methods study. *Digital health, 5*, 2055207619871808.
31. Oftedal, E. M., Foss, L., & Iakovleva, T. (2019). Responsible for responsibility? A study of digital e-health startups. *Sustainability, 11*(19), 5433.
32. Greenhalgh, T., Wherton, J., Shaw, S., & Morrison, C. (2020). Video consultations for covid-19. *BMJ, 368*, m998. https://doi.org/10.1136/bmj.m998
33. Moro Visconti, R., & Morea, D. (2020). Healthcare digitalization and pay-for-performance incentives in smart hospital project financing. *International Journal of Environmental Research and Public Health, 17*(7), 2318.
34. Smith, A. C., Thomas, E., Snoswell, C. L., Haydon, H., Mehrotra, A., Clemensen, J., & Caffery, L. J. (2020). Telehealth for global emergencies: Implications for coronavirus disease 2019 (COVID-19). *Journal of Telemedicine and Telecare, 26*(5), 309–313. https://doi.org/10.1177/1357633X20916567
35. Webster, P. (2020). Virtual health care in the era of COVID-19. *The Lancet, 395*(10231), 1180–1181. https://doi.org/10.1016/S0140-6736(20)30818-7
36. Kamarudin, S. F., Mustapha, M., & Kim, J. K. (2021). Green strategies to printed sensors for healthcare applications. *Polymer Reviews, 61*(1), 116–156.
37. Pley, C., Evans, M., Lowe, R., Montgomery, H., & Yacoub, S. (2021). Digital and technological innovation in vector-borne disease surveillance to predict, detect, and control climate-driven outbreaks. *The Lancet Planetary Health, 5*(10), e739–e745.
38. Brown, M. R., Knight, M., Peters, C. J., Maleki, S., Motavalli, A., & Nedjat-Shokouhi, B. (2023). Digital outpatient health solutions as a vehicle to improve healthcare sustainability—A United Kingdom focused policy and practice perspective. *Frontiers in Digital Health, 5*, 1242896.
39. Alfieri, F. M., da Silva Dias, C., de Oliveira, N. C., & Battistella, L. R. (2022). Gamification in musculoskeletal rehabilitation. *Current Reviews in Musculoskeletal Medicine, 15*(6), 629–636.
40. Nair, A. K., Raj, E., & Sahoo, J. (2022). An overview of artificial intelligence for advanced healthcare systems. *Digital Health Transformation with Blockchain and Artificial Intelligence*, 141–160.
41. Godinho, M. A., Ashraf, M. M., Narasimhan, P., & Liaw, S. T. (2023). Understanding the convergence of social enterprise, digital health, and citizen engagement for co-producing integrated person-centred health services: A critical review and theoretical framework. *International Journal of Medical Informatics, 178*, 105174.
42. Lehoux, P., Rocha de Oliveira, R., Rivard, L., Pacifico Silva, H., Alami, H., Mörch, C. M., & Malas, K. (2023). A comprehensive, valid, and reliable tool to assess the degree of

responsibility of digital health solutions that operate with or without artificial intelligence: 3-Phase mixed methods study. *Journal of Medical Internet Research, 25*, e48496. https://doi.org/10.2196/48496

43. Mezei, F., Horváth, K., Pálfi, M., Lovas, K., Ádám, I., & Túri, G. (2023). International practices in health technology assessment and public financing of digital health technologies: Recommendations for Hungary. *Frontiers in Public Health, 11*, 1197949.
44. Ndejjo, R., Kabwama, S. N., Namale, A., Tusubira, A. K., Wanyana, I., Kizito, S., et al. (2023). Harnessing digital technology for COVID-19 response in Uganda: Lessons and implications for future public health emergencies. *BMJ Global Health, 8*(Suppl 6), e013288.
45. Oo, K. T., Jonah, K. A. Z. O. R. A., & Thin, M. M. Z. (2023). A Systematic review of the pros and cons of digital pollution and its impact on the environment. *Journal of Sustainability and Environmental Management, 2*(1), 61–73.
46. Thomas, A. A., Yoshida, H., Keilman, A. E., Burns, B., McDade, J., Anderson, T., et al. (2023). Gamification of a low-fidelity paper doll to teach primary survey to pediatric residents. *Cureus, 15*(7), 1–4. e41996.
47. Tsagkaris, C., Nikolakea, M., Laskaratou, E. D., Samaras, C., Huang, H., Laubscher, L., & Bobirca, A. (2023). Environmental sustainability in healthcare: Time to make outpatient care in orthopaedics and rheumatology greener. *The International Journal of Health Planning and Management, 38*(3), 547–556.
48. Vărzaru, A. A., Bocean, C. G., Criveanu, M. M., Budică-Iacob, A. F., & Popescu, D. V. (2023). Assessing the contribution of managerial accounting in sustainable organizational development in the healthcare industry. *International Journal of Environmental Research and Public Health, 20*(4), 2895.
49. Ansari, R. S., Alfakeer, H., Arif, F., Bashir, M. A., Zehra, M., Rauf, S. A., et al. (2024). Exploring medical students' perceptions of telehealth in Pakistan: a cross-sectional study. *BMC Medical Education, 24*(1), 1093.
50. Chen, J., Mei, J., Li, X., Lu, Y., Yu, Q., Wei, Q., Luo, X., Xie, Y., Adeli, E., Wang, Y., Lungren, M. P., Zhang, S., Xing, L., Lu, L., Yuille, A., & Zhou, Y. (2024). TransUNet: Rethinking the U-Net architecture design for medical image segmentation through the lens of transformers. *Medical Image Analysis, 97*, 103280. https://doi.org/10.1016/j.media.2024.103280
51. Eckelman, M. J., Weisz, U., Pichler, P. P., Sherman, J. D., & Weisz, H. (2024). Guiding principles for the next generation of health-care sustainability metrics. *The Lancet Planetary Health, 8*(8), e603–e609.
52. Ijiga, A. C., Olola, T. M., Enyejo, L. A., Akpa, F. A., Olatunde, T. I., & Olajide, F. I. (2024). Advanced surveillance and detection systems using deep learning to combat human trafficking. *Magna Scientia Advanced Research and Reviews, 11*(01), 267–286.
53. Mani, Z. A., Naylor, K., & Goniewicz, K. (2024). Essential competencies of nurses for climate change response in Saudi Arabia: A rapid literature review. *Journal of Advanced Nursing*. https://doi.org/10.1111/jan.16372
54. Skogman-Lindqvist, C., Lapatto-Reiniluoto, O., Sirviö, M., & Sivén, M. (2023). Benefits and challenges of electronic package leaflet (ePL)-review of ePL pilots in hospital settings in Europe. *European Journal of Pharmaceutical Sciences, 191*, 106605.
55. McGain, F., & Naylor, C. (2014). Environmental sustainability in hospitals – a systematic review and research agenda. *Journal of Health Services Research & Policy, 19*(4), 245–252. https://doi.org/10.1177/1355819614534836
56. Moore, A. F., & Hawarden, V. (2020). Discovery digital health strategy: COVID-19 accelerates online health care in South Africa. *Emerald Emerging Markets Case Studies, 10*(3), 1–18. https://doi.org/10.1108/EEMCS-06-2020-0197
57. Virgolino, A., Antunes, F., Santos, O., Costa, A., de Matos, M. G., Bárbara, C., Bicho, M., Caneiras, C., Sabino, R., Núncio, M. S., Matos, O., Santos, R. R., Costa, J., Alarcão, V., Gaspar, T., Ferreira, J., & Carneiro, A. V. (2020). Towards a global perspective on digital health: Building a roadmap for worldwide research and development. *Sustainability, 12*(21), 8963. https://doi.org/10.3390/su12218963

58. Ye, J. (2020). The role of health technology and informatics in a global public health emergency: Practices and implications from the COVID-19 pandemic. *JMIR Medical Informatics, 8*(7), e19866. https://doi.org/10.2196/19866
59. Münzel, T., Sørensen, M., Lelieveld, J., Hahad, O., Al-Kindi, S., Nieuwenhuijsen, M., et al. (2021). Heart healthy cities: Genetics loads the gun but the environment pulls the trigger. *European Heart Journal, 42*(25), 2422–2438.
60. Chute, C., French, T., Raman, S., & Bradley, J. (2022). User requirements for comanaged digital health and care. *Journal of Medical Internet Research, 24*(6), e35337.
61. Lokmic-Tomkins, Z., Davies, S., Block, L. J., Cochrane, L., Dorin, A., von Gerich, H., et al. (2022). Assessing the carbon footprint of digital health interventions: A scoping review. *Journal of the American Medical Informatics Association, 29*(12), 2128–2139.
62. Saisó, S. G., Marti, M. C., Medina, F. M., Pascha, V. M., Nelson, J., Tejerina, L., et al. (2022). Digital transformation for more equitable and sustainable public health in the age of digital interdependence. *American Journal of Public Health, 112*(S6), S621–S624.
63. Agnello, D. M., Loisel, Q. E. A., An, Q., Balaskas, G., Chrifou, R., Dall, P., de Boer, J., Delfmann, L. R., Giné-Garriga, M., Goh, K., Longworth, G. R., Messiha, K., McCaffrey, L., Smith, N., Steiner, A., Vogelsang, M., & Chastin, S. (2023). Establishing a health CASCADE-curated open-access database to consolidate knowledge about co-creation: Novel artificial intelligence-assisted methodology based on systematic reviews. *Journal of Medical Internet Research, 25*, e45059. https://doi.org/10.2196/45059
64. Berniak-Woźny, J., & Rataj, A. (2023). Towards green and sustainable healthcare: A systematic literature review. *International Journal of Environmental Research and Public Health, 20*(2), 908. https://doi.org/10.3390/ijerph20020908
65. Hameed, F., & Hameed, K. (2023). The role of digital transformation in healthcare: A sustainability perspective, design and integration challenges, security and privacy challenges, blockchain technology, applications, and future research directions. *Healthcare Technology Advances*. (preprint on Preprints.org, version 1, posted 10 Aug 2023). https://doi.org/10.20944/preprints202308.0867.v1
66. Lapão, L. V., Correia, J. C., & Jevtic, M. (2023). Public health framework for smart cities within the comprehensive approach to sustainability in Europe: Case study of diabetes. *Sustainability, 15*(5), 4269.
67. Li, H., Alkahtani, M. E., Basit, A. W., Elbadawi, M., & Gaisford, S. (2023). Optimizing environmental sustainability in pharmaceutical 3D printing through machine learning. *International Journal of Pharmaceutics, 648*, 123561.
68. Rayan, R. A., Zafar, I., & Tsagkaris, C. (2023). Industry 4.0 technologies for healthcare: Applications, opportunities, and challenges. *Blockchain Technology Solutions for the Security of IoT-Based Healthcare Systems*, 23–44.
69. Sun, C., Chrysikou, E., Savvopoulou, E., Hernandez-Garcia, E., & Fatah gen. Schieck, A. (2023). Healthcare built environment and telemedicine practice for social and environmental sustainability. *Sustainability, 15*(3), 2697.
70. Almasri, A., El-Kour, T. Y., Silva, L., & Abdulfattah, Y. (2024). Evaluating the energy efficiency of popular US smartphone health care apps: Comparative analysis study toward sustainable health and nutrition apps practices. *JMIR Human Factors, 11*, e58311.
71. Bevere, D., & Faccilongo, N. (2024). Shaping the future of healthcare: Integrating ecology and digital innovation. *Sustainability, 16*(9), 3835.
72. Mountford, N., & Geiger, S. (2024). Public actor roles in market experiments: Innovating digital health markets in New York and Ireland. *Journal of Business Research, 183*, 114825.
73. Rowan, N. J. (2024). Digital technologies to unlock safe and sustainable opportunities for medical device and healthcare sectors with a focus on the combined use of digital twin and extended reality applications: A review. *Science of the Total Environment, 926*, 171672. https://doi.org/10.1016/j.scitotenv.2024.171672
74. Sepetis, A., Rizos, F., Pierrakos, G., Karanikas, H., & Schallmo, D. (2024, January). A sustainable model for healthcare systems: The innovative approach of ESG and digital transformation. In *Healthcare* (Vol. 12(2), p. 156). MDPI.

75. Tarpani, R. R. Z., & Gallego-Schmid, A. (2024). Environmental impacts of a digital health and well-being service in elderly living schemes. *Cleaner Environmental Systems, 12*, 100161.
76. Liverani, M., Hawkins, B., & Parkhurst, J. O. (2013). Political and institutional influences on the use of evidence in public health policy. A systematic review. *PLoS One, 8*(10), e77404.
77. Huang, F., Blaschke, S., & Lucas, H. (2017). Beyond pilotitis: Taking digital health interventions to the national level in China and Uganda. *Globalization and Health, 13*, 1–11.
78. Wallin, A. J., & Fuglsang, L. (2017). Service innovations breaking institutionalized rules of health care. *Journal of Service Management, 28*(5), 972–997. https://doi.org/10.1108/JOSM-04-2017-0099
79. Lennox, L., Maher, L., & Reed, J. (2018). Navigating the sustainability landscape: A systematic review of sustainability approaches in healthcare. *Implementation Science, 13*, 1–17.
80. Sadoughi, F., Khodaveisi, T., & Ahmadi, H. (2019). The used theories for the adoption of electronic health record: A systematic literature review. *Health and Technology, 9*, 383–400.
81. Ahmed, M. H., Bogale, A. D., Tilahun, B., Kalayou, M. H., Klein, J., Mengiste, S. A., & Endehabtu, B. F. (2020). Intention to use electronic medical record and its predictors among health care providers at referral hospitals, north-West Ethiopia, 2019: Using unified theory of acceptance and use technology 2 (UTAUT2) model. *BMC Medical Informatics and Decision Making, 20*, 1–11.
82. Burton-Jones, A., Akhlaghpour, S., Ayre, S., Barde, P., Staib, A., & Sullivan, C. (2020). Changing the conversation on evaluating digital transformation in healthcare: Insights from an institutional analysis. *Information and Organization, 30*(1), 100255.
83. Heinsch, M., Wyllie, J., Carlson, J., Wells, H., Tickner, C., & Kay-Lambkin, F. (2021). Theories informing eHealth implementation: Systematic review and typology classification. *Journal of Medical Internet Research, 23*(5), e18500.
84. Steinhauser, S. (2021). Enabling the utilization of potentially disruptive digital innovations by incumbents: The impact of contextual, organisational, and individual factors in regulated contexts. *International Journal of Innovation Management, 25*(02), 2150015.
85. Vărzaru, A. A. (2022). An empirical framework for assessing the balanced scorecard impact on sustainable development in healthcare performance measurement. *International Journal of Environmental Research and Public Health, 19*(22), 15155.
86. Carswell, C., Coventry, P. A., Brown, J. V., Alderson, S. L., Double, K., Gilbody, S., et al. (2023). Development of a supported self-management intervention for people with severe mental illness and type 2 diabetes: Theory and evidence-based co-design approach. *Journal of Medical Internet Research, 25*, e43597.
87. Denicolai, S., & Previtali, P. (2023). Innovation strategy and digital transformation execution in healthcare: The role of the general manager. *Technovation, 121*, 102555.
88. Carboni, C., Wehrens, R., van der Veen, R., & de Bont, A. (2022). Conceptualizing the digitalization of healthcare work: A metaphor-based Critical Interpretive Synthesis. *Social Science & Medicine, 292*, 114572.
89. Konopik, J., & Blunck, D. (2023). Development of an evidence-based conceptual model of the health care sector under digital transformation: Integrative review. *Journal of Medical Internet Research, 25*, e41512.
90. Mishra, A., & Pandey, N. (2023). Global entrepreneurship in healthcare: A systematic literature review and bibliometric analysis. *Global Business and Organizational Excellence, 42*(5), 9–21.
91. Priyadarshini, J., Singh, R. K., Mishra, R., & Dora, M. (2023). Application of additive manufacturing for a sustainable healthcare sector: Mapping current research and establishing future research agenda. *Technological Forecasting and Social Change, 194*, 122686.
92. Price, C., Suhomlinova, O., & Green, W. (2024). Researching big IT in the UK National Health Service: A systematic review of theory-based studies. *International Journal of Medical Informatics, 185*, 105395.

93. Rahat, N., Sahni, S., & Nasim, S. (2024). Mapping sustainability practices in the healthcare sector: A systematic literature review and future research agenda. *International Journal of Consumer Studies, 48*(1), e12997.
94. Schmitt, T. (2024). New governance of the digital health agency: A way out of the joint decision trap to implement electronic health records in Germany? *Health Economics, Policy and Law, 19*(2), 269–288.
95. Tan, A. J., Rusli, K. D., McKenna, L., Tan, L. L., & Liaw, S. Y. (2024). Telemedicine experiences and perspectives of healthcare providers in long-term care: A scoping review. *Journal of Telemedicine and Telecare, 30*(2), 230–249.
96. Tetteh, S. G., Agyeman, A. Y., & Mohammed-Nurudeen, S. (2025). Engineering Ghana's future: The impact of emerging technologies and digital transformation. *Journal of Engineering Research and Reports, 27*(5), 54–71. https://doi.org/10.9734/jerr/2025/v27i51492
97. Tenggono, E., Soedjipto, B. W., & Sudhartio, L. (2024). The effect of institutional pressures and dynamic managerial capability on strategic renewal: The case of strategic agility and digital readiness as mediators in healthcare industry. *Asian Journal of Business Research, 14*(1), 120–141. https://doi.org/10.14707/ajbr.230168
98. Okolo, C. A., Ijeh, S., Arowoogun, J. O., Adeniyi, A. O., & Omotayo, O. (2024). Reviewing the impact of health information technology on healthcare management efficiency. *International Medical Science Research Journal, 4*(4), 420–440.
99. Elendu, C., Elendu, T. C., & Elendu, I. D. (2024). 5G-enabled smart hospitals: Innovations in patient care and facility management. *Medicine, 103*(20), e38239.
100. Campbell, M. L., & Rankin, J. M. (2017). Nurses and electronic health records in a Canadian hospital: Examining the social organisation and programmed use of digitised nursing knowledge. *Sociology of Health & Illness, 39*(3), 365–379.
101. Ijeh, S., Okolo, C. A., Arowoogun, J. O., & Adeniyi, A. O. (2024). Theoretical insights into telemedicine and healthcare ICT: Lessons from implementation in Africa and the United States. *World Journal of Biology Pharmacy and Health Sciences, 18*(1), 115–122.
102. Doo, F. X., Parekh, V. S., Kanhere, A., Savani, D., Tejani, A. S., Sapkota, A., & Yi, P. H. (2024). Evaluation of climate-aware metrics tools for radiology informatics and artificial intelligence: Toward a potential radiology ecolabel. *Journal of the American College of Radiology: JACR, 21*(2), 239–247.
103. Adeghe, E. P., Okolo, C. A., & Ojeyinka, O. T. (2024). A review of emerging trends in telemedicine: Healthcare delivery transformations. *International Journal of Life Science Research Archive, 6*(1), 137–147.
104. Nassi, M., Riza, E., & Bouziani, E. (2023). Sustainably driven telemedicine for chronic illness patient satisfaction: Pre and post pandemic. *SDGs in the European Region*, 411–424.
105. Nti, I. K., Adekoya, A. F., Weyori, B. A., & Keyeremeh, F. (2023). A bibliometric analysis of technology in sustainable healthcare: Emerging trends and future directions. *Decision Analytics Journal, 8*, 100292.
106. Arega, A., & Sharma, D. P. (2023). Towards smart and green features of cloud computing in healthcare services: A systematic literature review. *Journal of Information Systems Engineering & Business Intelligence, 9*(2).
107. Ramírez-Saltos, D., Acosta-Vargas, P., Acosta-Vargas, G., Santórum, M., Carrion-Toro, M., Ayala-Chauvin, M., et al. (2023). Enhancing sustainability through accessible health platforms: A scoping review. *Sustainability, 15*(22), 15916.
108. Tsagkaris, C., Trygonis, N., Spyrou, V., & Koulouris, A. (2023). Telemedicine in care of sarcoma patients beyond the COVID-19 pandemic: Challenges and opportunities. *Cancers, 15*(14), 3700.
109. Verdejo Espinosa, A., Lopez, J. L., Mata Mata, F., & Estevez, M. E. (2021). Application of IoT in healthcare: Keys to implementation of the sustainable development goals. *Sensors, 21*(7), 2330.
110. Beck, S., Jasanoff, S., Stirling, A., & Polzin, C. (2021). The governance of sociotechnical transformations to sustainability. *Current Opinion in Environmental Sustainability, 49*, 143–152.

111. Ducret, M., Mörch, C. M., Karteva, T., Fisher, J., & Schwendicke, F. (2022). Artificial intelligence for sustainable oral healthcare. *Journal of Dentistry, 127*, 104344.
112. Mostepaniuk, A., Akalin, T., & Parish, M. R. (2023). Practices pursuing the sustainability of a healthcare organization: A systematic review. *Sustainability, 15*(3), 2353.
113. Ohalete, N. C., Ayo-Farai, O., Onwumere, C., Maduka, C. P., & Olorunsogo, T. O. (2024). Navier-stokes equations in biomedical engineering: A critical review of their use in medical device development in the USA and Africa. *World Journal of Advanced Research and Reviews, 21*(1), 1115–1131.
114. Lorena, A. (2018). The relation between corporate social responsibility and bank reputation: A review and roadmap. *European Journal of Economics and Business Studies, 4*(2), 7–21.

The ESG Rating Conundrum: A Bibliometric Analysis

Edgardo Bucciarelli, Alessia Regnicoli, and Aurora Ascatigno

Abstract In the current economic climate, ESG ratings are becoming an increasingly crucial consideration for investors. However, it is notable that the scores assigned by different agencies to the same company can vary significantly. This divergence in ratings is attributable to the disparate methodologies. In particular, ESG rating agencies employ different degrees of weight assigned to each criterion in their calculations. In this regard, the divergences observed in ESG ratings raise questions about their reliability. The existing literature indicates that these divergences result from a lack of standardisation. Moreover, subjectivity also influences how ESG rating agencies conduct ESG ratings. One of the principal consequences is the dissemination of misleading information and the occurrence of information asymmetry among stakeholders and investors. In light of this, the present study employs a bibliometric analysis to examine academic research on ESG rating, focusing on topics encompassing ESG rating divergences and disagreements. The analysis demonstrates a growing interest in ESG rating research, particularly concerning the divergences observed among ESG rating agencies. This indicates an increasing awareness of the challenges associated with ESG ratings, metrics, and final evaluations. Overall, this work highlights the increasing importance of ESG ratings while acknowledging the need to address standardisation. This study provides valuable insights for future research in this evolving field by exploring existing academic publications and identifying key trends.

Keywords ESG rating divergence · Bibliometric analysis · Sustainable development

---

E. Bucciarelli
University of Chieti-Pescara, Pescara, Italy
e-mail: edgardo.bucciarelli@unich.it

A. Regnicoli · A. Ascatigno (✉)
School of Advanced Studies, University of Chieti-Pescara, Chieti, Italy
e-mail: alessia.regnicoli@phd.unich.it; aurora.ascatigno@unich.it

M. Cipriano et al. (eds.), *Technologies for Organizations and Society*,
Lecture Notes in Information Systems and Organisation 80,
https://doi.org/10.1007/978-3-032-01697-3_11

1 Introduction

In recent years, there has been a global increase in the importance of considering environmental, social and governance (ESG) issues when measuring corporate performance [1]. This focus on environmental protection, social responsibility and good governance has pushed companies to look beyond financial metrics to understand how they are viewed by stakeholders [2]. In particular, ESG ratings have become integral to investors' financial decisions [3]. However, when it comes to the pivotal role of the ESG rating agencies, it arises, as well as the very different ESG scores these institutions address to the companies evaluated.

The aim of this study is to understand and examine the evolution of the academic literature on the contemporary discourse surrounding ESG rating agencies and, in particular, their divergences. The methodology used to achieve this goal is a bibliometric analysis. According to Ellili [3], this approach has recently witnessed a surge of interest, driven by the proliferation of software programmes and the increasing adoption of multidisciplinary approaches. The bibliometric analysis offers researchers an exciting tool for identifying trends within specific research fields and evaluating journal performance. By conducting a bibliometric analysis, we can identify the most frequently addressed ESG topics in the existing academic literature, potential gaps in current research, and possible avenues for future research directions. This study is guided by six specific research questions: (1) How has the number of publications on ESG ratings evolved over time? (1a) In particular, what has been the evolution of disagreement and divergence in ESG ratings over the years? (2) Which authors, organisations and countries have contributed most to academic research on ESG ratings? (3) What are the most cited documents on ESG rating? (4) What are the most cited references in ESG rating papers? (5) What are the most cited reference journals in ESG rating papers? (6) What are the most cited keywords and topics in ESG rating papers and their evolution over time? By reviewing the academic literature on ESG, it is possible to identify other studies that examine this broader area of research using a bibliometric analysis approach. For instance, Khan [4] carried out a bibliometric analysis in this direction, looking specifically at ESG performance in the banking sector; Demartini and Pagliei [5] carried out a bibliographic analysis of ESG disclosure; Kurbanova and Çalıyurt [6] used a bibliometric approach to investigate the quality of ESG data and the reliability of the ratings provided; Au et al. [7] carried out a bibliometric analysis focusing on the study of the global journey. In a more general sense, [8–10] carried out a bibliometric analysis on the evolution of ESG, shedding light on the evolution of publications over time in this emerging field of research. Among other existing studies, we can mention [3], which, in one way or another, has similarities with our work. In this respect, it is worth noting that [3] uses a similar methodological approach to ours, including using the Scopus platform to search for papers and the same software to perform analyses. However, it focuses primarily on ESG disclosure, which is different from the subject of our study. Building on the above, although we acknowledge the existence of various other works in the ESG field that use a bibliometric analysis approach, to the best of our knowledge, no previous research has used bibliometric analysis to specifically investigate ESG rating divergence and ESG rating disagreement within the Scopus database. This study addresses this gap in the academic literature by evaluating the most prominent research topics within ESG ratings. The analysis reveals a notable increase in publication volume, particularly since 2020. Furthermore, the findings identify Sustainability, an international academic journal, as a significant contributor to the field, as evidenced by its publication output and citation counts. In addition, this study sheds light on the most influential authors, countries, and institutions and cites references in the context of ESG rating research published on Scopus. Nevertheless, there are some limitations to this study. The exclusive use of Scopus in our study, to the exclusion of other academic research repositories, limits the generalisations that can be drawn from our findings.

The rest of this paper is structured as follows. Section 2 presents the methodology and the data. Section 3 presents and interprets the results of the bibliometric analysis. Section 4 presents the discussion, future research directions and concluding remarks.

1.1 Literature Review

The so-called ESG rating divergence issue [11–14], also referred to as ESG rating disagreement [15–17], has attracted much controversy. For instance, due to the diversity of ESG information, various studies have analysed different aspects of ESG rating criteria, indicators, metrics and methodologies [18–24]. Indeed, according to Chatterji et al. [25], we can consider two main reasons that are responsible for the divergence of ESG ratings, such as how rating agencies decide to make measurements (theorising) and the assessment of the consistency of the measurements made (commensurability). In line with the above, Dorfleitner et al. [18] provide an overview of the comparative methodologies used by different ESG rating agencies and an assessment of the correlation relationships observed within the scoring systems of the three leading players. In this context, Dorfleitner et al. [18] argue that there is little convergence between the concepts associated with the different ESG measures. Instead, Berg et al. [26] disaggregates the divergence in ESG ratings between six leading rating agencies into three contributing factors: Scope, Measurement and Weighting. Scope divergence arises from the use of different attribute sets by each agency. Measurement divergence reflects different perspectives on the relative importance of these attributes. Finally, weighting divergence results from different indicators quantifying the same attribute. Research suggests that measurement divergence is the most critical contributor to the observed divergence, exceeding the combined influence of scope and weight divergence. The approach taken by Dimson et al. [27] is somewhat different, where the scholars explore the extent and reasons for the observed divergence among prominent ESG raters. In particular, their analysis of the factors contributing to this divergence echoes the four reasons previously identified by Kotsantonis and Serafeim [20]. Christensen [16] identify a counterintuitive effect: Greater ESG disclosure by companies leads to more significant divergence in agency ESG ratings. In fact, this is particularly true for environmental and social disclosures due to the relative newness of these areas and the lack of consensus on the definition of good performance. Rating disagreements are also associated with market volatility and reduced access to external finance, highlighting the need for standardised ESG metrics and transparent performance criteria. In Bissoondoyal-Bheenick [28], we also noted that several other studies have examined the variation and divergence in ESG ratings. For instance, Gibson Brandon [22] examine the positive relationship between ESG rating divergence and stock returns, highlighting the implications for firms' cost of capital and investment strategies. Serafeim and Yoon [23] consensus ratings effectively predict future news, but significant disagreement weakens their predictive power. Berg [26], Lioui and Tarelli [29] and Gyönyörová et al. [30] contribute to understanding these differences by examining variations in rating methodologies. Research suggests that measurement divergence is the most important contributor to the observed divergence, exceeding the combined influence of scope and weight divergence. The approach taken by Dimson et al. [27] is somewhat different, where the researchers investigated the extent and reasons for the observed divergence among prominent ESG raters. The literature thus provides a clear framework for framing the controversial issue of ESG rating divergence. In short, the limitations of current ESG rating frameworks are a key concern for empirical researchers. According to Bissoondoyal-Bheenick et al. [28], these limitations stem from two key issues: Lack of standardisation [31–33] and inherent subjectivity [34] in the rating process. Regarding the latter issue, it is not uncommon to observe that different rating agencies may assign different ESG scores to the same company due to the subjective nature of their criteria. In addition, the voluntary disclosure of ESG information by companies (in the absence of legal requirements for standardised reporting) introduces a selection bias [35]; this, in turn, can facilitate greenwashing practices, whereby companies misrepresent their environmental risks to capitalise on the popularity of ESG investing [36].

2 Methodology and Procedures

This section outlines the methods and procedures employed in the bibliometric analysis of the following topics: "ESG rating", "ESG rating divergence" and "ESG rating disagreement". These topics are examined through the application of both quantitative and qualitative approaches. The methodology employed for the analyses and their representation is consistent with that described by Galletta [37]. The following sub-sections present an overview of the database and selection criteria, the tools and software employed, and the phases of analysis conducted. The phases of analysis reflect the sequence in which the results are presented for each topic.

2.1 Database and Selection Criteria

In accordance with the methodology followed by [38], all data were extracted from the Scopus database (https://www.scopus.com/search/form.uri?display=basic#basic) after a keyword search. The keywords used in the search include 'ESG rating', 'ESG rating divergence' and 'ESG rating disagreement', searched in the titles of articles, abstracts or keywords of works. The reference years considered are from 2000 to 2024. Once the search results were obtained, we selected all the available works and selected the variables (e.g., citation information such as author(s), document title, year, source title, volume, issues; bibliographical information such as affiliations, serial identifiers, language of original document; abstract, author keywords, indexed keywords) to be exported into the three separate datasets. The three datasets were exported, respectively, in two formats: BibTeX for analysis in Python and CSV Excel for analysis in VosViewer [39] as the two different tools required different data formats. Furthermore, it is necessary to consider that the analysis conducted in this work only concerns works extracted from the Scopus database, therefore, it is not generalised. Thus, the interpretation in the results is also subjugated to the works retrieved from the Scopus database.

2.2 Tools and Software Used

While most of the analyses were conducted using the pyBibX library [40] in Python 3, the network analyses were performed using the VosViewer software tool [39] to enable better visualisation of the networks. In essence, while the utilisation of the pyBibX library necessitates the employment of Python language codes, the utilisation of the VosViewer software, which is installed locally on the PC, avoids the necessity for code input in order to obtain output. Instead, the user is required only to load the dataset and select functions from the graphic interface and save the results.

2.3 Analysis of Publication Trends

For each topic, an analysis of publication trends was conducted, considering the type of works included in the analysis, the number of authors, countries and institutions. In particular, attention was also paid to the trend in the number of publications over time: This provides insight into what, who, when and where works on a given topic were published.

2.4 Analysis of the Most Influential Authors

An analysis of authors' citations and scientific productivity was carried out to assess the impact and relevance of researchers in the field of study. Indeed, the most influential and most cited authors were identified for each topic.

2.5 Analysis of Countries and Connections Between Scholars from Different Countries

We analysed the authors' countries of origin, taking into account the connections between authors on a global level together with the institutions they belong to. Overall, a fairly dense network of collaborations between authors and institutions around the world was weaved.

2.6 Analysis of Journals

The analysis of the journals made it possible to identify the main scientific journals of international relevance that most publish work on a related topic. As briefly mentioned, only journals found in the Scopus database are considered.

2.7 Analysis of Document Citations

For each topic, a citation analysis of the documents was conducted to determine the impact of the individual articles in the field of study. In this case, not the most cited authors but the most cited works were considered.

2.8 Analysis of the Most Frequently Used Words in Titles, Abstracts and Keywords

For each topic, we analysed the keywords and their evolution over time by means of network analysis. In particular, we considered the relatively most frequently used words in the titles, abstracts and as keywords in the studies considered.

2.9 *Analysis of Natural Language Processing (NLP)*

In accordance with the functionalities of the pyBibX library [40], a Natural Language Processing (NLP) analysis was conducted to ascertain the primary topics addressed in the works included in the bibliometric analysis. In particular, the contents of the abstracts were considered as input, and the following outputs were obtained: Firstly, an estimation of the most frequently treated topics in the various fields; secondly, a summary of the relatively more representative abstracts in a given field.

3 Bibliometric Analysis: ESG Rating

A search for keywords "ESG rating" in the international Scopus repository, with a reference time interval of 2000–2024, yielded 840 results. However, for the purposes of the bibliometric analysis, only 822 works published in the 20-year period 2004–2024 were considered. Of these, 677 were articles, 4 were books, 45 were book chapters, 71 were conference papers, 2 were conference reviews, 1 was an erratum, 3 were notes and 19 were reviews. Table 1 displays the main information about the works included in the bibliometric analysis.

3.1 *Trends in Publication*

The average number of documents per year is 48.35, with a mean of 2.15 documents per source. Figure 1 illustrates the trend in the publication of documents per year

Table 1 Summary table of the main information about the 822 works included in the bibliometric analysis

Main information	Results	Main information	Results
Total Number of Countries	76	Total Number of Authors	2105
Total Number of Institutions	1074	Total Number of Authors Keywords	2053
Total Number of Sources	383	Total Single-Authored Documents	111
Total Number of References	0	Total Multi-Authored Documents	711
Total Number of Languages	6	Average Collaboration Index	2.89
– Chinese (# of docs)	3	Max H-Index	4
– English (# of docs)	796	Total Number of Citations	15,786
– German (# of docs)	2	Average Citations per Author	7.5
– Korean (# of docs)	8	Average Citations per Institution	14.7
– Russian (# of docs)	12	Average Citations per Document	19.2
– Spanish (# of docs)	1	Average Citations per Source	41.22

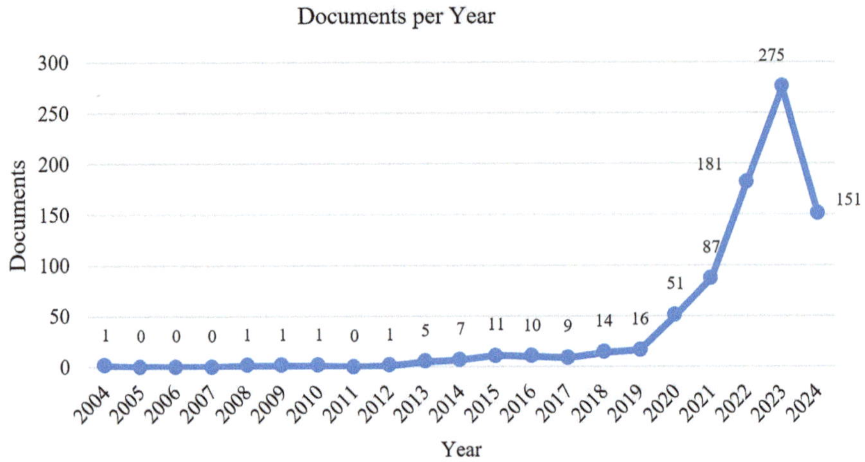

Fig. 1 The trend in the growth of the number of publications over time

(from 2004 to 2024). Upon initial examination it becomes evident that the trend is on the rise, particularly since the year 2020. The peak number of published documents per year is 2023 (no. 275).

3.2 *The Most Influential Authors*

Based on the works included in the analysis and considering the top 20 authors by citations, we can argue that the most influential author is George Serafeim (2135 citations). Instead, looking at the top 20 authors by document, the most influential authors are Christian Klein [41–45] and Gregor Dorfleitner [11, 46–49] both contributed five works to this in-depth study.

3.3 *The Most Influential Countries and the Authors' Connections*

The countries that exerted the greatest influence on the study are as follows (number of works in brackets): China (451); Russian Federation (232); Italy (218); Germany (130); United Kingdom (120) and South Korea (93). An analysis of the network connecting scholars from around the globe reveals that the countries from which the most connections originate are China, France, Germany, and the United Kingdom. It should be noted that these connections extend worldwide, particularly to Australia, Singapore, Indonesia, Canada, Russia, Italy, Spain, and South Africa.

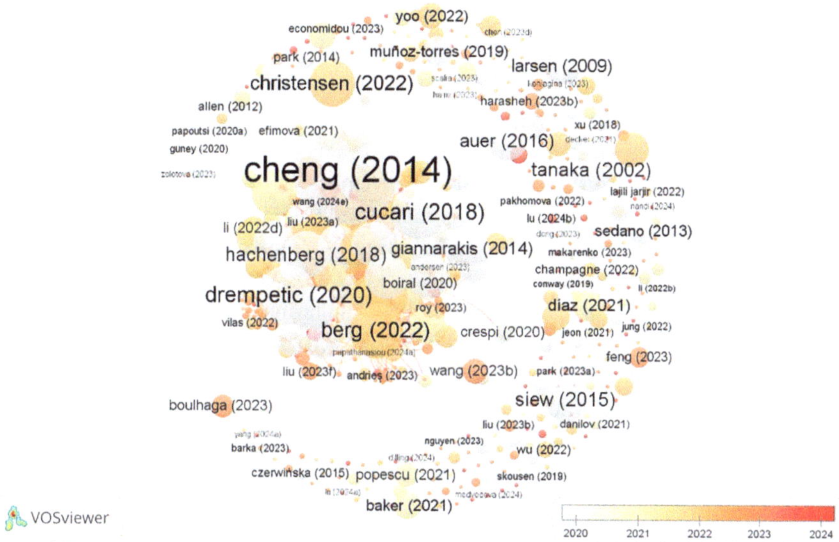

Fig. 2 Network representation of the most cited work over time

3.4 *The Most Influential Journals*

The most influential journals in the field of "ESG rating" are (number of works in brackets): Sustainability (59), Finance Research Letters (39), Corporate Social Responsibility and Environmental Management (30), Journal of Sustainable Finance and Investment (17), E3S Web of Conferences (16), and Journal of Corporate Finance Research (15).

3.5 *Top-Cited Works*

With regard to the study of the citations received by the works included in the analyses, it can be observed that the citation trend over time is increasing, particularly from 2013 to 2024. Nevertheless, lower peaks are observed between 2015 and 2017 and one in 2023. The highest number of citations was observed in 2022 (3949), although 2014 also exhibited a high number of citations (2210). Figure 2 illustrates the network of the most cited works over time, in accordance with the aforementioned observations. In particular, the most frequently cited work is [50] in 2020.

3.6 The Most Frequent Words in Titles, Abstracts and Keywords

A bibliometric analysis of the 822 works in question reveals that the most frequently occurring words in the titles are "ESG," "performance," "social," "environmental," "rating," "evidence," "corporate," and "governance." Instead, the abstracts demonstrate a different set of dominant terms, namely: "ESG," "performance," "social," "environmental," "corporate," "study," "rating," "company," and "corporation." Furthermore, the most frequently occurring keywords, considering their evolution over time (year in brackets), were as follows: The terms "green buildings" (2010), "corporate engagement" (2012), "US evidence" (2013), "Tinetti" (2014), "crowdsourcing" (2016), and "csr assessment" (2017), "mission investing" (2019), "ESG scores" (2020), "social" (2021), "firm value" (2022), "information asymmetry" (2023) and "ESG rating disagreement" (2024). It is noteworthy that in 2024, one of the most frequently used keywords is "ESG rating disagreement", which is also one of the most emerging themes and main topics covered in our work.

3.7 Applying NLP to Bibliometric Analysis

A typical Natural Language Processing (NLP) approach was applied to bibliometric analysis (for further details, please refer to [51]) using the pyBibX library [40] in Python. Thus, 13 topics were identified with their respective repetitions within the work under review. Table 2 summarises the topics, the number of repetitions and the most representative work on each topic.

Based on the above, we observed that the most correlated topics (with a correlation coefficient of 0.8 or above, indicated in yellow) in addition to the values

Table 2 Most representative work for each topic estimated using the NPL approach

Topic	# repetitions	Works
ESG funds portfolio investment	146	[52–54]
ESG financial sustainable development	111	[55, 56]
Sustainability companies reporting ESG	69	[57–59]
ESG governance rating disagreement	44	[6, 15, 60]
Green innovation corporate ESG	32	[5, 61, 62]
Credit ESG rating cds	31	[63–65]
CSR corporate social firm	25	[66–68]
Models ESG AI learning	23	[69–71]
Diversity gender female board	13	[72–74]
Corporate financing ESG enterprises	11	[75, 76]
Environmental firms corporate companies	10	[77–79]
Firms ESG targets defensive	10	[80–82]

reported on the diagonal are as follows: topics −1 and 0; topics −1 and 1; topics −1 and 2; topics −1 and 3. In total, based on 817 valid abstracts, the software generated and delivered the following abstract: "*Environmental, social, and governance (ESG) ratings have become an important issue in the corporate world, but their impact on green innovation has been poorly understood so far, and their impact on managers' self-interest has not been well understood in the Chinese market, where green innovation is a key priority for many Chinese companies, especially those in the energy and resources sector. The asymmetry of corporate green innovation activities is exacerbated by managers' self-interest, whereas the internal strategy adjustment channel is responsible for the impact of ESG rating disparity on green innovation efforts.*"

Building on the above, below we report the key findings from a relatively more specific bibliometric analysis considering first the ESG rating disagreement and then the ESG rating divergence.

4 ESG rating divergence

By entering the search term "ESG rating divergence" into the Scopus platform and selecting the reference time range 2000–2024, a total of 25 works published between 2018 and 2024 were identified. Of these, 23 were articles, one was a book chapter, and one was a review. In total, 14 countries and 36 institutions (e.g. universities and research centres) were involved in the production of the 25 works. All of the works were written in English, with 66 authors contributing to them and 84 keywords being used. Four of the works were single-authored, while 21 were mixed-authored. Based on these findings, the average collaboration index is 2.64, with a maximum value of 0 for the H-index.

4.1 Trends in Publication

On average, there are 5 documents published per year, with 1.19 documents per source. The total number of citations is 524. In particular, the average number of citations per author is 7.94, per institution is 14.56, per document is 20.96, and per source is 24.95. In consideration of the observed trend in the publication of documents per year (from 2018 to 2024), it was found that the trend exhibited an increasing pattern only from 2021 onwards. In point of fact, although only one publication was found in 2018, work on the subject of "ESG rating divergence" has only increased in recent years. The highest number of published documents per year is 2023 (no. 8). Overall, the limited number of works published on the topic in question allows us to argue that it is a relatively recent and developing topic.

4.2 The Most Influential Authors

Furthermore, the absence of identification of more influential authors per document suggests that there is still much to be discovered in this field. In fact, our analysis suggests that each of the 25 works considered was written by a different author, indicating that there are no cases in which the same author participated in a further work. Furthermore, an examination of the most influential authors per citation reveals that the most influential are Roberto Rigobon, Kölbel Julian and Berg Florian, each of whom has 326 citations.

4.3 The Most Influential Countries and the Authors' Connections

It is notable that the most influential countries are (number of works in parentheses): China (17), Italy (11), Russian Federation (11) and Germany (5). When we consider the network of scholars from around the globe, it becomes evident that the countries with the greatest number of connections (4) are Germany, Indonesia, Australia and Canada. It is notable that these connections are primarily between Germany and Indonesia and between Australia and Canada. Additionally, we studied all connections among authors, countries, institutions and languages concerning 20 of the 25 works included in our analysis. In support of the above, it can be observed that in the sources (authors), there are no authors who exert significant influence. From these sources, it is possible to ascertain the countries from which the majority of contributions originate. These are China, Italy, and the Russian Federation. Each author and country are linked to the institutions they belong to. The institution with the greatest number of links is the School of Business (China). All of the work was written in English.

4.4 The Most Influential Journals

Moreover, it is worth mentioning that the most influential journals are (number of works in parentheses): Business Strategy and the Environment (2); Corporate Social Responsibility and Environmental Management (2); Finance Research Letters (2) and Sustainability (2).

4.5 Top-Cited Works

With regard to the study conducted on the citations received by the works included in the analyses, it can be observed that the citation trend over time is only increasing in the period 2021–2022. In particular, the number of citations in both the periods 2018–2020 and 2023–2024 is notably low, with a range of 0–23. The greatest number of citations was observed in 2022 (370). By looking at the most cited works over time, in accordance with the previous observations, we can see that most frequently cited works are [19, 79, 80].

4.6 The Most Frequent Words in Titles and Abstracts

We then consider the most frequent words included within the titles of the 25 works under study. In detail, we observe that the relatively most frequent words are "ESG", "rating", "divergence", "sustainable", "social", "analysis", "corporate", "scores", "green", "innovation", "Governance", "comparative", "Transformation", "effect". When examining the evolution of the most frequent words used within the abstracts over time (from 2018 to 2024), it can be observed that in 2018 the most frequently used word was "instrumental", in 2021 it was "article", in 2022 it was "related", in 2023 it was "show" and in 2024 it was "wiley".

4.7 The Most Frequent Keywords and Their Evolution

Furthermore, we considered the most frequently used words in the abstracts are "ESG rating divergence" (used 25 times), "social and governance" (used 19 times), "of ESG rating" (used 16 times) and "and governance ESG" (used 16 times). Furthermore, the evolution of keywords over time is observed, with particular attention paid to the most frequent keywords used by the authors. In this regard, in 2018, these keywords can be grouped within the term "rating standards". In 2021, they are grouped within the term "Cee". In 2022, they are grouped within the term "environment". In 2023, they are grouped within the term "developed stock markets". Finally, in 2024, they are grouped within the term "information transparency". Upon initial observation, it becomes evident that the keywords that stand out the most in each group are "ESG rating," "environmental," "CSR," "ESG," "sustainability," "ESG rating," and "ESG rating divergence". A more clearly defined representation of the most frequently used keywords, along with their connections, is visible in Fig. 3. Several clusters are observed, grouping together the works with the most similar keywords. Each cluster is comprised of nodes (identified by the most representative keywords) and links connecting the various clusters, thereby indicating the interconnected nature of the topics addressed in the various works. From the figure, it can be observed that the most representative nodes (keywords) are: "geospatial modelling,", "biodiversity," "soil", "corporates", "ESG," "sustainability," "ESG ratings," "investment," and "environmental".

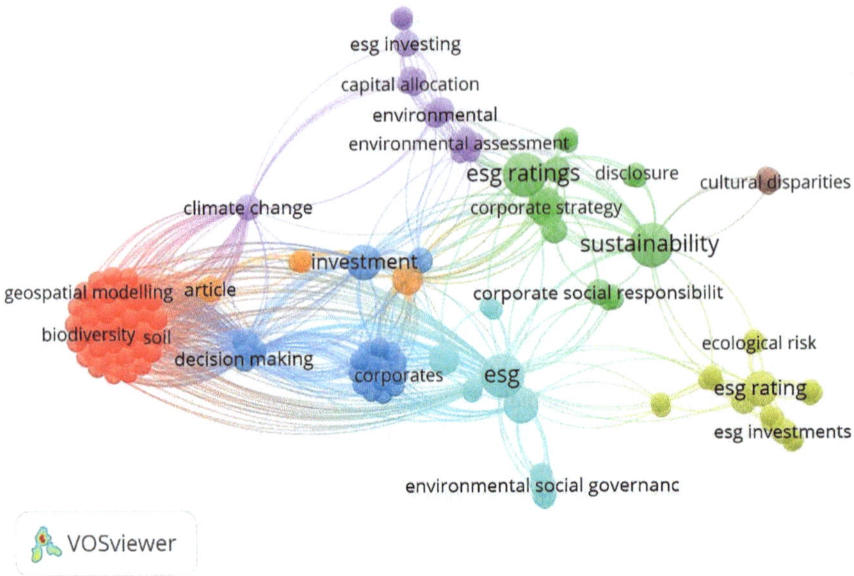

Fig. 3 Network representation of the most frequently used keywords (ESG rating divergence)

4.8 Applying NLP to Bibliometric Analysis

Following the typical approach of NLP, the common topic underlying all the works under consideration was identified. As might be expected, the term "esg rating and ratings divergence" appears 25 times. Building upon the 25 abstracts, the software has generated the identical abstract estimated for the general case of an ESG rating. It can therefore be concluded that, within the 25 works, some contribute significantly to the arguments, even when considered separately, in accordance with the general case.

5 ESG Rating Disagreement

A search via the Scopus platform for the keywords "ESG rating disagreement" and a reference time range of 2000–2024 yielded a total of 24 works published in the 2020–2024 period. Of these, 22 were articles, one was a conference paper and one was a review. In total, 13 countries and 39 institutions (e.g. universities and research centres) were involved in the 24 works. All works were written in English, with 67 authors and 80 keyword authors. There were two single-author papers and 22 double-author papers. Accordingly, the average collaboration index is 2.92, with a maximum value of the H-index of 1.

5.1 Trends in Publication

The average number of works per year is 4.8, with an average of 1.6 works per source. The total number of citations is 773. In particular, the average number of citations per author is 11.54, per institution is 19.82, per document is 32.21 and, finally, per source is 40.48. By looking at the trend of document publication per year (2020–2024), we can see that the trend is increasing, particularly from the year 2022. The highest number of documents published in a single year was in 2024 (no. 10).

5.2 The Most Influential Authors

In light of the works included in the analysis and the top 20 authors by citations, it can be argued that George Serafeim is the most influential author, with 300 citations. Instead, an analysis of the top 20 authors per paper reveals that the most influential authors are Wang Hongxia [13, 83], George Serafeim [9, 16] and Dong Minghua [13, 83], all of whom have two works included in the study.

5.3 The Most Influential Countries and the Authors' Connections

The most influential countries are (number of works in brackets): China (27); UK (7); Italy (7); Switzerland (3); Norway (3); Ireland (3) and South Korea (3). Overall, if we look at the network connecting scholars around the world, it is possible to observe that the countries from which the most connections start (7) are: China, Hong Kong, Egypt, Tunisia, Italy, Germany, and the United Kingdom. Note that these connections mainly concern China with Hong Kong, Italy with Germany and the UK with Tunisia and Egypt.

5.4 The Most Influential Journals

The most influential journals are (number of works in brackets): Corporate Social Responsibility and Environmental Management (4); Finance Research Letters (2) and Research in International Business and Finance (2).

5.5 Top-Cited Works

With regard to the analysis of the citations received by the works included in the analyses, it can be observed that the trend in citations over time is increasing in the first three years, with a particularly notable increase between 2020 and 2022. Subsequently, a decline in citations is observed up to the present day. The greatest number of citations was observed in 2022 (257). Moreover, it is noteworthy to consider that the most frequently cited works are [14–16, 20]. To summarise the above, it is possible to consider all connections among authors, countries, institutions, and languages concerning 20 of the 24 works included in our analysis. Specifically, we observed that Wang Hongxia, George Serafeim and Dong Minghua were the most influential authors in the sources. From these sources (authors), it is possible to ascertain the country of origin of each author. With regard to the three aforementioned authors, it can be observed that Wang Hongxia and Dong Minghua are affiliated with the Chinese academic institution, the College of Economics and Management, while George Serafeim is linked to the American academic institution, Harvard Business School. Finally, the language in which the work was written is indicated. All three works were written in English.

5.6 The Most Frequent Words in Titles and Abstracts

Subsequently, we consider the most frequent words included within the titles of the 24 works under study. In detail, we observe that the relatively most frequent words are "ESG", "rating", "disagreement", "China", "environmental", "stock", "Evidence", "performance", "return", "corporate", "external", "role", "impact", "risk". Similarly, when looking at the evolution over time (from 2020 to 2024) of the most frequently used words within the abstracts, it is observed that in 2020 the relatively most used word is "underpin"; in 2021 it is "environmental"; in 2022 it is "reduces"; in 2023 it is "corporate" and in 2024 it is "firms". Additionally, we observed that the most frequently used words in the abstracts are "ESG rating disagreement" (used 25 times); "environmental social and" and "social and governance" (both used 14 times).

5.7 The Most Frequent Keywords and Their Evolution

We also looked at the evolution of the keywords over time, taking into account the most frequent keywords used by the authors. In particular, in 2020 these keywords can be grouped under the heading "equity portfolio management", in 2021 under "emerging markets", in 2022 under "cost of equity", in 2023 under "esg" and in 2024 under "idiosyncratic return volatility". At first glance, we see that in all the keyword groups, the ones that stand out the most are "esg disclosure", "esg ratings",

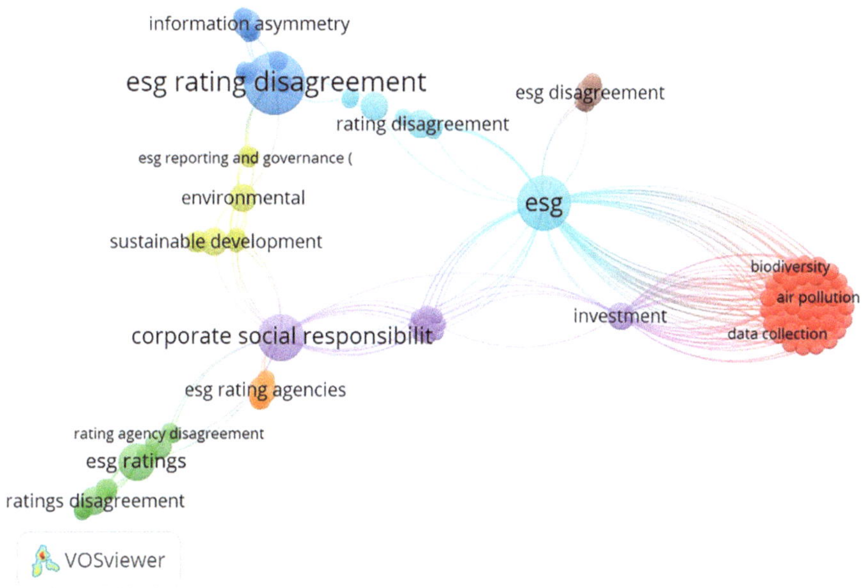

Fig. 4 A network representation of the most frequently used keywords within the documents (ESG rating disagreement)

"environmental", "rating disagreement", "esg" and "esg rating disagreement". A more clarified representation of the most frequently utilised keywords, along with their connections, is visible in Fig. 4. In particular, several clusters of varying colors are observed, grouping together the works with the most similar keywords. In each cluster, there are nodes (named by the most representative keywords) and links connecting the various clusters, suggesting the interconnected nature of the topics dealt with in the various works. From the Figure, it can be observed that the most representative keywords (nodes) are: "ESG rating disagreement," "ESG," "corporate social responsibility," "ESG ratings," "sustainable development," "ESG rating agencies," "investment," "biodiversity," "air pollution," "data collection".

5.8 Applying NLP to Bibliometric Analysis

A typical NLP approach to bibliometric analysis [51] was applied using the pyBibX library [40] in Python, which identified the topic common to all the works considered. As might be expected, the topic "ESG rating disagreement" appears 24 times. Building upon the 24 abstracts, the software has generated and provided this abstract: "*Environmental ratings and emissions scores for commercial airlines from several major environmental, social and governance ratings providers may be inconsistent, and may undermine trust in the ratings industry*".

6 Discussion and Future Research

This study uses a bibliometric analysis of ESG rating publications indexed in Scopus to assess their contribution to the existing body of ESG knowledge and to identify the central themes and theoretical underpinnings of the field, in particular, the themes of ESG rating divergence and ESG rating disagreement. This work has identified the most prolific authors, organisations, and countries contributing to the field through a multifaceted approach that includes bibliometrics, trend analysis, and content analysis. Furthermore, the analysis shows an increasing trend in publications for "ESG rating" since 2020, for "ESG rating divergence" since 2021 and finally for "ESG rating disagreement" since 2023. Furthermore, the results show that the international journal Sustainability has experienced an increasingly important growth in ESG rating research papers, especially in the field of "ESG rating", where we count 59 published papers, demonstrating its substantial advancement of knowledge in this field. This study has both theoretical and practical importance. First, it provides a comprehensive map of the ESG rating literature by highlighting the most influential studies and thematic areas within the field. Secondly, it provides scholars with insights into the latest ESG rating issues, particularly those related to the evolving landscape of ESG rating divergence and disagreement. It also identifies the most cited papers and relevant references. Finally, the findings presented here can serve as a valuable guide for ESG rating researchers in selecting future research studies. For instance, it has been explored that there is limited use in the academic literature of the associations between ESG rating divergence and the less commonly used keywords, such as 'CSR' and 'ESG disclosure', even if we look at the most cited research in the general field of 'ESG rating' [49], which focuses on corporate social responsibility (CSR) strategies. Based on our findings, we can conclude that the last two topics analysed ("ESG rating divergence" and "ESG rating disagreement") are a specific novelty of recent years in the broad field of ESG rating and are still at an early stage of research. For this reason, we can assume that there are no clear relationships between the most consolidated areas of academic research, such as CSR (and related areas), and ESG rating divergence and disagreement. In line with the research questions, this paper highlights the critical role of ESG rating agencies in guiding companies towards a more sustainable future. The growing influence of ESG ratings requires further research into their methodologies and impacts. An examination of the inherent characteristics and thematic focus of ESG ratings and benchmarks revealed that these ratings do not have a standardised and consistent system of measurement and analysis. In this sense, investors and policymakers will face several challenges when using ESG ratings. First, inconsistent ESG ratings from different rating agencies can make it difficult for investors to accurately assess the sustainability of companies. The second issue is the potential for greenwashing. Companies may manipulate ESG ratings through misleading practices, leading investors to make incorrect investment decisions. Finally, the third is the potential for increased costs. Investors may have to spend more time and money on due diligence or diversify their investments to mitigate the risks associated with inconsistent ESG ratings. Therefore, a significant academic research gap exists concerning the multifaceted nature of ESG ratings. While previous studies have mainly examined the impact of ESG ratings and scores on sustainable corporate development, a broader understanding of their influence and limitations is crucial. Future research should explore alternative databases to examine trends in ESG ratings over time and assess whether this area of research continues to expand. In addition, further research is needed on other aspects of the broad field of ESG ratings. For instance, it has been explored that there is limited use in the academic literature of the associations between ESG rating divergence and the less commonly used keywords, such as 'CSR' and 'ESG disclosure', even if we look at the most cited research in the general field of 'ESG rating' [49], which focuses on corporate social responsibility (CSR) strategies.

Disclosure of Interests The authors have no competing interests to declare that are relevant to the content of this article.

References

1. Zhai, Y., Cai, Z., Lin, H., Yuan, M., Mao, Y., & Yu, M. (2022). Does better environmental, social, and governance induce better corporate green innovation: The mediating role of financing constraints. *Corporate Social Responsibility and Environmental Management, 29*(5), 1513–1526.
2. Li, W., & Pang, W. (2023). The impact of digital inclusive finance on corporate ESG performance: Based on the perspective of corporate green technology innovation. *Environmental Science and Pollution Research, 30*(24), 65314–65327.
3. Ellili, N. O. D. (2022). Bibliometric analysis and systematic review of environmental, social, and governance disclosure papers: current topics and recommendations for future research. *Environmental Research Communications, 4*(9), 092001, 1–15.
4. Khan, M. A. (2022). ESG disclosure and firm performance: A bibliometric and meta analysis. *Research in International Business and Finance, 61*(101668), 1–19.
5. Demartini, P., & Pagliei, C. (2023). Can we trust ESG Ratings? Some insights based on a bibliometric analysis of ESG data quality and rating reliability. *Management Control, 2023*(2s), 165–174.
6. Kurbanova, M., & Çalıyurt, K. (2024). The concept of ESG in a global journey: Bibliometric analysis. In *New approaches to CSR, sustainability and accountability* (Vol. V, pp. 3–34). Springer Nature.
7. Au, A. K. M., Yang, Y. F., Wang, H., Chen, R. H., & Zheng, L. J. (2023). Mapping the landscape of ESG strategies: A bibliometric review and recommendations for future research. *Sustainability, 15*(24), 6592, 1–26.
8. Zhao, X., Nan, D., Chen, C., Zhang, S., Che, S., & Kim, J. H. (2023). Bibliometric study on environmental, social, and governance research using CiteSpace. *Frontiers in Environmental Science, 10*(1087493), 1–12.
9. Esposito De Falco, S., Montera, R., Leo, S., Laviola, F., Vito, P., Sardanelli, D., Basile, G., Nevi, G., & Alaia, R. (2024). Trends and patterns in ESG research: A bibliometric odyssey and research agenda. *Corporate Social-Responsibility And Environmental Management, 31*, 3703.
10. Khan, A., Goodell, J. W., Hassan, M. K., & Paltrinieri, A. (2022). A bibliometric review of finance bibliometric papers. *Finance Research Letters, 47*(102520), 1–9.

11. Dumrose, M., Rink, S., & Eckert, J. (2022). Disaggregating confusion? The EU taxonomy and its relation to ESG rating. *Finance Research Letters, 48*(102928), 1–8.
12. Chen, C., Fan, M., & Fan, Y. (2023). The impact of ESG ratings under market soft regulation on corporate green innovation: An empirical study from informal environmental governance. *Frontiers in Environmental Science, 11*(1278059), 1–12.
13. Wang, J., Wang, S., Dong, M., & Wang, H. (2024). ESG rating disagreement and stock returns: Evidence from China. *International Review of Financial Analysis, 91*(103043), 1–11.
14. Zhu, H. L., & Yang, K. Z. (2024). The spillover effect of ESG performance on green innovation—Evidence from listed companies in China A-shares. *Sustainability, 16*(8), 3238, 1–31.
15. Rubino, M., Mastrorocco, I., & Garegnani, G. M. (2024). The influence of market and institutional factors on ESG rating disagreement. *Corporate Social Responsibility and Environmental Management, 31*, 1–11. https://doi.org/10.1002/csr.2787
16. Christensen, D. M., Serafeim, G., & Sikochi, A. (2022). Why is corporate virtue in the eye of the beholder? The case of ESG ratings. *The Accounting Review, 97*(1), 147–175.
17. Lopez, C., Contreras, O., & Bendix, J. (2020). *Disagreement among ESG rating agencies: Shall we be worried?*. MPRA Paper 103027. University Library of Munich.
18. Dorfleitner, G., Halbritter, G., & Nguyen, M. (2015). Measuring the level and risk of corporate responsibility–An empirical comparison of different ESG rating approaches. *Journal of Asset Management, 16*(1), 450–466.
19. Semenova, N., & Hassel, L. G. (2015). On the validity of environmental performance metrics. *Journal of Business Ethics, 132*(1), 249–258.
20. Kotsantonis, S., & Serafeim, G. (2019). Four things no one will tell you about ESG data. *Journal of Applied Corporate Finance, 31*(2), 50–58.
21. Billio, M., Costola, M., Hristova, I., Latino, C., & Pelizzon, L. (2021). Inside the ESG ratings: (Dis)agreement and performance. *Corporate Social Responsibility and Environmental Management, 28*(5), 1426–1445.
22. Gibson Brandon, R., Krueger, P., & Schmidt, P. S. (2021). ESG rating disagreement and stock returns. *Financial Analysts Journal, 77*(4), 104–127.
23. Serafeim, G., & Yoon, A. (2023). Stock price reactions to ESG news: The role of ESG ratings and disagreement. *Review of Accounting Studies, 28*(3), 1500–1530.
24. Luo, D., Yan, J., & Yan, Q. (2023). The duality of ESG: Impact of ratings and disagreement on stock crash risk in China. *Finance Research Letters, 58*(104479), 1–8.
25. Chatterji, A. K., Durand, R., Levine, D. I., & Touboul, S. (2016). Do ratings of firms converge? Implications for managers, investors and strategy researchers. *Strategic Management Journal, 37*(8), 1597–1614.
26. Berg, F., Koelbel, J. F., & Rigobon, R. (2022). Aggregate confusion: The divergence of ESG ratings. *Review of Finance, 26*(6), 1315–1344.
27. Dimson, E., Marsh, P., & Staunton, M. (2020). Divergent ESG ratings. *The Journal of Portfolio Management, 47*(1), 75–87.
28. Bissoondoyal-Bheenick, B., Bennett, S., & Zhong, A. (2023). ESG rating disagreement: Implications and aggregation approaches. *Available at SSRN, 4515761*, 1–29.
29. Lioui, A., & Tarelli, A. (2022). Chasing the ESG factor. *Journal of Banking & Finance, 139*(106498), 1–77.
30. Gyönyörová, L., Stachoň, M., & Stašek, D. (2023). ESG ratings: relevant information or misleading clue? Evidence from the S&P Global 1200. *Journal of Sustainable Finance & Investment, 13*(2), 1075–1109.
31. Shanaev, S., & Ghimire, B. (2022). When ESG meets AAA: The effect of ESG rating changes on stock returns. *Finance Research Letters, 46*(102302), 1–7.
32. Avramov, D., Cheng, S., Lioui, A., & Tarelli, A. (2022). Sustainable investing with ESG rating uncertainty. *Journal of Financial Economics, 145*(2), 642–664.
33. Whelan, T., Atz, U., Van Holt, T., & Clark, C. (2021). ESG and financial performance. *Uncovering the Relationship by Aggregating Evidence from, 1*(1), 2015–2020.

34. Stubbs, W., & Rogers, P. (2013). Lifting the veil on environment-social-governance rating methods. *Social Responsibility Journal, 9*(4), 622–640.
35. Darnall, N., Ji, H., Iwata, K., & Arimura, T. H. (2022). Do ESG reporting guidelines and verifications enhance firms' information disclosure? *Corporate Social Responsibility and Environmental Management, 29*(5), 1214–1230.
36. Williams, Z. (2022). The materiality challenge of ESG ratings. *Economics and Culture, 19*(2), 97–108.
37. Galletta, S., Mazzù, S., & Naciti, V. (2022). A bibliometric analysis of ESG performance in the banking industry: From the current status to future directions. *Research in International Business and Finance, 62*(101684), 1–27.
38. Zainuldin, M. H., & Lui, T. K. (2022). A bibliometric analysis of CSR in the banking industry:A decade study based on Scopus scientific mapping. *International Journal of Bank Marketing, 40*(1), 1–26.
39. Van Eck, N., & Waltman, L. (2010). Software survey: VOSviewer, a computer program for bibliometric mapping. *Scientometrics, 84*(2), 523–538.
40. Pereira, V., Basilio, M. P., & Santos, C. H. T. (2023). pyBibX–A Python library for bibliometric and scientometric analysis powered with artificial intelligence tools. *arXiv preprint arXiv:2304.14516*, 1–30.
41. Stellner, C., Klein, C., & Zwergel, B. (2015). Corporate social responsibility and Eurozone corporate bonds: The moderating role of country sustainability. *Journal of Banking & Finance, 59*(1), 538–549.
42. Drempetic, S., Klein, C., & Zwergel, B. (2020). The influence of firm size on the ESG score: Corporate sustainability ratings under review. *Journal of Business Ethics, 167*(2), 333–360.
43. Cauthorn, T., Dumrose, M., Eckert, J., Klein, C., & Zwergel, B. (2023). Rating changes revisited: New evidence on short-term ESG momentum. *Finance Research Letters, 54*(103703), 1–6.
44. Dobrick, J., Klein, C., & Zwergel, B. (2023). Size bias in refinitiv ESG data. *Finance Research Letters, 55*(104014), 1–8.
45. Höck, A., Bauckloh, T., Dumrose, M., & Klein, C. (2023). ESG criteria and the credit risk of corporate bond portfolios. *Journal of Asset Management, 24*(7), 572–580.
46. Halbritter, G., & Dorfleitner, G. (2015). The wages of social responsibility—Where are they? A critical review of ESG investing. *Review of Financial Economics, 26*(1), 25–35.
47. Dorfleitner, G., Halbritter, G., & Nguyen, M. (2016). The risk of social responsibility–Is it systematic? *Journal of Sustainable Finance & Investment, 6*(1), 1–14.
48. Dorfleitner, G., Utz, S., & Wimmer, M. (2018). Patience pays off–corporate social responsibility and long-term stock returns. *Journal of Sustainable Finance & Investment, 8*(2), 132–157.
49. Dorfleitner, G., Kreuzer, C., & Sparrer, C. (2020). ESG controversies and controversial ESG: About silent saints and small sinners. *Journal of Asset Management, 21*(5), 393–412.
50. Cheng, B., Ioannou, I., & Serafeim, G. (2014). Corporate social responsibility and access to finance. *Strategic Management Journal, 35*(1), 1–23.
51. Masoumi, S., Amirkhani, H., Sadeghian, N., & Shahraz, S. (2024). Natural language processing (NLP) to facilitate abstract review in medical research: The application of BioBERT to exploring the 20-year use of NLP in medical research. *Systematic Reviews, 13*(107), 1–9.
52. Abate, G., Basile, I., & Ferrari, P. (2021). The level of sustainability and mutual fund performance in Europe: An empirical analysis using ESG ratings. *Corporate Social Responsibility and Environmental Management, 28*(5), 1446–1455.
53. Tan, Y. M., Szulczyk, K., & Sii, Y. H. (2023). Performance of ESG-integrated smart beta strategies in Asia-Pacific stock markets. *Research in International Business and Finance, 66*(102008), 1–15.
54. Dreyer, J. K., Moreira, M., Smith, W. T., & Sharma, V. (2023). Do environmental, social and governance practices affect portfolio returns? Evidence from the US stock market from 2002 to 2020. *Review of Accounting and Finance, 22*(1), 37–61.

55. Anikin, D., Finogenova, Y., Subbota, K., & Ermakova, A. (2023). Ensuring the efficiency of regulation and development of ESG rating methodology for Russian companies. *Relações Internacionais no Mundo Atual, 4*(42), 410–430.
56. Anikin, D., Finogenova, Y., Subbota, K., & Ermakova, A. (2023). Developing the ESG rating methodology for Russian companies. *Journal of Law and Sustainable Development, 11*(1), e0308–e0308.
57. Friske, W., Nikolov, A. N., & Morgan, T. (2023). Making the grade: An analysis of sustainability reporting standards and Global Reporting Initiative adherence ratings. *Corporate Social Responsibility and Environmental Management, 31*(3), 2098–2108.
58. Tenuta, P., & Cambrea, D. R. (2022). ESG measures and non-financial performance reporting. In *Corporate sustainability: Measurement, reporting and effects on firm performance* (pp. 27–57). Springer.
59. Papoutsi, A., & Sodhi, M. S. (2020). Does disclosure in sustainability reports indicate actual sustainability performance? *Journal of Cleaner Production, 260*(121049), 1–10.
60. He, F., Feng, Y., & Hao, J. (2023). Corporate ESG rating and stock market liquidity: Evidence from China. *Economic Modelling, 129*(106511), 1–13.
61. Wang, J., Ma, M., Dong, T., & Zhang, Z. (2023). Do ESG ratings promote corporate green innovation? A quasi-natural experiment based on SynTao Green Finance's ESG ratings. *International Review of Financial Analysis, 87*(102623), 1–14.
62. Wang, S., & Chang, Y. (2024). A study on the impact of ESG rating on green technology innovation in enterprises: An empirical study based on informal environmental governance. *Journal of Environmental Management, 358*(120878), 1–13.
63. Chodnicka-Jaworska, P. (2021). ESG as a Measure of Credit Ratings. *Risks, 9*(12), 226, 1–26.
64. Jin, Q. J. (2021). ESG factors as a determinant on credit ratings. *Journal of Finance, 34*(2), 31–65.
65. Bhattacharya, S., & Sharma, D. (2019). Do environment, social and governance performance impact credit ratings: A study from India. *International Journal of Ethics and Systems, 35*(3), 466–484.
66. Chan, C. Y., Chou, D. W., & Lo, H. C. (2017). Do financial constraints matter when firms engage in CSR? *The North American Journal of Economics and Finance, 39*(1), 241–259.
67. Malik, M., & Shim, E. D. (2022). Empirical examination of the direct and moderating role of corporate social responsibility in top executive compensation. *Pacific Accounting Review, 34*(5), 708–727.
68. Brooks, L. L. Z., Gill, S., Wong-On-Wing, B., & Yu, M. D. (2022). Does audit firm tenure enhance firm value? Closing the expectation gap through corporate social responsibility. *Managerial Auditing Journal, 37*(8), 1113–1145.
69. Choi, J. C., Chen, Q., & Lee, S. J. (2024). Predicting ESG ratings by machine learning and analyzing influencing factors by XAI. In *Proceedings of the 2024 7th international conference on software engineering and information management* (pp. 120–125). Association for Computing Machinery.
70. Svanberg, J., Ardeshiri, T., Samsten, I., Öhman, P., & Neidermeyer, P. (2023). Prediction of controversies and estimation of ESG performance: An experimental investigation using machine learning. In T. Rana, J. Svanberg, P. Öhman, & A. D. Lowe (Eds.), *Handbook of big data and analytics in accounting and auditing* (pp. 65–87). Springer Nature.
71. Svanberg, J., Ardeshiri, T., Samsten, I., Öhman, P., Neidermeyer, P. E., Rana, T., Maisano, F., & Danielson, M. (2023). Must social performance ratings be idiosyncratic? An exploration of social performance ratings with predictive validity. *Sustainability Accounting, Management and Policy Journal, 14*(7), 313–348.
72. Foster, B. P., Manikas, A. S., & Kroes, J. R. (2023). Which diversity measures best capture public company value? *Corporate Social Responsibility and Environmental Management, 30*(1), 236–247.
73. Nguyen, D. T., Hoang, T. G., Phi, N. T. M., & Truong, T. H. H. (2023). Do ESG ratings mediate the relationship between board gender diversity and firm financial performance? Evidence from the US Market. *The Economics and Finance Letters, 10*(2), 163–171.

74. Bristy, H. J., How, J., & Verhoeven, P. (2020). Gender diversity: The corporate social responsibility and financial performance nexus. *International Journal of Managerial Finance, 17*(5), 665–686.
75. Wang, C., Zhao, M., & Zhang, Z. (2021). Research on the relationship between corporate governance performance and financing cost under the background of ESG theory. In *2020 management science informatization and economic innovation development conference (MSIEID), MSIEID 2020, Guangzhou, China* (pp. 309–312).
76. Tian, H., & Tian, G. (2022). Corporate sustainability and trade credit financing: Evidence from environmental, social, and governance ratings. *Corporate Social Responsibility and Environmental Management, 29*(5), 1896–1908.
77. Kong, D., Liu, J., Wang, Y., & Zhu, L. (2024). Employee stock ownership plans and corporate environmental engagement. *Journal of Business Ethics, 189*(1), 177–199.
78. Ren, X., Zeng, G., & Sun, X. (2023). The peer effect of digital transformation and corporate environmental performance: Empirical evidence from listed companies in China. *Economic Modelling, 128*(106515), 1–12.
79. Zeng, H., Ren, L., Chen, X., Zhou, Q., Zhang, T., & Cheng, X. (2024). Punishment or deterrence? Environmental justice construction and corporate equity financing—Evidence from environmental courts. *Journal of Corporate Finance, 86*(102583), 1–24.
80. Dua, J., & Sharma, A. K. (2024). Unveiling the ESG-dividend nexus: The moderating role of investor protection and regulatory enforcement. *Journal of Indian Business Research, 16*(2), 265–286.
81. Liu, Y., Li, W., & Meng, Q. (2023). Influence of distracted mutual fund investors on corporate ESG decoupling: Evidence from China. *Sustainability Accounting, Management and Policy Journal, 14*(1), 184–215.
82. Bodhanwala, S., & Bodhanwala, R. (2023). Environmental, social and governance performance: Influence on market value in the COVID-19 crisis. *Management Decision, 61*(8), 2442–2466.
83. Dong, M., Li, M., Wang, H., & Pang, Y. (2024). ESG disagreement and stock price crash risk: Evidence from China. *Asia-Pacific Financial Markets, 32*, 1–33. https://doi.org/10.1007/s10690-024-09453-y

How to Measure the Social Impact of Renewable Energy Communities?

Michele Cipriano, Francesco Virili, and Stefano Za

Abstract This work-in-progress study examines the emergence and development of Renewable Energy Communities (RECs) in Europe, focusing particularly on the recent regulatory framework established in Italy. Supported by significant incentive policies, RECs aim to accelerate the sustainable transition of inner-country-localised ecosystems, building on a community-centric approach to redesigning energy production and consumption. Although many studies contribute to such scientific literature on renewable energy (especially from a technical perspective), very little research examines the characteristics and implications of RECs (especially considering the relevance of the social objective relative to the phenomenon). Moreover, while the necessity for a social impact evaluation model of RECs is increasingly emerging from the practical realm, little is known from an integrated perspective of organisational, managerial, and information systems (IS) aspects. Following in the footsteps of the IS tradition, this study seeks to contribute to such a discourse by considering technology as a component of the solution for addressing this need. We adopt a Design Science Research (DSR) approach for designing and developing an IT artefact crafted on RECs. At the same time, this artefact intends to enhance operational efficiency and establish a robust social impact evaluation system. The out-comes of this research are twofold: (1) to provide a comprehensive overview of the current landscape and challenges RECs face, and (2) to propose a novel IT-based solution for evaluating and maximising the social impact of RECs. This paper focuses particularly on the first two steps of the proposed DSR approach, providing the groundwork for the next steps.

M. Cipriano (✉) · F. Virili
Department of Economic and Social Sciences, Catholic University of the Sacred Heart, Piacenza, Italy
e-mail: michele.cipriano@unicatt.it; francesco.virili@unicatt.it

S. Za
Department of Management and Business Administration, University "G. D'Annunzio", Pescara, Italy
e-mail: stefano.za@unich.it

M. Cipriano et al. (eds.), *Technologies for Organizations and Society*,
Lecture Notes in Information Systems and Organisation 80,
https://doi.org/10.1007/978-3-032-01697-3_12

Keywords Renewable energy communities · Design science research approach · Social impact · Digital sustainability

1 Introduction

Sustainability still represents a global priority nowadays, expanding beyond environmental concerns and empowering economic and social aspects, emphasising the interdependencies among its three dimensions [1, 2]. By leveraging a paradigm for a sustainable society's development and resilience [3, 4], international governments committed to broader environmental goals and accounting for climate change mitigation and adaptation contribute to emerging initiatives promoted by several regulatory frameworks [5–7]. Renewable Energy Communities (RECs) represent a significant effort toward assessing sustainability across such three dimensions by involving citizens, governmental entities, private enterprises, and non-profit institutions. Although the idea for community-based energy projects already appeared decades ago [8, 9], nowadays, RECs are conceived to expedite the sustainable transition of localised ecosystems by fostering renewable energy production and consumption through a community-centric approach, in alignment with the SDGs goals, for example, as defined by the European Union (EU) [10, 11].

Then, a REC is supposed to facilitate the provision of environmental, economic, and social benefits to their members and local communities through renewable energy self-consumption [12, 13]. Given its purpose and value proposition to share renewable electricity first, as well as further resources and all the potential outcomes that could be produced by the REC, citizens, small and medium-sized enterprises, territorial bodies, and local authorities are intended to benefit and enhance their sustainable co-existence [14–16]. In this realm, among other state members, Italy emerges as one of the countries particularly committed to RECs development, considering also the regulatory framework and significant incentive policies the Italian Ministry of the Environment and Energy Security established [17].

Along with such a transforming energy system [18], while some authors suggest a roadmap for implementing RECs [19], addressing and measuring RECs benefits appears as one of the main challenges emerging from the practical realm. In particular, while various models have been developed for assessing the social impact of different organisations [7, 20–25], regarding RECs, it is evident that there is an urgent need to distinguish them from other institutions due to the diverse stakeholders' objectives, and their involvement in RECs design and development (i.e., including non-profit entities, municipalities, and religious bodies, according to regulations [17]). In the Italian realm, catholic institutions promote RECs among their several dioceses spread all around the country [26], also providing internal regulations (which should align with those established by the Italian government). Thus, the actual definition and measurement of such benefits, which are paramount for the promoters of RECs, is still an open issue.

From this perspective, we believe that RECs should be considered "complex systems" [27, 28] that, beyond more practical objectives, act as mechanisms of integration [27], community engagement [29], and as creative factors in terms of sense-making processes [30], form a social point of view. Accordingly, this study seeks to uncover the challenges, opportunities, and implications of leveraging digital tools to enhance sustainability in RECs through multidisciplinary research. By introducing new social impact evaluation systems, this research aims to advance both theoretical frameworks and practical applications. To this end, we propose the design and development of an IT artefact targeted explicitly at assessing the social impact of RECs. It emphasises the necessity of identifying and using appropriate measures to trigger, facilitate, develop, monitor, and evaluate community participation and positive outcomes.

This paper aims to contribute to such research by designing a comprehensive framework for evaluating the social impact of RECs, considering leveraging digital technologies to facilitate this process. Our approach is guided by the Design Science Research (DSR) tradition, which supports the creation of innovative artefacts that address real-world problems and advance theoretical knowledge [31–33]. Thus, we question:

- RQ1 (*how?*) *How can we evaluate the social impact of RECs using digital technology?* and
- RQ2 (*what?*) *What are the main measures, metrics, and theories relevant to social impact evaluation in the context of RECs?*

This work-in-progress study aims to provide a comprehensive overview of the current landscape and challenges RECs (and the various interested stakeholders) face. It also seeks to propose a novel IT-based solution for evaluating and maximising the social impact of RECs. The initial stages of the DSR approach will lay the groundwork for the subsequent development of a robust social impact evaluation system, leveraging technology as a crucial component of the solution.

The paper unfolds as follows. The next section provides a theoretical framework, including a literature review on social impact assessment, measures and metrics, and technologies (here, not necessarily intended as facilities to run RECs) supporting managing and evaluating procedures. Section 3 presents the methodology, detailing the protocol for progressing the DSR approach, data collection and analysis, and reference to the pilot cases under study. The subsequent sections discuss the results and outcomes of this work, providing a conclusion, implications, and future research directions.

2 Theoretical Framework

Exploring the literature, several authors started discussing RECs across many disciplines and perspectives, including case studies showing the first evidence of the design and development of establishing RECs [34–37]. Given the main objective of RECs (rooted in a community-based approach), particular attention has been given to the significant shift from centralised energy systems to decentralised ones, considering national innovations and related regional planning and optimisation of energy sources [38–41]. Besides, the majority of the evidence emerging from the literature is predominantly based on the environmental dimension or technical analyses [42–44] related to the energy domain and contextually similar ones (i.e., concerning climate change and other initiatives leveraging/integrating additional resources such as from biomass, geothermal, wind, hydroelectric) [45–48].

Delving deeply into RECs, some researchers focused on the different types and roles of stakeholders involved, the promoters, and the size of RECs, seeking to provide some classification [35, 49–51]. Further authors examined the power-sharing in such a context [16], the benefits and drivers [52], the relevance, purpose, and diversity of motivations behind RECs [53], as well as the public perceptions and opportunities for communities based on RECs [8]. Offering multidisciplinary insights on RECs are case studies reporting on the designing, planning, and development of RECs, such as Olivero's et al. [54] about one of the first RECs in Italy and Giampaolo et al. [55] about the Valle d'Aosta case. Micallef et al. [56] focus on a Maltase case, while Krug et al. [57] discuss RECs' drivers in Germany and Italy. Interestingly, increasingly scholarly attention is being given to the relevance of menage and, at the same time, measuring the social impact that RECs are supposed to generate [25, 34, 37, 39, 58].

Along with this transforming energy system, challenging the legitimacy and institutionalisation of such communities [18], recent studies attempt to reason and suggest a roadmap for the implementation of RECs [19], also remarking on the technological and organisational aspects [18, 59]. However, addressing and measuring REC benefits is particularly puzzling because of the specific social dimension driving RECs, including mitigating different social fragilities such as energy poverty and actively promoting community engagement (to mention some). Thus, in the following section, we first attempt to provide a thorough narrative useful for framing RECs. Afterwards, to identify the most significant research concerning RECs' social impact, we investigate measures, metrics, and approaches discussed in rigorous publications, considering only sources such as Articles and Literature Reviews published in Scientific Journals.

2.1 Energy Communities: Background Literature

A recent contribution by Gjorgievski et al. [60] analysed the state-of-the-art literature on energy communities while considering the different possible technical and social arrangements and their implications on impacts. RECs are depicted as groups of actors that produce and share renewable energy. These communities were officially recognised in the Clean Energy Package, a set of directives adopted by the EU in 2019 to facilitate the energy transition. RECs can include citizens, organisations, and businesses who collaborate to build facilities for renewable energy production.

By doing so, they contribute to environmental sustainability, economic benefits, and social well-being for all involved. In general, extant literature distinguishes four particular types of energy communities based on the technologies used: (1) shared solar PV (rooftop or collective, with or without individual batteries); (2) shared storage; (3) multi- and hybrid energy systems; and (iv) district heating and cooling systems.

This research focuses more specifically on the first REC type: shared solar photovoltaic sharing communities. In Europe, they are becoming increasingly prominent, approximatively ranging about 3500 such renewable energy cooperatives [61, 62]. Four main actor typologies are present in a typical shared solar REC, categorised as follows:

Consumers: Consumers within an energy community can be natural persons (households), schools, universities, non-governmental organisations, public utility companies, businesses (whose primary economic activity isn't energy-related), local authorities, municipalities, and more. Their role involves using energy services provided by the community.

Prosumers and Producers (Energy Service Providers): Prosumers both produce and consume energy. They generate energy (e.g., through solar panels) for their own use and can also share or trade excess energy with other community members. Besides prosumers, pure producers deal with energy-related services, including energy generation, distribution, storage, supply, and other related commodities. They may own and use infrastructure for energy generation, distribution, storage, and information and communication technologies (ICT).

Initiators: Initiators play a crucial role in organising and coordinating community energy projects. They set the project in motion, and their involvement is essential for successful implementation. Initiators may or may not directly benefit from the community energy service.

Community members exchange information, energy, and finance among themselves and external actors. The relationships with these external actors are graphically represented in Fig. 1 here below.

As a way of exemplification, in Fig. 1, the energy community is depicted as having only one consumer (C) and one prosumer (P). Accordingly, the depiction does not include the initiators, as the focus is on the established energy community.

Moreover, in Fig. 1, orange arrows indicate monetary flows, and blue arrows represent the flows of services and commodities. As per EU legislation, energy communities should have the right to access any suitable market and should be treated equally with other energy sector actors. This equality increases the likelihood of capturing the actual value that the community can provide to its members and the energy system.

An energy community can access a market directly, as a self-representative entity, or through a third-party energy service provider such as an aggregator.

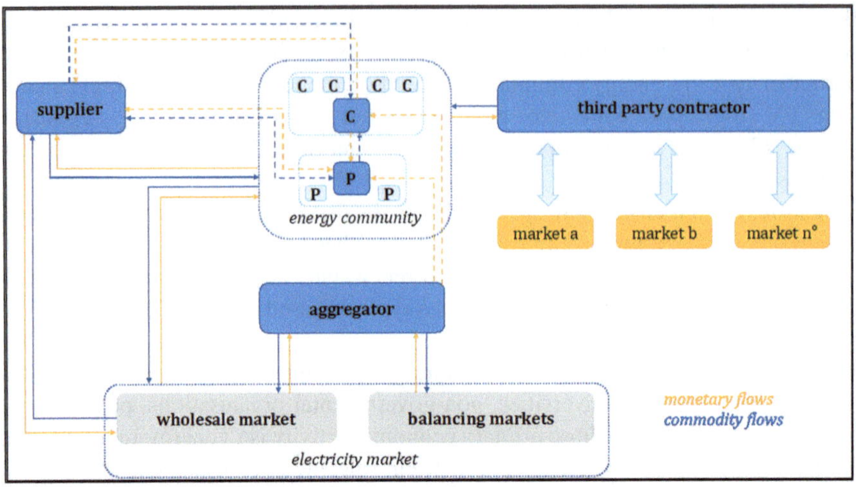

Fig. 1 Interplay between energy community with external actors from Gjorgievski et al. [60]

2.2 *Impact Evaluation of Energy Communities*

Based on the idea of leveraging digital technologies to enhance the assessment process and address the social dimensions effectively, this section attempts to outline the most relevant studies contributing to the initial discourse on assessing the social impact of RECs. To this end, although this paper does not aim to perform a literature review research, we sought to keep rigour also in this phase in line with the current ambition of this study (considering we will leverage this step as it will be explained in the methodology section). For this purpose, while we discuss only some articles recently published in Scientific Journal, attempting to provide an overview of the most recent state of the art, we report the list of all the previous literature reviews we were able to collect from the Scopus and Web of Science Databases in Appendix 1 (by running the same query search). Appendix 1, "Previous Literature Reviews", intends to outline an immediate understanding of the heterogeneity of focuses, main aspects, and domains discussed in concert with the RECs' social impact evaluation characteristics. This could be useful in recognising areas and stakeholders to be taken into account in the development of more accurate frameworks, selecting measures and metrics, and simultaneously addressing all the sustainability dimensions. Moreover, it highlights the actual need for research concerning the primary goal of the present study by carefully acknowledging the role of technology from various points of view.

In particular, we developed a crafted research query that we thoroughly refined in several steps according to the results we obtained. To our aim, we edited it with specific semantics in line with the guidelines provided by the two selected databases. As a way of explanation, we report hereafter the one used in the Scopus database:

(TITLE-ABS-KEY ("social impact" OR "evaluation" OR "assessment*" OR "measure*" OR "metric*" OR "KPI*" OR "Key performance indicator*") AND TITLE-ABS-KEY ("renewable" AND "energ*" AND "communit*") AND TITLE-ABS-KEY ("stakeholder*")) AND (LIMIT-TO (LANGUAGE, "English")).* This query retrieved 250 documents on Scopus (among the different document types, published 164 as Articles and 17 as Literature Reviews, respectively) and 229 documents on Web of Sciences (among the different document types, published 49 as Articles and 12 as Literature Reviews, respectively). In particular, we noticed that 133 documents were simultaneously retrieved from both databases; therefore, we ensured that duplicates were avoided in the final sample (last update in early May 2024). Appendix 1 lists the 29 literature reviews identified (that we are considering across the different stages of the DSR approach of the present research (for details, please see Sect. 3). Appendix 1 includes complete reference, document typology (i.e., Article (A), Review (R)), and the relative database of collection (i.e., Scopus (S), Web of Science (S), or (S and WoS) if appeared on both). In addition, while hereafter we provide a broader synthesis of some research strictly related to the various aspects characterising the present study, Appendix 2, "Integrated Synthesis of Previous Literature Reviews", summarises the main findings, theoretical underpinning, and methodologies, also reporting metrics and measures (if present) discussed in the selected list of articles in Appendix 1.

Then, delving deeply into the social impact discussions, Gjorgievski et al. [60] claim that existing studies on energy communities often lack a quantitative framework for evaluating social impacts and benefits (as a tool to assess enhanced social cohesion, improved energy literacy, the development of social networks, the promotion of global partnerships, and the reduction of energy poverty). Kumar et al. [63] and Santos et al. [64] incorporate social aspects into their design processes. For example, Kumar et al. [63] suggest key performance indicators like public acceptance, the Human Development Index, health issues, universal education, gender equality, and job creation. However, these studies do not offer methods for quantifying these social impacts, and the evaluations lack the quantitative rigour applied to economic, environmental, and technical impacts. At the same time, various approaches should be adopted to address such research gaps. Accordingly, Jones et al. [65] provide an overview of methods for measuring the socioeconomic impacts of renewable energy projects, while Nussbaumer et al. [66] and Li et al. [67] discuss measures relevant to energy and fuel poverty.

However, Charani Shandiz et al. [68] develop revised and extended resilience metrics and evaluation methods based on nine metrics (e.g., performance-based resilience index, probability of network performing its intended functions) and eight methods (e.g., analytic hierarchy process, spatial power outage duration model) from qualitative and quantitative perspectives. In comparison, Gruber et al. [69] propose a comparative analysis for optimising objective functions on overall energy community costs (as well as individual member costs) and resilience (technical goal) by integrating a distribution grid that could leverage high photovoltaic (PV) and electrical vehicle (EV) adoption. Elomari et al. [70] develop a data-driven model that combines Homer Pro with an in-house Python tool integrating a machine learning algorithm, life cycle cost (LCC), and life cycle assessment (LCA) calculations of a REC model. They establish a multi-objective optimisation model to minimise LCC and LCA parameters while maximising green energy, also proposing a multi-criteria decision-making approach using the Weighted Sum Model to assist stakeholders in selecting the optimal scenario for the desired energy community, considering the impact of various economic parameters on the sustainable performance of REC [70]. Sirviö et al. [71] suggest multi-objective value considerations and a value-sharing framework focusing on and examining the stakeholders' functionalities and analysis of them. In comparison, Heuninckx et al. [72] adopt the Multi Actor Multi Criteria Analysis stakeholders engagement tool in setting up an energy community as a participative decision-making methodology. Fleischhacker et al. [73] focus on portfolio optimisation, adopting clustering algorithms to improve two existing open source models with a Pareto optimisation concerning costs and carbon emissions objectives, eventually improving the models' scalability and performance. Moreover, Cultore et al. [74] propose a virtual energy-sharing scheme in Italy, allowing the energy community's electricity to cover the demands of members not physically connected to the production system (avoiding the need for a dedicated distribution network and reducing technical constraints and high investment costs).

Therefore, this research intends to build on these insights by developing a comprehensive framework for evaluating the social impact of Renewable Energy Communities (RECs) and IT Artefact (Abstract and Material).

3 Methodology

The Design Science Research (DSR) approach represents one of the most suitable methodologies in the information systems discipline for addressing a variety of problems and issues, particularly those that involve the creation and application of innovative solutions [33, 75–77]. Moreover, it is primarily helpful for addressing complex real-world problems and interdisciplinary challenges, impacting organisations and society [78] (e.g., concerning educational solutions [79], smart cities [80], and cybersecurity [81]). Accordingly, to ensure that the solutions are not only theoretically sound but also practically relevant and effective, in this research, we use the DSR approach to substantiate the process of developing an IT artefact for evaluating the social impact of RECs.

3.1 A Design Science Research Approach

We adopt the DSR approach as an optimal methodology to address this research challenge [31]. DSR provides a structured and rigorous framework for developing impactful information systems (IS) artefacts, promoting both technological and

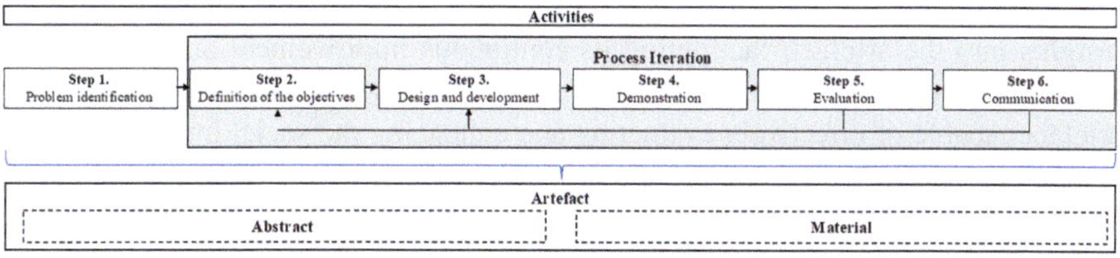

Fig. 2 DSR approach adapted from Peffer et al. [31] and Jones and Gregor [33]

scientific advancements [31–33]. This methodology encourages researchers to create innovative solutions that address real-world problems and enhance their operational environments [32, 33]. In this study, DSR enables us to systematically develop an IT artefact aimed at evaluating the social impact of Renewable Energy Communities (RECs).

Our objective is to investigate how a digital tool can facilitate ongoing social impact evaluation for RECs. To achieve this, we align with the assumptions proposed by Peffers et al. [31]. Additionally, we plan to implement an integrated DSR framework as suggested by Jones and Gregor [33], adapting it to design, develop, and evaluate abstract and material artefacts specific to RECs [32]. We propose a tailored DSR protocol for RECs (in Fig. 2), which guides the entire research and development process.

The DSR approach involves several stages: problem identification and motivation, objective definition, design and development, demonstration, evaluation, and communication. By following this structured process, we aim to create a robust and effective tool that not only assesses but also enhances the social impact of RECs. This methodology ensures that our research is grounded in both practical relevance and theoretical rigour, thereby contributing to the broader field of information systems and renewable energy community studies.

In alignment with the structured DSR approach, the artefact will be iteratively developed and refined over the five cycles following the Problem identification step (by performing the definition of the objectives, the design and development, demonstration, evaluation, and communication steps). These cycles involve continuous validation and revision with input from representatives of RECs (e.g., promoters, initiators, project partners, consulting organisations for REC development, and researchers) [31–33]. In addition, these cycles also contemplate the integration of mechanisms for continuous feedback from REC stakeholders, including the development process.

To achieve comprehensive evaluation and development, this multi-methodological approach develops on integrating conceptual and empirical iterations by leveraging information from existing literature and prior evidence in the first case alongside feedback and information from the practice realm in the second case. This iterative process ensures that the artefact is grounded in theoretical knowledge while being practically relevant and effective in real-world applications [31].

Furthermore, the iterative cycles enable the incorporation of feedback and insights into the artefact, facilitating its continuous improvement and ensuring its robustness. By following these steps, we aim to produce a validated and refined IT artefact capable of effectively evaluating and enhancing the social impact of RECs. In addition, such methodological rigour would strengthen the artefact's reliability and contribute to the broader knowledge base within management, organisations, information systems, and renewable energy community research. Thus, while we decided to provide relevant theoretical foundations in the theoretical background (seeking to provide a twofold contribution by reviewing the literature and supporting the first two steps presented in Fig. 2), the following section focuses on the empirical examination this paper focuses on.

3.2 Data Sampling, Collection and Analysis: RECs at the Core of the DSR Approach

Regarding the Italian context, it is possible to identify three-dimensional categories for RECs (generally established as PV RECs), depending on the size of the community contributing and participating in the REC establishing, that is, small, medium and large communities. We report the main characteristics of such dimensional categories of RECs in Table 1.

Table 1 Information concerning three-dimensional categories of RECs in Italy

Small: Micro-communities (such as condominiums and small parishes)	Installed power 20–200 kW Average potentially distributable incentives: 2500—10,000 euros/year Shared system and/or participants' systems Private individuals or small businesses with limited numbers and territory Strong participant involvement
Medium: Local communities (RECs affecting municipal/provincial territories)	Installed power 100 kW—1 MW Average incentives potentially distributable: 5000–50,000 euros/year Institutional founding members: Municipalities, Parishes, Third Sector Bodies PNRR financing specifically for municipalities <5000 inhabitants Medium direct involvement of participants
Large: Wide range (RECs affecting large territories and large populations)	Installed power 1–30+ MW (possibility of including multiple primary cab-ins) Average incentives potentially distributable: 50,000—1,500,000+ euros/year Often promoted by large energy companies and/or one or more dioceses/regions Standardisation of services, low direct involvement of participants

For this research, the observed sample is in the medium size dimensional category. Sample selection is still underway, taking into account both the project development stage, actual potential for completion in time, and data availability/collection issues.

The project partner is a consulting organisation for REC development: they have about 16 REC projects all around Italy. Among them, an initial prototype sample for our research could be composed of three REC projects with three different types of initiators: (1) non-profit initiator, (2) religious institution initiator, and (3) municipality initiator.

In the first exploratory phase, we collect project and initiator information, identifying different types of stakeholders, including beneficiaries and objectives for each stakeholder. We are also identifying possible stakeholders' objectives, assuming that there could be some that could be shared among distinct stakeholders, as well as we expect to encounter conflicting goals among the same or different objectives between stakeholders (because of their different roles with respect to the REC, or the particular social objective they represent/fit the most/should benefit from). Accordingly, we plan to carefully address the shared and conflicting objectives, as well as the unique objectives for specific categories of stakeholders or a specific stakeholder (attempting to mitigate any conflict) [82–84].

In parallel, we collect KPIs from the literature analysis in order to recognise specific measures to be used with respect to each objective. In particular, the adopted logic consists of finding a match: Objectives—Measure. From this perspective, we reason on the fact that objectives (e.g., (environmental, social, governmental, technical)) move stakeholders. However, we are interested in a more holistic understanding concerning RECs, focusing on how the community-based approach (the foundation of such a phenomenon) would be able to promote/could efficiently run a coordinated management of all the stakeholders' objectives and how it could maximise the benefits from this.

4 IT Artefact Design Process

To provide a preliminary frame concerning the second step of the DSR approach (as in Fig. 2), "definition of the objectives", this section represents an attempt to develop and instantiate design science (DS) principles (P) and requirements (R), in accordance with the piece of research described in the present study. Accordingly, we first present some principles of Design Science Research for RECs (DS.P) and then some requirements for the Design Science Artefacts for RECs (DS.R).

The DSR approach is grounded in several key principles that guide the research process. These principles are essential for ensuring the rigour and relevance of the artefacts developed. We provide eight design science principles in Table 2 and eight design science requirements in Table 3, briefly describing each. Next is Table 4, showing how such identified design science principles should be operationalised through specific requirements. For a straightforward representation and description,

Table 2 Principles of design science research for RECs

DS.P1	Relevance: The research should address a relevant problem faced by practitioners or society. In this case, the need for effective evaluation of the social impact of RECs is both a practical and a theoretical concern.
DS.P2	Rigour: The development process should be methodologically rigorous, drawing on existing theories and empirical evidence. This involves a thorough literature review and the use of robust data collection and analysis methods.
DS.P3	Design as an Artefact: The research must produce a viable artefact (in this case, a theoretical framework and a social impact dashboard) that solves the identified problem.
DS.P4	Design evaluation: The artefact must be evaluated to ensure it meets the intended goals and provides value. This involves iterative testing and refinement based on feedback from stakeholders.
DS.P5	Research contributions: The outcomes should contribute to the knowledge base, providing new insights or theoretical advancements. This research aims to extend existing theories on social impact measurement and offer practical tools for REC management. *(continued)*
DS.P6	Research rigor: The process should be rigorous, using established research methodologies to ensure validity and reliability.
DS.P7	Design as a search process: The development of the artefact involves a search for an effective solution through iterative design, testing, and refinement.
DS.P8	Communication of research: The findings and artefacts should be clearly communicated to both practitioners and academics, ensuring that the research has practical and theoretical impact.

we avoid using the complete names of principles and requirements and refer to related Tables that provide a specific ID for each (e.g., DS.P1).

Then, to align with these principles, the development of the theoretical framework and the social impact dashboard must meet specific requirements (see Table 3).

Afterwards, we attempt to explain how such principles could be operationalised through the identified requirements. For this purpose, we first provide Table 4, showing which requirements contribute to the achievement of the specific principles. Afterwards, we provide a brief narrative explaining how requirements development operationalises specific principles. It is worth noting that the requirements contribute to the achievement of one or more principles.

In particular, concerning DS.P1, Relevance, DS.R1 assumes that understanding who is involved in RECs and their objectives ensures the artefact addresses real-world needs. DS.R3 supposes that identifying appropriate metrics aligns the research with practical evaluation needs. DS.R4 assumes that gathering direct input from stakeholders ensures the artefact's relevance. Lastly, DS.R5 supposes that creating a policy-support framework ensures the research addresses significant practical concerns.

Regarding DS.P2, Rigor, DS.R1, assumes that a rigorous approach to identifying and analysing stakeholders ensures comprehensive understanding. DS.R3 supposes that a rigorous identification of metrics ensures the framework's validity. DS.R4 assumes that using structured methods to gather insights ensures methodological

Table 3 Requirements for the Design Science Artefacts for RECs

DS.R1	Stakeholder identification and analysis: Identify and categorise stakeholders involved in RECs, considering various configurations (e.g., private entities, associations, service suppliers). Understand their objectives and potential conflicts to ensure comprehensive stakeholder management.
DS.R2	Objective matrix development: Create a matrix listing objectives for each stakeholder, identifying shared, conflicting, and unique objectives. This matrix will help in designing strategies to mediate conflicts and align stakeholder goals.
DS.R3	Measure and metric identification: Review existing literature to identify relevant measures and metrics for evaluating the social impact of RECs. This will inform the development of the theoretical framework and the dashboard.
DS.R4	Focus group and interview insights: Conduct focus groups and semi-structured interviews with REC promoters and key stakeholders to gather insights and refine the framework and dashboard. This participatory approach ensures the artefacts are grounded in real-world needs and contexts.
DS.R5	Framework for supporting policy makers: Develop a framework that supports policymakers in understanding and evaluating the social impact of RECs. This framework should be practical, actionable, and aligned with policy objectives.
DS.R6	Dashboard development: Design and develop a social impact dashboard that allows REC managers and community members to monitor and maximise their social impact. The dashboard should be user-friendly, customisable, and capable of integrating diverse data sources.
DS.R7	Pre- and post-development evaluation: Describe and evaluate the situation before and after the development of the dashboard to demonstrate its effectiveness. This evaluation will include both quantitative and qualitative measures.
DS.R8	Iterative design and feedback loop: Implement an iterative design process, incorporating feedback from stakeholders to refine and improve the artefacts continuously. This approach ensures the artefacts remain relevant and effective over time

Table 4 Design science principles operationalised through specific requirements

DS.P	DS.R	DS.P	DS.R
DS.P1	DS.R1, DS.R3, DS.R4, DS.R5	DS.P6	DS.R3, DS.R4, DS.R7
DS.P2	DS.R1, DS.R3, DS.R4, DS.R7	DS.P7	DS.R2, DS.R6, DS.R8
DS.P3	DS.R2, DS.R6, DS.R5, DS.R8	DS.P8	DS.R5, DS.R7, DS.R8
DS.P4	DS.R7, DS.R8		
DS.P5	DS.R3, DS.R5, DS.R6		

rigour. DS.R7 supposes that systematic evaluation ensures the artefact's effectiveness.

Concerning DS.P3, Design as an Artefact, DS.R2 assumes that creating a detailed matrix is a tangible artefact that addresses stakeholder conflicts. DS.R6 supposes that developing a dashboard is a direct application of the artefact principle. DS.R5 assumes that the policy framework is a theoretical artefact aimed at practical application. DS.R8 supposes that continuous refinement produces a well-developed artefact.

Regarding DS.P4, Design Evaluation, DS.R7 assumes that assessing the artefact before and after implementation ensures it meets its goals. DS.R8 supposes that continuous evaluation and feedback improve the artefact's quality.

Concerning DS.P5, Research Contributions, DS.R3 assumes that identifying metrics contributes to the academic discourse on social impact. DS.R5 supposes that developing a new framework advances theoretical knowledge. DS.R6 assumes that creating a dashboard provides a practical tool for the community.

Regarding DS.P6, Research Rigor, DS.R3 supposes that using established methods to identify metrics ensures rigour. DS.R4 assumes that structured data collection methods ensure rigorous analysis. DS.R7 supposes that systematic evaluation processes ensure the research's rigour.

Concerning DS.P7, Design as a Search Process, DS.R2 assumes that developing the matrix through iterative processes embodies the search principle. DS.R6 supposes that creating and refining the dashboard is a search for an effective solution. DS.R8 assumes that continuous improvement reflects the search for optimal solutions.

Finally, regarding DS.P8, Communication of Research, DS.R5 supposes that the framework provides a clear communication tool for policymakers. DS.R7 assumes that documenting the evaluation process communicates the artefact's effectiveness, while DS.R8 supposes that sharing iterative improvements helps communicate the research process and outcomes.

5 Discussion, Expected Results, and Conclusions

In this paper, we present a structured research process intended to develop and adopt an IT artefact designed to monitor and enhance the social impact of RECs by means of a novel theoretical framework (abstract) and a REC social impact dashboard system (material). In particular, this research seeks to establish a novel theoretical framework for assessing the social impact of RECs and providing REC managers and community members with a tool to track and improve their social contributions effectively.

From this perspective, the expected results are at least twofold. On the one hand, it is a framework for supporting policymakers. On the other hand, this work should develop a dashboard that would measure and continuously monitor the REC's social impact in its different dimensions, showing how the REC is developing and pursuing the stakeholders' objectives. Thus, we would be able to describe and explain the improvements pre- and post-development of such a dashboard, showing how the use of the REC social impact dashboard would be helpful for REC development and management to maximise and continuously improve the benefits produced by the REC over time.

Besides, the present study contributes to advancing research on the theoretical frame concerning social impact measurement by focusing on the distinctive characteristics of RECs. By exploring and examining the literature, we started developing such a theoretical frame, providing Appendix 2 as a "meta-synthesis", integrating an understanding of approaches, methods, theoretical underpinnings and findings from previous literature reviews (strictly related to the objectives of this research). At the same time, we started recognising some studies discussing key metrics to foster community involvement and positive outcomes. Our research holds particular significance for REC community managers, as it would help define and monitor stakeholder activities related to sustainable renewable energy practices and evaluate the benefits associated with renewable energy production and distribution. The desired IT artefact will enable managers to assess REC contributions to sustainability across economic, social, and environmental dimensions, also allowing them to align to non-financial accounting requirements.

However, it is important to acknowledge the limitations of the present work. The current research only presents some preliminary outcomes of the initial two stages of the comprehensive DSR protocol. In future steps, supposing at the completion of a full cycle of the entire DSR protocol, more extensive research is planned to be presented and communicated while validating and refining the proposed frameworks and tools. Furthermore, while we are not considering the possibility of selecting cases from different countries (at the moment), we are assuming the possibility that some context-specific characteristics from different Italian regions could emerge from this research (considering that our consulting organisation for REC development is currently involved with about 16 REC projects across Italy). Additionally, we emphasise the value of conducting comparative studies across various European regions. Despite their complexity, such studies could offer valuable insights into the challenges and successes of different renewable energy community (REC) projects and their associated social impacts.

Beyond these limitations, this research is also intended to offer valuable contributions to the IS discipline by proposing such an integrated DSR framework tailored explicitly for evaluating the social impact of RECs, resulting in two main outputs: i) a specialised framework for social impact evaluation in RECs, and ii) an IT artefact for monitoring and measuring REC social impact.

Disclosure of Interests The authors have no competing interests to declare that are relevant to the content of this article.

Appendix 1: Previous Literature Reviews

Reference with [identifier (ID)]	Doc.Type/Database(es)
Zafar et al. [85]	R/S and WoS
Dirisu et al. [86]	R/S and WoS
Cai and Gou [87]	R/WoS
Kime et al. [88]	R/S and WoS
Shyu [89]	R/S and WoS
Caballero et al. [90]	R/S and WoS
Pasanec Preprotić et al. [91]	R/WoS
Mishra et al. [92]	R/WoS
Vallejos-Romero et al. [93]	R/WoS
Cerca et al. [94]	R/S and WoS
Amerson et al. [95]	R/S and WoS
Vuthi et al. [96]	R/S *(continued)*
Taormina et al. [97]	R/WoS
Zolfani et al. [98]	*R/WoS*
Copping et al. [99]	*R/S*
Moghaddasi et al. [100]	*R/S and WoS*
Rungcharoennan and Phoochinda [101]	*R/S*
Kuriqi et al. [102]	*R/S and WoS*
Mai-Moulin et al. [103]	*R/S and WoS*
Kumar and Cao [104]	*R/WoS*
Mazur et al. [105]	R/WoS
Ferrer-Martí et al. [106]	R/S and WoS
van Veelen and van der Horst [107]	R/WoS
Jamal et al. [108]	R/WoS
Huesca-Pérez et al. [109]	R/WoS
Whitton et al. [110]	R/WoS
Cosmi et al. [111]	R/S and WoS
Sinclair et al. [112]	R/S
Kermagoret et al. [113]	R/S and WoS

Appendix 2: Integrated Synthesis of Previous Literature Reviews

Reference [as in Appendix 1]	Methodological approach (M), theoretical underpinnings (T), major Findings and conceptual framework (F)
Zafar et al. [85]	– (M): Social life cycle assessment (SLCA) combining quantitative data (e.g., employee salaries, social risks) and qualitative methods (e.g., community questionnaires, compliance audits) to evaluate social performance against regional and universal social standards. – (T): Develops on the need for more comprehensive SLCA methodologies, proposing the use of detailed correlation methods and enhanced frameworks to provide deeper insights for managerial decision-making. – (F): Limitations in SLCA practices, recommending the inclusion of all relevant stakeholders and more thorough analysis to enhance social sustainability and increase public acceptance of renewable energy systems.
Dirisu et al. [86]	– (M): Forensic assessment combining a holistic review of bioenergy sources, impacts on sustainable development, and clean development mechanisms (CDM) to analyse energy use and emissions reduction. – (T): Relationship between energy sources, sustainable development, and population dynamics, with a focus on bioenergy's role in achieving global climate goals and sustainable economic growth. – (F): It identifies the potential for modern bioenergy to transform Africa's energy landscape by integrating bioenergy with agricultural and food security initiatives and emphasises the need for comprehensive policies to support bioenergy development.
Cai and Gou [87]	– (M): Literature review to refine flexure definitions and classifications and compares technologies for energy efficiency, generation, and storage based on cost and performance. – (T): Frames flexors, buildings with dynamic roles in energy consumption, generation, storage, and grid interaction, highlighting the need to address both static and dynamic energy balances. – (F): Four key energy functions for flexures and their applications, such as positive energy districts. Suggests further research on metrics for energy flexibility and embodied energy, and adapting technologies to local contexts.
Kime et al. [88]	– (M): Is based on a comprehensive literature review to identify and categorise metrics for evaluating equity in low-carbon energy transitions, analysing existing metrics across various disciplines and creating an analytical framework to assess equity impacts in four key areas: Renewable energy deployment, fossil fuel retirement, transportation electrification, and residential decarbonisation. – (T): Framework based on the vulnerability scoping diagram (VSD), adapted to categorise and evaluate equity outcomes in energy transitions. The framework is structured around three equity dimensions (health, access, and livelihood) each with specific indicators and metrics to guide stakeholders in assessing and addressing equity issues.

(continued)

	– (F): It highlights the need for a structured approach to evaluating equity in energy transitions, providing a framework with categorised dimensions and metrics. The study suggests that while the framework offers a practical starting point, further refinement of metrics and methods is necessary to address limitations and enhance the effectiveness of energy transition policies in achieving equity.
Shyu [89]	– (M): Review of 16 World Bank solar home system (SHS) projects in rural developing areas from 2000 to 2020, identifying key internal and external factors impacting project success. Internal factors include financial, technical, and project design barriers, while external factors cover political, institutional, and social-cultural barriers. – (T): It develop a framework to evaluate the implementation challenges of SHS projects, focusing on both internal and external barriers. It supports policy implications for overcoming these barriers and achieving sustainable development goal 7 (SDG7) by 2030, highlighting the need to address systemic and contextual issues in electrification efforts. – (F): Critical internal and external barriers affecting SHS project success and provide actionable policy recommendations. Key insights include addressing political and socio-cultural barriers, ensuring affordability, considering future energy integration, and adopting a holistic, multi-stakeholder approach for effective rural electrification.
Caballero et al. [90]	– (M): Interdisciplinary framework, the meaningful marine renewable energy (MRE) development framework, for integrating energy justice principles into the development of marine renewable energy (MRE) projects. It uses three theoretical approaches: Energy justice, the social framework for projects, and social life cycle assessment. – (T): Is based on current resources and implications for advancing energy justice within MRE projects. It helps translate theoretical concepts into practical guidelines, emphasising community involvement, and aligning with justice principles to improve project outcomes and equity. – (F): Potential consequences and opportunities in applying energy justice principles. Recommends a community-tailored approach to ensure equitable distribution of benefits and address potential injustices throughout project phases, guiding questions and resources to facilitate stakeholder engagement and informed decision-making.
Pasanec Preprotić et al. [91]	– (M): Reviews advancements in eco-efficient bookbinding through biodegradable materials and eco-advanced adhesive systems. Highlights the integration of non-toxic polymers and resins with ISO/TC130 standards to improve sustainability and efficiency in bookbinding. – (T): Adhesive technologies and the need for novel, sustainable solutions, eco-labelled adhesives and closed-loop recycling models to enhance productivity, reduce waste and meet environmental management standards. – (F): Identifies the need for continued innovation in adhesive systems to support eco-efficient practices in bookbinding. Recommends the development of sustainable workflow models, including circular resource management and stakeholder collaboration, to advance environmental, social, and economic sustainability in the graphic arts industry.
Mishra et al. [92]	– (M): Cooling technologies for photovoltaic thermoelectric (PV-TE) hybrid solar energy systems, including air-cooling, liquid cooling, nanofluids, and phase change materials. Analyses performance factors such as efficiency, coefficient of performance, and exergy efficiency.

(continued)

	– (T): Effectiveness of different cooling methods, noting that forced cooling offers about 30% better performance than natural cooling but is less cost-effective. Highlights that nanofluids significantly enhance exergy generation and thermal efficiency. – (F): Passive cooling techniques are cost-effective and simple, while active cooling provides superior performance. Integrating nanofluids and phase change materials (PCMs) can improve cooling efficiency and panel lifespan. Room for investigation refers to optimising cooling systems with advanced materials, improving cost-effectiveness, and addressing compatibility issues to enhance overall system performance and sustainability.
Vallejos-Romero et al. [93]	– (M): Article reviews in social science research on green hydrogen, analysing 78 articles from the web of science and SCOPUS published between 1997 and 2022. It identifies three main research areas: (a) risks, socio-environmental impacts, and public perception; (b) public policies and regulation; and (c) social acceptance. – (T): The review shows that Europe and Asia are leading in green hydrogen research. It highlights a strong focus on public policy and social acceptance but less on the social perception of risk and the social and environmental impacts on local and indigenous communities. The study also notes that a lack of integrated technical and social research and limited familiarity with green hydrogen technology impact acceptance. – (F): Research on green hydrogen needs to address gaps in socio-environmental impacts, integrate technical and social aspects, and enhance understanding of public perception and acceptance. Improved policies and case studies are essential for infrastructure, adoption, and governance. Expanding research to cover broader social and economic implications will support more effective and inclusive energy transitions.
Cerca et al. [94]	– (M): Systematic literature review of research on biorefineries to identify bottlenecks and social dimensions in the strategic planning of bio-based supply chains. It examines feedstocks from land and marine ecosystems and assesses current research trends. – (T): Predominant focus on techno-economic aspects in biorefinery research, with increasing attention to environmental aspects through life cycle assessments. Social dimensions remain underexplored, including employment, stakeholder engagement, and community impacts. – (F): Bottlenecks related to resource availability, logistics, and socio-ecological issues. Further research needs to integrate social sustainability into planning frameworks, by interdisciplinary approaches, and considering socio-technical-ecological systems for more effective and inclusive bio-based supply chains.
Amerson et al. [95]	– (M): Is based on triton field trials (TFiT) on marine energy environmental monitoring technologies and methods. It provides a guide for establishing effective environmental monitoring campaigns and discusses the importance of timing, tracking, and measuring the impact of these campaigns. – (T): It extends the TFiT findings to broader marine energy sustainability issues, life cycle assessment and sustainability methodologies. It emphasises the need for stakeholder collaboration and integrates environmental, economic, and social dimensions in marine energy research. – (F): Standardizing monitoring technologies, timing campaigns to coincide with critical species movements, and enhancing transparency and community engagement. For sustainability, it suggests expanding life cycle assessments to include marine-specific impacts and adopting design principles for environmental benefits. These measures aim to improve stakeholder trust, ensure equitable energy transitions, and optimize marine energy technologies.

(continued)

Vuthi et al. [96]	– (M): Literature review on agent-based modelling (ABM) applied to urban neighbourhood energy systems, focusing on models that explore local market mechanisms, renewable energy integration, heat transitions, and mobility. – (T): It employs ABM to understand complex interactions within energy systems, incorporating geographic information systems (GIS) and modelling approaches, including simulation, hybrid, optimization, and accounting models. – (F): Gap in current models, which often do not integrate heating, electricity, and mobility simultaneously. A consolidated ABM framework that integrates these sectors is proposed to address this. The findings reveal challenges in balancing local power grids with renewable energy and the significant role of battery-electric vehicles (BEVs) in local energy management. Additionally, the paper highlights the potential of energy communities to enhance self-sufficiency and proposes new business models that align with climate goals, providing a basis for evaluating social impact through energy community dynamics.
Taormina et al. [97]	– (M): Methods for assessing ecological modifications caused by artificial structures (AS) in marine environments. The review encompasses techniques for measuring changes in epibenthic and megafauna colonization and ecosystem functioning. It also evaluates existing indicators and methods, identifies gaps, and recommends new approaches for more reliable assessments. – (T): Existing research on ecological impacts of AS, focusing on biodiversity and ecosystem functioning. It highlights methods tailored for AS and others adapted for various uses, emphasizing the need for comprehensive and integrative indicators. – (F): While there are established methods for assessing megafauna and ecosystem changes, reliable methods for epibenthic colonization are lacking.
	Recommendations include developing new indicators and tools to fill these gaps. For effective assessments, stakeholders should prioritize integrated approaches but may need to select strategic methods based on specific objectives and available funding.
Zolfani et al. [98]	– (M): Literature review of multi-attribute decision-making (MADM) methodologies applied to site selection problems. It systematically analyses 425 studies, narrowing the focus to 217 relevant papers to examine trends and methodologies used in site selection across various domains. – (T): MADM approaches, integrating multiple criteria and stakeholder perspectives for site selection. It explores how these methodologies address diverse applications such as energy projects, transportation infrastructure, and environmental planning. – (F): Energy projects dominate the MADM research, covering renewable and non-renewable sources. Environmental planning and sustainable site selection are also significant but less explored. Need for further investigation into new trends and methodologies in site selection, emphasising the integration of stakeholder perspectives and strategic considerations. Social impact metrics are not explicitly detailed.
Copping et al. [99]	– (M): Literature review on current knowledge on the impacts of marine renewable energy (MRE) on fish populations by examining field and laboratory studies, focusing on measurement techniques and modelling tools used to assess fish interactions with MRE devices, collision risks and environmental changes.

(continued)

	– (T): Exploring how MRE devices, such as tidal and in-river turbines, might affect fish through mechanisms like collision, underwater noise, electromagnetic fields, habitat changes, and fish behaviour. It adopts modelling approaches. – (F): Collisions between fish and MRE devices are rare, and studies show minimal effects of turbine noise and electromagnetic fields on fish behaviour. The primary concerns are the risks associated with collision and the potential for changes in fish habitats. Research emphasises the need for improved methods to measure fish interactions and assess cumulative impacts alongside other environmental stressors. Social impact metrics are not specifically addressed, but the paper underscores the importance of ensuring fish population health while advancing renewable energy technologies.
Moghaddasi et al. [100]	– (M): Review of various net zero community (NZC) definitions, criteria, and case studies to understand the current state and challenges of NZC targets. It examines existing literature on energy efficiency measures, electrification, and renewable energy in power systems, buildings, and transportation. The review also considers climate projection models and planned NZC cases from international locations. – (T): It focuses on net zero community concepts, which aim to balance energy consumption with renewable energy production to achieve zero net emissions. It addresses challenges related to varied NZC definitions, lack of standardised metrics, data tracking and reporting. – (F): Significant barriers to achieving NZC targets, including inconsistent definitions, inadequate policy support, and insufficient data reporting. Key challenges include the need for standardised metrics and updated published data to track progress. It emphasises two main design requirements for NZC: Minimising total energy demand and maximising renewable energy use.
Rungcharoennan and Phoochinda [101]	– (M): Sustainability balanced scorecard (SBSC) framework to propose sustainability indicators for Thailand's community enterprises producing renewable energy. It develops on a literature review, a survey of community enterprises, and assessments by eighteen experts to identify and categorise nineteen sustainability indicators across six perspectives. – (T): The SBSC framework integrates financial, stakeholder, internal process, learning and growth, social and environmental perspectives to assess organisational sustainability. The study aligns these perspectives with Thailand's "Thailand 4.0" vision and the BCG (bioeconomy, circular economy, green economy) model to provide a set of indicators. – (F): Nineteen sustainability indicators categorised into financial (3), stakeholder (3), internal process (5), learning and growth (2), social (2), and environmental (4) perspectives. The indicators help community enterprises set operational goals and guide government policy formulation. It also notes that while all indicators are acceptable, the focus of community enterprises on self-reliance rather than profit maximisation affects the indicators' applicability. Further research refers to the types of renewable energy and the development of operational guidelines to enhance sustainability and self-reliance in community enterprises.
Kuriqi et al. [102]	– (M): Global review of the ecological impacts of small run-of-river (RoR) hydropower plants by analysing data from 146 peer-reviewed publications across 33 countries over the past 40 years. It categorises the impacts based on three main types of RoR schemes: Dam-toe, diversion weir, and pondage, focusing on biota, water quality, hydrologic alteration, and geomorphology.

(continued)

	– (T): Conceptual framework to evaluate how changes in the natural flow regime due to different types of small RoR hydropower schemes impact fluvial ecosystems, emphasising the need for environmental flows and mitigation strategies to balance hydropower development with ecological conservation. – (F): Diversion weir and pondage schemes have more severe ecological impacts than dam-toe schemes, including water depletion, habitat degradation, loss of connectivity, and water quality issues. Pondage schemes, in particular, cause significant problems like hydropeaking and sediment retention. Effective planning, management, and monitoring are essential to mitigate these impacts and support the sustainable development of small RoR hydropower plants.
Mai-Moulin et al. [103]	– (M): Review of the renewable energy directive recast (RED II) sustainability criteria, comparing them with national legislations and voluntary certification schemes. It proposes a set of more effective sustainability criteria validated through stakeholder interviews. – (T): Sustainability principles for bioenergy, focusing on environmental, socio-economic, and operational aspects. It critiques the RED II framework and integrates broader sustainability principles to propose more comprehensive criteria. – (F): The RED II framework, while a significant step forward, does not fully address issues like forest management, imported biomass, and socio-economic impacts. The proposed criteria include enhanced biodiversity protection, carbon stock preservation, and labour rights. These criteria are necessary for a more thorough approach to sustainability. Future work should involve better recognition of voluntary certification schemes, guidance on sustainability criteria, and alignment with the sustainable development goals (SDGs).
Kumar and Cao [104]	– (M): Review on positive energy buildings and communities (PECs). It covers definitions, energy supplies, demands, indicators, storage, management, and stakeholder roles and identifies bottlenecks. The review also differentiates between PEBs and PECs, examines the impacts of smart energy grids and new energy vehicles, and discusses the innovative approaches needed. – (T): Concepts of positive energy systems, contrasting them with zero energy systems (ZES). It integrates theories of energy efficiency, renewable energy generation, and the role of advanced energy management systems. It highlights the evolution from energy-efficient buildings to positive energy systems and examines various frameworks and initiatives aiming for energy positivity. – (F): Positive energy systems require generating more renewable energy than their annual demand and involve complex design and management approaches. Key differences between PEBs and PECs include the scale of renewable energy generation and storage, with PECs often being more cost-effective due to large-scale solutions. Challenges include ambiguous definitions, high capital costs, systems (ZES). It integrates theories of energy efficiency, renewable energy generation, and the role of advanced energy management systems. It highlights the evolution from energy-efficient buildings to positive energy systems and examines various frameworks and initiatives aiming for energy positivity.

(continued)

	– (F): Positive energy systems require generating more renewable energy than their annual demand and involve complex design and management approaches.
	Key differences between PEBs and PECs include the scale of renewable energy generation and storage, with PECs often being more cost-effective due to large-scale solutions. Challenges include ambiguous definitions, high capital costs, and the need for standardized criteria. Innovations such as smart grids and new energy vehicles are critical in optimizing performance and integrating with energy systems. Future research should focus on standardizing definitions, addressing off-site renewable energy use, and defining energy efficiency criteria.
Mazur et al. [105]	– (M): Existing resilience frameworks, key technological, social, and economic indicators. The framework includes 21 indicators for technical resilience, 8 for social resilience, and 13 for economic resilience, offering a comprehensive tool for stakeholders to enhance rural power system effectiveness. – (T): It extends traditional resilience concepts to include social and economic dimensions, adapting general and energy system resilience theories to the specific context of rural areas in emerging economies. – (F): Resilience involves more than technology; social and economic factors are crucial. The study highlights the need for local knowledge and stakeholder involvement in designing resilient systems. The proposed framework addresses current gaps and provides a structured approach for creating effective future resilience standards, supporting both technical and socio-economic goals.
Ferrer-Martí et al. [106]	– (M): Multi-criteria decision support tool for assessing household biogas digesters. It involves three decision levels: Prioritising rural communities, selecting digester models (masonry or plastic), and choosing designs (volume, materials). The tool, validated with case studies in the Peruvian Andes, integrates technical, environmental, and socio-economic criteria. – (T): Principles from multi-criteria decision analysis, tailored for sustainable energy solutions in rural settings. It incorporates theoretical concepts of resilience and sustainability, stressing the importance of context-specific evaluations that address socio-economic and environmental factors. – (F): Critical criteria for assessing biogas digesters: Socio-economic aspects (beneficiaries' ability to pay, investment costs), operational factors (availability of water, manure, and land), and digester reliability (ease of construction, operation, maintenance, and lifespan).
van Veelen and van der Horst [107]	– (M): Literature reviews across four dimensions: Aims ('why'), actors ('who'), material dimensions ('what'), and geographical focus ('where') about the concept of energy democracy. It advocates for a more inclusive, equitable, and decentralised electricity system and stresses the importance of citizen involvement and local self-organisation in achieving these goals. – (T): Energy democracy to broader social science and political theory discussions, identifying it as a movement rooted in the desire for localised decision-making and community involvement. It contrasts energy democracy with more academically developed concepts like energy justice and energy citizenship.

(continued)

	– (F): Energy democracy emphasises expanding access to electricity and broadening ownership to counteract monopolistic and corporate control. Need for more inclusive and locally driven approaches to energy systems, exploring how these democratic ideals can be practically implemented and how technological change intersects with political and social dimensions.
Jamal et al. [108]	– (M): Literature review on technical and non-technical challenges of integrating solar photovoltaic (PV) systems into remote networks, focusing on issues like power quality and system stability in Australian networks. – (T): The study relates its findings to broader research on PV integration, noting that the challenges and solutions are relevant to similar networks in Africa and Asia and that technical issues in diverse network contexts must be addressed. – (F): High PV penetration causes technical problems like reduced power quality and potential blackouts. Recommended solutions involve advanced control mechanisms and real-time monitoring, which address these challenges and enhance management strategies for remote networks with high PV levels.
Huesca-Pérez et al. [109]	– (M): Literature reviews on the social impacts of wind energy, focusing on the isthmus of Tehuantepec, Mexico, focusing on issues such as insufficient regulation, lack of stakeholder involvement, and socio-economic challenges, proposing improved participatory planning and policy development. – (T): It connects wind energy development with social science research, stressing the need for better public policies and governance to address conflicts and inequalities, particularly in disadvantaged areas. – (F): Inadequate local engagement and regulation lead to social conflicts and inequalities, recommending enhancing participatory planning, creating comprehensive public policies, and improving local governance for sustainable wind energy development.
Whitton et al. [110]	– (M): 2015 generic design assessment (GDA) public dialogue pilot for new nuclear reactors in the UK, contrasting it with a community-based, asset-focused approach to social sustainability, focusing on the tension between national and local engagement, with an emphasis on building social capital. – (T): Integrate local priorities into national engagement frameworks, given the conflict between national process requirements and local community needs, and more tailored direct communication to foster trust and effective dialogue. – (F): Conflict between national engagement strategies and local priorities, with participants valuing face-to-face interactions despite a preference for remote communication, and meaningful engagement requires addressing national and local concerns to build trust and improve decision-making processes.
Cosmi et al. [111]	– (M): Self-assessment (SAA) methodology to evaluate regional energy systems in nine European countries, focusing on local energy infrastructures, renewable potentials, and community attitudes to inform sustainable energy strategies, adopting the PEST (political, economic, social, technical) analysis. – (T): Integrates sustainability principles with policy, market, and community perspectives, aiming for a comprehensive view of energy development. – (F): Self-assessment identifies regional energy issues, sets goals, and improves community engagement. Metrics include community attitudes, policy effectiveness, market uptake, aiding in the development of sustainable energy strategies.

(continued)

Sinclair et al. [112]	– (M): Universal systems design process that uses a categorical language framework with mathematical mappings for decision support. The framework links English narratives to numbers concerning a UK bioenergy project, integrating environmental, economic, and social criteria. – (T): It combines narrative language with numeric data, aiming to enhance the communication and decision-making process in energy policy. It addresses the integration of verbal and numeric information in decision support systems. – (F): The process effectively translates narrative criteria into actionable objectives, improving decision-making efficiency. The approach helps to better manage energy goals and resources by leveraging a combined verbal and numeric system, contributing to more effective and sustainable development strategies.
Kermagoret et al. [113]	– (M): Qualitative discourse analysis to explore how institutional stakeholders perceive the impacts of a planned offshore wind farm on ecosystem services (ES), identifying six communities of practice (CoPs) – (T): Stakeholder theory and the "no-net-loss" principle, aiming to balance negative ES impacts with equivalent gains. It uses the CoP theory to understand stakeholder perspectives on impacts and compensation. – (F): Stakeholder discourses vary widely and are influenced by their interests and knowledge. Three compensation discourses are identified: Opportunistic (seeking compensation without significant impact), non-sequitur (using perceived impacts to demand compensation), and reasonable (matching compensation to accurately assessed impacts).

References

1. Kotlarsky, J., Corbett, J., Sutanto, J., Kude, T., & Tim, Y. (2024). Digital sustainability and information systems research: New challenges and theoretical perspectives. In *JAIS call for papers: Digital sustainability and information systems research.*
2. Khan, I. S., Ahmad, M. O., & Majava, J. (2021). Industry 4.0 and sustainable development: A systematic mapping of triple bottom line. Circular economy and sustainable business models perspectives. *Journal of Cleaner Production, 297*, 126655. https://doi.org/10.1016/j.jclepro.2021.126655
3. Geissdoerfer, M., Vladimirova, D., & Evans, S. (2018). Sustainable business model innovation: A review. *Journal of Cleaner Production, 198*, 401–416. https://doi.org/10.1016/j.jclepro.2018.06.240
4. Ghisellini, P., Cialani, C., & Ulgiati, S. (2016). A review on circular economy: The expected transition to a balanced interplay of environmental and economic systems. *Journal of Cleaner Production, 114*, 11–32. https://doi.org/10.1016/j.jclepro.2015.09.007
5. Calzolari, T., Bimpizas-Pinis, M., Genovese, A., & Brint, A. (2023). Understanding the relationship between institutional pressures, supply chain integration and the adoption of circular economy practices. *Journal of Cleaner Production, 432*, 139686. https://doi.org/10.1016/j.jclepro.2023.139686
6. Camodeca, R., & Almici, A. (2021). Digital transformation and convergence toward the 2030 agenda's sustainability development goals: Evidence from Italian listed firms. *Sustainability (Switzerland), 13*. https://doi.org/10.3390/su132111831

7. Fiandrino, S., Scarpa, F., & Torelli, R. (2022). Fostering social impact through corporate implementation of the SDGs: Transformative mechanisms towards interconnectedness and inclusiveness. *Journal of Business Ethics, 180*, 959–973. https://doi.org/10.1007/s10551-022-05189-9
8. Rogers, J. C., Simmons, E. A., Convery, I., & Weatherall, A. (2008). Public perceptions of opportunities for community-based renewable energy projects. *Energy Policy, 36*, 4217–4226. https://doi.org/10.1016/j.enpol.2008.07.028
9. Walker, G., & Devine-Wright, P. (2008). Community renewable energy: What should it mean? *Energy Policy, 36*, 497–500. https://doi.org/10.1016/j.enpol.2007.10.019
10. Hoicka, C. E., Lowitzsch, J., Brisbois, M. C., Kumar, A., & Ramirez Camargo, L. (2021). Implementing a just renewable energy transition: Policy advice for transposing the new European rules for renewable energy communities. *Energy Policy, 156*. https://doi.org/10.1016/J.ENPOL.2021.112435
11. Çeçen, H. (2021). "Renewable energy communities" as a new legal entity in the renewable energy law of the European Union. *Ankara Avrupa Calismalari Dergisi, 20*, 381–410. https://doi.org/10.32450/aacd.1050051
12. Lazaroiu, G. C., & Putrus, G. (2023). Renewable energy generation driving positive energy communities. *Renewable Energy, 205*, 627–630. https://doi.org/10.1016/j.renene.2023.02.001
13. Antwi, S. H., & Ley, D. (2021). Renewable energy project implementation in Africa: Ensuring sustainability through community acceptability. *Scientific African, 11*, e00679. https://doi.org/10.1016/J.SCIAF.2020.E00679
14. Pechancová, V., Pavelková, D., & Saha, P. (2022). Community renewable energy in The Czech Republic: Value proposition perspective. *Frontiers in Energy Research, 10*, 821706. https://doi.org/10.3389/fenrg.2022.821706
15. Kerr, S., Johnson, K., & Weir, S. (2017). Understanding community benefit payments from renewable energy development. *Energy Policy, 105*, 202–211. https://doi.org/10.1016/J.ENPOL.2017.02.034
16. Di Lorenzo, G., Martirano, L., Araneo, R., Cappello, L., Mingoli, G., & Ermellino, F. (2021). Democratic power sharing in renewable energy communities: Engaging citizens for sustainable energy transition. In *2021 IEEE international conference on environment and electrical engineering and 2021 IEEE industrial and commercial power systems Europe (EEEIC/I&CPS Europe)* (pp. 1–6). IEEE. https://doi.org/10.1109/EEEIC/ICPSEurope51590.2021.9584606
17. MASE: Energia: MASE, pubblicato decreto CER, https://www.mase.gov.it/comunicati/energia-mase-pubblicato-decreto-cer. Last accessed 2024/03/03.
18. Genus, A., & Iskandarova, M. (2020). Transforming the energy system? Technology and organisational legitimacy and the institutionalisation of community renewable energy. *Renewable and Sustainable Energy Reviews, 125*, 109795. https://doi.org/10.1016/J.RSER.2020.109795
19. Esposito, P., Marrasso, E., Martone, C., Pallotta, G., Roselli, C., Sasso, M., & Tufo, M. (2024). A roadmap for the implementation of a renewable energy community. *Heliyon., 10*, e28269. https://doi.org/10.1016/j.heliyon.2024.e28269
20. Ebrahim, A., & Rangan, V. K. (2014). What impact? A framework for measuring the scale and scope of social performance. *California Management Review, 56*, 118–141.
21. Cannatelli, B. (2017). Exploring the contingencies of scaling social impact: A replication and extension of the SCALERS model. *VOLUNTAS: International Journal of Voluntary and Nonprofit Organizations, 28*, 2707–2733. https://doi.org/10.1007/s11266-016-9789-x
22. Hadad, S., & Găucă, O. (2014). Social impact measurement in social entrepreneurial organisations. *Management & Marketing. Challenges for the Knowledge Society, 9*, 119–136.
23. Latané, B., & Wolf, S. (1981). The social impact of majorities and minorities. *Psychological Review, 88*, 438–453. https://doi.org/10.1037/0033-295X.88.5.438

24. Polonsky, M., & Grau, S. L. (2011). Assessing the social impact of charitable organisations—Four alternative approaches. *International Journal of Nonprofit and Voluntary Sector Marketing, 16*, 195–211. https://doi.org/10.1002/nvsm.407
25. Kah, S., & Akenroye, T. (2020). Evaluation of social impact measurement tools and techniques: A systematic review of the literature. *Social Enterprise Journal, 16*, 381–402. https://doi.org/10.1108/SEJ-05-2020-0027
26. Conferenza Episcopale Italiana. (2024). Le comunità energetiche rinnovabili: elementi etici, tecnici, economico-giuridici per gli enti religiosi, Italy.
27. Lawrence, P. R., & Lorsch, J. W. (1967). Differentiation and integration in complex organizations. *Administrative Science Quarterly, 12*, 1. https://doi.org/10.2307/2391211
28. Mumford, E. (1998). Problems, knowledge, solutions: Solving complex problems. In *International conference on information systems (ICIS)*. https://aisel.aisnet.org/icis1998/62
29. Lumpkin, G. T., & Bacq, S. (2019). Civic wealth creation: A new view of stakeholder engagement and societal impact. *Academy of Management Perspectives, 33*, 383–404. https://doi.org/10.5465/amp.2017.0060
30. Weick, K. E. (1979). *The social psychology of organizing*. McGraw-Hill.
31. Peffers, K., Tuunanen, T., Rothenberger, M. A., & Chatterjee, S. (2007). A design science research methodology for information systems research. *Journal of Management Information Systems, 24*, 45–77. https://doi.org/10.2753/MIS0742-1222240302
32. Za, S., Scornavacca, E., & Pallud, J. (2022). Enhancing workplace competence acquisition through a persuasive system. *Information Systems and e-Business Management, 20*, 819–846. https://doi.org/10.1007/s10257-022-00571-6
33. Jones, D., & Gregor, S. (2007). The anatomy of a design theory. *Journal of the Association for Information Systems, 8*, 312–335. https://doi.org/10.17705/1jais.00129
34. An, Y.-S., Kim, J., Joo, H.-J., Han, G., Kim, H., Lee, W., & Kim, M.-H. (2023). Retrofit of renewable energy systems in existing community for positive energy community. *Energy Reports, 9*, 3733–3744. https://doi.org/10.1016/j.egyr.2023.02.055
35. Canizes, B., Costa, J., & Vale, Z. (2023). Renewable energy communities classification. In *2023 IEEE power & energy society general meeting (PESGM)* (pp. 1–5). IEEE. https://doi.org/10.1109/PESGM52003.2023.10252824
36. Šahović, N., & da Silva, P. P. (2016). Community renewable energy - Research perspectives. *Energy Procedia, 106*, 46–58. https://doi.org/10.1016/j.egypro.2016.12.104
37. Ahmed, S., Ali, A., & D'Angola, A. (2024). A review of renewable energy communities: Concepts, scope, progress, challenges, and recommendations. *Sustainability (Switzerland), 16*, 1749. https://doi.org/10.3390/SU16051749
38. Trevisan, R., Mureddu, M., Ghiani, E., Galici, M., & Pilo, F. (2023). Transactive energy systems in decentralized autonomous renewable energy communities. In *2023 IEEE power & energy society general meeting (PESGM)* (pp. 1–5). IEEE. https://doi.org/10.1109/PESGM52003.2023.10252621
39. Queiroz, H., Lopes, R. A., Martins, J., Silva, F. N., Fialho, L., & Bilo, N. (2023). Assessment of energy sharing coefficients under the new Portuguese renewable energy communities regulation. *Heliyon, 9*, e20599. https://doi.org/10.1016/J.HELIYON.2023.E20599
40. Agostinelli, S., Neshat, M., Majidi Nezhad, M., Piras, G., & Astiaso Garcia, D. (2022). Integrating renewable energy sources in Italian port areas towards renewable energy communities. *Sustainability (Switzerland), 14*. https://doi.org/10.3390/SU142113720
41. Shahrom, S. F., Aviso, K. B., Tan, R. R., Saleem, N. N., Ng, D. K. S., & Andiappan, V. (2023). Regional planning and optimization of renewable energy sources for improved rural electrification. *Process Integration and Optimization for Sustainability, 7*, 785–804. https://doi.org/10.1007/s41660-023-00323-0
42. Lowitzsch, J., Hoicka, C. E., & van Tulder, F. J. (2020). Renewable energy communities under the 2019 European clean energy package—Governance model for the energy clusters of the future? *Renewable and Sustainable Energy Reviews, 122*, 109489. https://doi.org/10.1016/j.rser.2019.109489

43. Kabir, Z., Sultana, N., & Khan, I. (2022). Environmental, social, and economic impacts of renewable energy sources. In *Renewable energy and sustainability* (pp. 57–85). Elsevier. https://doi.org/10.1016/B978-0-323-88668-0.00009-7
44. Tiwari, G. N. (2024). Sustainable environment. In *Energy, ecology and environment* (pp. 175–218). Springer. https://doi.org/10.1007/978-981-99-3997-8_7
45. Ciric, R. M. (2019). Review of techno-economic and environmental aspects of building small hydro electric plants—A case study in Serbia. *Renewable Energy, 140*, 715–721. https://doi.org/10.1016/j.renene.2019.03.091
46. Salkuti, S. R. (2022). Modeling of various renewable energy resources for smart electrical power systems. In *Lecture notes in electrical engineering* (pp. 29–47). Springer. https://doi.org/10.1007/978-981-16-7794-6_2
47. Goodbody, C., Walsh, E., McDonnell, K. P., & Owende, P. (2013). Regional integration of renewable energy systems in Ireland—The role of hybrid energy systems for small communities. *International Journal of Electrical Power & Energy Systems, 44*, 713–720. https://doi.org/10.1016/j.ijepes.2012.08.012
48. Alam, M. F. B., Tushar, S. R., Debnath, B., Taghipour, A., Dinçer, H., Islam, A. R. M. T., Bari, A. B. M. M., & Tushan, S. S. (2024). Assessing the factors influencing the adoption of geothermal energy to support the national grid in emerging economies: Implications for sustainability. *Sustainable Operations and Computers, 5*, 167. https://doi.org/10.1016/j.susoc.2024.03.001
49. Canizes, B., Costa, J., Bairrão, D., & Vale, Z. (2023). Local renewable energy communities: Classification and sizing. *Energies (Basel), 16*, 2389. https://doi.org/10.3390/EN16052389
50. Strachan, P. A., Cowell, R., Ellis, G., Sherry-Brennan, F., & Toke, D. (2015). Promoting community renewable energy in a corporate energy world. *Sustainable Development, 23*, 96–109. https://doi.org/10.1002/sd.1576
51. Petrovich, B., & Kubli, M. (2023). Energy communities for companies: Executives' preferences for local and renewable energy procurement. *Renewable and Sustainable Energy Reviews, 184*, 113506. https://doi.org/10.1016/j.rser.2023.113506
52. Soeiro, S., & Ferreira Dias, M. (2020). Community renewable energy: Benefits and drivers. *Energy Reports, 6*, 134–140. https://doi.org/10.1016/J.EGYR.2020.11.087
53. Bauwens, T. (2016). Explaining the diversity of motivations behind community renewable energy. *Energy Policy, 93*, 278–290. https://doi.org/10.1016/J.ENPOL.2016.03.017
54. Olivero, S., Ghiani, E., & Rosetti, G. L. (2021). The first Italian renewable energy community of Magliano Alpi. In *2021 IEEE 15th international conference on compatibility, power electronics and power engineering (CPE-POWERENG)* (pp. 1–6). IEEE. https://doi.org/10.1109/CPE-POWERENG50821.2021.9501073
55. Giampaolo, C., Eleonora, C., Demetrio, M. F., Andrea, L., Matteo, M., & Marco, M. (2021). Renewable energy communities in Valle d'Aosta Region: Development perspectives. In *2021 IEEE 15th international conference on compatibility, power electronics and power engineering (CPE-POWERENG)* (pp. 1–7). IEEE. https://doi.org/10.1109/CPE-POWERENG50821.2021.9501172
56. Micallef, A., Spiteri Staines, C., & Licari, J. (2022). Renewable energy communities in islands: A Maltese case study. *Energies (Basel), 15*, 9518. https://doi.org/10.3390/en15249518
57. Krug, M., Di Nucci, M. R., Caldera, M., & De Luca, E. (2022). Mainstreaming community energy: Is the renewable energy directive a driver for renewable energy communities in Germany and Italy? *Sustainability, 14*, 7181. https://doi.org/10.3390/su14127181
58. Vecchi, F., Stasi, R., & Berardi, U. (2024). Modelling tools for the assessment of renewable energy communities. *Energy Reports, 11*, 3941–3962. https://doi.org/10.1016/J.EGYR.2024.03.048
59. Cuesta, M. A., Castillo-Calzadilla, T., & Borges, C. E. (2020). A critical analysis on hybrid renewable energy modeling tools: An emerging opportunity to include social indicators to optimise systems in small communities. *Renewable and Sustainable Energy Reviews, 122*, 109691. https://doi.org/10.1016/j.rser.2019.109691

60. Gjorgievski, V. Z., Cundeva, S., & Georghiou, G. E. (2021). Social arrangements, technical designs and impacts of energy communities: A review. *Renewable Energy, 169*, 1138–1156. https://doi.org/10.1016/J.RENENE.2021.01.078
61. Caramizaru, A., & Uihlein, A. (2020). *Energy communities: An overview of energy and social innovation* (pp. 1–43). European Commission. Joint Research Centre. EUR 30083 EN.
62. REScoop MECISE. (2020). Mobilising European citizens to invest in sustainable energy clean energy for all europeans final results oriented report of the Rescoop Mecise Horizon 2020 PROJECT.
63. Kumar, A., Singh, A. R., Deng, Y., He, X., Kumar, P., & Bansal, R. C. (2019). Integrated assessment of a sustainable microgrid for a remote village in hilly region. *Energy Conversion and Management, 180*, 442–472. https://doi.org/10.1016/j.enconman.2018.10.084
64. Santos, A., Ma, Z., Olsen, C., & Jørgensen, B. (2018). Framework for microgrid design using social, economic, and technical analysis. *Energies (Basel), 11*, 2832. https://doi.org/10.3390/en11102832
65. Jones, N., Malesios, C., Kantartzis, A., Zuluaga, S., Karney, B. W., Saxe, S., Karytsas, S., Mendrinos, D., & Karytsas, C. (2020). Measurement methods of socioeconomic impacts of renewable energy projects. *IOP Conference Series: Earth and Environmental Science, 410*, 012087. https://doi.org/10.1088/1755-1315/410/1/012087
66. Nussbaumer, P., Bazilian, M., & Modi, V. (2012). Measuring energy poverty: Focusing on what matters. *Renewable and Sustainable Energy Reviews., 16*, 231–243. https://doi.org/10.1016/j.rser.2011.07.150
67. Li, K., Lloyd, B., Liang, X.-J., & Wei, Y.-M. (2014). Energy poor or fuel poor: What are the differences? *Energy Policy, 68*, 476–481. https://doi.org/10.1016/j.enpol.2013.11.012
68. Charani Shandiz, S., Foliente, G., Rismanchi, B., Wachtel, A., & Jeffers, R. F. (2020). Resilience framework and metrics for energy master planning of communities. *Energy, 203*, 117856. https://doi.org/10.1016/j.energy.2020.117856
69. Gruber, L., Kockar, I., & Wogrin, S. (2024). Towards resilient energy communities: Evaluating the impact of economic and technical optimisation. *International Journal of Electrical Power & Energy Systems, 155*, 109592. https://doi.org/10.1016/J.IJEPES.2023.109592
70. Elomari, Y., Mateu, C., Marín-Genescà, M., & Boer, D. (2024). A data-driven framework for designing a renewable energy community based on the integration of machine learning model with life cycle assessment and life cycle cost parameters. *Applied Energy, 358*, 122619. https://doi.org/10.1016/j.apenergy.2024.122619
71. Sirviö, K., Motta, S., Rauma, K., & Evens, C. (2024). Multi-level functional analysis of developing prosumers and energy communities with value creation framework. *Applied Energy, 368*, 123496. https://doi.org/10.1016/j.apenergy.2024.123496
72. Heuninckx, S., Macharis, C., te Boveldt, G., Lode, M. L., & Coosemans, T. (2024). The impact of MAMCA as a stakeholder engagement tool during the setup of an energy community. *Heliyon, 10*, e23068. https://doi.org/10.1016/j.heliyon.2023.e23068
73. Fleischhacker, A., Lettner, G., Schwabeneder, D., & Auer, H. (2019). Portfolio optimisation of energy communities to meet reductions in costs and emissions. *Energy, 173*, 1092–1105. https://doi.org/10.1016/J.ENERGY.2019.02.104
74. Cutore, E., Volpe, R., Sgroi, R., & Fichera, A. (2023). Energy management and sustainability assessment of renewable energy communities: The Italian context. *Energy Conversion and Management, 278*, 116713. https://doi.org/10.1016/j.enconman.2023.116713
75. Gregor, S., Kruse, L., & Seidel, S. (2020). Research perspectives: The anatomy of a design principle. *Journal of the Association for Information Systems, 21*, 1622–1652. https://doi.org/10.17705/1jais.00649
76. Lacity, M., Willcocks, L., & Gozman, D. (2021). Influencing information systems practice: The action principles approach applied to robotic process and cognitive automation. *Journal of Information Technology, 36*, 216–240. https://doi.org/10.1177/0268396221990778
77. Pries-Heje, J., & Baskerville, R. (2008). The design theory nexus. *MIS Quarterly, 1*, 731.

78. Baranauskas, M., Pereira, R., & Bonacin, R. (2024). Socially aware systems design: A perspective towards technology-society coupling. *AIS Transactions on Human-Computer Interaction., 16*, 80–109. https://doi.org/10.17705/1thci.00201
79. John, B., Kurian, J. C., Fitzgerald, R., & Lian Goh, D. H. (2022). Students' learning experience in a mixed reality environment: Drivers and barriers. *Communications of the Association for Information Systems., 50*, 510–535. https://doi.org/10.17705/1CAIS.05024
80. Graf-Drasch, V., Keller, R., Meindl, O., & Röhrich, F. (2023). The design of citizen-centric green IS in sustainable smart districts. *Business & Information Systems Engineering, 65*, 521–538. https://doi.org/10.1007/s12599-023-00821-y
81. Scheider, S., Lauf, F., Möller, F., & Otto, B. (2023). A reference system architecture with data sovereignty for human-centric data ecosystems. *Business & Information Systems Engineering, 65*, 577–595. https://doi.org/10.1007/s12599-023-00816-9
82. Mini, T., & Widjaja, T. (2019). Tensions in digital platform business models: A literature review. In *40th international conference on information systems, (ICIS), Munich, Germany*.
83. Kouhizadeh, M., Zhu, Q., & Sarkis, J. (2020). Blockchain and the circular economy: Potential tensions and critical reflections from practice. *Production Planning & Control., 31*, 950–966. https://doi.org/10.1080/09537287.2019.1695925
84. Currie, W. L., Gozman, D. P., & Seddon, J. J. M. (2018). Dialectic tensions in the financial markets: A longitudinal study of pre- and post-crisis regulatory technology. *Journal of Information Technology, 33*, 304–325. https://doi.org/10.1057/s41265-017-0047-5
85. Zafar, I., Stojceska, V., & Tassou, S. (2024). Social sustainability assessments of industrial level solar energy: A systematic review. *Renewable and Sustainable Energy Reviews, 189*, 113962. https://doi.org/10.1016/j.rser.2023.113962
86. Dirisu, J. O., Salawu, E. Y., Ekpe, I. C., Udoye, N. E., Falodun, O. E., Oyedepo, S. O., Ajayi, O. O., & Kale, S. A. (2024). Promoting the use of bioenergy in developing nations: A CDM route to sustainable development. *Frontiers in Energy Research, 11*, 1184348. https://doi.org/10.3389/fenrg.2023.1184348
87. Cai, S., & Gou, Z. (2024). Defining the energy role of buildings as flexumers: A review of definitions, technologies, and applications. *Energy and Buildings, 303*, 113821. https://doi.org/10.1016/j.enbuild.2023.113821
88. Kime, S., Jacome, V., Pellow, D., & Deshmukh, R. (2023). Evaluating equity and justice in low-carbon energy transitions. *Environmental Research Letters, 18*, 123003. https://doi.org/10.1088/1748-9326/ad08f8
89. Shyu, C.-W. (2023). Lessons from the World Bank's solar home system-based rural electrification projects (2000–2020): Policy implications for meeting Sustainable Development Goal 7 by 2030. *Energy Reports, 9*, 2820–2838. https://doi.org/10.1016/j.egyr.2023.01.128
90. Caballero, M. D., Gunda, T., & McDonald, Y. J. (2023). Energy justice & coastal communities: The case for meaningful marine renewable energy development. *Renewable and Sustainable Energy Reviews, 184*, 113491. https://doi.org/10.1016/j.rser.2023.113491
91. Pasanec Preprotić, S., Vukoje, M., Petković, G., & Rožić, M. (2023). Novel approaches to enhancing sustainable adhesive system solutions in contemporary book binding: An overview. *Heritage, 6*, 628–646. https://doi.org/10.3390/heritage6010033
92. Mishra, A., Barat, B., Balaji, S., Singh, Y., & Senthil, R. (2023). A review of advanced cooling methodologies for solar photovoltaic and thermoelectric hybrid energy systems. *Energy Systems*, 1–32. https://doi.org/10.1007/s12667-023-00622-y
93. Vallejos-Romero, A., Cordoves-Sánchez, M., Cisternas, C., Sáez-Ardura, F., Rodríguez, I., Aledo, A., Boso, Á., Prades, J., & Álvarez, B. (2022). Green hydrogen and social sciences: Issues, problems, and future challenges. *Sustainability, 15*, 303. https://doi.org/10.3390/su15010303
94. Cerca, M., Sosa, A., Gusciute, E., & Murphy, F. (2022). Strategic planning of bio-based supply chains: Unlocking bottlenecks and incorporating social sustainability into biorefinery systems. *Sustainable Production and Consumption, 34*, 219–232. https://doi.org/10.1016/j.spc.2022.09.013

95. Amerson, A. M., Harris, T. M., Michener, S. R., Gunn, C. M., & Haxel, J. H. (2022). A summary of environmental monitoring recommendations for marine energy development that considers life cycle sustainability. *Journal of Marine Science and Engineering, 10*, 586. https://doi.org/10.3390/jmse10050586
96. Vuthi, P., Peters, I., & Sudeikat, J. (2022). Agent-based modeling (ABM) for urban neighborhood energy systems: Literature review and proposal for an all integrative ABM approach. *Energy Informatics, 5*, 55. https://doi.org/10.1186/s42162-022-00247-y
97. Taormina, B., Claquin, P., Vivier, B., Navon, M., Pezy, J.-P., Raoux, A., & Dauvin, J.-C. (2022). A review of methods and indicators used to evaluate the ecological modifications generated by artificial structures on marine ecosystems. *Journal of Environmental Management, 310*, 114646. https://doi.org/10.1016/j.jenvman.2022.114646
98. Zolfani, S. H., Hasheminasab, H., Torkayesh, A. E., Zavadskas, E. K., & Derakhti, A. (2022). A literature review of MADM applications for site selection problems — One decade review from 2011 to 2020. *International Journal of Information Technology and Decision Making, 21*, 7–57. https://doi.org/10.1142/s0219622021300019
99. Copping, A. E., Hemery, L. G., Viehman, H., Seitz, A. C., Staines, G. J., & Hasselman, D. J. (2021). Are fish in danger? A review of environmental effects of marine renewable energy on fishes. *Biological Conservation, 262*, 109297. https://doi.org/10.1016/j.biocon.2021.109297
100. Moghaddasi, H., Culp, C., & Vanegas, J. (2021). Net zero energy communities: Integrated power system, building and transport sectors. *Energies (Basel), 14*, 7065. https://doi.org/10.3390/en14217065
101. Rungcharoennan, Y., & Phoochinda, W. (2021). Sustainability indicators for community enterprises producing renewable energy in Thailand. *International Journal of Sustainable Development and Planning., 16*, 915–923. https://doi.org/10.18280/ijsdp.160512
102. Kuriqi, A., Pinheiro, A. N., Sordo-Ward, A., Bejarano, M. D., & Garrote, L. (2021). Ecological impacts of run-of-river hydropower plants—Current status and future prospects on the brink of energy transition. *Renewable and Sustainable Energy Reviews, 142*, 110833. https://doi.org/10.1016/j.rser.2021.110833
103. Mai-Moulin, T., Hoefnagels, R., Grundmann, P., & Junginger, M. (2021). Effective sustainability criteria for bioenergy: Towards the implementation of the european renewable directive II. *Renewable and Sustainable Energy Reviews, 138*, 110645. https://doi.org/10.1016/j.rser.2020.110645
104. Kumar, G. M. S., & Cao, S. (2021). State-of-the-art review of positive energy building and community systems. *Energies (Basel), 14*, 5046. https://doi.org/10.3390/en14165046
105. Mazur, C., Hoegerle, Y., Brucoli, M., van Dam, K., Guo, M., Markides, C. N., & Shah, N. (2019). A holistic resilience framework development for rural power systems in emerging economies. *Applied Energy, 235*, 219–232. https://doi.org/10.1016/j.apenergy.2018.10.129
106. Ferrer-Martí, L., Ferrer, I., Sánchez, E., & Garfí, M. (2018). A multi-criteria decision support tool for the assessment of household biogas digester programmes in rural areas. A case study in Peru. *Renewable and Sustainable Energy Reviews, 95*, 74–83. https://doi.org/10.1016/j.rser.2018.06.064
107. van Veelen, B., & van der Horst, D. (2018). What is energy democracy? Connecting social science energy research and political theory. *Energy Research and Social Science, 46*, 19–28 https://doi.org/10.1016/j.erss.2018.06.010
108. Jamal, T., Urmee, T., Calais, M., Shafiullah, G., & Carter, C. (2017). Technical challenges of PV deployment into remote Australian electricity networks: A review. *Renewable and Sustainable Energy Reviews, 77*, 1309–1325. https://doi.org/10.1016/j.rser.2017.02.080
109. Huesca-Pérez, M. E., Sheinbaum-Pardo, C., & Köppel, J. (2016). Social implications of siting wind energy in a disadvantaged region—The case of the Isthmus of Tehuantepec, Mexico. *Renewable and Sustainable Energy Reviews., 58*, 952–965. https://doi.org/10.1016/j.rser.2015.12.310
110. Whitton, J., Parry, I., Grundy, C., Lillycrop, A., & Ross, D. (2016). A review of the Generic Design Assessment (GDA) Public Dialogue Pilot (2015) for new nuclear build in the UK:

Lessons for engagement theory and practice. *Journal of Radiological Protection, 36*, S23–S44. https://doi.org/10.1088/0952-4746/36/2/s23

111. Cosmi, C., Dvarionienė, J., Marques, I., Di Leo, S., Gecevičius, G., Gurauskienė, I., Mendes, G., & Selada, C. (2015). A holistic approach to sustainable energy development at regional level: The RENERGY self-assessment methodology. *Renewable and Sustainable Energy Reviews, 49*, 693–707. https://doi.org/10.1016/j.rser.2015.04.094
112. Sinclair, P., Peters, M., & Fudge, S. (2015). Introducing "ecoputation": A universal systems design process. *Renewable and Sustainable Energy Reviews, 46*, 311–330. https://doi.org/10.1016/j.rser.2014.11.057
113. Kermagoret, C., Levrel, H., & Carlier, A. (2014). The impact and compensation of offshore wind farm development: Analysing the institutional discourse from a French case study. *Scottish Geographical Journal, 130*, 188–206. https://doi.org/10.1080/14702541.2014.922209

Toward a Data-Driven Social Intelligence System: Bridging Societal and Organizational Well-being

Francesca Mochi, Alessandra Lazazzara, Franca Maino, Asia Guerreschi, Alessandro Margherita, and Davide Antonioli

Abstract The aim of this research is to systematize existing knowledge on the social sustainability dimension of well-being by identifying and organizing its key constructs and related indicators. Although studies on social and organizational well-being have developed along separate paths, there is a growing interest in bridging these perspectives, particularly in light of recent transformations of work modalities that blur the boundaries between personal and professional life. Furthermore, the Strategic Human Resources Management (SHRM) literature urges consideration of the effects of HRM practices, including those related to organizational well-being, both inside and outside organizational boundaries. Through a systematic review, the research collects and analyzes contributions from both fields to clarify how well-being is defined and measured across different contexts. Particular attention is given to the variety of indicators used, the methodological approaches adopted, and the ways in which organizational practices and policy decisions influence individual and collective well-being.

This systematization serves as a foundation for future empirical work, which will be further developed and validated using a citizen science approach in the next phase of the research.

F. Mochi (✉) · F. Maino
Università degli Studi di Milano, Milan, Italy
e-mail: francesca.mochi@unimi.it; franca.maino@unimi.it

A. Lazazzara
Dipartimento di Scienze Sociali e Politiche, University of Milan, Milan, Italy
e-mail: alessandra.lazazzara@unimi.it

A. Guerreschi · D. Antonioli
Università degli Studi di Ferrara, Ferrara, Italy
e-mail: asia.guerreschi@unife.it; davide.antonioli@unife.it

A. Margherita
Università del Salento, Lecce, Italy
e-mail: alessandro.margherita@unisalento.it

M. Cipriano et al. (eds.), *Technologies for Organizations and Society*, Lecture Notes in Information Systems and Organisation 80,
https://doi.org/10.1007/978-3-032-01697-3_13

Keywords Sustainability · Well-being · Systematization

1 Introduction

Considering the ever-growing attention to sustainability, it is now an aim to raise awareness about it and identify the various types. Several significant events focusing on sustainability have been held in Italy. These include the Festival dello Sviluppo Sostenibile, Green Week—Festival della Sostenibilità, Fa' la cosa giusta, Climate Tech, Forum Sostenibilità, and the World Energy Transition Congress, among others. Similarly, a multitude of reports and indexes have been developed to understand better sustainability and its relationship with human well-being, such as the Sustainable Development Goals (SDG) Index Score [1], The Human Development Index Score [2] and the World Happiness Report [3].

Specifically, social sustainability and its measurements are gaining importance in society, politics and business, yet there is still no standardized, uniform and systematic approaches or frameworks that systematize the construct [4]. The multifaceted aspect of its "social" nature further complicates it, as it encompasses both analytical and normative dimensions, rendering social sustainability a multidimensional concept sensitive to temporal and spatial dynamics [5].

Various dimensions are related to social sustainability, including society and social policy, urban development, organizational performance, product design, well-being, and life cycle [5]. Our research focuses on the well-being dimension, specifically social well-being. Nevertheless, well-being has long been studied in the organizational realm as well, known as organizational well-being. However, this construct focuses only on employees' well-being perceived within the organization and related to work life, excluding the consideration of social well-being and the society context.

In the realm of strategic HRM literature and organizational one, the relationship between HRM practices and employees' well-being has long been a subject of research and debate within the organizational context. Indeed, well-being is considered an antecedent to individual and organizational performance, job satisfaction, employees' engagement and organizational climate, among other factors (e.g. [6]). On the other hand, interestingly, despite work being an important indicator of social well-being [7], there is a lack of research attention on social well-being from an organizational perspective. Thus, the research streams of social well-being and organizational well-being remain disconnected, despite the increasing prevalence of studies on remote work and other new ways of working and their effects on individuals' well-being in general [8].

However, organizations are open systems in continuous exchange with the external environment. It is therefore reasonable to assume that organizational and HRM practices influence not only the perceived well-being within the organization but also individual well-being more broadly (i.e. social well-being), just as external policies and events influence organizational well-being.

Considering the society, Juchnowicz and Kinowska ([9], p. 2), stated that "the notion of well-being can be analyzed from different standpoints. It includes dimensions such as life expectancy, poverty rates, and environmental factors as well as individuals' assessment of their quality of life, which is determined through three main aspects: physical, social, and psychological".

From an organizational perspective well-being is influenced by work-life balance, time management, workplace safety, hybrid working, leadership practices, reward systems, organizational communalities and social interactions, organizational culture and values, working practices, and organizational structures among others (e.g. [10, 11]).

However, Ilies, Schwind, & Heller [12] highlighted the importance of having a more dynamic model of well-being considering both personal and situational predictors, and both work and nonwork well-being indicators, and Renkema, Meijerink, and Bondarouk [13] highlighted the need for HRM literature to include an external perspective, considering the interconnections between HRM practices and their effects both inside and outside organizational boundaries, as well as the impact of external policies and events on working life. In the HRM literature, the adoption of this external perspective is still understudied.

Considering the construct of well-being, including extra-organizational perspective involves the understanding of how factors within and outside the organizational boundaries interact and impact the individuals' well-being.

Our aim is to systematize the construct of well-being by considering it both inside and outside the organizational boundaries, thus drawing closer the social well-being research stream and the organizational well-being one. Given that the research seeks to explore the potential connections between social well-being and organizational well-being, we will try to address two key questions: (1) does the concept of work emerge when social well-being is discussed?; (2) which stakeholders are involved, and at what levels (e.g., employees, citizens, organizations, institutions, government)?

We decided to adopt a systematic review as methodology given the large amount of scholarly research related to sustainability and well-being published; review articles also serve the purpose of facilitating researchers in keeping up with what has been discovered about their topic of interest. Indeed, the systematic approach would guarantee transparency, repeatability, and objectivity, by maximizing reliability and being less susceptible to bias than traditional reviews [14]. The systematic review is useful not only at a political level, but also at a professional level, for decision-making by practitioners [15] and thus is useful to untangle societal and organizational grand challenges.

We can assert that sustainable individual well-being represents a grand challenge for both organizations and society at large. In the context of grand challenges and complex, multifaceted issues that lack a singular solution and are perceived differently by various stakeholders, adopting a collective approach may be appropriate. A collective or social intelligence system leverages the knowledge and experience of a large group of individuals to support better decision-making or generate novel knowledge, ideas, and products. These systems utilize the "wisdom of crowds" concept, where the collective input from diverse individuals is aggregated to solve complex problems or innovate. Examples include platforms for ratings, reviews, user-generated content, and idea crowdsourcing [16].

In a subsequent phase of the research, as presented in the conclusions of this study, we will adopt a citizen science data approach conducive to a social intelligence system. Therefore, the systematization of the well-being construct in a comprehensive manner—one that accounts for both social and organizational contexts—is a necessary step toward validating the construct through a bottom-up approach that inclusively engages citizens via citizen science. This integration allows for a reconciliation between definitions emerging from academic literature and those arising from citizens themselves, thus contributing to the development of a *social intelligence system* on well-being. Such a system would reflect a dynamic and participatory understanding of well-being, grounded in both theoretical frameworks and lived experiences. The citizen science approach involves engaging citizens as active participants in the definition and validation of indicators and metrics that measure social sustainability and well-being.

2 Theoretical Framework

In the literature, there are numerous definitions of well-being [17]. The research project to which this systematic review is connected aims to offer policymakers and organizations insights on fostering sustainability, with a particular focus on its well-being dimension [17]. For this reason, we will consider definitions of well-being related to social well-being, which is tied to the social dimension of quality of life, and organizational well-being, which pertains to the organizational dimension.

Social well-being refers to the state of having positive relationships and a sense of belonging within a community. It includes aspects like strong social support networks, meaningful connections, and a feeling of being part of something larger. Social well-being is an integral part of overall health, affecting mental, emotional, and even physical aspects of life [17–19].

Social well-being refers to "how people see their relations to others and the wider community" ([18], p. 122). The inspiration for the scale comes from a World Health Organization document in which a definition of a person's well-being includes being able "to make a contribution to his or her community" ([18], p. 98). In the seminal work of Keyes [18] social well-being is defined as "the appraisal of one's circumstance and functioning in society" (p. 122), it refers to how people see their relations to others and the wider community. It comprises several dimensions: social acceptance (i.e. people hold favorable views of human nature and feel comfortable with others), social actualization (i.e. the belief in the evolution of society and the sense that society has potential which is being realized through its institutions and citizens), social contribution (i.e. the evaluation of one's social value, it includes the belief that one is a vital member of society, with something of value to give to the world), social coherence (i.e. the perception of the quality, organization, and operation of the social world), and social integration (i.e. the evaluation of the quality of one's relationship to society and community) [19].

Individual well-being is not solely relative to social well-being but can also be achieved within organizational boundaries.

Many research studies, particularly in HRM literature, consider organizational well-being and its impact on various organizational variables such as performance, organizational climate, employees' engagement, job satisfaction, and organizational climate (e.g. [13]). Organizational (or employee) well-being involves implementing strategies that reduce stress, prevent burnout, and encourage a supportive and inclusive workplace culture. Employee well-being is the state of individuals' mental, physical, and general health, and experiences of satisfaction at work. It is influenced by satisfaction of the job itself, as well as individuals' interactions with colleagues, relevant groups, and supervisors. It influences both psychological outcomes (e.g. burnout, anxiety, emotional exhaustion) and physiological ones (e.g. blood pressure, migraines, physical exhaustion) [20, 21].

Moreover, organizational well-being impact transcends the organizational boundaries and extends to an extra-organizational level. The article by Renkema and colleagues [13], to the stream of research this paper aims to contribute to, highlights the necessity of a multilevel approach to HRM practices that considers the organization as an open system, influenced by and influencing the external environment.

HRM phenomena are inherently multilevel, with micro-level behaviors embedded in macro-level contexts. The need to include the extra-organizational level in well-being research is especially pertinent given that the construct is examined by two research streams that remain largely detached, one of which is related to the external environment, i.e. the society.

Firstly, HRM practices, including those related to employees' well-being, do not operate in isolation but are influenced by broader external factors such as industry standards, economic conditions, and institutional pressures. Incorporating extra-organizational level can provide a more comprehensive understanding of how external factors affect well-being practices and their outcomes inside the organizational boundaries.

Furthermore, considering the extra-organizational level allows future well-being research to better address the dynamic nature of organizational settings and the interdependencies that exist beyond organizational boundaries. This approach facilitates a more accurate and holistic understanding of well-being. Integrating extra-organizational levels helps to account for the complexity and interconnectedness of modern organizational environments. It recognizes that HRM practices and outcomes are not solely determined by internal factors but are also shaped by interactions with other organizations, regulatory authorities, and the socio-economic environment [13].

Few studies addressed the importance of integrating social and organizational well-being [e.g. 22]. One notable example of research that considers well-being inside and outside the organizational boundaries is the one by Munzel et al. [23] which tried to understand the relationship between individual well-being and the use of social networking sites (SNS, here Facebook). They found that well-being is both a driver and an outcome of SNS use and social network characteristics.

Despite those few attempts, the research streams dedicated to social well-being and well-being within organizational boundaries are divided and unintegrated and an extensive multilevel approach has not been employed yet. Employees are consulted only for their opinions regarding well-being perceived during working hours and derived from organizational practices. However, they are not considered as citizens, and it is not taken into account that municipal policies influence the well-being perceived during working hours (for example, the promotion of efficient and sustainable transportation systems improves citizens' ability to commute to work), just as corporate policies affect well-being perceived outside of working hours (e.g., the promotion of agile working by the company enhances work-life balance). As the debate on sustainability and well-being is surging, it is even more germane to systematize social and organizational well-being research in a comprehensive framework. The complexity of a comprehensive approach derived from the difficulty to identify, capture and aggregate multi-stakeholders will benefit of a collective intelligence system, a structured approach able to leverage synergic or contrasting perspectives into a unique analysis and solution definition process. The systematization of the well-being construct—encompassing both societal and organizational dimensions—can serve as a foundational step toward the development of a collective intelligence system. By integrating perspectives from diverse contexts, this approach enables a more holistic and inclusive understanding of well-being that reflects both institutional knowledge and lived experiences. In particular, when well-being is conceptualized through inputs from both top-down (e.g., academic and policy frameworks) and bottom-up (e.g., citizen-driven insights) processes, it fosters the emergence of a dynamic knowledge ecosystem. Such a system supports collective sense-making, enhances responsiveness to complex socio-organizational challenges, and facilitates the co-creation of data-driven and socially attuned solutions. Ultimately, a comprehensive and participatory definition of well-being lays the groundwork for leveraging distributed knowledge, thereby reinforcing a collective intelligence model capable of informing policy, guiding organizational practices, and promoting sustainability and social resilience (e.g.[16, 24]).

3 Methodology

Following Tranfield et al. [25], Moher et al. [26], and Page et al. [27], we adopted the Preferred Reporting Items for Systematic Reviews and Meta-Analyses (PRISMA) statement and took a systematic approach characterized by transparency and reproducibility. The PRISMA statement provides updated reporting guidance for systematic reviews that reflects advances in methods to identify, select, appraise, and synthesize studies [27]. In accordance with Palumbo et al. [28], we chose the database with wider coverage leading us to select Scopus®.

The systematic literature review is employed to compile a comprehensive collection of articles delving into social and organizational well-being concepts, encompassing the various dimensions of well-being. We scrutinize articles from diverse sources and scientific disciplines, providing a means to construct a systematization of well-being [29].

As far as the inclusion/exclusion criteria are concerned, hereafter, in Table 1, we share the criteria and the literature review search strategy.

Our final query yielded 284 papers, which were downloaded, scanned, and analyzed during August 2024 to arrive to a final sample of 197 articles. Figure 1 presents the PRISMA flow diagram, detailing the articles that were included and excluded.

We carried out a bibliometric analysis using Biblioshiny derived from the RStudio Package Bibliometrix [30] and then a context analysis using Python with various packages further developed below. In particular, it should be noted that considering the small pool of studies included in the results on Python further analysis, such as sentiment analysis or more in-depth contextual analysis per key terms turned out limiting with zero to no valuable results. Hence, other forms of analysis were used employing Natural Language Processing (NLP) techniques, particularly topic modeling.

The purpose is to extract relevant themes (topics) that align with the research questions. The primary tools used include Python's pandas for data manipulation, scikit-learn for vectorization and topic modeling, and network for creating a relevance map.

Another challenge subsequent to the well-being systematization is related to the measurement of well-being. Aligned with the idea that well-being has to be investigated both inside and outside the organizational boundaries, we believe that consulting with citizens in the design of well-being measures and policies is fundamental to cultural and societal progress.

To validate the well-being definitions and measures adopting a social intelligence system, in a future research, as presented in the conclusions of this study, we will adopt a citizen science approach. As defined by Eitzel et al. [31], citizen science is a rather novel scientific field that engages members of the public in the process of creating scientific knowledge and addressing real-world problems (see also [32–37]. It can be implemented in a particularly effective way in urban environments to help tackle many "grand challenges", such as sustainable well-being.

Table 1 Literature review search strategy and criteria of inclusion and exclusion

SEARCH STRATEGY We use Scopus as data source. Keywords used for the queries are the following.	
Defining sustainability and well-being dimensions inside and outside the organization query (title, abstract, authors' keywords)	("social sustainability" OR "social sustainable development" OR "corporate social responsibility" OR "CSR") AND ("wellbeing" OR "well being" OR "well-being" OR "quality of life")
Defining indicators and metrics query (title, abstract, authors' keywords)	("measur*" OR "indicator*" OR "metric*" OR "analytic*" OR "assess*")
SELECTION CRITERIA	
Subject area limited to	Social sciences, Business, management and accounting, Computer science, Psychology, Arts and humanities, Decision sciences.
Study design	We do not apply exclusion criteria based on the type of study, considering quantitative, qualitative, mixed methods, and reviews. We are particularly interested in papers that concern sustainability and well-being, both inside and outside the organizational boundaries, and their measurements or indicators.
Population of studies	For this review, we consider all studies that focus on employees as well as on citizens. We consider individuals of all ages, genders, ethnicities, socio-economic backgrounds, and from any sector
Types of publications	We include only international papers. We exclude books, chapters, doctoral thesis, research report, executive summaries, conference proceedings and all the grey literature
Publication date	We include all papers published on this topic (no exclusion criteria)
Language	English
Location	We include all papers published on this topic (no exclusion criteria)
Query	(TITLE-ABS-KEY ("social sustainability" OR "social sustainable development" OR "corporate social responsibility" OR "CSR")) AND (TITLE-ABS-KEY ("wellbeing" OR "well being" OR "well-being" OR "quality of life")) AND (TITLE-ABS-KEY ("measur*" OR "indicator*" OR "metric*" OR "analytic*" OR "assess*")) AND (LIMIT-TO (SRCTYPE, "j")) AND (LIMIT-TO (DOCTYPE, "ar")) AND (LIMIT-TO (SUBJAREA, "SOCI") OR LIMIT-TO (SUBJAREA, "BUSI") OR LIMIT-TO (SUBJAREA, "PSYC") OR LIMIT-TO (SUBJAREA, "ARTS") OR LIMIT-TO (SUBJAREA, "COMP") OR LIMIT-TO (SUBJAREA, "DECI")) AND (LIMIT-TO (LANGUAGE, "English"))

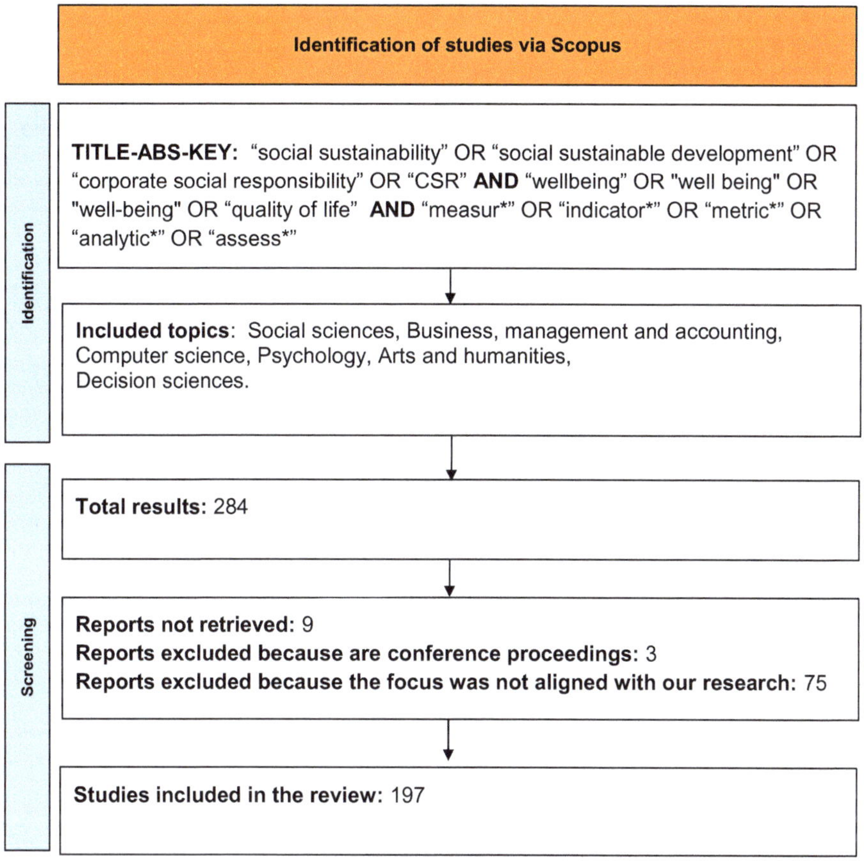

Fig. 1 PRISMA flow diagram for systematic reviews which included searches of databases only

4 Results

First, we present the results derived from the bibliometric analysis and the use of machine learning (Phyton) and second the results derived from the content analysis.

The first bibliometric result concerns the co-occurrence network (Fig. 2). The co occurrence analysis method enables to construct and visualize a network of emerging themes, i.e. connections within a body of text using linguistic analysis of relationships between words for pattern recognition [38] and nodes—representations of important terms, their weights and their location within the network [39]. We employ co-occurrence networks as a supportive tool to reveal patterns. For each theme, the size of the label circle and its font size mirror the theme's importance, and their proximities represent classification clusters.

From co-occurrence network we observe that the cluster of social sustainability includes the construct of quality of life but not that of well-being. The latter,

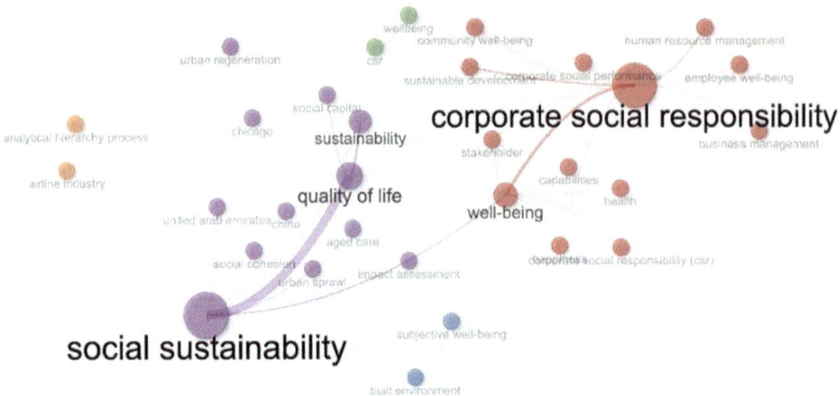

Fig. 2 Co-occurrence network by authors keywords

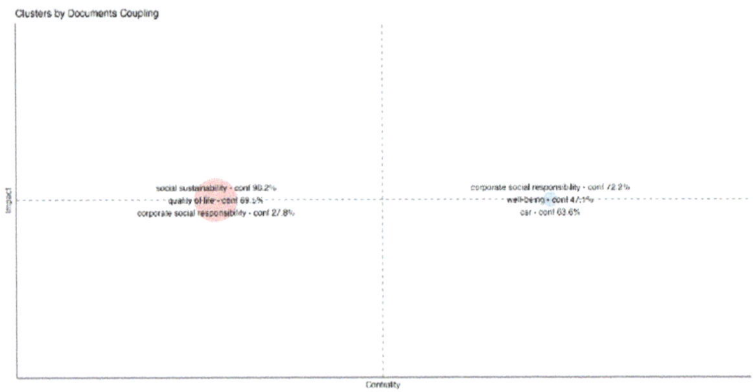

Fig. 3 Coupling map labeled by authors keywords

however, appears in the cluster related to corporate social responsibility. This suggests that even within the selected papers, there is a distinct clustering of the concept of quality of life that is socially oriented, contrary to well-being, that is more organizationally oriented. Supporting this observation, we note that the construct of subjective well-being is connected only to the social sustainability cluster and not to corporate social responsibility, while the opposite is true for the construct of employee well-being.

Similarly, the "coupling by references" map (Fig. 3) typically refers to the practice of connecting or associating different concepts, theories, or methods within a paper through citations or references to other works. This type of coupling helps to establish relationships between ideas, showing how they are interlinked, supportive of each other, or even how they contrast. In this map is even more clear the differences between the two clusters of social sustainability, associated with quality of life, and well-being, associated with corporate social responsibility.

It could be assumed that the scholarly literature takes two branches of research that do not unite the quality of life of an individual once it leaves the "corporate scenario" as observed by "aged care" node left next to quality of life, but not CSR, nor social capital further underlying that the quality of society is not united with the quality inside corporate boundaries. This is further enhanced by the node of human resource management being so far from the other nodes and connected to CSR but not to quality of life. Thus, these results let us wonder how the well-being of an employee is measured in a societal context and how in his personal and working sphere.

The observations drawn from Fig. 2 are further supported by the coupling map, which is a visualization technique used to identify and represent the relationships between different documents based on their shared references. In this context, centrality refers to the position of a document within the network formed by the coupling map, indicating how central or connected a document is relative to others in the network. On the other hand, the impact of a cluster reflects its influence or significance within the research domain, measured by the mean local citations. Specifically, the x-axis represents the cluster centrality (using Callon's Centrality index), while the y-axis indicates the cluster impact through the Mean Normalized Local Citation Score (MNLCS). The Normalized Local Citation Score (NLCS) for a document is calculated by dividing the actual number of local citations by the expected citation rate for documents published in the same year. It can be stated that Fig. 3 highlights not only that the two topics of well-being and social sustainability are not communicating, but overall their impact is average, meaning that the topics are not explored enough.

Contrary to the coupling map, that uses references, the factorial analysis, using the Multiple Correspondence Analysis (MCA) is a broader statistical tool used to explore and visualize relationships between categorical variables, helping to identify patterns or associations in diverse types of qualitative data. The factorial map (Fig. 4) shows us the centrality and impact of topics as well as different clusters. Once again, we can see that well-being is far from human development, thus indicating that the two topics are not considered together. Similarly, CSR and well-being, with the second having less centrality and impact.

While we expected a concentration on social well-being and CSR due to their inclusion in the query, the more significant finding lies in their relationships with other terms. Unlike earlier analyses that highlighted clusters with the highest density of terms based on the number of papers or the impact of their references, this factorial analysis reveals the strength and nature of these relationships within individual papers. Notably, inequality, which was absent in previous analyses, now appears, albeit in a lateral position, suggesting its focus may be geographically limited. Similarly, environmentally-focused terms, like air quality, emerge, indicating their potential relevance in the context of CSR. This is particularly interesting in the realm of citizen science, which typically concentrates on biodiversity and related topics.

The next analysis on Python allowed us to go more in-depth into the context in which these terms were inserted and understand the stakeholders involved. The first analysis aimed to observe when the term social well-being (and quality of life) was

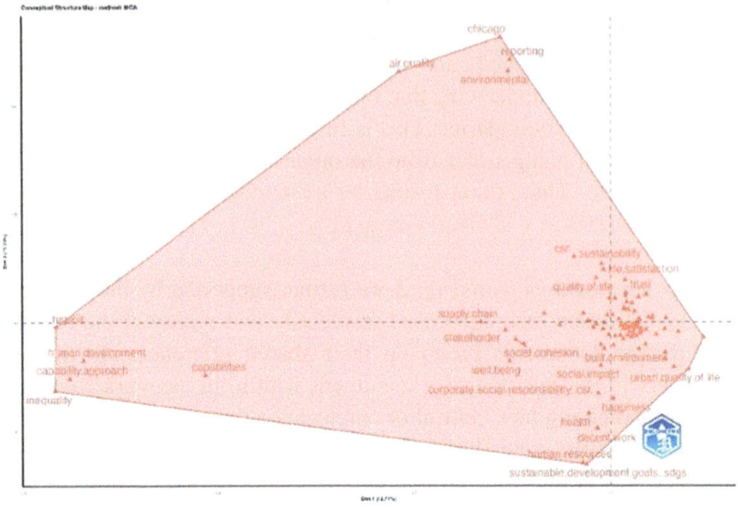

Fig. 4 Factorial map by authors keywords with MCA

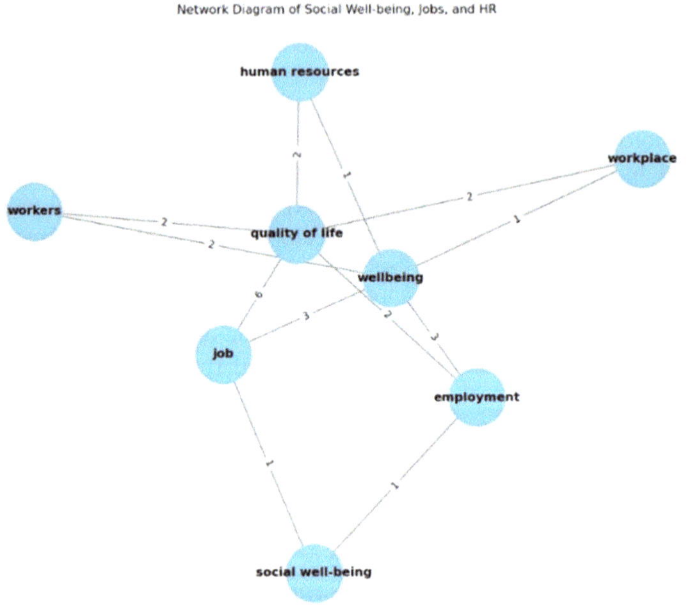

Fig. 5 Network diagram of Social well-being, Jobs and HR

mentioned, how the concepts of employment and HR were connected to it (Fig. 5). The idea behind this analysis is to better understand how many articles connect well-being with variables related to job. As the figure shows especially social well-being (the extra-organizational dimension of well-being) is not related to keywords such as workplace, workers, human resources. This result again highlights how the two well-being literatures are separated and the fact that employees are not considered as citizen in the majority of articles. That is, employees are considered only in organizational related papers.

The network was calculated by first filtering the dataset to identify papers that contain both keywords related to social well-being and those related to jobs or HRM. The relevant texts from these papers were then analyzed to identify co-occurrences of keywords from the two categories within the same text. For each instance where a keyword from the social well-being category appeared alongside a keyword from the jobs or HRM category, a keyword pair was recorded. The frequency of these keyword pairs was counted using the Counter function, which provided the basis for constructing the network. The network graph was then created by adding nodes for each keyword and edges between nodes based on the frequency of their co-occurrence, with edge weights reflecting how often each pair appeared together. Finally, the network was visualized, showing the relationships between concepts related to social well-being and jobs or HRM, with edge labels indicating the strength of these connections.

For the final part of the analysis we observed which stakeholders were mentioned, at which level and in relation to which topics.

Figure 6 identifies the stakeholders mentioned per frequency of mentions based on level of influence set by the authors. At the micro level of analysis (see Fig. 7) the main relevant stakeholders are employees, citizens, and consumers. Employees

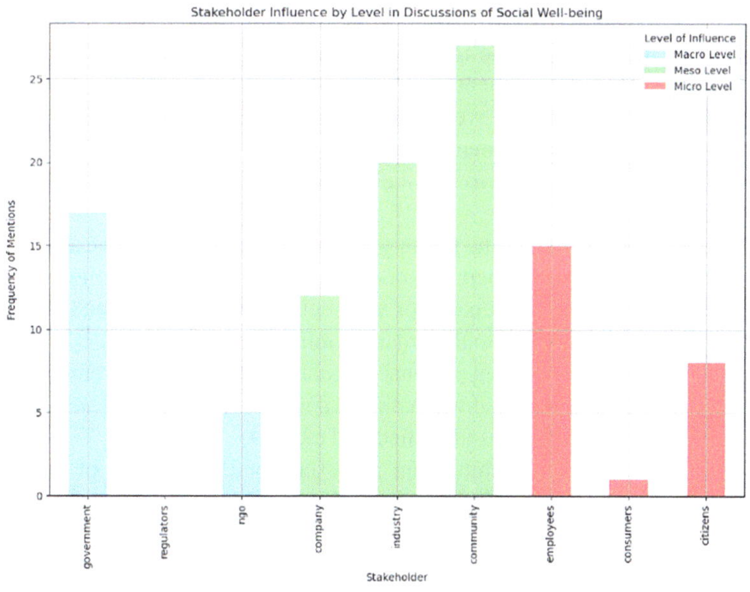

Fig. 6 Stakeholder influence by level of analysis

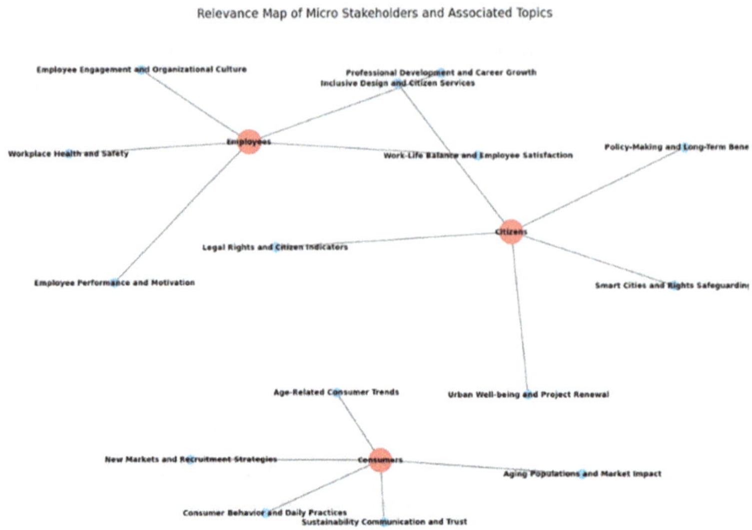

Fig. 7 Relevance map at the micro level about the stakeholders and associated topics

are related to concepts in the boundary of the organization, the only concept that transcends the organizational level is that of work-life balance. Citizens instead are related to concepts outside the organizational boundaries, with no relation to concepts related to work and working life.

At the meso level Fig. 8 shows that the primary stakeholders are companies, communities, and industries. Regarding companies and their impact on sustainability, the figure indicates that the focus is primarily on environmental responsibility and internal CSR, with no mention of an impact on the well-being of citizens. Community development and well-being are only addressed in papers where the community is considered the main stakeholder. However, when the community is the focus, there is no reference to well-being and sustainability within companies or the workplace dimension.

At the macro level (Fig. 9) the primary stakeholder identified in the articles is the government. In this context, there is a connection to both sustainability and quality of life topics. However, the concept of well-being is consistently understood at a social level, with no reference to the organizational one. Nonetheless, it is important to recognize that the government can enact regulations that influence corporate well-being. This raises the question of where the responsibility for societal well-being lies and which type of well-being is identified and tackled.

Below, we present the results from a partial content analysis of the first 20 papers manually reviewed. Table 2 will display the concepts of interest identified in these papers, categorized according to four levels of analysis: individual, team, organizational, and extra-organizational. The table is a first attempt to systematize results thus helping us develop a framework that will be accomplished when the process of the manual contest analysis will be finished. Although the content

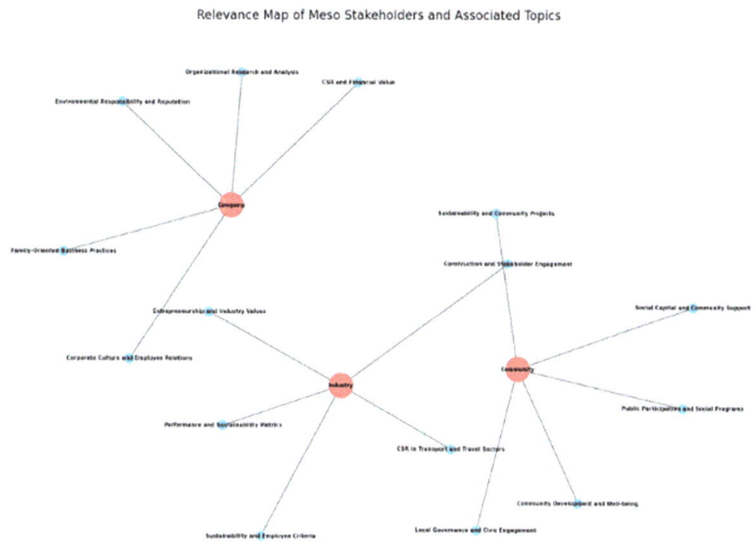

Fig. 8 Relevance map at the meso level about the stakeholders and associated topics

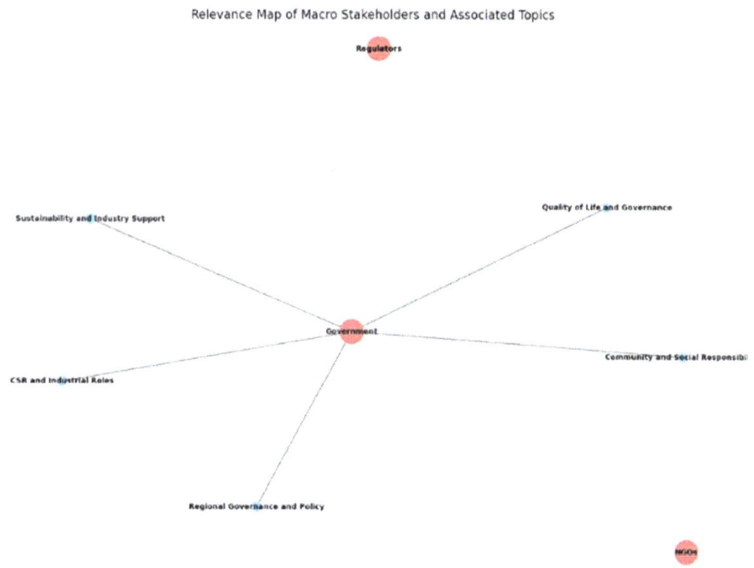

Fig. 9 Relevance map at the macro level about the stakeholders and associated topics

analysis is still partial, the table already provides some insights into the aspects of sustainable well-being at various levels of investigation and across different research streams (social and organizational).

Table 2 Content analysis systematic review

Level of analysis and focus	Representative studies (selection)
Micro level	
Social sustainability and well-being	
Individuals creating networks that increase happiness and quality of life in society (cohesion, integration, networks)	Acik Etike et al. [40]; Ahen [41]; Akbarinejad et al. [42]
Existence of common consciousness, responsibility, trust, and integrity in society (empathy, solidarity)	
Everyone benefitting from spatial and social activities, and human diversity is ensured in a heterogeneous society (D&I)	
The physical spaces and activities (urban development, infrastructures)	
Human health and dignity (included justice)	
Ecological literacy (awareness of environment and social events and related issues)	
Organizational sustainability and well-being	
Emotional and rational assessment by an employee of how his/her employer improves his/her wellness	Ahmad et al. [43]; Al Marzouqi et al. [44]
Work-life balance	
Internal communication for establishing effective relationships between the organization and employees.	
Practices to prevent burnout	
Meso level	
Social sustainability and well-being	
Social cohesion and group activities	Al Marzouqi et al. [44]
Organizational sustainability and well-being	
Management support	Al Marzouqi et al. [44]
Macro level	
Social sustainability and well-being	
Organizations development of effective partnerships for sustainability and well-being (e.g. with other organizations)	Alreshidi [45]
Organizational sustainability and well-being	
Organizational deployment of dynamic capabilities	Ahen [41], Alketbi & Ahmad [46]; Allam et al. [47]; Alreshidi [45]; Amato & Amato [48]; Ardito et al. [49]
Use of Metaverse to create job opportunities	
Sustainability practices that favor employees' well-being (e.g. workplace health and safety)	
Efficient use of resources	
Technological improvements inside the organization	
Female representation in the Board of Directors	

(continued)

Table 2 (continued)

Extra-organizational level	
Social sustainability and well-being	
Social equity (e.g. participation to decision-making process, formation of representative groups)	Akbarinejad et al. [42]; Allam et al. [47]; Arcagni et al. [50]
Environmental awareness (environment management)	
Health and environmental quality	
Safety measures	
Use of Metaverse (specifically digital twins) to predict and overcome urban challenges and improve residents' experience (e.g. equitable access to services)	
Interconnection of strategies (i.e. policy makers have to adopt both locally and globally strategies to foster sustainability and well-being)	
Organizational sustainability and well-being	
Material and non-material welfare of communities exploiting tourism and tourist organizations	Andrade-Valbuena et al. [51]

5 Implications, Future Results and Conclusions

From a theoretical standpoint, our research seeks to contribute in two ways: firstly, by attempting to reconcile the two literatures concerning the construct of well-being, namely social well-being and organizational well-being. Secondly, following the suggestions of Renkema and colleagues [13] we systematize definitions and factors influencing well-being both inside and outside organizational boundaries. In this way we consider the effect of HRM practices (in this case well-being practices) on the external environment, as well as how external policies and initiatives can impact the organization.

The results from the bibliometric analysis and the use of machine learning indicate that the two literatures have limited interaction. Additionally, the results from the content analysis highlight different aspects of well-being depending on the level of analysis considered. These aspects provide preliminary guidance for policymakers and HR managers to enhance the well-being of citizens and employees. In particular, the findings highlight certain aspects that are often overlooked by both policymakers and organizations, such as the importance of spaces both inside and outside the organizational boundaries, the use and development of dynamic capabilities, and the potential of the Metaverse as a tool for forecasting and designing spaces, activities, and policies aimed at social well-being.

A collective intelligence system refers to a socio-technical framework that harnesses the distributed knowledge, experiences, and problem-solving capacities of diverse actors—individuals, communities, organizations, and institutions—to generate insights and support informed decision-making. Such systems rely on the aggregation and synthesis of data and perspectives from multiple sources, enabling the co-creation of knowledge that is context-sensitive, adaptive, and oriented toward the public good [16, 24].

Through the integration of citizen science and the systematic conceptualization of well-being across both societal and organizational domains, it becomes possible to construct a collective intelligence system specifically focused on well-being. Citizen science facilitates the inclusion of citizens as active contributors to the research process, allowing for the collection of rich data that reflect real-life experiences and perceptions. At the same time, the systematization of the well-being construct ensures that the knowledge base underpinning the system is both academically grounded and socially relevant.

By combining these elements, a collective intelligence system on well-being can emerge, one that is capable of capturing the multidimensionality of well-being, identifying context-specific needs and priorities, and informing policies and organizational practices.

Thus, in a consequent phase of our research we will adopt the citizen science approach to implement a social intelligence system. Adopting the citizen science approach, we address the dynamic nature of well-being by regularly consulting employees and citizens thus continuously redesigning, monitoring and adapting well-being measures. Moreover, participants in the study may increase their scientific knowledge, gain intrinsic satisfaction from contributing to socially useful research, and connect with the scientific community, which had previously seemed distant from their concerns [52]. Furthermore, they will better understand the factors influencing their well-being both within and outside the organization. Finally, society as a whole will benefit from the citizen science approach due to more efficient and rapid scientific outcomes, as well as the increased literacy and engagement of citizens [53].

Next step of the research concerns adopting the citizen science approach, we will examine employees from three organizations located in different Italian regions: Bergamo, Ferrara, and Lecce. We will administer a questionnaire to these employees, based on the measures and metrics identified during our systematic review, and conduct in-depth qualitative interviews with a subset of participants. Selecting these three cities as a sample allows us to gather evidence on well-being across the northern, central, and southern parts of Italy. Additionally, these cities exhibit diverse well-being indicators. According to the 2023 quality of life ranking by Il Sole24Ore, Bergamo, Ferrara, and Lecce are ranked 5th, 60th, and 71st, respectively. Specifically, considering the business and employment indicator—which is of particular interest to us since our framework focuses on organizational and social well-being as perceived by workers—Bergamo is ranked 24th, Lecce 42nd and Ferrara 43rd. Therefore, we can consider these three cities as representative of well-being in the north, center, and south of Italy, accounting for their differences.

Acknowledgments This study was funded by European Union- Next Generation EU, Mission 4, Component 1, CUP G53D23004760006. This publication has been produced within the framework of the Project of Relevant National Interest (PRIN 2022), funded by the Italian Ministry of University and Research, project code PRIN202223ALAZA_01, CUP G53D23004760006, entitled "CITYBLE - Developing Two-Sided Citizen Analytics for the Sustainable Digital Society."

Disclosure of Interests The authors have no competing interests to declare that are relevant to the content of this article.

References

1. Sachs, J. D., Lafortune, G., Fuller, G., & Drumm, E. (2023). *Implementing the SDG Stimulus. Sustainable Development Report 2023. Paris: SDSN*. Dublin University Press.
2. UNDP (United Nations Development Programme). (2024). Human Development Report 2023–24: Breaking the gridlock: Reimagining cooperation in a polarized world.
3. Helliwell, J. F., Layard, R., Sachs, J. D., De Neve, J.-E., Aknin, L. B., & Wang, S. (2024). *World Happiness Report 2024*. University of Oxford: Wellbeing Research Centre.
4. Richter, F., Gawenko, W., Götze, U., & Hinz, M. (2023). Toward a methodology for social sustainability assessment: A review of existing frameworks and a proposal for a catalog of Criteria. *Schmalenbach Journal of Business Research, 75*(4), 587–626.
5. Kalfaoğlu, S. (2023). Social sustainability indicators from employees' perspective: A qualitative study on whether social sustainability in businesses is perceived as a necessity, preference, or dream. *Sustainability, 15*(10), 7954.
6. Li, M., Fu, N., Chadwick, C., & Harney, B. (2024). Untangling human resource management and employee wellbeing relationships: Differentiating job resource HR practices from challenge demand HR practices. *Human Resource Management Journal, 34*(1), 214–235.
7. Custodio, H. M., Hadjikakou, M., & Bryan, B. A. (2023). A review of socioeconomic indicators of sustainability and wellbeing building on the social foundations framework. *Ecological Economics, 203*, 107608.
8. Rudolph, C. W., & Zacher, H. (2025). Working from home: When is it too much of a good thing? *Human Resource Development Quarterly, 36*(1), 9–47.
9. Juchnowicz, M., & Kinowska, H. (2021). Employee well-being and digital work during the COVID-19 pandemic. *Information, 12*, 293.
10. Dale, G., Wilson, H., & Tucker, M. (2024). What is healthy hybrid work? Exploring employee perceptions on well-being and hybrid work arrangements. *International Journal of Workplace Health Management, 17*(4), 335–352.
11. Lindeberg, P., Saunila, M., Lappalainen, P., Ukko, J., & Rantanen, H. (2023). The relationship between various social work environment elements and hybrid worker well-being. *Facilities, 42*(15/16), 1–16.
12. Ilies, R., Schwind, K. M., & Heller, D. (2007). Employee well-being: A multilevel model linking work and non-work domains. *European Journal of Work and Organizational Psychology, 16*(3), 326–341.
13. Renkema, M., Meijerink, J., & Bondarouk, T. (2017). Advancing multilevel thinking in human resource management research: Applications and guidelines. *Human Resource Management Review, 27*(3), 397–415.
14. Haddaway, N. R., & Pullin, A. S. (2014). The policy role of systematic reviews: Past, present and future. *Springer Science Reviews, 2*, 179–183.
15. Hong, Q. N., & Pluye, P. (2018). Systematic reviews: A brief historical overview. *Education for information, 34*(4), 261–276.
16. Elia, G., & Margherita, A. (2018). Can we solve wicked problems? A conceptual framework and a collective intelligence system to support problem analysis and solution design for complex social issues. *Technological Forecasting and Social Change, 133*, 279–286.
17. Ly, A. M., & Cope, M. R. (2023). New conceptual model of social sustainability: Review from past concepts and ideas. *International Journal of Environmental Research and Public Health, 20*(7), 5350.

18. Keyes, C. L. M. (1998). Social well-being. *Social Psychology Quarterly*, 121–140.
19. Son, J., & Wilson, J. (2012). Volunteer work and hedonic, eudemonic, and social well-being. *Sociological Forum, 27*(3), 658–681.
20. Danna, K., & Griffin, R. (1999). Health and well-being in the workplace: A review and synthesis of the literature. *Journal of Management, 25*, 357–384.
21. Nielsen, K., Nielsen, M. B., Ogbonnaya, C., Känsälä, M., Saari, E., & Isaksson, K. (2017). Workplace resources to improve both employee wellbeing and performance: A systematic review and meta-analysis. *Work & Stress, 31*(2), 101–120.
22. Ng, E. C. W., & Fisher, A. T. (2013). Understanding well-being in multi-levels: A review. *Health, Culture and Society, 5*(1), 308–323.
23. Munzel, A., Meyer-Waarden, L., & Galan, J. P. (2018). The social side of sustainability: Well-being as a driver and an outcome of social relationships and interactions on social networking sites. *Technological Forecasting and Social Change, 130*, 14–27.
24. Malone, T. W., Laubacher, R. J., & Dellarocas, C. (2010). The collective intelligence genome. *MIT Sloan Management Review, 51*(3), 21–31.
25. Tranfield, D., Denyer, D., & Smart, P. (2003). Towards a methodology for developing evidence-informed management knowledge by means of systematic review. *British Journal of Management, 14*(3), 207–222.
26. Moher, D., Liberati, A., Tetzlaff, J., Altman, D. G., & PRISMA Group. (2009). Preferred reporting items for systematic reviews and meta-analyses: The PRISMA statement. *Annals of Internal Medicine, 151*(4), 264–269.
27. Page, M. J., McKenzie, J. E., Bossuyt, P. M., Boutron, I., Hoffmann, T. C., Mulrow, C. D., et al. (2021). The PRISMA 2020 statement: An updated guideline for reporting systematic reviews. *BMJ, 372*(71).
28. Palumbo, R., Fakhar Manesh, M., & Petrolo, D. (2024). What makes work smart in the public sector? Insights from a bibliometric analysis and interpretive literature review. *Public Management Review, 26*(6), 1449–1474.
29. Neuendorf, K. A. (2017). *The content analysis guidebook* (2nd ed.). Sage Publications Inc..
30. Aria, M., & Cuccurullo, C. (2017). Bibliometrix: An R-tool for comprehensive science mapping analysis. *Journal of Informetrics, 11*(4), 959–975.
31. Eitzel, M., Cappadonna, J., Santos-Lang, C., Duerr, R., West, S. E., Virapongse, A., et al. (2017). *Citizen science terminology matters: Exploring key terms* (pp. 1–20). Theory and practice.
32. Bonney, R., Cooper, C., & Ballard, H. (2016). The theory and practice of citizen science: Launching a new journal. *Citizen Science: Theory and Practice, 1*, 1–4.
33. Cohn, J. P. (2008). Citizen science: Can volunteers do real research. *Bioscience, 58*, 192–197.
34. Jordan, R., Crall, A., Gray, S., Phillips, T., & Mellor, D. (2015). Citizen science as a distinct field of inquiry. *Bioscience, 65*, 208–211.
35. Kosmala, M., Wiggins, A., Swanson, A., & Simmons, B. (2016). Assessing data quality in citizen science. *Frontiers in Ecology and the Environment, 14*, 551–560.
36. Ballerini, L., & Bergh, S. I. (2021). Using citizen science data to monitor the sustainable development goals: A bottom-up analysis. *Sustainability Science, 16*(6), 1945–1962.
37. Franzoni, C., & Sauermann, H. (2014). Crowd science: The organization of scientific research in open collaborative projects. *Research Policy, 43*(1), 1–20.
38. Godwin, A. (2016). Visualizing systematic literature reviews to identify new areas of research. *IEEE Frontiers in Education Conference (FIE)*, 1–8.
39. Van Eck, N. J., & Waltman, L. (2014). Visualizing bibliometric networks. In Y. Ding, R. Rousseau, & D. Wolfram (Eds.), *Measuring scholarly impact: Methods and practice* (pp. 285–320). Cham.
40. Acik Etike, B., & Erdonmez Dincer, M. E. (2024). Determining the interaction of social sustainability with the physical environment: A case study of Adana, Turkey. *Sustainability, 16*, 4947.
41. Ahen, F. (2018). Dystopic prospects of global health and ecological governance: Whither the eco-centric-humanistic CSR of firms? *Humanistic Management Journal, 3*, 105–126.

42. Akbarinejad, T., Salaj, A. T., & Johansen, A. (2023). Implementing the integrated social sustainability assessment to Norway: A citizen-centric and expert-weighted approach. *Sustainability, 15*(16), 12107.
43. Ahmad, N., Ullah, Z., Ryu, H. B., Ariza-Montes, A., & Han, H. (2023). From corporate social responsibility to employee well-being: Navigating the pathway to sustainable healthcare. *Psychology Research and Behavior Management*, 1079–1095.
44. Al Marzouqi, A. H., Khan, M., & Hussain, M. (2020). Employee social sustainability: Prioritizing dimensions in the UAE's airlines industry. *Social Responsibility Journal, 16*(3), 349–367.
45. Alreshidi, B. A. (2018) Green business operations for building eco-cities: Identifying the role of business and critical success factors for sustainability. *IBIMA Business Review Journal*, 592758.
46. Alketbi, M. S., & Ahmad, S. Z. (2024). Corporate social responsibility and sustainability practices: Mediating effect of green innovation and moderating effect of knowledge management in the manufacturing sector. *International Journal of Organizational Analysis, 32*(7), 1369–1388.
47. Allam, Z., Sharifi, A., Bibri, S. E., Jones, D. S., & Krogstie, J. (2022). The metaverse as a virtual form of smart cities: Opportunities and challenges for environmental, economic, and social sustainability in urban futures. *Smart Cities, 5*(3), 771–801.
48. Amato, C. H., & Amato, L. H. (2011). Corporate commitment to global quality of life issues: Do slack resources, industry affiliations, and multinational headquarters matter? *Business & Society, 50*(2), 388–416.
49. Ardito, L., Dangelico, R. M., & Messeni Petruzzelli, A. (2021). The link between female representation in the boards of directors and corporate social responsibility: Evidence from B corps. *Corporate Social Responsibility and Environmental Management, 28*(2), 704–720.
50. Arcagni, A., Fattore, M., Maggino, F., & Vittadini, G. (2021). Some critical reflections on the measurement of social sustainability and well-being in complex societies. *Sustainability, 13*(22), 12679.
51. Andrade-Valbuena, N., Baier-Fuentes, H., & Gaviria-Marin, M. (2022). An overview of sustainable entrepreneurship in tourism, destination, and hospitality research based on the web of science. *Sustainability, 14*, 14944.
52. Paul, K., Quinn, M. S., Huijser, M. P., Graham, J., & Broberg, L. (2014). An evaluation of a citizen science data collection program for recording wildlife observations along a highway. *Journal of Environmental Management, 139*, 180–187.
53. Cappa, F., Franco, S., & Rosso, F. (2022). Citizens and cities: Leveraging citizen science and big data for sustainable urban development. *Business Strategy and the Environment, 31*(2), 648–667.

Misalignments in the Digitalization of Proximity Health Care Services. A Case Study Upon Reforms in Italy

Gianluca Antonucci, Antonio D'Andreamatteo, and Pierpaolo Arquilla

Abstract The use of ICT resources in healthcare has been growing since the 2000s because can lead to cost saving, time saving, errors reduction, improvement of medical practice. In Italy, Mission 6 of the National Recovery and Resilience Plan (M6-PNRR) allocates 8.6 billions for disseminating telemedicine strengthening the healthcare system's information and digital tools. Considering the theories on ecosystem innovation in healthcare, this study, using a mixed-method approach, investigates the gaps between ideas and design by the policymakers and the correspondences by the side of health operators. Our results confirm that, a huge problem in the health sector is not innovation per se, but the dissemination of innovative concepts. Service innovation in healthcare is successful only if it can satisfy users' needs. A fundamental role has been found in the GPs, seen as strategical promoters. Another important aspect has been found in Covid health crisis as a buster of digitalization, thus confirming previous research. But another important aspect has been found in the need of "educating/training" patients, thus revealing the importance of really creating a co-production scheme for developing a real effective digitalized system. The commitment and active participation of patients represents indeed a prerequisite for obtaining high adherence, but if users are culturally not keen in contributing to the process, the potential of digitalization remains unexploited.

Keywords Digitalization · Telemedicine · Ecosystem innovation · Health policy

---

G. Antonucci (✉)
"G. d'Annunzio" University of Chieti-Pescara, Pescara, Italy
e-mail: gianluca.antonucci@unich.it

A. D'Andreamatteo
"G. d'Annunzio" University of Chieti-Pescara, Chieti, Italy

P. Arquilla
Azienda Sanitaria Locale Pescara, Pescara, Italy

M. Cipriano et al. (eds.), *Technologies for Organizations and Society*,
Lecture Notes in Information Systems and Organisation 80,
https://doi.org/10.1007/978-3-032-01697-3_14

1 Introduction

Healthcare systems, and public ones in particular, require nowadays a reform focused on Primary Care, as highlighted by the frame of reference on Primary Care by the EU Commission in 2014 [1], and by the 2018 Astana Declaration by the World Health Organisation [2]. Yet, adjustments in public healthcare systems seem to be insoluble, especially considering their persistent resistance to reforms [3–5].

Indeed, since the beginning of the 2010s (if not even before) western countries' governments have been looking for a way to improve quality and efficiency of health systems [6], but the different ways for optimisation, such as cost control and quality management, have been challenged by several tensions [7].

To overcome the difficulties for the actual implementation of the needed changes, a great role has been now allocated to Information and Communication Technology (ICT) and to digitalization [8]. The use of ICT resources in healthcare has been growing since the 2000s [9], given that digitalization can lead to cost saving [10], time saving [11, 12], errors reduction [13, 14], improvement of medical practice [15, 16]. Nowadays digitalisation of healthcare constitutes a central component of pervasive healthcare and represents an important instrument to increase health promotion, disease prevention, provision of care, and monitoring [17].

Moreover, the Covid health crisis challenged this ongoing progression, clarifying that the determination of the post pandemic is in our hands [18] as the reset of public sector system, after Covid, has been deemed the "hardest challenge of the century" [19]. Particularly, within public healthcare systems, the pandemic had two important effects. First, it led a positive change on the esteem of public health services and the respect of medical research [20]. The Covid19 crisis is indeed contributing, in requesting a tailored assessment of the value-based healthcare creation [21], necessitating the involvement of professionals, organizations, and public institutions in charge of the service supplying, together with an active role by the patients [22]. Secondly, the pandemic led to an increased use of digital tools, thus transforming our working arrangements as well as our interactions [23] and it was also a "booster" of innovation in the whole public sector [24–26] and in the healthcare in particular [27].

Consistently, among recent endeavors of improving healthcare systems, governments have launched policy initiatives to foster digitalization in healthcare (e.g [28]., even more in the post-pandemic era [29]. Health policy design and implementation have a relevant role in improving the performance of healthcare systems. Scholars recognize the power of policies to enhance the health and well-being of a population [30, 31], although not all the policies are implemented successfully [32]. Concomitantly, a growing body of research related to policy analysis has been developing to ascertain strength and pitfalls of such policies, both in the design and implementation phases. Health policy analysis is understood as <<a multi-disciplinary approach to public policy that aims to explain the

interaction between institutions, interests and ideas in the policy process>>[33:308], an approach that goes far beyond the mere technical content of the policy [30]. At present, the prevalent method of research used for such an analysis is the case study methodology [33].

Accordingly, this study investigates the alignment issues between policy-driven digital healthcare reforms and their practical implementation in a mainly public healthcare system: what are the challenges and barriers that could potentially impede the implementation of policy-driven digital healthcare reforms? In synthesis, we run our investigation with the aim of exploring and understanding possible causes and risks of misalignment between the reform plan on health digitalisation and its actual implementation in the field, especially at local level where primary proximity cares are delivered.

Rooting in the tradition of qualitative studies, we used case study research [34]. We chose the Italian National Health Service (INHS) as unit of analysis, essentially because the central Government has recently launched the massive Plan of investments of the EU Programme Next Generation EU, Mission 6 of the National Recovery and Resilience Plan (M6-PNRR) [35], with the aim of strengthening the healthcare system's information and digital tools [30]. The plan allocated approximately € 15.6 billion to support asset investments in Proximity Assistance and Telemedicine, having 8.6 billion for disseminating telemedicine. Further, the INHS has specific features that make it an interesting unit of analysis. First, Italy is one of the countries with the most aged population and with the necessity to modify its public National Health Service [36]. Second, it is a decentralized public health system, a setting which has great disparities among the territories in terms of quality and expenses [37]. Despite these disparities and problems, the systems had the potential to reach significant outcomes for its population. During Covid pandemic peaks, for example, the local branches of Italian National Health Services reacted promptly through a community co-production approach [25]. Third, the central Government recently launched a major reform redesigning primary healthcare in all the country, in which digitalization is one the levers to implement the reform.

To achieve our research aim we decided to focus on digitalization at the level of proximity caring, within a larger ongoing research upon Community Care Homes in Italy, and started from a desk analysis [38] to then run semi-structured interviews to high-qualified experts and finally managing two focus groups with GPs. To design our research and interpret results, we deemed useful to apply the theories on ecosystem innovation in healthcare [39, 40], searching for possible gaps between the different ideas and design by the policymakers and the correspondences by the side of health operators who actually deal with the proper digitalization of the public primary system, being in direct contact with their users.

Next section informs about the theoretical background, while Sect. 3 describes the research methodology. In Sect. 4 findings from the desk research, interviewees and focus group are presented. Section 5 contains discussion and conclusion.

2 Theoretical Background

In order to completely reform Healthcare systems, especially public ones, we ought to overturn the "in-hospital" paradigm. It is necessary to place primary health care as the core service of each caring system. For this reason we ought to manage the flows of the demand being able to maintain continuity of care for all [41]. It is therefore necessary to integrate caring among sectors [42], maintaining continuity of chronic care [43], and community-based health-services [44]. The point is that this target cannot be settled easily [45].

This is particularly factual in contexts having Public National Health Services which had, in the last years, reforms inspired by New Public Management theories and principles [44] whose effectiveness, in such a unique context as healthcare, has been contested [45]. This is because, especially since the new millennium, we are witnessing a ruining of public health services rather than their increase in efficiency and effectiveness, leading to an always changing complex, and thus impersonal, health system, not able to respond to citizens' needs and also difficult to be managed [46].

Indeed, the demand of caring services is transforming a lot because the aging of the population, particularly in more developed countries, is increasing the number of multi-pathological chronic diseases [47]. Moreover, nowadays most patients are more informed, thus claiming for better and personalized caring services according to advancement in medical knowledge [48]. The demand for more and better services has, on the other hand, to cope with financial sustainability, in a context of limited public resources [49]. It is therefore necessary to change public healthcare systems, aiming at both quality and efficiency, as well as equity and appropriateness [50].

In recent years, many studies have been increasing our knowledge and understanding about the notion of public value [48] and public value in healthcare [52] developing, issues concerning co-production in public health services [53, 54]. Additionally, many researchers are investigating the consequences of Covid 19 pandemic as a "booster" of innovation, both of services and strategies [25] especially linked with digitalization and telemedicine [24, 27].

Following this path, we aim at investigating both role and importance of proximity healthcare digitalisation and telemedicine implementation as planned within Italian healthcare reforms linked to PNRR.

Digitalisation and telemedicine services implementation had a fast growth during Covid crisis [55]. All healthcare systems are moving towards a setting with an intensive presence of virtual components in caring systems, modifying completely health services provision [56, 57]. This happened also to the Italian Public National Health Service that, before Covid, had "simply" formally transposed national guidelines launched in 2014 as a first attempt to give a "glossary" in a common national scheme [58]. Since Covid crisis, several regions (being Italian NHS governed at regional level) launched specific norms and regulatory statements to activate tele-examinations as interaction at distance between MD and patient [58].

This innovation is in line within the PNRR Mission 6 devoted to the primary care reorganisation, innovation, and implementation (M6-PNRR). It foresees, among the others, "Telemedicine to a better support to patients" allocating 1B€ (1.2.3 M6-PNRR) divided in 250 M€ to implement a national Platform for Telemedicine and 750 M€ to design and implement regional projects of telemedicine (Ministerial Decree 01/04/2022) meanwhile, with the Law 25/2022 (which modified previous Legislative Decrees) the National Agency for Regional Health Services [59] was attributed of the further role of National Agency for Digital Health (ASD) thus ratifying an evolution also in the governance of the regional health systems.

Starting from the above "new" definition of both the structure and especially the role of telemedicine within the Italian health service, we decided to analyze it within the studies upon innovation in health care [60] taking in particular consideration aspects regarding the health innovation ecosystems framework [39, 40].

Innovations in healthcare represents any improvement in the quality of services and/or life, being indeed a continual challenge to existing health care providers and systems [60]. This implies technologies, procedures, as well as forms of organization. Paradoxically, a huge problem in the health sector is not innovation per se, but the dissemination of innovative concepts [61]. Service innovation in healthcare implies new forms of logistics, advice, and reporting, and it is successful only if it can satisfy users' needs [60]. The so-called promoters cover a fundamental role in this sense: they are key persons who allow the implementation of the change, contributing to overcoming its barriers [62]. They can do that because they know "how things work" and thus comprehend the innovation and perceive its perspectives [63].

Innovation ecosystems in healthcare can be seen as the full potential, especially given by new technologies, to tackle unmet needs [64] by timely addressing patients' situations and thus being able to perform correct diagnosis, analyzing plentiful variables [65]. A great impulse in the development of innovations based upon these schemes was given by the research of solutions to fight Covid outbreak. The pandemic crisis led to the search for an ecosystem approach for new solutions, thus raising the competences of different stakeholders for achieving common important outcomes [66].

All the above considered, we decided to analyze the ongoing modifications of Italian public health systems looking at them as an innovation which could be probably effective if developed with a healthcare approach, and we decided to particularly address, in our investigation, not the digitalization and telemedicine design per se, rather than the path for its actual implementation, thus investigating the role of health operators as innovation promoters for an effective development of digitalization and telemedicine according to their foreseen outcomes.

3 Research Design and Method

Considering the multipurpose aim of our research, we chose to frame it using a mixed-method approach [67–69] informed by case study research [70]. We chose the INHS as a unit of analysis, on which we focused on two different steps.

The first step was represented by a desk analysis, i.e. a <<research strategy of using existing data sources>> [34:103], such as laws, policy briefs, commentaries, literature reviews, etc. Desk analysis is useful when trying to understand the context of the investigated phenomenon. Accordingly, we searched for laws, rules, and regulations, as well as preliminary possible published studies and reports regarding the digitalization and telemedicine within the reforms of the Italian Public Health Service stated in the PNRR. All read to see if, and especially how and for what, the ongoing process of digitalization could be seen as a health innovation ecosystem.

The second stage saw a qualitative explorative case sampling [34]. We investigated the prospective effects of digitalization in a proper reforming context, by collecting information from key informants involved in critical issues [70], through both semi-structured interviews and focus groups. Specifically, we managed exploratory targeted qualitative interviews [71] with privileged witnesses who were experts in the area [72].

We sketched the theoretical rationales for the interviews depicting the issues from the literature regarding community health services facilities [73]. We based our construct on the work by Srinivasan and Chandwani [74] who studied managers' role in an evolving health organization domain. We had as reference point also the research by Mergel et al. [8] upon digital transformation processes in public service facilities. We therefore create a specific questionnaire based on the following questions:

- Is the Italian public health sector changing? And how?
- What is the degree of digital skill in Italian public community services?
- Is there a positive attitude toward digital transformation?
- After the reform did your organization digitally transformed itself?

Within a larger, still ongoing, research upon Community Care Homes in Italy, we had the possibility to interview personnel belonging to two different Italian regions and to 4 different Local Public Health Territorial Services (ASL), in order to gather insights, not only for a specific case, but also about general indications coming from different contexts. Being the basic elements of a healthcare innovation ecosystem, we decided to select, for our interviews, personnel belonging to key roles in the implementation of the change. In other words, if GPs were found as promoters of the change (and therefore object of the two focus groups as showed later on in this section) we decided to interview the different points of entry of the change, that is those covering key roles in the management of local Italian NHS services.

In particular we interviewed:

- A Head of a unit of coordination and management of public primary care and local territorial services.

- A Responsible for public psychiatric territorial services.
- A Head of a public General Medicine Operating Unit.
- A MD and President of a Conference of Mayors for public local health services.

Moreover, considering the fundamental role of the promoters of the change, we run two focus groups with 9 GPs who represented the whole spectrum of the unions in Local Public Health Territorial Services (ASL). In other words, managing two focus groups with the different representatives of the category, we had the possibility to cover ideas, sentiments, experiences of the GPs of a whole local unit (ASL).

Interviews took place between June and November 2023 and were conducted (as well as the focus groups) in both the interviewers' and interviewees' native language (Italian). The average interview lasted about 20 min each.

Focus group one—dedicated to acquire information about the process services innovation—was managed in January 2024, lasting 85 min, while the Focus Group 2—specifically devoted on telemedicine issues as a deepening of previous investigation—took place in May 2024, lasting 40 min.

The records were firstly transcribed and then analyzed thanks to a content analysis [75], framed on deductive thematic analysis, obtained by theoretically-driven coding [76]. Specifically, the works by Winpenny et al. [73] and Srinivasan and Chandwani [74] allowed us to define the following items: (1) facility type; (2) expected outcomes; (3) staffing; (4) collaboration and networking among services; (5) users' centricity. Considering that we had no previous data to assist with coding, we opted not to use any specific computer-assisted software. The final results were translated in English to allow the final editing to this work.

4 Findings

Our investigation, in confirming that the ongoing reforms and digitalization of Italian public health system can be seen as a healthcare innovation ecosystem, showed also a kind of misalignment between policy-driven digital healthcare reforms and their practical implementation in a mainly public healthcare system. Particularly, we found a detachment between the reform plan on health digitalization and its actual implementation on the field, especially at local level, where primary proximity cares are delivered.

The findings show indeed that the real problem is not innovation per se, but the dissemination of the basic innovative concepts, those able to modify health services delivering in a successful way, namely really able to satisfy users' needs. In this sense we found the GPs as the crucial link, being them the strategical promoters of the change. A full commitment of them is essential, but if you want to have their commitment you first need to have their understanding of the change, and to have it you need to inform them. In synthesis without involvement, you cannot have commitment. On the contrary we discovered, for instance (see following paragraphs) that no GP knew that the electronic health record was already developed and that they could use it in assisting patients.

Moreover, our research found that you cannot see only at one side, but you need also to consider the other one, that is those of the recipients. Such a change, as a service digitalization, cannot indeed be unidirectional, but needs also an active role by the users' side. In this sense we found that an important aspect regards the need of "educating/training" patients, thus disclosing the relevance of creating a co-production scheme for really implementing operative digitalized systems. Indeed, the engagement of patients is important to have collaborative users, but if they are traditionally not keen in being part of the change, the potential of digitalization remains in name only.

This section about findings consists of two parts. We first present the results coming from the desk research, that is, as initially thought and designed by the policy makers. We then illustrate those coming from the content analysis of the interviews and the focus groups.

4.1 Digitalisation and Telemedicine in the PNRR as a Healthcare Innovation Ecosystem

The prominent result of our desk analysis regards the fact that, the ongoing reform, can be fully considered a strategic health innovation ecosystem. As previously mentioned, within the M6 PNRR panorama, there is a specific measure entitled "Telemedicine to a better support to patients". Furthermore, the National Agency for Regional Health Services (AGENAS) entrusted the additional role of National Agency for Digital Health (ASD), thus sanctioning the digitalized change, at national level, of the governance of the regional public health systems.

There is furthermore the clear aim to improve regional assistance in the area of primary and intermediate care, through technological and digital transformation [77]. This modernization aspires to define a strategic vision for telemedicine. It indeed starts giving a clear definition of regional strategies on digital health and governance of the relevant ecosystem [78]. Within this definition there is the implementation of a digitalized renewed information system in health service facilities to adapt and homogenize the that already in use, where territorial health services (maybe for the first time) are the core elements of these reforms [78].

A first important step can be found in the agreements between national Government and the different Regions, in December 2020. They clearly defined both the rights and responsibilities of the parties respecting the relevant general framework of the homogeneity of basic services within all the Italian territories, stating that [80]:

- the doctor is responsible for deciding in which situations tele-consultations can be employed in favor of the patient

Table 1 Glossary of the implemented digitalized health services

Tele-examination	Medical procedure in which the professional interacts remotely in real time with the patient, even with the support from a caregiver
Medical teleconsultation	Medical procedure in which the professional interacts with one or more doctors/specialists to discuss the clinic situation of a patient, via video call or even in asynchronous mode
Medical-care teleconsulting	Healthcare activity, not necessarily medical, which takes place remotely and is performed by two or more persons who have different responsibilities with respect to the specific case. It can be provided in the presence of the patient or in a deferred manner.
Tele-assistance	Professional act based on remote interaction between professional and patient/caregiver
Tele-monitoring	Telemedicine operating mode that allows continuously remote detection and transmission of vital and clinical parameters
Tele-control	Remote control of the patient through a regular series of contacts with the doctor, by means of video-call in association with the sharing of clinical data
Tele-rehabilitation	Remote provision of benefits and services intended to enable, restore, improve or otherwise maintain the psychophysical functioning of people with disabilities or disorders, or at risk of developing them

- during the tele-consultation it must always be guaranteed the ability to exchange on time real clinical data, medical reports, images, audio and video
- the activation of the service requires a prior intention of the patient that must be preceded by adequate information in so that the patient is aware and well informed about the visit methods, advantages, risks, and protection of his/her personal data.

Another relevant aspect is represented by the clear definition, at national level of the different assisted ICT interventions and caring both by a single specialist and by a team. This aspect has been stated at national level through the definition of a proper "glossary" of interventions [58] as reported in the following Table 1:

In brief, the programme "Telemedicine to a better support to patients" within M6 of the PNRR—as it has been thought and designed by the policymakers—can be definitively viewed as a relevant health innovation ecosystem, as it has been defined above. It can be seen at its full potential, given by new technologies, to tackle unmet needs [64].

But our investigation intended to deeper the analysis, taking into account the possible gaps between the planning, of an innovation in health services delivering, and its actual implementation. Particularly, we addressed the crucial role of the promoters of the change, that is the personnel working in public territorial health services, as illustrated hereafter.

4.2 *The Role of the Personnel and the Misalignments and Gaps in the Innovation Governance*

In this second part, we present the outcomes of the analysis upon the different items regarding the relevance of the personnel as change promoters in the implementation of the health innovation ecosystem, underlining the gaps between the two parties in governing this change.

Facility Type

The design of healthcare facilities should see the involvement of different stakeholders, being able to align clinical as well as operational and organizational objectives. This is because it ought to consider the dynamic and complex nature of public healthcare systems, which need an equilibrium, able of both improving population health and reducing costs, trying also to improve staff work life [81].

It is anyway evident the presence of a misalignment between what thought and designed in terms of infrastructure creation and the real implementation of the reform by those who should be the promoters of the change. All the interviewed people feel they tasks as "detached" from the current system modernization stimulated by the PNRR. One of the GPs, in the first focus group, even affirmed that "there continue to be parallel tracks and we do not know how to interact properly". Another one stated "They do not put the pieces together. There is no unique process line: the anamnesis is "productive" not detached". Lastly more than one highlighted referring to lack of tools: "It seems that everyday everything is urgent and must be done in extraordinary ways".

On the other hand, by the side of the service managers, it has been underlined the strategical importance of preliminary analysis of present pathologies in order to have different planning in different realities. Thus, being in line with the impossibility of implementing a telemedicine service if not tailored according to pathologies to then obviously tailor value-based interventions for any specific case. An example in this case was given by the following statement by the responsible for public psychiatric territorial services "Yes I know, it is easy for her (referring to another interviewed person) she is an oculist, but how could you think we might develop telemonitoring with people with psychiatric disorders?"

We found also territorial differences in our investigation, highlighting different stages of implementation as a consequence of different starting points, even in the same region. In one case local services had even implemented the so called "Unique medical electronic record", that is a virtual record which allows, all interested parties, to have a clear illustration of the actual medical situation of each patient, independently from the specialists that might have to intervene according to both previous and ongoing pathologies. But, nevertheless the system appeared implemented at the 90% at least, according to AGID, [82], that remained the only one we found, being, in all the other cases far from being activated.

Expected Outcomes

This revealed itself really a contested item. This was firstly because of a different interpretation, by interviewers and interviewee, of the word "outcome". Indeed, we designed our analysis, intending outcome as achievement of deliberated impacts, in line with the planned innovation. We therefore assumed to analyze aspects such as the extent of goals, level of accessibility by the target population, and the efficiency in the implementation [83]. But instead, by the side of health personnel, the meaning was specifically connected to health outcomes. They therefore initially intended the effects given by a proper cure and or medication delivered by the healthcare system [84].

This initial misunderstanding can be read positively, considering that, also taking a managerial position, health personnels focus on medical results for patients. Therefore, they consider digitalization and telemedicine as tools for achieving patients' wellbeing, and only secondarily as instruments to better manage health services in terms of cost and time efficiency.

Once clarified this aspect it has been possible to collect specific insights. The first important one, on which all the interviewees agreed, is that digitalization and telemedicine are opportunities, but much will depend on how the PNRR innovation will be actually implemented. In this sense some claims by our interviewees were indicative: "for having a result you need precise protocols, not just definitions!"; "there is nowadays what I named 'health consumerism' that is a misperception of the aims with the goals on one side and the "measured" interventions on the other one".

Moreover, the managers highlighted the need of a "different vision", stating that if it is true that digital innovation is an opportunity, it cannot be seen as the panacea for solving health local services problems. In other words, monitoring and caring of patients, especially those with chronic diseases, can be better assisted, but if you still have a system which remains linked to "old processes", innovations cannot be achieved nevertheless the expenditure in digitalization. This distrust in innovation is strictly linked to the staffing and collaboration items as illustrated hereafter.

Staffing

This item proved to be easily to be interpreted, but really sensitive. Indeed, it is absolutely not easy to handle a digitalized and telemedicine caring system, it is complicated because it must be cooperative and organizationally embedded at the same time. This means that it is necessary to correctly develop non-didactic training [84]. But the digitalization reform financed by the PNRR seems to be unreceptive to this aspect. Our analysis disclosed a lack of information and a complete absence of training.

We found that no GP knew that the electronic health record was already available to allow them to exchange information about patients' conditions. But above all, none of the interviewees had basic knowledge about telemedicine, starting from not being able to give a basic definition of it, as provided by the Ministry and presented in in 4.1. They had no information about the progress in the ongoing reform process. In this sense, a GP, in the second focus group declared "We are ill-informed, we have no capabilities, we don't know". Our analysis shows a peculiar misalignment: thanks to the PNRR funds technical tools were acquired, but the reform did not foresee proper training for the personnel. In this sense an interviewed GP claimed "it is not a matter of having inter"NET", you need a "NET"work of minds before technology"; another one stated "You first of all need to reorganize the operational system, otherwise, without knowing the process we will repeat twice or three times the same exam".

Lastly, most of the interviewees stressed on the persistence of digital divide problems, especially in aged workers, and this was linked to a lack of experience. One GP even affirmed "Before starting a battle, you have to know what forces you have, and it is not sufficient to have tools, you need personnel".

Collaboration and Networking Among Services

To be effective, a digitalized health system must consider: health data, electronic health record system, tele-health service [85]. The PNRR health reform appears not taking into account the relevance of designing and implementing a health innovation ecosystem as described above. On the contrary it look as if in the relevance of telehealth service quality is not properly taken into account. This last aspect points out that health providers ought to give an equal quality of care, according to the same principles, regardless of the type (i.e. at-distance or in-person visits) thus being always compliant with current protocols and procedures [85]. Unfortunately, our analysis uncovered some criticalities.

If it is true that both GPs and managers declare positively about having teleconsultations and telemonitoring to interact with specialists, even if staying far away, it is also true that they see its actual effective implementation as a utopia. This is due not only to the already described lack of retraining, but especially in the persistence of a bureaucratic system, nevertheless the reform designed by the PNRR. One GP affirmed "It would be great to have the possibility to interact at distance with specialists for a teleconsultation, but do you know that at the moment, if we want to prescribe a home assistance, we still have to fill specific forms which are given to us on printed on paper? What are you talking about? We dream simplification but we still have bureaucracy". Still a GP maintained "We'd like to exchange information, but the daily reality is that there are no specific protocols and especially no knowledge by the side of the personnel, and I'm referring to administrative ones. I saw screens left open with all sensible data while none was working in that specific moment!". Lastly, the majority of the interviewees stressed on the fact that "one thing is to work in urbanized areas, another is to assist people in internal ones (especially near mountains) were you would use more the possibility of teleconsultation, but you don't even have a stable connection".

But the crucial criticality was found in the system interoperability. We found that, there were still different operating software, not only among the regions, but even in local organizations of the same territory. One GP affirmed "They talk about the possibility of having interaction among the territories, but then my organization [referring to his one of GPs] suggested me a good management software, then the ASL [the territorial administrative branch of NHS] has another one, and the region another more! To account for our work and to allow the analysis of epidemiological data a good spreadsheet was more than enough. On the contrary we have to be linked to three licensed software providers! Where is the connection? How could we do networking?"

Users' Centricity
In drafting this item, we referred to the definition given by the EU Commission that is "putting users' needs at the centre when determining which public services should be provided and how they should be delivered" [86]. In contrast we discovered that the interviewees, especially the GPs, were bearing in mind the issue from another point of view.

They stressed about the need of "coaching" their patients. We actually collected several statements about uninformed and "demanding" patients. "Their expectations, in such a free of charge public system, as the Italian one, made the system inefficient. In several cases there are excessive requests"; "It is a cultural aspect. With the improper use of internet, a kind of 'self-diagnosis' is growing and if you say them they don't need that medical examination they tell you that you don't know your work"; "You are talking about monitoring at distance, but do you know that we spent hours answering to telephone calls that ask what to do if they have cold or cough". Initially we did not understand why they were portraying these criticalities while talking about telemedicine. We later comprehended that all these statements arrived at the same conclusion: "Can you imagine a patient to use a device to be monitored at distance?". In short, the interviewees intended to stress on the fact that, apart from retraining health personnel, it is fundamental to "educate" the users. Furthermore, they explained that telemonitoring might be really useful in assisting patients with chronic diseases, but most of these needing patients, being old, have serious digital divide problems. "They call me at the telephone because they forgot the posology... How could you think I might interact with them if SMS is the only way to remotely transmit information and only few can use WhatsApp?" and another added "And those who can use it are a problem. They send pictures of the results of their self-monitoring of blood pressure being worried. On the contrary, in the majority of the cases, this is due to an incorrect use of the machine. Could you imagine them having constant telemonitoring tools?"

5 Discussion and Conclusion

With the aim to study strengths and challenges of current policy driven digital healthcare reforms, we focused on the INHS as a unit of analysis, since two recent major reforms are reshaping the Italian context: fostering digitalization and reorganizing primary care.

A digitalization of the health system and the implementation of telemedicine services can contribute directly toward achieving (1) better health outcomes, (2) improved patient experience, (3) lower costs, and (4) improved clinician experience [87]. Telemedicine saves both the patient's and the healthcare providers' time and the cost of the treatment. Furthermore, due to its fast and advantageous characteristics, it can streamline the workflow of hospitals and clinics, thus being able to create a win-win situation [88].

Although one limit of case study analysis is the difficulty of generalizing results, our study confirms that a huge problem in the health sector is not innovation per se, but the dissemination of innovative concepts [61]. In the context of territorial services, a level of lack of homogeneity and fragmentation emerges of enormous services, recognizing the presence of a multiplicity of actors and care settings, equipped with different information and procedural tools, developed and used according to a performance logic, for activation and delivery of a specific health and social service [79].

Our investigation seems to show that the PNRR reform, regarding digitalization and telemedicine, is going on in a kind of double track. On one hand the technical components are going to be fully implemented [54, 82], on the other hand health personnel seem not to be involved in this change thus resulting in a not implemented reform. Our results, although having the limit of being based only on few interviews and two focus group, confirm that a full reflection of a strategic nature aimed at defining the objectives to be pursued through the implementation of telemedicine it is still immature [51].

Policy makers and practitioners should be aware that service innovation in healthcare is successful only if it can satisfy users' needs [60]. According to the conceptual model by Lepore et al. [40] designed to capture the key variables of a healthcare innovation ecosystem, some aspects are crucial. Particularly the way in which the key variables interact "investigating the emergence and evolution of focal actors and relationships among governmental institutions, academia and firms" [40] According to our analysis, while left part, according to the scheme reported in Fig. 1, as been developed, and it represents a central focus of the already ongoing strategy foreseen in the PNRR strategy, the other part seems, at least at the moment, set aside. Indeed, while the transformation of AGENAS has been realized and the different software by the companies have been developed, there has not been any involvement of the Academia, but most of all there is no investment yet on workers capabilities, first of all the GPs. In such a situation the success of the reform cannot be assured.

A fundamental role has been found in the importance to inform and retrain medical personnel (and GPs in particular) as strategical promoters of the change. But another important aspect has been found in the need of "educating/training" also patients, thus revealing the importance of really creating a co-production scheme for developing a real effective digitalized system. The commitment and active participation of patients represents indeed a prerequisite for obtaining high

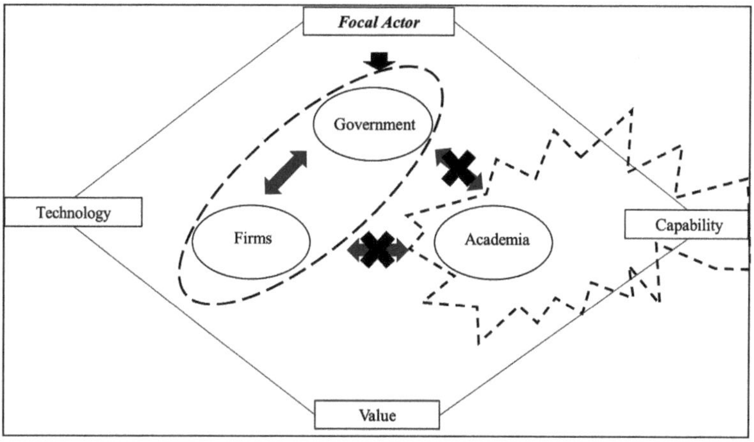

Fig. 1 Key variables in involvement in the ongoing innovation ecosystem reform Source: Adapted from [40]

adherence, but if users are culturally not keen in contributing to the process, the potential of digitalization remains unexploited. New policies should be designed thanks to a wider use of co-production approaches, whose solutions could be further adapted at the point of use according to the characteristics of the end user and/or the setting. Future policies should non underestimate the role of education and training, as well.

Moreover, in this sense our results are in line with the paradox according to which a huge problem in the health sector is not innovation per se, but the dissemination of innovative concepts [61]. The so-called promoters cover a fundamental role in this sense: they are key persons who allow the implementation of the change, contributing to overcoming its barriers [62]. Accordingly, policy makers should design policies first identifying key change agents. To design new plans, they should also adopt an ecosystem approach properly considering all its subsequent steps, and ought to rise the competences of different stakeholders for achieving common important outcomes [66]. But according to our results the above reported issues have not been taken into account by the ongoing reform, thus leading to the risk of spending PNRR money to implement a telemedicine system which few health personnel know, and no users is aware of.

Further research is needed. Comparative studies among different healthcare settings (secondary and tertiary care) and systems (intercountry comparison) could be useful to confirm our findings or highlight other issues in the design and implementation of policy driven digital healthcare reforms. Other studies could explore specific cultural factors and resistance patterns that hinder the adoption of digital healthcare tools among end-users. Further studies are needed to find strategies for better engagement of healthcare staff in digital initiatives. Finally, longitudinal studies of the implementation of such reforms could offer deeper insights on criticalities and the way to solve them.

Disclosure of Interests The authors have no competing interests to declare that are relevant to the content of this article. They did not receive support from any organization for the submitted work. No funds, grants, or other support was received.

References

1. EC. (2014). Report of the Expert Panel on Effective Ways of Investing in Health (EXPH) on Definition of a Frame of Reference in relation to Primary Care with a special emphasis on Financing Systems and Referral Systems European Commission, Brussels. Available at https://health.ec.europa.eu/system/files/2019-11/004_definitionprimarycare_en_0.pdf (Last accessed Jan 2024)
2. WHO. (2018). Declaration of Astana - Global Conference on Primary Health Care: Astana, Kazakhstan, 25 and 26 October 2018. Available at https://www.who.int/publications/i/item/WHO-HIS-SDS-2018.61 (Last accessed Jan 2024)
3. Broerse, J. E. W., & Grin, J. (Eds.). (2017). *Toward sustainable transitions in healthcare systems*. Routledge.
4. Dickinson, H., & Pierre, J. (2016). Between substance and governance: Healthcare governance and the limits to reform. *Journal of Health Organization and Management, 30*(1), 109–116.
5. Fineberg, H. V. (2012). A successful and sustainable health system—how to get there from here. *New England Journal of Medicine, 366*(11), 1020–1027.
6. Armitage, G. D., Suter, E., Oelke, N. D., & Adair, C. E. (2009). Health systems integration: State of the evidence. *International Journal of Integrated Care, 9*, e82.
7. Johansen, F., Loorbach, D., & Stoopendaal, A. (2018). Exploring a transition in Dutch healthcare. *Journal of Health Organization and Management, 32*(7), 875–890.
8. Mergel, I., Edelmann, N., & Haug, N. (2019). Defining digital transformation: Results from expert interviews. *Government Information Quarterly, 36*(4), 101–385.
9. Criswell, D. F., & Parchman, M. L. (2002). Handheld computer use in US family practice residency programs. *Journal of the American Medical Informatics Association, 9*, 80–86.
10. Silva, M. A., Tataronis, G. R., & Maas, B. (2003). Using personal digital assistants to document pharmacist cognitive services and estimate potential reimbursement. *American Journal of Health-System Pharmacy, 60*, 911–915.
11. d'Hemecourt, P. (2001). Assistance in the palm of your hand. *Healthcare Informatics, 18*, 102–103.
12. Rothschild, J. M., Lee, T. H., Bae, T., & Bates, D. W. (2002). Clinician use of a palmtop drug reference guide. *Journal of the American Medical Informatics Association, 9*, 223–229.
13. Grasso, B. C., Genest, R., Yung, K., & Arnold, C. (2002). Reducing errors in discharge medication lists by using personal digital assistants. *Psychiatric Services, 53*, 1325–1326.
14. Barrett, J. R., Strayer, S. M., & Schubart, J. R. (2004). Assessing medical residents' usage and perceived needs for personal digital assistants. *International Journal of Medical Informatics, 73*(1), 25–34.
15. Lapinsky, S. E., Weshler, J., Mehta, S., Varkul, M., Hallett, D., & Stewart, T. E. (2001). Handheld computers in critical care. *Critical Care, 5*(2001), 227–231.
16. Schneider, T. (2001). Easy access to a world of information: Using a handheld computer. *Journal of General Internal Medicine, 27*, 42–43.
17. Gagnon, M. P., Ngangue, P., Payne-Gagnon, J., & Desmartis, M. (2016). m-Health adoption by healthcare professionals: A systematic review. *Journal of the American Medical Informatics Association, 23*(1), 212–220.
18. Katzourakis, A. (2022). COVID-19: Endemic doesn't mean harmless. *Nature, 601*(7894), 485.
19. OECD. (2021). The territorial impact of COVID-19: Managing the crisis and recovery across levels of government OECD Policy Responses to Coronavirus (COVID-19). 10 May 2021. Available at: https://www.oecd.org/coronavirus/policy-responses/the-territorial-impact-of-covid-19-managing-the-crisis-and-recovery-across-levels-of-government-a2c6abaf/ (Last accessed Apr 2024).

20. Bargain, O., & Aminjonov, U. (2020). Trust and compliance to public health policies in times of COVID-19. *Journal of Public Economics, 192*, 104316.
21. Teisberg, E., Wallace, S., & O'Hara, S. (2020). Defining and implementing value-based health care: A strategic framework. *Academic Medicine : Journal of the Association of American Medical Colleges, 95*(5), 682–685.
22. Antonucci, G., Berardi, M., & Ziruolo, A. (2023). Not just targets: human prospects in health services for all - insights from an Italian case study on covid-19 vaccination and preventive services. In M. A. Pfannstiel (Ed.), *Human-centered service design for healthcare transformation* (pp. 353–373). Springer.
23. Berardi, M., et al. (2022). Trust and governance in a rethinking of classical knowledge management paradigms: Toolkits for public sector during the COVID-19 emergency. *The Electronic Journal of Knowledge Management, 20*(3), 167–178.
24. Agostino, D., Arnaboldi, M., & Lema, M. D. (2020). New development: COVID-19 as an accelerator of digital transformation in public service delivery. *Public Money and Management, 41*(1), 69–72.
25. Cepiku, D., Giordano, F., Bovaird, T., & Loeffler, E. (2021). New development: Managing the Covid-19 pandemic—from a hospital-centred model of care to a community co-production approach. *Public Money and Management, 41*(1), 77–80.
26. Sancino, A., Garavaglia, C., Sicilia, M., & Braga, A. (2021). New development: Covid-19 and its publics—implications for strategic management and democracy. *Public Money and Management, 41*(5), 404–407.
27. Leite, H., Hodgkinson, I. R., & Gruber, T. (2020). New development: 'Healing at a distance'—telemedicine and COVID-19. *Public Money and Management, 40*(6), 483–485.
28. Al Dahdah, M., & Mishra, R. K. (2023). Digital health for all: The turn to digitized healthcare in India. *Social Science & Medicine, 319*, 114968.
29. Özen, H., & Çetin, E. (2023). Contemporary strategy and approaches in healthcare policy, innovation and digitalization. In E. Çetin & H. Özen (A c. Di) (Eds.), *Healthcare policy, innovation and digitalization: Contemporary strategy and approaches* (pp. 3–8). Springer Nature.
30. Walt, G., & Gilson, L. (1994). Reforming the health sector in developing countries: The central role of policy analysis. *Health Policy and Planning, 9*(4), 353–370.
31. Baum, F. (2018). *Governing for health: Advancing health and equity through policy and advocacy*. Oxford University Press.
32. Kent, B., Nicholas, M., & Gill, W. (2012). *Making health policy*. McGraw-Hill Education (UK).
33. Walt, G., Shiffman, J., Schneider, H., Murray, S. F., Brugha, R., & Gilson, L. (2008). "Doing" health policy analysis: Methodological and conceptual reflections and challenges. *Health Policy and Planning, 23*(5), 308–317.
34. Patton, M. Q. (2002). *Qualitative evaluation and research methods*. SAGE Publications.
35. PNRR. (2021). Next Generation EU e il Piano Nazionale di Ripresa e Resilienza, Agenzia Coesione Territoriale. Available at: https://www.agenziacoesione.gov.it/dossier_tematici/790nextgenerationeu-e-pnrr/. Last accessed Mar 2024.
36. Mazzola, P., Rimoldi, S. M., Rossi, P., Noale, M., Rea, F., Facchini, C., Maggi, S., Corrao, G., & Annoni, G. (2016). Aging in Italy: The need for new welfare strategies in an old country. *The Gerontologist, 56*(3), 383–390.
37. Garattini, L., Badinella Martini, M., & Nobili, A. (2023). General practice in the EU: Countries you see, customs you find. *European Journal of Health Economics, 24*(n.d.), 153–156. https://doi.org/10.1007/s10198-022-01549-4
38. van Thiel, S. (2014). *Research methods in public administration and public management: An introduction*. Routledge.
39. Iyawa, G. E., Herselman, M., & Botha, A. (2016). Digital health innovation ecosystems: From systematic literature review to conceptual framework. *Procedia Computer Science, 100*, 244–252.

40. Lepore, D., Frontoni, E., Micozzi, A., Moccia, S., Romeo, L., & Spigarelli, F. (2023). Uncovering the potential of innovation ecosystems in the healthcare sector after the COVID-19 crisis. *Health Policy, 127*, 80–86.
41. OECD. (2021). Strengthening the frontline: How primary health care helps health systems adapt during the COVID-19 pandemic POLICY BRIEFS, OECD. Available at https://read.oecd-ilibrary.org/view/?ref=1060_1060243-snyxeld1ii&title=Strengthening-the-frontline-How-primary-health-care-helps-health-systems-adapt-during-the-COVID-19-pandemic (Last accessed Apr 2024)
42. Rosen, R., Mountford, J., Lewis, G., Lewis, R., Shand, J., & Shaw, S. (2011). *Integration in action: Four international case studies*. The Nuffield Trust.
43. Nicholson, C., Jackson, C., & Marley, J. (2017). Erratum to: A governance model for integrated primary/secondary care for the health reforming first world—results of a systematic review. *BMC Health Service Research, 17*, 569.
44. Cairney, P. (2002). New public management and the thatcher healthcare legacy: Enough of the theory, what about the implementation? *The British Journal of Politics and International Relations, 4*(3), 375–398.
45. Andrews, R., Beynon, M. J., & McDermott, A. (2019). Configurations of new public management reforms and the efficiency, effectiveness and equity of public healthcare systems: A fuzzy-set qualitative comparative analysis. *Public Management Review, 21*(8), 1236–1260.
46. Jackson, C. L., Nicholson, C., & McAteer, E. P. (2010). Fit for the future-a regional governance structure for a new age. *The Medical Journal of Australia, 192*(5), 284–287.
47. Hajat, C., & Stein, E. (2018). The global burden of multiple chronic conditions: A narrative review. *Preventive Medicine Reports, 12*(2018), 284–293.
48. Parker, R. M. (2006). What an informed patient means for the future of healthcare *Pharmaco. Economics, 24*(Suppl 2), 29–33.
49. Gabutti, I., Mascia, D., & Cicchetti, A. (2017). Exploring "patient-centered" hospitals: A systematic review to understand change. *BMC Health Services Research, 17*(1), 364.
50. Zaadoud, B., Chbab, Y., & Chaouch, A. (2021). The performance measurement frameworks in healthcare: Scopus study. *Journal of Health Management, 23*(2), 275–293.
51. Bracci, E., Papi, L., Bigoni, M., Deidda Gagliardo, E., & Bruns, H. J. (2019). Public value and public sector accounting research: A structured literature re-view. *Journal of Public Budgeting, Accounting & Financial Management, 31*(1), 103–136.
52. Heath, G., Wankhade, P. & Murphy, P. (2021) Exploring the wellbeing of ambulance staff using the 'public value' perspective: opportunities and challenges for research, *Public Money & Management*, n.d.(n.d.), 1–12 (E-pub ahead of print),
53. Loeffler, E., & Bovaird, T. (2019). Co-commissioning of public services and outcomes in the UK: Bringing co-production into the strategic commissioning cycle. *Public Money and Management, 39*(4), 241–252.
54. Cluley, V., & Radnor, Z. (2020). Rethinking co-creation: The fluid and relational process of value co-creation in public service organizations. *Public Money and Management, 41*(7), 1–10.
55. Shachar, C., Engel, J., & Elwyn, G. (2020). Implications for telehealth in a postpandemic future: Regulatory and privacy issues. *JAMA, 323*(23), 2375–2376.
56. Mann, D. M., Chen, J., Chunara, R., Testa, P. A., & Nov, O. (2020). COVID-19 transforms health care through telemedicine: Evidence from the field. *Journal of the American Medical Informatics Association, 27*(7), 1132–1135.
57. Wosik, J., Fudim, M., & Cameron, B. (2020). Telehealth transformation: COVID-19 and the rise of virtual care. *Journal of the American Medical Informatics Association, 27*(6), 957–962.
58. Bobini, M., Boscolo, P. R., Caccia, C., Petracca, F., & Rotolo, A. (2023). *La telemedicina verso il consolidamento: assetti organizzativi formalizzati ed emergent nel SSN, Rapporto OASI 2023*. CERGAS.
59. AGENAS. (2024). La telemedicina - Investimento PNRR M6C1I1.2.3, *Agenzia Nazionale per i Servizi Sanitari Regionali* Italian Ministry of Health. Available at https://www.agenas.gov.it/pnrr/componente-1?view=article&id=2329:rendicontazione&catid=85 (Last accessed, May 2024)

60. Flessa, S., & Huebner, C. (2021). Innovations in Health Care-A conceptual framework. *International Journal of Environmental Research and Public Health, 18*(19), 10026.
61. Berwick, D. M. (2003). Disseminating innovations in health care. *Journal of the American Medical Association, 289*(15), 1969–1975.
62. Gemünden, H. G., Salomo, S., & Hölzle, K. (2007). Role models for radical innovations in times of open innovation. *Creativity and Innovation Management, 16*(4), 408–421.
63. Goduscheit, R. C. (2014). Innovation promoters — A multiple case study. *Industrial Marketing Management, 43*(3), 525–534.
64. Javaid, M., & Haleem, A. (2019). Industry 4.0 applications in medical field: A brief review. *Current Medicine Research and Practice, 9*(3), 102–109.
65. Frontoni E., Romeo, L., Bernardini, M., Moccia, S., Migliorelli, L., Paolanti, M., Ferri, A., Misericordia, P., Mancini, A. & Zingaretti, P. (2020) A decision support system for diabetes chronic care models based on general practitioner engagement and EHR data sharing. *IEEE Journal of Translational Engineering in Health and Medicine*, *8*(n.d.), 1–12, Art no. 3000112.
66. Arribas-Ibar, M., Nylund, P. A., & Brem, A. (2021). The risk of dissolution of sustainable innovation ecosystems in times of crisis: The electric vehicle during the COVID-19 pandemic. *Sustainability, 13*(3), e1319.
67. Schoonenboom, J., & Johnson, R. B. (2017). How to construct a mixed methods research design. *Kolner Zeitschrift fur Soziologie und Sozialpsychologie, 69*(Suppl 2), 107–131.
68. Greene, J. C., Caracelli, V. J., & Graham, W. F. (1989). Toward a conceptual framework for mixed-method evaluation designs. *Educational Evaluation and Policy Analysis, 11*(3), 255–274.
69. Greene, J. C. (2007). *Mixed methods in social inquiry*. Jossey-Bass.
70. Yin, K. R. (2014). *Case study research: Design and methods* (5th ed.). SAGE publications Ltd.
71. Bailey, D. B. (1987). *Methods of Social Research*. Free Press.
72. Weiss, R. S. (1995). *Learning from strangers: The art and method of qualitative interview studies*. Simon and Schuster.
73. Winpenny, E. M., Corbett, J., Miani, C., King, S., Pitchforth, E., Ling, T., van Teijlingen, E., & Nolte, E. (2016). Community hospitals in selected high income countries: A scoping review of approaches and models. *International Journal of Integrated Care, 16*(4), Art. 13.
74. Srinivasan, V., & Chandwani, R. (2014). HRM innovations in rapid growth contexts: The healthcare sector in India. *The International Journal of Human Resource Management, 25*(10), 1505–1525.
75. Bauer, M. W., & Gaskell, G. (2000). *Qualitative researching with text, image and sound*. SAGE.
76. Braun, V., & Clarke, V. (2006). Using thematic analysis in psychology. *Qualitative Research in Psychology, 3*(2), 77–101.
77. Anessi Pessina, E., Cicchetti, E. A., Spandonaro, F., Polistena, B., D'Angelo, D., Masella, C., & Costa, G. (2021). Proposte per l'attuazione del PNRR in sanita: governance, riparto, fattori abilitanti e linee realizzative delle missioni. *Mecosan, 119*(Nov), 89–117.
78. Boscolo, P. R., Guerra, F., & Buongiorno Sottoriva, C. (2023). Sanità territoriale: come ripensare servizi e percorsi di cura col digitale, Agenda digitale.
79. Boscolo, P. R., & Longo, F. (2023). L'ecosistema digitale territoriale. In F. Longo & V. D. Tozzi (Eds.), *Management della Cronicità: Logiche aziendali per gestire i nuovi setting sanitari finanziati dal PNRR* (pp. 291–306).
80. Conferenza Stato-Regioni. (2020) Accordo, ai sensi dell'articolo 4, comma 1, del decreto legislativo 28 agosto 1997, n.281, sul documento recante "Indicazioni nazionali per l'erogazione di prestazioni in telemedicina". Repertorio atti n. 215/CSR del 17 dicembre 2020. Available at https://www.statoregioni.it/media/3221/p-3-csr-rep-n-215-17dic2020.pdf (last accessed April 2024)
81. Halawa, F., Madathil, S. C., Gittler, A., & Khasawneh, M. T. (2020). Advancing evidence-based healthcare facility design: A systematic literature review. *Health Care Management Science, 23*(3), 453–480.

82. AGID. (2024). Cos'è il Fascicolo Sanitario Elettronico? Agenzia per l'Italia Digitale, Italian Government. Available at https://www.fascicolosanitario.gov.it/ (Last accessed, May 2024)
83. World Bank. (2003). *Social analysis sourcebook: Incorporating social dimensions into bank-supported projects social development department*. World Bank (Ed.).
84. Greenhalgh, T., Payne, R., Hemmings, N., Leach, H., Hanson, I., Khan, A., Miller, L., Ladds, E., Clarke, A., Shaw, S. E., Dakin, F., Wieringa, S., Rybczynska-Bunt, S., Faulkner, S. D., Byng, R., Kalin, A., Moore, L., Wherton, J., Husain, L., & Rosen, R. (2023). Training needs for staff providing remote services in general practice: a mixed-methods study. *The British Journal of General Practice, 74*(738), e17–e26.
85. Zhang, X., & Saltman, R. (2022). Impact of electronic health record interoperability on telehealth service outcomes. *JMIR Medical Informatics, 10*(1), e31837.
86. EC. (2020). Glossary - User-centricity - NIFO - National Interoperability Framework Observatory. EU Commission Available at https://joinup.ec.europa.eu/collection/nifo-national-interoperability-framework-observatory/glossary/term/user-centricity#:~:text=User%2Dcentricity%20means%20putting%20users,how%20they%20should%20be%20delivered. (Last accessed, Mar 2024)
87. Bodenheimer, T., & Sinsky, C. (2014). From triple to quadruple aim: Care of the patient requires care of the provider. *Annals of Family Medicine, 12*(6), 573–576.
88. Haleem, A., Javaid, M., Singh, R. P., & Suman, R. (2021). Telemedicine for healthcare: Capabilities, features, barriers, and applications. *Sensors International, 2*, 100117.

Developing Social Sustainability in Higher Education: Evidence from a Framed Field Experiment with Causal Inference Analysis

Claudia Pelagatti, Manuel Di Francesco, Aurora Ascatigno, and Alessia Regnicoli

Abstract Social sustainability is increasingly important in higher education, especially concerning student employment and educational programmes. Educational institutions are incorporating sustainability into their curricula and aligning with the UN Sustainable Development Goals (SDGs) to enhance student learning and societal impact. However, measuring the impact of these initiatives on student employment and entrepreneurial attitudes is challenging. There are no standardised metrics, and it is difficult to isolate the effects of specific programmes from other factors influencing career paths. To address this, we conducted a framed field experiment. This experiment compared students, entrepreneurs, and university professors involved in the "Impresa IN Accademia" (IINA) project (treatment group) with those who were not (control group). The goal is to quantify differences in employment, motivation, and benefits between the two groups, focusing on students. The study aims to determine if participation in the IINA project has a measurable impact on students' career outcomes and overall university experience. The results of the data analysis indicate that the IINA project had a mixed effect on students, entrepreneurs, and university professors. Participation in the project did not significantly affect students' employment and motivation to work in companies. However, all categories showed substantial direct and indirect benefits from participation, con-firming the project's potential to bridge the gap between universities and the world of work.

Keywords Higher education · Sustainable development · Social sustainability · Field experimentation · Causal inference

C. Pelagatti · A. Ascatigno (✉) · A. Regnicoli
School of Advanced Studies, University of Chieti-Pescara, Chieti, Italy
e-mail: c.pelagatti@confindustriaabruzzoma.it; aurora.ascatigno@unich.it; alessia.regnicoli@phd.unich.it

M. Di Francesco
Toto Holding S.p.A, Chieti, Italy
e-mail: m.difrancesco@totoholding.it

M. Cipriano et al. (eds.), *Technologies for Organizations and Society*,
Lecture Notes in Information Systems and Organisation 80,
https://doi.org/10.1007/978-3-032-01697-3_15

1 Introduction

Social sustainability is increasingly recognised as a crucial aspect of higher education, particularly concerning employment and educational programmes for university students [1]. This connection can be explored through various dimensions, including the role of internships and training programmes, the commitment of market educational institutions to inclusivity, and the overall impact on employability. The effectiveness of social sustainability initiatives is also measured by how well sustainability concepts are integrated into the curriculum. Indeed, institutions evaluate the extent to which courses promote awareness and understanding of social sustainability among students. This includes assessing student engagement in sustainability-related projects and initiatives, which can enhance their learning experience and commitment to social issues (see more on [2]). Several market institutions align their social sustainability initiatives with the United Nations Sustainable Development Goals (SDGs). They measure progress by evaluating how their programmes contribute to achieving specific SDGs, such as promoting inclusive and equitable quality education or fostering lifelong learning opportunities for all. This alignment enhances accountability and provides a framework for assessing impact. Research has shown that aligning higher education strategies with the SDGs can significantly enhance institutional effectiveness and societal impact, as it promotes a structured approach to sustainability initiatives and ensures that educational outcomes are relevant to global challenges [3, 4]. However, there is a lack of consensus on which metrics to use to measure social sustainability outcomes related to employment effectively [5]. Institutions struggle to quantify the impact of their initiatives on students' employability and entrepreneurial attitudes. Indeed, it is challenging to directly attribute improvements in employment outcomes to specific social sustainability initiatives, as many factors influence career paths. Isolating the impact of these programmes is methodologically complex [6]. Overcoming these obstacles requires a concerted effort to develop robust frameworks and tools for assessing the impact of social sustainability initiatives on students' employment outcomes and entrepreneurial attitudes. Based on the above, measuring social impact is crucial for achieving positive societal change. Indeed, multiple studies [7–10] highlight the critical need to bridge the gap between education and the workforce. These studies emphasise the importance of equipping young people with relevant skills, improving orientation programmes, and providing support for a smoother entry into the working world. For these reasons, we conducted a framed field experiment which is *the same as an artefactual field experiment but with field context in either the commodity, task, or information set that the subjects can use*" (Harrison & List, [11], p. 1014). In this regard, it is noteworthy that the artefactual field experiment "*is the same as a conventional lab experiment but with a nonstandard subject pool*" (Harrison & List, [11], p. 1014). In this study, the framed field experiment is based on the "Impresa IN Accademia" project (see Sect. 1.1 for a more comprehensive description of the project), which involves the treatment and control groups for each specific category. Specifically, the treatment group consists of three categories: Students, entrepreneurs and university professors who participated in the "Impresa IN Accademia" project, while the control group consists of three other categories: Students, entrepreneurs and university professors who did not participate in the "Impresa IN Accademia" project. This study aims to identify and quantify any potentially significant differences between the two groups, considering the different categories, with a particular focus on students. These differences will be expressed in terms of employment, motivation, direct and indirect benefits of the chosen university programmes and participation in the project. Building on the above, we pose the following questions: Are students who have participated in the "Impresa IN Accademia" project more likely to be employed than those who have not? Does participation in the project motivate students to take an enterprise pathway? Are there any benefits to taking part in the project? Would students and entrepreneurs be willing to fund initiatives such as the "Impresa IN Accademia" project? If so, how much? Are there differences in willingness to contribute between the treatment and control groups? Do university professors promote this project to future and current students? If so, are there differences in promotion between university professors who participated in the project and those who did not? The rest of this study is organised as follows. Section 2 deals with the methods and procedures used to design and carry out the framed field experiment. Section 3 discusses the results. Section 4 presents a concluding discussion and future pathways.

1.1 Project "Impresa IN Accademia"

Confindustria Abruzzo Medio Adriatico has been running a project called "Impresa IN Accademia" (hereafter, IINA) since 2011, which aims to bring university students closer to the world of work. This project was designed to bridge the gap between academia and the professional world. The programme equips university students with the skills and knowledge necessary for personal and professional success. Running annually from March to October, IINA consists of two plenary workshops open to students from the University of Chieti-Pescara and Luiss Guido Carli in Rome. These workshop sessions foster dialogue between academia, industry, professional organisations and market educational institutions in which students can meet and interact with representatives of the working world and with educational and academic working people. For those students interested in pursuing the educational pathway, a competitive selection process managed by Randstad forms a class of twenty-one students who delve deeper into labour market dynamics and company insights through workshops, laboratories, and internships at company partners. The programme culminates in a group project focused on innovation, digital transformation, Industry 5.0, and sustainability. Students collaborate to develop solutions for real-world challenges presented by IINA partner companies. The winning team is recognised for their innovative and practical approach.

2 Methods and Procedures

This section outlines the methods and procedures adopted to design and carry out the framed field experiment based on the IINA project promoted by Confindustria Abruzzo Medio Adriatico in collaboration with other associations and local authorities in the Abruzzo region. The following sections address the recruitment and sampling of experimental subjects, providing information on the treatment and control groups for each respective category. The experimental design is then described in detail, with an illustration of the structure of the self-compiling and face-to-face surveys administered to the different groups. For additional insights on this point, see, among others [12].

2.1 Subjects' Recruitment and Sampling

To recruit the experimental subjects, we sent 112 invitation e-mails to all those who participated in the IINA project from 2011 to date (students, entrepreneurs and university professors). In addition, to randomly recruit university students and university professors who had not participated in the IINA project, we posted posters on the two university campuses of Chieti and Pescara, requesting all interested participants to send an e-mail to the experimenter by 31 March 2024 to express their voluntary willingness to participate in the experiment. In addition, to randomly recruit entrepreneurs who had not participated in the IINA project, 50 e-mails were sent by randomly extracting the e-mails of the entrepreneurs from the databases containing the data of the companies belonging to the Confindustria Abruzzo Medio Adriatico association. For further details on the random recruitment of experimental subjects, please refer to [13].

A total of 105 subjects expressed their willingness to participate in the experiment by sending an e-mail to the experimenter by 31 March 2024. In total, 105 subjects participated in the framed field experiment. Of these, 80 had participated in the IINA project, and 25 had not. Of the 80 participants, 50 were students, 15 were entrepreneurs, and 15 were university professors. Instead, of the 25 non-participants, 15 were students, 5 were entrepreneurs, and 5 were university professors. Based on this, the 80 who participated in the project were assigned to the treatment group, while the 25 who did not participate in the project were assigned to the control group. For both groups, the link containing the experimental task concerning the self-compiling survey was sent, which will be detailed in the following sub-section. Participants were given 3 days to complete the experimental task. The face-to-face survey took place at the University of Chieti-Pescara on 2 May 2024 and lasted approximately 1 h.

We first examine the details of the 50 students who participated in the treatment group. Although students in the age groups 19–21 to 36 or older were involved, a relatively higher percentage of students was in the 30–35 age group (43%). In terms of gender, 55.56% of the total were male, 41.66% female and 2.78% other gender. Of the 50 students, 36% had a Bachelor's degree, 56% had a Master's degree, and 8% had a Doctorate. The majority of students (94%) are from the economic field, with a minority (4%) from the humanities and a further minority (2%) from linguistics. Many students in the treatment group graduated in 2015 and 2016. A total of 96% of the students graduated from the University of Chieti-Pescara, 2% from LUISS and another 2% from the University of Teramo. The majority of students (26%) participated in the IINA project during their second and fourth years of university. Regarding the students forming the control group, it can be observed that most of them are between 26 and 29 years old (46.67%). Of the 15 students, 40% were male and 60% female. In general, 26.67% of the students have a Bachelor's degree, 66.67% have a Master's degree, and 6.67% have a Doctorate. All students were enrolled in economics programmes. A total of 26.67% of the students graduated in 2021. Despite having no prior involvement with the IINA project, 80% of them have had the opportunity to participate in other projects with a similar objective, namely bridging the gap between academia and the world of work in terms of supply and demand. The 15 firms in the treatment group exhibit a diverse range of sizes, including micro (13.33%), small (33.33%), medium (26.67%) and large (26.67%). Twenty percent of the forms are active in manufacturing, 6.67% in agri-food, 26.67% in ICT, 13.33% in health, 6.67% in fashion and 26.67% in services. In total, 66.67% of the firms participated in the IINA project for a period of 1 year, while 33.33% participated for a duration exceeding 1 year, from 2011 to the present. Similarly, the five firms included in the control group exhibit varying sizes: micro (20%), small (40%) and medium (40%). Forty percent of the firms operate in the food and beverage sector, 20% in the ICT sector, and the remaining 40% in the fashion sector. Notwithstanding their non-participation in the IINA project, 80% of the firms in question had previously engaged in other similar projects. In particular, 20% participated in similar projects for a period of 1 year, while 60% participated for a period exceeding 1 year. Finally, we will examine the category of university professors who, among other responsibilities, facilitate orientation for incoming students, provide information about the IINA project during orientation, and assist with placement.

2.2 *Experimental Design*

In this part of the work, we present the experimental design in which the framed field experiment we carried out is rooted. In this respect, it is necessary to consider the IINA project, promoted by Confindustria Abruzzo Medio Adriatico, started in 2011 with the aim of further bringing university students into contact with the professional world through classroom activities, internships and project work supported by firms. In particular, this project involves a wide range of territorial actors: associations, firms, students and universities. On this basis, we report on the structure of the project, divided into three phases in which the experimental subjects included in the treatment group participated. The first phase is an introductory phase in which the students, through various workshops, familiarise themselves with aspects of the professional world: From understanding their desires and ambitions to understanding the needs of firms. In the second phase, approximately 20 students are selected to participate in three specialised workshops that focus on specific topics related to the firms. Following these thematic workshops, the students attend sessions where they meet local and non-local firms and interact with industry experts to learn about their backgrounds, experiences and workforce needs. The aim of these sessions is to develop project work that is aligned with the needs of the forms and serves as an avenue for improvement ideas or business analysis, by fostering a valuable relationship between students and firms. The third phase is characterised by competition between project works. Students present their progress and projects to a dedicated panel of judges, resulting in a final ranking. The winners will have access to opportunities offered by the initiative's partners, such as free professional coaching. Completion of the three phases would enable students to acquire new knowledge and skills, and entrepreneurs to interact with young people and also acquire new knowledge. In carrying out the phases, the teachers will act as a bridge between the university and the world of work. To answer the research questions outlined in the introductory part of this work, a self-completed survey was conducted among the students and entrepreneurs who participated in the various editions of the project and those who did not participate, as outlined above. We used the SurveyMonkey® platform [14] to create the surveys and save the data. Instead, we administered a face-to-face survey to university professors who participated in the project and those who did not. The data were recorded manually in a spreadsheet. It should be noted that all experimental data were processed in aggregate form, in accordance with individual privacy policies. All survey questions were categorised to assess demographic information, objective and material benefits, and subjective, intangible and indirect benefits. Subjects who did not participate in the Project, in the experimental task, were asked to provide answers based on the viewing of a video explaining the functioning and purpose of the Project. Figure 1 depicts, in essence, the composition of the experimental subject pool, highlighting the existence of relationships between the members of the treatment group (students, entrepreneurs and university professors), indicated with the blue arrows, and the lack of intercurrent relationships between the subjects in the control group, highlighted with the shaded green circles.

For each subject category, the types of questions administered through the surveys are reported in the Appendix. In general, it should be noted that students, both participants and non-participants, were asked questions of a demographic nature (age, gender, level of education, etc.), motivational questions and questions aimed at expressing their opinion on the skills acquired both during their university studies and during their participation in projects such as IINA, providing relatively less argumentative answers. As for the questions addressed to entrepreneurs and university professors, as we shall see, they will be accompanied by relatively more critical and argumentative answers, especially those concerning the university

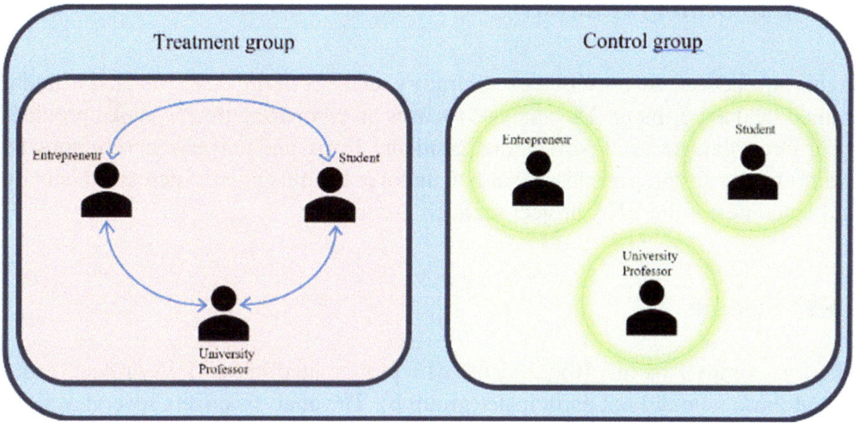

Fig. 1 A representation of the experimental subject pool, where the treatment group and the control group are characterised by different relationships between the categories involved

professors who answered the questions face-to-face. Overall, it is important to consider that some questions have a binary answer (e.g. yes/no), other questions have answers measured through the likert scale (for a discussion, see, among others, [15]) and other questions have open-ended answers, which will be summarised and discussed in the dedicated section. It is necessary to consider that the answers provided by each category to the respective questions in the online surveys are anonymous and were automatically recorded within separate datasets. Of course, although in the face-to-face surveys the experimenters had the opportunity to interact with the university professors, the names and generalities of the latter were not reported either in the dataset or in the analyses. Overall, the answers that populated the dataset were used by us to carry out statistical analyses of the data, the results of which are reported below.

3 Results

This section presents the results of the exploratory analyses which were conducted to obtain an overall framework on the differences in responses provided by the three categories of participants to the same questions. Subsequently, the results of the causal analysis are reported, which were conducted to investigate the effectiveness of the treatment (participation in the IINA Project) on the respective outcomes of each category. This was achieved by estimating the Average Treatment Effect (ATE).

3.1 *Exploratory Analysis*

In this subsection, we present the exploratory analysis of the data collected from the framed field experiment. The analysis focuses on comparing the responses provided by different categories of participants: Students, firms, and university professors. By examining these comparisons, we aim to uncover insights into the perceived benefits and outcomes of the IINA project for each group.

3.1.1 Students

The first comparison involves students who participated in the IINA project (group a) and those who did not participate (group b). The analysis covers several aspects, including motivation to start a career in a firm, current employment status, salary distribution, and perceived benefits of the project. Table 1 shows the comparison of the answers to the same questions provided by the student category (a) participants and (b) non-participants.

A comparison of the data in the table reveals significant discrepancies in the responses between the two groups. Firstly, it is evident that a greater proportion of participating students express a desire to pursue a career with the company, in comparison to non-participating students. Moreover, the mean level of motivation is higher among participants than among non-participants. A marginally higher proportion of non-participating students are currently in employment than participants. In total, only 25% of students initiated a career with the company with which they

Table 1 Comparison of the answers to the same questions provided by the student category (a) participants and (b) non-participants

Question	Answer (a)	Answer (b)
Number of students	50	15
Motivated to start a career in a firm	95.56%	85.72%
Average level of motivation	7.46/10	6.8/10
Currently employed	82.22%	85.71%
Monthly net salary (Bachelor's degree) $\leq$1322 euro	29.27%	28.57%
Monthly net salary (Master's degree) $\leq$1366 euro	43.90%	42.86%
Currently working in the firm	71.11%	78.57%
Current salary $\leq$1800 euro	51.11%	64.29%
Current salary >1800 euro	48.89%	35.71%
Transversal skills score (IINA)	6.32/10	6.04/10
University enrolment motivation score	6.37/10	6.83/10
Satisfaction of university services	4.59/10	4.31/10
Usefulness of participating in IINA	8.4/10	6.07/10
Willing to make an economic contribution	76.32%	26.67%
Economic contribution (200–500 euro)	48.15%	20%

had conducted the project, while 22.73% of them commenced careers with the other companies involved in the project in the same year. The types of contracts observed are as follows: Fixed-term employment (35.29%), curricular internship (23.53%), extracurricular internship (11.76%), apprenticeship (11.76%), and open-ended contract (11.76%). Regarding the monthly salary received, the percentages of students with a Bachelor's degree who receive a net monthly salary of ≤1322 euro are similar between the two groups. Furthermore, the proportion of Master's degree holders receiving a monthly net salary of up to 1366 euro is comparable. Nevertheless, a greater proportion of non-participants are in receipt of a current salary of up to 1800 euro than participants. Consequently, a higher percentage of participants have a salary greater than or equal to 1800 euro compared to non-participants. With respect to the acquisition of transversal skills and the level of motivation, it was observed that participants rated the transversal skills acquired through the IINA project slightly higher than non-participants (who provided responses based on hypothetical participation in the project). However, the non-participant group assigned a slightly higher mean score to the level of motivation for university enrolment than the participant group. Additionally, it is noted that levels of satisfaction with university services are marginally higher among participants than among non-participants. Moreover, participants perceive participation in the IINA project to be considerably more beneficial for their professional training than non-participants. Overall, it is observed that a significantly higher percentage of participants are willing to make a financial contribution to participate in the project, in comparison to non-participants. Moreover, a greater proportion of participants indicated a willingness to contribute between 200 and 500 euro, in comparison to non-participants. In conclusion, these differences suggest that students who participate in the IINA project tend to exhibit higher levels of motivation and satisfaction with the opportunities and skills acquired, compared to non-participants, despite both groups displaying similar employment rates.

3.1.2 Firms

In this part of the work, we analyse the responses of firms that participated in the IINA project (group a) and those that did not (group b). The comparison focuses on their opinions regarding the reduction of the gap between labour supply and demand, the promotion of entry into the labour market and the willingness to provide financial contributions to participate in the project. Table 2 shows the comparison of the answers to the same questions provided by the two groups in the same category.

The results presented in Table 2 indicate the existence of notable differences between the two groups with regard to the responses provided. In particular, a slightly higher percentage of participating firms indicated that they believe the project helps to reduce the gap between labour supply and demand than non-participating firms. In this regard, it was observed that the curricular internship and the open-ended contract were the most prevalent forms of contract utilised

Table 2 Comparison of the answers to the same questions provided by the firm category (a) participants and (b) non-participants

Question	Answer (a)	Answer (b)
Number of firms	15	5
Reducing the labour demand-supply gap	66.67%	60%
Promotes entry into the labour market	80%	60%
Willing to make an economic contribution	93.33%	100%
Economic contribution (250 euro)	40%	60%
Economic contribution (500 euro)	26.67%	40%

by participating firms to engage with participating students. Of the students participating, 26.67% and 20% were respectively hired under these contracts. With regard to the timing of employment, it is observed that 40% of the students were hired between one and 3 months after participation in the project. In general, a considerably higher proportion of participating firms hold the view that the project facilitates entry into the labour market than non-participating firms. With regard to the question of making an economic contribution in order to participate in the project, it was observed that all non-participating firms indicated their willingness to contribute, whereas 93.33% of participating firms expressed a similar intention. In particular, a greater proportion of non-participating companies are prepared to offer financial support of up to 250 euro than those that are participating. Similarly, a higher percentage of non-participating firms are willing to contribute up to 500 euro than participating firms. In conclusion, these differences suggest that participating firms perceive greater benefits from IINA in facilitating labour market entry and reducing the supply-demand gap, whereas non-participating firms demonstrate slightly greater willingness to economically contribute to the project.

3.1.3 University Professors

Ultimately, a comparison is made between the responses of university professors who participated in the IINA project (group A) and those who did not participate (group B). The comparison is made with regard to the knowledge of the participating students, their involvement in orientation and placement activities, the promotion of the project, and their perception of its usefulness for student retention. Table 3 presents a comparison of the responses to the identical questions provided by the two groups within the same category.

A comparative analysis of the responses provided by the two groups of university professors indicates that a higher proportion of participating professors demonstrated a clear knowledge of student involvement, in comparison to their non-participating counterparts. A larger proportion of participating professors employ student testimonials from the IINA project in their orientation activities than non-participating professors. Moreover, it is evident that a considerably higher proportion of participating professors engage in discourse pertaining to the IINA project

Table 3 Comparison of the answers to the same questions provided by the university professor category (a) participants and (b) non-participants

Question	Answer (a)	Answer (b)
Number of university professors	15	5
Knowledge of number of participating students	86.67%	60%
Testimonial during orientation	53.3%	40%
Discussion project during placement	66.67%	20%
Promotion of IINA	80%	40%
Usefulness of IINA for student retention	5.52/6	4.2/6

during placement activities, in comparison to their non-participating counterparts. In general, a greater proportion of participating professors promote the IINA project than non-participating professors. It can thus be concluded that participating professors tend to rate the usefulness of the IINA project for student retention higher on average than non-participating professors. In essence, these differences indicate that professors who participate in the IINA project are comparatively more engaged in the orientation and placement activities, promoting the project more and perceiving it as more useful for student retention than their non-participating counterparts.

In summary, the initial exploratory analyses indicate that within the various categories of students, entrepreneurs and professors, there are some perspectives that align with the responses provided and others that diverge. Nevertheless, these results do not provide a basis for understanding whether the treatment, namely participation in the IINA Project, is effective in terms of use, motivation and usefulness.

3.2 *Causal Inference Analysis*

In order to investigate the efficacy of the treatment, in response to the research questions posed in the initial part of this paper, we report below the results obtained from carrying out the causal inference analysis, where we calculate the Average Treatment Effect (ATE), by means of the Propensity Score Weighting approach (see, [16]), using the R software [17]. Firstly, the propensity score, which represents the probability of receiving the treatment given a set of covariates, was estimated as follows: (1)

$$e\left(X_i\right) = P\left(T_i = 1 \mid X_i\right) \tag{1}$$

where $T_i \in \{0, 1\}$ è is the treatment variable and X_i is the vector of covariates. Once the propensity score was estimated, we calculated the inverse probability weighting (IPW) weights as follows:

$$w_i = \frac{T_i}{e\left(X_i\right)} + \frac{1-T_i}{1-e\left(X_i\right)} \tag{2}$$

where w_i indicates the weight assigned to observation i on the basis of the previously estimated propensity score. Specifically, w_i was used to create a weighted sample balancing covariates between the treated and untreated groups (for additional insights on this point, see [18, 19]).

Subsequently, we performed a weighted regression of the outcome, Y_i, on the treatment, T_i, using the weighted sample to estimate the ATE, $\hat{\tau}$. In formula, the ATE estimate can be represented as follows:

$$\hat{\tau} = \frac{\sum_{i=1}^{n} w_i Y_i T_i}{\sum_{i=1}^{n} w_i Y_i} - \frac{\sum_{i=1}^{n} w_i Y_i \left(1-T_i\right)}{\sum_{i=1}^{n} w_i \left(1-T_i\right)} \tag{3}$$

Specifically, we estimated the ATE for each of the three categories separately, including participation in the IINA project as a binary variable 'treatment'.

In order to obtain better estimates of the weights, for each category we included specific variables as covariates and specified the outcomes as well as their linear relationship (see Table 4). The relationship between the covariates and the outcomes can be modelled as a linear relationship to estimate the Average Treatment Effect (ATE) using the Propensity Score Weighting method, balancing the covariates between the treated and untreated groups.

Tables 5, 6, and 7 show the estimate of the ATE for each category. The number of outcomes for each category is indicated in brackets. In each estimation of the ATE we have included the treatment variable "Participation in IINA". The estimate of each intercept represents the expected value of the outcome for subjects who did not participate in the project, while the estimate of the treatment variable indicates that participation in the project is associated with specific changes in the outcome. At first glance, we can see that the estimated average treatment effects of participating in the project on the outcomes of the student category are not statistically significant, as are those estimated for the entrepreneur category. However, statistically significant estimated average treatment effects are present when we look at the treatment and control groups formed by university professors. The discussion of these main statistically significant results is presented in the following section, where we also present the main views of entrepreneurs and professors on the IINA project.

4 Discussion and Future Research

This section discusses the results of the analysis, providing insights and suggesting improvements. The results reveal important differences in responses among students, firms, and university professors about the IINA Project.

Table 4 Specification of the covariates and outcomes included to estimate the ATE of each category

Category	Covariates	Outcomes
Students	–Age –Gender –Qualification –Level of motivation –Work in a firm –Current monthly net earnings –University ability to solve problems –University learn continuously –IINA ability to solve problems –IINA learn continuously –Usefulness of IINA for your professional training	1. Employed 2. Motivation 3. Usefulness of IINA for your professional training 4. Willingness to make an economic contribution to participation 5. Amount of contribution
Entrepreneurs	–Size –Sector	1. IINA fills the gap between demand and supply of work
		2. IINA promotes the entry of students in the world of work
		3. Willingness to make an economic contribution to participation
		4. Amount of contribution
University professors	–Incoming guidance –IINA is a professionalising educational activity –Department performs placement	1. Promotion on IINA 2. Usefulness of IINA 3. Explaining IINA during orientation 4. Utility of IINA for student retentions

Table 5 Estimated ATE, for each outcome, for the category of students

Category	Outcome	Coefficients	Estimate	Std. Error	t value	Pr(>|t|)
Students	(1)	Intercept	0.855	0.088	9.793	$3.48^{e-14***}$
		Participation in IINA	−0.125	0.101	−1.138	0.26
	(2)	Intercept	0.897	0.070	12.795	$<2^{e-16***}$
		Participation in IINA	0.081	0.079	1.019	0.312
	(3)	Intercept	6.012	0.550	10.930	$3.48^{e-16***}$
		Participation in IINA	1.498	0.652	2.298	0.0249^{*}
	(4)	Intercept	0.607	0.168	3.603	6.2^{e-4***}
		Participation in IINA	−0.093	0.185	−0.502	0.617
	(5)	Intercept	0.821	0.281	2.914	4.93^{e-3**}
		Participation in IINA	0.184	0.332	0.552	0.583

Significance codes: 0 '***' 0.001 '**' 0.01 '*' 0.05 '.' 0.1 ' ' 1

For students, those who participated in the IINA project show higher motivation, a greater willingness to make economic contributions, and perceive more benefits compared to non-participants. Interestingly, non-participating students report slightly higher employment rates and salaries. However, causal analysis shows

Table 6 Estimated ATE, for each outcome, for the category of entrepreneurs

Category	Outcome	Coefficients	Estimate	Std. Error	t value	Pr(>|t|)
Entrepreneurs	(1)	Intercept	5.671	0.251	22.625	$1.14e^{-14***}$
		Participation in IINA	−0.114	0.309	−0.368	0.717
	(2)	Intercept	5.849	0.136	42.95	$<2^{e-16***}$
		Participation in IINA	−0.095	0.197	−0.48	0.637
	(3)	Intercept	1.000	0.000	inf	$<2^{e-16***}$
		Participation in IINA	−0.052	0.053	−0.99	0.335
	(4)	Intercept	1.849	0.136	13.578	$6.74^{e-11***}$
		Participation in IINA	−0.022	0.278	−0.081	0.937

Significance codes: 0 '***' 0.001 '**' 0.01 '*' 0.05 '.' 0.1 ' ' 1

Table 7 Estimated ATE, for each outcome, for the category of university professors

Category	Outcome	Coefficients	Estimate	Std. Error	t value	Pr(>|t|)
University Professors	(1)	Intercept	0.242	0.212	1.140	0.269
		Participation in IINA	0.502	0.251	2.001	0.061.
	(2)	Intercept	4.857	0.319	15.224	$1.01^{e-11***}$
		Participation in IINA	1.143	0.319	3.583	0.002^{**}
	(3)	Intercept	0.177	0.187	0.946	0.357
		Participation in IINA	0.542	0.234	2.315	0.033^{*}
	(4)	Intercept	4.857	0.319	15.224	$1.01^{e-11***}$
		Participation in IINA	0.643	0.463	1.391	0.181

Significance codes: 0 '***' 0.001 '**' 0.01 '*' 0.05 '.' 0.1 ' ' 1

no statistically significant effect of participation on these outcomes, except for a slight increase in perceived professional training benefits. This suggests that while the IINA project boosts motivation and perceived benefits, it does not significantly impact employment rates or salaries. To improve them, the project could enhance career support services, focusing on job placements and practical skill development tailored to market demands. Participating firms believe the IINA project reduces the labor demand-supply gap and facilitates market entry more than non-participating firms. However, non-participating firms show a higher willingness to contribute economically. This difference might stem from differing expectations and experiences. Enhancing the project's visibility and demonstrating clear, measurable benefits can align expectations and increase economic support from all firms. University professors involved in the IINA project are more engaged in orientation and placement activities and perceive the project as more useful for student retention compared to their non-participating counterparts. Causal analysis indicates significant positive effects on university professors' perceptions of the project's usefulness. Active involvement of university professors is crucial for the success of educational projects like IINA. The project should encourage more participation by providing incentives and showcasing current benefits.

Overall, while the IINA project positively influences participants' perceptions and motivations, it does not significantly impact measurable outcomes such as employment rates and salaries. This gap highlights the need for a greater focus on practical career preparation. Increasing engagement from non-participating entities through targeted communication and incentives can bolster the project's effectiveness and sustainability.

While our study offers preliminary insights into the efficacy of the IINA project, we acknowledge that our work is not without limitations. One limitation is the difference in the number of experimental subjects included in the treatment and control groups. This constrained our capacity to undertake additional forms of statistical analysis, given the unbalanced structure of the data. A further limitation is the absence of a controlled experimental environment. Further details may be found in [20–22]. Moreover, it is important to highlight that the mode of administration of the experimental task was not consistent across all categories. It is therefore proposed that a similar study be conducted in the future, with the number of subjects in the two groups balanced and the experiment configured as a lab-in-the-field experiment (e.g., [23]). This will facilitate a more comprehensive evaluation of the impact of experimental variables on treatment efficacy and the standardisation of the mode of administration of the experimental task.

In conclusion, although there are some inherent limitations of the work, we believe that improving career support services and increasing stakeholder involvement can help the IINA project better achieve its goals of bridging the gap between education and employment by providing more substantial benefits to participants.

Disclosure of Interests The authors have no competing interests to declare that are relevant to the content of this article.

A.1 Appendix

Questions with answer options administered to students who participated in the project. U. means 'University'.

1. Age (from 19–21 to 36 or more)
2. Gender (male, female, other)
3. Qualification (e.g., bachelor's degree, master's degree, PhD)
4. Area of study (e.g., Economics)
5. Year of graduation (e.g., 2020, 2021)
6. University (name of the University)
7. Year of participation (from 2011 to 2024)
8. Sectors (e.g., manufacturing)
9. Motivation (yes/no
10. Level of motivation (from 0 to 10)
11. Work in a firm (yes/no)
12. After how long (e.g., 1–3 months, 1 year, etc)
13. Work with IINA firm (yes/no)
14. Work with other IINA firm (yes/no)
15. Working conditions (e.g., full time)
16. Employed (yes or no)
17. Profit (from 0 to 10)
18. Career (from 0 to 10)
19. Job stability (from 0 to 10)
20. Acquisition of professionalism (from 0 to 10)
21. Consistency with the studies (from 0 to 10)
22. Involvement and participation (from 0 to 10)
23. Flexibility of working hours (from 0 to 10)
24. Relationships with colleagues in the workplace (from 0 to 10)
25. Place of work (location) (from 0 to 10)
26. Correspondence to cultural interests (from 0 to 10)
27. Independence or autonomy (from 0 to 10)
28. Free time (from 0 to 10)
29. Social utility of work (from 0 to 10)
40. Prestige from work (from 0 to 10)
31. Opportunities for contacts abroad (from 0 to 10)
32. Continue to train (from 0 to 10)
33. Initial net monthly earnings (min/max of 1366€)
34. Work in a firm (yes/no)
35. Type of work (e.g., employee, freelancer)
36. Current monthly net earnings (min/max of 1800€)
37. U. ability to solve problems (from 0 to 10)
38. U. learn continuously (from 0 to 10)
39. U. analyse and synthesise information (from 0 to 10)
40. U. teamwork (from 0 to 10)
41. U. adaptability and flexibility (from 0 to 10)
42. U. ability to organise and plan (from 0 to 10)
43. U. to be independent (from 0 to 10)
44. U. making independent judgements (from 0 to 10)
45. U. communicating effectively (from 0 to 10)
46. IINA ability to solve problems (from 0 to 10)
47. IINA learn continuously (from 0 to 10)
48. IINA analyse and synthesise information (from 0 to 10)
49. IINA teamwork (from 0 to 10)
50. IINA adaptability and flexibility (from 0 to 10)
51. IINA ability to organise and plan (from 0 to 10)
52. IINA to be independent (from 0 to 10)
53. IINA making independent judgements (from 0 to 10)
54. IINA communicating effectively (from 0 to 10)
55. Interest in the course disciplines (from 0 to 10)
56. Interest in the employment opportunities (professionalising factors) (from 0 to 10)
57. U. Work orientation training initiatives (from 0 to 10)
58. U. Work search support (from 0 to 10)
59. U. Job placement service (from 0 to 10)
60. U. Work orientation training initiatives (from 0 to 10)
61. U. Work search support (with firm networks) (from 0 to 10)
62. U. Placement (from 0 to 10)
63. Usefulness of IINA for your professional training (from 0 to 10)
64. Willingness to make an economic contribution to participation (yes/no)
65. Amount of contribution (e.g., from 100€ over 1000€)

Questions with answer options administered to students who did not participate in the project. O. P. means 'Other Projects'; U. means 'University'.

1. Age (from 19–21 to 36 or more) 2. Gender (male, female, other) 3. Qualification (e.g., bachelor's degree, master's degree, PhD 4. Area of study (e.g., Economics) 5. Year of graduation (e.g., 2020, 2021) 6. University (name of the University) 7. Participation in other projects (yes/no) 8. Motivation (yes/no) 9. Level of motivation (from 0 to 10) 10. Employed (yes/no) 11. Profit (from 0 to 10) 12. Career (from 0 to 10) 13. Job stability (from 0 to 10) 14. Acquisition of professionalism (from 0 to 10) 15. Consistency with the studies (from 0 to 10) 16. Involvement and participation (from 0 to 10) 17. Flexibility of working hours (from 0 to 10) 18. Relationships with colleagues in the workplace (from 0 to 10) 19. Place of work (location) (from 0 to 10) 20. Correspondence to cultural interests (from 0 to 10) 21. Independence or autonomy (from 0 to 10) 22. Free time (from 0 to 10) 23. Social utility of work (from 0 to 10)	24. Prestige from work (from 0 to 10) 25. Opportunities for contacts abroad (from 0 to 10) 26. Continue to train (from 0 to 10) 27. Initial net monthly earnings (min/max of 1366€) 28. Work in a firm (yes/no) 29. Type of work (e.g., employee, freelancer) 30. Current monthly net earnings (min/max of 1800€) 31. O. P. ability to solve problems (from 0 to 10) 32. O. P. learn continuously (from 0 to 10) 33. O. P. analyse and synthesise information (from 0 to 10) 34. O. P. team work (from 0 to 10) 35. O. P. adaptability and flexibility (from 0 to 10) 36. O. P. ability to organise and plan (from 0 to 10) 37. O. P. to be independent (from 0 to 10) 38. O. P. making independent judgements (from 0 to 10) 39. O. P. communicating effectively (from 0 to 10) 40. IINA ability to solve problems (from 0 to 10) 41. IINA learn continuously (from 0 to 10)	42. IINA analyse and synthesise information (from 0 to 10) 43. IINA teamwork (from 0 to 10) 44. IINA adaptability and flexibility (from 0 to 10) 45. IINA ability to organize and plan (from 0 to 10) 46. IINA to be independent (from 0 to 10) 47. IINA making independent judgements (from 0 to 10) 48. IINA communicating effectively (from 0 to 10) 49. Interest in the course disciplines (from 0 to 10) 50. Interest in the employment opportunities (professionalising factors) (from 0 to 10) 51. U. Work orientation training initiatives (from 0 to 10) 52. U. Work search support (from 0 to 10) 53. U. Job placement service (from 0 to 10) 54. Usefulness of IINA for your professional training (from 0 to 10) 55. Willingness to make an economic contribution to participation (yes/no) 56. Amount of contribution (e.g., from 100€ over 1000€)

Questions with answer options administered to entrepreneurs who participated in the project (a) and those administered to entrepreneurs who did not participate in the project (b).

(a) Participating firms	(b) Non-participating firms
1. Firm name (e.g., firm "X") 2. Size (e.g, micro, small, medium, large) 3. Sector (e.g., manifacturing) 4. Year of participation (from 2011 to 2024) 5. IINA reduces the gap between work supply and demand (from 0 to 6) 6. IINA promotes the entry of graduates into the world of work (from 0 to 6) 7. Benefit from IINA (open-ended answers) 8. Work after IINA (yes/no) 9. Type of contract (e.g., full time) 10. After how long (e.g., 1–3 months, 1 year, etc) 11. Willingness to invest in IINA (yes/no) 12. How much to invest (e.g., from 100€ over 1000€)	1. Firm name (e.g., firm "X") 2. Size (e.g, micro, small, medium, large) 3. Sector (e.g., manifacturing) 4. Participation in initiatives similar to IINA (yes/no) 5. Year of participation (e.g., 2020, 2021, 2023) 6. IINA reduces the gap between work supply and demand (from 0 to 6) 7. IINA promotes the entry of graduates into the world of work (from 0 to 6) 8. Benefit from IINA (open-ended answers) 9. Work after IINA (yes/no) 10. Type of contract (e.g., full time) 11. After how long (e.g., 1–3 months, 1 year, etc) 12. Willingness to invest in I. (yes/no) 13. How much to invest (e.g., from 100€ over 1000€)

Questions with answer options administered to university professors who participated in the project (a) and those administered to university professors who did not participate in the project (b).

(a) Participating university professors	(b) Non-participating university professors
1. Incoming guidance (yes/no) 2. Promotion of initiatives that connect with the world of work during orientation (from never to 10 times a year) 3. Explained IINA during orientation (yes/no) 4. Assignment of cfu to IINA (yes/no) 5. IINA is a professionalising educational activity (yes/no) 6. Knowledge of the number of students participating in IINA (yes/no) 7. During orientation involve students who participated in IINA for a testimonial (yes/no) 8. Department performs placement activities (yes/no) 9. During placement explain IINA (yes/no) 10. During placement involve students for testimonials on IINA (yes/no) 11. Usefulness of initiatives such as IINA in terms of student activity and enrolment (from 0 to 6) 12. Promotion of IINA (yes/no) 13. Utility of IINA for student retention (from 0 to 6) 14. Benefit from IINA (open-ended answers)	1. Incoming guidance (yes/no) 2. Promotion of initiatives that connect with the world of work during orientation (from never to 10 times a year) 3. Explained IINA during orientation (yes/no) 4. IINA is a professionalising educational activity (yes/no) 5. Knowledge of the number of students participating in IINA (yes/no) 6. Promote IINA to your students (yes/no) 7. Involve students participating in IINA for a testimony during orientation (yes/no) 8. Department performs placement activities (yes/no) 9. During placement explain IINA (yes/no) 10. Explanation of IINA during the placement in the future (yes/no) 11. During placement involve students for testimonials on IINA (yes/no) 12. Involvement of students for testimonials on IINA in the future (yes/no) 13. Usefulness of initiatives such as IINA in terms of student activity and enrolment (from 0 to 6) 14. Promotion of IINA in the future (yes/no) 15. Utility of IINA for student retention (from 0 to 6) 16. Benefit from IINA (open-ended answers)

References

1. Isabel, N. C., Pociovalisteanu, D. M., & Iorgulescu, R. I. (2015). Social sustainability in higher education. The role of institutions from students' point of view. *Journal for Economic Forecasting, 3*, 166–180.
2. Wolff, L. A., & Ehrström, P. (2020). Social sustainability and transformation in higher educational settings: A utopia or possibility? *Sustainability, 12*(10), 4176.
3. Kioupi, V., & Voulvoulis, N. (2020). Sustainable development goals (SDGs): Assessing the contribution of higher education programmes. *Sustainability, 12*(17), 6701.
4. Serafini, P. G., de Moura, J. M., de Almeida, M. R., & de Rezende, J. F. D. (2022). Sustainable development goals in higher education institutions: A systematic literature review. *Journal of Cleaner Production, 370*, 133473.
5. Montalbán-Domingo, L., García-Segura, T., Sanz, M. A., & Pellicer, E. (2018). Social sustainability criteria in public-work procurement: An international perspective. *Journal of Cleaner Production, 198*, 1355–1371.
6. Shriberg, M. (2022). Institutional assessment tools for sustainability in higher education: Strengths, weaknesses, and implications for practice and theory. *Higher Education Policy, 15*(2), 153–167.
7. Ebrahim, A. (2005). *NGOs and organizational change: Discourse, reporting, and learning*. Cambridge University Press.
8. Holzer, H. (1997). Is there a gap between employer skill needs and the skills of the work force? In A. Lesgold, M. Feuer, & A. Black (Eds.), *Transitions in work and learning: Implications for assessment*. National Academy Press.
9. Stone, K. B., Kaminski, K., & Gloeckner, G. (2009). Closing the Gap: Education requirements of the 21st century production workforce. *Journal of Industrial Teacher Education, 45*(3), 5–33.
10. Oviawe, J. I., Uwameiye, R., & Uddin, P. S. (2017). Bridging skill gap to meet technical, vocational education and training school-workplace collaboration in the 21st century. *International Journal of Vocational Education and Training Research, 3*(1), 7–14.
11. Harrison, G. W., & List, J. A. (2004). Field experiments. *Journal of Economic Literature, 42*(4), 1009–1055.
12. Snowball, J. D., & Willis, K. G. (2011). Interview versus self-completion questionnaires in discrete choice experiments. *Applied Economics Letters, 18*(16), 1521–1525.
13. Greiner, B., & Stephanides, M. (2019). Subject pools and recruitment. In *Handbook of research methods and applications in experimental economics* (pp. 313–334). Edward Elgar Publishing.
14. SurveyMonkey Inc., www.surveymonkey.com, last Accessed 2024/23/05.
15. Joshi, A., Kale, S., Chandel, S., & Pal, D. K. (2015). Likert scale: Explored and explained. *British Journal of Applied Science & Technology, 7*(4), 396–403.
16. Rosenbaum, P. R., & Rubin, D. B. (1983). The central role of the propensity score in observational studies for causal effects. *Biometrika, 70*(1), 41–55.
17. R Core Team (2021). R: A language and environment for statistical computing. R Foundation for Statistical Computing, Vienna, Austria https://www.R-project.org/, last accessed 2024/25/05
18. Lopez, M. J., & Gutman, R. (2017). Estimation of causal effects with multiple treatments: A review and new ideas. *Statistical Science, 32*(3), 432–454.
19. Guo, R., Cheng, L., Li, J., Hahn, P. R., & Liu, H. (2020). A survey of learning causality with data: Problems and methods. *ACM Computing Surveys (CSUR), 53*(4), 1–37.
20. Roth, A. E. (1995). Introduction to experimental economics. *The Handbook of Experimental Economics, 1*, 3–109.
21. List, J. A., & Price, M. K. (2013). *Handbook on experimental economics and the environment*. Edward Elgar Publishing.
22. Davis, D. D., & Holt, C. A. (2021). *Experimental economics*. Princeton University Press.
23. Gneezy, U., & Imas, A. (2017). Lab in the field: Measuring preferences in the wild. In *Handbook of economic field experiments* (Vol. 1, pp. 439–464). North-Holland.

The Impact of Network Expansion, Developer's Activity and Seasonality on the Adoption of Cryptocurrencies

Leonardo Maria De Rossi and Nico Abbatemarco

Abstract Over the past decade, numerous studies have examined the remarkable appreciation of cryptocurrencies, typically focusing on their prices and predictive factors. In contrast, this paper posits that the success of a cryptocurrency is determined not only by its monetary value but also by its adoption, influenced by recurring seasonality. This study specifically examines the role of seasonality and the impact of developers' and miners' activities on cryptocurrency adoption. Utilizing Bitcoin data, we employ a seasonal autoregressive model to analyze 4632 daily observations, investigating the effects of miners and developer's activity on the number of end users. Our findings indicate that miners' activity plays a crucial role in cryptocurrency adoption. These results contribute to the conventional understanding of cryptocurrency success, highlighting the significance of seasonality. By elucidating the drivers of adoption and the influence of key stakeholders, this study provides valuable insights for researchers, practitioners, and policymakers in the evolving field of fintech adoption.

Keywords Bitcoin · Adoption · Seasonality · Network expansion · Developers' activity

1 Introduction

Often hailed as a seminal technological breakthrough of the twenty-first century, blockchain holds considerable disruptive potential across a spectrum of economic sectors [1, 2]. This innovation is part of a broader trend in financial technology, or FinTech, which is reshaping the way financial services are delivered [3]. Originally conceived as an underpinning technology for Bitcoin [4], blockchain has since expanded its scope significantly. It is now deemed instrumental in facilitating

L. M. De Rossi (✉) · N. Abbatemarco
SDA Bocconi School of Management, Milan, Italy
e-mail: leonardo.derossi@sdabocconi.it; nico.abbatemarco@sdabocconi.it

M. Cipriano et al. (eds.), *Technologies for Organizations and Society*,
Lecture Notes in Information Systems and Organisation 80,
https://doi.org/10.1007/978-3-032-01697-3_16

the evolution of the "Internet of Money" [5], where it serves as the cornerstone technology capable of establishing a worldwide infrastructure for peer-to-peer value exchange.

In the last years, cryptocurrencies have gained significant attention, creating a wave of discussions filled with both excitement and skepticism [6]. As this fintech opportunity is increasingly being recognized, many people view cryptocurrencies as a potential actor in the future financial market [7]. In stark contrast, critics perceive this movement as a fleeting bubble, expecting it to burst anytime soon [8]. Such contrasting opinions about the volatile nature of cryptocurrencies, propelled by the four-year seasonality of Bitcoin, are primarily influenced by fluctuations in their price [9]. Significantly, the prevailing discourse surrounding cryptocurrencies, whether characterized by positive or negative sentiment, frequently correlates with the price dynamics of cryptocurrencies. A rising price trajectory tends to instill optimism and excitement among market participants, fostering a sense of urgency and fear of missing out (FOMO). Conversely, downturns in the market elicit a wave of pessimism and apprehension. This behavior is consistent with the well-known psychological phenomenon of FOMO [10], wherein individuals experience anxiety or unease at the prospect of missing out on potential gains or opportunities.

Most scholarly discussions either revolve around the technological underpinnings of cryptocurrencies or their price volatility. However, it is crucial to note that price alone does not provide a holistic view of cryptocurrencies' success or failure. Alternative metrics such as the number of end users can offer valuable insights. Previous studies have suggested that the number of end users could serve as an effective success metric, a perspective that resonates with the approach of this study [11, 12]. Indeed, cryptocurrencies have exhibited significant network effects, driven by their technological foundations [13]. Factors like the computing power supporting cryptocurrencies and the quality of their underlying code have been acknowledged as influential variables in this context [11, 14].

However, there appears to be a gap in the literature concerning the interplay between the number of end users, the potential seasonality effects, and these technological components. This study aims to bridge this gap by examining the effect of developers' activity and miners' activity on the number of a cryptocurrency's end-users, considering seasonality effects. Thus, this paper explores the following research question:

RQ: What is the influence of miners' and developers' activities, in conjunction with seasonality, on the number of cryptocurrency user?

To answer this research question, we use Bitcoin as our subject of analysis. Being the leading cryptocurrency in terms of market capitalization and data availability, Bitcoin provides a rich and comprehensive cryptocurrency for this investigation. Through this study, we seek to contribute a nuanced understanding of cryptocurrencies' success metrics beyond the conventional focus on price.

2 Theoretical Background

2.1 Bitcoin's Inception and Functional Mechanics

The genesis of Bitcoin traces back to a whitepaper published in 2008 by an individual or group under the pseudonym Satoshi Nakamoto [4]. This revolutionary paper, titled "Bitcoin: A Peer-to-Peer Electronic Cash System", proposed a novel digital currency that operated on a decentralized network, bypassing the need for central authorities or financial institutions. The Bitcoin network officially began operations in 2009 when Nakamoto mined the inaugural block, famously known as the "genesis block" or "block 0". Central to Bitcoin's operation is blockchain technology. Essentially a chain of blocks or records, the blockchain is a distributed ledger that publicizes all Bitcoin transactions since the currency's inception. Each block in the chain contains a list of transactions, and these blocks are linked using cryptographic principles, which confer robust security to the transaction records.

As a digital currency, Bitcoin can be stored in digital wallets [15] and used for various purposes such as online purchases, investments, or even as a reward for certain online services [16]. It can also be exchanged for other currencies, digital or otherwise, through various online platforms.

Moreover, Bitcoin was designed to have a capped supply of 21 million coins, a feature aimed at creating scarcity, thereby lending value to the currency. As of May 2024, approximately 19.7 million Bitcoins have been mined [17]. The remaining coins are gradually introduced into the system through mining, a process expected to continue until the middle of the twenty-second century.

2.2 The Integral Components of Bitcoin: Developers and Miners

Bitcoin is primarily managed by two interconnected communities: the developer community and the miner community.

From one side, Bitcoin operates on an open-source program known as "Bitcoin Core", backed by continuous protocol upgrades [18]. Much like other free open-source software (F/OSSD) [19] projects such as Linux and Apache, Bitcoin Core is predominantly overseen by a public developer community via GitHub, a platform facilitating collaborative code improvement [20]. In Bitcoin, volunteer software developers work together within a hierarchical network, opting for tasks and roles that suit their skillset and interests. Key tasks tackled by developers on GitHub include commits, pull requests, and issues, as per GitHub's glossary. Developers without project commit rights must create a personal copy of the code, or "fork" it, and propose changes via pull requests. These changes can then be merged by a project owner or another commit rights holder.

From the other side, Bitcoin hinges on a distributed network comprising miners who collect, verify, and update transactions on a public, verifiable ledger [21]. The mining process entails using a cryptographic technique to aggregate new transactions into "blocks" of data. The lottery-like mining process often requires billions of attempts before finding a suitable verification solution and adding a block to the ledger. A miner's chances of providing the required "proof-of-work" are tied to their computational power. The difficulty of the cryptographic problem miners face alters every 2016 blocks based on the average computational power or "hash rate" to maintain a block mining rate of approximately every 10 min [4].

2.3 *Bitcoin's Success: From Price to Network*

Bitcoin's inherent visibility and disruptive nature have sparked widespread academic interest across various fields, with researchers keen on identifying what dictates its success. Buchholz et al. [22] were among the pioneers in this area, looking at factors such as Bitcoin circulation volume, daily transaction count, overall daily transaction volume, and the frequency of Bitcoin-related Google searches. Following this, other analysis [23] suggested a model pointing towards speculative elements in Bitcoin pricing, stating that investor interest—measured via Bitcoin-related Google searches and unique visits to the Bitcoin Wikipedia page—could explain price fluctuations. This hinted at Bitcoin's value as purely speculative, with parallels to bubble market dynamics. Others proposed a link between Bitcoin's price and its production cost, noting that incorporating the hash rate in predictive models could account for as much as 80% of Bitcoin price variance [24]. In a different vein, Trockman et al. [25] examined the link between developers' activity and cryptocurrency prices, but found no clear connection between them.

Over time, the academic discourse on Bitcoin has transitioned from viewing it as speculative asset to considering it as a network [11]. Given the accepted economic principle that a product's success is often tied to its user base, we believe that Bitcoin's success could be measured by its user adoption. The notion that a product's success increases as its user base expands is widely acknowledged in the field of economics, as evidenced by previous research [26–28]). Considering that Bitcoin is a OSS project, this concept is even more applicable [29].

In the Bitcoin context, users are identified by a unique cryptographic marker known as an address, akin to the beneficiary name on a cheque [30]. Therefore, the number of addresses within the Bitcoin system appears to be as an additional measure of Bitcoin's success.

2.4 *Bitcoin's Seasonal Variations*

Bitcoin has garnered significant attention since its inception, primarily due to its substantial price volatility. Its price fluctuations have been observed on multiple occasions, indicating the unpredictable nature of Bitcoin's price dynamics. However, amidst these various factors influencing Bitcoin's price, one intrinsic and predictable factor has been identified to have a significant impact—the halving event. The halving refers to the reduction in the amount of new Bitcoin that miners can generate when they successfully mine a new block. Bitcoin operates on a fixed inflation schedule, with the amount of new Bitcoin issued halving approximately every 210,000 blocks. Initially set at 50 Bitcoin per block, the halving reduces the reward to 25, then 12.5, and currently 6.25 Bitcoin per block. On average, the time taken to mine 210,000 blocks is approximately 4 years. This intrinsic feature of Bitcoin's inflation has been found to be associated with changes in its price. Indeed, research has demonstrated a correlation between the level of miner remuneration from mining activities and the market price of Bitcoin [9].

The reduction in the supply of new Bitcoin resulting from the halving event contributes to a potential imbalance between supply and demand, ultimately influencing the market price. This relationship between the halving event and Bitcoin's price dynamics provides a predictable and significant factor to consider when analyzing cryptocurrency's price. However, to our knowledge, no previous studies have investigated the existence of a seasonal effect in the context of end users' adoption.

3 Data Collection

We collected three types of data for our analysis in alignment with previous research papers in this field [11]. Firstly, we evaluated the adoption of Bitcoin's by end users by determining the total number of Active Addresses. Secondly, we quantified the miners' activity by measuring the total computing power of the Bitcoin network, i.e., the Hash Rate. Finally, we assessed the developers' activity by measuring the overall coding activities on the Bitcoin GitHub page, proxied by the number of Commits (Table 1).

To collect these data, a Python script was developed to extract data from two sources: CoinMetrics and the GitHub. The script utilized various libraries including requests, JSON, time, datetime, and openpyxl. All the collected data were stored in a consolidated database to facilitate subsequent data analysis. The openpyxl package was utilized to create and manipulate these files.

The data series encompassed daily data from July 18th, 2010, to March 23rd, 2023. It was divided into two samples: a regression sample covering the period from July 18th, 2010, to March 23rd, 2022, and a test sample spanning from March 24th, 2022, to March 23rd, 2023.

Table 1 Variables and measures

Measure	Variable	Description	Source
Adoption by End-Users	Active Addresses	Number of addresses with at least 1 transaction per day	CoinMetrics
Miners' activity	Hash Rate	Hash Rate (Hash/s)	CoinMetrics
Developers' activity	Commits	Number of commits of GitHub Bitcoin repository	GitHub

4 Descriptive Analysis

In order to gain a comprehensive understanding of the data series and assess its characteristics before and after pre-processing, a descriptive analysis was conducted on three variables: Active Addresses, Hash Rate, and Commits. This analysis followed a standardized approach, which involved several steps. Firstly, the raw data series was visualized by plotting graphs using the matplotlib library. This initial analysis provided an initial insight into the data. Secondly, descriptive statistics were computed for the original data series. This allowed for a comprehensive overview of the main characteristics of the data series. The scipy.stats package was utilized for this purpose. Lastly, the Autocorrelation Function (ACF) correlograms of each data series were examined to identify any potential autoregressive and moving average effects. This was achieved by employing the plot_acf and plot_pacf from the statsmodels library.

4.1 Active Addresses

Throughout the years, there has been a notable increase in the number of Active Addresses within the Bitcoin Network. A consistent growth pattern can be observed from 2010 to 2018, characterized by regular increments in the data series. However, from 2018 to 2021, the growth patterns exhibit greater variability, resulting in more inconsistent trends. Subsequently, between 2021 and 2022, the number of Active Addresses in the network reached a stabilization point, hovering around approximately 1,000,000 daily Active Addresses (Fig. 1).

The analysis of the Active Addresses reveals a slight positive skewness, indicating a denser distribution towards the left side (Table 2). Additionally, the kurtosis value below 3 suggests a platykurtic distribution, characterized by lighter tails and a lower presence of outliers compared to a normal distribution. Furthermore, the Jerque Bera test demonstrates significant deviation of the data from a normal distribution.

The analysis of the ACF reveals a significant seasonality pattern in the data, characterized by a recurring pattern that repeats every 7 lags. This observation is indicative of a weekly seasonality. The presence of such patterns suggests

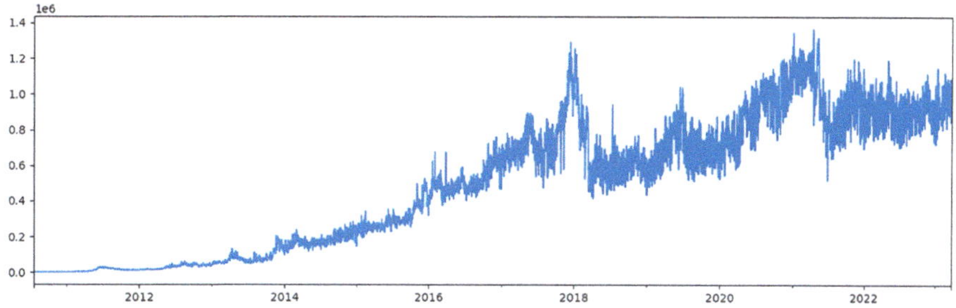

Fig. 1 Active Addresses—Daily Data, 2010–2023

Table 2 Active Addresses—Descriptive Statistics

Statistic	Value
Number of observations n	4632
Mean value	494,701.348
Median	534,874.5
Standard deviation	372,491.6443
Skewness	0.0736
Kurtosis	−1.3797
Jarque Bera value	3689.4016
Maximum value	1,366,494
Minimum value	408

the existence of Seasonal Autoregressive (SAR) and Seasonal Moving Average (SMA) components in the data. The magnitude of the seasonal spikes in the ACF signifies the greater importance of the Seasonal Autoregressive and Seasonal Moving Average processes compared to the traditional Autoregressive (AR) and Moving Average (MA) components.

4.2 *Hash Rate*

The Hash Rate of the Bitcoin network has exhibited a consistent upward trend over recent years. It has experienced a steady increase, culminating in the highest recorded value of approximately 834 EH/s at the pinnacle of block 844,894 on May 24, 2024 (Fig. 2).

The analysis of skewness reveals a slight positive skewness, indicating that the distribution is more densely concentrated towards the left side (Table 3). In contrast to the Active Addresses data series, the positive kurtosis of the Hash Rate data suggests that its distribution has thinner tails compared to a normal distribution. Furthermore, the Jarque-Bera test demonstrates significant deviation of the Hash Rate data from a normal distribution, similar to the findings observed for the Active Addresses data series.

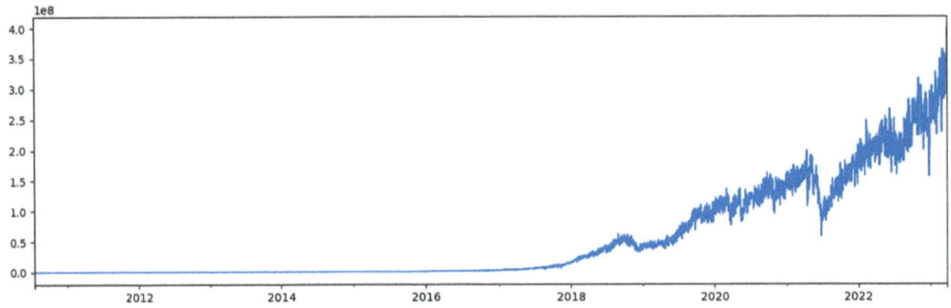

Fig. 2 Hash Rate—Daily Data, 2010–2023

Table 3 Active Addresses—Descriptive Statistics

Statistic	Value
Number of observations n	4632
Mean value	52,190,501.9404
Median	2,043,815.1143
Standard deviation	78,036,876.0263
Skewness	1.4910
Kurtosis	1.3401
Jarque Bera value	2250.1891
Maximum value	398,970,829.7257
Minimum value	0.002

The ACF exhibits a distinctive sinusoidal pattern with a rapid decline which is indicative of an ARMA (Autoregressive Moving Average) process. Furthermore, the ACF reveals a recurring pattern repeating every 7 lags, suggesting the presence of a weekly seasonality. These patterns imply the existence of SAR and SMA components in the data.

4.3 *Commits*

Over the course of time, the Commits exhibits a gradual upward trend. However, it is important to note that the number of daily Commits displays a highly irregular pattern, with significant variations observed from 1 day to another. These variations can range widely, fluctuating between 0 and 30 over short periods, highlighting the unpredictable nature of the data series (Fig. 3).

Regarding the Commits data, the skewness analysis reveals that the distribution exhibits a left-skewed pattern, indicating a greater concentration of data towards the lower end (Table 4). Furthermore, the kurtosis value below 3 suggests that the distribution is platykurtic, indicating lighter tails and a lower likelihood of extreme outliers compared to a normal distribution.

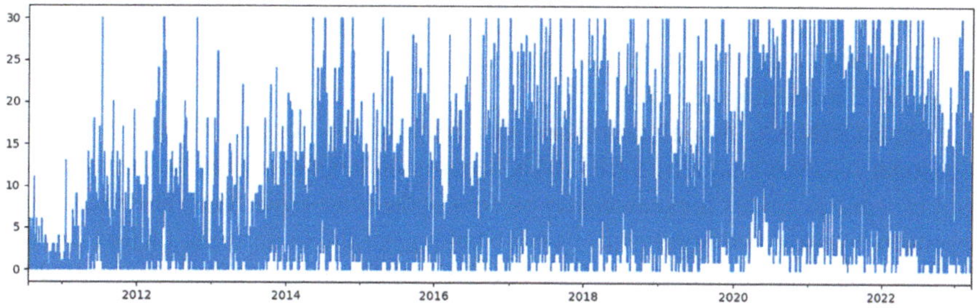

Fig. 3 Commits—Daily Data, 2010–2023

Table 4 Active Addresses—Descriptive Statistics

Statistic	Value
Number of observations n	4632
Mean value	7.8284
Median	6
Standard deviation	7.3081
Skewness	1.1867
Kurtosis	0.8809
Jarque Bera value	1953.7562
Maximum value	30
Minimum value	0

The presence of a damped sinusoidal pattern in the Partial Autocorrelation Function (PACF), along with the slow exponential decay, is indicative of ARMA process. Moreover, the ACF function demonstrates a pronounced weekly seasonal pattern, suggesting the presence of Seasonal Autoregressive and Seasonal Moving Average components.

5 SARIMAX Model

In this section, we present the preliminary analysis and introduction to the Seasonal AutoRegressive Integrated Moving Average with Exogenous Variables (SARIMAX) modelling approach. Then we proceed with the analysis of the developed model.

5.1 *Preliminary Analysis and Introduction to SARIMAX Modelling*

The data series underwent a series of transformations to facilitate the implementation of the SARIMAX model, with specific transformations applied to the collected data. In particular, we used differencing and hyperbolic transformation to enhance the stationarity and linearity of the data, aligning with the assumptions required for SARIMAX modelling [31, 32].

The SARIMAX model combines the features of ARIMAX and SARIMA (Seasonal ARIMA) models. SARIMAX accommodates the inclusion of exogenous variables and accounts for seasonality present in the time series data. This modelling approach enables a comprehensive understanding of the underlying factors driving the observed trends and patterns [33]. The SARIMAX model can be represented by the following equation:

$$Y_t' = \varepsilon_t + \sum_{i=1}^{p} \varphi_i Y_{t-i}' + \sum_{i=1}^{q} \theta_i \varepsilon_{t-i} + \sum_{i=1}^{P} \eta_i Y_{t-mi}' + \sum_{i=1}^{Q} \omega_i \varepsilon_{t-mi} + \sum_{i=1}^{r} \beta_i X_{it} \quad (1)$$

- Y′_t represents the differenced dependent variable under analysis (i.e., Active Addresses on day t).
- ε_t denotes the error term, assumed to be independent and identically distributed (i.i.d.) specific to each observation.
- Y′_(t-i) refers to the differenced past observations (e.g., Active Addresses on the previous days t-i).
- φ_i and θ_i represent the weights applied to the past observations in the AR (AutoRegressive) and MA (Moving Average) components, respectively.
- ε_(t-i) denotes the past observations of white noise, assumed to be i.i.d. normal random variables.
- η_i and ω_i represent the weights applied to the past seasonal observations, capturing the seasonal AR and MA components.
- X_i_t represents the exogenous variables (i.e., Hash Rate and Commits).
- β_i represents the weights applied to the exogenous variables.

This equation encapsulates the SARIMAX model's ability to incorporate autoregressive, moving average, seasonal autoregressive, seasonal moving average, and exogenous components in modeling Bitcoin time series data.

5.2 SARIMAX Model: Hash Rate and Commits as Exogenous Variables

The optimal SARIMAX model is determined by considering various orders and selecting the lag orders that yield the best fit to the data. In this analysis, the optimal SARIMAX model is characterized by a maximum autoregressive lag order of 3, a maximal moving average order of 1, a maximal seasonal autoregressive order of 1, a maximal seasonal moving average order of 1 (Fig. 4). Upon examining the significance of the lags in the model, it was found that the AR(2) and

```
Dep. Variable:                Diff_Active_Addresses    No. Observations:                  4266
Model:             SARIMAX(3, 0, 1)x(1, 0, 1, 7)    Log Likelihood                 3455.335
Date:                          Tue, 18 Apr 2023    AIC                           -6892.670
Time:                                  18:22:36    BIC                           -6835.444
Sample:                              07-19-2010    HQIC                          -6872.451
                                   - 03-23-2022
Covariance Type:                            opg
=========================================================================================
                          coef    std err          z      P>|z|      [0.025      0.975]
-----------------------------------------------------------------------------------------
Diff_Hashrate           0.2872      0.014     20.249      0.000       0.259       0.315
Inv_Hyp_Sine_Commits    0.0003      0.001      0.499      0.617      -0.001       0.001
ar.L1                   0.4699      0.010     48.580      0.000       0.451       0.489
ar.L2                   0.0144      0.009      1.593      0.111      -0.003       0.032
ar.L3                   0.0069      0.012      0.582      0.561      -0.016       0.030
ma.L1                  -0.9072      0.007   -132.503      0.000      -0.921      -0.894
ar.S.L7                 0.9620      0.005    198.379      0.000       0.952       0.971
ma.S.L7                -0.8333      0.010    -85.845      0.000      -0.852      -0.814
sigma2                  0.0116    9.9e-05    116.869      0.000       0.011       0.012
===================================================================================
Ljung-Box (L1) (Q):                   0.38   Jarque-Bera (JB):             58808.68
Prob(Q):                              0.54   Prob(JB):                         0.00
Heteroskedasticity (H):               0.22   Skew:                             1.05
Prob(H) (two-sided):                  0.00   Kurtosis:                        21.07
===================================================================================

Warnings:
[1] Covariance matrix calculated using the outer product of gradients (complex-step).
```

Fig. 4 SARIMAX Model—Result

AR(3) lags were not statistically significant. However, all the other lags, including AR(1), MA(1), AR.S(1), and MA.S(1), were found to be statistically significant. Furthermore, the lags, except for AR(2) and AR(3), exhibited substantial weights in the model, suggesting their importance in capturing the dynamics of the time series. Regarding the exogenous variable, the analysis revealed that Hash Rate demonstrated both statistical significance and a significant weight (0.2872) in the model. Conversely, Commits did not exhibit statistical significance and had an insignificant weight (0.0003) in the model.

Overall, the findings highlight the significance of certain lag orders and the role of Hash Rate as an exogenous variable in the SARIMAX model. The analysis also provides insights into the correlation, heteroscedasticity, skewness, and kurtosis of the residuals, contributing to a comprehensive understanding of the model's performance and limitations (Fig. 4).

The plot (Fig. 5) comparing the predicted and actual values demonstrates good performance of the model on the training sample. The predicted values closely align with the actual values, indicating a high level of accuracy and reliability in capturing the underlying patterns and dynamics of the data. This suggests that the SARIMAX model captures the relationships between the variables and provides reliable predictions within the training period. Figure 6 illustrates this plot, highlighting the model's effectiveness in capturing the patterns and trends present in the training sample.

The plots (Figs. 6 and 7) depicting the predicted and actual values illustrates the performance of the SARIMAX (1) model on the test sample, indicating a satisfactory level of accuracy.

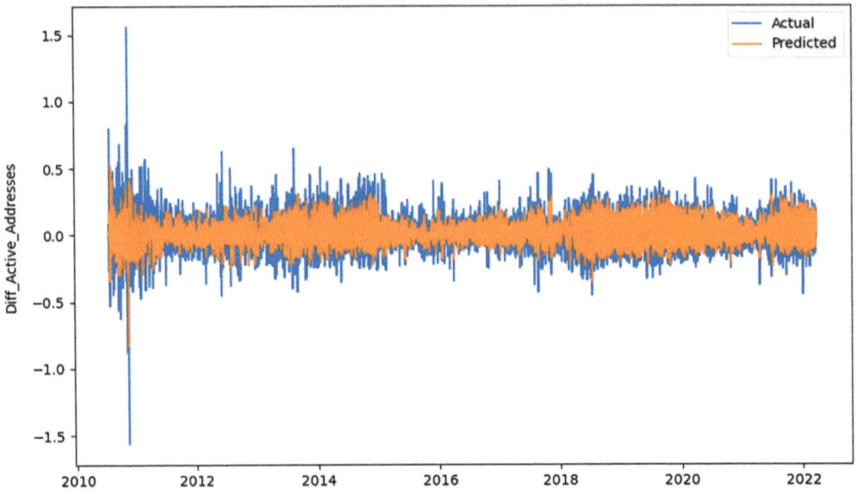

Fig. 5 Actual vs Predicted In-Sample Values

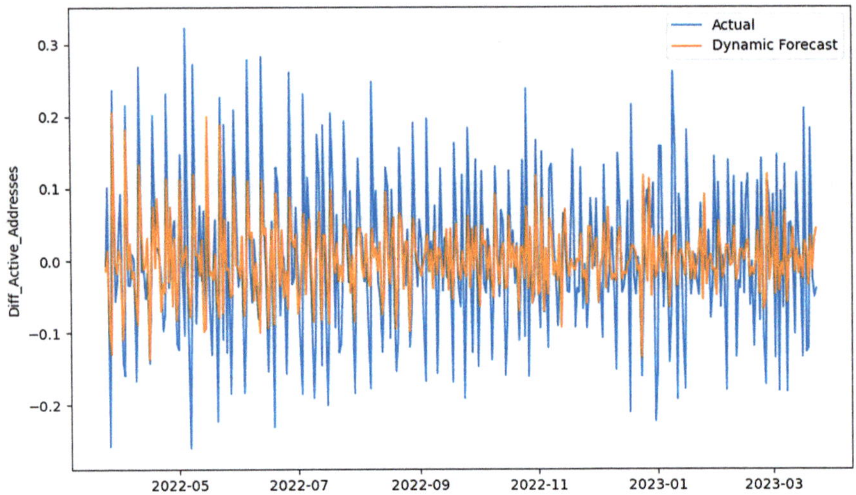

Fig. 6 Actual vs Dynamic Forecast

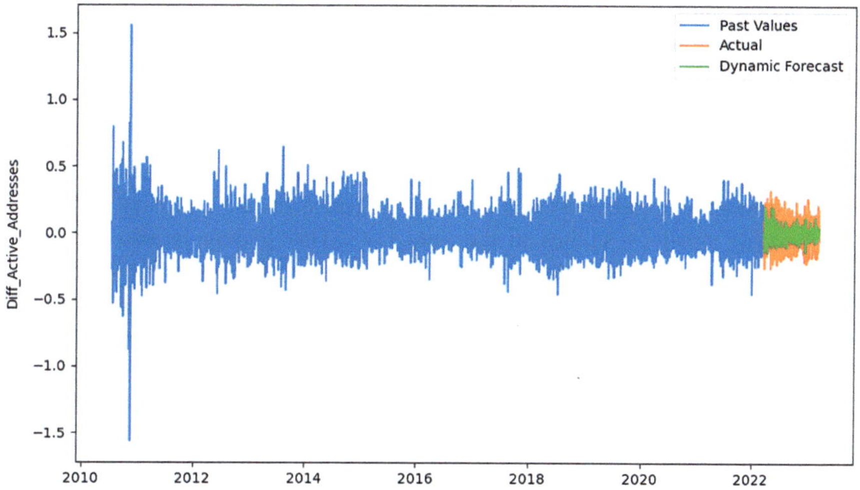

Fig. 7 Past and Actual Values and Dynamic Forecast

Table 5 Prediction Results

Result	Value
In-sample prediction MSE:	0.011645
In-sample prediction MAE:	0.073967
In-sample prediction RMSE:	0.107914
In-sample prediction R-squared:	0.426478
Dynamic prediction MSE:	0.007189
Dynamic prediction MAE:	0.06767
Dynamic prediction RMSE:	0.084788
Dynamic prediction R-squared:	0.404302

As we can see in Table 5, The SARIMAX model with the two exogenous variables performs well both on the regression sample ($R^2 = 0.426478$) and on the test sample ($R^2 = 0.404302$).

6 Discussion

This study provides valuable insights into the seasonality of Bitcoin and its end-users' adoption, specifically focusing on the role of miners' and developers' activity in this context. By employing SARIMAX models and conducting thorough statistical analyses, we have shed light on the underlying dynamics of Bitcoin's key variables, including Active Addresses, Hash Rate, and Daily Commits.

Our findings reveal a clear seasonality pattern in Bitcoin, as evidenced by the recurring weekly cycles observed in the data series. This weekly seasonality suggests that certain factors, possibly influenced by market and investor behavior, play a significant role in shaping Bitcoin's activity levels. The presence of seasonal autoregressive and seasonal moving average components further emphasizes the importance of seasonality in understanding Bitcoin's dynamics.

Interestingly, our analysis highlights the predominant role of miners' activity in the adoption of Bitcoin, as evidenced by the significant weight and impact of Hash Rate in our models. This finding suggests that the computational power dedicated to mining activities has a strong influence on the adoption of Bitcoin corroborating previous studies in the field [14]. This finding is also consistent with prominent research in the field of Information Systems, which establishes a link between system quality and the overall success of Information Systems [34]. Moreover, considering the number of end users as a success factor, open interesting considerations around the importance of network effects in this field [11, 12]. On the other hand, our results indicate that the level of developers' activity, as captured by Commits, holds relatively little relevance in explaining the final adoption of Bitcoin. This suggests that while developers contribute to the technical aspects and evolution of the Bitcoin network, their activity may not be a primary perceived driver of broader adoption. The insights provided by this study contribute to a deeper understanding of the factors influencing cryptocurrencies' adoption and highlight the importance of considering seasonality and miner activity in modelling models.

Furthermore, the implications of our research transcend the scope of cryptocurrencies and hold relevance for other phenomena within the realm of Fintech. Notably, the concept of financial inclusion is of utmost importance in the Fintech sector [35]. Understanding the factors that drive the adoption of one of the most widely discussed Fintech technologies aligns with this discourse and sheds light on the requirements for enhancing inclusion. By examining the seasonality and network computing power as key drivers of cryptocurrency adoption, our study contributes to the broader understanding of Fintech's role in promoting financial inclusion. The insights obtained through our research have the potential to contribute to the formulation of strategies and initiatives that seek to enhance access to financial services for marginalized populations. By introducing new elements to the current discourse on fintech strategy, our findings can provide valuable guidance for the development and implementation of approaches that effectively address the financial needs of underserved communities [36]. Recognizing the factors that encourage the adoption of cryptocurrencies can guide the development of inclusive Fintech solutions that address barriers to financial participation and empower individuals in marginalized communities.

7 Limitations and Further Research

Despite the valuable insights gained from this study, it is important to acknowledge certain limitations that may have influenced the findings. These limitations provide opportunities for future research and should be taken into consideration when interpreting the results.

Firstly, the SARIMAX modelling approach has its own limitations. While SARIMAX models are widely used in time series analysis, they assume linearity and stationarity in the data. Alternative modelling techniques, such as machine learning algorithms or advanced econometric models, could be explored to address these limitations and provide more accurate predictions.

Secondly, this study focused on a specific set of variables. Factors such as regulatory developments, social media sentiment, or macroeconomic indicators could be considered as additional variables in future studies to provide a more comprehensive analysis of Bitcoin adoption.

Lastly, the analysis in this study was focused solely on Bitcoin. Although Bitcoin is the most well-known and widely adopted cryptocurrency, the findings may not necessarily generalize to other cryptocurrencies. Different cryptocurrencies may exhibit distinct adoption patterns and drivers.

8 Conclusions

This paper presents a comprehensive analysis of cryptocurrencies from the perspective of user adoption, with a particular emphasis on the influence of seasonality. The research employs a SARIMAX modelling approach to explore the relationship between user adoption and miners' and developers' activity. The results of the analysis highlight the significant impact of miners' activity on end-user adoption of cryptocurrencies. This finding emphasizes the critical role played by the computing power of the network in driving user adoption. The study's findings have implications for the IS field, particularly in the domain of Fintech, as they provide valuable insights into the factors that influence the adoption of cryptocurrencies. By understanding the drivers of user adoption, researchers, practitioners, and policymakers can develop strategies and initiatives aimed at increasing the accessibility and utilization of cryptocurrencies.

Disclosure of Interests The authors have no competing interests to declare that are relevant to the content of this article.

References

1. Beck, R., Avital, M., Rossi, M., & Thatcher, J. B. (2017). Blockchain technology in business and information systems research. *Business & Information Systems Engineering, 59*, 381–384. https://doi.org/10.1007/s12599-017-0505-1
2. Tapscott, D., & Tapscott, A. (2016). *Blockchain revolution: How the technology behind bitcoin is changing money, business, and the world*. Penguin.
3. Gomber, P., Kauffman, R. J., Parker, C., & Weber, B. W. (2018). On the fintech revolution: Interpreting the forces of innovation, disruption, and transformation in financial services. *Journal of management information systems., 35*, 220–265.

4. Nakamoto, S. (2008). *Bitcoin: A peer-to-peer electronic cash system*. https://bitcoin.org/bitcoin.pdf. 4, 21260.
5. Antonopoulos, A. M. (2016). *The internet of money*. Merkle Bloom LLC Columbia.
6. Bunjaku, F., Gjorgieva-Trajkovska, O., & Miteva-Kacarski, E. (2017). Cryptocurrencies–advantages and disadvantages. *Journal of Economics, 2*, 31–39.
7. Wilson, C. (2019). Cryptocurrencies: The future of finance? *Contemporary Issues in International Political Economy, 359–394.*
8. Geuder, J., Kinateder, H., & Wagner, N. F. (2019). Cryptocurrencies as financial bubbles: The case of bitcoin. *Finance Research Letters., 31.*
9. Meynkhard, A. (2019). Fair market value of bitcoin: Halving effect. *Investment Management and Financial Innovations., 16*, 72–85.
10. Przybylski, A. K., Murayama, K., DeHaan, C. R., & Gladwell, V. (2013). Motivational, emotional, and behavioral correlates of fear of missing out. *Computers in Human Behavior, 29*, 1841–1848.
11. De Rossi, L.M., Avital, M., Gleasure, R. (2022). The proliferation of end users as a success metric for cryptocurrencies. In: *The 55th Hawaii International Conference on System Sciences: HISS 2022.*
12. De Rossi, L.M., Avital, M., Gleasure, R., & Solcia, R. (2022). *The impact of layer 2 technologies on the adoption and security of Blockchain.*
13. Gandal, N., & Halaburda, H. (2016). Can we predict the winner in a market with network effects? Competition in cryptocurrency market. *Games (Basel), 7.* https://doi.org/10.3390/g7030016
14. Abbatemarco, N., De Rossi, L.M., Salviotti, G. (2018). An econometric model to estimate the value of a cryptocurrency network. The bitcoin case. In: *26th European Conference on Information Systems: Beyond Digitization - Facets of Socio-Technical Change*, ECIS 2018.
15. Meiklejohn, S., Pomarole, M., Jordan, G., Levchenko, K., McCoy, D., Voelker, G.M., & Savage, S. (2013). A fistful of bitcoins: characterizing payments among men with no names. In: *Proceedings of the 2013 conference on Internet measurement conference*. pp. 127–140.
16. Polasik, M., Piotrowska, A. I., Wisniewski, T. P., Kotkowski, R., & Lightfoot, G. (2015). Price fluctuations and the use of bitcoin: An empirical inquiry. *International Journal of Electronic Commerce, 20*, 9–49.
17. Coinmarketcap: Today's Cryptocurrency Prices by Market Cap, https://coinmarketcap.com.
18. Hsieh, Y. Y., Vergne, J. P., Anderson, P., Lakhani, K., & Reitzig, M. (2018). Bitcoin and the rise of decentralized autonomous organizations. *Journal of Organization Design., 7.* https://doi.org/10.1186/s41469-018-0038-1
19. Von Krogh, G. (2003). Open-source software development. *MIT Sloan Management Review., 44*, 14.
20. Dabbish, L., Stuart, C., Tsay, J., & Herbsleb, J. (2012). Social coding in GitHub: Transparency and collaboration in an open software repository. In: *Proceedings of the ACM Conference on Computer Supported Cooperative Work, CSCW.* https://doi.org/10.1145/2145204.2145396.
21. Ammous, S. (2018). *The bitcoin standard: The decentralized alternative to central banking.* John Wiley & Sons.
22. Buchholz, M., Delaney, J., Warren, J., & Parker, J. (2012). Bits and bets: Information, price volatility, and demand for bitcoin. *Economics, 312.*
23. Kristoufek, L. (2015). What are the main drivers of the bitcoin price? Evidence from wavelet coherence analysis. *PLoS One, 10.* https://doi.org/10.1371/journal.pone.0123923
24. Hayes, A. S. (2017). Cryptocurrency value formation: An empirical study leading to a cost of production model for valuing bitcoin. *Telematics and Informatics, 34*, 1308–1321.
25. Trockman, A., Van Tonder, R., & Vasilescu, B. (2019). Striking gold in software repositories? An econometric study of cryptocurrencies on GitHub. In: *IEEE International Working Conference on Mining Software Repositories.* https://doi.org/10.1109/MSR.2019.00036.
26. Farrell, J., & Saloner, G. (1985). Standardization, compatibility, and innovation. *The Rand Journal of Economics, 16.* https://doi.org/10.2307/2555589

27. Oren, S. S., & Smith, S. A. (1981). Critical mass and tariff structure in electronic communications markets. *The Bell Journal of Economics, 12*. https://doi.org/10.2307/3003567
28. Rohlfs, J. (1974). Theory of interdependent demand for a communications service. *Bell Journal of Economics and Management Science, 5*. https://doi.org/10.2307/3003090
29. Sen, R., Singh, S. S., & Borle, S. (2012). Open source software success: Measures and analysis. *Decision Support Systems, 52*, 364–372.
30. Narayanan, A., Bonneau, J., Felten, E., Miller, A., & Goldfeder, S. (2016). *Bitcoin and cryptocurrency technologies: A comprehensive introduction*. Princeton University Press.
31. Pierce, D. A. (1971). Distribution of residual autocorrelations in the regression model with autoregressive–moving average errors. *Journal of the Royal Statistical Society: Series B (Methodological)., 33*, 140–146.
32. Pierce, D. A. (1971). Least squares estimation in the regression model with autoregressive-moving average errors. *Biometrika, 58*, 299–312.
33. Vagropoulos, S. I., Chouliaras, G. I., Kardakos, E. G., Simoglou, C. K., & Bakirtzis, A. G. (2016). Comparison of SARIMAX, SARIMA, modified SARIMA and ANN-based models for short-term PV generation forecasting. In: *2016 IEEE international energy conference (ENERGYCON)*. pp. 1–6.
34. DeLone, W. H., & McLean, E. R. (1992). Information systems success: The quest for the dependent variable. *Information Systems Research, 3*, 60–95.
35. Lagna, A., & Ravishankar, M. N. (2022). Making the world a better place with fintech research. *Information Systems Journal., 32*, 61–102.
36. Ng, E., Tan, B., Sun, Y., & Meng, T. (2023). The strategic options of fintech platforms: An overview and research agenda. *Information Systems Journal., 33*, 192–231.

Design in the Wild: Novel Insights into High School Students Identification and Perception of Misleading Data Visualisations

Nidia Guadalupe López Flores, Inga Karen Ingólfsdóttir, Anna Sigridur Islind, and María Óskarsdóttir

Abstract Design best practices for creating reliable visualisations have been extensively researched. However, such design practices are not always present in the visualisations we interact with in our everyday lives. Visualisations influence how information is interpreted and understood, so evaluating them critically is a valuable skill. High school students are constantly exposed to visual content, so understanding how they process visualisations is crucial. This study explores the ability of 396 students to identify misleading graphical and textual elements and their perceptions of deceiving elements in real-world and synthetic visualisations. Results suggest high school students are limited in their ability to identify misleading elements. Furthermore, the way components are perceived can lead to deception even when no explicit errors exist. The study highlights the need to improve students' critical analysis of visualisations, providing a basis for future research to empower young individuals to critically engage with visualisations and enhance ethical design practices.

Keywords Misleading visualisations · Ethical design · High school students · Information systems

1 Introduction

Data is one of the most valuable resources in modern life. As a result, data visualisations and the way data is represented become vital [40]. Data visualisations, referred to as 'visualisations' from now on, outline the representation of data in a visual manner through various means [42]. They constitute powerful tools for communicating information, summarising results, and presenting findings. The

N. G. López Flores (✉) · I. K. Ingólfsdóttir · A. S. Islind · M. Óskarsdóttir
Department of Computer Science, Reykjavik University, Reykjavik, Iceland
e-mail: nidiaf@ru.is; islind@ru.is; mariaoskars@ru.is

M. Cipriano et al. (eds.), *Technologies for Organizations and Society*,
Lecture Notes in Information Systems and Organisation 80,
https://doi.org/10.1007/978-3-032-01697-3_17

ability to interpret findings accurately can be impacted if visualisations are created with misleading elements, whether intentionally or due to a lack of expertise [30, 41, 47]. Further, designing visualisations and engaging with them involves a complex interplay of social and technical factors [44].

The general public increasingly seeks more autonomy in self-governance and personal choices in areas like health and education. This desire is paired with a need for better data and information literacy through meaningful visualisations [58, 59]. To make informed decisions aligned with their values and priorities, people need a better understanding of how to evaluate and interpret data through visualisations. Additionally, as the average attention span declines, the value of sharing information visually, such as through infographics and visualisations, increases [13]. These resources are expected to easily capture the audience's attention and convey complex ideas simply and clearly [2]. Unfortunately, the current digital landscape is plagued by misleading practices, often categorised as malinformation, misinformation, or disinformation [3], making difficult for people to comprehend and understand the information available to them [39, 46] and decreasing their ability to genuinely make informed decisions based on their best interest [35]. As this trend is likely to grow, it is an important research topic that needs serious attention. Additionally, children and young adults are more susceptible to misleading practices, unlike adults who may apply a critical filter to data visualisations [56]. Particularly, high school students' exposure to misleading information and overreliance on online platforms can not only potentially harm their decision-making skills [11] but also, favour the development of negative psychological consequences [51].

Using a four-module case study, our work explores Icelandic high school students' visual data literacy and the potential influence of misleading visualisations' elements on their decision-making skills from an ethical design perspective. To that end, we review two research questions (RQs): (1) *What is the degree to which high school students are able to identify misleading graphical and textual elements in visualisations?* and (2) *What are the differences between the way high school students perceive textual and graphical elements in visualisations?*. From a socio-technical perspective, these RQs attest to the importance of both technical and social factors involved in visualisations' ethical design [25]. On the technical side, they allow us to explore the impact of elements involved in the visualisations design, namely graphical and textual elements. Complementing this on the social side, the RQs emphasise on students' identification and perception of such elements, allowing us to gain a better understanding of their influence on this demographic.

Our empirical data is based on a questionnaire featuring a set of real-life and synthetic misleading visualisations. The questionnaire targeted Icelandic high school students and was distributed via high schools' social media accounts, receiving 396 responses which outline the basis of the empirical data in this paper. Our main contribution is two-fold. Firstly, we assess how misleading visualisations can influence high school students' decision-making. Secondly, we provide implications for ethical design guidelines to promote transparency, truthfulness, and accuracy in visualisations.

The rest of the paper is organised as follows. Section 2 outlines the related work on misleading visualisations and ethical design. In Sect. 3 the research approach adopted and visualisations utilised are presented, followed by the results in Sect. 4. The paper concludes with a discussion on the implications, limitations, directions for future work and final conclusions in Sects. 5 and 6.

2 Related Work

2.1 Misleading Visualisations

The impact of misleading elements in visualisations has been extensively studied in the past, usually with the intention to identify and prevent misleading practices when creating visualisations. While an individual's educational background can influence their ability to interpret data visualisations [53], there is not always a direct correlation between higher education and better chart comprehension. O'Brien & Lauer [52] found that participants who had taken a data visualisation course were, somewhat counterintuitively, more susceptible to being misled by distorted axes than those without prior training. This suggests that those comfortable with reading charts might have a disadvantage by taking a more heuristic approach, making more assumptions, and potentially overlooking important details that require thorough reading [16, 31, 52]. In contrast, Fan et al. [22] assessed people's visual literacy and found that the participants' educational level had no significant effect on the visual literacy scores related to line graphs.

Design choices can clearly influence attribution biases and deficit thinking, even catering to harmful stereotypes. For instance, Holder and Xiong [32] investigated how displaying variability within groups affects audience perceptions of stereotypes. They found that (1) readers tend to agree more with personal explanations if within-group variability is downplayed, and less if it is emphasised, and (2) the type of graphic selected also influences reader interpretation. Solid bars using averages led to more confidence in generalising about a group, while dot and boxplots displaying variability led to external reasoning. Dimara et al. [19] research on cognitive biases examined the effect of labels when comparing groups. It showed that neutral labels are more effective in countering racist preconceptions, allowing for fair, prejudice-free evaluations, unlike labels that explicitly indicate the groups' ethnicity.

Although evidence suggests that various attributes and design choices can influence the memorability of visuals and readers' comprehension and conclusions [31, 38, 53], factors like pre-existing attitudes also affect decision-making, highlighting the need for in-depth research on the impact of visualisation elements on non-expert audiences.

2.2 Ethical Design

Misleading representations of data, whether intentional or not, have become a significant problem in modern society, with numerous real-world examples encountered every day (e.g. [1]). The problem is magnified by the ease of access to online mass communication platforms with enormous reach, potentially exposing users to manipulative and obstructive experiences [15, 27]. Moreover, the severity of the impact is amplified by confirmation biases [14, 50], echo chambers [18, 49], and ambiguous algorithms designed persuasively to conceal biases [26, 45]. In this paper, we evaluate the scope of our findings from an ethical design standpoint. Islind and Willermark [34] conceptualise ethical design from a practical perspective, accounting for both the designer's understanding of moral guidelines influencing him or her, and the need to ensure that the end result is ethically sound and considers the well-being of the users. Investigating human-centric ethical design practices, in alignment with socio-technical theories for exploring the interplay between individuals and technology [7], have the potential to improve accuracy, fairness, and trust in data representation, ultimately supporting decision-making [25, 44].

On the one hand, research on the implications of designers' decision-making highlights the need for a better understanding of ethics from a practitioner perspective to support the development of guidelines and best practices to enhance reliable visualisations [23]. Nonetheless, problems arise when these practices are absent from the visualisations we encounter in everyday life. In this context, the question *Who is designing?* takes particular importance, as the efforts on incorporating ethical design instruction on education and research [34] might still be limited when such best practices are not fully adopted. On the other hand, the second element addressing the creation of ethically sound outputs, relates to the question: *For whom is the output being designed?* One ethical dilemma in visualisation research is determining the appropriate level of guidance and transparency to incorporate [17], which may vary between target groups. Visualisations are often used in settings like business or academia, where audiences have prior experience in communicating information and interpreting visualisations effectively. However, these resources have also become common for communicating information to the general public, who might not share the designer's background. To cope with this lack of knowledge, the public likely relies on the written information alongside the visualisation without questioning it or contrasting it with the visual; exposing them to deception if the text does not match the chart's information [43]. As a result, one key factor in the internet age is the unpredictability of the audience. A message can be clear to one demographic with specific skills or prior knowledge, yet completely misleading to others [39].

There is a growing need to deepen our understanding of how these questions connect. Research suggests various means to this goal, including creating guidelines to address designers' dilemmas and exploring data literacy in different audiences [43]. In this paper, we contribute to this effort by examining how high school students identify and perceive misleading elements in visualisations that were not created by experts and were openly shared to the general public.

3 Research Approach

This paper is based on a case study, consisting of four modules. The four modules (outlined below) were selected through abductive engagement [4]. Abduction herein refers to the interplay between the observations of real-world problems in combination with framing these problems with theory [28]. In other words, we have viewed "reality from the theoretical viewpoint or perspective" [60] and done our analysis accordingly. More specifically, our abductive approach entailed shifting between inductive and deductive reasoning as a way to continuously revise, sharpen, and re-formulate the selection of the modules, which we then presented in the questionnaire. Moreover, when arriving at our conceptual contribution in this paper, our abductive engagement included several rounds of analysis [28, 60]. Ergo, each module was developed to shed light on different elements of unfaithful data visualisations. As mentioned in the introduction, our targeted study cohort was high school students, due to the fact that they have been identified as being heavily exposed and potentially influenced by data visualisations that may be unfaithful but our focal point in the analysis, was to adbuctively arrive at an in-depth understanding of how misleading visualisations can influence high school students' decision-making and implications for ethical design guidelines to promote transparency, truthfulness, and accuracy in visualisations.

3.1 Case Study Design

In this paper, we explore the identification and perception of graphical and textual misleading elements in visualisations. The case study is divided into four modules, each of them including one visualisation (Fig. 1). Modules 1 and 2 focus on assessing the extent to which high school students identify the presence of misleading graphical and textual elements in visualisations, respectively. In contrast, modules 3 and 4 focus on high school students' perception of textual and graphical representations, respectively. Table 1 presents information about the modules along with their visualisations' features, source, and the description of the graphical or textual elements assessed. The visualisations included are displayed and described in Sect. 3.3.

3.2 Data Collection

The target group for this study was high school students, so the primary distribution of the survey was through various high school student associations. Invitations to participate, along with a link, were sent by email and through Instagram to all association members. Participation was voluntary. The study targeted native-

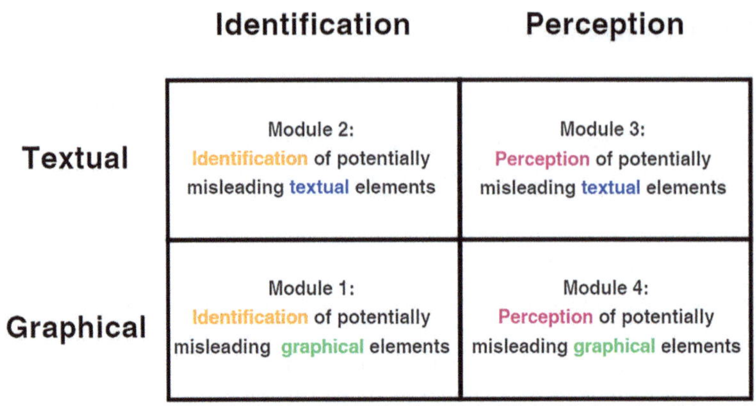

Fig. 1 Four modules included in the case study

Table 1 Modules' names, sources, and descriptions

Module	Name	Abbreviation	Source	Description of graphical or textual element evaluated
1	Identification of graphical elements	IG	Real	Y-axis is truncated and in a logarithmic scale
2	Identification of textual elements	IT	Real	Inconsistent headings: Message reversal
3	Perception of textual representations	PT	Real	Inconsistent phrasing: Message exaggeration and change of concept
4	Perception of graphical representations	PG	Synthetic	Data aggregation

speaking students, with both the invitation and the questionnaire distributed in Icelandic. However, the visualisations shown to the participants and their answers were translated into English retrospectively for this paper. The questionnaire was created with the online survey tool QuestionPro. Participants accessed the questionnaire on their own devices, designed to be easy to navigate and engaging. None of the questions were mandatory, so participants could skip any they were uncomfortable answering. Informed consent was obtained before starting. After a disclaimer stating the purpose and estimated duration of the questionnaire, participants were asked their age, gender, and other demographic information. Each question was optional, and multiple-choice options were displayed in random order to prevent biases [5]. Along with the background questions, participants were asked about their perception of the terms 'disgusting' and 'repulsive': "Is 'repulsive' and 'disgusting' exactly the same in your opinion?" This question was intentionally placed at the beginning of the questionnaire to assess the visualisation in module 3 (see Table 1). Afterwards, and before presenting the visualisations, the participants received a message stating that the data provided could be real or synthetic, and that the questionnaire's objective was to explore the visualisations and perception and not to judge their performance.

A total of 396 responses (276 partial and 120 complete) to the questionnaire were received, all of them were valid and accessed through social media posts. Regarding their demographics, about 84% ($n = 297$ out of 359 responses received for the question) declared they were younger than 25 years old. Gender distribution was 73% female participants ($n = 263$), 25% male participants ($n = 90$), and 2% non-binary participants ($n = 7$). Regarding the language, 99% ($n = 367$) of total participants declared they were native speakers, or understood enough Icelandic to answer the questionnaire. The metadata showed 96% of the answers were collected in Iceland ($n = 379$ out of 396 responses).

3.3 Visualisations Included

3.3.1 Module 1: Identification of Graphical Elements

Participants were presented with visualisation seen in Fig. 2. The visualisation showed a line chart with the y-axis representing plasma concentration on a logarithmic scale and the x-axis representing time in hours since the Q12h dose was administered. Participants were asked, "Do you see anything irregular about the graph?" with the options: (1) Yes, (2) No, (3) The image quality was too poor to evaluate, and (4) Prefer not to answer. The y-axis was truncated and displayed on a logarithmic scale. For those who answered "yes," an extra question provided a multiple-row free text field asking them to explain what they felt was irregular.

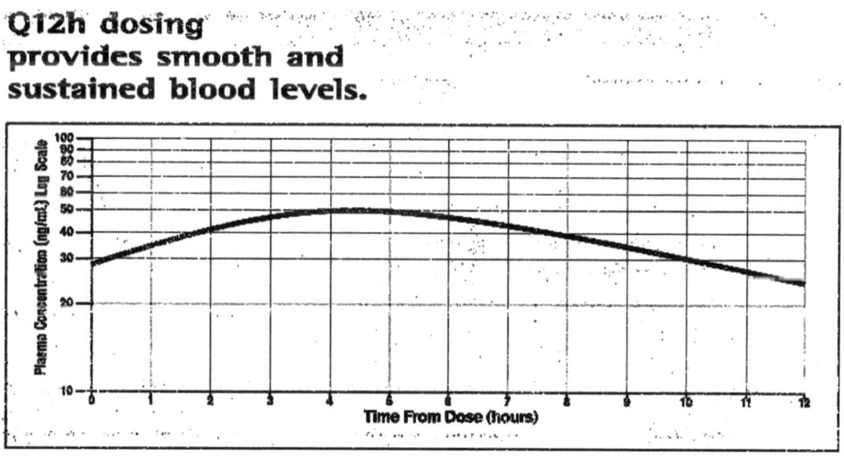

Fig. 2 Module 1 visualisation. Line chart displaying the plasma concentration since the Q12h dose administration

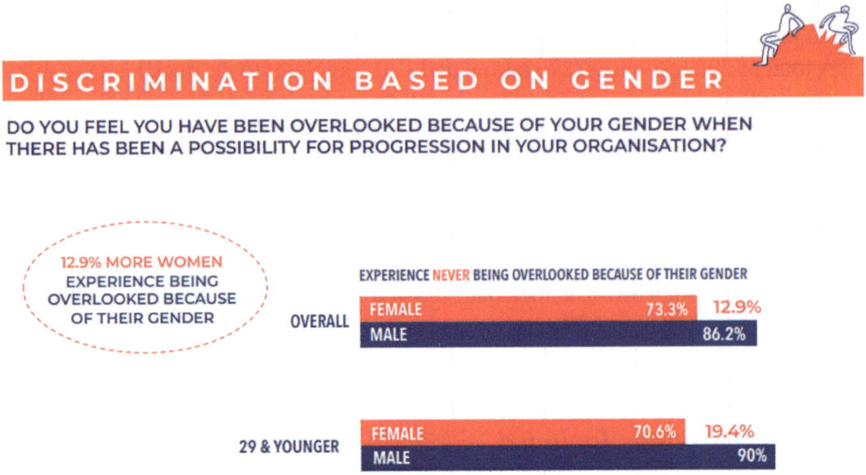

Fig. 3 Module 2 visualisation. Results from a survey about gender bias in the workplace are presented

3.3.2 Module 2: Identification of Textual Elements

Participants were asked to examine the visualisation in Fig. 3, which showed a horizontal bar chart from a survey on gender bias. The heading read, "Do you feel you have been overlooked because of your gender when there has been a possibility for progression in your organisation?" However, the chart emphasised those who never felt overlooked. Although labelled with explanatory text, the axes had been inverted, relative to the title of the visualisation and the original question. Participants were asked, "Did you feel you understand the picture?" with the options: (1) Yes, I understand, (2) No, I do not understand, (3) Unsure, (4) The image quality was too poor to evaluate, and (5) Do not want to answer. A page break was inserted between the visualisation and the question to reduce the likelihood of participants putting extra effort into understanding it.

Similarly to the previous visualisation, an extra question provided a multiple-row free text field asking participants to explain what they saw in the visualisation. Skipping those who did not want to answer or claimed poor image quality, the next question inquired about the inverted axis: "Did you notice that people were asked if they felt they had experienced discrimination, but the columns showed the responses of those who did not feel they had experienced discrimination?" The options were: (1) Yes, immediately, (2) Yes, at a second glance, (3) Yes, but not immediately, (4) No, and (5) Other (Free text option). Despite mitigating factors like anonymity and a low-stress environment, few participants study such visualisations for a long time. Consequently, if they do not notice immediately, they are likely to miss it entirely.

3.3.3 Module 3: Perception of Textual Representations

The participants were shown Fig. 4. The visualisation was based on an online survey distributed to middle and high school students in Iceland about their attitudes towards pornography. It included a highlighted survey conclusion at the top and bar charts at the bottom representing the distribution of answers. This visualisation included two misleading textual elements. First, there was an inconsistency between the survey's question, which asked students about the last time they watched porn, and the visualisation's phrasing, which generalised to all watching behaviour. Second, the word "disgusting" found in the answers distribution was changed to "repulsive" in the visualisation text. They were asked to choose words they felt described the highlight (top) as an illustration of the bar charts (bottom). Options included *Honest, dishonest, fair, unfair, correct, incorrect, misleading, and descriptive*. Similarly to the previous visualisation, participants were asked about the extent to which they noticed the change in phrasing: 'Did you notice that the charts ask about the last time you watched porn, but the visualisation insinuated general opinion?' The options were: (1) Yes, immediately, (2) Yes, at a second glance, (3) Yes, but not immediately, (4) No, (5) Other (Free text), and (6) Prefer not to answer.

3.3.4 Module 4: Perception of Graphical Representations

In this module, synthetic data were presented with the following prompt: "Let's say that girls in a high school were asked to choose one answer to describe their experience the last time they watched porn. Their answers were distributed as: 29% Don't care at all, 21% Liked it, 15% Exciting, 15% Unsure, 9% Disgusting, 9% Uncomfortable, 2% Other." Participants were then informed they would see nine different pie charts illustrating the described data, each representing the data based on different aggregations. Each pie chart in Fig. 5, was displayed to the participants along with nine descriptive terms including honest, dishonest, fair, unfair, misleading, descriptive, I would use this chart, I would absolutely not use this chart, and other. Participants were instructed to select all options they felt applied to each pie chart displayed.

4 Results

4.1 Results Module 1: Identification of Graphical Elements

In regards of the first module's visualisation, 140 participants provided an answer to the question "Do you see anything irregular about the graph?'. Of them, 48% ($n = 67$) declared they noticed an irregularity. In contrast, 34% ($n = 48$) declared

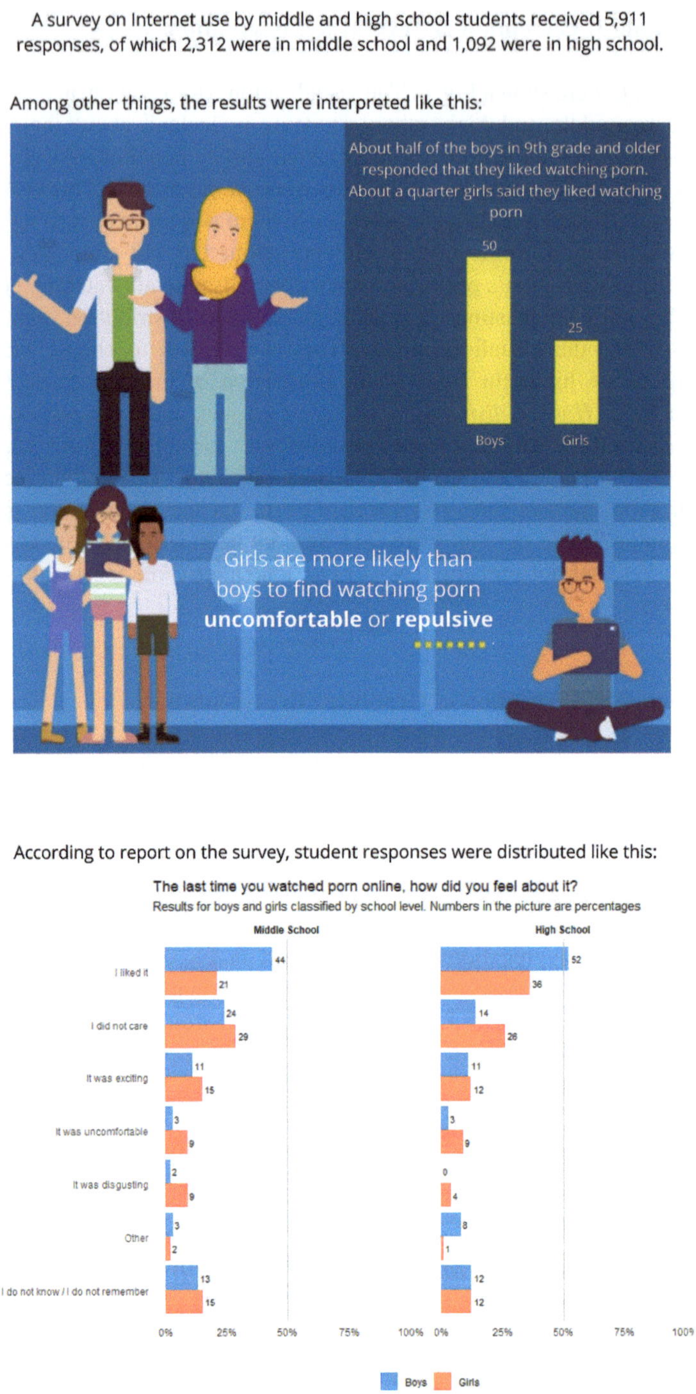

Fig. 4 Module 3 visualisation. Results from a survey about middle and high school students' attitudes towards pornography are presented, with a highlighted conclusion at the top and the answer distribution at the bottom

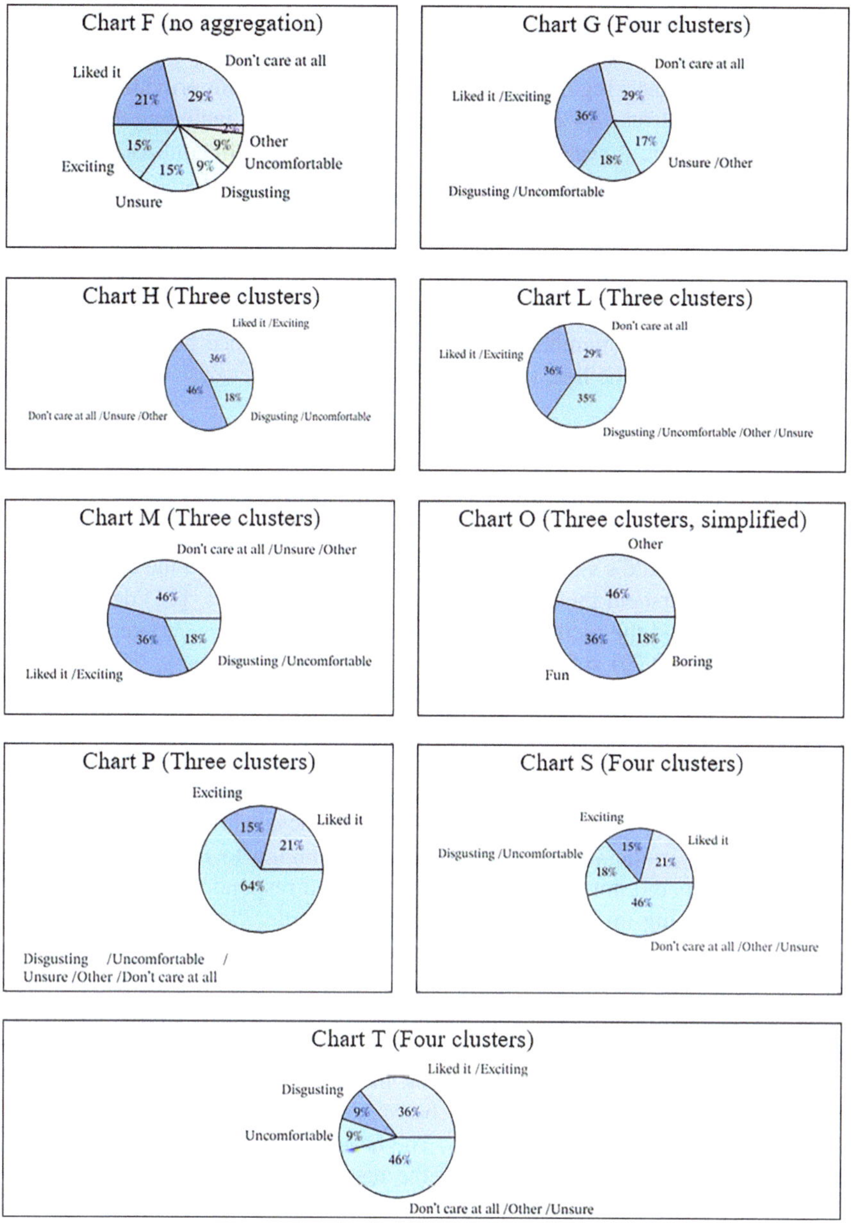

Fig. 5 Module 4 visualisation. Nine pie charts displayed to the participants one at a time. Charts named form F to T as shown, along with the number of clusters created and the aggregation adopted in each plot

no irregularities identified, and 18% ($n = 25$) declared the image quality was insufficient. As described, the 67 participants who answered 'Yes', had the option to provide details on the irregularities identified, with 58 of them providing a written answer. In their answers, 74% ($n = 44$) referred to the axes, including the concepts 'y-axis', 'logarithmic', 'scales', 'spacing', and 'flattening'. In contrast, just one of the participants mentioned the y-axis was truncated: "It does not start with zero, and the length between 10-20 is much greater than 20-30 which is greater than 30-40". Regarding the logarithmic scale indicated on the y-axis label, multiple responses described the y-axis scale and how different it appeared to the participants, for example "Why there are such big boxes at 10-20 and 20-30? It is kinda weird", "It is weird that as the numbers on the y-axis rise, the space between them gets smaller, which affects the line, [...]".

4.2 Results Module 2: Identification of Textual Elements

For the second module's visualisation, 195 participants answered the question 'Did you feel you understand the picture?'. Out of them, 62% ($n = 121$) declared they felt they understood the picture. In contrast whereas 18% ($n = 35$) declared to be unsure, 15% ($n = 29$) stated they did not understand it. Finally, 5% ($n = 10$) considered the quality of the image insufficient. Similarly, the 156 participants who answered 'Yes' or 'Unsure' were given the opportunity to provide insights about the visualisation. Among the 85 participants who filled in the free text field, responses were divided. Some participants wrote their conclusions based on the visualisation without noting any inconsistency, while others highlighted specific features in the visualisation. Answers belonging to the first group show some participants did not notice the bars represented respondents who were never overlooked, drawing mistaken conclusions, for example, "I see 73.3% of women are overlooked because of gender". Other participants drew wrong conclusions due to the way the information in the bars were split, for example: "12.9 percent of women feel they are not targeted at work because of their gender. So of the women 29 or younger who took the survey, 19.4 percent felt they weren't being targeted because of their gender". Among the answers belonging to the second group, eight indicated the inconsistency between the title and the bars' heading, for example, "Very confusing presentation. The headline and question are in contrast to each other, and the interpretation of the result too", "I totally understood the publication, but it took me a relatively long time to realize that it was showing how many people did NOT experience gender differences in work environments", or "I understand the graph that, for example, 73.3% of women experience that they are not 'overlooked' so I don't understand when the result says that 12.9% feel that they are 'overlooked'". In regards to the second question, 'Did you notice that people were asked if they felt they had experienced discrimination, but the columns showed the responses of those who did not feel they had experienced discrimination?', it received 149 answers. Out of them, 37% ($n = 55$), 28% ($n = 42$), and 14%

($n = 21$) answered 'Yes, immediately', 'Yes, at a second glance', and 'Yes, but not immediately', respectively. About 20% ($n = 30$) recognised not noticing the change. One participant answered 'Other' and provided a free text input.

4.3 Results Module 3: Perception of Textual Representations

A total of $n = 112$ participants provided answers to the questions related to the third visualisation. The first question required participants to select the words that best described the visualisation in relation to the corresponding bar charts. Figure 6 displays the percentage of participants who selected each of the descriptive words. There is no clear tendency in the participants' opinions. Similar percentages indicated both positive and negative views about the visualisations (e.g., descriptive vs. misleading, and honest vs. dishonest), showing that visualisations are highly influenced by public perception.

In regards of the second question, 'Did you notice the charts ask about the last time you watched porn, but the visualisation insinuated general opinion?' about half of the respondents, 48% ($n = 54$) recognised not realising the inconsistency. In contrast, 21% ($n = 23$), 17% ($n = 19$), and 14% ($n = 16$) indicated they noticed it, answering 'Yes, immediately', 'Yes, but not immediately', and 'Yes, at a second glance', respectively. Finally, as described above, at the beginning of the questionnaire, the participants were asked about their perception of the words 'disgusting' and 'repulsive'. The question was answered by 306 participants, with only 20% ($n = 62$) indicating that the words have the exact same meaning. In contrast, 76% ($n = 234$) of them indicated 'repulsive' is worse than 'disgusting', and 3%($n = 10$) considered 'disgusting' worse than 'repulsive'. Despite the majority of participants stating that "disgusting" and "repulsive" have different meanings, the change from "disgusting" to "repulsive" in the visualisation did not significantly affect their perception. There was an even split between positive and negative descriptions.

4.4 Results Module 4: Perception of Graphical Representations

In the final module, the participants were asked to evaluate the nine different pie charts based on given hypothetical data. Table 2 summarises the results for the nine pie charts. The first row indicates the number of participants taking part in the question for each of the plots. A Chi-squared test for independence confirmed that the differences between the answers each chart got are statistically significant (χ-squared = 441.45, df = 56, p-value $< 2.2e{-16}$).[1] In Table 2, percentages

[1] Option 'other' was not included in the Chi-squared test.

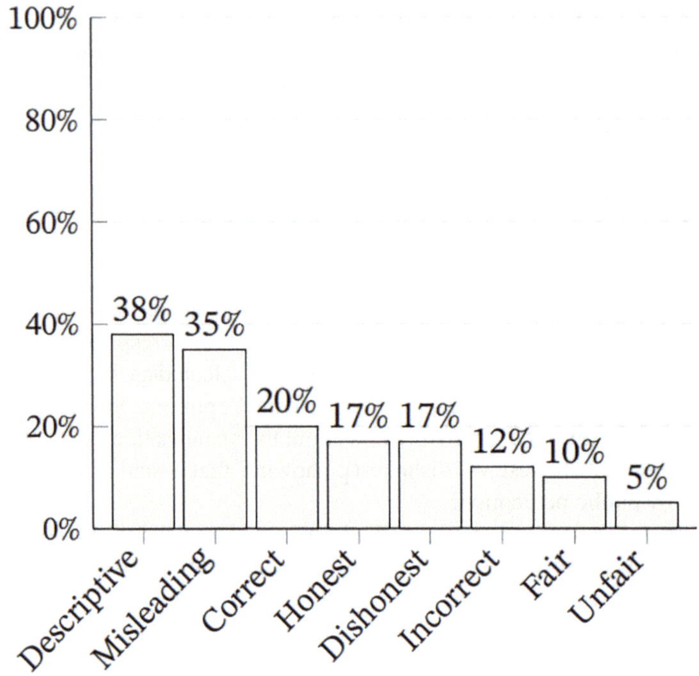

Fig. 6 Percentage of participants (out of $n = 112$) that selected the descriptive word to characterise the visualisation in Fig. 4

indicate the proportion of participants marking the word as representative. Further, the standardised residuals for each of the descriptive words for all the charts are displayed under their respective percentages, with significant residuals marked with an asterisk (*). From the standardised residuals corresponding to the terms 'honest', 'fair', and 'descriptive', we note that out of the nine aggregations, only in charts F and G these terms were selected more frequently than we would expect if the choice of descriptive words were independent of the charts. However, although the values for the term 'I would absolutely not use this chart' are both significant and negative, the values for 'I would use this chart' differ, as just chart F was selected more than expected. In contrast to those charts, values for charts L, O, and P, show these terms were selected less than expected. The only chart where all residuals were significant and consistent was chart F, which displayed all categories separately without any aggregation. This indicates that chart F was perceived as the most reliable and usable. On the contrary, residuals for charts L,O, and P indicate they are perceived as less adequate and usable. No significant residuals were observed in charts H, M, S, and T.

Table 2 Summary of results for the nine pie charts displayed in Fig. 5. Each chart was assessed separately by the participants. Significant residuals indicated as (*).

Chart	F	G	H	L	M	O	P	S	T
Participants	104	101	99	99	98	96	94	91	92
Honest	36% (6.76)*	19% (2.21)*	7% (−1.18)	4% (−2.21)*	7% (−1)	6% (−1.74)	3% (−2.56)*	10% (−0.17)	9% (−0.56)
Dishonest	5% (−4.25)*	20% (−0.89)	23% (−0.01)	31% (1.34)	22% (0.08)	40% (2.46)*	35% (1.59)	22% (−0.04)	22% (−0.15)
Fair	39% (6.19)*	24% (2.5)*	12% (−0.46)	5% (−2.49)*	11% (−0.51)	6% (−2.36)*	1% (−3.6)*	12% (−0.28)	16% (0.77)
Unfair	3% (−3.88)*	14% (−1.05)	17% (−0.12)	24% (1.28)	16% (−0.1)	30% (2.18)*	34% (2.98)*	16% (−0.08)	12% (−1.19)
Descriptive	54% (6.21)*	40% (3.71)*	20% (−0.26)	14% (−1.78)	16% (−0.87)	9% (−2.99)*	13% (−2.3)*	12% (−1.75)	18% (−0.46)
Misleading	7% (−5.4)*	22% (−2.56)*	43% (1.23)	49% (1.84)	36% (0.27)	55% (2.14)*	52% (1.65)	38% (0.68)	38% (0.53)
I would use this chart	43% (6.45)*	23% (1.76)	18% (0.74)	5% (−2.75)*	16% (0.49)	4% (−3.12)*	4% (−3.06)*	11% (−0.89)	15% (0.12)
I would absolutely not use this chart	12% (−4.88)*	23% (−2.69)*	35% (−0.46)	54% (2.05)*	42% (0.93)	51% (1.09)	60% (2.33)*	46% (1.55)	40% (0.52)
Other	5%	2%	2%	0%	2%	1%	1%	2%	1%

5 Discussion

This paper presents a case study based on four modules exploring the identification and perception of misleading visualisations elements. First, we investigate how graphical (module 1) and textual (module 2) misleading elements impact young audiences' ability to identify inconsistencies in visualisations. High school students were presented with real images used to summarise and communicate information to the public. Furthermore, we examined their perception of the reliability of textual (module 3) and graphical (module 4) elements in representing numerical data. To evaluate these elements, participants were shown real and synthetic visualisations. The questionnaire targeted native-speaking high school students and was distributed online, receiving 396 responses.

Several implications can be drawn based on the results presented. First, regarding our research questions, we show that high school students' ability to understand data is impaired when visualisations with misleading graphical and textual elements are presented. However, the extent to which they identify misleading elements differs between graphical and textual elements. In module 1, while the majority of participants who identified an irregularity mentioned the y-axis scale as a factor impairing the visualisation, just one mentioned the truncated axis, which has been found to be a common issue in visualisations [43]. In contrast, module 2 focused on identifying textual misleading elements. Only eight participants indicated they noticed the visualisation's message reversal [53]. Regarding the second research question, participants' answers to module 3 show variability in audience perceptions of textual elements. The descriptive words chosen to characterise the visualisation were almost equally distributed between positive and negative, despite the over-generalisation and message exaggeration [53]. In contrast, participants showed a higher agreement in module 4 regarding different aggregations, showing a preference for no aggregation.

Our work also has practical implications. Firstly, the results of our work are relevant for those interested in sharing information with young audiences using visualisations. This demographic is high consumer of social media resources [6], which had been found to be attention drivers, influencing information viewership [54]. Moreover, considering social media's limitations due to device screen size, the time a resource is available, and the volume of simultaneous content, research on effective ways to summarise and share information is essential to prevent the spread of misleading information to this audience. While our study offers insights into the effects of misleading visualisation elements, it also highlights this demographic's limited understanding, underscoring the need to enhance high school students' data and visualisation literacy [8]. To accomplish this goal, various methods can be used to integrate data and visualisation literacy into the curriculum; including workshops featuring digital and physical resources that allow the students to interact and engage with data, create and experiment with data visualisations, and explore the impact of technologies such as machine learning and artificial intelligence [20, 21, 24, 36, 55]. Moreover, ethical design tools and socio-technical systems can be helpful as a means of assessing and enhancing young students' data literacy. The integration of these resources into the curriculum would also favour the enhancement of critical thinking skills in this demographic by relying on real world examples and the analysis of the systems and stakeholders involved [9, 55, 61].

Concerning research implications, an essential element in the agenda of information systems research is the ethical use of technology. This is a fundamental aspect of design research and a critical process component [48, 62]. The design process must be approached with caution as multiple elements combine to make it an ill-structured and complex endeavour [33]. A socio technical perspective of the practical aspects of ethical design should also be considered to enhance ethical design learning [25, 34, 44]. Regarding data visualisations, although multiple frameworks and guidelines to prevent misinformation through deceptive visualisations have been developed [12, 57], several studies focus on developing guidelines for visualisation practitioners without adequately considering how people are deceived by misleading elements [37]. It is essential that ethical design takes into account the ethical challenges and dilemmas encountered in the visualisation research streams, such as the acknowledgement of hidden information, the collection of data, and the issue of power [17]. Moreover, due to the interplay between power and responsibility, unethical practices and outcomes can also result [17]. This calls for further investigation on the moral character of visualisation research and other ethical practices in information systems research [10]. Linked to this discourse, our work provides insights for ethical design implications. More specifically, we provide empirical evidence on four ways a young audience can be manipulated to misunderstand information through misleading visualisations without explicitly using false data. This issue is particularly problematic because individuals can be intentionally led to draw incorrect conclusions, despite not being presented with false claims. As a result, it is often challenging to identify and hold creators of misleading visualisations accountable. In our work, when the participants were asked if they noticed the inconsistencies, only 48%, 37%, and 21% declared they immediately did so in modules 1, 2 and 3, respectively. Nonetheless, the primary purpose of visualisations presented to the general public is to relay information graphically so that an audience can quickly grasp the message without needing to scrutinise it [2]. Therefore, although most participants answered 'yes' to some extent when asked if they noticed the inconsistencies, arguably more than 50% would not have noticed them in real-world contexts such as advertisements or social media. Consequently, our work contributes to ethical design by investigating the variability of elements within digital artefacts, outlining one of the multiple elements needed for cultivating ethical design, along with reflecting on vulnerabilities, needs and expectations [34].

Thereupon, our study explored design and visualisation practices *'in the wild'*, illustrating their impact when neither the questions *Who is designing?* nor *For whom is the output being designed?* correspond to those who are experts in the creation and interpretation of visualisations, as is common in our everyday lives. Moreover, our work extends to challenges in visualisations research in information systems and socio-technical systems, namely data collection of public input [44], influence of personal factors and cognitive factors [29]. In particular, the adoption of socio-technical perspectives that acknowledge the importance of the social system where visualisations are embedded, has the potential to benefit both the development of ethical design practices and the students awareness of the impact of deceiving visualisations. From the standpoint of ethical design, our study shows the stakeholders' perspective is helpful to provide insights into the potential that visualisation's elements have to mislead a particular audience, informing the designers' understanding of such effects. On the other hand, socio-technical approaches to data and visualisation literacy in educational settings would also benefit from insights on the students' understanding of technology and artefacts they are exposed to in their everyday lives, by which they may gain a greater understanding of ethical and societal implications [55].

A number of factors limit our research. Firstly, since most respondents were female, their answers might not extend to their male counterparts, who tend to prefer different social media platforms [6]. In addition, for the purposes of this research, the questionnaire was targeted primarily at high school students, which limits our ability to draw conclusions from subjects from diverse age groups and educational backgrounds. Further, in our work we assume the students have had similar prior training in interpreting graphs, which is an assumption we could not verify. Regarding the language, the study was conducted completely in Icelandic, leaving participants who do not speak Icelandic excluded from the study. Additionally, the authors translated the questions, answers, and visualisations, which could have led to minor ambiguities in concept and perception across languages. Finally, since all questions were optional, the insights into specific sub-demographics were limited. Future work will address these shortcomings, including reaching a wider audience of male students, improving the questionnaire design to facilitate contrasting different groups, including control graphs, and conducting a qualitative assessment of the participants' perspectives and their answers to the open ended questions. Focus groups, workshops, and interviews will also be conducted to collect richer data to inform the development of pedagogical strategies to support Icelandic high school students' data and visualisation literacy.

6 Conclusion

This paper contributes to the growing interest in the literature on misleading visualisations and ethical design within information systems. We examine both the degree to which high school students are able to identify misleading graphical and textual elements in visualisations as well as outlining the differences between the way they perceive misleading textual and graphical elements in visualisations. We present a four-module case study, each module focusing on a different element and featuring relevant visualisations. Our two-fold contribution comprises: (1) we provide empirical evidence of how graphical and textual misleading elements are identified and perceived by a young audience, highlighting differences and how such elements may influence decision-making, and (2) we reflect on the practical and ethical implications, as well as the need for more comprehensive research on ethical design that takes into consideration the stakeholders' perceptions to promote responsible and trustworthy visualisations. Furthermore, our findings and contributions highlight the relevance of socio-technical perspectives to support both the development of ethical design practices, as well as the enhancement of data and visualisation literacy in young audiences.

Disclosure of Interests The authors have no competing interests to declare that are relevant to the content of this article.

References

1. https://www.deceptive.design/
2. Albers, M. J. (2015). Infographics and communicating complex information. In A. Marcus (Ed.), *Design, user experience, and usability: Users and interactions* (pp. 267–276). Lecture Notes in Computer Science. Springer International Publishing. https://doi.org/10.1007/978-3-319-20898-5_26
3. Alexander, J., & Smith, J. (2011). Disinformation: A taxonomy. *IEEE Security & Privacy Magazine*, *9*(1), 58–63. https://doi.org/10.1109/MSP.2010.141
4. Alvesson, M., & Sköldberg, K. (2018). *Reflexive methodology: New vistas for qualitative research* (3rd ed.). Sage.
5. Arslan, R. C., Reitz, A. K., Driebe, J. C., Gerlach, T. M., & Penke, L. (2021). Routinely randomize potential sources of measurement reactivity to estimate and adjust for biases in subjective reports. *Psychological Methods*, *26*(2), 175–185. https://doi.org/10.1037/met0000294
6. Atske, S. (2022). Teens, social media and technology 2022. https://www.pewresearch.org/internet/2022/08/10/teens-social-media-and-technology-2022/
7. Bednar, P. M., & Welch, C. (2020). Socio-technical perspectives on smart working: Creating meaningful and sustainable systems. *Information Systems Frontiers*, *22*(2), 281–298. https://doi.org/10.1007/s10796-019-09921-1
8. Bergstrom, C. T., & West, J. D. (2020). *Calling bullshit: The art of skepticism in a data-driven world* (1st ed.). Random House.
9. Bilstrup, K. E. K., Kaspersen, M. H., Lunding, M. S., Schaper, M. M., Van Mechelen, M., Tamashiro, M. A., Smith, R. C., Iversen, O. S., & Petersen, M. G. (2022). Supporting critical data literacy in k-9 education: Three principles for enriching pupils' relationship to data. In *Proceedings of the 21st Annual ACM Interaction Design and Children Conference, IDC '22* (pp. 225–236). Association for Computing Machinery. https://doi.org/10.1145/3501712.3530783. https://dl.acm.org/doi/10.1145/3501712.3530783
10. Bock, A. C., España, S., Gulden, J., Jahn, K., Nweke, L. O., & Richter, A. (2021). The ethics of information systems: The present state of the discussion and avenues for future work. ECIS 2021 Research-in-Progress Papers. https://api.semanticscholar.org/CorpusID:235428206
11. Bristol, T. (2005). Not telling the whole story: Teen deception in purchasing. *Journal of the Academy of Marketing Science*, *33*(1), 79–95. https://doi.org/10.1177/0092070304269754. http://link.springer.com/10.1177/0092070304269754
12. Cabanski, C., Gilbert, H., & Mosesova, S. (2018). Can graphics tell lies? A tutorial on how to visualize your data. *Clinical and Translational Science*, *11*(4), 371–377. https://doi.org/10.1111/cts.12554
13. Cairo, A. (2019). *How charts lie: Getting smarter about visual information*. WW Norton & Company.
14. Calero-Valdez, A., Ziefle, M., & Sedlmair, M. (2018). *Studying biases in visualization research: Framework and methods* (pp. 13–27). Springer International Publishing. https://doi.org/10.1007/978-3-319-95831-62. http://link.springer.com/10.1007/978-3-319-95831-62

15. Camba, J. D., Company, P., & Byrd, V. (2022). Identifying deception as a critical component of visualization literacy. *IEEE Computer Graphics and Applications*, *42*(1), 116–122. https://doi.org/10.1109/MCG.2021.3132004
16. Cho, I., Wesslen, R., Karduni, A., Santhanam, S., Shaikh, S., & Dou, W. (2017). The anchoring effect in decision-making with visual analytics. In *2017 IEEE Conference on Visual Analytics Science and Technology (VAST)* (pp. 116–126). IEEE. https://doi.org/10.1109/VAST.2017.8585665. https://ieeexplore.ieee.org/document/8585665/
17. Correll, M. (2019). Ethical dimensions of visualization research. In *Proceedings of the 2019 CHI Conference on Human Factors in Computing Systems* (pp. 1–13). ACM. https://doi.org/10.1145/3290605.3300418. https://dl.acm.org/doi/10.1145/3290605.3300418
18. Cossard, A., De Francisci Morales, G., Kalimeri, K., Mejova, Y., Paolotti, D., & Starnini, M. (2020). Falling into the echo chamber: The italian vaccination debate on twitter. *Proceedings of the International AAAI Conference on Web and Social Media*, *14*, 130–140. https://doi.org/10.1609/icwsm.v14i1.7285
19. Dimara, E., Franconeri, S., Plaisant, C., Bezerianos, A., & Dragicevic, P. (2020). A task-based taxonomy of cognitive biases for information visualization. *IEEE Transactions on Visualization and Computer Graphics*, *26*(2), 1413–1432. https://doi.org/10.1109/TVCG.2018.2872577
20. DiPaola, D., Payne, B. H., & Breazeal, C. (2020). Decoding design agendas: An ethical design activity for middle school students. In *Proceedings of the Interaction Design and Children Conference, IDC '20* (pp. 1–10). Association for Computing Machinery. https://doi.org/10.1145/3392063.3394396. https://dl.acm.org/doi/10.1145/3392063.3394396
21. Estevez, J., Garate, G., & Graña, M. (2019). Gentle introduction to artificial intelligence for high-school students using scratch. *IEEE Access*, *7*, 179027–179036. https://doi.org/10.1109/ACCESS.2019.2956136. https://ieeexplore.ieee.org/document/8915693
22. Fan, A., Ma, Y., Mancenido, M., & Maciejewski, R. (2022). Annotating line charts for addressing deception. In *CHI Conference on Human Factors in Computing Systems* (pp. 1–12). ACM. https://doi.org/10.1145/3491102.3502138. https://dl.acm.org/doi/10.1145/3491102.3502138
23. Fansher, M., Chivukula, S. S., & Gray, C. M. (2018). #darkpatterns: Ux practitioner conversations about ethical design. In *Extended Abstracts of the 2018 CHI Conference on Human Factors in Computing Systems, CHI EA'18* (pp. 1–6). Association for Computing Machinery. https://doi.org/10.1145/3170427.3188553. https://dl.acm.org/doi/10.1145/3170427.3188553
24. Fernandez, C., Blikstein, P., & Lopes, R. D. D. L. (2024). Design failures in data visualization programming activities. In *Proceedings of the 23rd Annual ACM Interaction Design and Children Conference, IDC '24* (pp. 574–586). Association for Computing Machinery. https://doi.org/10.1145/3628516.3663348. https://dl.acm.org/doi/10.1145/3628516.3663348
25. Fiore, E. (2020). Ethics of technology and design ethics in socio-technical systems: Investigating the role of the designer. *FormAkademisk - forskningstidsskrift for design og designdidaktikk, 13*(1). https://doi.org/10.7577/formakademisk.2201. https://journals.oslomet.no/index.php/formakademisk/article/view/2201
26. Ghai, B., & Mueller, K. (2022). D-bias: A causality-based human-in-the-loop system for tackling algorithmic bias. *IEEE Transactions on Visualization and Computer Graphics*, 1–10. https://doi.org/10.1109/TVCG.2022.3209484
27. Gray, C. M., Kou, Y., Battles, B., Hoggatt, J., & Toombs, A. L. (2018). The dark (patterns) side of ux design. In *Proceedings of the 2018 CHI Conference on Human Factors in Computing Systems* (pp. 1–14). ACM. https://doi.org/10.1145/3173574.3174108. https://dl.acm.org/doi/10.1145/3173574.3174108
28. Gregory, R., & Muntermann, J. (2011). Theorizing in design science research: Inductive versus deductive approaches. In *ICIS 2011 Proceedings*. https://aisel.aisnet.org/icis2011/proceedings/engagedscholarship/2
29. Gulden, J., Van Der Linden, D., & Aysolmaz, B. (2016). A research agenda on visualizations in information systems engineering. In *Proceedings of the 11th International Conference on Evaluation of Novel Software Approaches to Software Engineering* (pp. 234–240). SCITEPRESS - Science and Technology Publications. https://doi.org/10.5220/0005898702340240. http://www.scitepress.org/DigitalLibrary/Link.aspx?doi=10.5220/0005898702340240

30. Hardesty, K. S., & Hardesty, C. (2020). Math matters in communication: Manipulation and misrepresentation in data displays. In *2020 IEEE International Professional Communication Conference (ProComm)* (pp. 61–67). IEEE. https://doi.org/10.1109/ProComm48883.2020.00016. https://ieeexplore.ieee.org/document/9201218/
31. Healey, C. G., & Enns, J. T. (2012). Attention and visual memory in visualization and computer graphics. *IEEE Transactions on Visualization and Computer Graphics*, *18*(7), 1170–1188. https://doi.org/10.1109/TVCG.2011.127
32. Holder, E., & Xiong, C. (2023). Dispersion vs disparity: Hiding variability can encourage stereotyping when visualizing social outcomes. *IEEE Transactions on Visualization and Computer Graphics*, *29*(1), 624–634. https://doi.org/10.1109/TVCG.2022.3209377
33. Islind, A. S., & Lundh Snis, U. (2018). From co-design to co-care: Designing a collaborative practice in care. *Systems, Signs & Actions*, *11*(1), 1–24.
34. Islind, A. S., & Willermark, S. (2022). Becoming a designer: The value of sensitive design situations for teaching and learning ethical design and design theory. *Scandinavian Journal of Information Systems*, *34*(1). https://aisel.aisnet.org/sjis/vol34/iss1/1
35. Islind, A. S., & Willermark, S. (2022). *Polite interaction design: Capturing the users attention without compromising their experienced trust. AMCIS 2022 Proceedings*. https://aisel.aisnet.org/amcis2022/sig_hci/sig_hci/1
36. Johnson, E., Bae, S. S., & Do, E. Y. L. (2023). Supporting data visualization literacy through embodied interactions. In *Proceedings of the 15th Conference on Creativity and Cognition, C&C'23* (pp. 346–348). Association for Computing Machinery. https://doi.org/10.1145/3591196.3596607. https://dl.acm.org/doi/10.1145/3591196.3596607
37. Lauer, C., & O'Brien, S. (2020). The deceptive potential of common design tactics used in data visualizations. In *Proceedings of the 38th ACM International Conference on Design of Communication, SIGDOC '20* (pp. 1–9). Association for Computing Machinery. https://doi.org/10.1145/3380851.3416762. https://doi.org/10.1145/3380851.3416762
38. Lauer, C., & O'Brien, S. (2020). How people are influenced by deceptive tactics in everyday charts and graphs. *IEEE Transactions on Professional Communication*, *63*(4), 327–340. https://doi.org/10.1109/TPC.2020.3032053
39. Liao, Q. V., & Fu, W. T. (2014). Age differences in credibility judgments of online health information. *ACM Transactions on Computer-Human Interaction*, *21*(1), 1–23. https://doi.org/10.1145/2534410
40. Lisnic, M., Lex, A., & Kogan, M. (2024). "yeah, this graph doesn't show that": Analysis of online engagement with misleading data visualizations. In *Proceedings of the CHI Conference on Human Factors in Computing Systems* (pp. 1–14).
41. Lisnic, M., Polychronis, C., Lex, A., & Kogan, M. (2023). Misleading beyond visual tricks: How people actually lie with charts. In *Proceedings of the 2023 CHI Conference on Human Factors in Computing Systems* (pp. 1–21).
42. Lo, L. Y. H., Gupta, A., Shigyo, K., Wu, A., Bertini, E., & Qu, H. (2022). Misinformed by visualization: What do we learn from misinformative visualizations? *Computer Graphics Forum*, *41*, 515–525. Wiley Online Library.
43. Lo, L. Y. H., Gupta, A., Shigyo, K., Wu, A., Bertini, E., & Qu, H. (2022). Misinformed by visualization: What do we learn from misinformative visualizations? *Computer Graphics Forum*, *41*(3), 515–525. https://doi.org/10.1111/cgf.14559
44. Mahyar, N., Jasim, M., & Sarvghad, A. (2020). Designing technology for sociotechnical problems: Challenges and considerations. *IEEE Computer Graphics and Applications*, *40*(6), 76–87. https://doi.org/10.1109/MCG.2020.3017405. https://ieeexplore.ieee.org/document/9238543
45. Manresa-Yee, C., & Ramis, S. (2021). Assessing gender bias in predictive algorithms using explainable ai. In *Proceedings of the XXI International Conference on Human Computer Interaction* (pp. 1–8). ACM. https://doi.org/10.1145/3471391.3471420. https://dl.acm.org/doi/10.1145/3471391.3471420
46. Mantri, P., Subramonyam, H., Michal, A. L., & Xiong, C. (2022). How do viewers synthesize conflicting information from data visualizations? *IEEE Transactions on Visualization and Computer Graphics*, 1–11. https://doi.org/10.1109/TVCG.2022.3209467

47. McClure Haughey, M., Muralikumar, M. D., Wood, C. A., & Starbird, K. (2020). On the misinformation beat: Understanding the work of investigative journalists reporting on problematic information online. *Proceedings of the ACM on Human-Computer Interaction*, *4*(CSCW2), 1–22. https://doi.org/10.1145/3415204
48. Müller, S., Jonsson, K., Pirkkalainen, H., Parmiggiani, E., & Tona, O. (2023). The anatomy of scandinavian journal of information systems. *Scandinavian Journal of Information Systems*, *35*(1). https://aisel.aisnet.org/sjis/vol35/iss1/1
49. Morstatter, F., Wu, L., Yavanoglu, U., Corman, S. R., & Liu, H. (2018). Identifying framing bias in online news. *ACM Transactions on Social Computing*, *1*(2), 1–18. https://doi.org/10.1145/3204948
50. Nalcaci, A. A., Girgin, D., Balki, S., Talay, F., Boz, H. A., & Balcisoy, S. (2019). Detection of confirmation and distinction biases in visual analytics systems. In *EuroVis Workshop on Trustworthy Visualization (TrustVis)* (5 pp.). https://doi.org/10.2312/TRVIS.20191185
51. Oberst, U., Wegmann, E., Stodt, B., Brand, M., & Chamarro, A. (2017). Negative consequences from heavy social networking in adolescents: The mediating role of fear of missing out. *Journal of Adolescence*, *55*(1), 51–60. https://doi.org/10.1016/j.adolescence.2016.12.008. https://onlinelibrary.wiley.com/doi/10.1016/j.adolescence.2016.12.008
52. O'Brien, S., & Lauer, C. (2018). Testing the susceptibility of users to deceptive data visualizations when paired with explanatory text. In *Proceedings of the 36th ACM International Conference on the Design of Communication* (pp. 1–8). ACM. https://doi.org/10.1145/3233756.3233961. https://dl.acm.org/doi/10.1145/3233756.3233961
53. Pandey, A. V., Rall, K., Satterthwaite, M. L., Nov, O., & Bertini, E. (2015). How deceptive are deceptive visualizations?: An empirical analysis of common distortion techniques. In *Proceedings of the 33rd Annual ACM Conference on Human Factors in Computing Systems* (pp. 1469–1478). ACM. https://doi.org/10.1145/2702123.2702608. https://dl.acm.org/doi/10.1145/2702123.2702608
54. Ren, J., Dong, H., Popovic, A., Sabnis, G., & Nickerson, J. (2022). Digital platforms in the news industry: How social media platforms impact traditional media news viewership. *European Journal of Information Systems*, 1–18. https://doi.org/10.1080/0960085X.2022.2103046
55. Schaper, M. M., Tamashiro, M. A., Smith, R. C., Van Mechelen, M., & Iversen, O. S. (2023). Five design recommendations for teaching teenagers' about artificial intelligence and machine learning. In *Proceedings of the 22nd Annual ACM Interaction Design and Children Conference, IDC '23* (pp. 298–309). Association for Computing Machinery. https://doi.org/10.1145/3585088.3589366. https://dl.acm.org/doi/10.1145/3585088.3589366
56. Selnes, F. N. (2023). Fake news on social media: Understanding teens' (dis)engagement with news. *Media, Culture & Society*, 01634437231198447. https://doi.org/10.1177/01634437231198447
57. Sheppard, S. R. (2001). Guidance for crystal ball gazers: Developing a code of ethics for landscape visualization. *Landscape and Urban Planning*, *54*(1–4), 183–199. https://doi.org/10.1016/S0169-2046(01)00135-9
58. Tripodi, F. B. (2019). Radicalism, authoritarianism, and the role of new media. *New Media & Society* , *21*(4), 1021–1026. https://doi.org/10.1177/1461444818816085
59. Tripodi, F. B., Stevenson, J. A., Slama, R., & Reich, J. (2023). Libraries combating disinformation: From the front line to the long game. *The Library Quarterly*, *93*(1), 48–71.
60. Van de Ven, A. H. (2007). *Engaged scholarship: A guide for organizational and social research*. Oxford University Press.
61. Williams, R., Ali, S., Devasia, N., DiPaola, D., Hong, J., Kaputsos, S. P., Jordan, B., & Breazeal, C. (2023). Ai+ethics curricula for middle school youth: Lessons learned from three project-based curricula. *International Journal of Artificial Intelligence in Education*, *33*(2), 325–383. https://doi.org/10.1007/s40593-022-00298-y. https://doi.org/10.1007/s40593-022-00298-y
62. Zhang, J. (2011). Ethical issues in information systems. In *2011 International Conference of Information Technology, Computer Engineering and Management Sciences* (pp. 321–323). https://doi.org/10.1109/ICM.2011.24

Developing a Framework for Shared Responsibility: The Role of Digital Technology

Shiting Wang and Haiat Perozzo

Abstract In the realm of Information Systems (IS), shared responsibility is a crucial yet ambiguously defined concept. This study addresses the research gap by applying the Gioia Methodology to a dataset of first-order concepts derived from a systematic literature review. These concepts were distilled into second-order concepts and further aggregated into three overarching dimensions: Technological Adoption and Resistance, Information Control and Power Dynamics, and Trust and Transparency. Our findings emphasize the critical role of digital technologies in mediating shared responsibility. By comparing Internet of Things (IoT) and Generative Artificial Intelligence (Generative AI) technologies, we illustrate how each influence these aggregated dimensions differently. IoT enhances operational efficiency and transparency but can reinforce existing power structures, while Generative AI democratizes access to advanced capabilities yet complicates accountability due to its black-box nature. This study contributes to the IS field by providing a structured framework for understanding and defining shared responsibility, highlighting the evolving dynamics of human-technology interaction. Future research should focus on developing robust frameworks to support transparent and trustworthy relationships in digital ecosystems.

Keywords Shared responsibility · Digital technology · IoT · Generative AI

S. Wang (✉)
Copenhagen Business School, Frederiksberg, Denmark
e-mail: ws.digi@cbs.dk

H. Perozzo
LIUC – Cattaneo University, Castellanza, Italy
e-mail: hperozzo@liuc.it

M. Cipriano et al. (eds.), *Technologies for Organizations and Society*,
Lecture Notes in Information Systems and Organisation 80,
https://doi.org/10.1007/978-3-032-01697-3_18

1 Introduction

In the digital era, the concept of "shared responsibility" has transcended its traditional boundaries, becoming a pivotal theme in the Information Systems (IS) community. Shared responsibility refers to the collective accountability of multiple stakeholders in managing, implementing, and sustaining technological solutions and data governance frameworks [1]. Despite its importance, there is a conspicuous absence of a unified definition of shared responsibility in the IS field. This lack of consensus hinders the development of standardized frameworks and best practices, leading to confusion and misaligned expectations among stakeholders [2].

The urgency to define shared responsibility in IS is driven by the increasing complexity of digital ecosystems and the pivotal role that technology plays in modern organizational structures. As digital technologies evolve, they not only offer unprecedented opportunities for innovation and efficiency but also introduce new challenges and risks. This duality underscores the need for a robust understanding of how shared responsibility operates in the context of digital transformation [3].

To address this research gap, the primary research question guiding this investigation is: "What are the key variables and dimensions that define shared responsibility in the Information Systems community, and how do digital technologies influence these dimensions?"

Our research seeks to address this gap by exploring the key variables and dimensions that define shared responsibility within the IS community. We aim to elucidate how digital technologies, specifically Internet of Things (IoT) and Generative AI, influence these dimensions, shaping the dynamics of shared responsibility among stakeholders [4]. Our research is grounded in the socio-technical model, which emphasizes the interdependence between social and technical factors in organizational settings [5]. The socio-technical model posits that both social and technical elements must be considered to fully understand and effectively manage complex systems. In the context of shared responsibility, this means recognizing how social dynamics, such as trust and power relationships, interact with technical aspects, like data governance and technological capabilities [6].

Through the application of the Gioia Methodology, we identified several first-order concepts from a comprehensive literature review, which were then distilled into second-order concepts and finally aggregated into broader dimensions [7]. These aggregated dimensions represent both the social and technical spheres of the socio-technical model, providing a holistic view of the factors influencing shared responsibility in the IS field [5].

2 Theoretical Background

Existing literature on shared responsibility emphasizes the benefits of making collective decisions between humans [8], and examines how decisions are made between humans and computers [4, 9]. Making accurate decisions is crucial, so it is important to understand the variables that might affect the accuracy of decisions made under shared responsibility.

Responsibility entails the ability to be held accountable, whether through blame or praise, for an action or its outcome, in accordance with a legal or moral norm from which a duty arises [3]. Moreover, an individual cannot be deemed responsible for an act if they do not have the ability to make a decision concerning that action [2]. Shared responsibility, therefore, refers to allocating obligations among multiple individuals or entities within a society [1]. Understanding the definition of responsibility helps us identify stakeholders in shared responsibility scenarios. Therefore, a prerequisite for sharing responsibility is that stakeholders must have the ability to make choices and act with intent [2].

When multiple stakeholders take intentional actions that collectively contribute to a state of affairs, they share responsibility for the outcome, with the degree of responsibility assigned to each stakeholder depending on their specific level of intentionality and causal contribution. Furthermore, this intentionality can be triggered under different conditions. (1). Shared responsibility is triggered by the legal obligation [10], which is mandatory for companies and individuals to comply. For example, when an organization complies with a consumer privacy act, it shares the responsibility of protecting consumer data with other stakeholders, such as users and regulatory bodies. Therefore, shared responsibility can also serve as a goal advocated in policy analyses [11]. However, conflicts can also arise in such situation.

For instance, companies need to invest more resources in upgrading their data protection infrastructure, hiring dedicated privacy protection personnel, or seeking external legal advice to ensure compliance [12]. These additional expenses can impact their profitability. To avoid these extra costs, some companies might choose to abandon certain data-intensive businesses or move them to jurisdictions with more lenient privacy regulations [13]. This leads to a decline in service quality or reduced user adoption. On another hand, if companies shift the responsibility to users (such as requiring users to manage their privacy settings themselves), it causes inconvenience to users and potentially lead to users abandoning the service [14]. Additionally, a lack of security awareness among users increases the likelihood of data breaches. Meanwhile, regulatory bodies also needs to invest more resources in monitoring and enforcing compliance, which require additional budget and personnel allocation [15].

These conflicts can affect the interests of the entire ecosystem, including organizations, users, and regulatory authorities. In order to mitigate these conflicts, it is important for regulatory bodies to engage in communication and consultation with various stakeholders when formulating regulations to ensure a reasonable distribution of responsibilities and costs [16]. Regulations should provide clear guidance and reasonable transition periods for companies to reduce the compliance burden [17]. Companies should view privacy protection as a long-term investment rather than merely a compliance cost. By building user trust and loyalty, they can gain a long-term competitive advantage [18]. Ultimately, mitigating these conflicts can only be accomplished through shared responsibility that involves all stakeholders. Shared responsibility, within the context of legal obligations, serves as a protective mechanism [8] aims to balance the interests of all stakeholders.

2.1 Shared Responsibility Triggers: The Common Goals

When multiple stakeholders are involved in a project, they often share a common goal but may prioritize tasks differently, leading to conflicts, reduced productivity, and increased costs. Each stakeholder brings their perspective, expertise, and interests, resulting in disagreements over resource allocation, timelines, and task importance [19, 20].

For example, marketing stakeholders prioritize features that enhance user experience, while manufacturing stakeholders focus on technical feasibility and system stability. The complexity of a project often necessitates the involvement of multiple stakeholders, such as vendors, manufacturers, and end-users, which adds additional perspectives and expectations, complicating decision-making [21].

Effective data sharing is crucial for mitigating conflicts and fostering collaboration among stakeholders. By implementing robust data sharing practices, organizations can ensure all stakeholders access the same information, reducing misunderstandings and enabling informed decision-making [22]. Cloud-based platforms and collaborative tools facilitate real-time data sharing, allowing stakeholders to access updates, share insights, and provide feedback regardless of location [23]. Standardized data formats and protocols improve the efficiency of information exchange, ensuring shared data is accurate and easily interpretable [24]. Promoting transparency and trust through effective data sharing creates a more collaborative environment [25]. Regular meetings, workshops, and training sessions help align stakeholders' expectations and foster a shared understanding of project objectives [26]. Open communication facilitates problem-solving and enables stakeholders to appreciate each other's roles and contributions [27]. However, data sharing raises significant concerns regarding security and privacy. To mitigate these issues, the concept of shared responsibility has emerged, encouraging collaboration and collective accountability among stakeholders [28].

A well-designed shared responsibility model helps align stakeholders' interests and priorities, ensuring data-sharing initiatives support the organization's goals. This model balances benefits and risks, incorporating mechanisms for dispute resolution and continuous improvement [29].

2.2 Digital Technology Instrument in Shared Responsibility

Digital technological instruments are available to implement the concept of shared responsibility, which refers to the practical application of scientific knowledge to solve problems or enhance processes [30]. In the context of shared responsibility, technology plays a crucial role in facilitating collaboration, ensuring compliance, and monitoring the actions of various stakeholders. While private companies often develop and implement technology, governments and non-governmental organizations also play a significant role in shaping technological policies and standards [31].

Technological instruments for shared responsibility can include secure data sharing platforms, blockchain-based systems for transparency and accountability, and AI-powered tools for monitoring and auditing [32, 33]. Secure data sharing platforms enable different stakeholders to collaborate and share information while maintaining data privacy and security [34], while blockchain technology can create tamper-proof records of transactions and agreements, ensuring that all parties are held accountable for their actions [35]. AI-driven tools can automate compliance monitoring and detect potential violations, reducing the burden on human auditors [36].

In addition to facilitating collaboration and ensuring compliance, technology can also serve as a mediator in mitigating conflicts across multiple stakeholders in a shared responsibility model. By providing a neutral platform for communication and decision-making, technological tools can help stakeholders find common ground and resolve disputes more efficiently [37]. For example, online dispute resolution (ODR) platforms can use AI-powered algorithms to analyze the positions of different parties and suggest fair solutions [38].

Moreover, digital technology can help level the playing field for stakeholders with varying levels of power and resources. By providing access to information and tools that were previously unavailable or too costly, digital platforms can empower weaker parties and ensure that their voices are heard in the decision-making process [39]. This can lead to more equitable outcomes and reduce the risk of conflicts arising from power imbalances [40].

However, the deployment of these technological instruments is not solely the domain of private companies. Governments and non-governmental organizations have a crucial role to play in setting technological policies, standards, and regulations [31]. These policies ensure that the technology used for shared responsibility is secure, reliable, and aligned with the interests of all stakeholders. Furthermore, non-governmental organizations can use these policies to hold technology companies accountable for their actions and ensure that they are meeting their obligations under the shared responsibility framework [41].

2.3 Shared Responsibility in Information System

In the field of Information Systems (IS), the concept of shared responsibility is particularly significant due to the collaborative nature of technology development, implementation, and usage. However, despite its importance, there is no consensus on a single definition of shared responsibility within this domain. Shared responsibility often emerges in discussions about cybersecurity, data management, and system development. In cybersecurity, shared responsibility frameworks delineate the roles and duties of cloud service providers and users in ensuring data security and compliance [42], clarifying the boundaries of responsibility between the provider, who secures the infrastructure, and the user, who manages data and applications [43].

Data management also highlights shared responsibility, particularly concerning data governance and data quality. Organizations must collaborate internally among departments and externally with stakeholders to ensure the accuracy, consistency, and security of data. Shared responsibility in this context ensures that all parties involved understand their roles in maintaining data integrity [44]. The importance of data stewardship and collaborative data practices is well documented in the literature [45, 46].

System development within IS further illustrates the concept of shared responsibility through methodologies like Agile and DevOps, which promote a collaborative environment where developers, operations teams, and business stakeholders share responsibility for the successful delivery and maintenance of software systems [47, 48]. The principles of continuous integration and continuous delivery (CI/CD) also reinforce the shared responsibility model in software engineering [49].

Despite these examples, the absence of a unique and unified definition of shared responsibility in IS poses challenges, such as confusion and misalignment of expectations among stakeholders, and complications in developing standardized frameworks and best practices [50, 51]. The existing literature on shared responsibility across various disciplines, including IS, underscores its complexity and context-specific nature. However, the lack of a unified definition within the IS field highlights a critical research gap that needs to be addressed.

First, there is a need for a systematic analysis of how shared responsibility is currently defined and implemented in IS practices. This analysis should examine the various contexts in which shared responsibility is applied, such as cybersecurity, data management, and system development, as discussed in the previous paragraphs. Understanding the nuances and commonalities across these contexts can provide valuable insights into the core components of shared responsibility in IS [6]. Second, empirical research is necessary to identify the key variables that practitioners and organizations consider most relevant when discussing shared responsibility. These variables might include factors such as the distribution of roles, communication channels, accountability mechanisms, and the impact of digital technologies, which were highlighted in the context of technological instruments for shared responsibility. By analyzing these variables, researchers can develop a more precise and comprehensive definition that reflects the practical realities of the IS field [5, 52]. Third, it is crucial to explore the role of digital technologies in shaping and facilitating shared responsibility. As mentioned earlier, digital technologies such as secure data sharing platforms, blockchain-based systems, and AI-powered tools play a significant role in enabling shared responsibility. However, as digital technologies evolve, they introduce new dynamics and complexities into the concept of shared responsibility. For example, the rise of cloud computing, artificial intelligence, and Internet of Things (IoT) technologies presents new challenges and opportunities for distributing and managing responsibility among various stakeholders [53, 54]. Understanding these dynamics is essential for developing a relevant and forward-looking definition. Finally, addressing this research gap will contribute to the development of standardized frameworks and best practices that can enhance collaboration and accountability in IS. Such frameworks can help organizations navigate the complexities of shared responsibility, ensuring that all stakeholders are aligned and equipped to fulfill their roles effectively [55, 56]. By building upon the existing examples of shared responsibility in IS, such as those found in cybersecurity, data management, and system development, researchers can develop a more comprehensive and universally applicable definition.

While the concept of shared responsibility is widely recognized and applied in various aspects of IS, such as cybersecurity, data management, and system development, its definition within the IS field remains fragmented and underexplored. By conducting empirical research to identify key variables, examining the role of digital technologies, and analyzing the existing examples of shared responsibility in IS, this study aims to propose a unified and comprehensive definition of shared responsibility in IS. This definition will not only clarify the concept but also provide practical guidance for organizations seeking to implement shared responsibility in their technological endeavors.

3 Methodology

The main purpose of this systematic literature review is twofold. First, we develop a transdisciplinary synthesis model that aims to define the concept of 'shared responsibility' and the role of digital technologies. Second, we formulate recommendations for future research based on this new model. As many of the concepts relevant to this model are scattered in different literature streams, this study requires a broad and multidisciplinary literature search. To increase coverage and facilitate access to isolated concepts [57], we therefore adopted a three-step strategy.

3.1 The First Step: Systematic Literature Review

For the first step, we conducted a Systematic Literature Review (SLR) with bibliographic network analysis to explore and define the concept of shared responsibility and the role of digital technologies within it. This methodology unfolds in two phases (Fig. 1). The initial phase involves conducting a SLR, which is defined as "a specific methodology that locates existing studies, selects and evaluates contributions, and synthesizes data" [58]. This method aims to avoid bias, ensure rigor, and provide replicable and significant findings [59]. The main steps of this methodology are outlined as follows [60].

Scope of the Analysis To frame a robust literature review, it is crucial to formulate the research question accurately. Denyer and Tranfield [61] recommend using the CIMO framework, addressing Context, Intervention, Mechanism, and Outcome, to define the scope:

- Context: Shared Responsibility. The primary objective is to understand the concept of shared responsibility as it emerges from the literature. This involves identifying key variables and dimensions that describe shared responsibility. The objective is to identify the key variables and dimensions that describe shared responsibility as it appears in the literature.
- Intervention: Role of Digital Technologies. Examining how digital technologies facilitate or impact shared responsibility. This includes understanding how technologies enable collaboration, data sharing, and joint decision-making among stakeholders.

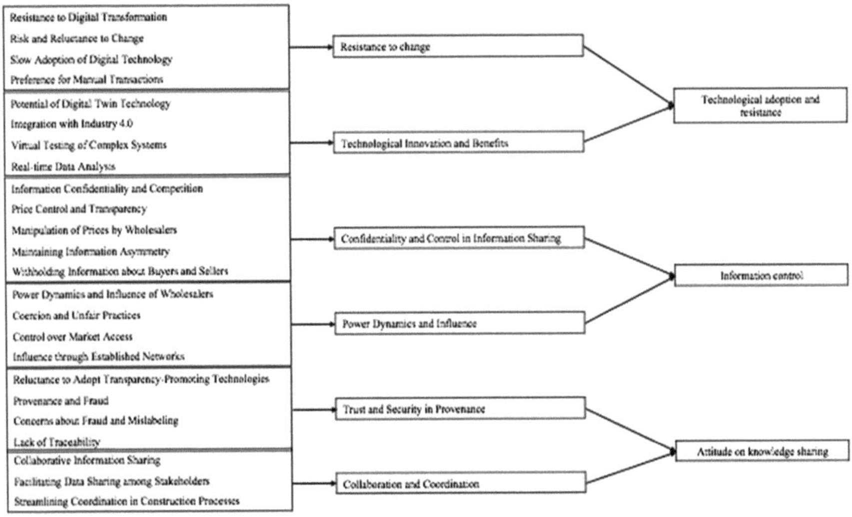

Fig. 1 Structure of coding

- Mechanism: Framework Development. Developing a theoretical framework that encompasses the variables identified. This framework should explain how shared responsibility operates and the role of digital technologies in enhancing it.

Locating Studies Studies are located using keywords related to the identified CIMO areas through databases such as Scopus and ISI Web of Knowledge. However, this study relies primarily on Scopus due to the comprehensive coverage of peer-reviewed literature it offers, including over 57 million records (www.elsevier.com/engb/solutions/scopus).

Studies are located using keywords related to the identified CIMO areas through databases such as Scopus. However, this study relies primarily on Scopus due to the comprehensive coverage of peer-reviewed literature it offers, including over 57 million records [62–64].

Keywords relevant to shared responsibility and digital technologies were identified and refined through expert consultation. This process ensures the selection of appropriate literature, using a comprehensive search string: ("shared responsibil*" OR "data shar*" OR "information shar*") AND ("digital technolog*" OR "collaboration tool*").

Study Selection and Evaluation Study selection and evaluation with the identification of inclusion criteria [59, 63]: Inclusion criteria are identified to select relevant studies [59, 63]. The selection process ensures that only pertinent literature contributing to the understanding of shared responsibility and digital technologies is included.

A set of selected papers will be obtained as a result. The data used in this work were collected from the Scopus database, which is the largest abstract and citation database of peerreviewed literature: scientific journals, books and conference proceedings, for over 57 million records (www.elsevier.com/engb/solutions/scopus). The use of ISI Web of Knowledge database was also explored for retrieving papers. However, in our case, we found that the number of retrieved works was smaller, and these articles were already included in the sample retrieved from Scopus. Hence, we decided to rely on Scopus only. Inclusion criteria are identified to select relevant studies [59, 63]. The selection process ensures that only pertinent literature contributing to the understanding of shared responsibility and digital technologies is included (Table 1).

First, the search was performed looking for papers published in peer-reviewed scientific journals only. This choice is based on the assumption that by limiting the search to peer-reviewed journals, it is possible to enhance the quality control of search outcomes thanks to the rigorous review process that articles undergo before publication in such journals, as argued by Newbert [65], Pereira et al. [64] and Ali et al. [63]. The retrieval of papers from Scopus database ensured that this criterion is met. Additionally, papers were selected without restriction on publication year (i.e. setting "All years" in the Data range field). This allowed taking into account the widest possible time window in accordance with the purpose of this study, that is,

Table 1 Inclusion criteria for study selection and evaluation [63]

Inclusion criteria	Rationale
Published in peer-reviewed journals	Peer-reviewed journals are considered to be of higher quality than non-peer-reviewed articles
Selection of papers without restriction on publication year	Widest possible time window to comply with the purpose of the study, that is, focus on the evolutionary view of the field
Selection of papers with restriction on the Search Field, that is, "Title-Abstract-Keywords" Selected articles present high relevance, since keywords must be present in the articles' title, abstract or keywords	Selected articles present high relevance, since keywords must be present in the articles' title, abstract or keywords
Published in English	English is the dominant language in the field of supply chain management research

focus on the evolutionary view of the field, without introducing a subjective starting date of the analysis. The identified keywords were used as a search string in Scopus at the end of May 2024, resulting in 414 articles retrieved. The selection of papers was then refined by restricting the search field to "Title-Abstract-Keywords". This inclusion criterion ensured that the selected articles presented a high relevance to the field under study [63] by requiring the presence of at least three keywords in the articles' title, keywords or abstract, that is, one keyword from each area composing our search string. This alignment appraisal criterion is effective in making sure that the selected papers are focused on the topic under investigation [64]. Finally, only papers published in English were selected, as English is the dominant language in the field of research. This led to obtaining 213 works as a final search outcome, dated from 2002 to 2024.

3.2 The Second and Third Step: Snowballing Techniques and Coding

As the second step of our search strategy, we proceeded to use a snowballing technique to identify articles similar to the key documents that might not have been captured by during our initial search. We performed backward and forward searches [66].

Third, we coded the sampled literature to identify key concepts. We iteratively developed first order concepts and second-order themes, as well as aggregate dimensions [7]. We used these themes and dimensions to characterize and integrate findings from a range of study domains. We continuously revisited articles until we reached saturation (i.e., we could not find new components that did not overlap with our existing themes), focusing mostly on our set of documents, but also drawing from our reserved documents whenever needed. A few examples can help illustrate our analytical approach: among the articles about shared responsibility and digital technology. Figure 1 presents a visual summary of our coding. After extensive coding, peer debriefing, and several rounds of iterations, we developed a synthesis of the literature that captures the main variables that define the concept of Shared Responsibility and the role of digital technologies.

This section presents the application of the first phase of the adopted methodology to the field under study. The steps of the SLR are performed and a description of the process is provided.

4 The Building Blocks of Shared Responsibility Concept and the Role of Digital Technologies: A Transdisciplinary Synthesis Model

The extensive analysis of articles from SCOPUS, focusing on keywords related to shared responsibility, data sharing, digital technology, and collaboration, has yielded valuable insights into the dynamics of shared responsibility in the digital age. Through the Gioia Methodology, the first-order concepts were refined into second-order concepts and ultimately into three overarching aggregated dimensions: Technological Adoption and Resistance, Information Control and Power Dynamics, and Trust and Transparency. These dimensions provide a comprehensive framework for understanding the factors that influence shared responsibility.

From the outset, it was evident that the first-order concepts encapsulated a diverse range of themes, each reflecting various aspects of digital technology adoption, information control, power dynamics, trust, and collaboration. For instance, concepts related to the resistance to digital transformation highlighted how entrenched traditional practices and a preference for manual operations posed significant barriers. Similarly, issues of information confidentiality and control surfaced, revealing how wholesalers often resist transparency to maintain a competitive edge.

As we delved deeper, these first-order concepts began to coalesce into more refined, second-order concepts. The theme of resistance and risk aversion emerged, underscoring the hesitancy among stakeholders to embrace digital changes due to fears of disrupting established relationships and practices. Simultaneously, the critical role of information control and the inherent power dynamics within supply chains became apparent. Trust and security, particularly concerning provenance and food fraud, also stood out as pivotal concerns. Moreover, the promise and potential of technological innovations like digital twin technology and Industry 4.0 initiatives offered a glimpse into the future of enhanced efficiency and collaboration. Finally, the necessity for robust collaboration and coordination mechanisms to facilitate seamless information sharing was a recurrent theme.

These second-order concepts naturally led us to identify three overarching aggregated dimensions: Technological Adoption and Resistance, Information Control and

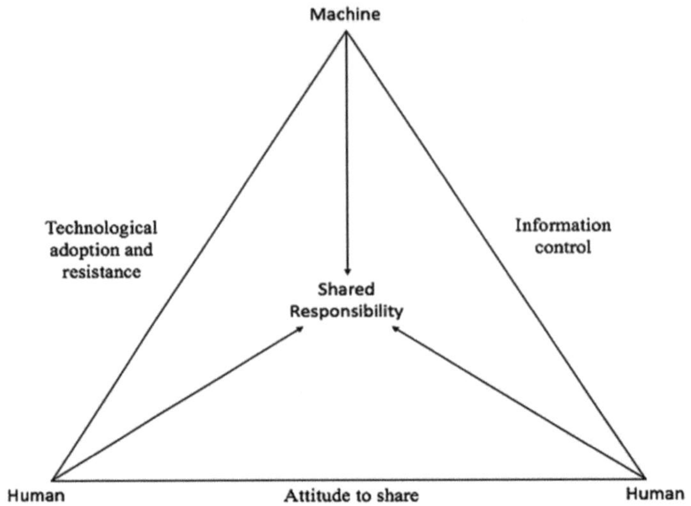

Fig. 2 Shared responsibility model

Power Dynamics, and Trust and Transparency. These dimensions encapsulate the broader themes derived from our analysis and provide a holistic view of the factors influencing shared responsibility in the digital age.

The shared responsibility model, as depicted in Fig. 2, illustrates the interplay between human actors, machines, and the key dimensions that shape their interactions. At the core of this model lies the concept of shared responsibility, which is influenced by the relationships between human actors, the adoption and resistance to technology, the attitude to share and the control of information.

The dimension of Technological Adoption and Resistance, positioned between the machine and human actors, highlights the dual nature of technology's impact. While digital technologies offer opportunities for innovation and enhanced transparency, they are often met with resistance due to risk aversion and entrenched practices. The adoption of Internet of Things (IoT) technologies exemplifies this dynamic, as organizations gradually embrace these tools for their potential to improve efficiency and transparency, while also grappling with the perceived risks and challenges of integration. Generative AI, while promising significant innovation, encounters resistance due to its opacity and the unpredictable nature of its outputs, which can heighten anxiety around control and accountability.

Information Control, situated on the other side of the machine-human relationship, underscores the delicate balance of maintaining confidentiality and exercising control within competitive environments. IoT devices often reinforce existing power structures by providing granular control and data insights to those who manage them. This control can enhance transparency but may also exacerbate existing power imbalances. The advent of Generative AI further complicates these dynamics, as its opaque decision-making processes can shift power dynamics in unpredictable ways, often centralizing control with those who understand and can manipulate these systems. The black-box nature of Generative AI can erode trust, making stakeholders wary of relying on its outputs without understanding the underlying logic.

At the base of the shared responsibility model, connecting the human actors, lies the crucial element of attitude to share. This dimension emphasizes the importance of trust and transparency in fostering effective collaboration and ensuring the security and integrity of shared information. Trust is the foundation upon which shared responsibility thrives, enabling stakeholders to engage openly and collaboratively. IoT technologies generally foster trust through improved traceability and real-time data sharing. However, excessive user control can lead to data breaches, placing responsibility on the vendor. Generative AI, due to its opaque decision-making processes, can erode trust, making stakeholders wary of relying on its outputs without understanding the underlying logic. This erosion of trust places an even greater emphasis on the need for transparency and accountability in technological mediation.

As digital technologies become increasingly integrated into organizational processes, they play a critical role in mediating shared responsibility. IoT devices and Generative AI systems act as intermediaries between human actors, shaping the flow of information and influencing power dynamics. However, this technological mediation introduces a paradox in human-machine interaction, as responsibility becomes shared not only among human actors but also with the technology itself. The opacity of Generative AI, in particular, complicates the assignment of responsibility when issues arise, often leading to the technology being held accountable rather than the human stakeholders.

Technological Adoption and Resistance speaks to the dual nature of technology's impact—where opportunities for innovation are often met with significant resistance due to risk aversion and entrenched practices. Information Control and Power Dynamics highlight the delicate balance of maintaining confidentiality and exercising control within competitive environments, underscoring the significant influence wielded by powerful actors. Trust and Transparency, perhaps the most crucial dimension, focus on the essential elements needed to foster collaboration and ensure the security and integrity of shared information.

These second-order concepts naturally led us to identify three overarching aggregated dimensions: Technological Adoption and Resistance, Information Control and Power Dynamics, and Trust and Transparency. These dimensions encapsulate the broader themes derived from our analysis and provide a holistic view of the factors influencing shared responsibility in the digital age.

The aggregated dimensions identified in this study form the bedrock of defining shared responsibility within the IS community. At its core, shared responsibility thrives on a foundation of trust and transparency, where stakeholders are willing to engage openly and collaboratively. However, this balance is delicate and requires careful management of information control and power dynamics.

Technology plays an indispensable role in mediating shared responsibility. Consider the relationship between a vendor and a user. Shared responsibility flourishes when there is a high level of trust and an openness to sharing knowledge. For instance, if a vendor provides the user with greater control and flexibility, it enhances transparency but also introduces potential risks such as data breaches. In such scenarios, even with high trust levels, the user may hold the vendor accountable for any issues arising from the granted flexibility.

This is where technology becomes a crucial mediator, protecting shared responsibility by balancing control and security. However, this mediation introduces a paradox in human-machine interaction. As technology evolves, responsibility is increasingly shared not only among human actors but also with the technology itself. For instance, when Internet of Things (IoT) devices moderate interactions between a vendor and a user, any problems due to excessive user control typically result in the user holding the vendor accountable.

With the advent of Generative AI, this dynamic shifts further. Generative AI is often perceived as a black-box technology, complicating the assignment of responsibility. When Generative AI mediates interactions, issues that arise are more likely to be attributed to the technology rather than to human stakeholders. This shift underscores the complex interplay between trust, technology, and responsibility in modern digital ecosystems.

5 Conclusions and Further Research

The integration of digital technologies into organizational processes redefines the landscape of shared responsibility. Trust and transparency are central to effective collaboration, but technology's role as a mediator introduces new complexities. Our analysis reveals that technologies like IoT and Generative AI significantly impact how responsibility is perceived and managed. IoT is generally embraced for its ability to enhance transparency and operational efficiency, although it can reinforce existing power dynamics. In contrast, Generative AI, while offering significant innovation potential, poses challenges due to its opacity and unpredictable outputs, shifting the burden of responsibility away from human actors to the technology itself.

The comparison between IoT and Generative AI within the aggregated dimensions underscores the nuanced ways in which technology shapes, mediates, and sometimes complicates shared responsibility. IoT devices typically foster trust through improved traceability and real-time data sharing. However, issues like data breaches due to excessive control granted to users often place responsibility on the vendor. Conversely, Generative AI's black-box nature erodes trust, making stakeholders hesitant to rely on its outputs without understanding the underlying logic. This erosion of trust highlights the need for greater transparency and accountability in technological mediation.

As digital technologies evolve, so too must our frameworks for managing shared responsibility. The ongoing evolution of human-machine interaction necessitates continuous adaptation to ensure accountability and trust in digital interactions. Our study lays the groundwork for future research to develop robust frameworks that support transparent and trustworthy relationships in increasingly complex digital ecosystems. The paradox of human-machine interaction exemplifies the shifting dynamics of responsibility, emphasizing the importance of balancing technological advancements with ethical and practical considerations to maintain trust and effective collaboration among stakeholders.

Disclosure of Interests The authors have no competing interests to declare that are relevant to the content of this article.

References

1. McLennan, B., & Eburn, M. (2014). Exposing hidden-value trade-offs: Sharing wildfire management responsibility between government and citizens. *International Journal of Wildland Fire, 24*(2), 162–169.
2. Sacconi, L. (2011). From individual responsibility to 'Shared' Social responsibilities: Concepts for a new paradigm.
3. Hart, H. L. A. (2008). *Punishment and responsibility: Essays in the philosophy of law*. Oxford University Press.
4. Zhai, S., Wang, L., & Liu, P. (2023). Human and machine drivers: Sharing control, sharing responsibility. *Accident Analysis & Prevention, 188*, 107096.
5. Bostrom, R. P., & Heinen, J. S. (1977). MIS problems and failures: A socio-technical perspective. Part II: The application of socio-technical theory. *MIS Quarterly, 1*(4), 11–28.
6. Cram, W. A., Brohman, M. K., & Gallupe, R. B. (2017). HCI research in the management information systems discipline. *Communications of the Association for Information Systems, 40*(1), 36.
7. Gioia, D. A., Corley, K. G., & Hamilton, A. L. (2013). Seeking qualitative rigor in inductive research: Notes on the Gioia methodology. *Organizational Research Methods, 16*(1), 15–31.
8. El Zein, M., Bahrami, B., & Hertwig, R. (2019). Shared responsibility in collective decisions. *Nature Human Behaviour, 3*(6), 554–559.
9. Kirchkamp, O., & Strobel, C. (2019). Sharing responsibility with a machine. *Journal of Behavioral and Experimental Economics, 80*, 25–33.
10. Lukasiewicz, A., Dovers, S., & Eburn, M. (2017). Shared responsibility: The who, what and how. *Environmental Hazards, 16*(4), 291–313.
11. McLennan, B., & Handmer, J. (2012). Changing the rules of the game: Mechanisms that shape responsibility-sharing from beyond Australian fire and emergency management. *Australian Journal of Emergency Management, 27*(2), 7–13.
12. Sirur, S., Nurse, J. R., & Webb, H. (2018). Are we there yet?: Understanding the challenges faced in complying with the general data protection regulation (GDPR). In *Proceedings of the 2nd International Workshop on Multimedia Privacy and Security* (pp. 88–95).
13. Koops, B. J. (2014). The trouble with European data protection law. *International Data Privacy Law, 4*(4), 250–261.
14. Obar, J. A., & Oeldorf-Hirsch, A. (2020). The biggest lie on the internet: Ignoring the privacy policies and terms of service policies of social networking services. *Information, Communication & Society, 23*(1), 128–147.
15. Raab, C. D., & Koops, B. J. (2009). Privacy actors, performances and the future of privacy protection. In *Reinventing data protection?* (pp. 207–221). Springer.
16. Reding, V. (2011). The upcoming data protection reform for the European Union. *International Data Privacy Law*, 1(1), 3–5. https://doi.org/10.1093/idpl/ipq007

17. Tankard, C. (2016). What the GDPR means for businesses. *Network Security, 2016*(6), 5–8. https://doi.org/10.1016/S1353-4858(16)30056-3
18. Martin, K. (2020). Breaking the privacy paradox: The value of privacy and associated duty of firms. *Business Ethics Quarterly, 30*(1), 65–96.
19. Jergeas, G. F., Williamson, E., Skulmoski, G. J., & Thomas, J. L. (2000). Stakeholder management on construction projects. In *AACE international transactions*, P12A.
20. Olander, S., & Landin, A. (2005). Evaluation of stakeholder influence in the implementation of construction projects. *International Journal of Project Management, 23*(4), 321–328.
21. Mishra, A., & Mishra, D. (2013). Applications of stakeholder theory in information systems and technology. *Engineering Economics, 24*(3), 254–266.
22. Kache, F., & Seuring, S. (2017). Challenges and opportunities of digital information at the intersection of Big Data Analytics and supply chain management. *International Journal of Operations & Production Management, 37*(1), 10–36.
23. Attaran, M., Attaran, S., & Kirkland, D. (2019). The need for digital workplace: Increasing workforce productivity in the information age. *International Journal of Enterprise Information Systems (IJEIS), 15*(1), 1–23.
24. Wang, X., Williams, C., Liu, Z. H., & Croghan, J. (2019). Big data management challenges in health research—a literature review. *Briefings in Bioinformatics, 20*(1), 156–167.
25. Sivarajah, U., Kamal, M. M., Irani, Z., & Weerakkody, V. (2017). Critical analysis of Big Data challenges and analytical methods. *Journal of Business Research, 70*, 263–286.
26. Pemsel, S., & Wiewiora, A. (2013). Project management office a knowledge broker in project-based organisations. *International Journal of Project Management, 31*(1), 31–42.
27. Aakhus, M., & Bzdak, M. (2015). Stakeholder engagement as communication design practice. *Journal of Public Affairs, 15*(2), 188–200.
28. Felici, M., Koulouris, T., & Pearson, S. (2013, December). Accountability for data governance in cloud ecosystems. In *2013 IEEE 5th international conference on cloud computing technology and science* (Vol. 2, pp. 327–332). IEEE.
29. Ansell, C., & Gash, A. (2008). Collaborative governance in theory and practice. *Journal of Public Administration Research and Theory, 18*(4), 543–571.
30. Brey, P. (2018). The strategic role of technology in a good society. *Technology in Society, 52*(C), 39–45.
31. Cath, C., Wachter, S., Mittelstadt, B., Taddeo, M., & Floridi, L. (2018). Artificial intelligence and the 'good society': The US, EU, and UK approach. *Science and Engineering Ethics, 24*, 505–528.
32. Biswas, K., & Muthukkumarasamy, V. (2016, December). Securing smart cities using blockchain technology. In *2016 IEEE 18th international conference on high performance computing and communications; IEEE 14th international conference on smart city; IEEE 2nd international conference on data science and systems (HPCC/SmartCity/DSS)* (pp. 1392–1393). IEEE.
33. Mendoza, I., & Bygrave, L. A. (2017). The right not to be subject to automated decisions based on profiling. EU internet law*:* Regulation and enforcement, 77–98.
34. Yang, Y., Wu, L., Yin, G., Li, L., & Zhao, H. (2017). A survey on security and privacy issues in internet-of-things. *IEEE Internet of Things Journal, 4*(5), 1250–1258.
35. Reijers, W., O'Brolcháin, F., & Haynes, P. (2016). Governance in blockchain technologies & social contract theories. *Ledger, 1*, 134–151.
36. Romeu, P. C., Hashmi, M., & de Koker, L. (2019). Legal compliance through design: Preliminary results. In *CEUR workshop proceedings* (pp. 59–72).
37. Liang, F., Yu, W., An, D., Yang, Q., Fu, X., & Zhao, W. (2018). A survey on big data market: Pricing, trading and protection. *IEEE Access, 6*, 15132–15154.
38. Katsh, M. E., & Rabinovich-Einy, O. (2017). *Digital justice: Technology and the internet of disputes*. Oxford University Press.
39. Hegel, F., Muhl, C., Wrede, B., Hielscher-Fastabend, M., & Sagerer, G. (2009, February). Understanding social robots. In *2009 Second International Conferences on Advances in Computer-Human Interactions* (pp. 169–174). IEEE.

40. Kitchin, R. (2014). The real-time city? Big data and smart urbanism. *GeoJournal, 79*(1), 1–14.
41. Taeihagh, A. (2017). Crowdsourcing, sharing economies and development. *Journal of Developing Societies, 33*(2), 191–222.
42. Amazon Web Services. (2021). *Shared Responsibility Model*. Retrieved from https://aws.amazon.com/compliance/shared-responsibility-model/
43. Jansen, W., & Grance, T. (2011). *Guidelines on security and privacy in public cloud computing* (pp. 800–144). NIST Special Publication.
44. Khatri, V., & Brown, C. V. (2010). Designing data governance. *Communications of the ACM, 53*(1), 148–152.
45. Otto, B. (2011). A morphology of the organisation of data governance. In *Proceedings of the 19th European Conference on Information Systems.*
46. Redman, T. C. (2008). *Data driven: Profiting from your Most important business asset*. Harvard Business Press.
47. Beck, K., Beedle, M., van Bennekum, A., Cockburn, A., Cunningham, W., Fowler, M. et al. (2001). *Manifesto for Agile Software Development*. Retrieved from http://agilemanifesto.org/
48. Kim, G., Humble, J., Debois, P., & Willis, J. (2016). *The DevOps handbook: How to create world-class agility, reliability, & security in technology organizations*. IT Revolution Press.
49. Fowler, M. (2006). *Continuous Integration*. Retrieved from https://martinfowler.com/articles/continuousIntegration.html
50. Boehm, B. (2006). A view of 20th and 21st century software engineering. In *Proceedings of the 28th International Conference on Software Engineering* (pp. 12–29).
51. Sommerville, I. (2007). *Software engineering* (8th ed.). Addison-Wesley.
52. Alter, S. (2004). A work system view of DSS in its fourth decade. *Decision Support Systems, 38*(3), 319–327.
53. Evans, D. (2011). *The internet of things: How the next evolution of the internet is changing everything*. CISCO white paper.
54. Weinman, J. (2012). *Cloudonomics: The business value of cloud computing*. John Wiley & Sons.
55. Gregor, S., & Hevner, A. R. (2013). Positioning and presenting design science research for maximum impact. *MIS Quarterly, 37*(2), 337–355.
56. Hevner, A. R., March, S. T., Park, J., & Ram, S. (2004). Design science in information systems research. *MIS Quarterly, 28*(1), 75–105.
57. Raghuram, S., Hill, N. S., Gibbs, J. L., & Maruping, L. M. (2017). Virtual work: Bridging research clusters. *Academy of Management Annals, 13*(1), 308–341.
58. Denyer, D., & Tranfield, D. (2009). Producing a systematic review. In D. A. Buchanan & A. Bryman (Eds.), *The Sage handbook of organizational research methods* (pp. 671–689). Sage.
59. Kembro, J., Selviaridis, K., & Näslund, D. (2014). Theoretical perspectives on information sharing in supply chains: A systematic literature review and conceptual framework. *Supply Chain Management: An International Journal, 19*(5/6), 609–625.
60. Colicchia, C., & Strozzi, F. (2012). Supply chain risk management: A new methodology for a systematic literature review. *Supply Chain Management: An International Journal, 17*(4), 403–418.
61. Denyer, D., Tranfield, D., & Van Aken, J. E. (2008). Developing design propositions through research synthesis. *Organization Studies, 29*(3), 393–413.
62. Colicchia, C., Creazza, A., Noè, C., & Strozzi, F. (2019). Information sharing in supply chains: A review of risks and opportunities using the systematic literature network analysis (SLNA). *Supply Chain Management: An International Journal, 24*(1), 5–21.
63. Ali, A., Mahfouz, A., & Arisha, A. (2017). Analysing supply chain resilience: Integrating the constructs in a concept mapping framework via a systematic literature review. *Supply Chain Management: An International Journal, 22*(1), 16–39.
64. Pereira, J. A., Constantino, K., & Figueiredo, E. (2014). A systematic literature review of software product line management tools. In *International Conference on Software Reuse* (pp. 73–89). Springer.

65. Newbert, S. . L. (2007). Empirical research on resource-based view of the firm: An assessment and suggestions for future research. *Strategic Management Journal, 28*, 121–146.
66. Watson, R. T., & Webster, J. (2020). Analysing the past to prepare for the future: Writing a literature review a roadmap for release 2.0. *Journal of Decision Systems, 29*(3), 129–147.

Entrepreneurial Perspective of AI Bias: A Preliminary Investigation

Marco Smacchia, Michele Cipriano, and Stefano Za

Abstract Artificial Intelligence (AI) technology is becoming increasingly pervasive in our daily lives, facilitating a wide range of tasks. However, the expanded deployment of AI also broadens the spectrum of potential problems that can impact both individuals and organizations. In this paper, we present a multiple case study based on semi-structured interviews to explore entrepreneurs' perceptions of AI bias within the solutions designed and developed by their firms. Our results reveal two distinct interpretations of bias: the first based on technical (computational) bias and the second based on societal (systemic) bias. In particular, a coding analysis of such empirical evidence is provided. Then, drawing on these assumptions, we propose a matrix useful to assess the potential negative outcomes that different types of bias (technical vs social) can have at various decision levels. This work contributes to research by providing insights and practical tools for understanding and mitigating AI bias and a lens of analysis to foster more equitable and effective AI implementations in organizational contexts.

Keywords AI bias · Artificial intelligence · Case study · AI artifacts · AI fairness

M. Smacchia (✉) · S. Za
Department of Management and Business Administration, University "G. D'Annunzio", Pescara, Italy
e-mail: marco.smacchia@unich.it; stefano.za@unich.it

M. Cipriano
Department of Economic and Social Sciences, Catholic University of the Sacred Heart, Piacenza, Italy
e-mail: michele.cipriano@unicatt.it

M. Cipriano et al. (eds.), *Technologies for Organizations and Society*,
Lecture Notes in Information Systems and Organisation 80,
https://doi.org/10.1007/978-3-032-01697-3_19

1 Introduction

1.1 A Subsection Sample

The importance and relevance of Artificial Intelligence (AI) have amplified exponentially in recent years. This growth has been driven by the increased availability of data, advancements in AI techniques, and the rise in computational power, facilitating its adoption across various fields globally [1, 2]. In addition, AI technology is highly multidisciplinary and is being more and more adopted by organizations on a large scale to solve a great variety of tasks.

AI can be used in almost any organizational function, supporting a great variety of decision or automation-based tasks, and it is likely to become an essential part of many jobs in the future [3]. At the same time, however, users should ensure that AI decisions do not reflect discriminatory and unfair behaviors due to social or technical shortcomings [4, 5]. In particular, AI algorithms, when applied to solve problems, could sometimes worsen the scenario by threatening rights, opportunities, and wealth not only by creating new inequalities but also by amplifying the existing ones [6]. Moreover, as many organizations and governments are beginning to use AI applications, the decisions of such systems could influence many people simultaneously, increasing the scope of potential problems related to ethics, fairness, and algorithmic bias [7].

Addressing ethical concerns in AI systems represents a significant challenge for users who implement such systems. As a matter of fact, traditional AI approaches are being reevaluated by innovative methodologies to ensure algorithmic fairness [8]. Governments are also taking proactive steps to mitigate fairness and ethical problems by establishing comprehensive regulations and guidelines, which are essential for the responsible design, development, and use of AI technologies [9]. From an organizational point of view, companies that design and deploy AI technologies are accountable for addressing these issues, thereby improving the explainability and transparency of AI systems [10]. As a result, the widespread adoption of AI in various sectors has significantly increased academic interest, contributing to the development of new research, theoretical advancements, and emerging questions that drive the field forward [11].

In light of the increasing importance that ethics and fairness assume in the AI domain, recent research has shifted from focusing solely on technical solutions to incorporating social and ethical dimensions, emphasizing the need for a socio-technical perspective [12–14]. Applied to such a domain, a socio-technical approach serves to account for not only computational aspects but also the values, behaviors, and environmental contexts of developers, organizational processes, and user interactions [15, 16]. Specifically, considering that the context in which an AI system is developed (including organizational ideals and practices) significantly impacts the design and fairness of AI outcomes [17, 18], addressing AI bias deserves optimizing and harmonizing technical and social elements (as components) of "socio-technical" systems [19]. However, although abundant conceptual studies on AI bias emerge in the literature, there is still an urgent need for empirical research to understand and mitigate AI bias effectively [20].

Drawing on these assumptions, this study aims to investigate how entrepreneurs involved in the design and development of AI solutions perceive AI bias. More specifically, our objective is to answer the following research questions (RQ):

- RQ1: *How do entrepreneurs perceive AI bias in the AI artifacts designed and developed by their companies?*
- RQ2: *How do decision-making processes impact the types and perceptions of AI bias in organizational contexts?*

To this end, we develop a multiple case study that includes qualitative semi-structured interviews with entrepreneurs of start-up companies involved in designing and developing AI artifacts. By adopting this approach, we aim to gather insights and diverse perspectives on the perceived biases and decision-making processes within different organizational contexts.

Then, the paper is structured as follows: the subsequent section concerns the relevant theoretical underpinnings. Subsequently, the methodology used to perform the study. Afterward, the results are presented and discussed. Finally, implications and contributions, including limitations and future research directions, close the paper.

2 Theoretical Background

Alongside the technological advancements in AI, there is a growing interest in addressing ethical and fairness aspects by mitigating bias within AI solutions [15]. While AI provides numerous advantages to society and organizations, users are also increasingly experiencing the need to address potential biases that could undermine the effectiveness of these solutions and lead to significant errors. By mitigating AI bias, firms can better identify opportunities to benefit society and prevent critical mistakes, ensuring the responsible and equitable deployment of AI technologies [21]. Although several academics elaborate on the definition of AI bias as a discrepancy between the outcomes produced by a system and the established ground truth, resulting in imbalanced advantages (or disadvantages) for specific groups or individuals [5, 13], the conceptualization of AI bias remains complex and problematic. Among various challenging factors are historical, geographical, and ideological influences that usually complicate establishing a universally accepted ground truth. Moreover, AI bias could be present in various stages of the AI lifecycle comprising the design, development, and deployment of AI artifacts.

In the literature, many studies provide classifications and mitigation strategies to address AI bias. Kordzadeh and Ghasemaghaei [18] develop a framework based on eight theoretical concepts influenced by contextual dimensions such as individual and organizational factors, arguing that algorithmic bias impacts perceived fairness and user behavior. Mehrabi et al. [5] categorize biases by context, data, algorithm, and user interaction, offering corresponding mitigation strategies. Akter et al. [13] classify AI bias into three distinct sources: data bias, method bias, and societal bias. Data bias arises from issues related to the data used to train AI algorithms, such as sample inadequacy, sample selection bias, or incomplete datasets, all of which can lead to underperformance and inherent biases in AI artifacts [13]. Method bias refers to the impact of the methods employed in the design and development of AI systems, with examples including correlation fallacies, overgeneralization, and confirmation bias [13]. Lastly, societal bias encompasses biases embedded within society that often appear in the training data, reflecting historical and institutional behaviors [13]. In comparison, the US National Institute of Standards and Technology (NIST) identifies categories of bias based on three different sources [14]. The first category, "Systemic bias", refers to the influence of societal customs and institutional beliefs on AI design and development, encompassing social, historical, and institutional biases [14]. The second category, "Computational bias", arises from issues in the underlying data and methods, affecting the performance and outcomes of AI artifacts, including measurement, representation, label, and feedback biases [14]. The third category, "Human bias", involves the impact of human perceptions and heuristics on the use of AI artifacts, such as deployment, anchoring, availability, and confirmation biases [14]. Interestingly, this classification follows in the footsteps of the socio-technical traditions emphasizing the relevance of the human-centric perspective, especially highlighting the importance of involving domain experts in AI design and development [14]. Thus, we adopt this last classification provided by NITS as a theoretical baseline to inspect and classify the perceptions about AI bias concerning the Italian landscape (for details, see the methodology section).

3 Methodology

To perform our research, we adopted an exploratory approach using multiple case study methodology [22]. This methodology enabled us to gather diverse perspectives and identify patterns and insights across different contexts. Figure 1 depicts the protocol we adopted to perform this case study. Specifically, we adapted the framework of Yin [22] and opted for an iterative cycle because every step has to be refined during the entire process. Moreover, as this is a preliminary study, we will iterate the various steps in order to perform a more comprehensive design and collection of data. Notwithstanding that, the preliminary interviews presented in this paper represent an initial pilot step contributing to refining the semi-structured interview protocol and the sample of such research. Then, we thoroughly describe the cases analyzed in the first sub-section while focusing on the data collection and analysis in the second sub-section.

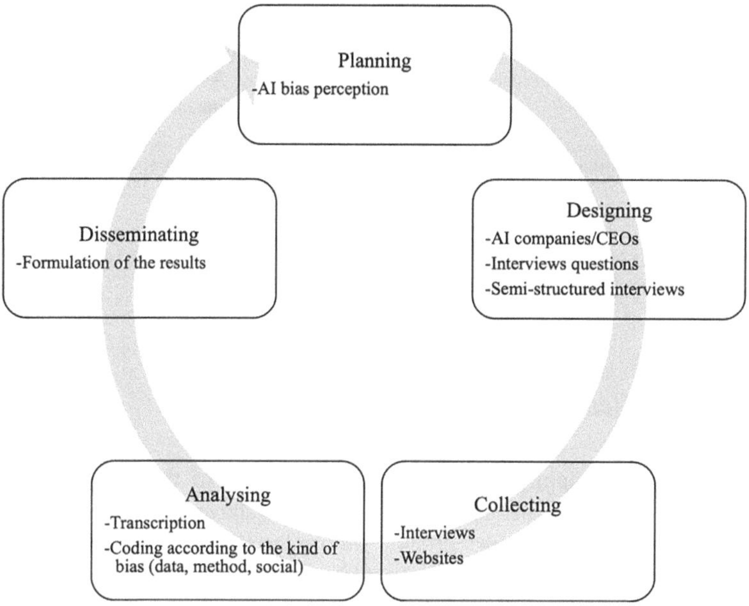

Fig. 1 Research framework (adapted from Yin [22])

3.1 Case Selection

Concerning our sample, we selected only firms that are focused on the design and development of AI artifacts. To conduct the interviews, we scheduled appointments with two entrepreneurs at the Confindustria branch in Pescara-Chieti[1] during an event focused on educating high school students about AI technology. The companies interviewed in this research are Oltrematica S.r.l. and Diskover S.r.l. The first case, represented by Oltrematica S.r.l., is a small-medium enterprise focused on the design of custom-made software and the implementation of network architectures and servers. The solutions offered by Oltrematica S.r.l. encompass many fields at a corporate level. Moreover, such a company is located in the Italian municipality of Pescara. Concerning the second case, Diskover S.r.l. is an innovative start-up that provides AI solutions to be implemented mainly in manufacturing plants to predict machinery operations (e.g., predictive maintenance and performance assessment). This company is also located in Pescara. We chose these two companies because they are deeply involved in the digitalization process of the territory in which they are based, and the management is well aware of the risks related to AI technology.

[1] Confindustria, information about Confindustria Abruzzo Branch. URL: https://www.confindustria.it/en/associative-network/local-associations/association?id=4B0031A114C95CA3C1258AA7004806D4 (Retrieved on: 28/08/2024).

Table 1 Information concerning the characteristics of the two cases under study

Company	Company size	Objective(es)/markets
Oltrematica S.r.l.	Small enterprise < 50 employees	Tailored AI software: decision support systems, business intelligence and data mining
Diskover S.r.l.	Small enterprise < 50 employees	Predictive AI: manufacturing

Table 1 summarizes the main characteristics of the companies in terms of size and objectives.

3.2 *Data Collection and Analysis*

This study focuses mainly on how the entrepreneurs of the cases under study perceive bias inside the AI applications that they have developed. As already mentioned in the theoretical background, we use the framework given by the NIST [14] as a theoretical lens because we want to inspect the perception of the three kinds of bias (i.e., systemic, computational, and human) in different contexts. To this end, we adopted a qualitative multiple-case study research design that allow us to inspect the phenomena more widely and to have more robust and heterogeneous results [22]. Our aim is to conduct in-depth semi-structured interviews to examine how entrepreneurs perceive the bias related to the AI solutions their company designs and develops. In particular, this study consists of preliminary research in which we performed two pilot interviews ranging from 30 to 60 min in which we asked basic questions reported in Table 2.

In line with our research objectives, the questions were developed to assess the entrepreneurs' knowledge and perception of bias and to determine whether their views align with all or part of the framework we adopted. Additionally, the questions aimed to explore the types of decisions made when biases are detected within the firm and the subsequent impact of these decisions on the design and development processes of AI artifacts. Regarding the respondent, we selected the two entrepreneurs of the cases, presenting different backgrounds, with the idea of reasoning on distinct organizational behaviors given the possible diverse perspectives people might have about the investigated phenomena. Table 3 summarizes information about the interviews and the participants.

4 Results

This section presents some results emerging from the interviews that were conducted. In particular, we describe and interpret excerpts, seeking to develop an understanding by examining the interviews. Interestingly, the presence of systemic

Table 2 Interview questions and motivations

Question	Focus	Objective
What are AI biases (from your perspective), and what practical impact do they have on your firm?	The first question is to break the ice with entrepreneurs and see their perspective on the phenomena inspected	General knowledge about AI biases and their classification
Have you experienced bias inside the solutions you developed?	We begin to go deeper and ask questions referred to the company. If the answer is affirmative, we proceed and ask the following three questions; otherwise (if not), we simply ask the last two	Organizational aspects about AI bias: consistency/discrepancy with the perception of bias
What kind of bias you have encountered?	The following question helps us to understand what kind of bias the respondent describes according to our selected framework	
What have you done about it?	We want to understand the processes and practices that they have done to address the bias	
What are the consequences that the presence of this bias has brought to the firm decision process?	To investigate if the presence of bias could affect the way processes and decisions are made after being found	Organizational aspects about AI bias: mitigation strategy and decision making
With the implementation of your solutions, have you contributed to the resolution of bias present inside systems that were already implemented?	We also take into account the possibility that their solution helps to solve an existing bias inside the firm	
What is your academic and working background?	We want to understand if academic and working backgrounds affect how people perceive AI bias	Background influence on AI bias perception

Table 3 Interview information

Company	Participants	Role	Background	Duration
Oltrematica S.r.l.	1 participant	CEO	Technical	40 min
Diskover S.r.l.	1 participant	CEO	Social science	50 min

and computational biases clearly emerged in different contexts and industry fields. In comparison, no evidence emerged with regard to Human bias during such a preliminary wave of interviews. Then, considering the pilot nature of this study, the following findings are limited to the data gathered at this point (based on only two interviews). Thus, in this specific instance, the diverse backgrounds of the interviewees and the preliminary structure of the interview allowed us to identify only two types of AI bias. Moreover, each interviewee focused on a distinct type of bias. Accordingly, we used this data to conduct a preliminary analysis, leading to the development of a prototype framework. This framework will be refined and enriched as we acquire additional data, allowing for a more comprehensive and structured analysis. Then, the following sub-section focuses on the computational bias, while the systemic bias is examined in the second sub-section.

4.1 Potential Bias Emerging from the Algorithm (Relative to Computational Bias)

The founder of Diskover S.r.l. was focused on his previous experience as well as on the current solution that the company developed. More specifically, a platform based on a predictive algorithm exploiting neural networks was examined. The system could be implemented in various manufacturing plants. It can manage historical data to predict the operations of a given machine and when it is most likely to need maintenance. In this scenario, the biggest issue is to identify all the variables that compose and are necessary for the correct operation of the plant. Some plants are characterized by a high degree of complexity, containing machines that incorporate various components. The interrelation of these variables causes the emergence of a variety of situations, all different from each other. An AI system capable of predicting these situations must explore and investigate all the correlations between the variables by studying the cause-and-effect links that occur between them. Since some correlations may be hidden and difficult to detect, there is a risk of overlooking these correlations, which can lead to the emergence of bias. This bias may result in false positives by incorrectly attributing the problem to a component that is (actually) functioning correctly. For example, it was stated that: "*If the production depends on the speed at which the machine performs a certain task, and that task depends on the speed of the machine's engine, then in the event of a decrease in production, you are prone to increase the engine speed. What you don't know is that a particular filter might give problems and decrease the engine speed*" (Diskover S.r.l.).

Professional experts, acting as a "prompt" manager, operate by studying the results of AI systems, identifying hidden correlations, and training the algorithm to eliminate the bias given by the lack of necessary information. Every AI system initially presents a number of problems because it fails to recognize the various correlations between the different devices it has to take into account. It is commonly expected that the first results are affected by a high error rate (false positives), which is gradually corrected over time, resulting in the continuous learning and improvement of the artifact.

The presence of bias within the algorithm has different impacts on the operational and strategic decisions of the enterprise, depending on the core function of the AI system. When used to make predictions on strategic enterprise dimensions (investments, optimal production quantities), it has a very high impact on decisions and relative outcomes. Accordingly, as a result of the presence of a bias, overproduction or underproduction could occur, in some cases, leading to a considerable loss of resources. When the AI artifact is implemented to enhance the performance of operations, it could represent an important resource even if it is biased, considering it can still make predictions that allow for saving time and resources (e.g., predict that a machine needs maintenance). In other words, the algorithm positively contributes to enhancing the processes. However, it cannot make predictions that take into account all the variables and the correlations beneath them. For example, this is an explanatory extract: "*In my previous job, I had to predict exactly the quantity to be produced with a 99% confidence interval because even a small error could result in a loss of market share. With our solution, even if we can initially predict the interventions to make with low accuracy, it still saves the company time, and the management is impressed because it allows them to save money*" (Diskover S.r.l.). Moreover, thanks to the work of the prompt manager and the learning capabilities of the algorithm, the AI artifact will be more and more accurate and reliable over time, improving the efficiency of the entire plant.

4.2 Potential Bias Emerging from the Society (Relative to Systemic Bias)

The interviews reveal an emerging awareness of the increasing societal issues deriving from AI [15, 23]. In the past, the research mainly focused on inspecting AI from a technical point of view, enhancing its performance and reliability, and finding possible application fields. Nowadays, AI artifacts are more popular and useful thanks to improved techniques, the availability of vast amounts of data, and computational capabilities [24]. The increased use of AI has led to an increased sensitivity to social and ethical problems such as work replacement, discrimination, and social inequality [3, 6]. Hence, AI has two principal components: procedural and emotional. From a procedural point of view, management works to implement this technology inside the operation by adjusting and modifying the processes (flow of communications, information management, internal procedures), as emerged from the case of Oltrematica S.r.l.: "*This technological shift affects roles, responsibilities, and competencies*". From an emotional point of view, AI implementation often leads to some forms of employee resistance and worries [25]. Everyone has a different attitude towards change, depending on various factors (e.g., age, culture, education). In this scenario, the managers must cope with difficult challenges. Firstly, they must understand the benefits of the digital transition and help raise awareness among employees about the opportunity they will have after the AI implementation, avoiding possible contrasting behaviors. For example, in the case of Oltrematica S.r.l., it was claimed that: "*Managers must not only implement technology within the company but also have it accepted by the employees through an approach that can be bottom-up or top-down*".

Other factors could also impact the correct implementation of AI technology; for example, it could revolutionize the sector in which it is implemented, causing a "*closure*" for individuals working within. This adversity could be due to many factors, such as fear of replacement and lack of trust. That is, people external to the company that adopts an AI system could additionally hinder the use of the technology and engage in opposing behaviors that could be explicit or implicit. That is: "*We can take the example of a company operating in the legal sector with whom we worked. After implementing our system, which could predict the outcome of lawsuits, the Italian Lawyers' Association tried to oppose this solution in every way. Something similar happened with the introduction of Uber in Italy and the taxi driver associations*" (Oltrematica S.r.l.).

In this scenario, the company that supplies the AI artifact must rethink the implementation process, not the objective. More specifically, when facing some kind of resistance, more resources (e.g., communication, financial) are needed to sensitize the stakeholders to see the technology shift as an opportunity to augment the work, not as a menace. This effort is required for different reasons. First, it is necessary to reduce the adoption time and enhance the outcome of the project. Second, it could be an opportunity to find new customers willing to implement AI in their activities. For example, it was stated that: "*More work must certainly be done, gathering alliances or partnerships that were not previously foreseen. Biases often bring higher adoption costs but can be an opportunity to build new relationships*" (Oltrematica S.r.l.).

Beside such preliminary description, in Table 4, we present an initial coding of the data obtained from the interviews [26]. This table reports the concepts expressed by the interviewees, along with their absolute frequency (A.f.), highlighting relevant aspects that we subsequently categorized into distinct themes. These themes were then classified into four primary categories based on decision level and the nature of AI bias. This further step provides a structured analysis of the interview data and an understanding of the different dimensions of AI bias and their impact on decision-making processes.

5 Discussion

This work-in-progress research presents a preliminary analysis concerning AI bias by exploring how entrepreneurs perceive and address AI issues in their companies, as well as in the external environment.

Drawing on the data we gathered during the preliminary interviews, we then attempted to develop a matrix summarizing the potential interaction between the two main variables analyzed (as emerged in Table 4). Specifically, we consider the level of the decision shifting from operational to strategical to be assigned to the y-axis and the nature of AI bias (i.e., technical to social) to the x-axis. Accordingly,

Table 4 The data structure of the coding analysis

First order concepts	A.f.	Themes	Macro-themes
Inefficiencies	3	Operative shortcomings	Operational decision-making
Productivity loss	2		
Unnecessary or missed maintenance	1		
Roles and competences	3	AI impact on operations and work	
Employees training	2		
New professional roles	1		
Exploitation of opportunities	4	Strategic communication	Strategical decision-making
Forming alliances	1		
Internal and external communication	3		
Redefinition of strategies	2	Process management	
Process innovation and restructuring	3		
Reputational risks	3	Strategical shortcomings	
Loss of market share	1		
Financial loss	2		
Communication issues	2	Internal and communication challenges	AI social bias
Opposing behaviors	1		
Resistance to AI	1		
Cultural aversion	3		
Institutional resistance	1	Institutional challenges	
Legal issues	1		
Protests	1		
Influence of past data	2	Systemic shortcomings	
Data processing and validation	1	AI design and development	AI technical bias
Algorithmic training and monitoring	2		
Process structure	1		
Forecast issues	3	AI technical challenges	
AI Solution accuracy	1		
Hidden correlations	1		
Techniques of optimization	2		

it is possible to identify four different quadrants from this matrix. To instantiate our proposed framework, we provide a practical example by associating some evidence that emerged from the cases analyzed within each quadrant. This attempt would offer further insights, serve as an initial classification of cases, and identify potential clusters representative of certain organizations. Hence, in Fig. 2, we report the exemplification cases we analyzed for each quadrant, highlighting the possible negative outcomes that could verify if AI bias is present (see Fig. 2). In addition, we

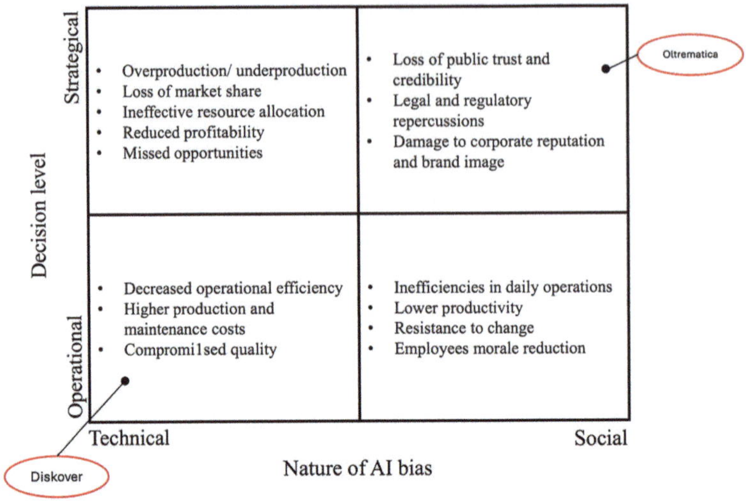

Fig. 2 A framework for evaluating negative outcomes based on the decision level and the nature of AI bias

describe each quadrant and propose potential mitigation strategies according to the literature and the data we gathered from the interviews.

Upper Right Quadrant This quadrant represents the cases where the decision-making level is strategic, and the nature of bias is social, highlighting a significant risk of repercussions from both the external and internal environments. Protests or legal actions could arise, potentially undermining the company's reputation, stakeholder trust, and market position. These consequences could lead to resource loss and some challenges, such as impacting the organization's long-term sustainability and success. Focusing on the interviews, a reported example is the resistance by sector associations toward a company deciding to implement an AI system. This opposition can hinder the technological transition, potentially stalling innovation and progress within the industry.

In such cases, organizations or users should actively engage with opposing entities to demonstrate the potential benefits of the AI solution. Additionally, an approach that emphasizes transparency in both communication and the functioning of the AI artifact while adopting appropriate ethical and fairness frameworks can significantly enhance trust among various internal and external stakeholders [21, 27]. Implementing specific guidelines designed to achieve these objectives can improve overall outcomes and ensure compliance with ethical and fairness standards [14].

Upper Left Quadrant This quadrant represents the cases in which accuracy is essential as decisions are made at the managerial and strategic levels. In this configuration, technical bias in algorithms, arising from errors in data selection or processing or the use of an inappropriate algorithm, can lead to misleading decisions. These decisions can result in a loss of market share and resources, affecting stakeholders negatively. For instance, consider a company's decision on production levels for the upcoming year. If the AI algorithm fails to meet production requirements, the consequences could include overproduction, leading to a surplus and subsequent price reduction. Conversely, underproduction could drive customers to switch to similar or substitute products, resulting in a loss of market share.

Addressing these issues includes a strong focus on technical solutions. Given that related challenges primarily refer to computational shortcomings within the data or the algorithms used to train the AI solution, users should adopt effective bias mitigation techniques. This task includes ensuring that data is adequately cleaned, processed, and validated to avoid underrepresentation or imbalance [28]. Additionally, algorithms must be carefully selected and validated through continuous benchmarking activities [5]. During this phase, technical mitigation techniques suitable for the specific data and methods of the AI artifacts should be employed, in addition to continuous monitoring routines that enable the highest reliability and accuracy of the artifact.

Lower Left Quadrant This quadrant represents the cases in which, concerning operational decisions, a high level of bias inside the algorithm could result in failed predictions (i.e., maintenance when is not needed, missed maintenance when is needed), resulting in loss of money and time. For instance, an algorithm that fails to identify all correlations within a specific system may struggle to recognize the occurrence of a particular event, leading to prediction errors. This lack of accurate correlation detection can compromise the reliability of the algorithm's predictions and potentially result in significant operational inefficiencies.

In this situation, organizations and users should consider to employ domain experts and dedicated professionals. These professionals should work alongside the AI solution to provide continuous monitoring and training, ensuring the ongoing improvement of the algorithm and its outcomes. Their expertise is apt for reducing possible errors and enhancing the accuracy and effectiveness of predictions and error signals. Additionally, to achieve highly accurate simulations, uncertainty and complexity in manufacturing complex systems should be properly managed [29]. By leveraging specialized knowledge and continuous oversight, organizations can significantly improve the reliability and precision of their AI solutions, ultimately leading to better efficiency and cost reduction.

Lower Right Quadrant This quadrant represents the cases where operational decisions influenced by social bias, both implicit and explicit opposing behaviors may emerge, potentially disrupting the company's workflow and causing dissatisfaction and fear among employees. For example, employees may be reluctant to utilize an AI solution, leading to resistance and inefficiencies in the implementation process. This resistance can hinder the adoption of new technologies, create friction within teams, and ultimately impact the overall productivity and morale of the workforce.

Addressing these challenges includes communicating and demonstrating the AI solution to the workforce effectively, such as introducing comprehensive employee training programs in such a process. Organizations must ensure that employees are well-equipped to collaborate with AI systems by providing thorough training programs and the necessary tools to understand and manage the implemented solutions. This approach fosters an appropriate level of control and trust, ultimately enhancing the integration and acceptance of AI technologies within the company [30].

To summarize, starting from the data gathered in the interview process, we have started recognizing the potential negative outcomes that can arise from various types of AI bias at different decision levels. At the same time, we have proposed potential mitigation strategies that can effectively address these biases and contribute to designing and developing more reliable and fair AI systems. Furthermore, these techniques underscore the importance of a socio-technical approach, emphasizing the pivotal role of human involvement in the design, development, and deployment of AI systems [14].

Besides, we also highlighted the positions of the two analyzed cases into a framework (see Fig. 2) that we developed intending to support managers in evaluating negative outcomes based on the decision level and the nature of AI bias (based on the preliminary data acquired during the interviews. As a result, Diskover S.r.l. focuses on developing and enhancing its algorithm to counter bias in operational contexts, such as manufacturing plants. In contrast, Oltrematica S.r.l. appears more concerned with addressing institutional and social issues that could undermine its market presence.

The analysis of the interviews and the development of such a matrix-based framework highlights a clear distinction in how AI bias is classified across different sectors, as illustrated by the examples provided by the interviewees. Specifically, we observed disparities between the legal sector, which uses technology less intensively and primarily focuses on the social aspects of AI bias, and the manufacturing sector, which requires a high intensity of technology and predominantly concentrates on technical aspects of AI bias. In the preliminary analysis, we chose not to delve deeper into these distinctions due to potential misinterpretations stemming from the varying backgrounds of the entrepreneurs and the limited data available. However, as a next step, we plan to incorporate an examination of the intensity level of technology as a third dimension in our matrix to enhance understanding of how sector-specific factors influence AI bias.

6 Conclusion

This work represents a preliminary step of a broader project intended to examine the entrepreneur's perception of AI bias in the products their companies design and develop. To this end, we started developing multiple case analyses by performing two pilot interviews with the CEOs of two Italian companies focused on the development of AI artifacts. We used the NIST framework concerning the categorization of AI bias [14] to analyze the data gathered from the interviews. Interestingly, although preliminary and limited, results show two approaches to interpreting the bias. The first approach is more focused on the bias that could be detected inside the algorithm or the data of the AI artifact (computational bias). In comparison, the second approach is more related to bias that arises within society (systemic bias). Concerning computational bias, the main aim of the company was to iteratively train the artifact in order to enhance its performance and reliability. Systemic bias, instead, required more attention from the communication sphere to sensitize all stakeholders to the opportunities the new technologies bring. From this perspective, such assumptions lay the groundwork for further reasoning on the fact that there could be patterns, emergencies, or a lack of awareness concerning AI biases among entrepreneurs (and managers) of small and medium-sized enterprises in Italy.

From a theoretical point of view, we provide an empirical case exploiting the NIST framework that contributes to advancing research on AI bias and their perception inside Italian organizations. The debate on such a domain has developed over the last 4 years, and more research is needed to investigate possible issues arising from AI design, development, and implementation. Moreover, the proposed matrix could be helpful for mapping the different nature of a bias and whether and how it affects various decision levels of an organization. Drawing on such assumptions, our discussions show that adopting and using a socio-technical approach is functional to mitigate AI bias and ensure fairness in AI solutions.

From a practical point of view, this contribution could help entrepreneurs and managers become more aware of the different kinds of bias they could encounter when dealing with AI systems inside their company. There aren't only internal difficulties and challenges that arise from the external environment. That is, AI bias could impact many spheres of the organization. Some examples could be made by taking into account the legal sphere and the issues that arise concerning AI norms that are still lacking. Technical problems are not to be underestimated as well, especially at the managerial and strategic levels, considering they could lead to serious damages at the financial and human resource levels. Finally, ethical and societal issues are becoming central to the AI debate, and managers, policymakers and designers of AI artifacts will have to address increasingly common awareness that AI could amplify and challenge aspects such as social inequality, lack of trust, privacy concerns, and discrimination.

This work presents some limitations. Considering the number of interviews and cases analyzed, this research is restricted in the generalizability of the results, also challenging the possibility of elaborating and proposing a comprehensive conceptual framework (aimed to conceptualize our findings). Accordingly, in further research steps, we could increase the sample taken into account by conducting more structured interviews (also increasing the number of interviews for the same company), eventually developing more rigorous and robust research. To this end, we will use these preliminary interviews as a foundation to refine and expand our semi-structured questionnaire, ensuring broader coverage of AI bias topics. At the same time, we could further develop the theoretical background to provide a more robust context for our study (for example, we could adopt additional perspectives and theoretical groundwork in addition to the socio-technical lens adopted in this study).

More specifically, we aim to leverage the network of Confindustria to engage with firms that are actively engaged in both the development and application of AI solutions. This collaborative project will entail conducting comprehensive interviews with various companies to investigate the implications of AI bias, particularly considering recent regulatory frameworks and guidelines, including the European AI Act. The latter legislation represents one of the most comprehensive frameworks for regulating AI design, development, and usage.[2] Thus, our research will focus on assessing the impact of these regulations within these firms concerning bias mitigation. We are supposed to examine the operational and strategic changes experienced by both developers and users subsequent to the Act's enactment. Besides, based on the findings from our study, it would be interesting to establish a discussion on non-EU legislation regarding AI bias. This discourse could consider the insights gained from our interviews to evaluate the comparative effectiveness and scope of international regulatory approaches to AI bias. It could then be used as a starting point for other comparative analyses.

Moreover, our long-term ambition is to expand and enrich such research, focusing on the influence of the manager's background and the influence of the vision and mission of a company in perceiving AI bias (in addition to providing a more generalizable set of findings). From our initial analysis, we observed a significant variation in how AI bias is classified based on the entrepreneur's background. Since these preliminary findings are not comprehensive, we also plan to delve deeper into how diverse entrepreneurial backgrounds affect the detection and subsequent mitigation of AI bias.

Disclosure of Interests The authors have no competing interests to declare that are relevant to the content of this article.

References

1. Shobana, V., & Kumar, N. (2015). Big data—A review. *International Journal of Applied Engineering Research, 10*, 1294–1298. https://doi.org/10.26634/jit.6.1.13507
2. Collins, C., Dennehy, D., Conboy, K., & Mikalef, P. (2021). Artificial intelligence in information systems research: A systematic literature review and research agenda. *International Journal of Information Management, 60*, 102383. https://doi.org/10.1016/j.ijinfomgt.2021.102383
3. Huang, M. H., & Rust, R. T. (2018). Artificial intelligence in service. *Journal of Service Research, 21*, 155–172. https://doi.org/10.1177/1094670517752459
4. Hunkenschroer, A. L., & Luetge, C. (2022). Ethics of AI-enabled recruiting and selection: A review and research agenda. *Journal of Business Ethics*. https://doi.org/10.1007/s10551-022-05049-6
5. Mehrabi, N., Morstatter, F., Saxena, N., Lerman, K., & Galstyan, A. (2021). A survey on bias and fairness in machine learning. *ACM Computing Surveys, 54*(6), 1–35. https://doi.org/10.1145/3457607

[2] European Commission, The EU Artificial Intelligence Act: Up-to-date developments and analyses of the EU AI Act. URL: https://artificialintelligenceact.eu/ (Retrieved on: 16/08/2024).

6. Hoffmann, A. L. (2019). Where fairness fails: data, algorithms, and the limits of antidiscrimination discourse. *Information, Communication & Society, 22*, 900–915. https://doi.org/10.1080/1369118X.2019.1573912
7. Zuiderwijk, A., Chen, Y. C., & Salem, F. (2021). Implications of the use of artificial intelligence in public governance: A systematic literature review and a research agenda. *Government Information Quarterly, 38*. https://doi.org/10.1016/j.giq.2021.101577
8. Ntoutsi, E., Fafalios, P., Gadiraju, U., Iosifidis, V., Nejdl, W., Vidal, M. E., Ruggieri, S., Turini, F., Papadopoulos, S., Krasanakis, E., Kompatsiaris, I., Kinder-Kurlanda, K., Wagner, C., Karimi, F., Fernandez, M., Alani, H., Berendt, B., Kruegel, T., Heinze, C., ... , Staab, S. (2020). Bias in data-driven artificial intelligence systems—An introductory survey. *Wiley Interdisciplinary Reviews: Data Mining and Knowledge Discovery 10*, 1–14. https://doi.org/10.1002/widm.1356.
9. Haenlein, M., Huang, M. H., & Kaplan, A. (2022). Guest editorial: Business ethics in the era of artificial intelligence. *Journal of Business Ethics*. https://doi.org/10.1007/s10551-022-05060-x
10. D'Cruz, P., Du, S., Noronha, E., Parboteeah, K. P., Trittin-Ulbrich, H., & Whelan, G. (2022). Technology, megatrends and work: Thoughts on the future of business ethics. *Journal of Business Ethics, 180*, 879–902. https://doi.org/10.1007/s10551-022-05240-9
11. Makarius, E. E., Mukherjee, D., Fox, J. D., & Fox, A. K. (2020). Rising with the machines: A sociotechnical framework for bringing artificial intelligence into the organization. *Journal of Business Research, 120*, 262–273. https://doi.org/10.1016/J.JBUSRES.2020.07.045
12. Dignum, V. (2018). Ethics in artificial intelligence: introduction to the special issue. *Ethics and Information Technology, 20*, 1–3. https://doi.org/10.1007/s10676-018-9450-z
13. Akter, S., McCarthy, G., Sajib, S., Michael, K., Dwivedi, Y. K., D'Ambra, J., & Shen, K. N. (2021). Algorithmic bias in data-driven innovation in the age of AI. *International Journal of Information Management*. https://doi.org/10.1016/j.ijinfomgt.2021.102387
14. Schwartz, R., Vassilev, A., Greene, K., Perine, L., Burt, A., & Hall, P. (2022). *Towards a standard for identifying and managing bias in artificial intelligence*. US Department of Commerce, National Institute of Standards and Technology. 3. https://doi.org/10.6028/NIST.SP.1270.
15. Smacchia, M., & Za, S. (2023). Exploring artificial intelligence bias, fairness and ethics in organisation and managerial studies. In *ECIS 2023 research papers* (p. 362).
16. Dignum, V. (2023). Responsible artificial intelligence-from principles to practice: A keynote at TheWebConf 2022. In *ACM SIGIR Forum, New York* (pp. 1–6).
17. Someh, I., Davern, M., Breidbach, C. F., & Shanks, G. (2019). Ethical issues in big data analytics: A stakeholder perspective. *Communications of the Association for Information Systems., 44*, 718–747. https://doi.org/10.17705/1CAIS.04434
18. Kordzadeh, N., & Ghasemaghaei, M. (2022). Algorithmic bias: review, synthesis, and future research directions. *European Journal of Information Systems, 31*, 388–409. https://doi.org/10.1080/0960085X.2021.1927212
19. Sarker, S., Chatterjee, S., Xiao, X., & Elbanna, A. (2019). The sociotechnical axis of cohesion for the IS discipline: Its historical legacy and its continued relevance. *MIS Quarterly, 43*, 695–719. https://doi.org/10.25300/MISQ/2019/13747
20. Mikalef, P., Conboy, K., Lundström, J. E., & Popovič, A. (2022). Thinking responsibly about responsible AI and 'the dark side' of AI. *European Journal of Information Systems*. https://doi.org/10.1080/0960085X.2022.2026621
21. Floridi, L., Cowls, J., Beltrametti, M., Chatila, R., Chazerand, P., Dignum, V., Luetge, C., Madelin, R., Pagallo, U., Rossi, F., Schafer, B., Valcke, P., & Vayena, E. (2018). AI4People—An ethical framework for a good AI society: Opportunities, risks, principles, and recommendations. *Minds and Machines (Dordrecht), 28*, 689–707. https://doi.org/10.1007/s11023-018-9482-5
22. Yin, R. K. (2018). *Case study research and applications*. Sage.
23. Smacchia, M., & Za, S. (2022). Artificial intelligence in organisation and managerial studies: A computational literature review. In *ICIS 2022 proceedings* (Vol. 6, pp. 0–17).

24. Moore, P. V. (2019). Jerry Kaplan artificial intelligence: What everyone needs to know. *Organization Studies, 40*, 466–470. https://doi.org/10.1177/0170840618792173
25. Glikson, E., & Woolley, A. W. (2020). Human trust in artificial intelligence: Review of empirical research. *Academy of Management Annals, 14*, 627–660. https://doi.org/10.5465/annals.2018.0057
26. Corbin, J. M., & Strauss, A. (1990). Grounded theory research: Procedures, canons, and evaluative criteria. *Qualitative Sociology, 13*, 3–21. https://doi.org/10.1007/BF00988593
27. Diakopoulos, N. (2016). Accountability in algorithmic decision making. *Communications of the ACM, 59*, 56–62. https://doi.org/10.1145/2844110
28. Suresh, H., & Guttag, J. V. (2019). A framework for understanding sources of harm throughout the machine learning life cycle. In *EAAMO '21: Proceedings of the 1st ACM conference on equity and access in algorithms, mechanisms, and optimization*. https://doi.org/10.1145/3465416.3483305.
29. Lee, J., Wu, F., Zhao, W., Ghaffari, M., Liao, L., & Siegel, D. (2014). Prognostics and health management design for rotary machinery systems—Reviews, methodology and applications. *Mechanical Systems and Signal Processing, 42*, 314–334. https://doi.org/10.1016/j.ymssp.2013.06.004
30. Burr, C., Taddeo, M., & Floridi, L. (2020). The ethics of digital well-being: A thematic review. *Science and Engineering Ethics*. https://doi.org/10.1007/s11948-020-00175-8

(Ir)Responsible Uses of Digital Technologies in Business Education. Interruptions or Engagement?

Leonardo Caporarello, Massimo Magni, and Iuliia Trabskaia

Abstract The study addresses a crucial question regarding the (ir)responsible use of digital technology in education. By "responsible use of technology," we refer to an approach that integrates technology into the educational process, carefully considering its impacts (both positive and negative) on the state of the educational process's stakeholders. To gauge the extent of responsible technology use in education, this research contrasts digital technology's positive and negative effects in business education settings. Furthermore, we focused on the student-centered perspective since students are major stakeholders in education.

The paper utilizes a survey of students (n = 285) and applies partial least squares structural equation modelling (PLS-SEM).

The results confirm that digital technology in business education context has a dual effect. On one hand, digital technology enhances engagement; on the other hand, it increases the level of distraction. The engagement has then a positive impact on task performance, while the link from distraction to task performance is positive and not statistically significant. This supports our perspective that technology exerts a complex and multifaceted impact. We argue that responsible use of technology necessitates studying and accounting for these diverse effects.

The research attempts to extend the framework of responsible use of technology by deepening understanding of digital technology's impact on student performance. Furthermore, the study compared the positive and negative impacts of digital technology use. Lastly, we explore the phenomenon in business education settings.

Keywords Digital technologies · Interruptions · Engagement · Task performance · Business education

L. Caporarello (✉)
SDA Bocconi School of Management, Bocconi University, Milan, Italy

Department of Management and Technology, Bocconi University, Milan, Italy
e-mail: leonardo.caporarello@unibocconi.it

M. Magni · I. Trabskaia
SDA Bocconi School of Management, Bocconi University, Milan, Italy

M. Cipriano et al. (eds.), *Technologies for Organizations and Society*,
Lecture Notes in Information Systems and Organisation 80,
https://doi.org/10.1007/978-3-032-01697-3_20

1 Introduction

Today, digital technologies have become an essential part of our lives. In this vein, the past decade has seen rapid advances in the role played by digital technology in education [1–3]. The COVID-19 lockdown pushed universities to implement digital innovation. During the pandemic period, universities had no choice but to apply technology-driven innovation to continue the educational process and communicate with students and colleagues [4, 5]. However, in the post-COVID period, the question has arisen regarding the extent to which digital technologies should remain an important part of education [6]. Digital technologies, along with benefits, pose new risks [7]. This raises the question of how to draw the line between responsible and irresponsible use of digital technologies. Too often, the primary motivation for adopting new technologies into the educational process is to adopt modern trends, stay competitive, or create an image of an innovative university. However, the effects on the stakeholders of educational process are frequently overlooked. Therefore, the authors of this study define responsible use of technology as the implementation of technological innovations, with careful consideration of their impact on stakeholders. Accordingly, by irresponsible use of technology, we refer to the opposite situation, where the introduction of technology into the educational process does not take into account the reactions and behaviour of stakeholders. Thus, the introduction of technology should contribute to the sustainable development of education [8]. The responsible use of technology must be human-centered, and student responses must be considered to understand whether digital technology positively contributes to the student learning process. The student is a key stakeholder in the education system and a consumer of the educational product; therefore, the student-centric view is relevant for analyzing the impact of digital processes on education [9].

Despite the debate, most of the existing literature emphasizes the positive impacts of digital technologies on education (e.g., [10–12]). In contrast, significantly fewer studies have explored the negative effects (e.g., [13–16]). Furthermore, comparing the positive and negative effects of technologies' adoption are almost ignored. Additionally, previous studies have mostly focused on the impact of individual technologies on the educational process. For instance, scholars explored the effect of mobile technology (e.g., [17–19]); the AI-education link (e.g., [20–22]), the augmented reality impact on the educational process [23, 24]. In contrast, we propose to examine the overall impact of technologies. By "overall impact of technologies," we refer to the aggregate of all technologies that influence the educational process. Indeed, today's technologies are deeply integrated into both education and our daily lives. These technologies are intertwined and exert their influence not in isolation but collectively. This interconnectedness explains the focus of our research on the overall impact of technology.

So far, in this study, we aim to close the shortcomings of the previous literature and better understand the (ir)responsible use of technology by contrasting the positive and negative impacts of digital technology in business education settings. We observe technology use through the lens of Affordance Theory since it provides relevant framework for understanding the motivations for technology use. Furthermore, engagement represents the positive impact of digital technology, showing how technologies can improve students' experience and stimulate their involvement. On the other hand, destruction represents the negative effect of digital technologies and shows how technology takes away students' attention and interrupts their primary tasks. So far, the research examines the following questions: (1) How does digital technology impact students' engagement and destruction? (2) How does digital technology influence task performance? (3) Is there a mediating role between student engagement and distractions about technology use and task performance? Additionally, we aim to apply a holistic approach to technology use and measure its overall impact.

The structure of the paper is as follows: We begin with a literature review on how digital technology use shapes students' performance. This is followed by a methodological part. We proceed with results on the effect of digital technology use on students' performance, moderated by students' engagement and destruction. Finally, the paper ends with a concluding section that summarizes and discusses the study's key findings.

2 Theoretical Foundation

Affordance Theory is widely used in the study of the effects of technology and human-computer interaction. The concept originated from the field of ecology and was later introduced to analyze the technology-user relationship [25]. In human-computer interaction, Affordance Theory focuses on the action possibilities provided by the object [26] and explains how technologies are selected and used. Despite the relatively long history and significant interest it has garnered, discussions about the meaning of the phenomenon of affordances and the application of the theory persist [27]. In general, as Caws and Hamel [28] observed, the various perspectives on the essence of affordance generally align with either cognitivist or post-cognitivist viewpoints. The cognitivist perspective holds to the view of affordance as attributes of technologies. A post-cognitivist perspective focusing on the interaction between the technology and the user. We adopt a post-cognitivist perspective, believing that true affordance emerges only through interaction with technology; it is shaped by the dynamic relationship between the user and the technology. This approach to Affordance Theory also allows for the consideration of the social context surrounding this interaction. Therefore, based on this understanding, affordances can be defined as a combination of the actual and perceived properties of an object that determine how it can be used in the process of technology-user interaction [25].

Karahanna et al. [29] further developed Affordance Theory in the context of technology use by proposing a needs-affordances-features framework. This approach compels us to consider why people use technology by emphasizing how physiological needs influence user behavior. According to this approach, physiological needs influence perceptions of technology use if the technology is able to satisfy these needs (needs for autonomy, relatedness, competence, having a place, and self-identity [29]. Thus, for example, certain technologies are perceived positively and used because they satisfy physiological needs for self-identity (e.g., FB), relatedness (mobile technologies, communication platforms), and so on.

Clearly, physiological needs are unique to everyone, making this framework broadly applicable. In the context of studying the responsible use of technology, Affordance Theory is particularly relevant, as it considers how physiological needs (related to a person's overall well-being) influence their interaction with technology. By doing so, we emphasize the various actions that technology facilitates within a learning environment.

3 Literature Review and Hypothesis Development

Digital technologies have profoundly influenced the educational landscape [1, 30], shaped student-educator communication models [31, 32], learning outcomes [33, 34], design of educational systems and curriculum [35–37]. Ever-evolving digital technologies have unfolded new horizons and impacted universities and the overall future of education [6, 30].

The introduction of digital technology in education, a relatively new phenomenon, raises problem of (ir)responsible use of technology. By responsible use of technology, we refer to a deliberate approach to introducing technologies that considers the responses of educational stakeholders and carefully consider the positive and negative effects that digital technologies may bring to the educational process.

Despite the high interest in the topic, the issue of (ir)responsible use of digital technology in education and comparing positive and negative effects remains controversial. Scholars mainly examine the positive impact of digital technologies on education. For instance, Kearney and Maakrun [10] posit that 95% of contributions to the Australasian Journal of Educational Technology centre around extolling the advantages of technologies on the educational process. Undoubtedly, digital technologies bring many favourable trends in education. Technologies empower students to increase autonomy and enhance self-regulated learning [38, 39], enable students to independently manage the allocation of study time [40]. Moreover, digital technologies promote collaboration in the learning process [12, 41], serve as a driver for transformations in the academic landscape [42], increase the accessibility of education [43], create personal learning environments [37, 38].

Considering the positive impact of digital technologies on education from a student-centered perspective, an important mechanism is increase of student engagement through digital technologies. Engagement is broadly understood as the increase of motivation, activity, and participation (e.g., [44]). Overall, incorporating digital technology into the learning process can make it more exciting and interactive, further enhancing engagement; for instance, business education can be different business simulation games. Thus, we hypothesize:

H1: Digital technology use positively influences students' engagement

In turn, engagement leads to increased academic performance [45]. When a student is engaged, spends more time on education, and invests cognitive and emotional resources in education, this leads to increased task performance [46]. Thus, in line with previous studies, we assume that:

H2: Engagement positively influences task performance

Returning to digital technologies, we should underline that along with the bright side of digital technology in the context of education, it also provides adverse effects (e.g., [47]). For instance, digital technologies may be associated with a sense of isolation [48]. Among the negative effects of digital technologies on education is that technologies may trigger disruptive interruptions [11] and require time for recovery [49]. The introduction of digital technologies does not automatically lead to its effective application in the context of the learning process [6]. Students can see introduced technologies as an entertainment element, distracting from acquiring new knowledge [50].

Brady, Kim and Cutshall [51] noted that integrating technology into the learning process is an intense distraction that affect learning outcomes. So far, one of the significant negative effects of using digital technology is interruptions. Overall, we hypothesize that:

H3: Digital technology use positively influences distraction

The disruptive nature of interruptions and their negative impacts is debated [47, 52]. For instance, cognitive and emotional dimensions of interruptions have been explored across diverse contexts —work environments (e.g., [53]), personal lives (e.g., [54]), educational settings (e.g., [55–57]). Interruptions have negative effect, and can lead to the loss of time, the reduction of memory functions [58–60], negative emotions [61, 62], decrease of satisfaction [49, 63] and raise of stress levels [64, 65].

Although interruptions have many negative implications, it is also essential to consider the possible positive effects. Several studies have reported that interruptions enhance mental agility and efficiency [62, 66]. Furthermore, interruptions can lead to the development of the ability to quickly shift attention from one task to another [67]. Mochi and Madjar [66] noted that interruptions stimulate the development of creativity. Finally, following the cognitive load theory (e.g., [68]), using technology as a means of distraction and a change of activity allows for relaxation and reduces cognitive overload; it may foster greater performance reach through digital recreation. In turn, all the above factors contribute to increasing task performance. We follow a positive view on the effect of interruptions, and our hypothesis is that:

H4: Distraction positively influences task performance

Given the above, we suggest that digital technologies have both positive and negative effects on students' performance both indirectly through engagement (positive effect); through disruption (negative effect):

H5: Digital technology use has dual effect on task performance in business education settings

Further, there are several unexplored and controversial issues in the field of studying interruptions and their role in education. Various technologies have been examined as potential stimuli for interruptions in the context of education. Notably, researchers have delved into the impact of diverse technological tools, such as mobile phones [69], mobile blogs [25], social media [56, 70], and communication platforms [71]. Despite these individual explorations, there exists a lack of research addressing the collective influence of these technologies. (For instance, Dontre [72] investigates the effects of digital devices on student learning and academic performance, emphasizing the technological distractions posed by laptops, smartphones, and social media applications). The holistic approach is paramount as technologies exert their impact not in isolation (e.g., solely through emails or phone calls) but collectively and concurrently. Therefore, a comprehensive examination of this combined effect is imperative.

4 Methodology

4.1 Measurement of Constructs

The positive effect of using technology is measured as an increase in student engagement in the educational process stimulated by digital technology use and its further impact on task performance. The negative effect is measured as an increase in interruptions in the educational process stimulated by the use of digital technologies and the impact of interruptions on task performance, furthermore, we also estimate indirect impact of digital technology on task performance (Fig. 1).

When measuring technology use in the classroom as mentioned above, we were based on Affordance Theory. In doing so we focuses on the different actions that technology enables in the learning context (e.g., access learning material, looking for materials related to the class, upload class assignment, exchange emails).

We measure interruptions by looking at the degree to which the technology distracts the individual from the class main activity such as "During class, technology-based distractions (phone call, email, and messaging) distract my concentration in class". In particular we relied on a four-item scale.

Henrie, Halverson and Graham's [73] review highlighted a large body of publications on student engagement and various methods for measuring it. In our study, engagement was determined by vigour as vigour shows positive energy in the classroom. Specifically, we relied on four items in which individuals indicated their degree to which they felt across different adjectives such as energetic, vigorous, and active.

Since learning orientation reflects the individual performance in a learning process, we measured performance by relying on four items learning orientation

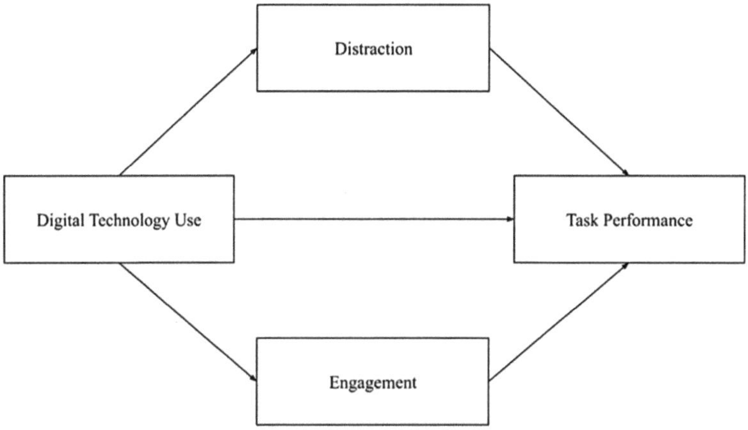

Fig. 1 The hypothesised model. Source: authors' own elaboration

scale adapted by Bunderson and Sutcliffe [74]. We used learning orientation because it may represent a proxy of "performance" in a learning environment.

Interruptions, engagement and learning orientation were measured using established scales, which have been adapted to fit the context. To catch technology use we applied the self-developed scale relying on the affordance theory which focus on the kind of activities that the technology enables). So, the studies using affordances most of the studies rely on self-developed scales based on the context.

All items were measured using a five-point Likert scale. Respondents were read a statement and were asked to evaluate the degree of agreement on a scale of 1–5, where 1 indicated 'Strongly disagree' and 5 'Strongly agree' or 1 'Non use' and 5 'Very heavy'.

4.2 Sampling and Data Collection

This study is based on a quantitative data collection method and utilizes standardized questionnaire. We collected data using an online questionnaire. The questionnaire was approved by the ethical committee of Bocconi University. Respondents are university students belonging to different degrees programs. Overall, we received 285 responses.

It is widely recognized that self-reported surveys have a problem when respondents attempt to give answers that are expected or considered as correct and desirable by the community [75]. To mitigate these risks, the survey was anonymized, and participants were warned that all responses are anonymous.

5 Data Analysis and Results

To address the research questions and estimate the theoretical model, partial least squares structural equation modeling (PLS-SEM) was utilized. This approach was selected for several reasons. First, PLS-SEM is causal-predictive approach that allow to "overcomes the apparent dichotomy between explanation—as typically emphasized in academic research—and prediction" ([76], p. 3). Second, PLS-SEM is a suitable method when the dataset is quite small, as in our case (298 observations). In addition, PLS-SEM is valuable for studies requiring the evaluation of complex models with numerous constructs and subconstructs, especially when variables can influence one another [76].

The results of the analysis are presented in Fig. 2. The model has supported the first hypothesis regarding the positive and statistically significant relationship between digital technology use and students' engagement ($\beta = 0.325$, $p < 0.001$). Statistical results also confirm the positive relationship between engagement and task performance ($\beta = 0.233$, $p < 0.001$). However, the link from distraction to task performance is positive and not statistically significant ($\beta = 0.071$; $p = 0.361$). Results confirm the fourth hypothesis, the analysis demonstrates the positive and statistically significant relationship between digital technology use and distraction ($\beta = 0.272$, $p < 0.001$). We partly confirmed the fifth hypothesis, according to which digital technology use positively and statistically significant impact task performance ($\beta = 0.095$, $p < 0.001$). We did not observe any negative or dual impacts of digital technologies on task performance in business education settings.

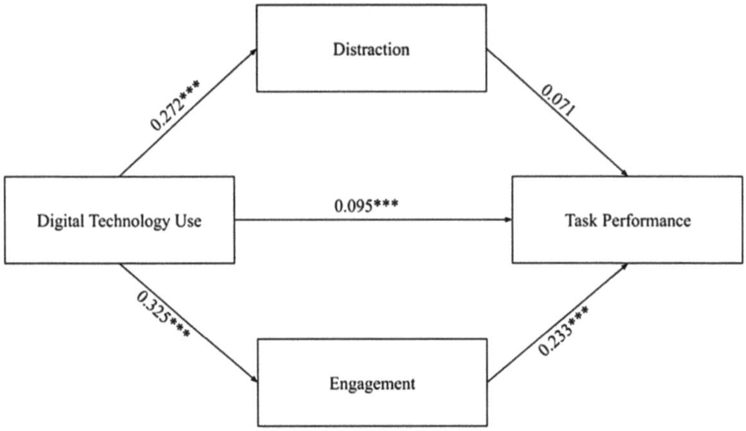

Fig. 2 The structural model. Source: authors' calculations based on the online survey results. Notes: Cronbach's alpha of the variables were above the suggested threshold of .7, suggesting good reliability of our scales

6 Conclusion and Discussion

The study helps to understand how to consider the reactions of the key stakeholder in education (students) in order to implement responsible use of technology.

We contribute to the ongoing discussions on the role of digital technologies in business education, including their effects on students' performances. Our findings are based on a survey of students conducted in Italy. The data allowed us to shed light on the importance of using digital technology as a stimulus for interruptions and engagement, which in turn affect task performance. This creates a valuable tool that allows for considering students' opinions when implementing technologies, making the use of technology more responsible.

Our results supported the hypothesis that digital technology use positively influences students' engagement. Thus, in line with previous studies (e.g., [44]) we believe that technology increases students' motivation, makes the educational process more interesting and thus increases engagement. Also, in line with previous studies [45, 46] we confirmed the relationship between engagement and task performance. Thus, a student who is engaged tends to have a more positive outlook on education, which increases their motivation and interest in the material. As a result, the student spends more time studying, which ultimately has a positive impact on task performance.

A special focus is placed on interruptions; the novelty of this research lies in the fact that we look at interruptions impact in a nuanced way, both positive and negative. In the discussion about negative and positive effects of distractions, we found the positive (and not statistically significant) effect of distraction on task performance. That contrasts with researchers that reported negative effects of distraction on task performance [61, 62, 77]. This result (positive impact of distraction on task performance) is somewhat unexpected, as we initially hypothesized that digital technologies would perform a dual effect. However, these findings align with a body of research that highlights the positive effects of digital technologies [62, 66, 67]. The presence of solely positive effects of digital technologies on task performance can be attributed to several factors. For instance, when considering technologies as a source of interruptions, they may also contribute to a range of positive outcomes, such as enhancing creativity, reducing cognitive overload, and increasing efficiency.

Furthermore, the positive and negative impacts of using digital technology were compared, which is another novel aspect of the study. As we mentioned earlier, most researchers tend to focus either on the negative or positive effects of technology. However, it is extremely rare to compare both effects. This approach allows for a comprehensive assessment of the impact of technology on student behavior.

Moreover, in contrast with previous studies [56, 68, 78] we consider the overall impact of digital technologies, without highlighting the impact of individual technologies. So, if previous studies consider it important to evaluate the effect on education of individual technologies, e.g., mobile technology [18] the AI [21], the augmented [23, 24], social media [79]. It is extremely important to consider the comprehensive impact of all technologies. Today, in both everyday life and education, technologies are highly pervasive, interconnected, and no longer exist in isolation. As a result, technologies exert their influence in a collective manner, and isolating their effects based on individual types of technology seems somewhat artificial. We believe it is fundamentally important to analyze the overall impact of technology, as this approach allows for a more comprehensive understanding of the phenomenon of technology and its responsible use in education.

In terms of practical implications, first, educational managers can develop strategies of education by considering the positive and negative effects of digital technologies. Thus, we propose an applied tool for assessing the impact of technologies on students and, consequently, for the responsible use of technologies. Second, the results have implications for educators, as teachers can consider the impact of technology as an engaging element of the educational experience.

The study has several limitations. We consider the impact of digital technologies on students' performance; however, we did not examine the impact of digital technologies on students' outcomes and well-being. Furthermore, different types of tasks in terms of tasks complexity and characteristics (e.g., routine and creative tasks) were overlooked. Finally, our data also has some limitations; since we consider the phenomenon in the context of business education only, it would be interesting to test whether the level of education influences the studied phenomenon. Additionally, we analyzed the phenomenon from the student's perspective, but adopting a multi-stakeholder approach in future studies would be valuable. This would involve assessing the positive and negative impacts of digital technologies from the viewpoints of various business education stakeholders (including professors, industry partners, administrative staff, students of continuing education programs, etc.). Also, a further direction for research could involve exploring models and approaches that effectively account for both the positive and negative effects of integrating technology into education. Another direction for future research is to conduct a comparative analysis of which technologies stimulate engagement and which lead to interruptions.

Acknowledgements This publication was developed within the MUSA—Multilayered Urban Sustainability Action—project CUP B43D21011010006, funded by the European Union—NextGenerationEU, under the National Recovery and Resilience Plan (NRRP) Mission 4 Component 2 Investment Line 1.5: Strengthening of research structures and creation of R&D "innovation ecosystems", set up of "territorial leaders in R&D".

Disclosure of Interests The authors have no competing interests to declare that are relevant to the content of this article.

References

1. Alfaro, L., Rivera, C., Luna-Urquizo, J., Castaneda, E., Zuniga-Cueva, J., & Rivera-Chavez, M. (2021). New trends in e-technologies and e-learning. In *IEEE world conference on engineering education 2021, EDUNINE, Guatemala* (pp. 1–6). https://doi.org/10.1109/edunine51952.2021.9429120.

2. Bond, M., Zawacki-Richter, O., & Nichols, M. (2018). Revisiting five decades of educational technology research: A content and authorship analysis of the British Journal of Educational Technology. *British Journal of Educational Technology, 50*(1), 12–63. https://doi.org/10.1111/bjet.12730
3. De Oliveira, L. C., Guerino, G. C., De Oliveira, L. C., & Pimentel, A. R. (2022). Information and communication technologies in education 4.0 paradigm: a systematic mapping study. *Informatics in Education, 22*(1), 71–98. https://doi.org/10.15388/infedu.2023.03
4. Ng, D. T. K., Ching, A. C. H., & Law, S. W. (2023). Online learning in management education amid the pandemic: A bibliometric and content analysis. *The International Journal of Management Education, 21*(2), 100796. https://doi.org/10.1016/j.ijme.2023.100796
5. Vergara-Rodríguez, D., Antón-Sancho, Á., & Fernández-Arias, P. (2022). Variables influencing professors' adaptation to digital learning environments during the COVID-19 pandemic. *International Journal of Environmental Research and Public Health, 19*(6), 3732. https://doi.org/10.3390/ijerph19063732
6. Hannan, A. S. (2023). Development of digital transformation in higher education institutions. *Journal of Computer Science & Computational Mathematics, 13*(1), 1–8. https://doi.org/10.20967/jcscm.2023.01.001
7. Polly, D., Martin, F., & Guilbaud, T. C. (2021). Examining barriers and desired supports to increase faculty members' use of digital technologies: perspectives of faculty, staff and administrators. *Journal of Computing in Higher Education, 33*(1), 135–156. https://doi.org/10.1007/s12528-020-09259-7
8. Qureshi, M. I., Khan, N., Raza, H., Imran, A., & Ismail, F. (2021). Digital technologies in education 4.0. Does it enhance the effectiveness of learning? A systematic literature review. *International Journal of Interactive Mobile Technologies (IJIM), 15*(04), 31–47. https://doi.org/10.3991/ijim.v15i04.20291
9. Rajaram, K., & Rajaram, K. (2021). Student-centric learning: A transformation in the learning culture. In K. Rajaram (Ed.), *Evidence-based teaching for the 21st century classroom and beyond: Innovation-driven learning strategies* (pp. 175–198). Springer.
10. Kearney, S., & Maakrun, J. (2020). Let's get engaged: The nexus between digital technologies, engagement and learning. *Education Sciences, 10*(12), 357. https://doi.org/10.3390/educsci10120357
11. Orhan Göksün, D., & Gürsoy, G. (2019). Comparing success and engagement in gamified learning experiences via Kahoot and Quizizz. *Computers & Education, 135*, 15–29. https://doi.org/10.1016/j.compedu.2019.02.015
12. Pinto, M., & Leite, C. (2020). Digital technologies in support of students learning in higher education: Literature review. *Digital Education Review, 37*, 343–360. https://doi.org/10.1344/der.2020.37.343-360
13. Addas, S., & Pinsonneault, A. (2015). The many faces of information technology interruptions: a taxonomy and preliminary investigation of their performance effects. *Information Systems Journal, 25*(3), 231–273.
14. Haughton, N. A., Yeh, K. C., Nworie, J., & Romero, L. (2013). Digital disturbances, disorders, and pathologies: A discussion of some unintended consequences of technology in higher education. *Educational Technology, 53*(4), 3–16
15. Purnamaningsih, I. R., & Amalia, D. (2021). The negative impact of long-term online learning in educational innovation on students. *Journal of Research and Innovation in Primary Education, 1*(1), 18–23.
16. Silva, I., Rodrigues, L., & Sampayo, M. (2020). The bad and the ugly: a systematic review of technology's negative impacts' mentions in literature from 2005 to 2020. In *6th international conference on higher education advances (HEAd'20), 30* (pp. 819–829). Editorial Universitat Politècnica de València.
17. Gong, X., Kannan, S., & Ramakrishnan, K. (2023). Impact of mobile technology on collaborative learning in engineering studies. *European Journal of Educational Research, 12*(1).
18. Poçan, S., Altay, B., & Yaşaroğlu, C. (2023). The effects of mobile technology on learning performance and motivation in mathematics education. *Education and Information Technologies, 28*(1), 683–712.

19. Saif, N., Khan, I. U., & Khan, G. A. (2020). Investigating the impact of mobile application on learning among teachers based on technology acceptance model (TAM). *Global Educational Studies Review, 5*(2), 45–54.
20. Berendt, B., Littlejohn, A., & Blakemore, M. (2020). AI in education: Learner choice and fundamental rights. *Learning, Media and Technology, 45*(3), 312–324.
21. Wu, Y. (2023). Integrating generative AI in education: how ChatGPT brings challenges for future learning and teaching. *Journal of Advanced Research in Education, 2*(4), 6–10.
22. Zhang, K., & Aslan, A. B. (2021). AI technologies for education: Recent research & future directions. *Computers and Education: Artificial Intelligence, 2*, 100025.
23. Garzón, J., Baldiris, S., Gutiérrez, J., & Pavón, J. (2020). How do pedagogical approaches affect the impact of augmented reality on education? A meta-analysis and research synthesis. *Educational Research Review, 31*, 100334.
24. Low, D. Y. S., Poh, P. E., & Tang, S. Y. (2022). Assessing the impact of augmented reality application on students' learning motivation in chemical engineering. *Education for Chemical Engineers, 39*, 31–43.
25. Norman, H., Din, R., Nordin, N., & Ryberg, T. (2013). A review on the use and perceived effects of mobile blogs on learning in higher educational settings. *Asian Social Science, 10*(1), 209–222. https://doi.org/10.5539/ass.v10n1p209
26. Volkoff, O., & Strong, D. M. (2017). Affordance theory and how to use it in IS research. In R. Galliers & M.-K. Stein (Eds.), *The Routledge companion to management information systems* (pp. 232–245). Routledge.
27. Chemero, A. (2018). An outline of a theory of affordances. In *How shall affordances be refined?* (pp. 181–195). Routledge.
28. Caws, C., & Hamel, M. J. (2016). *Language-learner computer interactions: Theory, methodology and CALL applications*. John Benjamins.
29. Karahanna, E., Xu, S. X., Xu, Y., & Zhang, N. (2018). The needs–affordances–features perspective for the use of social media. *Mis Quarterly, 42*(3), 737–A23.
30. Bonfield, C. A., Salter, M., Longmuir, A., Benson, M., & Adachi, C. (2020). Transformation or evolution?: Education 4.0, teaching and learning in the digital age. Higher Education. *Pedagogies, 5*(1), 223–246. https://doi.org/10.1080/23752696.2020.1816847
31. Bojović, Ž., Bojović, P. D., Vujošević, D., & Šuh, J. (2020). Education in times of crisis: Rapid transition to distance learning. *Computer Applications in Engineering Education, 28*(6), 1467–1489. https://doi.org/10.1002/cae.22318
32. Scherzinger, M., & Wettstein, A. (2018). Classroom disruptions, the teacher–student relationship and classroom management from the perspective of teachers, students and external observers: a multimethod approach. *Learning Environments Research, 22*(1), 101–116. https://doi.org/10.1007/s10984-018-9269-x
33. Biagi, F., & Loi, M. (2013). Measuring ICT Use and Learning Outcomes: evidence from recent econometric studies. *European Journal of Education, 48*(1), 28–42.
34. Jayakumar, P., Suman Rajest, S., & Aravind, B. R. (2022). An empirical study on the effectiveness of online teaching and learning outcomes with regard to LSRW skills in COVID-19 pandemic. In A. Hamdan, A. E. Hassanien, T. Mescon, & B. Alareeni (Eds.), *Technologies, artificial intelligence and the future of learning post-COVID-19: The crucial role of international accreditation* (pp. 483–499). Springer. https://doi.org/10.1007/978-3-030-93921-2_27
35. Bennett, S., Lockyer, L., & Agostinho, S. (2018). Towards sustainable technology-enhanced innovation in higher education: Advancing learning design by understanding and supporting teacher design practice. *British Journal of Educational Technology, 49*(6), 1014–1026. https://doi.org/10.1111/bjet.12683
36. Novakovich, J., Miah, S., & Shaw, S. (2017). Designing curriculum to shape professional social media skills and identity in virtual communities of practice. *Computers and Education, 104*, 65–90. https://doi.org/10.1016/j.compedu.2016.11.002

37. Wilson, S., Liber, O., Johnson, M., Beauvoir, P., Sharples, P., & Milligan, C. (2007). Personal learning environments: Challenging the dominant design of educational systems. *Journal of e-Learning and Knowledge Society, 3*(3), 27–23.
38. Dabbagh, N., & Kitsantas, A. (2012). Personal learning environments, social media, and self-regulated learning: A natural formula for connecting formal and informal learning. *The Internet and Higher Education, 15*(1), 3–8. https://doi.org/10.1016/j.iheduc.2011.06.002
39. Rashid, T., & Asghar, H. M. (2016). Technology use, self-directed learning, student engagement and academic performance: Examining the interrelations. *Computers in Human Behavior, 63*, 604–612. https://doi.org/10.1016/j.chb.2016.05.084
40. Aresta, M., Pedro, L., & Santos, C. (2015). Mobile learning and higher education: A theoretical overview. *Journal of Mobile Multimedia, 11*(1–2), 147–156.
41. Wihlborg, M., Friberg, E. E., Rose, K. M., & Eastham, L. (2017). Facilitating learning through an international virtual collaborative practice: A case study. *Nurse Education Toda, 61*, 3–8. https://doi.org/10.1016/j.nedt.2017.10.007
42. Gegenfurtner, A., Schmidt-Hertha, B., & Lewis, P. (2020). Digital technologies in training and adult education. *International Journal of Training and Development, 24*(1), 1–4. https://doi.org/10.1111/ijtd.12172
43. Cavanaugh, C., Repetto, J., Wayer, N., & Spitler, C. (2013, January). Online learning for students with disabilities: a framework for success. *Journal of Special Education Technology*. ISBN 978-3-030-93920-5, ISBN 978-3-030-93921-2 (eBook). https://doi.org/10.1007/978-3-030-93921-2.
44. Kahn, P. E. (2014). Theorising student engagement in higher education. *British Educational Research Journal, 40*(6), 1005–1018.
45. Delfino, A. P. (2019). Student engagement and academic performance of students of Partido State University. *Asian Journal of University Education, 15*(1), 1–16.
46. Trowler, V. (2010). Student engagement literature review. *The Higher Education Academy, 11*(1), 1–15.
47. Rennecker, J., & Godwin, L. (2005). Delays and interruptions: A self-perpetuating paradox of communication technology use. *Information and Organization, 15*(3), 247–266.
48. Parte, L., & Herrador-Alcaide, T. (2021). Teaching disruption by COVID-19: Burnout, isolation, and sense of belonging in accounting tutors in E-learning and B-learning. *International Journal of Environmental Research and Public Health, 18*(19), 10339. https://doi.org/10.3390/ijerph181910339
49. Altmann, E. M., & Trafton, J. G. (2007). Time course of recovery from task interruption: Data and a model. *Psychonomics Bulletin and Review, 14*(6), 1079–1084.
50. Buzzard, C., Crittenden, V. L., Crittenden, W. F., & McCarty, P. (2011). The use of digital technologies in the classroom: A teaching and learning perspective. *Journal of Marketing Education, 33*(2), 131–139. https://doi.org/10.1177/0273475311410845
51. Brady, A. C., Kim, Y., & Cutshall, J. (2021). The what, why, and how of distractions from a self-regulated learning perspective. *Journal of College Reading and Learning, 51*(2), 153–172. https://doi.org/10.1080/10790195.2020.1867671
52. Borst, J. P., Taatgen, N. A., & van Rijn, H. (2015). What makes interruptions disruptive? A process-model account of the effects of the problem state bottleneck on task interruption and resumption. In *Proceedings of the 33rd annual ACM conference on human factors in computing systems, Groningen* (pp. 2971–2980). https://doi.org/10.1145/2702123.2702156.
53. Yin, P., Ou, C. X. J., Davison, R. M., & Wu, J. (2018). Coping with mobile technology overload in the workplace. *Internet Research, 28*(5), 1189–1212.
54. McDaniel, B. T., & Drouin, M. (2019). Daily technology interruptions and emotional and relational well-being. *Computers in Human Behavior, 99*, 1–8. https://doi.org/10.1016/j.chb.2019.04.027
55. Federman, J. E. (2019). Interruptions in online training and their effects on learning. *European Journal of Training and Development, 43*(5/6), 490–504. https://doi.org/10.1108/ejtd-10-2018-0100

56. Gupta, N., & Irwin, J. D. (2016). In-class distractions: The role of Facebook and the primary learning task. *Computers in Human Behavior, 55*, 1165–1178. https://doi.org/10.1016/j.chb.2014.10.022
57. Leonard, L. J. (2003). Optimising by minimising: interruptions and the erosion of teaching time. *The Journal of Educational Enquiry, 4*(2), 15–29.
58. Edwards, M. B., & Gronlund, S. D. (1998). Task interruption and its effects on memory. *Memory, 6*(6), 665–687. https://doi.org/10.1080/741943375
59. Foroughi, C. K., Werner, N. E., McKendrick, R., Cades, D. M., & Boehm-Davis, D. A. (2016). Individual differences in working-memory capacity and task resumption following interruptions. *Journal of Experimental Psychology: Learning, Memory, and Cognition, 42*(9), 1480–1488. https://doi.org/10.1037/xlm0000251
60. Gould, S., Brumby, D., & Cox, A. L. (2013). What does it mean for an interruption to be relevant? An investigation of relevance as a memory effect. *Proceedings of the Human Factors and Ergonomics Society Annual Meeting, 57*(1), 149–153. Sage.
61. Bailey, B. P., & Konstan, J. A. (2006). On the need for attention-aware systems: Measuring effects of interruption on task performance, error rate, and affective state. *Computers in Human Behavior, 22*(4), 685–708.
62. Leroy, S., Schmidt, A., & Madjar, N. (2020). Interruptions and task transitions: Understanding their characteristics, processes, and consequences. *Academy of Management Annals, 14*(2), 661–694. https://doi.org/10.5465/annals.2017.0146
63. Barnová, S., Krásna, S., & Gabrhelová, G. (2019). Application of digital technologies as a factor influencing university students' academic satisfaction. In *ICERI2019 proceedings, Spain* (pp. 11146–11151). https://doi.org/10.21125/iceri.2019.2752.
64. Keller, A. C., Meier, L. L., Elfering, A., & Semmer, N. K. (2020). Please wait until I am done! Longitudinal effects of work interruptions on employee well-being. *Work & Stress, 34*(2), 148–167.
65. Kushlev, K., & Dunn, E. W. (2015). Checking email less frequently reduces stress. *Computers in Human Behavior, 43*, 220–228. https://doi.org/10.1016/j.chb.2014.11.005
66. Mochi, F., & Madjar, N. (2018). Interruptions and multitasking: Advantages and disadvantages for creativity at work. In R. Reiter-Palmon, V. L. Kennel, & J. C. Kaufman (Eds.), *Individual creativity in the workplace* (pp. 103–127). Academic Press.
67. Jett, Q. R., & George, J. M. (2003). Work interrupted: A closer look at the role of interruptions in organizational life. *Academy of Management Review, 28*(3), 494–507.
68. Paas, F., Renkl, A., & Sweller, J. (2016). *Cognitive load theory: A Special issue of educational psychologist*. Routledge.
69. Chen, Q., & Yan, Z. (2016). Does multitasking with mobile phones affect learning? A review. *Computers in Human Behavior, 54*, 34–42. https://doi.org/10.1016/j.chb.2015.07.047
70. Kross, E., Verduyn, P., Demiralp, E., Park, J., Lee, D. S., Lin, N., Shablack, H., Jonides, J., & Ybarra, O. (2013). Facebook use predicts declines in subjective well-being in young adults. *PLoS One, 8*(8). https://doi.org/10.1371/journal.pone.0069841
71. Chen, S.-Y., & Liu, S.-Y. (2020). Using augmented reality to experiment with elements in a chemistry course. *Computers in Human Behavior, 111*, 1–12. https://doi.org/10.1016/j.chb.2020.106418
72. Dontre, A. J. (2021). The influence of technology on academic distraction: A review. *Human Behavior and Emerging Technologies, 3*(3), 379–390.
73. Henrie, C. R., Halverson, L., & Graham, C. (2015). Measuring student engagement in technology-mediated learning: A review. *Computers & Education, 90*, 36–53.
74. Bunderson, J. S., & Sutcliffe, K. M. (2003). Management team learning orientation and business unit performance. *Journal of Applied Psychology, 88*(3), 552–560. https://doi.apa.org/doi/10.1037/0021-9010.88.3.552
75. Podsakoff, P. M., MacKenzie, S. B., Lee, J. Y., & Podsakoff, N. P. (2003). Common method biases in behavioral research: a critical review of the literature and recommended remedies. *Journal of Applied Psychology, 88*(5), 879.

76. Hair, J., Risher, J., Sarstedt, M., & Ringle, C. (2019). When to use and how to report the results of PLS-SEM. *European Business Review, 31*(1), 2–24. https://doi.org/10.1108/EBR-11-2018-0203
77. Orhan, M. A., Castellano, S., Khelladi, I., Marinelli, L., & Monge, F. (2021). Technology distraction at work. Impacts on self-regulation and work engagement. *Journal of Business Research, 126*, 341–349. https://doi.org/10.1016/j.jbusres.2020.12.048
78. Zureick, A. H., Burk-Rafel, J., Purkiss, J. A., & Hortsch, M. (2017). The interrupted learner: How distractions during live and video lectures influence learning outcomes. *Anatomical Sciences Education, 11*(4), 366–376. https://doi.org/10.1002/ase.1754
79. Boateng, R., & Amankwaa, A. (2016). The impact of social media on student academic life in higher education. *Global Journal of Human-Social Science, 16*(4), 1–8.

Organizational Change in Social Cooperatives: Implementing the Shared Administration Paradigm in Italy

Walter Castelnovo and Nicola Basile

Abstract The Italian Third Sector Code established the shared administration paradigm as a new mode of relationship between Public Administration and non-profit organizations based on a collaborative mode of governance. Under the new paradigm, third sector organizations can be involved in *co-programmazione* (co-planning) and *co-progettazione* (co-design) exercises with public sector organizations, different from the traditional client-provider contractual relationship. The exploratory paper investigates whether the shift from the contractual to the collaborative mode of relationship with Public Administration requires social cooperatives, as a particular type of third sector organizations, to undergo organizational change processes, and what such processes entail. The study is based on semi-structured interviews with eight highly reputed expert of shared administration belonging to social cooperatives that experienced both the contractual and the collaborative mode of relationship with Public Administration. From the interviews it emerges that the establishment of the shared administration paradigm is perceived by social cooperatives as an environmental evolution that requires them to change their mindset, their strategies, their operational modalities, and their management system. Fostering organizational flexibility and inter-functional (horizontal) integration, developing better planning and design capabilities, and improving management practices to support organizational and social entrepreneurship are the measures that social cooperatives should implement under the new regime.

Keywords Social cooperative · Shared administration · Organizational change · Co-planning · Co-design · Managerialism

W. Castelnovo (✉) · N. Basile
Department of Human Sciences, Innovation and Territory, University of Insubria, Como, Italy
e-mail: walter.castelnovo@uninsubria.it; nicola.basile@uninsubria.it

M. Cipriano et al. (eds.), *Technologies for Organizations and Society*,
Lecture Notes in Information Systems and Organisation 80,
https://doi.org/10.1007/978-3-032-01697-3_21

1 Introduction

Third sector organizations (TSOs) have acquired an increasing relevance in the Italian local welfare system starting at least from the late '80s [1–3], which made them a fundamental component of the today 'welfare mix' system i.e., a complementary regime of mutual cooperation between the state and the third sector [3, 4]. During the years, the relationship between local government organizations (LGOs) and third sector organizations underwent some transformations, from the mutual accommodation model of the '80s, to the contracting-out model typical of the New Public Management era, to the more collaborative model based on the involvement of LGOs and third sector organizations in co-planning and co-design activities that has been institutionalized in 2017 with the reform of the Third Sector Code (TSC).

The TSC frames co-planning and co-design within the 'shared administration' paradigm that makes the collaborative mode the preferred arrangement for the relationship between LGOs and third sector organizations enrolled in the *Registro Unico Nazionale del Terzo Settore* (Third Sector Single National Register—RUNTS). The establishment of the shared administration paradigm shifts the axis of that relationship from a client-provider market scheme (contractual) to a collaborative relationship between a plurality of subjects placed on the same level and equally entitled to contribute to the framing of issues and solutions in the production of goods and services of general interest [5].

Based on a general inductive approach [6, 7], the aim of the exploratory study is to investigate whether the shift of their role from providers to service co-planners and co-designers requires third sector organizations to undergo organizational change processes, and what such processes should amount to. The study is focused on social cooperatives as a particular type of third sector organizations (social cooperatives are enrolled in the RUNTS by law) and is based on eight semi-structured interviews with key testimonials selected for their high reputation as shared administration experts.

There are several reasons that make social cooperatives an interesting domain to study with respect to the shared administration topic. First, social cooperatives had already had a long tradition of collaboration with LGOs as local welfare service providers under contractual agreements long before the establishment of the shared administration paradigm [3, 8, 9]. Hence, it could be expected that for them acting in the new scenario requires some organizational change. Second, since social cooperatives are hybrid organizations that also incorporate a business orientation in their vision [9–12], they could be expected to be somewhat acquainted with business tools and concepts, including entrepreneurial and organizational planning [13]. Hence, it can be hypothesized that with respect to other kinds of third sector organizations they are better equipped to manage innovation and change [14]. Third, social cooperatives are social enterprises [15] and this makes it possible for those interested in comparative studies to compare the results of our exploratory study with the literature on organizational change in social enterprises, i.e. a specific and clearly identifiable type of TSOs [16].

That said, there are some reasons that, in our view, make investigating organizational change in social cooperatives a relevant and timely endeavour. First, organizational innovation and change in social cooperatives are still quite underexplored topics, since existing organizational change models and frameworks have been developed from research undertaken largely within the for-profit sector, with little reference to the unique challenges of third sector [13, 17–20]. Second, theories and approaches to organizational change often lack empirical evidence [21] and this is even more true in the case of change in social cooperatives. Third, 7 years after the TSC institutionalization of the shared administration paradigm (and 4 years after the Italian Constitutional Court's judgment stating that the shared administration—and its tools, i.e. co-planning and co-design—represents one of the more substantial implementations of the horizontal subsidiarity constitutional principle), it is now time to consider what impact the shared administration model had on social cooperatives. Finally, to the best of our knowledge, our is one of the first studies that investigate the organizational impacts of the establishment of the shared administration paradigm in Italy.

The paper is structured as follows. Section 2 describes the study motivation and introduces the research question the study intends to address, based on the theoretical frame described in Sect. 3. The methodological approach is described in Sect. 4, whereas the results of the study are reported in Sects. 5 and 6 in which the role of digital technologies as perceived by the testimonials is discussed. Finally, the last section drives some conclusions, highlights the limitation of the study, and describes some further research directions.

2 Motivation of the Study

As a new administrative paradigm, the foundation of shared administration within the Italian administrative system lays on the reform of the article 118 of the Italian Constitution in 2001. The article states the principle of horizontal subsidiarity and requires LGOs to collaborate on equal terms with "civil society organizations, starting with those with the entrepreneurial capacity to produce goods and services capable of satisfying diverse needs and demands that would otherwise go unmet" [5, p. 3].

The 2017 reform of the TSC incorporates the shared administration principles and tools in the article 55 that states that "in implementation of the principles of subsidiarity and cooperation (...) public administrations ensure the active involvement of third sector entities, through forms of co-planning and co-design", alternative to the traditional mechanism of calls for proposals and tenders. This introduces a double regime in the relationship between LGOs and third sector organizations: the traditional market-oriented contractual arrangements and the shared administration collaborative practices. These two modes of relationship materialize two alternative institutional logics [22–24], that determine incompatible prescriptions, and inform different "practices in use" [24, 25].

By making the collaborative practices of co-planning and co-design the preferred mode of relationship between LGOs and third sector organizations, article 55 of the TSC induces a paradigm shift in the Italian welfare system [26] that can be expected to impact on both structural (assets, roles, resources, etc.) and cultural (habits, self-representation, voice capacity, etc.) organizational dimensions [27, 28]. LGOs and third sector organizations cannot operate business as usual in the new context shaped by the principles of shared administration. Rather, they should be expected to implement organizational transformation processes, similar to those required by the shift from a New Public Management inspired mode of governance (contractual) to a New Public Governance inspired mode (collaborative) [29].

This motivates the research question our exploratory study intends to address, i.e. *(a) whether the establishment of the shared administration paradigm forced social cooperatives, as a particular type of third sector organizations, to implement organizational change processes, and (b) what such changes should amount to.*

3 Theoretical Framework

Cooperative enterprises are different from other typical profit-oriented organisations as they "follow social solidarity principles of pursuing social, environmental and redistributive justice through cooperative, associative and solidarity relations" [30, p. 8]. Nevertheless, cooperatives are enterprises, and, as such, besides pursuing social goals, focusing on democratic values and principles such as solidarity, equality and inclusion [31], cooperatives also pursue business goals [32]. This makes cooperative enterprises typical hybrid organisations.

In organisational studies, hybridity refers to the coexistence, within the same organisation, of different (sometimes even conflicting) institutional logics, typically related to the public, private or third-sector domain [33–35]. For cooperatives, the coexistence of plural logics is a permanent phenomenon [11, 14, 32, 35, 36]. It represents a positive aspect [35], since "operating in institutional interstices and combining multiple logics (. . .) allows them to be innovative, to create new products and services and to pioneer new ways of organizing" [14, p. 715].

As hybrid organizations, cooperatives can adapt to different local economic opportunities, different legal arrangements and governance models. From this point of view, it could be expected that their ability to manage distinctly different institutional logics will enable cooperatives to respond strategically to external pressures and opportunities [13, 37].

For decades before the introduction of co-planning and co-design practices, in Italy cooperatives acted as welfare service providers by answering to competitive tenders issued by LGOs. Even in case the tender was reserved to third sector organizations, the procurement procedure had to comply with the Public Procurement Code, as it is required for the public procurement procedures open to private sector organizations. Operating in a context shaped by a market-oriented institutional logic and by leveraging their hybrid nature, social cooperatives had been able to adopt operational modalities typical of for-profit organizations, which allowed them to compete with profit-oriented organizations. In other words, in the pre-TSC context, the need to manage contractual relationships with LGOs within a competitive context led social cooperatives to define a hybrid equilibrium between different institutional logics oriented toward market practices at the operational level [19, 38], while nevertheless maintaining their fundamental pro-social orientation at the strategic level.

By establishing the shared administration paradigm, the TSC determined a change in the context in which social cooperatives operate, which requires them to adapt to new contextual opportunities and constraints. However, as Soparnot [39] reminds us, adaptation should be considered as an organizational change process that varies in its depth and vigour depending upon the environmental change taking place (p. 642). The establishment of shared administration as a new institutional paradigm informing the relationship between LGOs and social cooperatives, requires social cooperatives to overcome their traditional contractual-based mode of relating with LGOs and to shift towards new systems, beliefs, values and practices [13] informed by a collaborative institutional logic. The establishment of the shared administration paradigm can thus be considered as an environmental evolution [39] that broke the previous institutional hybrid equilibrium, pushing social cooperatives to search for a new hybrid equilibrium under an exogenous pressure [40].

In the effort to gain a new equilibrium state in a complex institutional environment, changes in and among institutional logics may occur [41] that can be considered as triggers of change at organizational level [14, 42–44]. According to the TSC, in their relationships with social cooperatives LGOs can decide on a case-by-case basis whether to activate a shared administration procedure or to resort to a traditional contractual arrangement. Hence, in their interactions with LGOs, social cooperatives have to be prepared to manage both types of relationship, which requires them to confront with institutional complexity [44], to balance change and stability [28] and to ultimately operate according to a double standard. This can have consequences on the cooperatives capacity to manage change and to establish a new hybrid equilibrium under the shared administration paradigm.

Following Al-Haddad and Kotnour [45], organizational change can be considered as situational and contingent, with a high variation between organizations undergoing change to achieve "optimum fit" with the changing environment. Since it impacted on consolidated operating procedures informed to the previously dominant contractual logic, the establishment of the shared administration paradigm determined a discontinuous change in social cooperatives' operating context. This motivates our exploratory study that intends to investigate whether to absorb the shift from the contractual to the collaborative institutional logic social cooperatives need to implement organizational change processes, and what changes should be implemented.

In our exploratory study we do not assume any of the many specific change models and frameworks available in the literature (see [45] for an extensive classification) to explore the social cooperatives' responses to the shared administration paradigm shift. This choice is motivated by the general inductive approach assumed in the study that requires researchers to "stay open to the emergent and to earned relevance" [46, p. 1] and avoid the risk of being misled by "the tendency to cling to a particular theoretical perspective" (p. 3). For this reason, we assume a quite general definition of organizational change like that suggested by Soparnot [39, p. 641] that defines it as the ability of the organization to produce solutions (content) that respond to environmental evolution (external context) and to implement those change processes successfully within the organization (process).

Moreover, since, as observed by Rosenbaum, More and Steane [17, p. 77], in much of the extant research on organizational change views of change from the perspective of those who experience it is missing [17, 47, 48], in our research we investigate how the dimensions of organizational change are perceived by the individuals that within the social cooperatives are directly involved in change processes related to the shared administration paradigm.

4 Methodological Approach

The exploratory study involves eight highly reputed experts in co-planning and co-design of welfare services with LGOs that hold top positions within social cooperatives (founder, president, CEO, project manager). These key testimonials have been selected for their recognized role within second level associations in the welfare domain and for their contributions to the debate on shared administration within highly valued Italian professional journals (Animazione Sociale, Prospettive Sociali e Sanitarie, Lombardia Sociale), which makes them "individuals with a view to secure greater insight into the practical aspects of the problem" [49, p. 13].

The profiles of the testimonials involved in the study are summarized in Table 1.

The study has been carried out through in-depth semi-structured interviews based on the methodology for semi-structured interviews described in [49, 50]. The interviews have been designed with the aim of exploring subjective viewpoints and gather in-depth accounts from the testimonials [51]. More specifically, during the interviews, questions have been submitted to the testimonials to collect information concerning the dimension of change defined by Soparnot [39]. More specifically:

- The perceived impact of the establishment of the shared administration paradigm on the social cooperatives' operating context (the environmental evolution dimension)
- How social cooperatives should change to operate effectively in the new context shaped by the shared administration collaborative paradigm (the content of change dimension)
- How the change process can/should be implemented (the process dimension)

Table 1 Testimonials involved in the study

Testimonial	Profile
T1	Founder and past president of a social cooperative
T2	Founder of a social cooperative and long-term collaborator of the ACLI (Christian Associations of Italian Workers)
T3	President of a social cooperative and long-term collaborator of the CNCA—Coordinamento Italiano delle Comunità di Accoglienza (Italian Coordination of Care Communities)
T4	Community worker in a social cooperative and territorial development facilitator
T5	Area manager in a social cooperative and expert in the management of complex co-planning and co-design projects
T6	CEO in a social cooperative and member of the Forum del Terzo Settore (Third Sector Forum) in a province of Lombardy
T7	Manager responsible of all the planning activities of the social cooperative he belongs to
T8	President of a social cooperative

- Finally, since shared administration practices require a continuous interaction between social cooperatives and LGOs, we also asked our informants whether they consider digital tools and platforms as useful supporting tools for co-planning and co-design activities

The interviews, that lasted about one hour each, took place between April 2024 and May 2024 and have been conducted online by involving two researchers, one acting as the interviewer and the other acting as an observer. The interviews have been recorded, transcribed, anonymized and codified individually by each researcher using Microsoft Office tools. The coding of the interview has been based on the general inductive approach that is frequently reported in health and social science research [6, 7]. By using a 'in vivo' coding methodology [52], the transcripts were read several times by each researcher to identify topics and themes, which involved grouping segments of text (topics) by theme. If new themes emerged the coding was changed, and the transcripts were reread according to the new structure. At the end of this step, the results of the individual coding have been discussed and compared by the two researchers, addressing any interpretive variations and selecting the main themes for subsequent analysis. At the end of the coding process, 190 topics have been identified in the interviews, grouped around the themes listed in Table 2.

5 The Establishment of Shared Administration as an Environmental Transformation

All the testimonials involved in the study consider the establishment of the shared administration paradigm as an environmental evolution that, notwithstanding the persistence of problems in its implementation on the ground, is going to radically transform the Italian welfare system [T6]. Even testimonial T1, who declared that

Table 2 The themes identified with the coding process

Dimensions of change	Themes
Environmental evolution	Transformational impact of shared administration
Content	Development of new competences and capacities
	Direction of the change required
	The role of organizational culture
	The role of management
	The role of leadership
Process	Change strategies
	Implementation of change
	Difficulties of change/barriers to change
	Enabling elements for change
Use of digital technologies	

the cooperative he belongs to already had such an extensive experience in co-design projects with LGOs that for them very little has changed after the issuing of the TSC, recognized an important element of novelty in a normative framework that combines the social dimension of active participation with the legislative dimension of the proceduralization of shared administration.

According to our testimonials, the materialization of the collaborative logic of shared administration in 'practices in use' challenges social cooperatives in many ways, forcing them to change their mindset, their strategies, their organizational arrangements, as well as their management and operational modalities [T2]. This answers positively to the first part of our research question: by reshaping their operating context, the establishment of the shared administration paradigm forces social cooperatives to change. By summarizing the main findings emerged from the interviews, the following subsections will provide an answer also to the second part of the research question, i.e. what needs to be changed under the new paradigm.

5.1 Develop Better Strategic, Planning and Design Capabilities

Under the traditional contractual regime, all was required to social cooperatives was acting as providers implementing projects and delivering services someone else had already defined. This impacted critically on the cooperatives' planning capacity, progressively reducing their capacity (and the required competences) to develop a vision for the future and to act as social innovators [T5].

The establishment of the shared administration paradigm radically changes this situation. In co-planning and co-design exercises social cooperatives and LGOs are placed on the same level and equally entitled to contribute to the framing of issues and solutions. This requires social cooperatives to recover their social entrepreneurship role for local welfare and sustainable development [T7]. To actively participate in co-planning and co-design initiatives, social cooperatives should develop the capacity to elaborate a vision, to design a strategy, to plan the measures necessary to implement it and to define the criteria to evaluate the outcomes of the interventions [T2]. Managerial, methodological and planning competences are required to contextualize the object of co-planning and co-design exercises with respect to a vision of the local development [T5].

To exert social entrepreneurship, social cooperatives must be open to an entrepreneurial logic and implement an effective managerial system, which one of the testimonials reports could risk being perceived by the cooperative members as a shift of the cooperative mission toward a profit-oriented logic [T3]. This is a cultural barrier that needs to be removed to advance the social cooperatives' entrepreneurial and managerial capacity [T6].

5.2 *Redefine the Management System*

The establishment of the shared administration model also impacts the cooperatives' management and governance systems that may need to be redefined under the new paradigm. According to our testimonials, this is one of the major challenges for social cooperatives for several reasons.

First, the traditional provider role assigned to social cooperatives in the past limited the development of a managerial culture beyond what is required for administrative matters. In the new scenario, what is needed is a management oriented to change and innovation, able to define new directions, implement new strategies, tools and methods and to renew the cooperative's value proposition [T2].

Second, a traditional authoritative top-down management style does not fit well with the shared administration underlying collaborative logic [T7]. Rather, managers should move from a steering and directing to a leadership-based management style to foster engagement and empowerment [T4].

Third, the new role of cooperatives as co-planners and co-designers with LGOs requires to extend responsibility to the middle levels of the organization who are those more directly involved in co-planning and co-design exercises. This is not easy to do for the cooperative's management [T3], but it is nevertheless critical for social cooperatives participation in shared administration exercises. You can have highly competent managers in your organization, but are your middle level operators able to manage co planning and co-design? As one testimonial reported, middle level operators in social cooperatives can be very good in managing services (even critical ones), but they are often reluctant to assume planning and managing responsibilities [T5]. These operators should be empowered to develop these capacities. What is needed is spreading the strategic vision at all the organizational levels and enable the middle levels to manage the complexity of the organization and of its activities [T7].

5.3 Develop Interaction and Lateral Communication Capabilities

To comply with the collaborative institutional logic underlying the shared administration paradigm, social cooperatives need to develop new interaction capabilities to interact on a peer-to-peer basis with LGOs within shared administration exercises [T4]. This is another critical challenge shared administration poses to social cooperatives [T3]. Developing more collaborative-oriented organizational culture and operational practices (both internally and externally), create networks and working as a system is perceived by all the testimonials as the direction of the change required by the new regime.

Social cooperatives often lack interaction and lateral communication capabilities, also due to the past general tendency to implement vertical organizational structures [T4]. For instance, as pointed out by testimonial [T8], within the cooperative there is traditionally a rigid separation between those involved in the design and implementation of projects and those responsible for the administrative and financial aspects. Maintaining this separation in co-planning and co-design exercises can have critical consequences.

Different from a traditional contractual arrangement, in which the amount of the financial resources available for a project has already been established by the contracting authority (LGO), under the new regime also the budget should be defined collaboratively. Without a careful ex-ante financial analysis, critical problems could emerge since the solutions agreed on during a collaborative exercise may end up financially unsustainable when implemented. To avoid this critical outcome, the cooperative planning and administrative teams must work together in all the phases, from planning to implementation and evaluation [T8].

Being a highly cooperative exercise, co-planning and co-design require cooperatives to change their operational approach to the design, implementation and, even more importantly, evaluation of the outcomes of the projects [T4]. This requires social cooperatives to redefine their organizational structure, improve HR capabilities, foster horizontal collaboration, and make roles and responsibilities clearer [T2]. Resorting to cross-functional coordination groups to which all the members of the cooperative involved in shared administration procedures participate, irrespective of the organizational structure and level they belong to, is reported as an organizational arrangement social cooperatives could implement under the shared administration regime [T6].

5.4 Implementing Change

Beside highlighting the organizational changes that the shared administration paradigm shift requires social cooperatives to implement, our testimonials also reported some enabling factors and some critical elements that can affect the change process.

Engagement, empowerment and leadership are generally recognized by all our testimonials as fundamental tools to sustain the change process.

The role of leadership has been mentioned by our testimonials with reference to both the capacity to moderate all the participants, to establish a collaborative climax and to foster open communication during collaborative exercises [T5], and the capacity to activate and sustain the internal change process in all its phases [T4]. However, individual leadership by itself is not enough. Engagement and an appropriate organizational context are necessary too [T2]. Change can be difficult and laborious. Advancing a positive narrative to maintain engagement at the lower levels of the cooperative can facilitate it [T3]. Flexibility, knowledge sharing and learning are the main organizational characteristics that have been reported as enabling factors for change processes [T4].

Concerning the critical factors, the main problem reported in the interviews concerns the role of management in sustaining the change process. On the one hand, not always the managers of the cooperatives have a clear vision of how their organizations should change under the shared administration paradigm: for the management is difficult to give up the contractual logic they are used to [T3]. On the other hand, the cooperatives managers perceive the risk to break a fragile equilibrium and to harm the organization that organizational change always entails [T2].

Another critical factor that has been highlighted in the interviews concerns the cooperative managers' scarce acquaintance with methodologies and tools for organizational change management [T7]. Most often, in the implementation of change processes social cooperatives are compelled to proceed tentatively, by trials and errors without a clear direction [T2]. Alternatively, they have to resort to external resources (consultants), which implies a cost that not always they can afford [T6].

6 The Role of Digital Technologies

In the study we also explored whether, according to our testimonials, the materialization of the new collaborative institutional logic underlying the shared administration paradigm could be supported by digital tools and what these tools could be. This is a relevant point to explore, also considering that third sector organizations often encounter difficulties and resistance to implement and use digital technologies in their strategic and operational activities [18, 53, 54].

These difficulties affect the social cooperatives too, as confirmed by the data collected by the Italian National Institute of Statics [55] that show only a moderate use of mobile applications, digital platforms and cloud services, and a scarce use of advanced digital technologies (data analytics, IoT). Moreover, considering the reported motivations for the limited use of digital technologies, besides the more obvious motivations related to the lack of internal ICT competences and financial resources, also motivations related to the irrelevance of digital technologies for their activities and to the necessity of dealing with more pressing problems have been indicated by social cooperatives.

Our interviews partially confirm the data collected by ISTAT. None of the testimonials reported a strategic use of digital technologies within the social cooperative they belong to. The most often used digital technologies are office automation tools, cloud-based platform for storage and document sharing, and video-conferencing systems.

Cipriano and Za [18] observed that the adoption and use of digital technologies can be challenging for third sector organizations since "it may represent both a driver and an obstacle in a non-profit-based organisational scope" (p. 17). The interviews we collected for our study confirm this perceived 'double sword' nature of digital technologies also with respect to co-planning and co-design.

On the one hand, some of our testimonials (T1, T3, T4) see little or no positive value on their use in co-planning and co-design that, to be effective, should be based exclusively on face-to-face meetings. For them the use of digital technologies would make the interaction less effective and the definition of shared solutions more difficult.

On the other hand, other testimonials (T2, T5, T6, T7) point to a possible positive role of digital technologies to support shared administration exercises, although the tools they report as potentially useful are mainly the same simple cloud platforms for document sharing they already use in their intra-organizational activities.

Moreover, notwithstanding their contrasting views of the usefulness of digital technologies, all the testimonials agree on reporting that in none of the collaborative exercises they have been involved specific digital tools have been adopted beside basic office productivity tools.

From the data collected with the interviews two provisional conclusions can be hypothesized concerning the social cooperatives' perceived relevance of digital technologies for organizational change under institutional pressure. First, a scarce awareness emerged concerning the strategic role digital technologies can exert in organizational change processes. Their view of digital technologies is still informed to a conception of IT-related changes as mainly oriented toward increased productivity. Second, although all the testimonials agree that in a complex process of organizational de-institutionalization and re-institutionalization social cooperatives cannot operate business as usual, they seem to think that under the shared administration paradigm shift social cooperatives can nevertheless operate "technologies as usual".

7 Final Remarks, Limitations and Further Research Directions

The exploratory study was intended to investigate whether the establishment of the shared administration paradigm in Italy requires social cooperatives (as a particular type of TSOs) to implement organizational change processes to absorb the shift from the traditional contractual logic to a new collaborative logic in their relationship with LGOs, and what the content of those processes should be.

From the interviews, it emerges quite clearly that the establishment of the shared administration paradigm really represents a challenge for social cooperatives in their relationship with LGOs. All our testimonials acknowledge this and agree on the view that to achieve optimum fit with the new scenario social cooperatives must undergo a process of organizational change.

Although social cooperatives had already been occasionally involved in co-design exercises even before the establishment of shared administration in the TSC, it is only recently that LGOs started to resort quite extensively to this collaborative mode of relationship. This increases the pressure on social cooperatives (and on TSOs more generally) that most often are neither used nor equipped to manage extensive and rapid multidimensional organizational changes as illustrated in the preceding section.

The testimonials involved in the study converged on the identification of some organizational challenges that social cooperatives have (possibly) to deal with under the new collaborative scenario, which can be considered as the content of the organizational change processes that should be implemented. They include:

- Developing better strategic, planning and design capabilities.
- Developing new interaction and lateral communication capabilities.
- Implementing horizontal integrated inter-functional organizational structures.
- Fostering organizational flexibility, organizational learning, and the sharing of knowledge across all the organizational structures and levels.
- Transforming the internal mode of governance from a steering and directing to a leadership style.
- Developing an entrepreneurial culture and more effective management styles.
- Redefining the management structure to distribute responsibilities and empower the middle levels.

Our study concerned only social cooperatives that, as hybrid organizations, can be hypothesized to be somewhat acquainted with business tools and concepts, including entrepreneurial and organizational planning. However, especially when their primary, or even unique, market are LGOs, social cooperatives show a tendency to organizational inertia and stability, which sensibly weakens incentives for endogenous change with critical consequences for their structural change capabilities and preparedness.

In the pre-TSC scenario, social cooperatives were simply required to reactively answer to tenders issued by LGOs. This generally limited the development of an appropriate managerial culture within the cooperatives, beyond what is required for administrative matters and to adopt market practices at the operational level to compete in competitive tenders issued by LGOs. In the absence of exogenous pressures, social cooperatives (especially the small-to-medium ones) were not compelled to develop a more managerial-oriented organizational culture, which many cooperators would have perceived (and still would perceive) as an unacceptable shift toward a logic typical of private sector organizations. Thus, in a context not favourable to the development of institutional and organizational entrepreneurship capabilities, social cooperatives maintained a hybrid equilibrium strategically more oriented to social entrepreneurship and less sensitive to the principles of good management [56].

The new scenario shaped by the shared administration paradigm magnifies the cooperatives' social entrepreneurship role. However, according to our testimonials, to exert social entrepreneurship in the new scenario social cooperatives are required to re-consider their organization, their operational practices and, most importantly, to develop an appropriate managerial culture. This does not mean adhering to a managerialist ideology and rhetoric though.

This is a critical point for cooperatives since managerialism is not only the use of managerial tools within organizations. It is also an ideology [57], "a strong faith in the virtues of corporate management knowledge and practices as well as a firm belief in the power of professional managers to improve organizations" [58, p. 227]. For cooperatives, uncritically embracing the principles of managerialism could make them too much business-like organizations, which could entail mission drift and loss of idealism. This would transform social cooperative in 'conforming hybrids', strongly identified with one specific institutional logics (the market oriented one) [14].

As Hvenmark [59] points out, the concept of managerialism is so broadly defined that runs the risk of losing its analytical power. To avoid this risk, it is convenient to distinguish between managerialism as an ideology, management as a set of managerial practices, and managerialization as an organizational change process. As referred to this distinction, what emerges quite clearly from our interviews is the need for cooperatives to implement a change process (managerialization) to introduce appropriate managerial practices and tools (management) to improve programs and services and contribute to rationalization [60]. All this without "*behaving like a profit-oriented organizations to pursue a bad profit*", as one of our testimonials stressed. In this context managerialization should then be understood with reference to the concepts of social entrepreneurship and entrepreneurial orientation, focusing on the entrepreneurial behaviours of cooperatives, that is, behaviours that involve high degrees of innovation, risk-taking, and pro-activeness [61, p. 71].

A new hybrid equilibrium must be pursued by social cooperatives under the shared administration scenario, one in which managerialization and organizational entrepreneurship are reinforced to become instrumental to strengthen their social entrepreneurship capabilities in a sustainable way. This means that they do not strongly identify with a specific logic, but selectively couple elements prescribed by different logics and adopt hybridity for substantive reasons, what Mair, Mayer, and Lutz [14] define 'dissenting hybrids'.

How this objective can be achieved and what this new hybrid equilibrium could amount to is still an open question. Although all our testimonials share a clear perception about the necessity of implementing better managerial practices within their organizations, they see this still as an objective to be achieved.

Our exploratory study has been based on interviews with eight highly informed key testimonials. Although eight interviews can be an acceptable basis for formulating some hypothesis concerning the organizational change processes required to social cooperatives under the shared administration collaborative paradigm, they are not enough to drive generalizable conclusions. To this end, further research is needed.

First, further evidence can be derived with more interviews, also involving people from different organizational levels within the cooperatives. Second, it would be interesting to verify whether the evidence we collected represent personal opinions of the testimonials or derive from a collective reflection within the cooperatives they belong to. Third, the study should be extended involving also different types of third sector organizations to verify whether they are subjected to the same pressure toward organizational change as social cooperatives are. Finally, in the study we did not consider whether, how and with what results the organizational measures that have been indicated by the testimonials have been, are being or will be implemented within the cooperatives. In other words, we did not examine in depth the process dimension of organizational change. This is the main limitation of the study that should be removed with further research.

However, notwithstanding these limitations, our study can help highlighting the organizational impacts of a fundamental transformation of the Italian Third Sector, one holding a constitutional status, that is still a topic quite underexplored.

Disclosure of Interests The authors have no competing interests to declare that are relevant to the content of this article.

References

1. Gasparre, A., & Bassoli, M. (2019). Governance beyond the rhetoric: Organizational action, change, and illusion in the Italian local welfare system. *Administration & Society, 52*(6), 927–958.
2. Ranci, C. (1994). The third sector in welfare policies in Italy: the contradictions of a protected market. *VOLUNTAS: International Journal of Voluntary and Nonprofit Organizations, 5*(3), 247–271.
3. Ranci, C. (2015). The long-term evolution of the government–third sector partnership in Italy: Old wine in a new bottle? *VOLUNTAS: International Journal of Voluntary and Nonprofit Organizations, 26*(6), 2311–2329.
4. Ascoli, U., & Ranci, C. (2003). *Dilemmas of the welfare mix*. Springer.
5. Sacchetti, S., & Salvatori, G. (2023). *"Shared administration" as a new relationship between the public sector and the social economy* (Euricse Working Paper Series).
6. Fereday, J., & Muir-Cochrane, E. (2006). Demonstrating rigor using thematic analysis: A hybrid approach of inductive and deductive coding and theme development. *International*

Journal of Qualitative Methods, 5(1), 80–92.
7. Thomas, D. R. (2006). A general inductive approach for analyzing qualitative evaluation data. *American Journal of Evaluation, 27*(2), 237–246.
8. Rensi, S., & Zandonai, F. (2015). *Per chi e per quanti opera la cooperazione sociale?* EURICSE.
9. Thomas, A. (2004). The rise of social cooperatives in Italy. *VOLUNTAS: International Journal of Voluntary and Nonprofit Organizations, 15*(3), 243–263.
10. Battilana, J., & Lee, M. (2014). Advancing research on hybrid organizing—Insights from the study of social enterprises. *Academy of Management Annals, 8*(1), 397–441.
11. Battilana, J. (2018). Cracking the organizational challenge of pursuing joint social and financial goals: Social enterprise as a laboratory to understand hybrid organizing. *M@n@gement, 21*(4), 1278–1305.
12. Doherty, B., Haugh, H., & Lyon, F. (2014). Social enterprises as hybrid organizations: A review and research agenda. *International Journal of Management Reviews, 16*(4), 417–436.
13. Eti-Tofinga, B., Singh, G., & Douglas, H. (2018). Facilitating cultural change in social enterprises. *Journal of Organizational Change Management, 31*(3), 619–636.
14. Mair, J., Mayer, J., & Lutz, E. (2015). Navigating institutional plurality: organizational governance in hybrid organizations. *Organization Studies, 36*(6), 713–739.
15. Hernâdez Cáceres, D. (2023). Social enterprises in the social cooperative form. In H. Peter, C. Vargas Vasserot, & J. Alcalde Silva (Eds.), *The international handbook of social entreprise law. Benefit corporations and other purpose-driven companies* (pp. 173–191). Springer-VDI.
16. Salamon, L. M., Haddock, M. A., & Toepler, S. (2023). Conceptualizing, measuring, and theorizing the third sector: Embedding statistical and methodological developments awaiting broader scholarly take-up. *VOLUNTAS: International Journal of Voluntary and Nonprofit Organizations, 34*(1), 115–125.
17. Rosenbaum, D., More, E., & Steane, P. (2017). A longitudinal qualitative case study of change in nonprofits: Suggesting a new approach to the management of change. *Journal of Management & Organization, 23*(1), 74–91.
18. Cipriano, M., & Za, S. (2023). Non-profit organisations in the digital age: A research agenda for supporting the development of a digital transformation strategy. *Journal of Information Technology, 39*(4).
19. Laurett, R., & Ferreira, J. J. (2018). Strategy in nonprofit organisations: A systematic literature review and agenda for future research. *VOLUNTAS: International Journal of Voluntary and Nonprofit Organizations, 29*(5), 881–897.
20. do Adro, F. J. N., & Leitão, J. C. C. (2020). Leadership and organizational innovation in the third sector: A systematic literature review. *International Journal of Innovation Studies, 4*(2), 51–67.
21. By, R. T. (2005). Organisational change management: A critical review. *Journal of Change Management, 5*(4), 369–380.
22. Friedland, R., & Alford, J. (1991). Bringing society back. In W. Powell & P. J. Di Maggio (Eds.), *Symbols, practices, and institutional contradictions, in the new institutionalism in organizational analysis* (pp. 232–263). University of Chicago Press.
23. Ocasio, W., Thornton, P. H., & Lounsbury, K. (2017). Advances to the institutional logics perspective. In R. Greenwood et al. (Eds.), *The Sage handbook of organizational institutionalism* (pp. 509–531). Sage.
24. Smets, M., Greenwood, R., & Lounsbury, M. (2015). An institutional perspective on strategy as practice. In D. Golsorkhi et al. (Eds.), *Cambridge handbook of strategy as practice* (pp. 283–300). Cambridge University Press.
25. Smets, M., Aristidou, A., & Whittington, R. (2017). Towards a practice-driven institutionalism. In R. Greenwood et al. (Eds.), *The Sage handbook of organizational institutionalism* (pp. 365–391). Sage.
26. De Tommaso, C. V., & Maino, F. (2023). Le pratiche collaborative: fattori facilitanti e ostacolanti, sfide e opportunità della coprogettazione. In *Agire insieme: Coprogettazione e coprogrammazione per cambiare il welfare: Sesto Rapporto sul secondo welfare* (pp. 100–128). Percorsi di secondo welfare.

27. Busso, S., Reggiardo, A., & Sciarrone, R. (2023). L'amministrazione condivisa: nuovi assetti istituzionali e ruolo dei contesti locali. *Rivista trimestrale di scienza della amministrazione, 2*, 1.
28. Meyer, C. B., & Stensaker, I. G. (2006). Developing capacity for change. *Journal of Change Management, 6*(2), 217–231.
29. Osborne, S. P. (Ed.). (2010). *The (new) public governance: A suitable case for treatment?* Routledge.
30. ILO. (2019). *Financial mechanisms for innovative social and solidarity economy ecosystems*. International Labour Organization.
31. Kerlin, J. (2010). A comparative analysis of the global emergence of social enterprise. *VOLUNTAS: International Journal of Voluntary and Nonprofit Organizations, 21*(2), 162–179.
32. Camargo Benavides, A. F., & Ehrenhard, M. (2021). Rediscovering the cooperative enterprise: A systematic review of current topics and avenues for future research. *VOLUNTAS: International Journal of Voluntary and Nonprofit Organizations, 32*, 964–978.
33. Brandsen, T., van de Donk, W., & Putters, K. (2005). Griffins or chameleons? Hybridity as a permanent and inevitable characteristic of the third sector. *International Journal of Public Administration, 28*(9–10), 749–765.
34. Evers, A. (2008). Hybrid organisations—Background, concept, challenge. In S. Osborne (Ed.), *The third sector in Europe* (pp. 279–292). Routledge.
35. Ebrahim, A., Battilana, J., & Mair, J. (2014). The governance of social enterprises: Mission drift and accountability challenges in hybrid organizations. *Research in Organizational Behavior, 34*(C), 81–100.
36. Besharov, M. L., & Smith, W. K. (2014). Multiple institutional logics in organizations: Explaining their varied nature and implications. *Academy of Management Review, 39*(3), 364–381.
37. Petrella, F., Simsa, R., Pape, U., Pahl, J. B., Brandsen, T., Richez-Battesti, N., & Zimmer, A. (2021). Dealing with paradoxes, manufacturing governance: Organizational change in European third-sector organizations. *Nonprofit and Voluntary Sector Quarterly, 51*(2), 237–259.
38. Lie, M., & Baines, S. (2007). Making sense of organizational change: Voices of older volunteers. *VOLUNTAS: International Journal of Voluntary and Nonprofit Organizations, 18*(3), 225–240.
39. Soparnot, R. (2011). The concept of organizational change capacity. *Journal of Organizational Change Management, 24*(5), 640–661.
40. Koning, E. A. (2016). The three institutionalisms and institutional dynamics: understanding endogenous and exogenous change. *Journal of Public Policy, 36*(4), 639–664.
41. Ponte, D., & Pesci, C. (2022). Institutional logics and organizational change: the role of place and time. *Journal of Management and Governance, 26*(3), 891–924.
42. Canales, R. (2013). Weaving straw into gold: Managing organizational tensions between standardization and flexibility in microfinance. *Organization Science, 25*(1), 1–28.
43. Jay, J. (2012). Navigating paradox as a mechanism of change and innovation in hybrid organizations. *Academy of Management Journal, 56*(1), 137–159.
44. Greenwood, R., Raynard, M., Kodeih, F., Micelotta, E. R., & Lounsbury, M. (2011). Institutional complexity and organizational responses. *Academy of Management Annals, 5*(1), 317–371.
45. Al-Haddad, S., & Kotnour, T. (2015). Integrating the organizational change literature: a model for successful change. *Journal of Organizational Change Management, 28*(2), 234–262.
46. Glaser, B. G. (2013). Staying open: The use of theoretical codes in GT. *The Grounded Theory Review, 12*(1).
47. Oreg, S., Michel, A., & By, R. T. (2013). *The psychology of organizational change: Viewing change from the employee's perspective*. Cambridge University Press.
48. Isett, K. R., Glied, S. A. M., Sparer, M. S., & Brown, L. D. (2013). When change becomes transformation. *Public Management Review, 15*(1), 1–17.
49. Kothari, C. R. (2004). *Research methodology: Methods and techniques*. New Delhi.

50. Adams, W. C. (2015). Conducting semi-structured interviews. In K. E. Newcomer, H. P. H. P. Hatry, & J. S. Wholey (Eds.), *Handbook of practical program evaluation* (pp. 492–505). Wiley.
51. Flick, U. W. E. (2009). *An introduction to qualitative research*. Sage.
52. Saldaña, J. (2014). Coding and analysis strategies. In P. Leavy (Ed.), *The Oxford handbook of qualitative research* (pp. 581–598). Oxford.
53. Nahrkhalaji, S. S., Shafiee, S., Shafiee, M., & Hvam, L. (2018). Challenges of digital transformation: The case of the non-profit sector. In *2018 IEEE international conference on industrial engineering and engineering management (IEEM)*.
54. Vogelsang, K., Packmohr, S., & Brink, H. (2021). Challenges of the digital transformation—Comparing nonprofit and industry organizations. In *Innovation through information systems*. Springer.
55. ISTAT. (2024, July 31). Censimento permanente delle istituzioni non profit. Available from: https://www.istat.it/tavole-di-dati/censimento-permanente-delle-istituzioni-non-profit-2021/.
56. Calabrese, G. G., & Falavigna, G. (2024). Do social cooperatives stimulate social change? An investigation on Italian firms based on DEA-Malmquist approach. *Technological Forecasting and Social Change, 199*.
57. Pollitt, C. (2016). Managerialism redux? *Financial Accountability & Management, 32*(4), 429–447.
58. Hvenmark, J. (2013). Business as usual?: On managerialization and the adoption of the balanced scorecard in a democratically governed civil society organization. *Administrative Theory & Praxis, 35*(2), 223–247.
59. Hvenmark, J. (2016). Ideology, practice, and process? A review of the concept of managerialism in civil society studies. *VOLUNTAS: International Journal of Voluntary and Nonprofit Organizations, 27*(6), 2833–2859.
60. Shirinashihama, Y. (2019). The positive and negative consequences of "managerialization": Evidence from Japanese nonprofit elderly care service providers. *Nonprofit and Voluntary Sector Quarterly, 48*(2), 309–333.
61. Maier, F., Meyer, M., & Steinbereithner, M. (2014). Nonprofit organizations becoming business-like: A systematic review. *Nonprofit and Voluntary Sector Quarterly, 45*(1), 64–86.

Bridging the Gap: Analyzing Collaboration Between Practitioners and Researchers Across Different Stages of the Design Science Research Process

Simon Michael Schmid

Abstract Design Science Research (DSR) projects significantly increase the knowledge base while delivering practical results. These projects involve collaboration between practitioners seeking functional solutions and researchers aiming to contribute to knowledge generation. This difference in goals can lead to challenges. To date, there is little research on the collaboration between researchers and practitioners during the different phases of DSR. As the start of a larger research initiative, this paper provides preliminary insights into practitioner-researcher collaborations within DSR projects. The work is structured around four core areas of investigation: first, the project phase in which the collaboration occurs; second, the parties involved; third, the kind of artifact developed; and fourth, the challenges encountered during the collaboration between practitioners and researchers. The aim of this research initiative is to explore these collaborations in depth and to develop implications and innovative procedural models for DSR. This paper represents the first phase of an ongoing research initiative. Preliminary findings suggest that the documentation of these collaborations lacks precision and adequate oversight. The purpose of this study is to highlight the need for further research in this area, with the final goal of establishing a framework to guide future research efforts in practitioner-researcher collaborations.

Keywords Design science research (DSR) · Collaboration in DSR · Practice impacts · Researcher and practitioner collaboration · University–business collaboration · Academic-practitioner relationships

---

S. M. Schmid (✉)
University of St. Gallen, St. Gallen, Switzerland
e-mail: simonmichael.schmid@student.unisg.ch

M. Cipriano et al. (eds.), *Technologies for Organizations and Society*,
Lecture Notes in Information Systems and Organisation 80,
https://doi.org/10.1007/978-3-032-01697-3_22

1 Introduction

Design Science Research (DSR) takes the approach of creating innovative artifacts to solve real-world problems and generate design knowledge [1, 2]. The design of artifacts has both scientific and practical relevance, as it always involves multiple stakeholders, such as researchers and practitioners [2–4]. As ongoing research, as part of a larger research project, this research paper provides an initial contribution to the question of how practitioners and researchers work together in DSR projects. This endeavour represents an attempt to design and establish a comprehensive and exhaustive knowledge base. Several stakeholders, such as experts, decision-makers and researchers, must work together on a project [5, 6]. However, these different groups naturally do not always pursue the same goals [1]. DSR research must always fulfill the criteria of both scientific rigor and relevance [3, 7]. While the focus for practitioners is on a functional and effective solution, research attempts to generate (design) knowledge through the construction and evaluation of artifacts and to incorporate this into the knowledge base and thereby expanding it [1, 4]. DSR therefore faces many challenges in meeting the different needs of practitioners and researchers as described by Sein et al. [8] that "researchers bring their knowledge of theory and technological advances, while the practitioners bring practical hypotheses and knowledge of organizational work practices" (p. 43). DSR projects include the generation of scientific knowledge on the one hand and practical implications on the other [1]. Often, these different interests lead to a DSR project being carried out with either a focus on impact on practice or a focus on knowledge contributions [1]. Achieving a balance between these conflicting goals is difficult [2]. A comprehensive understanding of the levels of abstraction of design artifacts in practical contributions and the role of scientific contributions in defining theory has already been established within the field of DSR [4], but the question remains as to how this is possible in the context of the tension between practice and research, and what the nature of the collaboration between researchers and practitioners is, as well as the challenges and problems encountered.

The determined research gap concerns the manner in which design artifacts are constructed in DSR projects, particularly focusing on their scientific and practical contributions. This raises the question of how collaboration between researchers and practitioners unfolds within the inherent tension between practice and research, as well as the challenges and problems that arise in this context. The objective of this research is to address the existing research gap by examining a range of DSR projects in relation to the collaboration between researchers and practitioners. This will enable the identification of the individuals involved, the phases during which collaboration occurred, the outcomes of the collaboration, and the challenges encountered during the process. Conclusions are drawn based on this analysis, and implications for the collaboration between practice and research, as well as for the methodology of DSR, are derived and recognized. The aim is to guide future efforts in improving practitioner-researcher collaborations. This results in the following research question:

RQ: *"How does collaboration between practitioners and researchers take place in complex DSR projects?"*

As a first step, this research paper provides an abstract of the related literature, which gives an overview of DSR research and artifacts and highlights the collaboration between practitioners and researchers. This is followed by an explanation of the methodology of the literature analysis. In the findings and conclusion section, the results of the literature analysis are analyzed regarding the research questions and the contribution of the research. Finally, further research is outlined, and the limitations of this work are described. This paper is the first part of a larger research project and therefore is an attempt to design and set the knowledge base for an exhaustive and comprehensive work representing a preliminary exploration.

2 Related Literature

2.1 Design Science Research

Design science research (DSR) is a design-oriented problem-solving research paradigm that deals with the systematic design and evaluation of artifacts to generate knowledge. DSR has its roots in engineering and the artificial sciences [9]. It is based on methods from various scientific disciplines, such as business administration, engineering and computer science [9]. DSR seeks to enhance human knowledge with the creation of innovative artifacts and the generation of design knowledge via innovative solutions to real-world problems [1]. DSR is an iterative approach to the design and evaluation of an artifact, where the iteration stages consider both relevance (i.e. importance to the application domain) and rigor (i.e. alignment with the scientific state of the art) [1, 3]. Hevner et al. [1] elucidates the pivotal distinction between behavioral science and design science, noting that "The goal of behavioral science in truth. The goal of design science is utility" (p. 80). The objective of a DSR research project is to extend the boundaries of human and organizational capabilities by designing new and innovative artifacts, represented by constructs, models, methods and instantiations [1, 4]. DSR aims to generate knowledge through human action about how things can and should be constructed or arranged (i.e. designed) to achieve a desired set of goals, this is referred to as design knowledge. In DSR, knowledge and understanding of a problem are achieved through the development and application of a solution that aims to improve existing practices and research findings [1, 10]. However, based on the fundamental assumptions of the DSR approach [4], various process models have been developed to structure the research in terms of methodology and content. The underlying aim is to design, implement, analyze, manage and use information systems (IS) effectively and efficiently [1].

2.2 The Output of DSR: Artifact

The output of a DSR solution takes the form of an artifact or set of artifacts. In DSR, the development of artifacts is a central element that serves to address both theoretical and practical problems [1, 2, 4]. Artifacts in DSR can be diverse, including models, methods, frameworks or software and system prototypes [4, 11]. The output of DSR research, the artifact, pursues various goals. Essentially, these include understanding and improving existing practices, generating knowledge, improving human performance and achieving an improvement in organizational capabilities [1, 4]. The objective is to serve the human purpose [11]. The development process of an artifact typically follows an iterative cycle. It starts with identifying the problem and defining the goals, which is followed by the design and development phase, in which the artifact is designed and created. This phase often comprises several iterations in which the artifact is continuously improved. After development, a rigorous evaluation takes place, which aims to check the effectiveness and efficiency of the artifact in relation to the requirements [1, 3].

2.3 Researcher and Practitioner Collaboration

The contributions of DSR projects include both scientific findings and effects on application practice [1]. In DSR projects, specific challenges often arise from the collaboration between practitioners and researchers, which result from the different goals, working methods and communication styles of the two groups [3, 4]. The tensions arise from the different backgrounds of the stakeholders, different expectations and approaches. This results in different objectives: While the practitioners are looking for good solutions with measurable improvements for the practical problem, the aim of the scientists is to gain generalizable design knowledge through the creation, evaluation, and use of the artifact. This theoretical knowledge can be generalized and is valid beyond the individual application [12]. Similarly, practitioners try to achieve quick results by making efficient decisions, while research takes an iterative and explorative approach. Consequently, the fundamentally different interests of the stakeholders mean that a DSR research project will either focus on the impact on practice or on the contributions to knowledge. Achieving a possible balance between the two contributions is difficult [10].

3 Research Methodology

To the best of the author's knowledge, there is currently no existing literature that focuses on analyzing and reviewing the collaboration between practitioners and researchers, nor on identifying potential issues in such collaborations. As the presentation of the results of a research project naturally focuses on the results, the collaboration between researchers and practitioners that took place during the project is briefly mentioned in the paper but not explicitly and in detail elaborated. To gain a deeper insight into this topic, a literature review was conducted on projects in which collaboration between practitioners and researchers took place. The following criteria will be used to examine this: (1) the project phases in which the collaboration took place, (2) the parties involved, (3) the nature of the developed artefact, and (4) the challenges encountered during the collaboration.

In order to identify existing literature regarding the collaboration between practitioners and researchers in DSR projects, a comprehensive search of academic sources was conducted. The databases for the literature search were AISel, ACM, Ebsco IEEE, Scopus and Science Direct. Databases such as AISel, ACM and IEEE were chosen because they reflect established traditions and research priorities in Information Systems and Engineering. These traditions influence the way in which researchers and practitioners in these disciplines collaborate and thus contribute to the relevance of the knowledge gained.

The keywords listed below, were selected to ensure that this is a Design Science Research project and that a complex and real artifact (not just a theoretical artifact) has been developed. They are derived from the DSR context [1, 3, 4] on the one hand, and from the research question and the requirements of the overall research project on the other. The keywords also reflect efforts to identify potential challenges to collaborating and to generate learning.

"Design Science Research" OR "DSR"
AND ("Artifact" OR "System" OR "Solution" OR "Product" OR "Innovation")
AND (Complex* OR difficult OR complicat* OR Challeng*)
AND (Knowledge OR Expertise OR Insights OR Understanding OR Learn Or Understand)

Only English-language publications that had undergone a peer review process and were published between 2004 and 2024 were considered. Starting in 2004 was chosen deliberately, as the publication of Hevner et al. [1] published in 2004, was a key milestone in DSR research. Much of the DSR literature that has been published since then has been strongly influenced by this paper. The initial search identified 109 hits. Based on these results, a title and abstract screening was carried out according to the following criteria. A paper was excluded if it did not meet both of the following criteria: (1) the development of a complex artifact, and (2) the existence of a practical collaboration. In this way, all publications that did not contain a complex artifact or only contained a theoretical artifact with no practical relevance were excluded.

A total of 76 results were excluded through title and abstract screening, leaving 33 publications. The next step is to carry out a full paper screening. The ATLAS.ti software is employed for a more detailed analysis of the collaboration between practitioners and researchers. First, the full paper examines for the inclusion criteria mentioned above. Consequently, a further 33 publications are excluded from the

Table 1 Databases and literature analysis

Source	Results	After abstract screening	After full paper screening
IEEE	32	4	2
ACM	5	2	1
Scopus	4	1	1
Science Direct	20	11	6
AISel	6	3	1
EBSCO	42	16	5
Total	**109**	**37**	**16**

analysis, leaving 16 publications for a more detailed examination. Table 1 provides an overview of the papers that were analyzed and subsequently discarded. The remaining papers are then subjected to a more detailed analysis based on the following four criteria, which are reflected in the structure of Sect. 4:

(i) In which of the phases described by Peffers et al. [3] and elucidated in greater detail in Sect. 4.1 did documented collaboration between practitioners and researchers occur
(ii) Which stakeholders were involved in the DSR project
(iii) What kind of artifact was developed and
(iv) What problems occurred in the collaboration between researchers and practitioners and how, or if at all, were these documented

The aim is not to analyze all the literature on each topic, but to obtain a synthesis of content for each area. Therefore, the search was limited to complex artifacts in DSR research in practical collaboration. This literature search should only serve as a starting point to identify possible problems in the collaboration between practitioners and researchers, as well as their documentation.

4 Findings and Discussion

In this section, the results of the literature analysis are presented and analyzed. The results are divided into four specific aspects in order to address the research question posed at the beginning. The objective is to elucidate the temporal, personnel, technical, and problematic dimensions of cooperation, thereby facilitating a comprehensive understanding of the multifaceted aspects of cooperation.

Section 4.1 provides a structured analysis of the collaboration between practitioners and researchers. A comprehensive understanding of how interactions between researchers and practitioners take place in the course of a project is developed by analyzing the different phases of collaboration according to Peffers et al. that typically occur in a DSR project [3]. An in-depth understanding of these phases, through which the collaboration of the interacting groups and individuals passes, forms the essential basis for identifying and evaluating specific factors influencing the effectiveness of the collaboration.

Section 4.2 then analyzes the stakeholders involved. This section will present an analysis of the stakeholder groups involved in the collaborative process.

Since the development of the artifact is the central aspect of DSR, a detailed analysis of the development of the artifact follows in Sect. 4.3. Here, prior screening of the papers ensured that the artifact was (1) real and (2) complex. The type of artifact development is central to the understanding of practitioner-researcher collaboration. The different types of artifacts, such as software or prototypes, have different implications for practice, which have a decisive influence on the collaboration between researchers and practitioners.

Finally, Sect. 4.4 discusses various problems that have arisen in research-practice cooperation. Identifying and documenting the problems encountered is the basic prerequisite for understanding the challenges and obstacles in the collaboration and learning from them in order to achieve significant optimization for future projects.

These four aspects are suitable for offering potential problems, challenges and solutions, as they cover the essential aspects of DSR processes and thus make it possible to comprehensively map the dynamics and challenges that form the initial question for this work.

4.1 Phases of the Collaboration

The analysis of the results is based on the process model proposed by Peffers et al. [3] which consists of six phases (1) Identify Problem and Motivate, (2) Define Objectives of a Solution, (3) Design and Development, (4) Demonstration, (5) Evaluation and (6) Communication. The process model proposed by Peffers et al. [3] was selected for its comprehensive structure and its relevance to design science research. The model provides a clearly defined framework that enables the systematic analysis of collaboration between researchers and practitioners. In particular, this model allows the differentiation of specific phases in the development of artifacts, thereby facilitating a more precise analysis. According to Peffers et al. [3], DSR projects progress through six phases. Phase six (communication), however, is not subjected to a more detailed analysis. This is because the analysis is based on scientific publications, which inherently reflect communication originating from scientists. This point will be addressed in greater detail in the limitations section. Table 2 illustrates the collaborative efforts between practitioners and researchers, as evidenced by the research work analysed in the previously introduced phases. The "X" symbol denotes instances of joint cooperation. The individual phases are elucidated in the subsequent sections.

The first phase of collaboration typically starts with problem identification, which enables practitioners and researchers to work together to define the problem. Therefore, the problem is usually defined and narrowed down by expert interview(s) [22, 24, 25]. Different experts are used to identify the problem(s). For example

Table 2 Phases of collaboration

Source	Identify problem	Define objectives of a solution	Design & development	Demonstration	Evaluation
Bagheri et al. [13]					X
Bodendorf et al. [14]					X
Bagheri et al. [15]			X		X
Iaksch and Borsato [16]	X			X	X
Ge et al. [17]	X		X		X
Palomar et al. [18]			X		X
Inan and Beydoun [19]	X		X	X	X
Widjaja and Gregory [20]	X	X	X	X	X
Brendel et al. [21]	X		X	X	X
Große et al. [22]	X				X
Mikkelsen et al. [23]	X				X
Schacht et al. [24]	X				X
Guggenberger et al. [25]	X				X
Behutiye et al. [26]	X		X		X
Ramtahalsing et al. [27]	X	X	X		X
Rosa et al. [28]	X			X	X
Total	**12**	**2**	**8**	**5**	**16**

semi-structured workshops with project managers from different companies are used [23] or a combination of literature, expert interviews and internal company literature is used as a starting point for the collaboration [24]. A mixed approach consisting of theoretical and practical data is used as a starting point [14, 18]. For example the "users of the platform" and the "providers of the platform" give an insight into the different orientations of the experts [22]. The Delphi method is used to provide participants from different value networks, as well as from different geographical areas, with the opportunity to share existing ideas, free from the risk of being influenced by group effects [15]. For this purpose, semi-structured expert interviews are conducted with each individual expert [23]. This approach creates a common understanding of the problem, which can facilitate and improve future communication. However, in addition to the practical aspects, research always begins with an analysis of the existing literature.

In the second phase, the Define Objectives of a Solution phase, the particular objectives of the artifact to be developed are defined. In Ramtahalsing et al. [27], for instance, the question is posed: What should the design accomplish? The design is divided into several sub-goals. The "how" is addressed through a detailed analysis in this phase. In Widjaja and Gregory [20], the problem is standardized in the initial phase in order to address the objectives of a solution at a later stage.

In the third phase, the Design and Development the artifacts are constructed. In this phase, the theoretical concepts and requirements that were previously identified are translated into a concrete design [3]. Palomar et al. [18] created an online platform in the source artifact to standardize and synchronize information about historical architecture. The objective of the platform is to facilitate the integration of disparate information sources and enhance collaboration between stakeholders engaged in heritage conservation and architectural heritage [16]. In Ge at al. [17] a River Basin Sustainable Development Decision Support System is developed. This system develops and evaluates a design science research perspective, which is then used to address a range of sustainability issues in endorheic catchments. A decision support system is currently being developed with the objective of promoting sustainability. This integrates disparate systems and provides a decision-making framework for the sustainable management of water resources in these specific geographical regions [20].

In the fourth, demonstration phase the developed artifact is tested in a real or simulated environment to check its functionality and effectiveness. The aim of this phase is to demonstrate the applicability of the artifact and to evaluate its performance [3]. For example, in Rosa et al. [28], the demonstration phase involves implementing the developed method in a real industrial context. This includes the digital evaluation of the suitability of the current production system for adapting to changes in product design. Real data and scenarios are used to test the effectiveness of the method and demonstrate its benefits in a practical use case. In Brendel et al. [21] the developed crowd-based system will be tested in a simulated environment to evaluate its effectiveness in optimizing the distribution of car-sharing vehicles. Widjaja and Gregory [20] describe in the demonstration phase how the developed IT artifact, which is used to monitor and analyze the complexity of IT architectures, is used in a real business environment. Iaksch and Borsato describe in the demonstration phase how the developed digital evaluation method is tested through a case study in a real production environment within the automotive industry and is applied to existing production systems to evaluate their suitability and flexibility in relation to changes in product development [16].

The evaluation, which follows in the fifth phase, is usually also carried out in collaboration between the researchers and practitioners to test the built solution's functionality. Various methods are used here. Examples include "why questions" and "real-life discussions" [13]. There is also the option of conducting an evaluation through expert interviews with "domain experts" and "managing directors" [21]. The practitioners were able to evaluate the causal effect of each input on the defined target variable [13]. In several iterations, the design principles are evaluated ex-ante and the development of the artifact is evaluated ex-post with various experts [22]. Evaluations are also carried out using a combination of technical evaluation tools and expert interviews [25]. The evaluations were also realized with the help of questionnaires and an open discussion [26].

The final phase, communication, was carried out exclusively by the scientists.

4.2 Stakeholders Involved

The second analytical step concerns the examination of the stakeholders involved in the collaboration between researchers and practitioners. The stakeholder categories are derived from the works of vom Brocke and Lippe [5] and vom Brocke and Maedche [6], and are augmented by pertinent stakeholders identified in the analysed papers.

Table 3 shows the results from the analysed literature. A distinction is made here between (a) external stakeholders, such as suppliers, external experts and developers, and (b) internal stakeholders, such as decision makers, business departments and internal experts.

Only two papers explicitly mentioned cooperation with suppliers as stakeholders; for example, in Bodendorf et al. [14] "first-tier supplier [...] in the automotive industry" (p. 4) is mentioned as an important partner in the research project. There are different variants of decision makers, like for example decision makers from the area of "watershed management" [17]. Examples of business departments are the "product development department" [16]. Engineers and technical staff are also mentioned as further stakeholders [17]. In some cases, the collaboration took place not only with one company but also with several companies over a longer period of time. Examples of this include collaboration with five different companies over a period of 8 years [20] or with two companies, such as those from the car-sharing provider sector [21] or Agile Software Development [26], as well as with 15 different companies [23].

It is worth noting that in 50% of the studies analyzed, the collaboration took place between the researchers and the relevant business unit within the company. In about

Table 3 Involved stakeholders

Source	Research and academic institutions	Supplier	Industrial partner: Decision maker	Industrial partner: Business departments	Industrial partner: Experts	External Experts	Developer
Bagheri et al. [13]	X		X				
Bodendorf et al. [14]	X	X					
Bagheri et al. [15]	X	X			X		
Iaksch and Borsato [16]	X			X			
Ge et al. [17]	X		X				X
Palomar et al. [18]	X					X	
Inan and Beydoun [19]	X		X			X	
Widjaja and Gregory [20]	X		X				
Brendel et al. [21]	X		X	X	X	X	X
Große et al. [22]	X			X			
Mikkelsen et al. [23]	X		X	X			
Schacht et al. [24]	X			X	X		
Guggenberger et al. [25]	X			X	X	X	
Behutiye et al. [26]	X			X			
Ramtahalsing et al. [27]	X				X		
Rosa et al. [28]	X			X	X		
Total	**16**	**2**	**6**	**8**	**6**	**4**	**2**

a third of the studies analyzed, additional decision-makers or internal company experts were involved in the collaboration. Internal company experts are technical experts from different departments of the company who are not employed in the department with which the project is carried out. This group of people includes, for example, lawyers or security experts [27]. In only 25% of the cases analyzed are experts from outside the company consulted, such as researchers in specific fields, for example experts in "historic buildings" [18] or experts from research institutes on health [25]. In three of the cases analyzed, suppliers such as automotive suppliers [14] or health technology suppliers [25] were also explicitly mentioned. Overall, it can be seen that in most cases the collaboration took place between researchers and the respective business unit, often complemented by internal experts.

4.3 Artifact Development

In the DSR process, the initially developed artifact goes through a varying number of iterations of further development and refinement. The number of iterations through which the artifact evolves ranges from one iteration [14, 15, 26], to two iterations [22], to three iterations [19, 20, 29], to four iterations [21], to five iterations [28]. In essence, the artifact undergoes a process of refinement and improvement with each iteration. However, in Widjaja and Gregory [20], the artifact does not improve with each iteration; rather, it oscillates between two levels of IT artifact creation and problem-solving. On the one hand, this involves collaboration with the company, and on the other, it entails the accumulation of abstract knowledge. This results in a "reverse loop," which allows for the adjustment of the artifact. Following the demonstration and evaluation phase, the artifact is deemed to have undergone an improvement before entering the communication phase.

4.4 Problems in Collaboration Between Practitioners and Researchers

The problem of different perspectives between practitioners and researchers is addressed by Ge et al. [17] at this point: "The dilemma is rooted in the different perspectives from which scientists and decision-makers explain phenomena" (p. 2). In general, however, the problems encountered by researchers in working together are not described in detail, but in general terms, including Iaksch et al. [16] "that process engineers do not follow a pre-established flow of activities" (p. 4) and "product engineering [...] does not consider the requirements [...] in a structured way" (p. 4). Such circumstances have the potential to result in delays and complications. The problems arise from the different perspectives from which scientists and decision-makers explain phenomena. Here, as stated by Ge et al.

[17] "scientific methods are focused on the nature of a phenomenon and are used to explore and quantitatively describe the interaction mechanism of internal elements based on assumptions drawn from a methodological perspective" (p. 2), while on the other hand practitioners seek a solution from a simple and available approach. Bringing together experts with different backgrounds and from different organisations can provide diverse insights [27].

In order to conclude, it can be stated that the research question, which was posed at the outset of this study, namely, "How does collaboration between practitioners and researchers take place in complex DSR projects?" can be answered by recognising that there is no clear pattern that can always be identified. It can be stated that collaboration typically occurs between researchers and the respective company department, as illustrated in Sect. 4.2. In such instances, a decision-maker and/or experts from the company are frequently involved. There is also the possibility that other stakeholders, such as other companies or external experts, are also involved in the process. With these stakeholders, the problem is identified and defined at the beginning, usually through expert interviews. As shown the process in which the artifact is built and evaluated is often carried out by the research team. In some cases, there is also collaboration with practitioners in the "design and development" and "demonstration" phases. However, the development is often the responsibility of the researchers and co-operation only takes place again at the time of evaluation. This is mostly carried out on the basis of expert interviews with practitioners. There is usually no mutual communication. Also, only a few research studies record whether the same employees were responsible for the requirements at the beginning and for the evaluation at the end [25] or whether other employees were used for this purpose. Furthermore, the number of iterations observed does not appear to exhibit a discernible correlation with the interaction between the Parkers and the researchers. All in all, it can be stated that in some cases the collaboration is very close and well documented [20, 24], but in most cases it is not described in great detail.

5 Discussion and Conclusion

The purpose of this paper is to provide an initial insight into a larger research project on practitioner-researcher collaboration in the context of DSR. The initial findings and the necessity for further research were derived from an analysis of the existing literature. The findings presented here show that the process of documentation between practitioners and researchers is described only to a limited extent and not in great detail, with the two exceptions [20, 24].

Basically, it can be recognized that the relevant problem is often described, narrowed down and defined in collaboration with practitioners. Research teams then build a solution artifact over several iterations, which is then presented and tested in practice. Between the starting point of the collaboration and the collaborative problem identification and the final evaluation of the artifact, little collaboration seems to take place or be documented, which means that the researchers build and further develop the artifact. However, it seems hardly plausible that little or no collaboration takes place between problem identification and definition and the testing and evaluation of the finished artifact. It often seems as if the collaboration is not precisely documented in every phase, as the focus of the publication remains on the result, the developed artifact and its application and evaluation. Collaboration may take place but is not described in detail or not mentioned. Research projects in the field of design science present particular challenges, as different interest groups with different requirements and objectives are involved. While practitioners want contextualized solutions for real and complex problems, researchers focus on the generation of knowledge. Problems and conflicts that (possibly) arise from these conflicting objectives are not addressed in the research papers analyzed. Overall, DSR should focus more on a continuous dialogue between researchers and practitioners.

Current DSR research, such as Design Science Research Methodology (DSRM) [3] and Action Design Research (ADR) [8, 30], provides limited methodological guidance to balance the activities and collaboration of practitioners and researchers and their different project goals. DSR should always generate design knowledge and provide solutions to real-world problems. In order to gain insight into the role of academics and practitioners and their impact on DSR projects, this study was undertaken. The initial objective is to comprehend the manner in which the collaboration is structured and documented, the parties involved, and the influence of the collaboration on the various phases of the project and the different artifacts. The objective is to be able to address these points in greater depth in the subsequent phase of the overarching research project.

Based on a review of the literature, the study shows that there is evidence that practitioners and researchers collaborate only at certain stages of DSR research. It also shows that the process of collaboration and the problems that arise in this context are described only marginally and with little detail. This paper contributes to the research by showing that there is a need for in-depth analysis. The focus should be on examining and analysing the cooperation that has actually taken place, as well as identifying the problems that arise and comparing them with the documentation of DSR research. As DSR in IS research offers a good opportunity to bridge the gap between scientific rigor and practical relevance, a precise understanding of the cooperation between practitioners and researchers is needed.

6 Future Research and Limitation

The aim of this paper is to take the initial phase in a larger research project with the overarching theme of analyzing the current state of collaboration between practitioners and researchers in DSR, in order to identify and develop further research needs. The research is subject to several limitations. It should be noted that the databases selected for the literature review represent a targeted selection and a suitable sample, and therefore only represent a selection. It is, however, suitable for deriving initial hypotheses. Future research could start here and extend the literature search to other databases, for example, and integrate the aspect of professional literature in order to gain a more comprehensive insight and thereby expand and analyze the communication phase as described in Sect. 4.1. Another process model could also be used to enable comparisons with the process model used [3]. As stated at the beginning, this paper does not claim to provide a comprehensive overview. It is limited to pointing out the vaguely defined and not very detailed documentation of the collaboration between practitioners and researchers that was evident in the results. As the focus of the publications is naturally on the results, the artifacts developed and the evaluation of these artifacts, the collaboration between the actors involved has not been well documented. This is an important starting point for further research to analyze in more detail what the actual interaction and cooperation between researchers and practitioners looks like. To this end, it seems useful to conduct interviews with the researchers and experts involved in order to analyze how cooperation actually took place in practice, what problems arose, how these were solved and how the whole process could be improved in order to achieve an even better result for all involved. Furthermore, interviews could be conducted with the stakeholders identified in Sect. 4.2. This can provide valuable information that can form the basis of a framework for future research. Another limitation is the choice of factors to be analyzed. The aim in this section was also to gain initial indications of where cooperation should be improved in order to further optimize the DSR methodology through further research and thereby achieve the overarching goal of providing further research activities with a clear set of rules. Further research is needed to address the different interests, backgrounds, motivations and languages of practitioners and researchers and to support meaningful collaboration.

This article provides an overview of the collaboration between researchers and practitioners in DSR projects, as well as the complexity of the tasks and problems that arise in the context of this collaboration. The aim of this paper is to provide a direction for further steps in research in order to promote constructive scientific dialogue and improve the interaction between researchers, experts and practitioners and to make an important contribution to supporting and improving the transfer of knowledge from research to practice and vice versa.

Acknowledgments No acknowledgments.

Disclosure of Interests The author has no competing interests to declare that are relevant to the content of this article.

References

1. Hevner, A. R., March, S. T., Park, J., & Ram, S. (2004). Design science in information systems research. *MIS Quarterly, 28*, 75–105.
2. Vom Brocke, J., Winter, R., Hevner, A., & Maedche, A. (2020). Special issue editorial—Accumulation and evolution of design knowledge in design science research: a journey through time and space. *Journal of the Association for Information Systems, 21*, 9.
3. Peffers, K., Tuunanen, T., Rothenberger, M. A., & Chatterjee, S. (2007). A design science research methodology for information systems research. *Journal of Management Information Systems, 24*, 45–77.
4. Gregor, S., & Hevner, A. R. (2013). Positioning and presenting design science research for maximum impact. *MIS Quarterly, 37*, 337–355.
5. vom Brocke, J., & Lippe, S. (2010). Taking a project management perspective on design science research. In *Global perspectives on design science research: 5th International conference, DESRIST 2010, St. Gallen, Switzerland, June 4–5. Proceedings* (pp. 31–44). Springer.
6. Vom Brocke, J., & Maedche, A. (2019). The DSR grid: six core dimensions for effectively planning and communicating design science research projects. *Electronic Markets, 29*, 379–385.
7. Hevner, A. R. (2007). A three cycle view of design science research. *Scandinavian Journal of Information Systems, 19*, 4.
8. Sein, M. K., Henfridsson, O., Purao, S., Rossi, M., & Lindgren, R. (2011). Action design research. *MIS Quarterly, 35*(1), 37–56.
9. Simon, H. (1996). *The sciences of the artificial.* MIT Press.
10. Baskerville, R., Baiyere, A., Gregor, S., Hevner, A., & Rossi, M. (2018). Design science research contributions: Finding a balance between artifact and theory. *Journal of the Association for Information Systems, 19*, 3.
11. March, S. T., & Smith, G. F. (1995). Design and natural science research on information technology. *Decision Support Systems, 15*, 251–266.
12. Drechsler, A., & Hevner, A. (2015). Effectuation and its implications for socio-technical design science research in information systems. In *At the Vanguard of design science: First impressions and early findings from ongoing research research-in-progress papers and poster presentations from the 10th international conference, DESRIST 2015. Dublin, Ireland, 20–22 May*.
13. Bagheri, S., Kusters, R. J., & Trienekens, J. J. M. (2019). Customer knowledge transfer challenges in a co-creation value network: Toward a reference model. *International Journal of Information Management, 47*, 198–214.
14. Bodendorf, F., Sauter, M., & Franke, J. (2023). A mixed methods approach to analyze and predict supply disruptions by combining causal inference and deep learning. *International Journal of Production Economics, 256*, 108708.
15. Bagheri, S., Kusters, R. J., Trienekens, J. J. M., & Grefen, P. W. P. J. (2019). A reference model-based user requirements elicitation process: Toward operational business-IT alignment in a co-creation value network. *Information and Software Technology, 111*, 72–85.
16. Iaksch, J. S., & Borsato, M. (2019). Method for digital evaluation of existing production systems adequacy to changes in product engineering in the context of the automotive industry. *Advanced Engineering Informatics, 42*, 100942.
17. Ge, Y., Han, F., Wu, F., Zhao, Y., Li, H., Tian, Y., Zheng, Y., Luan, W., Zhang, L., Cai, X., Ma, C., & Li, X. (2024). Sustainable decision making based on systems integration and decision support system promoting endorheic basin sustainability. *Decision Support Systems, 179*, 114169.
18. Palomar, I. J., García Valldecabres, J. L., Tzortzopoulos, P., & Pellicer, E. (2020). An online platform to unify and synchronise heritage architecture information. *Automation in Construction, 110*, 103008.

19. Inan, D. I., & Beydoun, G. (2017). Disaster knowledge management analysis framework utilizing agent-based models: Design science research approach. *Procedia Computer Science, 124*, 116–124.
20. Widjaja, T., & Gregory, R. W. (2020). Monitoring the complexity of IT architectures: design principles and an IT artifact. *Journal of the Association for Information Systems, 21*, 4.
21. Brendel, A. B., Lichtenberg, S., Morana, S., Prinz, C., & Hillmann, B. M. (2022). Designing a crowd-based relocation system—The case of car-sharing. *Sustainability, 14*(12), 7090.
22. Große, N., Möller, F., Schoormann, T., & Henke, M. (2024). Designing trust-enabling blockchain systems for the inter-organizational exchange of capacity. *Decision Support Systems, 179*, 114182.
23. Mikkelsen, M., Venable, J., & Aaltonen, K. (2020). Researching navigation of project complexity using action design research. *International Journal of Managing Projects in Business, 14*(1), 108–130. Ahead-of-print.
24. Schacht, S., Morana, S., & Maedche, A. (2015). The evolution of design principles enabling knowledge reuse for projects: an action design research project. *Journal of Information Technology Theory and Application (JITTA), 16*, 2.
25. Guggenberger, T., Schweizer, A., & Urbach, N. (2020). Improving interorganizational information sharing for vendor managed inventory: Toward a decentralized information hub using blockchain technology. *IEEE Transactions on Engineering Management, 67*, 1074–1085.
26. Behutiye, W., Rodríguez, P., & Oivo, M. (2022). Quality requirement documentation guidelines for agile software development. *IEEE Access, 10*, 70154–70173.
27. Ramtahalsing, M., Haanstra, W., Braaksma, J., Rajabalinejad, M., & van Dongen, L. (2023). MOSAIC: A structured multidisciplinary analysis for managing the integration of inter-organizational changes. *Engineering Management Journal, 35*, 405–419.
28. Rosa, T. D. O., Guerra, E. M., Correia, F. F., & Goldman, A. (2023). CharM—Evaluating a model for characterizing service-based architectures. *Journal of Systems and Software, 206*, 111826.
29. Lepmets, M., Mesquida, A. L., Cater-Steel, A., Mas, A., & Ras, E. (2014). The evaluation of the IT service quality measurement framework in industry. *Global Journal of Flexible Systems Management, 15*, 39–57.
30. Mullarkey, M. T., & Hevner, A. R. (2019). An elaborated action design research process model. *European Journal of Information Systems, 28*, 6–20.

Unveiling the Behaviour: Analysing Isomorphic Forces in the Emilia-Romagna Industrial Ecosystem

Michele Cipriano, Francesco Virili, Franca Cantoni, and Diego Boerchi

Abstract This study investigates non-financial accounting novelties within the "ECOSISTER: Ecosystem for Sustainable Transition in Emilia-Romagna" project, aligned with and funded by the "NextGeneration EU" plan. Sustainability is still an urgent challenge for organisations increasingly compelled to acknowledge the significance of integrating environmental, social, and governance (ESG) factors into their operations. In addition, accounting for non-financial purposes often appears as a voluntary, self-crafted practice that organisations develop to gain competitive advantage and visibility. In light of this, the European Union (EU) Taxonomy emerges as one of the latest methodologies the EU defines for accounting and measuring industrial ecosystems toward the transition to sustainable activities. This work aims to examine whether the Emilia-Romagna regional industrial ecosystems recognise and align to such new metrics. We aim to explore organisational and managerial implications for enterprises and how these regulations influence their actions. Contributing to developing and interpreting an extensive survey questionnaire intersecting various academic disciplines, this work draws on the literature based on isomorphism and institutional theories. We design a framework to examine the three isomorphic forces: normative, coercive, and mimetic. The outcomes of this work are twofold: (1) to qualitatively describe the existing research interconnecting isomorphic forces, information technology, and non-financial accountability practices; (2) to recognise the main drivers that could contribute to targeting the Italian production ecosystem toward sustainable transition. Hence, this preliminary study lays the groundwork for examining a large-scale survey, building theoretical and

M. Cipriano (✉) · F. Virili · F. Cantoni
Department of Economic and Social Sciences, Catholic University of the Sacred Heart, Piacenza, Italy
e-mail: michele.cipriano@unicatt.it; francesco.virili@unicatt.it; franca.cantoni@unicatt.it

D. Boerchi
Department of Psychology, Catholic University of the Sacred Heart, Milan, Italy
e-mail: diego.boerchi@unicatt.it

M. Cipriano et al. (eds.), *Technologies for Organizations and Society*,
Lecture Notes in Information Systems and Organisation 80,
https://doi.org/10.1007/978-3-032-01697-3_23

methodological foundations for examining the "alignment" of Italian's industrial ecosystems to the EU Taxonomy.

Keywords EU taxonomy · ESG · Non-financial measures · Isomorphism · Twin transformation

1 Introduction

The Italian region Emilia Romagna is characterised by one of Europe's most relevant innovation ecosystems. This dynamic network composed of shared resources, institutions, organisations, and projects acts as a powerful ecosystem for regional growth. By fostering collaboration, supporting research and development (R&D), and supporting entrepreneurship, such a regional innovation ecosystem benefits Italy and extends its impact beyond national borders [1, 2].

In this context, the Ecosister project, funded under the "NextGeneration EU plan" and Italy's "Piano Nazionale Ripresa e Resilienza" (PNRR), represents a flagship research endeavour involving various research institutions, six universities, four public research centres and thirteen private research and innovation centres. The project aims to invest 110 million € over 3 years (2023–2025), collaborating over 800 researchers to leverage the innovation ecosystem for Emilia-Romagna's sustainable transition.

Specifically, research activities encompass critical areas such as sustainable materials, clean energy production, green manufacturing, intelligent mobility solutions, and ecological transitions driven by high-performance computing and data technology. This research refers to the sub-area of the Ecosister project dedicated to exploring the measurement and reporting of sustainability, where the EU Taxonomy [1], alongside (and in conjunction with) other EU regulations (such as the Corporate Sustainability Reporting Directive (CSRD) [2], and the Sustainable Finance Disclosure Regulation (SFDR) [3]), aims to innovate and transform sustainable finance [4–8].

Exploring the literature, some scholars have examined practical and political traits related to such innovative frameworks, exploring the link interconnecting financing transition through sustainable investments [4]. Others have focused on the potential impact of such a reporting regime with regard to the primary goal of investing capital for mitigating climate change [6]. Further researchers have studied the effect of such financial and non-financial regulations [1–3] on financial institutions and the banking realm [8]. Recent studies have also examined innovations and digitalisation initiatives, focusing on digital technologies and strategies for carrying sustainable output [9, 10]. Interestingly, scholarly attention is rapidly developing on the concept of "twin transformation" [11], intending to reflect the mutually reinforcing relationships given the digital and sustainability transition that organisations are called to put to the top of their agendas [12, 13]. From this perspective, the convergence of digital technologies and accounting information systems (AISs) has revolutionised the way organisations process, store, and report information in the digital era [12, 14–25].

In particular, non-financial accounting has emerged as a crucial element in the transition towards sustainability [26, 27]. As organisations face increasing pressure from stakeholders, regulators, and the broader society to account for their environmental, social, and governance (ESG) impacts, non-financial reporting has become a significant aspect of corporate accountability and transparency [28, 29]. Non-financial accounting refers to measuring and reporting an organisation's performance in areas that are not strictly financial but essential for long-term sustainability. This includes reporting on environmental impact, social responsibility, and governance practices. Non-financial accounting provides a more comprehensive view of an organisation's performance, complementing traditional financial reports with information that reflects the company's impact on society and the environment [26, 27].

As a result, besides the emphasis on coping with societal challenges at all levels of innovative ecosystems, contemporary organisations must increasingly align their operations toward less environmental impact activities [12, 13, 30]. This often requires organisations not only to undergo sustainability transformation but also to disclose information on how and to what extent their activities are associated with environmentally sustainable economic activities [31]. However, while the EU Taxonomy [1] is currently producing effects on companies that are required to publish information on sustainability issues, for smaller non-financial companies, this remains a voluntary decision, whether referring or not to such a directive and, therefore, releasing disclosure on sustainability matters or not. At the same time, such "smaller companies" that do not fall under the scope of CSRD can decide to disclose this information on a voluntary basis to get access to sustainable financing or for other business-related reasons.[1]

Based on such assumptions, this study would contribute to such an emerging discourse by exploring the institutional factors [32–34] affecting the adoption of non-financial accounting practices among heterogeneous organisations. This study sets forth designing and developing theory-grounded empirical research based on a large-scale survey to recognise the main drivers that contribute to targeting the Italian production ecosystem (with a particular focus on the Emila-Romagna region) toward sustainable transition. The underlying research questions are therefore:

- RQ1 (what?) *What factors drive companies towards alignment with the EU taxonomy of sustainable activities?* And
- RQ2 (how?) *How can these factors be interpreted as isomorphic behaviours?*

Drawing on the literature based on isomorphism and institutional theories [32–34], we identify a set of questions developing a framework to examine the three isomorphic forces: normative, coercive, and mimetic [35–38]. Accordingly, our long-term ambition is to examine an extensive survey investigation (that we

[1] https://ec.europa.eu/sustainable-finance-taxonomy/

contribute to develop) based on the intersection of various academic disciplines, including organisational and information systems focuses. In this paper, we design and propose a foundation based on some of the questions belonging to the mentioned large-scale survey. We also integrate additional items from previous studies [39–42], ensuring specific sets of questions address all three isomorphic forces.

The paper unfolds as follows. The next section provides an overview of the relevant EU regulations. Subsequently, the theoretical background includes literature analysis on isomorphic forces, evidencing the prominence of non-financial accounting. Section 4 proposes the methodological underpinnings of the data collection and analysis. Afterwards, information concerning the empirical analysis is reported, and the questionnaire scheme is developed on the basis of our interdisciplinary large-scale survey, integrated with extant studies investigating isomorphism in organisations. Expected outcomes, final remarks, and conclusions close the paper.

2 Regulatory Background

In the last two decades, sustainability reporting has represented a multifunctional tool for governments, companies, investors, and third-sector organisations to share and understand performance and impacts on a wide range of sustainability topics [43–45]. Among others, one of the pioneer ambitions toward sustainability reporting has been the Global Reporting Initiative (GRI), playing a pivotal role by proposing a standardised framework intended to help organisations communicate their environmental risks, opportunities, and practices to stakeholders such as investors, regulators, partners, employees, and customers [46–48]. In particular, in the realm of social and environmental accounting, several regulations and directives, such as the Carbon Disclosure Project (CDP) and the Non-Financial Reporting Directive (NFRD), have rapidly followed given the commitment of international associations and governments in such matter (e.g., the International Sustainability Standards Board (ISSB)) [43, 49–51].

In line with the aim of this paper, and focusing strictly on non-financial reporting directives, the EU recently introduced the Corporate Sustainability Reporting Directive (CSRD), which came into effect in 2023, introducing modernised and strengthened requirements for companies regarding social and environmental reporting [2]. The CSRD was introduced to enhance the disclosure process previously settled with the NFRD [51] by addressing the emerging issue of inconsistent and non-comparable data, which could have hindered sustainable investments and increased data costs for stakeholders [31]. By providing such a more straightforward and consistent framework, the CSRD allows investors and consumers to better understand and compare an organisation's ESG impact, enabling more informed decision-making based on sustainability data [31]. Specifically, the CSRD aims to ensure that investors and other stakeholders have the necessary information to evaluate the impact of companies on both people and the environment, as well

Table 1 Organisations or companies that will need to comply with the CSRD by 2028

Type/dimension	Criteria
Publicly listed companies, including all those listed on an EU-regulated stock ex-change, except for "micro-enterprises" that do not meet at least two of three criteria over consecutive balance sheet dates	(i) A total asset value of at least 450,000 € (ii) A net turnover of at least 900,000 € (iii) An average of at least 10 employees throughout the year
Large EU-based companies, whether listed or not, that meet at least two of the three criteria over two consecutive balance sheet dates	(i) A total asset value of at least 25 million € (ii) A net turnover of at least 50 million € (iii) An average of at least 250 employees throughout the year
Non-EU companies with an EU-based parent and an annual turnover of at least 150 million € in the EU over the past 2 years Non-EU ("third-country") companies that have an annual turnover in the EU of at least 150 million € over the past 2 years and meet one of three criteria	(i) A large EU-based subsidiary (ii) An EU-based subsidiary with securities listed on an EU-regulated stock exchange (iii) An EU-based subsidiary with at least 40 million € in net turnover

as to assess the financial risks and opportunities related to climate change and other sustainability issues. By standardising the required disclosures, the directive is expected to reduce company reporting costs over the medium to long term [2, 31]. In particular, compliance with the CSRD will be introduced gradually between 2024 and 2029, primarily building on the foundations of the NFRD or the size of the company and, therefore, becoming effective with the financial year 2024, with reporting starting in 2025. As a way of explanation, Table 1 reports the organisations or companies that must comply with the CSRD by 2028 that have been obligated to disclose sustainability information accordingly [2, 51].

Moreover, compliance with the CSRD requires companies to follow the European Sustainability Reporting Standards (ESRS). In this scenario, the European Financial Reporting Advisory Group (EFRAG) was established in 2001 with the support of the EU. EFRAG is a private association dedicated to serving the public interest. In 2022, it expanded its mission to align with the new responsibilities assigned under the CSRD. Hence, as part of this expanded role, EFRAG is currently entitled to provide the EU with technical advice, including a fully developed draft of the ESRS and proposals for amendments to these standards.[2]

Besides this, the EU introduced an industrial strategy in March 2020 in response to the challenges posed by the COVID-19 pandemic [52]. In particular, attention has been given to the concept of ecosystem, intending to emphasise the strong connections among diverse economic stakeholders (vertically and horizontally), underscoring the integration of ancillary activities like research and innovation, distribution networks, and business services with core industry sectors. Drawing on these premises, the EU taxonomy was defined upon six climate and environmental

[2] https://www.efrag.org/en

objectives, with the aim to categorise economic activities based on their sustainability performance, aligning with the goals of decarbonisation, digitalisation, and resilience within the EU economy.

2.1 The EU Taxonomy: A Component of the System of Sustainability Reporting Standards

The EU Taxonomy[3] is a regulatory framework establishing a standardised classification system for sustainable economic activities as part of the European Green Deal. Such a taxonomy aims to facilitate sustainable investment by clarifying which economic activities can be considered environmentally sustainable [1].

The primary role of the EU Taxonomy is to support the EU member states in advancing the EU's sustainability agenda by promoting investment in environmentally sustainable activities, fostering economic growth, and contributing to achieving climate and environmental objectives. Specifically, the six environmental objectives are (1) climate change mitigation, (2) climate change adaptation, (3) sustainable use and protection of water and marine resources, (4) transition to a circular economy, (5) pollution prevention and control, and (6) protection and restoration of biodiversity and ecosystems. Accordingly, activities are assessed against these objectives to determine their contribution to sustainability [53].

Beyond providing investors, businesses, and policymakers with a common language and framework for identifying sustainable economic activities (what constitutes environmentally sustainable investment), this framework is also intended to reduce greenhouse gas emissions and promote resource efficiency [1]. At the same time, the taxonomy would serve as a tool for enhancing transparency and accountability in sustainable finance by providing standardised information on the sustainability performance of investment opportunities. Specifically, in addition to its goal of accelerating financial flows to address the climate and environmental challenges [31], the EU Taxonomy was introduced to complement the EU's NFRD [51] and the more recent CSRD [2]. As a result, organisations subject to the CSRD (as in Table 1) are now also required to disclose the alignment of their activities or investments with the criteria established by the EU Taxonomy [2, 31]. Then, the taxonomy would encourage organisations to align their activities with sustainable principles, driving innovation and fostering the transition to a low-carbon, resource-efficient economy.

As a way of explanation, a total of 14 ecosystems were identified based on their technological and economic relevance and for their expected contribution to the decarbonisation, digitalisation and resilience of the EU economy. The latter are: Aerospace and Defence, Agri-food, Construction, Cultural and Creative

[3] https://finance.ec.europa.eu/sustainable-finance/tools-and-standards/eu-taxonomy-sustainable-activities_en

Industries, Digital, Electronics, Energy Intensive Industries, Energy-Renewables, Health, Mobility-Transport-Automotive, Proximity, Social Economy and Civil Security, Retail, Textiles, and Tourism. They account for approximately 70% of the EU economy and 80% of the business economy as a share of value added [54]. Interestingly, these ecosystems are interlinked (e.g., the Retail ecosystem provides services to all other ecosystems) and overlap with each other, as some activities are relevant for more than one ecosystem (e.g., professional services, waste management) [30].

3 Theoretical Framework

In the post-pandemic era, sustainability still represents a major concern for individuals and organisations [55], especially considering the unavoidable interconnections linked with economic and social factors [56]. As a result, the paradigm for a sustainable society's development and resilience goes far beyond environmental purposes [57, 58], as it is increasingly emerging from both academic and practice realms. For example, scholarly attention has recently been given to the role of digital technologies in addressing sustainability challenges in business, particularly through the concept of twin transitions [12]. This dual transformation involves the interplay between digital and green (sustainable) transitions, where the effective application of digital technologies is believed to enhance resource efficiency, support circular economies, and contribute to climate neutrality [13]. Moreover, achieving these twin transformations requires an organisation to comprehensively understand the synergies between digital and environmental advancements coupled with proactive and inclusive policies, considering the public sector and civil society should also be involved to maximise the benefits and minimise any negative side effects of digitisation and greening processes [11–13].

3.1 Twin Transformation: A Sustainable Perspective

Focusing on the industrial ecosystems [42, 59], this phenomenon has represented a significant effort of organisations to integrate environmental, social, and governance (ESG) objectives into their daily operations [55]. International governments committed to broader environmental goals in addition to accounting for climate change mitigation and adaptation contribute to this emerging pressure [40, 60–62]. For example, the growing traction among EU member states is facilitated by national regulations implementing EU norms and incentivising investment to accelerate the transition towards efficient production and consumption [63] as a response to the challenges posed by the COVID-19 pandemic [53].

Affecting industrial ecosystems is one of the latest significant efforts from the EU, represented by the EU Taxonomy, establishing a standardised classification system for sustainable economic activities [53]. This framework is intended to act as a catalyst for organisational sustainability (including digitalisation focuses), and at the same time, it represents an accounting tool for non-financial purposes [30]. Accordingly, this innovative system presents both challenges and opportunities for organisations [30], particularly concerning integrating financial and non-financial information [31, 51] while implementing sustainability [64–67].

From this perspective, the performance of an organisation's "sustainable economic activities" under the EU Taxonomy is presented through specific Key Performance Indicators (KPIs), which differ between financial and non-financial organisations. For financial undertakings, the primary KPI is the Green Asset Ratio (GAR), while non-financial undertakings focus on KPIs related to (1) Turnover, (2) Capital Expenditure (CapEx), and (3) Operational Expenditure (OpEx) [1, 2]. These KPIs are derived by aggregating the contributions of all EU' taxonomy-aligned economic activities within the organisation [31]. To begin this process, it is essential to identify which economic activities are taxonomy-eligible, with eligibility being a necessary condition for alignment, as required by the EU Taxonomy Regulation [31]. The EU Taxonomy categorises activities into three types: (1) primary activities that directly contribute to one of the six environmental objectives (such as climate change mitigation or adaptation), (2) transitional activities that support the shift to a climate-neutral economy, and (3) enabling activities that indirectly facilitate primary activities [31]. For an eligible activity to be considered taxonomy-aligned, it must meet three criteria: (1) it must substantially contribute to one of the six environmental objectives according to the Technical Screening Criteria (TSC), (2) it must do no significant harm (DNSH) to the other environmental objectives, and (3) it must comply with minimum social safeguards (MSS) [31]. As of July 2022, organisations have 88 activities to choose from in Climate Change Mitigation and 95 in Climate Change Adaptation for reporting their alignment with the EU Taxonomy [31]. Accordingly, such a reporting process involves identifying eligible activities, determining which of these are aligned, mapping their performance to the relevant EU Taxonomy KPIs, and then reporting these KPIs.

3.2 Twin Transformation: A Digital Perspective

Focusing on the other side of such twin transition [11–13], the rapid advancement of digital technologies presents opportunities to address these challenges and support sustainability initiatives [14–16, 23, 68]. For example, the convergence of digital technologies and accounting information systems (AISs) has revolutionised the way organisations process, store, and report information [22, 69]. Considering that the transformative potential of digital technologies enhances organisations empowering their data management process, digital AISs could enable organisations to identify, assess, and mitigate sustainability risks and opportunities, foster responsible business practices and enhance stakeholder trust [70, 71].

In this perspective, Zwaid et al. [72] examine the implementation of AISs and IT in the sustainability of developed economic units. Interestingly, these authors demonstrate the positive impact of effective AISs and IT implementation on economic unit performance, including improved decision-making capabilities, streamlined operations, and enhanced financial reporting [72]. Conversely, by conducting a case study analysis, Beretta and Demartini [73] claim that collecting and reporting data for non-financial disclosure by using digital AIS represents a significant challenge for the company analysed. Although they recognise the pivotal role of such systems for the data collection and the programming phase, these authors argue that managers should pay more attention to how organisations can collect information more securely [73].

In addition, advances in AI and machine learning are further enhancing the capabilities of AISs, providing deeper insights into non-financial performance, integrating financial and non-financial reporting, and providing a holistic view of organisational performance. For example, Villiers et al. [44] investigate the use of AI assistants in the domain of text generation (such as ChatGPT) and processing for developing and improving sustainability reporting [44]. Harden et al. [74] compare the ESG ratings of chosen companies reported by three different AI systems (i.e., Microsoft's Bing, OpenAI's ChatGPT and Google's Bard) to evaluate the abstract concept of ESG accounting and reporting based on AI. In comparison, Ge [75] examine Virtual Reality (VR) and Augmented Reality (AR) technologies as potential tools for assisting financial systems to overcome possible problems provided by unforeseen events and crises.

However, operationalising AISs and digital technologies is challenging, and further concerns depend on the adoption of new accounting frameworks, such as the EU taxonomy [70, 76]. Besides data quality and consistency issues, interoperability concerns, and the need for specialised skills and expertise, organisational and managerial implications could further influence enterprises' actions in response to such regulations [16, 17, 22].

3.3 An Institutional Analysis: Isomorphism Towards EU Taxonomy Alignment

Organisational behaviours and decision-making processes play a key role in effectively integrating and leveraging the twin transition of digital and sustainable transformations [11, 13] into organisations. These processes could not only influence the adoption of new accounting frameworks towards non-financial reporting but also play a pivotal role in enhancing long-term value creation [77, 78] by aligning operations with sustainability goals. Often observed in organisational settings, isomorphic behaviours play a pivotal role in shaping companies' structures, strategies, and behaviours [79, 80]. Similarly, the approach to sustainability can also appear in isomorphic behaviours [32, 33, 35, 81, 82]. The concept of isomorphism, rooted in institutional theory [34], describes the process by which organisations within a particular field or industry begin to resemble each other over time. This convergence can occur due to various pressures, leading organisations to adopt similar structures, practices, and policies. In the context of sustainability, isomorphic behaviours can significantly shape how organisations implement and standardise sustainable practices.

As conceptualised in institutional theory, isomorphic forces exert pressure on organisations to conform to prevailing norms, practices, and regulations [32, 35, 83–85]. These forces, categorised as coercive, mimetic, and normative [34, 42, 80], could influence organisational behaviours and decision-making regarding adopting new accounting frameworks like the EU taxonomy.

From this perspective, Coercive isomorphism arises from formal and informal pressures exerted on organisations by other entities on which they depend or by societal expectations. For example, regulatory compliance often drives organisations to adopt sustainable practices to meet government regulations, environmental laws, or international standards for environmental management [37]. Additionally, supply chain requirements can act as coercive forces; large companies may mandate that their suppliers adhere to specific sustainability standards, thereby compelling these suppliers to adopt similar practices.

Mimetic isomorphism occurs when organisations imitate or model themselves after others who are perceived as more legitimate or successful. In terms of sustainability, this can manifest through benchmarking against industry leaders' best practices. If a leading company implements a robust recycling program, other organisations in the industry may replicate this initiative to remain competitive and maintain credibility [36, 86]. Similarly, organisations often adopt widely recognised sustainability frameworks and certifications. For instance, the Sustainability Accounting Standards Board (SASB) provides industry-specific disclosures about sustainability-related risks and opportunities that could reasonably be expected to affect entities' cash flows, access to finance, or cost of capital over the short, medium, or long-term [87–89]. The Task Force on Climate-related Financial Disclosures (TCFD) is structured around four thematic areas (i.e., governance, strategy, risk management, and metrics and targets) that represent core elements of organisational operations [90–92]. In comparison, the GRI standards for sustainability reporting as a form of mimetic behaviour [93–96].

Normative isomorphism stems from professionalisation and the standardisation of norms and practices through education and professional networks. Sustainability professionals typically share common educational backgrounds and adhere to industry standards, which leads to the dissemination of similar practices across organisations [97]. Furthermore, participation in industry associations and sustainability networks, such as the Italian Network for Business Reporting (NIBR) [98, 99] and the Global Compact Network [100–102], can lead to the adoption of common sustainability strategies due to shared resources and guidelines.

Accordingly, practical examples of isomorphic behaviours in sustainability include the widespread publication of Corporate Social Responsibility (CSR) reports. Many companies follow the GRI standards for these reports, driven by normative pressures from professional standards and mimetic behaviours modelled after industry leaders. The adoption of renewable energy sources [63, 103] across various industries illustrates the influence of coercive pressures (such as regulatory incentives and mandates), mimetic behaviours (emulating successful companies), and normative pressures (industry norms advocating for renewable energy). Similarly, waste reduction initiatives often result from regulatory requirements, the successful implementation of similar programs in peer organisations, and industry best practices promoted through professional networks [104–107].

Therefore, we believe that isomorphic forces play a significant role and could act as drivers for organisations in adopting non-financial accounting disclosure practices [38, 108, 109]. Then, we build on the institutional theory tradition [32, 35, 83–85], intending to explore how these forces might impact the organisation's approach to aligning its economic activities with the EU Taxonomy, specifically regarding the shift towards "taxonomy-aligned" economic activities [31].

4 Methodology

In line with the ECOSISTER project aims (i.e. producing knowledge and fostering innovation and collaboration in the Emilia-Romagna production ecosystem), a survey was designed to collect and extensively examine data among the ecosystem actors.

This study is a work in progress, and we are currently at the final stage of survey design, consolidating and testing the survey questionnaire with small focus groups before the first stage of extensive data collection. In accordance with Sects. 2 and 3, the final sample of the leading project will include large companies and listed small and medium-sized enterprises (SMEs), that have been obligated to disclose sustainability information, as well as "smaller companies" that do not fall under the scope of CSRD, but that can decide to disclose this information on a voluntary basis.

As a way of explanation, hereafter, we provide a representative sample of the enterprises of Emilia-Romagna that were formed in the following industries in Table 2. Accordingly, this section is dedicated to the design and development of the survey analysis and comprises two subsections. After a description of the composition of the observed sample and data collection procedure, the first subsection delineates the study design, outlining the groundwork underpinning the development of such a questionnaire. The second subsection delineates the questionnaire, encompassing its structure, inquiries, and pertinent details regarding the items adopted from previous studies.

4.1 Study Design

The measurement and analysis of the adoption drivers is just a section of a more extensive data collection effort about the alignment with the EU Taxonomy of sustainable activities in the regional ecosystem.

Table 2 Information concerning the composition of the observed sample

Population	Companies with at least one production unit in the Emilia-Romagna region Number of employees greater than 5
Sampling	Stratified random sampling Economic activities of the enterprises included in the sample according to the NACE Revision 2 [110]: section a (agriculture, forestry and fishing); section c (manufacturing); section d (electricity, gas, steam and air conditioning supply); section e (water supply; sewerage, waste management and remediation activities); section f (construction); section h (transportation and storage) Size classes of enterprises considered: small (5–20 employees); medium (21–100 employees); large (> 100 employees) Provinces of the region (if there is more than one local unit, the one with the highest number of employees is considered)
Respondent	Small enterprises: entrepreneur Medium and Large Enterprises: managers involved in the production activities
Target	2000 Enterprises operating in the Emilia-Romagna region

The main survey is structured in the following major parts: (A) General information about the company; (B) company ownership structure; (C) employees and labour; (D) knowledge and perceptions about the EU taxonomy; (E) Company actions/investments in each of the six major environmental objectives of the EU taxonomy; (F) drivers for new Circular Economy (CE) activities; (G) Financing obtained for CE; (H) Sustainability metrics, reporting and communication; (I) Further info (innovation, internationalisation, emergency handling), (J) Further info (general, company), (details follow hereafter).

Accordingly, although these parts refer to a more extensive data collection effort (given the survey's involvements of researchers from different disciplines), we refer to such more generic parts by selecting only relevant questions (included in the different parts from A to J), depending on whether they fit or not within our objectives to examine measurement, analysis of the adoption drivers, isomorphic forces, and an organisation's approach to aligning its economic activities with the EU Taxonomy.

1. Factors driving companies towards alignment with EU taxonomy

   The analysis of the factors driving companies towards taxonomy alignment can be based on data collected in a specific section (F) focused on Circular Economy activities (target 4 of the EU Taxonomy). This section, combined with more general information on knowledge and perception of the EU taxonomy collected in section (D) has been designed with the aim of exploring the most important factors behind the ongoing taxonomy alignment process. Moreover, we expect to identify different actors assuming prominence in our analysis, such as suppliers, competitors, customers, financers, top management, and employees, as well as more general pressures from the market and society.

   Then, analysing the picture above would serve to give relevant and urgent informative elements on the ongoing sustainable transition process in the Emilia Romagna regional ecosystem, identifying various paces of industrial, economic,

Table 3 The most relevant questionnaire items from an institutional viewpoint

Isomorphism	Normative	Coercive	Mimetic
Positive	D1; D1a.; D1b.; F4.1c.; F4.1d.; F4.1f.; F4.1h.; F4.1i.; F4.1k.; F4.1l.; F4.1m.; F4.3v.; F4.3x.; G2.; G4.; G5.; H2.1.; H2.2.; H2.3.; H2.10.	F4.1a.; F4.1b.	F4.1e.
Negative	F5.6.; F5.14.	F5.5.; F5.7.	

and organisational transformation in different areas and understanding different degrees of development.

The expected answer to RQ1 from data collection and analysis should show how the different degrees of alignment of the companies to the six EU environmental objectives are not necessarily connected with enforcing laws. Still, they are the outcome of pressures at many different levels by different actors, with varying degrees of implementation also connected to the distinct nature and context of production activities.

2. Interpreting factors as isomorphic behaviors

A further step of understanding based on a solid theoretical framework could be done by interpreting the survey data with an institutional approach, as discussed in the theoretical background above. The institutional theory analyses isomorphic convergence processes within specific organisational fields. Therefore, the first step of analysis would require identifying homogeneous organisational fields for the isomorphic convergence process towards taxonomy alignment.

Besides identifying the relevant organisational fields, it would serve to trace down the empirical signs of the three main pillars of an isomorphic convergence process: Normative, Coercive, and Mimetic. To this aim, Table 3 identifies specific items in the survey questionnaire that can be used to instantiate the three fundamental institutional pillars (also considering the positive and negative effects on organisations). Besides, with respect to the project's disclosure of interest, we provide only the essential sections of the survey relevant to the current study in Appendix "*Survey Questionnaire (Excerpt)*".

4.2 Survey: Additional Questionnaire Items and Data Analysis

In general, the operationalisation of institutional forces is a relatively novel field of investigation, and it is often crafted to specificities of different contexts and data availability and collection issues. For example, Zeng et al. [42] used a measurement instrument of seven items, three for coercive, two for normative and two for mimetic forces, while Vanalle et al. [41] and Zhu et al. [111] used a measurement instrument of sixteen items, six for coercive, seven for normative and three for mimetic forces.

Accordingly, for this study, we are looking forward to eventually integrating further questions, including additional items from previous studies [39–42]. In particular, we are considering the seven items reported in Table A1, "Measurement items and references" by Zeng et al. [42], and the 16 items reported in Appendix (questionnaire items) section 2. "Institutional pressures" by Zhu et al. [111].

The ongoing focus groups are dedicated to verifying such aspects in the field, with the possibility of asking qualitative questions, interacting with test subjects, and progressing preliminary tests on first data samples.

In due course, our aim is to develop a statistical model for the analysis of the relationships between the three main institutional forces constructs (given the questionnaire items presented in Table 3 and potentially further items as mentioned above) and the degree of alignment of each company. Regarding the latter, the measurement of the degree of alignment of each company is planned to be done using the items in section E of the large-scale survey mentioned in Sect. 4.1 for each of the six Taxonomy objectives.

5 Expected Results

Given the work-in-progress nature of this research, in this section, we attempt to underline some expected results with regard to the two research questions we claimed at the beginning of the paper.

Regarding the expected outcomes for the first research question, we assume that the drivers of alignment to the EU taxonomy will provide a comprehensive overview of the sustainable transition within the Emilia-Romagna industrial ecosystem. From this perspective, insights should be analysed and discussed concerning the emerging actions and initiatives that organisations undertake or plan to develop. Thus, such an investigation will elucidate how various companies across different industries and contexts are achieving or fostering varying levels of alignment with the six EU environmental objectives.

For the second research question, based on institutional analysis, we anticipate uncovering the distinct types of isomorphic pressures that influence such a sustainable alignment process. In particular, although this assumption could be reasonably common among researchers, for this research, we expect that companies' behaviours are less driven by enforced regulations and more by unwritten norms, values, and the imitation of pioneering first movers.

From this perspective, various actors can exert isomorphic pressures at multiple levels, and the unique circumstances and nature of production activities will likely impact the extent to which these forces are applied.

6 Conclusions

This study represents a preliminary exploration into the integration of the EU Taxonomy and non-financial accounting novelties focusing on the "ECOSISTER: Ecosystem for Sustainable Transition in Emilia-Romagna" project, funded by the "NextGeneration EU" plan. Our long-term ambition is to examine whether regional industrial ecosystems in Emilia-Romagna recognise and adopt new sustainability metrics and investigate the organisational and managerial implications emerging from organisations' alignment and adoption of such regulatory frameworks.

This study remarks on the novelty implications and awareness the EU Taxonomy will gradually trigger to interested parties, considering it provides a structured framework for accounting ESG factors resulting from daily practices run by organisations. Therefore, it is notable that such a reporting tool can enhance organisational transparency and accountability objectives, enhancing several organisational dynamics.

From this perspective, managers should prioritise upskilling their workforce to handle such new accounting systems and ESG reporting tools (also from a technological point of view, considering the adoption of digital technologies and the availability of innovative digital accounting systems, such as AISs). To this end, the role and inclusion of a sustainability manager is becoming of paramount importance for organisations where expertise is also required in managing and developing non-financial reporting and related evaluations. It should be noted that the EU Taxonomy simultaneously represents a compulsory accounting tool for banks and financial institutions (considering the SFDR [3] requires financial market participants to disclose how their products, services, and activities (more in general) align with the EU Taxonomy [31]), which they are increasingly adopting to evaluate and manage the loans and credits for enterprises (e.g., resulting in providing lower loan costs the greater an organisation is aligned and compliant with such a taxonomy). Besides, adopting these practices can improve decision-making processes, boost stakeholder confidence, and ultimately provide a competitive edge in the market. Organisations that effectively integrate these metrics might better identify sustainability risks and opportunities, leading to more responsible and informed strategic decisions.

From a theoretical point of view, drawing on the recent conceptualisation of "twin transformation", digital and sustainable [11–13], this study contributes to the literature on isomorphism and institutional theory [32–34] by linking these concepts with non-financial accounting practices [26–29]. By examining normative, coercive, and mimetic forces, we aim to design a crafted protocol to develop an understanding of how organisations respond to external pressures to adopt sustainability metrics. Beyond the proposed lens of analysis, this work would contribute to research by highlighting the dynamic interplay between regulatory requirements and organisational practices in the context of sustainability. Specifically, this study lays the groundwork for future empirical investigations by defining a comprehensive set of questions aimed at exploring the three isomorphic forces. The design of these questions serves as a preliminary effort for developing a larger-scale survey, providing a robust basis for eventually examining the impact of the EU Taxonomy on organisational behaviour. The adopted interdisciplinary approach, combining insights from accounting, management, organisational, information systems, and sustainability studies, offers an integrated perspective with respect to previous frameworks available in the literature for studying non-financial accounting practices.

This paper also presents some limitations that should be acknowledged. Firstly, as a pilot study, the scope of this work is limited due to its work-in-progress nature (i.e., considering empirical analyses are still in progress). Moreover, the sample size and geographic focus on the Emilia-Romagna region may not fully seize the diversity of practices across different contexts, restricting the generalizability of the results of such research. Additionally, the study relies on qualitative descriptions and theoretical constructs, which need to be validated through empirical data collection and analysis.

Drawing on such assumptions, future research is expected to address these limitations, given the large-scale surveys we are conducting across various industries. However, in further additional steps, it could be helpful considering the chance to run large-scale surveys in other Italian regions. Accordingly, the empirical investigations could serve to validate and expand upon the preliminary findings of this study, providing more generalizable insights. At the same time, longitudinal studies would also be beneficial in understanding how the adoption of the EU Taxonomy and other sustainability metrics evolves over time. Thus, we plan to conduct a second wave of such research with the same organisations selected in the first run. Furthermore, we also contemplate the importance of comparative studies between different European regions and international contexts, considering that although demanding, they could provide a broader perspective on the challenges and successes of integrating sustainability, non-financial accounting systems, accounting information systems, and the EU taxonomy.

In addition, while this research focused on the institutional analysis of the adoption of non-financial accounting practices, we claim that an area of further analysis concerns the role of IT and digital technologies in driving organisations towards sustainability and non-financial accounting practices [26–29] (as emerged in the theoretical background). In particular, recent research shows that by leveraging cloud computing, artificial intelligence, blockchain, big data analytics, and machine learning technologies, AISs will likely support organisations in enhancing automated information processes, overcoming data-related challenges, and supporting sustainability initiatives [12, 18–21]. However, to the best of our knowledge, only a few studies have explored the links between the complex relationship between accounting, non-financial reporting, and information systems [22, 23].

For example, Efimova et al. [112] explore the eXtensible Business Reporting Language (XBLR) technology adoption for enabling the existing system of financial and non-financial information disclosure of companies, noticing that its application could ensure their effective management and business processes and high-quality meetings of stakeholder information requests. Nerantzidis et al. [113] focus on social media accounting research, noticing that previous studies focus on (publicly listed) corporate use of social media (mainly Twitter and Facebook) to disseminate financial and non-financial information in the North American and European regions and claiming for further investigations how social media interactions among various parties could push for greater transparency in different forms of organisations and in countries where stakeholder interests are less protected. Brijesh Singh et al. [114] examine the adoption and use of data mining technology, proposing a model for the design of financial management and financing of enterprises. Further attention is paid to how such systems could support enterprises in developing the information for more specific management processes and production systems [115].

By highlighting the managerial, theoretical, and methodological contributions, as well as acknowledging the limitations, we set the stage for more comprehensive future research projects. In conclusion, we argue that integrating sustainability metrics into accounting (information) systems represents a crucial step for promoting responsible business practices and achieving long-term sustainability goals towards sustainable transition of productive ecosystems.

Acknowledgments This study was funded by the "National Recovery and Resilience Plan (NRRP), Mission 04 Component 2 Investment 1.5—NextGenerationEU, Call for tender n. 3277 dated 30/12/2021, Award Number: 0001052 dated 23/06/2022".

Disclosure of Interests The authors have no competing interests to declare that are relevant to the content of this article.

Appendix. Survey Questionnaire (Excerpt)

Section A. General Information About the Company

Questions: A1., A2., A3., A4., A5.

Section B. Company Ownership Structure

Questions: B1., B2., B3., B4., B5., B6., B7., B8.

Section C. Employees and Labour

Questions: C1., C2., C3., C4., C5., C6.

Section D. Knowledge and Perceptions About the EU Taxonomy

D1. Are you aware of Regulation 852/2020 ("Taxonomy Regulation" for sustainable investments)?

D1a. If yes, I become aware of it . . .
D1b. If you became aware of the Regulation through financial intermediaries, which aspects did they highlight in relation to the 'Taxonomy Regulation'? Select all that apply:

Section E. Company Actions/Investments in Each of the Six Major Environmental Objectives of the EU Taxonomy

E1. Have you undertaken specific actions related to the sustainability areas outlined in the Regulation? [Summary of areas: (1) climate change mitigation; (2) climate change adaptation; (3) sustainable use and protection of water and marine resources; (4) transition to a circular economy; (5) pollution prevention and reduction; (6) protection and restoration of biodiversity and ecosystems]
E2. [If E1 = Yes] Why have you not undertaken specific actions in these areas yet? [Multiple answers possible]
E3. [If E1 = Yes] Have these actions led to changes in the company organization? [For 'yes', both answers are possible]
E4. "Type of past and/or future interventions: specify if you have invested or plan to invest in the next 5 years in actions related to the following sustainability areas outlined in the Regulation?" (Table E4)
E5. Can you estimate the percentage of total revenue, the percentage of total capital expenditure, and total operating expenses resulting from the set of actions undertaken within the sustainability areas outlined in Regulation (see E4) today and in 5 years? (Table E5)
E6. Have you activated consultations related to the sustainability areas outlined in the Regulation?

Section F. Drivers for New Circular Economy (CE) Activities

Questions: F1., F2., F3.

F4. [If at least one answer to E4.14–E4.25] What are the motivational factors/drivers have driven or will drive you to carry out activities related to circular economy practices? (Table F4)
F5. What are your company's most significant barriers to implementing circular economy practices? (Table F5)

Table E4 Type of past and/or future interventions

Area	Has the company invested in the last 5 years? (2019/2023) [If E1 = Yes]	Will the company invest in the next 5 years? (2024/2028)
Area 1: Climate change mitigation *answer to (1., 2., 3., 4., 5., 6., 7.)*		
Area 2: Adaptation to climate change *answer to (8., 9., 10.)*		
Area 3: Sustainable use and protection of water and marine resources *answer to (11., 12., 13.)*		
Area 4: Transition towards a circular economy *answer to (14., 15., 16., 17., 18., 19., 20., 21., 22., 23., 24., 25)*		
Area 5: Prevention and reduction of pollution *answer to (26., 27., 28.)*		
Area 6: Protection and restoration of biodiversity and ecosystems *answer to (29., 30.)*		

Table E5 Estimations

Type	Now	In 5 years
1. Revenue	%	%
2. Capital expenditures (Capex)	%	%
3. Operating expenses (Opex)	%	%

Section G. Financing Obtained for CE

G1.

G2. Have financial intermediaries you work with ever proposed: [Possible multiple answers]

G3.

G4. Are you aware of financial incentives available through government programs to support activities related to the circular economy? [single answer]

G5. Which of the following incentives or subsidies has the company benefited from in the last 5 years [2019–2023]? [Possible multiple answers]

Table F4 Factors/drivers

Drivers	Answer
1. General Area	
(a) Regulatory constraints for sustainability and cleaner energy	
(b) European and national incentivization (e.g., support funds, subsidies, taxation, and facilitative policies)	
(c) Improvement of the company's image	
(d) Competitive advantage	
(e) Imitation of competitors	
(f) Increasing awareness among customers and suppliers about the recyclability and/or sustainability of the product	
(g)	
(h) Explicit requests from partners along the supply chain (e.g., suppliers, customers)	
(i) Owners/managers feel environmental/social responsibility	
(j)	
(k) The market demands green products	
(l) The community demands the adoption of circular economy practices	
(m) Financial institutions require environmental parameters	
2. Economic Area	
(n)	
(o)	
(p)	
(q)	
(r)	
3. Environmental area	
(s)	
(t)	
(u)	
(v) Better compliance with environmental standards	
(x) Environmental awareness and the resulting opportunity to reduce environmental impact	

Section H. Sustainability Metrics, Reporting and Communication

H1.

H2. What are the tools used to communicate externally elements related to developed sustainability processes? [multiple answers possible] (Table H2)

Table F5 Barriers

Obstacles/barriers	Answer
1. General area	
2.	
3.	
4.	
5. Complex and overlapping regulations (European, national, and/or regional) Complex administrative or legal procedures	
6. Low environmental awareness among stakeholders	
7. Lack of government support	
8.	
9.	
10.	
11.	
12.	
13.	
14. Lack of support from top management	
15.	
16.	
17.	

Table H2 Tools used to communicate externally.

Tools	Is used
1. Annual report	
2. Social reporting	
3. Environmental report	
4.	
5.	
6.	
7.	
8.	
9.	
10. Recognised certifications	

Section I. Further Information (Innovation, Internationalization, Emergency Handling)

Questions: I1., I2., I3., I4., I5., I6., I7., I8., I9., I10., I11.

Section J. Further Information (General, Company)

Questions: J1., J2.

References

1. European Commission. (2020). Regulation (EU) 2020/852 of the European Parliament and of the Council of 18 June 2020 on the establishment of a framework to facilitate sustainable investment, and amending Regulation (EU) 2019/2088 (Text with EEA relevance). *Official Journal of the European Union*.
2. European Commission. (2022). Directive (EU) 2022/2464 of the European Parliament and of the Council of 14 December 2022 amending Regulation (EU) No 537/2014, Directive 2004/109/EC, Directive 2006/43/EC and Directive 2013/34/EU, as regards corporate sustainability reporting (Text with EEA relevance). *Official Journal of the European Union*.
3. European Commission. (2019). I (legislative act) Regulation (EU) 2019/2088 of the European Parliament and of the Council of 27 November 2019 on sustainability-related disclosures in the financial services sector (Text with EEA relevance). *Official Journal of the European Union*.
4. Viñes Fiestas, H. (2023). The EU taxonomy: Financing the transition through sustainable investing. *ICE, Revista de Economía*. https://doi.org/10.32796/ice.2023.932.7658
5. European Commission. Factsheet: How does the EU taxonomy fit within the sustainable finance framework? Last retrieved June 4, 2024, from https://finance.ec.europa.eu/document/download/413e545a-c839-4b70-a1bc-136e266f82b8_en.
6. Cochran, I., Mackenzie, C., & Brander, M. (2024). EU's sustainable finance disclosure regulation: does the hybrid reporting regime undermine the goal to reorient capital to climate action? *Climate Policy*, 1–13. https://doi.org/10.1080/14693062.2024.2353115
7. Moadeli, S. (2022). Risky business: It is considered sustainable, right?: Examining the EU Taxonomy and its implications of legally classifying what economic activities are sustainable. https://urn.kb.se/resolve?urn=urn:nbn:se:su:diva-205380. https://doi.org/urn:nbn:se:su:diva-205380.
8. Poulle, J.-B., Kannan, A., Spitz, N., Kahn, S., & Sotiropoulou, A. (2024). *EU banking and financial regulation*. Edward Elgar. https://doi.org/10.4337/9781035301959
9. Neligan, A., Baumgartner, R. J., Geissdoerfer, M., & Schöggl, J. P. (2023). Circular disruption: Digitalisation as a driver of circular economy business models. *Business Strategy and the Environment, 32*, 1175–1188. https://doi.org/10.1002/bse.3100
10. Jayakodi, S., Senaratne, S., & Perera, S. (2024). Circular economy business model in the construction industry: A systematic review. *Buildings*. https://doi.org/10.3390/buildings14020379
11. Christmann, A.-S., Crome, C., Graf-Drasch, V., Oberländer, A. M., & Schmidt, L. (2024). The twin transformation butterfly. *Business & Information Systems Engineering, 66*, 489–505. https://doi.org/10.1007/s12599-023-00847-2
12. Graf-Drasch, V., Kauffeld, L., Kempf, L., Maria Oberländer, A., Teuchert, A., & Maria A. (2023). Driving twin transformation: The interplay of digital transformation and sustainability transformation. In: *31st European conference on information systems (ECIS), Kristiansand, Norway, 2023*.
13. Burinskienė, A., & Nalivaikė, J. (2024). Digital and sustainable (twin) transformations: A case of SMEs in the European Union. *Sustainability, 16*, 1533. https://doi.org/10.3390/su16041533
14. Ixmeier, A., Wagner, F., & Kranz, J. (2024). Leveraging information systems for environmental sustainability and business value. *MIS Quarterly Executive*. https://doi.org/10.17705/2msqe.00090

15. Schwartz, D., & Te'eni, D. (2024). AI for knowledge creation, curation, and consumption in context. *Journal of the Association for Information Systems, 25*, 37–47. https://doi.org/10.17705/1jais.00862
16. Elmagrhi, H., Diavastis, I. E., Chrysafis, K. A., & Papadopoulou, G. C. (2024). Determinants of accounting information systems success: The case of the Greek hotel industry. *International Journal of Financial Studies, 12*, 42. https://doi.org/10.3390/IJFS12020042
17. Jarvenpaa, S., & Klein, S. (2024). New frontiers in information systems theorizing: Human-gAI collaboration. *Journal of the Association for Information Systems, 25*, 110–121. https://doi.org/10.17705/1jais.00868
18. Kwilinski, A., Lyulyov, O., & Pimonenko, T. (2023). Unlocking sustainable value through digital transformation: An examination of ESG performance. *Information (Switzerland), 14*. https://doi.org/10.3390/info14080444
19. ElMassah, S., & Mohieldin, M. (2020). Digital transformation and localizing the sustainable development goals (SDGs). *Ecological Economics, 169*, 106490. https://doi.org/10.1016/j.ecolecon.2019.106490
20. Elgohary, E. M. (2022). The role of digital transformation in sustainable development in Egypt. *The International Journal of Informatics, Media and Communication Technology (IJIMCT), 4*, 71–106.
21. Graf, A. (2024). Negotiating social sustainability in the course of organisations' digital transformation. In S. Jebseng & K. Lueg (Eds.), *Social sustainability and good work in organizations*. Routledge. https://doi.org/10.4324/9781003306436
22. Hoang Nguyen, L., Lins, S., Renner, M., Sunyaev, A., & Hoang, L. (2024). Unraveling the nuances of AI accountability: A synthesis of dimensions across disciplines. In: *32nd European conference on information systems (ECIS)*.
23. Quang Huy, P., & Kien Phuc, V. (2024). Sustainable decision making in the time of uncertainty: Does moral intelligence make it different? *Pacific Asia Journal of the Association for Information Systems, 16*, 144–174. https://doi.org/10.17705/1pais.16108
24. Gil, M. A., & Montoya, M. A. (2020). Digital transformation and corporate sustainability accounting. In S. H. Park, M. A. Gonzalez-Perez, & D. E. Floriani (Eds.), *The Palgrave handbook of corporate sustainability in the digital era* (pp. 651–669). Palgrave Macmillan. https://doi.org/10.1007/978-3-030-42412-1_33/TABLES/1
25. Lombardi, R., & Secundo, G. (2021). The digital transformation of corporate reporting—A systematic literature review and avenues for future research. *Meditari Accountancy Research, 29*, 1179–1208. https://doi.org/10.1108/MEDAR-04-2020-0870
26. Stolowy, H., & Paugam, L. (2018). The expansion of non-financial reporting: an exploratory study. *Accounting and Business Research, 48*, 525–548. https://doi.org/10.1080/00014788.2018.1470141
27. Tsagas, G., & Villiers, C. (2020). Why "less is more" in non-financial reporting initiatives: Concrete steps towards supporting sustainability. *Accounting, Economics and Law: A Convivium, 10*. https://doi.org/10.1515/AEL-2018-0045/MACHINEREADABLECITATION/RIS
28. Esposito, D., & Cecchin, M. (2022). EU taxonomies on ESG regulation. Research Paper Series. 2022.
29. Delgado-Ceballos, J., Ortiz-De-Mandojana, N., Antolín-López, R., & Montiel, I. (2023). Connecting the sustainable development goals to firm-level sustainability and ESG factors: The need for double materiality. *BRQ Business Research Quarterly, 26*, 2–10. https://doi.org/10.1177/23409444221140919
30. Turci, L., Rizzi, P., & Timpano, F. (2023). Regional industrial ecosystems in Emilia Romagna: An analysis for a sustainable transition. Project funded under the National Recovery and Resilience Plan (NRRP), Mission 04 Component 2 Investment 1.5—NextGenerationEU, Call for tender n. 3277 dated 30/12/2021, Award Number: 0001052 dated 23/06/2022. 1–28.
31. European Commission. (2023). A user guide to navigate the EU Taxonomy for sustainable activities. https://doi.org/10.2874/561427EV-03-21-657-EN-N.

32. Kwabena Amoako, G., Adam, A. M., Lamboi Arthur, C., & Tackie, G. (2021). Institutional isomorphism, environmental management accounting and environmental accountability: a review. *Environment, Development and Sustainability, 23*, 11201–11216. https://doi.org/10.1007/s10668-020-01140-y
33. Srikantia, P., & Bilimoria, D. (1997). Isomorphism in organization and management theory. *Organization & Environment, 10*, 384–406. https://doi.org/10.1177/192181069701000404
34. DiMaggio, P. J., & Powell, W. W. (1983). The iron cage revisited: Institutional isomorphism and collective rationality in organizational fields. *American Sociological Review, 48*, 147. https://doi.org/10.2307/2095101
35. Anlesinya, A., Amponsah-Tawiah, K., Dartey-Baah, K., Adeti, S. K., & Brefo-Manuh, A. B. (2023). Institutional isomorphism and sustainable HRM adoption: a conceptual framework. *Industrial and Commercial Training, 55*, 62–76. https://doi.org/10.1108/ICT-03-2021-0013
36. Haveman, H. A. (1993). Follow the leader: Mimetic isomorphism and entry into new markets. *Administrative Science Quarterly, 38*, 593. https://doi.org/10.2307/2393338
37. Yusoff, R., Yusoff, H., Amran, S., Rahman, A., & Darus, F. (2019). Investigating sustainability reporting from the lens of stakeholder pressures and isomorphism. *Journal of Asia-Pacific Business*. https://doi.org/10.1080/10599231.2019.1684170
38. Mejía, L. M. C., Val, M. P. D., & Coscollar, À. D. (2020). The institutional isomorphism in the context of organizational changes in higher education institutions. *International Journal of Research in Education and Science, 6*, 61–73.
39. Bansal, P. (2005). Evolving sustainably: a longitudinal study of corporate sustainable development. *Strategic Management Journal, 26*, 197–218. https://doi.org/10.1002/smj.441
40. Calzolari, T., Bimpizas-Pinis, M., Genovese, A., & Brint, A. (2023). Understanding the relationship between institutional pressures, supply chain integration and the adoption of circular economy practices. *Journal of Cleaner Production, 432*, 139686. https://doi.org/10.1016/j.jclepro.2023.139686
41. Vanalle, R. M., Ganga, G. M. D., Godinho Filho, M., & Lucato, W. C. (2017). Green supply chain management: An investigation of pressures, practices, and performance within the Brazilian automotive supply chain. *Journal of Cleaner Production, 151*, 250–259. https://doi.org/10.1016/j.jclepro.2017.03.066
42. Zeng, H., Chen, X., Xiao, X., & Zhou, Z. (2017). Institutional pressures, sustainable supply chain management, and circular economy capability: Empirical evidence from Chinese eco-industrial park firms. *Journal of Cleaner Production, 155*, 54–65. https://doi.org/10.1016/j.jclepro.2016.10.093
43. Wagenhofer, A. (2024). Sustainability reporting: A financial reporting perspective. *Accounting in Europe, 21*, 1–13. https://doi.org/10.1080/17449480.2023.2218398
44. de Villiers, C., Dimes, R., & Molinari, M. (2024). How will AI text generation and processing impact sustainability reporting? Critical analysis, a conceptual framework and avenues for future research. *Sustainability Accounting, Management and Policy Journal, 15*, 96–118. https://doi.org/10.1108/SAMPJ-02-2023-0097
45. Hardiyanto, N., Ahmar, N., & Etty Merawati, E. (2023). Internet financial report and determinants of the quality of financial statements of non-profit organizations. *Devotion Journal of Community Service, 4*, 186–201. https://doi.org/10.36418/dev.v4i1.369
46. Dumay, J., Guthrie, J., & Farneti, F. (2010). Gri sustainability reporting guidelines for public and third sector organizations. *Public Management Review, 12*, 531–548. https://doi.org/10.1080/14719037.2010.496266
47. Isaksson, R., & Steimle, U. (2009). What does GRI-reporting tell us about corporate sustainability? *The TQM Journal, 21*, 168–181. https://doi.org/10.1108/17542730910938155
48. Guthrie, J., & Farneti, F. (2008). GRI sustainability reporting by Australian public sector organizations. *Public Money & Management, 28*, 361–366. https://doi.org/10.1111/j.1467-9302.2008.00670.x
49. Anguiano-Santos, C., Salazar-Ordóñez, M., Tornel-Vázquez, R., & Rodríguez-Entrena, M. (2024). Sustainability reporting harmonisation? A utopian endeavour for European agri-food companies. *Journal of Policy Modeling, 46*, 354–368. https://doi.org/10.1016/j.jpolmod.2024.01.008

50. Parrondo, L., & Amat, O. (2024). *Research handbook on financial accounting*. Edward Elgar. https://doi.org/10.4337/9781803920597
51. European Commission. (2014). Directive 2014/95/EU of the European Parliament and of the Council of 22 October 2014—amending Directive 2013/34/EU as regards disclosure of non-financial and diversity information by certain large undertakings and groups. *Official Journal of the European Union*.
52. The European Parliament and of the Council. Regulation—2020/852—EN—taxonomy regulation—EUR-Lex. Last retrieved May 15, 2024, from https://eur-lex.europa.eu/legal-content/EN/TXT/?uri=CELEX:32020R0852.
53. The European Parliament and of the Council. (2020). Regulation (EU) 2020/852 of The European Parliament and of The Council of 18 June 2020 on the establishment of a framework to facilitate sustainable investment, and amending Regulation.
54. European Commission. (2021). Accompanying the communication from the Commission to the European Parliament, the Council, the European Economic and Social Committee and the Committee of the Regions Updating the 2020 New Industrial Strategy: Building a stronger Single Market for Europe's recovery.
55. Kotlarsky, J., Oshri, I., & Sekulic, N. (2023). Digital sustainability in information systems research: Conceptual foundations and future directions. *Journal of the Association for Information Systems, 24*, 936–952. https://doi.org/10.17705/1jais.00825
56. Khan, I. S., Ahmad, M. O., & Majava, J. (2021). Industry 4.0 and sustainable development: A systematic mapping of triple bottom line, circular economy and sustainable business models perspectives. *Journal of Cleaner Production, 297*, 126655. https://doi.org/10.1016/j.jclepro.2021.126655
57. Geissdoerfer, M., Savaget, P., Bocken, N. M. P., & Hultink, E. J. (2017). The circular economy—A new sustainability paradigm? *Journal of Cleaner Production, 143*, 757–768. https://doi.org/10.1016/j.jclepro.2016.12.048
58. Ghisellini, P., Cialani, C., & Ulgiati, S. (2016). A review on circular economy: The expected transition to a balanced interplay of environmental and economic systems. *Journal of Cleaner Production, 114*, 11–32. https://doi.org/10.1016/j.jclepro.2015.09.007
59. Bag, S., & Pretorius, J. H. C. (2022). Relationships between industry 4.0, sustainable manufacturing and circular economy: proposal of a research framework. *International Journal of Organizational Analysis, 30*, 864–898. https://doi.org/10.1108/IJOA-04-2020-2120
60. Camodeca, R., & Almici, A. (2021). Digital transformation and convergence toward the 2030 agenda's sustainability development goals: Evidence from Italian listed firms. *Sustainability, 13*, 11831. https://doi.org/10.3390/su132111831
61. Fiandrino, S., Scarpa, F., & Torelli, R. (2022). Fostering social impact through corporate implementation of the SDGs: Transformative mechanisms towards interconnectedness and inclusiveness. *Journal of Business Ethics, 180*, 959–973. https://doi.org/10.1007/s10551-022-05189-9
62. Stephenson, M., Hamid, M. F. S., Peter, A., Sauvant, K. P., Seric, A., & Tajoli, L. (2021). More and better investment now! How unlocking sustainable and digital investment flows can help achieve the SDGs. *Journal of International Business Policy*. https://doi.org/10.1057/s42214-020-00094-2
63. Cipriano, M., Virili, F., & Za, S. (2024). Evaluating the social impact of renewable energy communities: A design science research approach. In *32nd European conference on information systems (ECIS)*.
64. Adelekan, A., & Sharmina, M. (2024). Collaborative digitally-enabled business models for a circular economy: Sustaining, managing and protecting value in the UK plastics sector. *Journal of Cleaner Production, 438*, 140770. https://doi.org/10.1016/j.jclepro.2024.140770
65. Akberdina, V., Strielkowski, W., Linder, N., Kashirin, S., & Shmeleva, L. (2023). Information technology and digital sufficiency for building the sustainable circular economy. *Energies (Basel), 16*. https://doi.org/10.3390/en16031399
66. Luoma, P., Toppinen, A., & Penttinen, E. (2021). The role and value of data in realising circular business models—A systematic literature review. *Journal of Business Models, 9*, 44–71. https://doi.org/10.5278/JBM.V9I2.3448

67. Zhao, Q., Li, X., & Li, S. (2023). Analyzing the Relationship between digital transformation strategy and ESG performance in large manufacturing enterprises: The mediating role of green innovation. *Sustainability (Switzerland), 15*. https://doi.org/10.3390/su15139998
68. Kotlarsky, J., Corbett, J., Sutanto, J., Kude, T., & Tim, Y. (2024). *Digital sustainability and information systems research: New challenges and theoretical perspectives*. JAIS Call for Papers.
69. Al-Okaily, M. (2024). Assessing the effectiveness of accounting information systems in the era of COVID-19 pandemic. *VINE Journal of Information and Knowledge Management Systems, 54*, 157–175. https://doi.org/10.1108/VJIKMS-08-2021-0148
70. Andi, Bahiroh, E., & Mulyani, A. S. (2024). A systematic literature review of accounting information systems implementation success factors. *Accounting Studies and Tax Journal (COUNT), 1*, 182–194. https://doi.org/10.62207/zs6wm395
71. Booker, A., Chiu, V., Groff, N., & Richardson, V. J. (2024). AIS research opportunities utilizing Machine Learning: From a Meta-Theory of accounting literature. *International Journal of Accounting Information Systems, 52*, 100661. https://doi.org/10.1016/j.accinf.2023.100661
72. Zwaid, J. G., Kareem, H. B., Abed, R. A., & Fatima, K. (2023). Implementation of accounting information systems and information technology (IT) in the sustainability of the developed economic units. *Eastern-European Journal of Enterprise Technologies, 4*, 79–86. https://doi.org/10.15587/1729-4061.2023.286380
73. Beretta, V., Demartini, M. C., & Trucco, S. (2023). Digital accounting information system for non-financial disclosure: A case study analysis. In *Lecture notes in information systems and organisation* (pp. 11–22). Springer. https://doi.org/10.1007/978-3-031-15770-7_2
74. Harden, G., Noe, K., & Ross, S. (2023). Using artificial intelligence to identify and analyze ESG investments. In *29th annual Americas conference on information systems (AMCIS), Panama*. Association for Information Systems.
75. Ge, X. (2024). Design of an enterprise financial information management system based virtual reality for hypertext system interactive devices. *Computer-Aided Design and Applications*, 270–288. https://doi.org/10.14733/cadaps.2024.S17.270-288
76. Schiavi, G. S., Behr, A., & Marcolin, C. B. (2024). Institutional theory in accounting information systems research: Shedding light on digital transformation and institutional change. *International Journal of Accounting Information Systems, 52*, 100662. https://doi.org/10.1016/j.accinf.2023.100662
77. Lardo, A., Mancini, D., Paoloni, N., & Russo, G. (2020). The perspective of capability providers in creating a sustainable I4.0 environment. *Management Decision, 58*, 1759–1777. https://doi.org/10.1108/MD-09-2019-1333
78. de Villiers, C., Kuruppu, S., & Dissanayake, D. (2021). A (new) role for business—Promoting the United Nations' sustainable development goals through the internet-of-things and blockchain technology. *Journal of Business Research, 131*, 598–609. https://doi.org/10.1016/j.jbusres.2020.11.066
79. Findik, M., & Bedük, A. (2014). Organizational isomorphism in the context of institutional theory. *International Journal of Social and Economic Sciences, 4*, 27–33.
80. Choi, Y., & Woo, H. (2021). Understanding diverse types of performance information use: evidence from an institutional isomorphism perspective. *Public Management Review*. https://doi.org/10.1080/14719037.2021.1955953
81. Martínez-Ferrero, J., & García-Sánchez, I.-M. (2016). Coercive, normative and mimetic isomorphism as determinants of the voluntary assurance of sustainability reports. *International Business Review*. https://doi.org/10.1016/j.ibusrev.2016.05.009
82. Gauthier, J. (2013). Institutional theory and corporate sustainability: Determinant versus interactive approaches. *Organization Management Journal, 10*, 86–96. https://doi.org/10.1080/15416518.2013.801741
83. Davidson, E. J., & Chismar, W. G. (2007). The interaction of institutionally triggered and technology-triggered social structure change: an investigation of computerized physician order entry. *MIS Quarterly, 31*, 739. https://doi.org/10.2307/25148818

84. Hinings, B., Gegenhuber, T., & Greenwood, R. (2018). Digital innovation and transformation: An institutional perspective. *Information and Organization, 28*, 52–61. https://doi.org/10.1016/j.infoandorg.2018.02.004
85. Weerakkody, V., Omar, A., El-Haddadeh, R., & Al-Busaidy, M. (2016). Digitally-enabled service transformation in the public sector: The lure of institutional pressure and strategic response towards change. *Government Information Quarterly, 33*, 658–668. https://doi.org/10.1016/j.giq.2016.06.006
86. Hwang, K., & Choi, M. (2017). Effects of innovation-supportive culture and organizational citizenship behavior on e-government information system security stemming from mimetic isomorphism. *Government Information Quarterly*. https://doi.org/10.1016/j.giq.2017.02.001
87. Gasparyan, V. (2024). The evolution of standardization of sustainable development reporting. *Economics, Finance and Accounting, 1*, 65. https://doi.org/10.59503/29538009-2024.1.13-65
88. Hedley, T., Porco, B., Keiningham, T. L., Aksoy, L., Statuto, L. A., & Amin, M. (2024). Beyond apples and oranges: unraveling the complexity in corporate sustainability reporting. *Journal of Service Management*. https://doi.org/10.1108/JOSM-12-2023-0505
89. IEEE. (2019, January). *IEEE approved draft recommended practice for the planning and design of the microgrid*. IEEE P2030.9/D10 (pp. 1–44).
90. Chua, W. F., James, R., King, A., Lee, E., & Soderstrom, N. (2022). Task Force on Climate-related Financial Disclosures (TCFD) implementation: An overview and insights from the Australian Accounting Standards Board dialogue series. *Australian Accounting Review, 32*, 396–405. https://doi.org/10.1111/auar.12388
91. O'Dwyer, B., & Unerman, J. (2020). Shifting the focus of sustainability accounting from impacts to risks and dependencies: researching the transformative potential of TCFD reporting. *Accounting, Auditing & Accountability Journal, 33*, 1113–1141. https://doi.org/10.1108/AAAJ-02-2020-4445
92. Ding, D., Liu, B., & Chang, M. (2023). Carbon emissions and TCFD aligned climate-related information disclosures. *Journal of Business Ethics, 182*, 967–1001. https://doi.org/10.1007/s10551-022-05292-x
93. Jain, K., & Tripathi, P. S. (2024). GRI-aligned disclosures of Indian corporates: a study on environmentally sensitive industries. *International Journal of Indian Culture and Business Management, 31*, 16–36. https://doi.org/10.1504/IJICBM.2024.136594
94. Massari, G. F., & Giannoccaro, I. (2023). Adopting GRI standards for the circular economy strategies disclosure: The case of Italy. *Sustainability Accounting, Management and Policy Journal, 14*, 660–694. https://doi.org/10.1108/SAMPJ-07-2021-0284
95. Nial, N., & Parashar, P. (2024). A comparative study on sustainability standards with specific reference to GRI standards and BRSR framework. *International Journal of Quality & Reliability Management*. https://doi.org/10.1108/IJQRM-02-2023-0028
96. Kaminioti, E., Kottaridi, C., & Economidou, C. (2022). Bioeconomy and corporate GRI reporting: A case study analysis. *Circular Economy and Sustainability, 2*, 383–399. https://doi.org/10.1007/s43615-021-00114-0
97. Peng, X., & Zhang, R. (2022). Corporate governance, environmental sustainability performance, and normative isomorphic force of national culture. *Environmental Science and Pollution Research, 29*, 33443–33473. https://doi.org/10.1007/s11356-022-18603-6
98. Baldarelli, M.-G., Cosentino, A., Del Baldo, M., & Magistro, A. (2020). Theory of the firm and integrated reporting model: First essay from NIBR guidelines for SMES in Italy. *International Journal of Business and Management, 15*, 84. https://doi.org/10.5539/ijbm.v15n6p84
99. Del Baldo, M. (2018). Integrated reporting in small and medium enterprises: Issues and perspectives from Italy. In S. O. Idowu, C. Sitnikov, D. Simion, & C. G. Bocean (Eds.), *Current issues in corporate social responsibility*. Springer. https://doi.org/10.1007/978-3-319-70449-4_13
100. Schembera, S. (2018). Implementing corporate social responsibility: Empirical insights on the impact of the UN global compact on its business participants. *Business Society, 57*, 783–825. https://doi.org/10.1177/0007650316635579/FORMAT/EPUB

101. Rasche, A. (2009). Toward a model to compare and analyze accountability standards—The case of the UN Global Compact. *Corporate Social Responsibility and Environmental Management, 16*, 192–205. https://doi.org/10.1002/csr.202
102. Ruggie, J. G. (2002). The theory and practice of learning networks: Corporate social responsibility and the global compact. *The Journal of Corporate Citizenship, 5*, 27–36.
103. MASE. Energia: MASE, pubblicato decreto CER. Last retrieved March 3, 2024, from https://www.mase.gov.it/comunicati/energia-mase-pubblicato-decreto-cer.
104. Haque, F., Fan, C., & Lee, Y.-Y. (2023). From waste to value: Addressing the relevance of waste recovery to agricultural sector in line with circular economy. *Journal of Cleaner Production, 415*, 137873. https://doi.org/10.1016/j.jclepro.2023.137873
105. Khawar Balwan, W., Singh, A., & Kour, S. (2022). 5R's of zero waste management to save our green planet: A narrative review. *European Journal of Biotechnology and Bioscience, 10*, 7–11.
106. Secondi, L., Principato, L., Ruini, L., & Guidi, M. (2019). Reusing food waste in food manufacturing companies: The case of the tomato-sauce supply chain. *Sustainability, 11*, 2154. https://doi.org/10.3390/su11072154
107. Boccia, F., Di Donato, P., Covino, D., & Poli, A. (2019). Food waste and bio-economy: A scenario for the Italian tomato market. *Journal of Cleaner Production, 227*, 424–433. https://doi.org/10.1016/j.jclepro.2019.04.180
108. Velte, P. (2023). Which institutional investors drive corporate sustainability? A systematic literature review. *Business Strategy and the Environment, 32*, 42–71. https://doi.org/10.1002/bse.3117
109. Mosconi, F., & D'Ingiullo, D. (2023). Institutional quality and innovation: evidence from Emilia-Romagna. *Economics of Innovation and New Technology, 32*, 165–197. https://doi.org/10.1080/10438599.2021.1893140
110. European Commission. (2022). II of the European Parliament and of the Council establishing the statistical classification of economic activities NACE Revision 2 (Text with EEA relevance). *Official Journal of the European Union*.
111. Zhu, Q., Sarkis, J., & Lai, K. (2013). Institutional-based antecedents and performance outcomes of internal and external green supply chain management practices. *Journal of Purchasing and Supply Management, 19*, 106–117. https://doi.org/10.1016/j.pursup.2012.12.001
112. Efimova, O., Rozhnova, O., & Gorodetskaya, O. (2020). XBRL as a tool for integrating financial and non-financial reporting. In *Advances in intelligent systems and computing* (pp. 135–147). Springer. https://doi.org/10.1007/978-3-030-37737-3_13
113. Nerantzidis, M., Tampakoudis, I., & She, C. (2024). Social media in accounting research: A review and future research agenda. *Journal of International Accounting, Auditing and Taxation, 54*, 100595. https://doi.org/10.1016/j.intaccaudtax.2024.100595
114. Singh, B., Swathi, P. K., & Sinha, S. (2023). Design of financing strategy model of financial management based on data mining technology. In *2023 second international conference on smart technologies for smart nation (SmartTechCon)* (pp. 67–71). IEEE. https://doi.org/10.1109/SmartTechCon57526.2023.10391329.
115. Lytneva, N., & Krestov, V. (2023). Developing the informatization of the technological waste management process in the lean production system of an enterprise. In *Lecture notes in networks and systems* (pp. 416–430). Springer. https://doi.org/10.1007/978-3-031-32719-3_32

Motivation and Risk-Opportunity Dynamics in Big Data Ecosystems

Giulia Renzi, Paula Ungureanu, and Selini Natalia Hadjidimitriou

Abstract Data-sharing ecosystems offer a transformative approach to addressing critical societal challenges through multi-stakeholder collaboration. However, existing literature suggests a need to explore how diverse perceptions and practices influence the functioning of these ecosystems. This study addresses the following research questions: what factors shape data-sharing practices in big data ecosystems, and how do they do so? We emphasize the importance of understanding how different actors influences sharing practices, particularly in relation to differing perceptions of the opportunities and risks of data sharing and the motivations behind these practices. Through a qualitative study within a data sharing ecosystem, we identified three distinct categories of data-sharing practices: diving, scaffolding, and pushing. These practices are shaped by stakeholders' attitudes toward data sharing, which are influenced by cognitive and social evaluations of risks and opportunities, as well as their motivational orientations (whether utilitarian or socially driven). Our findings reveal that stakeholders' data sharing behaviors vary significantly depending on whether they prioritize utilitarian benefits or broader societal impacts. Notably, we found no significant correlation between stakeholders' socio-demographic attributes and their data-sharing practices. This research contributes to the literature on data-sharing ecosystems and the dynamics of sharing data in complex multi-stakeholder organizations.

Keywords Data sharing · Data ecosystems · Motivation to share

G. Renzi (✉) · P. Ungureanu · S. N. Hadjidimitriou
Department of Sciences and Method for Engineering, University of Modena and Reggio Emilia, Reggio Emilia, Italy
e-mail: giulia.renzi@unimore.it; Paula.ungureanu@unimore.it; selini@unimore.it

M. Cipriano et al. (eds.), *Technologies for Organizations and Society*,
Lecture Notes in Information Systems and Organisation 80,
https://doi.org/10.1007/978-3-032-01697-3_24

1 Introduction

The world faces numerous social problems, including the exploitation of natural resources, inequalities in access to education and health services, and unequal living conditions [1, 2]. While still developing, big data holds the potential to improve social conditions [3]. Data ecosystems can unify efforts to address systemic problems and foster cooperation among stakeholders for societal benefit [4].

There have been both successes and failures in data sharing ecosystems [5, 6] and understanding of data sharing dynamics in these ecosystems remains limited [4]. Recent studies have started to treat data sharing ecosystems as distinct phenomena [7, 8] and one of their main findings shows that despite efforts to create common frameworks and standards [9], data sharing ecosystems often face challenges due to the diversity of stakeholders. Different actors, such as cross-sectoral organizations, policymakers, and civil society, in fact, have varying understandings and practices related to big data. For example, the European Commission funds projects on data sharing and standardization to create a unified framework, while private organizations focus on business opportunities, often overlooking the need for common rules [10]. Governments balance the benefits of collaboration with regulatory risks, and citizens are concerned with privacy and the need to adopt new skills [11].

The coexistence of different goals and motivations for data sharing significantly shapes behaviors in big data ecosystems. Research has begun to identify key factors influencing sharing practices, such as collaborative attitudes, financial incentives, power dynamics, legal barriers, and self-promotion interests [12]. However, an integrated perspective is still lacking. While there is growing attention to data governance [13], most studies focus on structural factors rather than motivational and relational aspects like mutual trust and collaboration [6]. Furthermore, little is known about how diverse perceptions, expectations, and practices of data sharing coexist and shape ecosystems. Some argue that greater stakeholder diversity increases organizational challenges, such as coordination costs and responsibility issues, leading to performance challenges [9]. Others suggest that diversity can foster creativity and innovation but also result in conflicts and delays [14, 15].

Building on this overview of the potential and challenges of big data sharing ecosystems, we explore how motivational, relational, and structural factors influence sharing behaviors and ecosystem functioning. Our study reveals that data-sharing practices in a big data ecosystem depend on a combination of motivational factors, cognitive and social appraisals of data sharing opportunities and risks, and stakeholders' attitudes towards data sharing.

2 Theoretical Framing

2.1 *Big Data Ecosystems: Shifting from Data Governance to Data Sharing Objectives, Practices and Motivation*

Numerous sources generate data, from internet clicks and mobile transactions to user-generated content and business activities like sales and purchases [16]. To handle the vast and diverse data, collaborative big data management and big data ecosystem have become a key societal trend and research area.

Despite a lack of universally agreed definitions, efforts are ongoing to clarify concepts and provide integrated definitions [13]. For example, Oliveira et al. [17] defined a data ecosystem as a network of actors involved in the consumption, production, or provision of data, fostering innovation, and creating value.

Big Data Ecosystems are positioned within the broader and more extensively studied context of ecosystems and platform ecosystems. Ecosystems represent a complex network of interconnected actors that typically collaborate and compete within a shared platform to create collective value. Thomas et al. [18] emphasize the importance of platforms as architectural leverage points for orchestrating these ecosystems. Platforms serve not only as technological foundations but also enable various forms of interaction among participants, fostering innovation and co-creation through a set of modules and interfaces that allow for shared use and customization to meet the diverse needs of the involved actors. This architectural approach leverages economies of scale and scope, generating network effects that can significantly enhance the ecosystem's potential for growth and innovation.

Even if the big data ecosystems are strongly linked with platform ecosystems, the complexity of big data ecosystems arises from data characteristics such as incompleteness, scalability, timeliness, privacy, and security, as well as the variety of involved actors [6, 19]. While much focus has been on understanding these properties, recent studies highlight the importance of data governance as data volumes and stakeholder numbers grow. However, literature often emphasizes structural aspects of data governance, like the roles and models of involved parties [4, 20, 21]. These studies provide a static view of data ecosystems, seeing data as assets managed by stakeholders with defined roles. Yet, human intentions play a significant role, as stakeholders share data based on specific goals and interests. The alignment of these interests is crucial for value creation and ecosystem growth, but motivational orientations in data ecosystems have been less explored. Organizations may share data to accumulate resources, support innovation, improve quality and security, evolve culture, gain legitimacy, or achieve social impact. The performance of an ecosystem and its actors is interdependent, but this interdependence needs further exploration. Thus, a practice-based view of data sharing is necessary to understand how big data ecosystems form and evolve over time through the interaction of different sharing motivations and relationships.

Although less explored, motivational orientations, such as personal interests and familiarity with the topic, are significant. Familiarity fosters trust and increases the willingness to collaborate, expecting reciprocation. Conversely, some studies show that the motivation is driven by the perception of contributing to the greater good, like social welfare or public health. Contextual factors like governance arrangements and legal requirements also play a role [22–24].

Understanding how perceived advantages and disadvantages of big data shape the motivation to share remains a gap.

Navigating big data complexities may require negotiation to improve data quality and address issues like inconsistency and incompleteness. Furthermore, motivation and perceptions of risks and benefits vary among stakeholders such as businesses, governments, and citizens. Finally, it is unclear how different levels of motivation may shape an ecosystem.

These gaps hinder a comprehensive understanding of big data-sharing ecosystems, and greater clarity on how various factors influence motivation is essential for advancing the study of these ecosystems.

3 Methods

3.1 Context

Our analysis is grounded in the MobiDataLab project, an initiative supported by the Horizon 2020 Research and Innovation Programme (H2020). Operating from January 2021 to January 2024, the MobiDataLab project aimed to foster data sharing practices among mobility stakeholders.

It structured its approach around four main pillars: the Open Knowledge Base, the Transport Cloud, Living and Virtual Labs, and impact assessment of the data sharing culture. The Open Knowledge Base served as a web-based repository of resources concerning data sharing challenges and best practices in the mobility sector. Drawing insights from leading projects, it provided recommendations for enhancing data quality, accessibility, and usability across various sharing models. The cloud-based prototype platform was developed to facilitate seamless sharing of transport data among stakeholders. Embracing federated cloud principles, this platform offered a unified interface for accessing both internal and external resources. Living and Virtual Labs offered open innovation ecosystems for nurturing a culture of data sharing. Furthermore, living labs facilitated real-time data exchanges and collaborative sessions among local stakeholders, addressing immediate challenges within specific territorial contexts. On the other hand, virtual labs provided a digital hub for remote participants, fostering engagement and collaboration in a virtual setting. Lastly, the impact assessment of the data sharing culture evaluated the ramifications of digitalization and data sharing in the transport sector. It explored how these innovations could drive new business models, enhance societal benefits, and mitigate environmental impacts.

Overall, MobiDataLab succeeded in cultivating a dynamic ecosystem where stakeholders collaborated, innovated, and advanced the culture of data sharing in the mobility sector.

3.2 Data Collection

We gathered data from various sources to facilitate the theory-building process, specifically through semi-structured interviews and archival records.

Our aim was to interview key stakeholders within the MobiDataLab ecosystem to explore their views, motivations, and engagement with data sharing in the context of integrated mobility solutions. Since we had no predefined criteria for selecting stakeholder categories, we began with interviews involving MobiDataLab partners. One author's direct involvement in various phases of the project facilitated access to these initial contacts, helping us connect not only with project partners and coordinators but also with other relevant actors within the ecosystem.

Using a snowball sampling strategy, we gradually extended our outreach beyond the original partners to include stakeholders involved in the project's living labs and virtual labs. This allowed us to involve a wider range of companies, individuals, and organizations. In total, we conducted 40 semi-structured interviews between May 2022 and December 2023, covering representatives from 19 different actor categories. All interviews were fully recorded, anonymized, and transcribed.

The interview protocol was structured into four main parts. The first section collected general background information about the interviewees and their organizations, with a focus on their motivations, objectives, and data-sharing practices. The second section addressed perceptions of data quality, aiming to understand how aspects such as accuracy, reliability, and completeness influence data-sharing efforts. The third section examined collaboration practices, highlighting the methods and forms of data exchange used in organizational contexts. This helped reveal key mechanisms that facilitate collaboration. The final section explored stakeholders' perspectives and experiences related to data sharing within the partnership, shedding light on their ambitions, practical actions, and the broader dynamics of cooperation.

Furthermore, we analysed certain archival data, starting from the MobiDataLab Grant Agreement, the official contract outlining the legal rights and responsibilities of the European Commission and the project partners. Additionally, we compiled and conducted preliminary analyses of the 24 deliverables generated within MobiDataLab to gain insight into the project's scope, primary activities, objectives, and obligations. Finally, in order to provide a comprehensive context for the MobiDataLab project and its operations, we also scrutinized 12 previous and ongoing European, national, and international projects and initiatives related to big data sharing. This analysis helped us to clarify ambiguities in the regulatory framework governing big data sharing, expand the range of anticipated benefits, underscore the importance of collaborative governance for systemic transformation, and enhance our understanding of fully-funded participation. The selection of initiatives for this examination was guided by a project review conducted by the authors, supplemented by recommendations provided by interviewees.

3.3 Data Analysis

After being transcribed word-for-word and anonymized, the interviews were further contextualized by incorporating the researchers' observations during the conversations and by referencing relevant project documentation. These enriched materials were then uploaded into DEDOOSE, a QACDAS platform, to support systematic qualitative analysis.

Employing a grounded theory methodology, we began by organizing the material into meaningful segments to uncover recurring patterns and relationships between concepts and the theoretical framework [25]. The analysis started with an open coding phase, where we identified prominent ideas and grouped them into initial codes. These first-order codes laid the groundwork for the emergence of broader conceptual themes, which we then refined through second-order analysis, following a more abstract, theory-driven lens.

In the open coding phase, we cataloged a wide array of views—both positive and negative—on the sharing of big data, including anticipated challenges, perceived risks, desirable changes to enable sharing, and notions of what defines high-quality data. We also examined ideas related to what stakeholders saw as essential for enabling collaborative data exchange.

Axial coding involved moving back and forth between the initial codes, interview transcripts, and conceptual frameworks to identify overarching patterns. This iterative process revealed a recurring contrast in how stakeholders articulated their reasons for participating in or refraining from data sharing—initially described as perceived benefits and drawbacks. These were later reframed through a theoretical lens as *cognitive evaluations of potential gains and risks*.

A notable insight emerged from repeated references to evaluative behaviors—interviewees often described informal vetting processes used to assess the credibility and reliability of potential data-sharing partners. These informal checks led us to identify a set of decision-making cues we termed *social proof heuristics*, some of which aligned with instrumental objectives and others with social value-driven goals.

As the coding evolved, we were also able to trace various motivations driving stakeholders' motivation to contribute data to the ecosystem, which we labeled as *motivation to share*. Alongside these, we identified concrete practices and strategies that actors employed in relation to data exchange, which we grouped under the theme *data sharing practices*. These practices were frequently linked to how individuals interpreted risks, opportunities, and their underlying motivations.

Through further abstraction and comparison of these second-order themes, we mapped out how different concepts were interrelated. The analysis suggested that perceptions of risk and opportunity shaped stakeholders' motivations, which in turn influenced the strategies they adopted for sharing data. Two central types of goals—utilitarian and social impact-oriented—emerged as key organizing dimensions of stakeholder behavior.

4 Findings

We found evidence of a variety of data sharing practices in the ecosystem, which we divided into three categories: *pulling*, *scaffolding*, and *pushing*. These depended on the stakeholders' attitudes towards data sharing, which in turn depend on how each stakeholder performs cognitive and social appraisals of the account of opportunities and risks regarding data sharing, together with each stakeholders' data sharing motivational orientations. Most importantly, we found that data-sharing motivation, evaluation, and practices differ according to whether risk appraisals and opportunities relate to utilitarian or social impact motivations, pushing the stakeholders to create different strategies to cope with opportunity-risk appraisals.

The diverse practices of data sharing seem to emerge from a complex process that initiates with motivational orientations towards data sharing, leading into a cycle of cognitive and social evaluation encompassing risks and opportunities. This cycle, in turn, is influenced by varying degrees of motivation to share, which shapes the data sharing practices adopted by different actors within a big data sharing ecosystem. Throughout our analysis, we observed no significant correlation between sharing practices and the socio-demographic attributes of stakeholders (e.g., their sector or industry background) or their roles within the ecosystem.

4.1 Data Sharing Motivations

Within the analyzed ecosystem, we consistently observed two primary motivational orientations concerning sharing. While some stakeholders prioritize the social impact stemming from data sharing, others perceive it as a utilitarian tool to fulfill their predetermined objectives. Regarding the social impact perspective, participants expressed a deep appreciation for the transformative potential inherent in data sharing during our interviews. They viewed it as a catalyst for effecting significant and positive changes on a global scale. There was a unanimous belief among interviewees that data sharing is crucial for contributing to societal well-being, with a specific emphasis on advancing environmental sustainability. Through active engagement in the ecosystem, in fact, both individuals and organizations aspire to play a central role in addressing urgent global challenges, aiming to improve the overall quality of life for current and future generations. This sentiment is vividly reflected in the following excerpt, where interviewee articulate his perception of the data sharing ecosystem as a tool for instigating beneficial societal transformations.

> I really think that the social community feeling helps a lot in an ecosystem (...): data is the new gold, and you have to believe that it is used for the right reason (Airline 1).

In contrast to stakeholders who prioritize broader societal goals, those adhering to a utilitarian approach tend to place greater emphasis on objectives directly linked to the essential functions of their respective organizations. This entails prioritizing the fulfillment of their organizational needs over considerations of the collective welfare. The utilitarian stance is characterized by a focus on maximizing individual or corporate advantages, typically driven by a practical assessment of self-interest and economic objectives. The following excerpt exemplifies this utilitarian perspective, illustrating how stakeholders prioritize their company's core objectives above broader societal concerns.

> The main goal for business is to make money (municipality, 1).

This approach emphasizes strategic measures aimed at enhancing internal processes, resource allocation, and decision-making to strengthen the organization's competitive position and financial stability. By adopting such a standpoint, stakeholders may show a tendency to favor outcomes aligned with the immediate interests of the company, potentially neglecting broader societal or ethical considerations. This utilitarian inclination reflects a pragmatic and self-centered mindset, where corporate success takes precedence, sometimes overshadowing contributions to the broader collective welfare.

It is noteworthy that we observed the presence of both orientations across various types of organizations (private and public) and roles within the ecosystem (policymakers, data orchestrators, providers, and users). Through interviews, we discerned how these orientations influenced stakeholders' attitudes towards data sharing. For instance, some interviewees articulated a data sharing strategy grounded in principles of transparency, accessibility, and a dedication to collaborative openness. By embracing an open data approach, these organizations demonstrate a conscious endeavor to provide specific information to the public. Conversely, some entities are motivated to share data due to strategic factors, especially smaller organizations, newcomers to an industry, or those aiming to carve out a unique market position. These entities may recognize that engaging in collaborative data exchange can strategically position them and set them apart in a competitive market environment.

The motivations behind data sharing influence behaviors, visions, expectations, and desires associated with it, guiding stakeholders to adopt particular data sharing practices.

4.2 *Cognitive Evaluation*

In our interviews with stakeholders, we found that they engaged in cognitive assessments regarding the risks and opportunities associated with data sharing within the ecosystem. Aligned with their motivational orientations, some stakeholders focused their evaluations primarily on societal impacts and potential changes, while others centered on business-related opportunities and risks. Interestingly, we noted that the emphasis on either social impact or utilitarian ones did not exhibit a clear-cut division but rather manifested along a continuum, with many assessments falling somewhere in between.

Stakeholders envisioned data sharing as a catalyst for fostering collective efforts toward environmental sustainability within the transportation sector. They anticipated optimizing resource usage, reducing pollution, and promoting sustainable practices, ultimately contributing to a globally ecologically conscious system. Additionally, they envisaged streamlined logistics and transportation operations resulting from data sharing, leading to reduced resource consumption, minimized noise pollution, and alleviated traffic congestion, thereby enhancing overall quality of life. Shared data was viewed as a valuable asset facilitating collaboration among diverse entities, leading to the development of digitized processes and operational efficiencies across industries, with a collective aim of continual process improvement. Comprehensive data sharing was deemed essential for policymakers to assess policy impacts, particularly regarding job creation and workforce diversification, enabling informed decision-making aligned with societal goals. Stakeholders anticipated the emergence of new business opportunities, particularly in vehicle manufacturing, driven by shared data's potential to fuel innovation, improve customer service, and yield positive societal outcomes.

The examination of potential risks linked to data sharing, considering diverse viewpoints from stakeholders, has unveiled a multifaceted landscape of risks. These risks span various dimensions, including socio-cultural, legal, technical, and economic considerations. First and foremost, the absence of a unified and cohesive long-term strategy to address complex societal challenges, often depicted as wicked problems, presents a significant risk. In fact, differing rates of engagement and levels of commitment among stakeholders may impede collaborative efforts on a national scale, potentially limiting the collective impact on intricate societal issues.

Collaboration hurdles arise from the diverse makeup of stakeholders, each bringing their unique perspectives to the forefront. The challenge lies in reconciling these varying viewpoints, with doubts about transparency and integrity potentially obstructing the establishment of common objectives. Furthermore, the risk of unsuccessful implementation of collaborative projects is heightened within such a diverse environment.

Legal complexities emerge as a significant risk factor in data sharing initiatives. The absence of clear regulatory frameworks presents challenges in defining acceptable datasets, ensuring interoperability, and crafting agreements for data sharing. This legal uncertainty poses a potential barrier to the seamless integration and data exchange.

From a technical standpoint, challenges such as the lack of standardized procedures for data collection are perceived as significant risks. Inaccuracies in user-contributed data and the absence of common standards require extensive data analysis before effective utilization. These technical challenges may impede the efficiency of shared information, particularly in the context of mobility solutions. Economic considerations, particularly concerns about potential organizational losses through data sharing, are identified as notable risks too. Stakeholder reluctance stems from fears of potential economic consequences, presenting a significant barrier to open collaboration and hindering the realization of collective benefits.

4.3 Social Evaluation

The dialogue around data-sharing opportunities and risks is enriched by various social indicators from diverse ecosystem stakeholders. These perspectives provide insights into the dynamics of shared vision, collaboration reliability, legal safeguards, and the capabilities and motivation of individual stakeholders.

Social assessments, in line with cognitive evaluations, seek to determine how collaboration can mitigate data-sharing risks and help achieve established objectives. A shared vision, a crucial social indicator, is linked to community building and exchanges among ecosystem participants, fostering transparency and effective cooperation. While not mandatory, it emphasizes collaboration's role in advancing collective goals. Similarly, the capacity for efficient collaboration among partners is essential, as technology alone cannot guarantee a successful ecosystem.

Legal mechanisms like robust regulations and contracts can mitigate the risks of data misuse by ensuring alignment with intended purposes. Interviews reveal the diverse roles and attitudes of stakeholders, highlighting the significance of community in building trust, especially in data sharing. These insights stress the balance between data value, trust, and commitment in collaboration. Other critical indicators for risk mitigation focus on stakeholders' capacity and motivation to find solutions and set common standards. Alignment of motivation is a key driver for collaboration, intertwining shared interests with innovative solutions. Stakeholders' testimonies provide a comprehensive view of shared vision, collaboration reliability, legal protection, and individual capabilities, essential for decision-making in data-sharing ecosystems.

Cognitive and social assessments are closely linked, each influencing the other: social evaluation measures collaboration's effectiveness in bridging gaps to achieve goals, while cognitive appraisal shapes engagement strategies to balance opportunities and risks.

4.4 Data Sharing Practices

Various data sharing practices were identified. The excerpt below illustrates how motivation to share correlates with different types of data sharing practices:

> Collaboration is more important than the risks out there (Researcher 2).

Based on the interview findings, we have categorized the primary practices into three main groups: *diving* (highlighted by a multi-stakeholder approach, collaboration, and trust), *scaffolding* (marked by institutional advocacy, the establishment of legal agreements, and the development of specialized tools for data sharing) and *pushing* (distinguished by standardization and incentives).

The "Diving practice" in data sharing is characterized by an active commitment to what we refer to as "diving behaviors". These behaviors demonstrate a proactive stance toward collaborative design and cooperation, with a strong focus on governance and nurturing collaborative relationships within the ecosystem. The objective is to work collectively with other stakeholders, prioritizing the development of shared solutions to drive progress across the entire ecosystem. One aspect of the diving practice entails the collaborative design of solutions through a multi-stakeholder approach. Stakeholders recognize the unique insights and expertise offered by various urban contexts, municipalities, policymakers, and other stakeholders, viewing them as partners rather than competitors. This recognition of each actor's diverse perspectives, stemming from their distinct technologies, experiences, expertise, and approaches, underscores the importance of fostering community building and exchanges among all stakeholders involved in diving practices. As articulated by a Software Provider (1):

> Without community building, without exchanges between all the actors of the ecosystem, you could not go far.

Another pivotal aspect of the diving practice is the enhancement of collaboration and the fostering of trust among stakeholders. Unlike more transactional or technology driven approaches, diving behavior emphasizes the irreplaceable value of human connection and collective effort. While practices as data analytics and machine learning offer powerful tools for processing information and identifying patters, they fall short in capturing the nuanced, relational dynamics that drive successful collaboration. The diving practice acknowledges that these technologies, while advanced, cannot fully substitute the deep, trust-based relationships that are crucial for effective collaboration.

As articulated by an interviewee the human elements of cooperation—such as trust, mutual understanding, and shared goals—are central to the success of data-sharing ecosystems. He highlights the necessity of ongoing collaboration and suggests that, despite technological advancements, the future of data-sharing relies on human-centered approaches. The diving practice, therefore, not only involves the exchange of data but also the co-creation of solutions, where diverse perspectives are valued, and stakeholders work hand in hand to navigate challenges and capitalize on opportunities. This collective effort is seen as the foundation for building robust and sustainable ecosystems that can adapt and thrive in an increasingly complex world.

The essence of the diving practice lies in recognizing that trust and collaboration are fundamental pillars for successful data sharing, transcending mere technological solutions to embrace human-centered approaches. This practice aligns with a comprehensive approach to data sharing, wherein stakeholders actively participate in co-designing solutions and prioritize collaboration and trust-building. This proactive and collaborative mindset distinguishes the diving practice from alternative approaches, underscoring the interconnectedness of stakeholders and their shared commitment to advancing the ecosystem through collaborative solutions and mutual understanding.

The "Scaffolding practice" within the domain of data sharing is characterized by stakeholders demonstrating a moderate inclination towards data sharing. In this practice, actors strategically establish structured frameworks to facilitate the growth of the ecosystem while safeguarding their own interests and vulnerabilities. Our interviews have revealed three distinct types of scaffolding practices: institutional lobbying behavior, creation of legal agreements, and development of specific tools. Concerning the institutional lobbying behavior, where stakeholders actively collaborate with external entities such as the European Commission and the EU Parliament, their objective is to influence legislation pertaining to data sharing, engaging in activities related to European policy to anticipate forthcoming regulations.

> We share ideas, and we work with apparatus like EU commission, with the EU parliament, about legislation of data sharing (Vehicle manufacturer, 1).

Within the creation of legal agreements, stakeholders emphasize the importance of regulatory compliance to ensure ethical and legal conduct. They advocate for adherence to regulations as a means to facilitate data sharing by establishing standardized legal agreements among diverse actors. In this approach, stakeholders place significant trust in legal frameworks, even pioneering the implementation of new laws.

For instance, an ITS provider highlighted the impact of EU regulations on sustainability in supply chains, indicating her commitment to compliance and the broader societal benefits derived from adhering to legal agreements.

Finally, the development of specific tools practice included the creation of platforms and Application Programming Interfaces (APIs) designed to streamline data sharing processes. A representative from a municipality highlighted the pivotal role of platforms in managing transportation networks and aligning with policy objectives. Despite harboring doubts regarding the motivation of other partners, scaffolding actors adopt a cautious approach and exhibit a moderate motivation to share. Consequently, their data sharing practices predominantly revolve around developing tools for collaboration, with the expectation that these tools will be effectively utilized. This strategic stance allows them to actively contribute to the partnership within a controlled framework, minimizing exposure while operating within the collaborative loop. Unlike stakeholders with higher levels of motivation to share, they refrain from adopting a more collaborative approach to resolving doubts, tensions, and skepticism within the partner network.

Finally, the "Pushing practice" involves partners with limited motivation to share engaging in strategic behaviors aimed at exerting influence on others while minimizing their own exposure. This approach encompasses two distinct pushing practices: a focus on standardization and the implementation of participation incentives. Within the Standardization-Driven Behavior, stakeholders advocate for the adoption of standardized practices throughout the ecosystem. The goal is to regulate the behaviors of others and address perceived challenges, conflicts, and inconsistencies within the ecosystem. Importantly, each stakeholder seeks to promote their own practices as the standard to be adopted. Additionally, the incentive-creation behavior entails strategically designing incentives to encourage others' involvement and steer the development of the ecosystem, all while minimizing personal engagement costs. In the domain of pushing practices, stakeholders with limited motivation to share employ standardization and incentive creation tactics to influence the ecosystem's trajectory while protecting their own interests.

5 Discussion

This research aimed to understand the factors influencing actors' decisions on sharing big data in a data sharing ecosystem. Our findings highlight how these decisions are contingent upon the cognitive and sociocultural assessments of the potential benefits and risks associated with data sharing.

A key insight was the complex spectrum of attitudes toward data sharing, differing from a simple "share" or "not share" dichotomy. Managing these ecosystems requires considering diverse perspectives and interactions among actors to navigate this nuanced gradient effectively. It is crucial to address this complexity to achieve a collective vision of data sharing that accommodates diverse actor inclinations. Failing to understand and manage these complexities in ecosystems can undermine stakeholders' performance.

Our contribution extends the emerging literature on big data ecosystems and addresses the motivation to share big data within complex multi-stakeholder organizations. We suggest that decision-making processes regarding data sharing are underpinned by a delicate balance between perceived risks and opportunities. This equilibrium initiates an evaluative process where choices tend towards either data sharing or abstention. We have shown that a key factor of a favorable attitude towards data sharing is the focus on the social impact of the partnership, rather than on personal utility. Those who envision societal change are more willing to engage in sharing behaviors even when they see serious risks and limitations in the partnership. On the contrary, when the perceived risks are more tightly related to personal goals, partners are less likely to put their competence and motivation to the test, and in case they do not receive positive answers, they are less likely to adopt proactive sharing strategies in the partnership.

5.1 Limitations and Implication for Practice

The research presented provides valuable insights into Big Data Ecosystems, while also acknowledging its limitations and suggesting avenues for future research.

Firstly, our investigation into Big Data Ecosystems is not exhaustive. Future studies should include a broader range of ecosystems to validate the patterns identified here and uncover new ones. It would be useful to explore the relational dynamics within these ecosystems, particularly how the practices of diving, scaffolding, and pushing interact and influence each other. This involves analyzing how stakeholders perceive and respond to these practices during their interactions.

Theoretically, governance has been primarily viewed as a means of exerting control in our paper. However, recent literature suggests that it also involves the creation and management of artifacts that encode governance with the goal of fostering "generativity" [26]. In the context of these ecosystems, generativity can be understood as the motivation to share, contribute, and innovate. Future research could investigate how governance mechanisms can be crafted to strike a balance between control and openness, thereby encouraging a diverse range of actors to actively engage and co-create value within the ecosystem.

Although we have identified specific risks and opportunities perceived by stakeholders—both in cognitive and social evaluations—other factors might also significantly shape data-sharing practices [27].

Our study does not aim to create a comprehensive taxonomy of practices and acknowledges that these practices can vary across different ecosystems.

Another limitation is the lack of direct observation of stakeholder interactions and the specific practices implemented within Big Data Ecosystems.

The evolving nature of ecosystems must also be considered, as their development over time can affect the relevance of our findings.

The research contributes to both theoretical and practical understanding. Theoretically, it adds depth to the literature on ecosystems, data sharing, and data governance. It aims to provide a realistic view of the benefits and risks of participating in Big Data Ecosystems, challenging idealized or overly negative perceptions. Practically, the study offers insights for potential participants in Big Data Ecosystems, including private and public organizations, citizens, stakeholders, and policymakers. Managers can use these insights to focus on risk management by developing strategies to mitigate associated risks. Effective relationship management is crucial, requiring regular reassessment and adaptation of strategies as ecosystems evolve, and ensuring clear communication and alignment of goals among partners, as noted by James et al. [28]. Building and maintaining trust through transparency, consistent communication, and adherence to data governance standards is also essential [28]. For policymakers, the study suggests promoting standardization and regulation by creating frameworks for data sharing that ensure security, privacy, and interoperability. This would reduce friction and build trust among stakeholders. Finally, involving stakeholders in the decision-making process can positively influence their perceptions [29–31]. Highlighting successful big data ecosystem initiatives can shift views from skepticism to optimism. Empowering stakeholders with access to information allows for more informed decisions and fosters trust. Such involvement can also drive innovation, leading to new applications or services that address local needs and enhance community well-being, especially for drivers.

To address the study's limitations, future research should broaden the exploration of big data ecosystems to include a wider variety of contexts.

Acknowledgments This work is part of MobiDataLab which has received funding from the European Union under the Horizon 2020 Research and Innovation program (Grant Agreement N° 101006879). The content reflects only the authors' views, and the European Commission is not responsible for any use that may be made of the information it contains.

Disclosure of Interests The authors have no competing interests to declare that are relevant to the content of this article.

References

1. Farquharson, C., McNally, S., & Tahir, I. (2022). Education inequalities. *IFS Deaton Review of Inequalities*.
2. Sidze, E. M., Wekesah, F. M., Kisia, L., & Abajobir, A. (2022). Inequalities in access and utilization of maternal, newborn and child health services in sub-Saharan Africa: A special focus on urban settings. *Maternal and Child Health Journal, 26*(2), 250–279.
3. Hansen, J., & Pang, Y. S. (2023). Opening industry data: The private sector's role in addressing societal challenges. *Data & Policy, 5*, e19.
4. Susha, I., van den Broek, T., van Veenstra, A. F., & Linåker, J. (2023). An ecosystem perspective on developing data collaboratives for addressing societal issues: The role of conveners. *Government Information Quarterly, 40*(1), 101763.
5. Chaudhari, S. L., & Sinha, M. (2021). A study on emerging trends in Indian startup ecosystem: Big data, crowd funding, shared economy. *International Journal of Innovation Science, 13*(1), 1–16.
6. Wang, Z., Zheng, Z., Jiang, W., & Tang, S. (2021). Blockchain-enabled data sharing in supply chains: Model, operationalization, and tutorial. *Production and Operations Management, 30*(7), 1965–1985.
7. Munoz-Arcentales, A., López-Pernas, S., Pozo, A., Alonso, Á., Salvachúa, J., & Huecas, G. (2019). An architecture for providing data usage and access control in data sharing ecosystems. *Procedia Computer Science, 160*, 590–597.
8. Sifah, E. B., Xia, Q., Agyekum, K. O. B. O., Xia, H., Smahi, A., & Gao, J. (2021). A blockchain approach to ensuring provenance to outsourced cloud data in a sharing ecosystem. *IEEE Systems Journal, 16*(1), 1673–1684.
9. Hayashi, T., Ishimura, G., & Ohsawa, Y. (2021). Structural characteristics of stakeholder relationships and value chain network in data exchange ecosystem. *IEEE Access, 9*, 52266–52276.
10. Janhunen, T. (2019). Why do companies fail to create data driven B2B ecosystems? Case study on a data sharing ecosystem initiative.
11. Jäckle, A., Burton, J., Couper, M. P., & Lessof, C. (2019, April). Participation in a mobile app survey to collect expenditure data as part of a large-scale probability household panel: Coverage and participation rates and biases. *Survey Research Methods, 13*(1), 23–44.
12. Devriendt, T., Borry, P., & Shabani, M. (2021). Factors that influence data sharing through data sharing platforms: A qualitative study on the views and experiences of cohort holders and platform developers. *PLoS One, 16*(7), e0254202.
13. Micheli, M., Ponti, M., Craglia, M., & Berti Suman, A. (2020). Emerging models of data governance in the age of datafication. *Big Data & Society, 7*(2), 2053951720948087.
14. Bühler, M. M., Nübel, K., Jelinek, T., Riechert, D., Bauer, T., Schmid, T., & Schneider, M. (2023). Data cooperatives as a catalyst for collaboration, data sharing and the digital transformation of the construction sector. *Buildings 2023, 13*(2), 442.

15. Curtis, S. K., Singh, J., Mont, O., & Kessler, A. (2020). Systematic framework to assess social impacts of sharing platforms: Synthesising literature and stakeholder perspectives to arrive at a framework and practice-oriented tool. *PLoS One, 15*(10), e0240373.
16. George, G., Haas, M. R., & Pentland, A. (2014). Big data and management. *Academy of Management Journal, 57*(2), 321–326.
17. Oliveira, M. I., Barros Lima, G. D. F., & Farias Lóscio, B. (2019). Investigations into data ecosystems: A systematic mapping study. *Knowledge and Information Systems, 61*, 589–630.
18. Thomas, L. D., Autio, E., & Gann, D. M. (2014). Architectural leverage: Putting platforms in context. *Academy of Management Perspectives, 28*(2), 198–219.
19. Kitsios, F., Papachristos, N., & Kamariotou, M. (2017, July). Business models for open data ecosystem: Challenges and motivations for entrepreneurship and innovation. In *2017 IEEE 19th Conference on Business Informatics (CBI)* (Vol. 1, pp. 398–407). IEEE.
20. Gupta, A., Panagiotopoulos, P., & Bowen, F. (2020). An orchestration approach to smart city data ecosystems. *Technological Forecasting and Social Change, 153*, 119929.
21. Pikkarainen, M., Ervasti, M., Hurmelinna-Laukkanen, P., & Nätti, S. (2017). Orchestration roles to facilitate networked innovation in a healthcare ecosystem. *Jultika. Oulu.Fi, 7*(9), 30–43.
22. Leon, P. G., Ur, B., Wang, Y., Sleeper, M., Balebako, R., Shay, R., et al. (2013, July). What matters to users? Factors that affect users' willingness to share information with online advertisers. In *Proceedings of the ninth symposium on usable privacy and security* (pp. 1–12).
23. Struminskaya, B., Toepoel, V., Lugtig, P., Haan, M., Luiten, A., & Schouten, B. (2020). Understanding willingness to share smartphone-sensor data. *Public Opinion Quarterly, 84*(3), 725–759.
24. Ziefle, M., Halbey, J., & Kowalewski, S. (2016). Users' willingness to share data on the internet: Perceived benefits and caveats. In *IoTBD* (pp. 255–265).
25. Strauss, A., & Corbin, J. (1998). *Basics of qualitative research techniques*.
26. Staub, N., Haki, K., Aier, S., & Winter, R. (2022). Governance mechanisms in digital platform ecosystems: Addressing the generativity-control tension. *Communications of the Association for Information Systems, 51*(1), 43.
27. Kazantsev, N., Islam, N., Zwiegelaar, J., Brown, A., & Maull, R. (2023). Data sharing for business model innovation in platform ecosystems: From private data to public good. *Technological Forecasting and Social Change, 192*, 122515.
28. James, R., Tsosie, R., Sahota, P., Parker, M., Dillard, D., Sylvester, I., et al. (2014). Exploring pathways to trust: A tribal perspective on data sharing. *Genetics in Medicine, 16*(11), 820–826.
29. Ballerini, L., & Bergh, S. I. (2021). Using citizen science data to monitor the Sustainable Development Goals: A bottom-up analysis. *Sustainability Science, 16*(6), 1945–1962.
30. Cappa, F., Franco, S., & Rosso, F. (2022). Citizens and cities: Leveraging citizen science and big data for sustainable urban development. *Business Strategy and the Environment, 31*(2), 648–667.
31. Åström, J. (2020). Participatory urban planning: What would make planners trust the citizens? *Urban Planning, 5*(2), 84–93.

Collaborative Data Sharing Partnership in Mobility: Transformations, Sustainability, and Hidden Challenges

Giulia Renzi, Paula Ungureanu, and Selini Natalia Hadjidimitriou

Abstract Leveraging big data in the mobility sector can help address some of today's most significant challenges, from enhancing sustainability to optimizing mobility services and improving the quality of life for users. However, despite the recognized potential of data sharing to generate social impact, those entering data sharing partnerships often express concerns regarding cost-benefit uncertainties, data use risks, and the operational and organizational challenges associated with collaboration. Our research adopts a collaborative perspective on data sharing, investigating how perceptions of the benefits and risks influence participation strategies in such partnerships. We conducted empirical research within the context of the European project MobiDataLab, which aims to prototype new solutions for mobility data sharing, increasing data sharing culture. This study involved collecting archival data and conducting semi-structured interviews with key actors in the transport sector, analyzed using the grounded theory approach. Our findings underscore the role of trust and satisfaction in shaping attitudes toward data sharing and behaviors within large cross-sectoral partnerships. These attitudes and behaviors are influenced by perceptions of data sharing risks and opportunities, leading to varied satisfaction levels with the status quo and trust in data sharing processes and partners. These factors, in turn, pave the way for three attitudes and corresponding data sharing strategies: refraining, improving, and maintaining. By elucidating how different attitudes and beliefs regarding data sharing impact strategies at the partnership level and thus influence a partnership's trajectory and outcomes, we contribute to the literature on cross sectoral partnerships and the collaborative dynamics of data sharing.

Keywords Data sharing partnerships · Willingness to share · Grounded theory

G. Renzi (✉) · P. Ungureanu · S. N. Hadjidimitriou
Department of Sciences and Method for Engineering, University of Modena and Reggio Emilia, Reggio Emilia, Italy
e-mail: giulia.renzi@unimore.it; paula.ungureanu@unimore.it; selini@unimore.it

M. Cipriano et al. (eds.), *Technologies for Organizations and Society*,
Lecture Notes in Information Systems and Organisation 80,
https://doi.org/10.1007/978-3-032-01697-3_25

1 Introduction

The potential of data sharing is undeniable: the Organization for Economic Cooperation and Development (OECD) has recognized data use and reuse across the economy as a new form of capital. Furthermore, sharing and reusing open data is creating new opportunities for economic growth and generating societal benefits for various actors, including data providers, suppliers, data users, and the overall economy [1].

Despite living in the Age of Data [2], numerous challenges remain before we can achieve a flourishing shared culture of data. There is a need to increase awareness of the importance and value of data, and a significant knowledge gap exists regarding the necessary organizational aspects [3]. As industries and public bodies produce data at an unprecedented rate [2], there is significant expectation and investment to understand how this data can create value [4]. This value can benefit society, improving social well-being in education, healthcare [5, 6], public safety and security [7], as well as enhance business efficiency, revenue, and market share [8–12].

While still in its nascent stages, the potential for enhancing societal conditions through data sharing is tangible and substantial [13]. For example, initiatives promoting open data have been initiated to enhance transparency, combat corruption in public governance, bolster law enforcement, facilitate smart urban planning, improve healthcare, and tackle climate change [14]. Presently, data partnerships are viewed as promising avenues to realize a collective vision addressing these systemic challenges, fostering collaboration among stakeholders for the betterment of society [15]. Creating a data culture, rather than an information-sharing culture, risks misleading participants into believing they can achieve more than is feasible, affecting the pace of societal data sharing and the success of large-scale partnerships [16, 17]. We know much about cross-sector partnership dynamics and outcomes [18–21], yet relatively little about how these dynamics influence data-sharing strategies and behaviors.

Hence, we assert that for a deeper comprehension of data sharing partnerships' trajectories, increased emphasis is necessary on how various elements, encompassing perceptions of data sharing (including both advantages and risks), expectations, and behaviors, coexist and mold these partnerships. While structural factors (like participant characteristics and organizational setups) have garnered significant attention, less insight exists regarding motivational inclinations, such as individual and collective objectives, and relational dynamics, such as mutual trust or attitudes toward sharing, and the intricate interplay among structural, motivational, and relational factors impacting data sharing practices within multi-stakeholder partnerships.

For data sharing to reach its full potential, data must be collected and shared by various sources and actors [22]. This will foster innovative products, services, and business opportunities [23, 24], while improving operations, optimizing supply chain flows, and selecting the right people for specific tasks and jobs [2, 25].

In response to these challenges, we embarked on a qualitative inquiry situated within a data sharing partnership centered on integrated mobility solutions. Our investigation embraces a practice-oriented lens, delving into how perceptions, anxieties, and relational anticipations sculpt strategies for sharing data. What emerged from our exploration are discernible patterns of data sharing behaviors—namely refraining, improving, and maintaining—each influenced by what we term as the stakeholders' perception-action loop.

This loop, akin to a finely tuned instrument, comprises two key components: the perceived benefits and risks associated with sharing data, and the conceptual contrast between idealistic partnership aspirations and pragmatic realities. Through our study, we endeavor to unravel the intricacies of this perception-action loop, aiming to enrich our collective comprehension of how stakeholders engage in data-sharing practices within partnerships.

The thrust of our research extends beyond mere academic discourse; it seeks to make substantive contributions to the burgeoning literature on data sharing and the willingness to share. By unearthing fresh insights into the dynamic interplay of data sharing among diverse stakeholders, we aspire to illuminate pathways for informed decision-making and policy formulation.

In casting light on the varied practices of data sharing within these partnerships, our work holds relevance for policymakers and stakeholders alike. Much like a beacon guiding ships through treacherous waters, our findings serve to inform and empower those navigating the complexities of data sharing within contemporary landscapes.

2 Theoretical Framework

Within data sharing partnerships, notable diversity prevails, potentially influencing the disparate efficacy of endeavors within these realms. Grasping this spectrum demands more than a cursory glance at governance frameworks and shared datasets: it mandates a thorough exploration of stakeholders' outlooks, inclinations, and perceptions, particularly regarding their inclination to collaborate. Thus, we immersed ourselves in the literature surrounding data sharing partnerships, aiming to decipher their architecture, the impetuses propelling their genesis, and the alliances forged therein. Moreover, we tapped into research dedicated to unraveling the propensity to share data, with a keen eye on the relational dynamics among stakeholders.

2.1 *From Data to Value*

With technological development, data has gained significant momentum in both the business and academic worlds [25, 26]. While cutting-edge technologies are necessary to manage large and varied volumes of data [4], it is clear that data is essential for companies to develop innovative products and services, expand business opportunities, and enhance networking and market reach [23]. The potential of data is so vast that Baesens et al. [27] referred to it as "the mother lode of disruptive change in a networked business environment" (p. 629).

The value of data is not only economic but also sociological. Data improves social well-being in various sectors, including education [28], healthcare [6], public safety and security [7], government [29], and employment [30]. Although the literature strongly focuses on the opportunities data brings to organizations [31], the associated problems and lack of clarity can hinder the effective achievement of value. Relying solely on data risks misleading stakeholders into believing they can achieve more than is realistically possible [16, 17].

In the transport sector, the lack of a clear vision of the value-data relationship, combined with the lack of and poor-quality data, is a major constraint. This issue prevents progress that could be economically, environmentally, and socially sustainable [32].

2.2 Data Sharing

Data sharing offers significant potential to accelerate scientific innovation, enhance the efficiency of research investment, and improve the quality of analysis [33]. Even recognizing these clear benefits, there is an emerging consensus on the need to develop policies, infrastructures, and best practices for data sharing [34].

Although most data-sharing activities have been concentrated in high-income regions [35], the European Commission (EU) has recognized the importance of spreading data culture across all sectors in member countries to foster economic, environmental, and societal advancements. To this end, the EU has begun financing data-centric projects, aiming to become a model society that demonstrates how fundamental data is to build a free, sustainable, fair, safe, democratic, and inclusive environment. While encouraging and financing projects related to data culture and data governance, the EU is also working on establishing a robust legal framework regarding data protection, fundamental rights, safety, and cybersecurity [36].

Data sharing will only reach its full potential if data can be collected and shared by multiple sources and actors [22]. This approach enables the development of innovative products, services, and business opportunities [23, 24], while improving operations, optimizing supply chain flows, and selecting the right people for specific tasks and jobs [2, 25]. Modern data sharing surpasses traditional methods (e.g., using pre-installed sensors) but introduces issues of trust and control [22].

The challenges of data sharing in the transport sector remain understudied, highlighting a gap in the literature. Describing in detail the problems and challenges of a complex phenomenon like data sharing is the first, albeit intricate, step toward developing innovations, solutions, and collaborations aimed at overcoming existing obstacles.

2.3 Data Governance

Although we have not found a widely recognized definition of "data governance," for the purposes of this article, we have decided to refer to the definition proposed by Abraham:

> Data governance specifies a cross-functional framework for managing data as a strategic enterprise asset. In doing so, data governance specifies decision rights and accountabilities for an organization's decision-making about its data. Furthermore, data governance formalizes data policies, standards, and procedures and monitors compliance ([37]; p. 425–426).

This definition encompasses several concepts related to data governance reported in the literature [35, 38, 39], offering a broad and inclusive view of key concepts. Major areas of research related to data governance include governance mechanisms, the scope of data governance, the antecedents of data governance, and the consequences of data governance [37]. Our research fits into the scope of data governance, specifically investigating data governance in interorganizational settings, such as platform partnerships, following Lee's studies [40].

For defining our interviews, particularly regarding data governance, we followed the guidance of Abraham [37], who argued that new research should focus on understanding the data governance mechanisms that help organizations support both individuals and groups in sharing data. This includes co-determining how their data is governed, used, and reused.

2.4 Willingness to Share: Challenges and Opportunities

Which aspects are important to encourage data sharing? What can influence the willingness to share? To offer a comprehensive picture of how problems, challenges, prerequisites, and changes are closely related to the willingness to share, we analyzed the literature on the factors influencing decisions to share data.

To achieve an efficient and effective operational system, data needs to be shared. Although data and information sharing have gained research attention in recent years (among the others [14]), the willingness to share, whether spontaneous or predetermined, has not been sufficiently explored [2, 41].

Willingness to share includes several key aspects as timeliness, accuracy, adequacy, completeness, and reliability: these features affect the quality of the decisions made by a firm [42]. Sharing at the organizational level involves disclosing private and closely guarded financial and strategic information to partners and collaborators. Consequently, actors are cautious about what they share, to what extent, and with whom. When defining the possibilities for sharing, actors, organizations, and stakeholders base their decisions on trust and commitment in the partnership, making these elements crucial for the willingness to share [41].

Although we acknowledge new research fields that focus on the influence of personality on the willingness to share data (e.g., [43]), we have decided not to include this aspect in our research. Instead, we focus on categories of actors rather than individuals.

3 Methodology

3.1 Research Setting: The MobiDataLab Project

This study draws upon the MobiDataLab project, a European initiative funded under the Horizon 2020 Research and Innovation Programme (H2020). MobiDataLab was selected as a reference case for its demonstrative value in establishing a collaborative data-sharing framework, involving a wide array of stakeholders who jointly contributed to the achievement of the project's objectives through the effective exchange and use of data to foster innovation. Implemented between January 2021 and January 2024, the project sought to promote data-sharing practices within the mobility sector.

By leveraging data analytics, MobiDataLab addressed urban mobility and transportation challenges through the collection, processing, and interpretation of extensive transportation datasets. These datasets were derived from diverse sources, including GPS devices, mobile applications, public transport systems, and traffic sensors. Advanced analytical techniques, such as machine learning and statistical modeling, were employed to extract insights related to mobility patterns, congestion, and infrastructure usage, with the overarching aim of enhancing efficiency, sustainability, and accessibility in urban environments.

As a Horizon 2020 initiative, MobiDataLab integrated research, dissemination, and practical application, while engaging a heterogeneous set of stakeholders. These included academic researchers investigating emerging mobility trends, private-sector actors aiming to identify inefficiencies and create added value, public authorities involved in urban and transport planning, and local communities interested in improving mobility and quality of life. Over the course of its implementation, MobiDataLab evolved into a comprehensive data-sharing ecosystem. Initially composed of ten partners from various sectors—ranging from ITS providers and academic institutions to public bodies and associations—the project expanded through its Living and Virtual Labs, which facilitated broader stakeholder engagement. These collaborative environments enabled participants to articulate data and service needs, identify barriers to the deployment of new mobility solutions, and address critical challenges related to interoperability, connectivity, and standardization.

The multiplicity of actors and practices involved in MobiDataLab offered a unique opportunity to investigate the development and governance of data-sharing partnerships. The project provided empirical insights into stakeholders' perceptions, expectations, and concerns regarding data exchange, while also contributing to a deeper understanding of the structural, motivational, and relational dimensions that underpin such collaborative arrangements.

Although MobiDataLab officially concluded in January 2024, its findings continue to be disseminated through academic publications and conference presentations. The project's prototype and its contributions to the understanding of data-sharing cultures in Europe—particularly those emerging from stakeholder interactions during hackathons—constitute a valuable foundation for future research on collaborative data governance.

3.2 Data Collection

We gathered data from diverse sources to facilitate the theory-building process, encompassing semi-structured interviews and archival data.

3.2.1 Interviews

The objective of our inquiry was to capture the perspectives, visions, and openness to data sharing among key actors involved in the MobiDataLab partnership, with a focus on integrated mobility solutions. We did not impose predefined actor categories at the outset: initially, we engaged with MobiDataLab's core partners—an approach facilitated by the involvement of one of the authors in various phases of the project, which allowed direct access to coordinators and participants—we then broadened the sample to include additional stakeholders who joined the ecosystem later, particularly those involved in the Living and Virtual Labs.

Between May 2022 and December 2023, we conducted 40 semi-structured interviews with representatives from 19 different stakeholder categories. This number was determined based on three criteria: (i) data saturation, as later interviews yielded no substantial new information; (ii) representativeness, with sufficient diversity of perspectives across stakeholder types; and (iii) analytical manageability, which allowed for in-depth analysis without excessive data redundancy [44–46].

All interviews were audio-recorded, anonymized, and fully transcribed. The interview guide consisted of four main sections. The first addressed general background information on the interviewees and their organizations, including motivations and objectives related to data sharing. The second focused on perceptions of data quality—specifically, the role of accuracy, reliability, and completeness in enabling effective data exchange. The third explored collaboration and data-sharing practices, examining the mechanisms used to facilitate stakeholder cooperation. The final section investigated future visions and operational strategies for data sharing within the partnership, uncovering motivations, challenges, and success factors that shaped the governance and implementation of shared data practices.

3.2.2 Archival Data

Archival data collection began with the analysis of the MobiDataLab Grant Agreement—the formal contract outlining the legal roles and responsibilities of both the European Commission, as the funding body, and the project's consortium partners. In parallel, we collected and conducted an initial review of the 24 project deliverables produced within MobiDataLab. These documents provided valuable insights into the project's core activities, stated goals, and operational commitments.

To situate MobiDataLab within a broader context, we examined relevant European, national, and international initiatives—both completed and ongoing—that addressed data-sharing in mobility and related sectors. This review included an analysis of official project websites, social media content, and publicly available reports detailing their objectives, outcomes, and activities. Through this process, we developed a comparative understanding of different types of data-sharing partnerships across Europe, encompassing research-focused, market-oriented, and hybrid models. We also considered distinctions between initiatives funded internally (e.g., industry-led) and those supported by external public or private sources.

This comparative analysis enhanced our understanding of the regulatory, institutional, and organizational environments in which data-sharing partnerships operate. It also enabled us to identify key differences in governance mechanisms, stakeholder involvement, and participation strategies. The selection of these initiatives was informed by a thorough review carried out by the research team and further refined through recommendations offered by interview participants. This method allowed us to position MobiDataLab within the wider landscape of European data-sharing efforts and better interpret its operational choices and governance arrangements.

3.3 Methods of Analysis

Once interviews were transcribed and anonymized, we used archival materials to further investigate references, implicit connections, and contextual elements mentioned by participants. The anonymized transcripts were imported into a centralized database using the QACDAS platform DEDOOSE. Adopting a grounded theory approach, we carried out a systematic categorization of the textual material to identify clusters of meaning, drawing connections between empirical evidence, established theoretical frameworks, and the emergence of new conceptual insights [47, 48].

In parallel to the interview analysis, we conducted an in-depth review of European, national, and international projects and initiatives, both concluded and ongoing, that addressed data sharing. By examining their websites, social media content, and publicly available documentation, we gained a broader understanding of their goals, outputs, and key achievements. This comparative review provided a valuable reference point for interpreting the MobiDataLab case, allowing us to contextualize its dynamics within a wider spectrum of data-sharing initiatives. It also contributed to our understanding of the regulatory and institutional factors shaping such partnerships and revealed the diversity of governance models and stakeholder configurations.

Following the procedures of grounded theory, our analytical process began with open coding to extract recurring concepts and themes from the data. We then applied axial coding to develop second-order themes, linking categories and subcategories identified in the earlier phase [48]. This iterative process allowed us to surface a range of perceived benefits and concerns associated with data sharing, identify enabling conditions for collaborative practices, and articulate shared criteria for assessing data quality.

4 Results

The grounded model outlined in this study delineates the interplay among perceived risks and advantages of data sharing, trust and satisfaction concerning collaborative data sharing, and the approaches and strategies of data sharing embraced within the partnership. Figure 1 provides an overview of our grounded model.

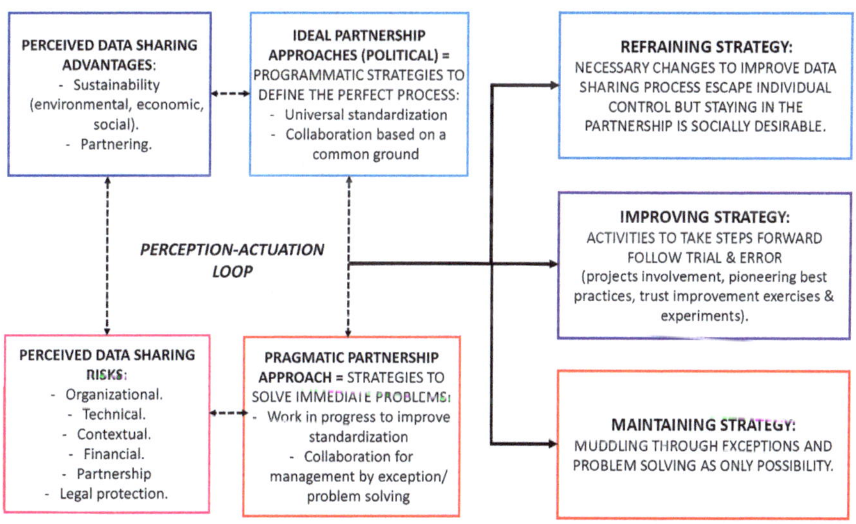

Fig. 1 A grounded model of the impact of perception-actuation loops on the process of partnering for data sharing

4.1 Perceived Data Sharing Advantages and Ideal Partnership Approaches

We discovered that partners' perception of the benefits associated with data sharing significantly influenced their attitudes and behaviors toward data sharing within the partnership. Specifically, we observed a recurring pattern in which partners oscillated between recognizing the advantages and disadvantages of data sharing and determining ideal versus pragmatic strategies for engaging in data sharing partnerships. Our analysis revealed two primary categories of perceived benefits: sustainability and collaboration, as shown in the following excerpts:

> The main opportunity (of data sharing) is to contribute with digital information that is shared to a more climate-friendly environment and to a better and more effective mobility system. If you know what the current information is about what's going on in the traffic, you'll not have delays in public transport, nor traffic jams. The data exchange can contribute to effectiveness and to more sustainability. (ITS provider 2)

> (When you set up data sharing systems) having a collective vision is not a prerequisite, but I think this collaboration and this knowledge sharing is super helpful because you generate transparency, you learn from each other. (. . .) It is super helpful to have a fruitful and efficient collaboration, and therefore I think the initiatives like MobiDataLab are super helpful for that (. . .). In my view (this) is what distinguishes successful cases of sharing from not so successful ones (ITS provider 1).

Firstly, our examination of sustainability included improving quality of life, enhancing safety and inclusivity, optimizing economic efficiency, and promoting environmental sustainability within transportation systems. Secondly, many perceived benefits were related to fostering collaboration for societal improvement. Partners highlighted the opportunity to expand knowledge networks through enriching collaborative experiences, which ideally facilitated a continuous process of mutual learning. These perceived benefits, driven by aspirations for positive societal change, significantly influenced partners' attitudes toward data sharing, often outweighing perceived drawbacks.

4.2 Perceived Data Sharing Risks and Pragmatic Partnership Approaches

Our interviews also revealed various challenges voiced by our informants, which we categorized into six main areas of perceived risks: organizational, technical, contextual, financial, partnerships, and legal protection. The following excerpts are an example of the legal and financial perceived risks:

> Well, I can speak for the work we are doing, so there are a lot of legal challenges. (. . .) What datasets can be provided and how to integrate them? There are also interoperability issues. How to make sure that the different datasets work and communicate with each other to make the systems work? Then there is again legal issue about contracting on how to share the data. (Researcher 1)

Although our informants emphasized the risks and challenges associated with data sharing, even those expressing pessimism remained committed to the partnership. Their attachment to sustainable and collaborative ideals motivated them to continue engaging in data sharing collaborations, despite lingering doubts and dissatisfaction. Just as we observed a continuum between perceptions of benefits and risks, we also identified a spectrum of partnership strategies, ranging from idealistic to pragmatic approaches.

Partners' strategies were influenced by their perceptions of benefits and risks, leading to what we term the perception-action loop. While idealistic approaches focused on long-term visions and programmatic actions aimed at achieving universal standardization, pragmatic strategies were more grounded in day-to-day collaboration experiences and problem-solving efforts. The following excerpts are reported as an example of the idealistic approach (the first one) and the pragmatic view (the second one):

> The data can improve life in so many ways. It is clear that if I have a more massive, punctual, and efficient data exchange, and I can make my work more efficient, I can save on consumption and pollute less. I will have fewer running trucks waiting outside the terminal, I will make the cranes work a lot less, because I have the data on the position of the containers, it is a cascade effect. The train, if I know it arrives earlier, I can arrange the means to work it, I can better organize people's shifts, fewer people who drive on the street with the car. A more efficient data transmission has a positive effect on sustainability and on social issues, less acoustic noise, and less traffic. (CEO 1, railway transport operator).

Partners' attitudes toward data sharing, shaped by their perceptions of benefits and risks, as well as their levels of trust and satisfaction, influenced the strategies they adopted within the partnership. Trust emerged as a central theme in our interviews, with varying degrees of trust observed among informants. While trust motivated partners to address challenges and mitigate risks collaboratively, a lack of trust prompted a reliance on standardization and legal safeguards. Satisfaction, both with data quality and partnership dynamics, also influenced partners' strategies.

4.3 Strategies for Data Sharing: Maintaining, Improving, Refraining

Based on the interplay between perceptions, trust, satisfaction, and resulting strategies, we identified three overarching approaches to partnering for data sharing: maintaining, improving, and refraining. Overall, our analysis highlights the complex interplay between perceptions, trust, satisfaction, and partnership strategies within data sharing partnerships, shedding light on the nuanced dynamics of collaborative endeavors.

Maintaining Strategy

The maintaining approach, characterized by a pragmatic focus on the status quo, involved partners prioritizing immediate problem-solving efforts over long-term idealizations. Despite recognizing areas for improvement, partners were generally satisfied with the current state of affairs and thus focused on addressing immediate challenges without pursuing radical changes.

Improving Strategy
Conversely, the improving approach combined pragmatic problem-solving with a proactive desire for progress. Partners adopting this approach were dissatisfied with certain aspects of the partnership but maintained trust and confidence in the potential for improvement. They actively sought opportunities to enhance collaboration and drive toward their ideal vision of data sharing. In contrast, the refraining approach was marked by a programmatic and cautious stance toward data sharing, lacking empirical grounding in collaborative experiences.

Refraining Strategy
Partners refraining from active engagement perceived both risks and benefits but were reluctant to invest efforts in improving the status quo. Instead, they relied on preconceived notions and external factors to inform their decision-making, exhibiting hesitancy to fully commit to data sharing initiatives.

5 Conclusion

Data-sharing partnerships offer a fresh perspective on tackling societal issues through collaborative engagement from diverse stakeholders. Existing studies underscore the significance of comprehending the array of factors influencing data-sharing practices, including social dynamics, sharing perceptions, and motivations (among the others, [13]). Our research aimed to bridge this knowledge gap by exploring the drivers behind the coexistence of diverse data-sharing practices within such partnerships.

Through qualitative inquiry within a data-sharing partnership, our findings suggest that data sharing practices are shaped by an interplay between stakeholders' perceptions and partnership views. Our contribution enriches the evolving literature on data sharing and willingness to share by delving into data sharing governance within intricate multi-stakeholder environments, while also redefining the concept of willingness to share data within these contexts.

Our research aims to illuminate the dynamics of data sharing partnerships within the transport sector. We delve into the intricate interplay of various factors that shape the behaviors of stakeholders involved in these partnerships, offering insights into the diverse attitudes and strategies driving data sharing initiatives.

Our model underscores the significance of perception-action loops in data sharing partnerships, particularly in shaping stakeholders' attitudes and behaviors. We argue that stakeholders' perceptions of the advantages and risks associated with data sharing, coupled with their approach to partnership, serve as key determinants influencing their levels of trust, satisfaction, and overall strategies in data sharing collaborations.

We posit that stakeholders' perceived benefits and drawbacks, along with their partnering strategies, drive distinct attitudes and approaches to data sharing partnerships: namely, maintaining the status quo, seeking improvement, or refraining from active engagement.

These findings contribute to the literature on cross-sectoral partnerships and meta-organizations, shedding light on the complex dynamics underlying attitudes toward data sharing and the efficacy of data sharing initiatives (among the others: [18–21].

From a practical standpoint, our research reveals the diverse strategies employed in data sharing partnerships within the transport sector. It underscores the evolving nature of data sharing processes, characterized by a spectrum of approaches. Understanding the underlying beliefs, attitudes, and strategies guiding these actions is crucial for fostering awareness, negotiation, and alignment within complex collaborative endeavors such as mobility data sharing.

Furthermore, our study offers insights into the nuanced aspects of socially desirable goals, such as sustainability and collaborative partnerships, highlighting both their positive and negative implications. By understanding these dynamics, stakeholders can move beyond the dichotomy between idealized aspirations and practical experiences, fostering more effective and sustainable data sharing practices in the transport sector.

5.1 Limitations and Implication for Practice

The research presented offers valuable insights into data-sharing partnerships, while also acknowledging its limitations and suggesting directions for future exploration.

Firstly, our study's examination of data-sharing practices is not exhaustive. Future studies should explore a broader range of data-sharing partnerships to validate the patterns identified here and potentially uncover additional ones. Further research could delve into the relational dynamics of the data-sharing practices discussed, specifically examining how refraining, improving, and maintaining practices interact and influence each other within partnership contexts. This includes analyzing how stakeholders interpret and respond to these practices during their interactions.

In addition, while we have identified certain risks and opportunities perceived by stakeholders, other factors may also significantly impact data-sharing and partnership practices.

Our study does not aim to provide a complete taxonomy of data-sharing practices, and we recognize that different partnerships may exhibit varying practices. Another limitation is our inability to directly observe stakeholder interactions and collaborations, as well as the specific data-sharing and partnership practices implemented within the partnerships themselves. Finally, the dynamic nature of partnerships should be considered, as their evolution over time can impact the relevance of our findings.

Our research aims to contribute both theoretically and practically.

Theoretically, it enriches the information systems literature on partnerships, data sharing, willingness to share, and data governance. The primary objective is to provide a realistic portrayal of the advantages and risks of participating in data-sharing partnerships, moving beyond current idealized or negative perceptions.

Practically, it offers insights for potential participants in data-sharing partnerships, including private and public organizations, citizens, stakeholders, and policymakers.

Managers and policymakers can draw several implications from this study. Managers need to focus on risk management by developing strategies to mitigate risks associated with data-sharing partnerships, such as establishing clear data governance frameworks. Dynamic relationship management is also crucial, requiring managers to regularly reassess and adapt their strategies as partnerships evolve, ensuring strong communication channels and goal alignment among partners as previously stated by James et al. [49]. Furthermore, managers should work on building and maintaining trust through transparency, consistent communication, and adherence to data governance standards [49].

For policymakers, our study suggests promoting standardization and regulation by creating standardized frameworks for data sharing that ensure security, privacy, and interoperability, thereby reducing friction and increasing trust among stakeholders. Policymakers should also consider offering incentives for participation, such as tax breaks, grants, or public recognition for organizations engaging in data-sharing partnerships (in line with [50]). Additionally, establishing legal and ethical guidelines would be important to protect sensitive data and prevent misuse or exploitation (in line with Meyer [51]).

Finally, we claim that involving stakeholders and citizens in the decision-making process can positively influence their perception (in line with [52–54]). Highlighting success stories where data sharing has led to tangible benefits can also shift views from skepticism to optimism and empowering citizens and stakeholders with access to information allows them to make more informed decisions. Furthermore, engaging them in data sharing initiatives, such as through participatory data governance models, can build trust between the public and institutions, as when citizens are involved in the decision-making process, they are more likely to trust that their data is being used responsibly. Citizens and stakeholders can foster innovation, as access to data may lead to the development of new applications or services that address local needs, thereby contributing to the community's overall well-being.

To address the study's limitations, future research should expand the scope of data-sharing practices by exploring a wider range of partnerships. There is also a need to examine the relational dynamics of data-sharing practices, investigating how different practices interact and influence each other within partnerships. Future research should aim to include direct observations of stakeholder interactions to better understand the dynamics at play. Lastly, considering the evolution of partnerships over time is crucial, as this can impact data-sharing practices and outcomes, offering more dynamic insights for managers and policymakers.

Acknowledgments This work is part of MobiDataLab which has received funding from the European Union under the Horizon 2020 Research and Innovation program (Grant Agreement N° 101006879). The content reflects only the authors' views, and the European Commission is not responsible for any use that may be made of the information it contains.

Disclosure of Interests The authors have no competing interests to declare that are relevant to the content of this article.

References

1. Deloitte, L. L. P. (2017). *Assessing the value of TfL's open data and digital partnerships.*
2. McAfee, A., Brynjolfsson, E., Davenport, T. H., Patil, D. J., & Barton, D. (2012). Big data: The management revolution. *Harvard Business Review, 90*(10), 60–68.
3. Gupta, M., & George, J. F. (2016). Toward the development of a big data analytics capability. *Information & Management, 53*(8), 1049–1064.
4. Constantiou, I. D., & Kallinikos, J. (2015). New games, new rules: Big data and the changing context of strategy. *Journal of Information Technology, 30*(1), 44–57.
5. Cazier, J., Cech, T., & Spaulding, T. (2015). *Applying business analytic methods to improve organizational performance in the public school system.*
6. Raghupathi, W., & Raghupathi, V. (2014). Big data analytics in healthcare: Promise and potential. *Health Information Science and Systems, 2*(1), 1–10.
7. Newell, S., & Marabelli, M. (2015). Strategic opportunities (and challenges) of algorithmic decision-making: A call for action on the long-term societal effects of 'datification'. *The Journal of Strategic Information Systems, 24*(1), 3–14.
8. Griffin, J. (2010). Action record – four critical principles of data governance success. *Journal of Pediatric, Maternal & Family Health Chiropractic, 20*(1), 29.
9. Smallwood, R. F. (2014). Information governance, IT governance, data governance: What's the difference? In *Information governance: Concepts, strategies, and best practices*. Wiley.
10. Begg, C., & Caira, T. (2011). Data governance in practice: The SME quandary reflections on the reality of data governance in the small to medium enterprise (SME) sector. In *Proceedings of 5th European Conference on Management Information and Evaluation System* (pp. 75–83).
11. van Bommel, P., Hoppenbrouwers, S. J. B. A., Proper, H., & van der Weide, T. (2006). Giving meaning to enterprise architectures: Architecture principles with ORM and ORC. In R. Meersman, Z. Tari, & P. Herrero (Eds.), *OTM 2006 Workshops* (LNCS) (Vol. 4278, pp. 1138–1147). Springer.
12. Coleman, C., Yeh, C., Mussmann, S., Mirzasoleiman, B., Bailis, P., Liang, P., ... & Zaharia, M. (2019). *Selection via proxy: Efficient data selection for deep learning*. arXiv preprint arXiv:1906.11829.
13. Hansen, J., & Pang, Y. S. (2023). Opening industry data: The private sector's role in addressing societal challenges. *Data & Policy*. https://doi.org/10.1017/dap.2023.15
14. Davidson, E., Wessel, L., Winter, J. S., & Winter, S. (2023a). Future directions for scholarship on data governance, digital innovation, and grand challenges. *Information and Organization, 33*(1), 100454.
15. Susha, I., van den Broek, T., van Veenstra, A. F., & Linåker, J. (2023). An ecosystem perspective on developing data collaboratives for addressing societal issues: The role of conveners. *Government Information Quarterly, 40*(1), 101763.
16. Ransbotham, S., Kiron, D., & Prentice, P. K. (2016). Beyond the hype: The hard work behind analytics success. *MIT Sloan Management Review, 57*(3).

17. Ross, J. W., Beath, C. M., & Quaadgras, A. (2013). You may not need big data after all. *Harvard Business Review, 91*(12), 90–98.
18. Austin, J. E., & Seitanidi, M. M. (2012). Collaborative value creation: A review of partnering between nonprofits and businesses. Part 2: Partnership processes and outcomes. *Nonprofit and Voluntary Sector Quarterly, 41*(6), 929–968.
19. Waddock, S. A. (1988). Building successful social partnerships. *MIT Sloan Management Review, 29*(4), 17.
20. Gray, B. (1996). Cross-sectoral partners: Collaborative alliances among business, government and communities. *Creating Collaborative Advantage*, 57–79.
21. Van Tulder, R., & Pfisterer, S. (2013). Creating partnering space: Exploring the right fit for sustainable development partnerships. In *Social partnerships and responsible business* (pp. 105–124). Routledge.
22. Cao, Q. H., Khan, I., Farahbakhsh, R., Madhusudan, G., Lee, G. M., & Crespi, N. (2016, May). A trust model for data sharing in smart cities. In *2016 IEEE international conference on communications (ICC)* (pp. 1–7). IEEE.
23. Davenport, T. H., Barth, P., & Bean, R. (2012). *How 'big data' is different.*
24. Davenport, T. H., & Kudyba, S. (2016). Designing and developing analytics-based data products. *MIT Sloan Management Review, 58*(1), 83.
25. Chen, H., Chiang, R. H., & Storey, V. C. (2012). Business intelligence and analytics: From big data to big impact. *MIS Quarterly*, 1165–1188.
26. Fichman, R. G., Dos Santos, B. L., & Zheng, Z. (2014). Digital innovation as a fundamental and powerful concept in the information systems curriculum. *MIS Quarterly, 38*(2), 329–A15.
27. Baesens, B., Bapna, R., Marsden, J. R., Vanthienen, J., & Zhao, J. L. (2016). Transformational issues of big data and analytics in networked business. *MIS Quarterly, 40*(4), 807–818.
28. Cech, T. G., Spaulding, T. J., & Cazier, J. A. (2015, August). Applying business analytic methods to improve organizational performance in the public school system. In *Proceedings of the Twenty-First Americas Conference on Information Systems, Puerto Rico* (pp. 13–15).
29. Kim, G. H., Trimi, S., & Chung, J. H. (2014). Big-data applications in the government sector. *Communications of the ACM, 57*(3), 78–85.
30. Loebbecke, C., & Picot, A. (2015). Reflections on societal and business model transformation arising from digitization and big data analytics: A research agenda. *The Journal of Strategic Information Systems, 24*(3), 149–157.
31. Clarke, H. D., Kellner, P., Stewart, M. C., Twyman, J., & Whiteley, P. (2016). *Austerity and political choice in Britain*. Palgrave Macmillan.
32. Wismadi, A., Soemardjito, J., & Sutomo, H. (2013). *Transport situation in Jakarta. Study on Energy Efficiency Improvement in the Transport Sector through Transport Improvement and Smart Community Development in the Urban Area* (pp. 29–58).
33. Mello, M. M., Francer, J. K., & Wilenzick, M. (2013). Preparing for responsible sharing of clinical trial data. *The New England Journal of Medicine, 369*, 1651–1658. https://doi.org/10.1056/NEJMhle1309073
34. Merson, L., Phong, T. V., Nhan, L. N. T., Dung, N. T., Ngan, T. T. D., Kinh, N. V., et al. (2015). Trust, respect, and reciprocity: Informing culturally appropriate data-sharing practice in Vietnam. *Journal of Empirical Research on Human Research Ethics, 10*(3), 251–263.
35. Korhonen, J. J., Melleri, I., Hiekkanen, K., & Helenius, M. (2014). Designing data governance structure: An organizational perspective. *GSTF Journal on Computing (JoC), 2*(4).
36. Plan, A. (2011). *Communication from the Commission to the European Parliament, the Council, the European Economic and Social Committee and the Committee of the Regions.* European Commission.
37. Abraham, R., Schneider, J., & Vom Brocke, J. (2019). Data governance: A conceptual framework, structured review, and research agenda. *International Journal of Information Management, 49*, 424–438.
38. Dyché, J., & Levy, E. (2011). *Customer data integration: Reaching a single version of the truth.* Wiley.
39. Morabito, V. (2015). *Big data and analytics. Strategic and organisational impacts.*

40. Lee, S. U., Zhu, L., & Jeffery, R. (2017). *Data governance for platform ecosystems: Critical factors and the state of practice*. arXiv preprint arXiv:1705.03509.
41. Du, T. C., Lai, V. S., Cheung, W., & Cui, X. (2012). Willingness to share information in a supply chain: A partnership-data-process perspective. *Information & Management, 49*(2), 89–98.
42. Gosain, A., & Mann, S. (2014). Empirical validation of metrics for object oriented multidimensional model for data warehouse. *International Journal of System Assurance Engineering and Management, 5*, 262–275.
43. Linek, S. B., Fecher, B., Friesike, S., & Hebing, M. (2017). Data sharing as social dilemma: Influence of the researcher's personality. *PLoS One, 12*(8), e0183216.
44. Guest, G., Bunce, A., & Johnson, L. (2006). How many interviews are enough? An experiment with data saturation and variability. *Field Methods, 18*(1), 59–82.
45. Maxwell, J. A. (2012). *A realist approach for qualitative research*. Sage.
46. Morse, J. M., Barrett, M., Mayan, M., Olson, K., & Spiers, J. (2002). Verification strategies for establishing reliability and validity in qualitative research. *International Journal of Qualitative Methods, 1*(2), 13–22.
47. Strauss, A., & Corbin, J. M. (1997). *Grounded theory in practice*. Sage.
48. Strauss, A., & Corbin, J. (1998). *Basics of qualitative research*.
49. James, R., Tsosie, R., Sahota, P., Parker, M., Dillard, D., Sylvester, I., et al. (2014). Exploring pathways to trust: A tribal perspective on data sharing. *Genetics in Medicine, 16*(11), 820–826.
50. Tenopir, C., Palmer, C. L., Metzer, L., van der Hoeven, J., & Malone, J. (2011). Sharing data: Practices, barriers, and incentives. *Proceedings of the American Society for Information Science and Technology, 48*(1), 1–4.
51. Meyer, M. N. (2018). Practical tips for ethical data sharing. *Advances in Methods and Practices in Psychological Science, 1*(1), 131–144.
52. Ballerini, L., & Bergh, S. I. (2021). Using citizen science data to monitor the Sustainable Development Goals: A bottom-up analysis. *Sustainability Science, 16*(6), 1945–1962.
53. Cappa, F., Franco, S., & Rosso, F. (2022). Citizens and cities: Leveraging citizen science and big data for sustainable urban development. *Business Strategy and the Environment, 31*(2), 648–667.
54. Åström, J. (2020). Participatory urban planning: What would make planners trust the citizens? *Urban Planning, 5*(2), 84–93.

MIX
Papier aus verantwortungsvollen Quellen
Paper from responsible sources
FSC® C105338

If you have any concerns about our products,
you can contact us on
ProductSafety@springernature.com

In case Publisher is established outside the EU,
the EU authorized representative is:
Springer Nature Customer Service Center GmbH
Europaplatz 3, 69115 Heidelberg, Germany

Printed by Libri Plureos GmbH
in Hamburg, Germany